The Egyptian Campaign, 1882 & The Mahdist Campaigns, Sudan 1884-98

Two Volumes in One Edition

The Egyptian Campaign, 1882 & The Mahdist Campaigns, Sudan 1884-98

Two Volumes in One Edition
The British Army at War in North Africa
During the 19th Century

Charles Royle

The Egyptian Campaign, 1882 & The Mahdist Campaigns, Sudan 1884-98
Two Volumes in One Edition
The British Army at War in North Africa During the 19th Century
by Charles Royle

First published under the title
The Egyptian Campaigns 1882 to 1885 Revised Edition

Leonaur is an imprint of Oakpast Ltd
Copyright in this form © 2013 Oakpast Ltd

ISBN: 978-1-78282-150-2 (hardcover)
ISBN: 978-1-78282-151-9 (softcover)

http://www.leonaur.com

Publisher's Notes

The views expressed in this book are not necessarily those of the publisher.

Contents

Preface	9
Egyptian Finance	13
Ismail Pasha	19
The Military Movement	24
Triumph of the Army	29
Foreign Intervention	34
Critical Position	43
The Riots at Alexandria	55
The Alexandria Bombardment	70
Observations on the Bombardment	88
The Day After the Bombardment	98
Alexandria During the Bombardment	103
Events on Shore	111
The Situation	119
Military Operations	126
The Conference	133
The Porte and the Powers	140
Wolseley's Move to the Canal	145
De Lesseps and the Canal	151

Seizure of the Suez Canal	158
Tel-El-Mahuta to Mahsameh	168
Kassassin	174
Tel-El-Kebir	183
Capture of Cairo and Collapse of the Rebellion	195
England and the Porte	209
Restoration of Tewfik and Exile of Arabi	214
The Soudan and the Mahdi	226
Arrangements for the Future	235
Operations Against the Mahdi	248
The Destruction of Hicks' Army	258
Abandonment of the Soudan—Osman Digna	266
Baker's Defeat at El-Teb.	275
Gordon's Mission	283
Souakim Expedition, 1884	289
Graham's Victory At El-Teb.	294
Graham's Victory at Tamaai	307
The Gordon Relief Expedition	325
Progress to Dongola	333
Advance to Korti	343
Stewart's Desert March	352
The Battle of Abu Klea	360
The Advance on Metammeh	366
Gordon's Journals	373
Wilson's Voyage to Khartoum	381
The Fall of Khartoum	391
The Retreat from Gubat	406

The Nile Column	413
Wolseley and the Prosecution of the Campaign	422
The Souakim Expedition of 1885	430
The Attack on McNeill's Zeriba	439
Graham's Advance and Withdrawal from the Eastern Soudan	453
Evacuation	461
Continuation	468
The Mahdist Invasion	471
Finance, the Suez Canal, and the Army of Occupation	477
The Eastern Soudan	484
The Nile Frontier	491
Wad-En-Nejumi and Collapse of the Invasion	498
The Eastern Soudan Again	511
In Lower Egypt	519
The Dongola Expedition	527
The Reconquest of Dongola	538
The Advance to Berber	544
On the River—Kassala	549
From the Nile to the Atbara	555
The Battle of the Atbara	565
The Advance on Omdurman	575
The Battle of Omdurman	583
The Capture of Omdurman	598
Fashoda	608
Destruction of the Khalifa	614
Conclusion	619

Preface

In the new and revised edition of *The Egyptian Campaigns*, the history of the military operations in Egypt has been brought down to the present time, so as to include all the recent fighting in the Soudan. This has been accompanied by a slight alteration in the title of the book, as well as by the elimination of such details contained in the original work as are no longer of general interest. The space thus gained has been utilised for the purpose of bringing before the reader the chief events of a military character which have occurred in the interval which has elapsed since the book first appeared.

It has been the object of the author to make the work in its present form a complete narrative of the rise and fall of the Arabist and Mahdist movements, as well as a history of England's intervention in Egypt, this last a subject on which many persons entertain somewhat vague and indistinct ideas.

C. R.

Cairo,
December, 1899.

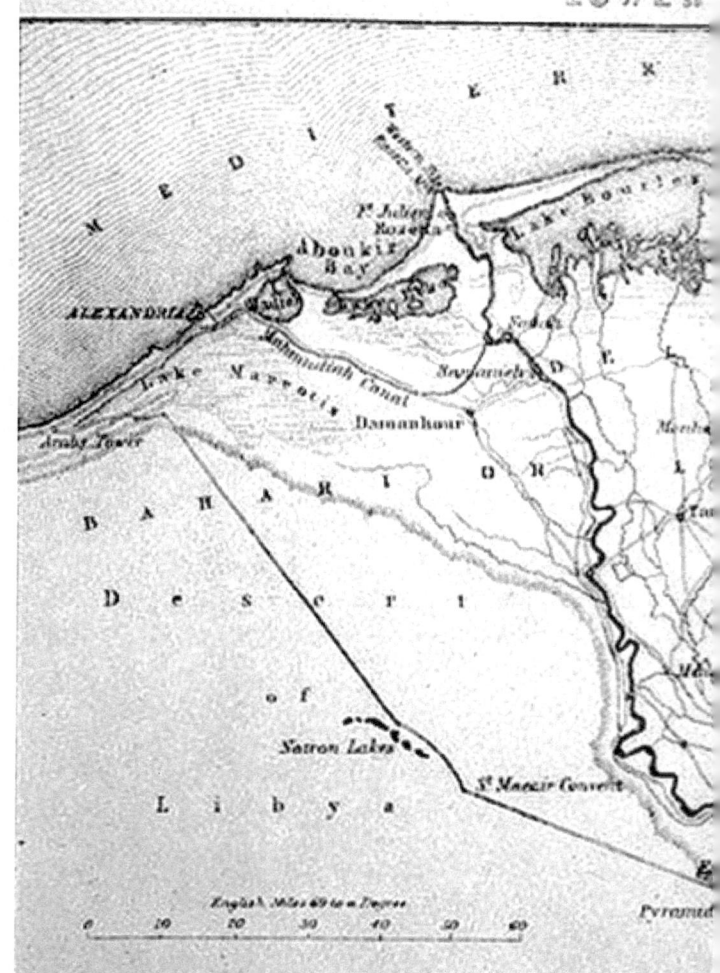

EGYPT
Damietta
Lake Menzaleh
Menzaleh
Salahieh
Belbeis
CAIRO
Suez
RED SEA
French Leagues 25 to a Degree
0
5
10
15
20

Chapter 1

Egyptian Finance

Towards the close of the year 1875, Ismail Pasha, then *khedive* of Egypt, had about got to the end of his resources. His liabilities on loans, contracted either in his own name or in that of his government, amounted to £55,332,609; in addition to this there was a "Floating Debt" of £21,334,960—and £1,000,000—due for the expenses of the war with Abyssinia. The Treasury Bills were being daily protested, the salaries of the government officials were in arrear, and everything pointed to impending bankruptcy.

This was the situation when Ismail sold to the British Government the shares in the Suez Canal Company which he had inherited from his predecessor, Said Pasha.[1]

By the transaction, which was due to the genius of the late Lord Beaconsfield, England made an excellent investment of capital. She also acquired an important interest in the great maritime highway to India, and indirectly in Egypt herself.

Attentive observers regarded what had taken place as only a prelude to a more intimate connection of England with Egyptian affairs, and the financial mission of Mr. Cave, an important Treasury official, undertaken about the same period, naturally strengthened this impression, notwithstanding Lord Derby's declaration that sending the mission to Egypt "was not to be taken to imply any desire on the part of Her Majesty's Government to interfere in the internal affairs of that country."

There is no reason to doubt the sincerity of the Foreign Secretary in the matter. The policy of Lord Beaconsfield's Cabinet, as well as

---

1. The exact number of shares was 176,602, and the "mess of pottage" for which Ismail bartered away his birthright was £3,976,582. The same shares at today's prices are worth just £25,077,484.

that of Mr. Gladstone, which succeeded it, was originally one of non-intervention, and it was only the force of circumstances which led to its modification. England's first wish was that no power should interfere in Egypt; her second, that in the event of interference becoming necessary, England should not be left out in the cold. When this is borne in mind, the attitude which Her Majesty's Ministers from time to time assumed in regard to Egyptian affairs becomes comparatively intelligible.

In confirmation of the preceding, the reader will observe that, although one of the causes which eventually led to England's action in the valley of the Nile was her mixing herself up with questions of Egyptian finance, all attempts to induce her to move in this direction met for a long time with failure.

When Mr. Cave's report, and, later on, that of Messrs. Goschen and Joubert, revealed the embarrassed condition of the country, and the necessity for the adoption of the financial scheme set forth in the Decrees of May and November, 1876, Her Majesty's Government declined to take any part in the arrangement. They even refused to nominate the Englishmen who were to fill the various posts created by the decrees.

The French, Italian and Austrian members of the Commission of the Public Debt were nominated by their respective governments as early as May, 1876, but their British colleague up to the end of the year remained unappointed. France, on the other hand, throughout the whole of the negotiations, appears to have been singularly ready to come to the front, and when in December, 1876, the Duke Decazes, the French Minister of Foreign Affairs, was asked to nominate one of the Controllers of Finance, he declared "that he felt no difficulty whatever on the subject." Lord Derby, however, persisted in his policy of abstention, and eventually the *khedive* was under the necessity of himself appointing the Englishmen required.

At last the financial scheme came into operation, and, combined with other reforms, for some time seemed likely to secure to Egypt and her creditors a fair share of the blessings intended. This, however, was not destined to last. As early as June, 1877, it became evident that the revenues set apart to meet the Interest and Sinking Fund of the Public Debt were insufficient.

In fact, the estimates on which the decrees were founded proved simply fallacious—a deficit of no less than £820,000 appeared in the revenues assigned to the service of the Unified Debt, and of £200,000 on those set apart for the Privileged Debt. Moreover, there was strong reason to suppose that considerable portions of the receipts were being secretly diverted from their legitimate channel by Ismail and his agents.

At the same period serious difficulty arose in satisfying the judgments obtained against the government in the newly-established Mixed Tribunals. These courts, having been instituted by treaties with the powers, partook largely of an international character, and when the European creditors, on issuing execution, found that it was resisted by force, they sought the aid of their respective consuls-general.

The Honourable H. C. Vivian, then British Consul-General in Cairo, a diplomatist who took a prominent part in this stage of Egypt's history, had, as England's representative, to remonstrate with the *khedive*. The advice which Mr. Vivian gave, that the amounts of these judgments should be paid, was excellent, but, under the circumstances, about as practical as if he had counselled His Highness to take steps to secure an annual high Nile.

Early in 1878, when things were going from bad to worse, Mr. Vivian wrote that the whole government of the country was thrown out of gear by financial mismanagement, and that affairs were becoming so entangled as to challenge the interference of foreign governments. This very sensible opinion was backed up by M. Waddington, who had become French Minister of Foreign Affairs, and who, addressing Lord Derby on the financial and political situation, made the significant observation that if England and France did not exert themselves at once, the matter would slip out of their hands. This suggestion, pointing obviously to the probable intervention of other powers, was not without effect, and the British Foreign Secretary in reply went a little further than he had yet done, and stated that "Her Majesty's Government would be happy to co-operate with that of France in any useful measure not inconsistent with the *khedive's* independent administration of Egypt."

This was followed by Mr. Vivian pressing upon the *khedive* the necessity for "a thorough and exhaustive inquiry into the finances of the country."

This constituted a fresh departure in the policy of England with regard to the Egyptian question, and, as will be seen, ultimately led to that complete interference in Egyptian affairs which the British Cabinet had so much desired to avoid.

Of course, Ismail had to yield, and the famous Commission of

Inquiry instituted by the decree of 30th March, 1878, assembled in Cairo under the presidency of Mr. (afterwards Sir C.) Rivers Wilson, and revealed the most startling facts relating to the finances of Egypt. The commission had no easy task before it, and it only attained its object through the dogged resolution of its chairman, backed by the moral support of the representatives of the powers.

At the outset, the late Cherif Pasha, the *khedive's* Minister of Foreign Affairs and of Justice, refused point-blank to obey the decree, and submit to be personally examined by the commission.

As Cherif was a statesman who will be frequently referred to in the following pages, it may be opportune to briefly describe him. He was then about sixty years of age, and, like most of those who have held the highest posts in Egypt, of Circassian origin. He was amongst the favoured individuals who had been sent to France by Mehemet Ali to be educated. He gradually passed through nearly every post in the State with that facility which is so frequently seen in Egypt, where a man is one day a station-master on the railway, the next a Judge in the Tribunals, and eventually a Master of Ceremonies, or a cabinet minister.

Cherif had pleasing manners, spoke French fluently, and was in every respect a gentleman. A Mahomedan by religion, he was, from an early period in Ismail's reign, a prominent character in Egyptian history. He soon became a rival of Nubar Pasha (referred to further on), and he and Nubar alternated as the *khedive's* prime ministers for many years.

Of a naturally indolent character, Cherif always represented the *laissez aller* side of Egyptian politics. With an excellent temper, and a supremely apathetic disposition, he was always willing to accept almost any proposition, provided it did not entail upon him any personal exertion, or interfere with his favourite pastime, a game of billiards.

Cherif's notion in refusing to appear before the commission was of a two-fold character. Educated with Oriental ideas, and accustomed to regard Europeans with suspicion, it is not unlikely that he resented the appointment of the commission as an unwarrantable intrusion on the part of the Western Powers.

"Here," thought he, "were a number of people coming to make disagreeable inquiries, and to ask indiscreet questions. Others might answer them; he, for his part, could not, and for two reasons: first, because he couldn't if he would; and second, because he wouldn't if he could. Was he, at his time of life, to be asked to give reasons for all he had done? It was ridiculous; all the world knew that he had no reasons."[2]

Probably, also, Cherif had his own motives for not wishing to afford too much information. Though enjoying a deservedly high reputation for honesty, he belonged to what must be regarded as the "privileged class" in the country. For years this class had benefited by certain partial immunities from taxation, and these advantages the work of the commission threatened to do away with. Further, Cherif's love of ease and comfort, and absence of energy, indisposed him to give himself unnecessary trouble about anything in particular. Be this as it may, Cherif, though expressing his readiness to reply in writing to any communications which the commission might address to him, declined to do more.

The decree, however, provided that every functionary of State should be bound to appear before the commission. This might have placed a less astute minister in a dilemma. Cherif at once evaded the difficulty by resigning office, rightly calculating on again returning to power when the commission should have become a thing of the past. Riaz Pasha, then second vice-president of the commission, succeeded Cherif as minister, and the inquiry proceeded without him.[3]

It will not have escaped notice that in authorizing Rivers Wilson, who held a high post in the Office of the National Debt, to sit on the commission, and in granting him leave of absence for the purpose, the British Government had allowed itself to advance one stage further in its Egyptian policy. The significance of the event was only partially disguised by Lord Derby's cautious intimation that "the *employé* of the British Government was not to be considered as invested with any official character."

In April of the same year, whilst the commission was still sitting, it became evident that there would be a deficit of £1,200,000 in the amount required to pay the May coupon of the Unified Debt. Further influences were brought to bear, and Mr. Vivian was instructed to join the French Consul-General in urging upon the *khedive* the necessity of finding the requisite funds at whatever cost to himself. Ismail pointed out that this could only be done by ruinous sacrifices, which he promised should nevertheless be made if it was insisted on. The representatives of England and France remained firm, and the

---
2. *khedives and Pashas*, by C. Moberly Bell.
3. Cherif, who was as good a sportsman as he was a billiard player, went to his "long rest" at Aix-les-Bains, on the 19th April, 1887.

bondholders got their money. By what means this was accomplished it is needless to inquire. Rumours of frightful pressure being put on the unfortunate *fellaheen*, of forced loans and other desperate expedients, were prevalent in Cairo, and were probably only too well founded. It is said that even the jewellery of the ladies of Ismail's harem was requisitioned in order to make up the sum required.

Meanwhile the inquiry proceeded.

It would require too much space to give at length the details of the report which the commission presented. Suffice it to say that it showed confusion and irregularity everywhere. Taxes were collected in the most arbitrary and oppressive manner, and at the most unfavourable periods of the year. The land tenures were so arranged that the wealthier proprietors evaded a great portion of the land tax, and the *corvée*, or system of forced labour, was applied in a way which was ruinous to the country. Further, the *khedive* and his family had amassed, at the expense of the State, colossal properties, amounting, in fact, to as much as one-fifth of the whole cultivable land of Egypt, and this property the commission declared ought to be given up. On every side the most flagrant abuses were shown to prevail. In conclusion, it was found that the arrangements made by the Financial Decrees of 1876 could not possibly be adhered to, and that a fresh liquidation was inevitable.

Ismail, after every effort to make better terms for himself, yielded to Rivers Wilson's requisitions, and accepted the conclusions of the commission. He acquiesced with as good grace as he could in making over to the State the landed property of himself and family. He went even further, and in August, 1878, approved the formation of a cabinet under the presidency of Nubar Pasha, with Rivers Wilson as Minister of Finance and M. de Blignières (the French member of the Commission of the Public Debt) as Minister of Public Works. At the same time, as if to show Europe that he had seriously entered on the path of reform, the *khedive* proclaimed his intention to renounce personal rule and become a constitutional sovereign, governing only through his Council of Ministers.

Chapter 2

Ismail Pasha

Any history of Egyptian affairs at the time of the events referred to in the present chapter would be incomplete without a sketch of Ismail Pasha himself. He was then forty-six years of age, short in stature, and heavily and squarely built. He was corpulent in figure, of dark complexion, and wore a reddish brown beard closely clipped. With one eye startlingly bright and the other habitually almost closed, he gave one the idea of a man of more than ordinary intelligence.

Speaking French fluently, and possessed of a peculiarly fascinating manner, Ismail exercised an almost mesmeric influence on those who came in contact with him. His business capacity was unbounded, and not the smallest detail, from the purchase of a coal cargo to the sale of a year's crop of sugar, was carried out without his personal direction. He was entitled to the denomination of Merchant Prince more than anyone who ever bore the title, combining the two characters profitably for a long time, but in attempting to add to them that of a financier also he ended by wrecking his country.

The three great passions of Ismail were, his ambition to render Egypt independent of the *Porte*, his desire to accumulate landed property, and his mania for building palaces. His prodigality was unbounded, and as a result the indebtedness of Egypt was raised in fifteen years from £3,292,000, at which his predecessor left it, to over £90,000,000 at the time now referred to.

To do Ismail justice, it must be admitted that a large part of this money was spent in the construction of railways, canals, and other improvements, and in beautifying Cairo, which it was his aim to convert into a sort of Oriental Paris. But after allowing for all this, and for the two millions sterling spent in the *fêtes* which attended the opening of the Suez Canal, there is still a large balance left unaccounted for.

One of the great defects of Ismail's character was his absolute insincerity. When his reckless administration had brought his country to the brink of ruin, he instituted the system of financial control set forth in the decrees of 1876. It must not be supposed that he ever meant that the system should be carried into effect, or at most that it should be more than a temporary expedient. When he promulgated reforms and enlisted a number of Europeans in his service, did he intend that the reforms should become realities, or that the European officials should exercise the functions nominally intrusted to them? Not for an instant. All that he desired was to throw dust in the eyes of Europe. For a while he succeeded, but it was not to last. After a time it dawned on the powers that they were being played with, and from that moment Ismail's downfall was assured.

In nominally transforming himself into a constitutional ruler, Ismail was only following out his habitual policy. The change, at any rate, looked well on paper. It would, he expected, possess a further advantage—Ismail, by his personal rule, had brought Egypt to the brink of ruin, and by posing as a constitutional sovereign, he hoped to transfer his responsibility to his ministers.

The nomination of Rivers Wilson to the post of Egyptian Minister of Finance was so unprecedented an event that it required all the care of the Marquis of Salisbury, who had now succeeded Lord Derby, to attenuate its political importance. To save appearances it was arranged that Her Majesty's Ministers should do nothing more than give their consent to the appointment.

As a consequence of the installation of constitutional government, with European ministers in the Cabinet, the English and French controllers were deemed unnecessary, and the dual control was declared suspended. On the adoption of the new order of things, a hint was given to the *khedive* that Her Majesty's Government relied on his steady support being given to the new Cabinet, and that the position of himself and his dynasty might become seriously compromised in the event of a contrary course being adopted.

It would have been well for the *khedive* had he taken the advice given. Unfortunately, he was too much steeped in Eastern intrigue, and too fond of the authority which he had nominally surrendered, to bend to the new order of things.[1]

The earliest symptom of this was the military outbreak which took

---

1. The Arabs have a proverb, "*A dog's tail will never stand straight,*" meaning that evil habits, once acquired, cannot be got rid of.

place in Cairo on the 18th February, 1879, when 400 officers and 2,000 discharged soldiers mobbed Nubar Pasha and the European members of his Cabinet at the Ministry of Finance. The ostensible grievance was the non-payment of their salaries; the real one was the reduction in the army, a measure which had been forced on the *khedive* by his new advisers. Both Nubar and Wilson were actually assaulted, and the cry of "Death to the Christians" was raised. What further events might have taken place it is hard to say, but, all at once, Ismail personally appeared on the scene, and as if by magic order was restored.

Everything tended to show that Ismail himself had arranged this little comedy; but be this as it may, he speedily took advantage of it to inform the Consuls-General that the new state of things was a failure, and that he could no longer retain his position without either power or authority. Finally he declared that unless a change were made he would not be answerable for the consequences. This was followed by the resignation of his prime minister, Nubar, and the despatch of British and French vessels of war to Alexandria.

The progress made in the direction of British interference in Egyptian affairs will not fail to strike the reader.

Ismail's motive in bringing about the military disturbance of the 18th February was to demonstrate, in the same manner as Arabi Pasha did later on, that he was the only real power in the country. In doing this, however, he played a dangerous game, and one which shortly after cost him his vice-regal throne.

For the moment, a *modus vivendi* was found in the appointment of his son Prince Tewfik (afterwards *khedive*) as prime minister, *vice* Nubar, and the Western Powers accepted the solution, at the same time giving Ismail another warning, namely, that any further disturbance would be regarded as the result of his action, and the consequences to him would be very serious.

The financial difficulties of the country now became so grave, that a decree suspending payment of the interest of the debt was issued at the end of March, by the advice of the ministers. Then Ismail all at once turned round and declared that the measure was unnecessary, and proposed a financial scheme of his own. How far this could be reconciled with his declaration that he was a constitutional ruler is not clear. This event was followed by the arbitrary dismissal of his ministers and the formation of a purely native Cabinet under Cherif Pasha. So secretly had the change been brought about, that the former ministers only discovered it when, on going to their offices, they found their places already occupied by their successors.

This veritable *coup d'état* placed the English and French representatives in a position of some difficulty. On the one hand, the right of the *khedive* to change his ministers, even under the reformed regime, could not be contested; on the other, the change was of so radical a nature, and so much opposed to the moral obligations which he had contracted with the Western Powers, that it could hardly be permitted. The two consuls-general therefore waited on the *khedive*, and plainly told him that the precipitate dismissal of ministers whose services he had solicited from the governments of England and France constituted an act of grave discourtesy, and warned him of the necessity of adopting the course which they recommended to him. Ismail had by this time become so used to warnings of this character, that the intimation produced but little effect. On the contrary, he at once ordered the army to be increased to 60,000 men, and followed this up by a decree of the 22nd April, 1879, reducing the interest of the debt, and otherwise modifying the arrangements made by the Financial Decrees of 1876.

It was scarcely to be expected that Ismail's action, conceived in defiance of all Europe, would be tolerated, but it might, nevertheless, but for another circumstance, namely, the continued non-payment of the sums due on the judgments of the tribunals. both England and France addressed strong representations to the *Porte* on the subject. Though anxious that Ismail should be taken to task, neither power was prepared to go so far as to demand his deposition. At length the hands of both were forced by a statesman who had more will and less hesitation, namely, Prince Bismarck. He plainly intimated that if England and France did not demand Ismail's removal, Germany would. This decided the matter, and the two powers, seeing the danger of the matter being taken out of their hands, summoned up sufficient resolution to apply to the *sultan* for the removal of the man who had so long trifled with them.

Meanwhile intrigues of all kinds had been going on at Constantinople. Ismail was privately sounded on the subject, and was given his choice, either to abdicate or to be deposed. He was reluctant to come to any decision, and in this he was strengthened by the information which he received from his agent, Ibraim Pasha, at Constantinople. The latter, from time to time, misled his unfortunate principal. When things looked at their very worst, Ibraim repeatedly assured Ismail that if only sufficient money were transmitted to Stamboul, everything would yet be made right. Animated by this hope, the deluded *khedive* sent fabulous sums to the *sultan*, up to the moment when the latter threw him over. It is not, therefore, to be wondered at, that, when the storm actually burst, and the news of his deposition arrived, he was simply thunderstruck. At four in the morning of the 25th June, 1879, the English and French consuls-general sought out Cherif Pasha, and made him accompany them to the palace, and after some difficulty succeeded in finding Ismail. They then communicated to him despatches from Constantinople, and insisted on his abdication as the only means of saving his dynasty. Ismail at first refused point-blank, but later on, he qualified his refusal by stating that he would only yield to a formal order from the *Porte* itself.

The *dénouement* was not far off, for, only a few hours later, a telegram arrived, addressed to "Ismail Pasha, late *khedive* of Egypt," informing him that the *sultan* had deposed him, and nominated his son Tewfik in his place.

There was nothing for the fallen ruler to do but to bow to the inevitable, although he did not acquiesce with good grace. He showed himself most *exigeant* as to the conditions on which he would consent to leave Egypt. He wished for a large sum in ready money. He wanted Smyrna selected as his place of residence. He wished to take with him all his followers, including a *harem* of at least three hundred women. He also demanded that an Egyptian steamer should be placed at his disposal. In fact, he asked so many things that the consuls-general were at their wits' end to know what to do. The great object was to get rid of him at any price, and he was, in effect, told that he could have almost anything he wanted if he would only go at once.

Eventually the parties came to terms, Ismail was given the money he demanded, he was allowed to choose Naples in place of Smyrna as a residence, and at the end of the month, accompanied by seventy ladies of his *harem*, he quitted Alexandria in the *khedivial* yacht *Maharoussa* under a royal salute from the batteries and ships of war.[2]

---

2. Ismail landed at Naples, and resided in many places in Europe, principally in Paris and London, till in December, 1887, he was permitted to settle at Constantinople, where he died in 1895. His body was brought back to Egypt and interred with great ceremony.

CHAPTER 3

The Military Movement

No sooner was Egypt rid of Ismail Pasha, than the *firman* of investiture of Tewfik was solemnly read at the Citadel in Cairo with great state and ceremony.

The powers having insisted on the restoration of the control, Major Baring (afterwards Lord Cromer) and M. de Blignières were appointed Controllers-General by the English and French Governments respectively, on the 4th September. Riaz Pasha, on the 23rd, became Prime Minister.

Riaz is a statesman who has played an important part in Egypt for many years, and is therefore deserving of a passing notice. He is of Circassian family and of Hebrew extraction, possesses a strong will, tenacious perseverance, and business-like habits, and he has always been remarkable for his independence. Riaz is a master of detail, and has all the ins and outs of Egyptian administration at his fingers' ends, and he was, therefore, all the more fitted for taking public affairs in hand at this period. His experience as President of the Council of Ministers in past times rendered his services especially valuable. Gifted with natural foresight, he was shrewd enough to see that, when the control was re-established, England and France seriously intended to take Egyptian affairs in hand, and he accepted the situation accordingly. This led him to work cordially with the controllers, with the happy result that, during the two years that his ministry lasted, Egypt attained an unprecedented degree of prosperity.

In April, 1880, what was styled the Commission of Liquidation was appointed, and under its advice the Public Debt was subjected to various modifications, and other financial changes were made, including a reduction of taxation and other reforms.

How long this pleasant state of things would have lasted it is impossible to say, had not trouble arisen in another direction, and the military revolt under Arabi supervened and upset all previous calculations.

In order to understand the nature and causes of this movement, it is necessary to know something of the Egyptian military organization at the time referred to. The army, which had achieved such great things under Mehemet Ali, had gradually declined under his successors, and when Ismail came to power was represented by a total force of 10,000 fighting men. Ismail raised the number to 45,000, but the *firman* of Tewfik's investiture limiting the number to 18,000, the force had to be reduced to that number. The soldiers were all brought into the ranks by the system of conscription. Those recruited from the Soudan were men possessed of considerable endurance and warlike qualities, but those taken from the other districts, that is, the ordinary *fellah* or agricultural class, had no taste for war.

This is not to be wondered at when the character and habits of the latter are considered. The Egyptian *fellah* is a type in himself. Possessed of no national pride or patriotic aspirations, he cares nothing about politics, and till less for fighting. All that he asks is to be let alone, to till in peace and quietness his little plot of land on the banks of his beloved Nile. Do not vex him too much with forced labour, or tax him beyond his means, and he remains peaceful and fairly law-abiding from the moment of his birth till the day comes for him to be carried out to the little cemetery, the white tombs of which brighten the borders of the desert.

In the preceding observations the Egyptian soldier is spoken of as he was at the period under consideration. What he is capable of becoming, when placed under English officers, and properly trained under humane and just treatment, subsequent events will show.

Amongst the soldiers at the time of the occurrence of Arabi's outbreak there was a fair amount of subordination, and but little jealousy prevailed. Amongst the officers, however, the state of things was entirely different. The majority of them were of Egyptian or *fellah* origin, whilst the others were of Turkish or Circassian extraction. The latter, as belonging to the same race as the reigning family, naturally constituted the dominant caste; when there was a campaign in the Soudan, or any other unpleasant duty to be taken in hand, the *fellah* officers were selected for it. When, on the other hand, it was a question of taking duty in Cairo or Alexandria, the Circassians were employed.

Naturally, a good deal of jealousy was thus created, though, as long as Ismail was in power, it was not openly manifested, and discipline was maintained, except where it answered that ruler's purpose (as in the case of the demonstration against Nubar and Rivers Wilson) that it should be otherwise. With the young and inexperienced Tewfik, however, things were different—a spirit of insubordination developed itself, and the two sets of officers entered upon a struggle for the mastery.

Among the prominent *fellah* officers was a certain Ali Fehmi, who was a favourite of the *khedive*, and in command of the guards at the palace. In this capacity he was frequently called on to convey orders to Osman Pasha Rifki, the Minister of War. Osman was a Circassian, and felt hurt at receiving orders from a *fellah* officer. By what means the change was effected is uncertain, but eventually Ali fell into disfavour, and became one of a group of discontented officers belonging to the same class. There were two others, Abdel-el-Al, and Ahmed Arabi, subsequently known as Arabi Pasha. These three, afterwards known as "The Colonels," were joined by Mahmoud Sami Pasha, a politician, and, thus associated, they formed the leaders of what began to be known as "The National Party."

As Arabi forms one of the chief actors in the events which followed, some details relating to him may not be out of place here.

In person, Arabi was a big, burly specimen of the *fellah* type—his features were large and prominent, and his face, though stern, had a good-natured expression. He was born about the year 1840, in the Province of Charkieh, in Lower Egypt. His father was a *fellah* possessing a few acres of land, and working it himself. Arabi was one of four sons, and he got such education as could be afforded by the village school. In due time he was drafted by conscription into the army, and became an officer. At Said Pasha's death he was a captain, and one of the officers of the guard at the palace at Cairo. He was once rather boisterous under the palace windows, and Ismail Pasha, exclaiming that he was more noisy than the big drum, and less useful, ordered him to be removed and to receive punishment.

This was his first grievance against Ismail, and it induced Arabi to join a secret society of native officers. The objects which this society proposed to itself were the abolition of the invidious favouritism shown to Circassian officers, and the deposition of Ismail, the sovereign.

War broke out between Egypt and Abyssinia; Arabi was in charge of the transports at Massowah, and a charge of corruption being made against him, he fell into disgrace. This fact strengthened his dislike to Ismail, and, with time lying idle on his hands, he took to attending lectures at the religious university, known as the Mosque El Azhar, in Cairo, where he acquired a certain degree of eloquence superior to that of most persons in his position. After a time, Ismail, always working to increase the army, allowed him to join a regiment, and he resumed his connection with the secret society, and soon became the head of it.

One of its members informed the *khedive* of the aims and intentions of the society, upon which Ismail sent for some of the chiefs, and Arabi and his confederates waited on him. They went as his enemies in fear and trembling, and left as his friends; seventy native officers were, in one day, made lieutenant-colonels, including Arabi and his companions. Arabi, in addition, received the high honour of having one of the *khedivial* slaves as his wife.

When the question of the deposition of Ismail came to the front, Arabi took a formal oath to defend him with his life, but this did not prevent him, forty-eight hours after, going to do obeisance to Tewfik as the new *khedive* of Egypt. The latter let it be known that there was a tacit amnesty for the past, and made Arabi a full colonel.

Of Arabi's mental gifts it is impossible to form a high estimate. Ignorant of any language but his own, his forte seemed to be the enunciating of any number of quotations from the *Koran*, quite regardless of their relevancy. He had, however, original ideas at times, and must be credited, at all events, with the quality of sincerity. To Europeans and European influences he was strongly opposed. On one occasion he presided at a meeting of natives assembled for the purpose of founding a free school at Zag-a-zig.

He pointed out the changes which European civilization had wrought in Egypt, and observed that, "before the native was brought in contact with Europe, he was content to ride on a donkey, to wear a blue gown, and to drink water, whereas now he must drive in a carriage, wear a Stambouli coat, and drink champagne. Europeans," he said, "are ahead of us, but why? Is it because they are stronger, better, or more enduring than we? No; it is only because they are better taught. Let us, then, be educated, and the boasted supremacy of the Christians will disappear." The result of this appeal was a large subscription, and the school was established.

Mahmoud Sami Pasha, unlike his associates, was not a *fellah*, but of Turkish descent. He was a man of consummate cunning, and of great personal ambition; basing his calculations on the power of the military movement, and not believing in the disposition of the English and French to resist it, he proposed to use the simple-minded Arabi and his friends as a means of bringing himself into power.

The crisis was brought about by agitators among the *fellaheen* officers, who objected to a proposed reduction of the army; petitions on the subject were presented, not only to the Minister of War, but to the *khedive* himself, setting forth all their grievances, and demanding that an Egyptian should be appointed Minister of War. Osman Rifki, the actual Minister of War, could not brook this, and at a Cabinet Council, at which Mahmoud Sami was present, it was decided to put the three ringleaders, Ali Fehmi, Abdel-el-Al, and Arabi, under arrest.

According to Arabi, a steamer was in readiness to take the prisoners away, and iron boxes were prepared in which they were to be placed and dropped into the Nile, but of this there is no proof beyond his statement. Mahmoud Sami took care to warn "the Colonels" of what was going to happen, and it was arranged that if they did not by a certain time return from Kasr-el-Nil Barracks, to which they were summoned, the soldiers of their respective regiments should march down and liberate them.

It turned out exactly as provided for. On arriving at the barracks on the 1st February, 1881, "the Colonels" found themselves before a court-martial, but hardly had the proceedings begun before a turbulent crowd of soldiery broke in, upset the tables and chairs, ill-treated the members of the court, and carried off the prisoners in triumph to the palace. Here the three colonels interviewed the *khedive*, and demanded the substitution of Mahmoud Sami for Osman Rifki as Minister of War, an increase of the army to 18,000 men, and the establishment of a new system of promotion, which should exclude favouritism to the Circassian officers.

Tewfik having no force wherewith to resist, yielded all that was asked of him, and there the matter for the time ended.

CHAPTER 4

Triumph of the Army

Matters progressed for some time pretty quietly after the events referred to in the previous chapter, but in July, 1881, two incidents occurred which were followed by important results.

A native artilleryman was run over and killed in the streets of Alexandria. His comrades bore the dead body to the palace and forced an entrance in defiance of the orders of their officers. They were tried, and the ringleaders were condemned to severe sentences. Next, nineteen Circassian officers brought charges against the colonel of their regiment, Abdel-el-Al, already mentioned. The charges were inquired into and found to be unfounded, whereupon the nineteen officers were removed from the active list of the army, but were restored subsequently by order of the *khedive*.

These measures gave great umbrage to "the Colonels," who believed that the order was given with a view to encourage the insubordination of the officers towards them; and a letter was written by "the Colonels" to the Minister of War, contrasting the leniency shown towards the nineteen officers with the severity towards the soldiers in the case of the artilleryman.

The *khedive* by this time had become completely dissatisfied with his new Minister of War, and alarmed at the bearing of "the Colonels." He determined to see if energetic measures would not be successful, and appointed his brother-in-law, Daoud Pasha, a Circassian, to the Ministry of War, in the place of Mahmoud Sami. Measures were at the same time taken for getting the disaffected regiments out of Cairo.

These steps were viewed with the greatest possible dissatisfaction by Arabi and his colleagues. Not only so, but they began to entertain considerable fear for their own personal safety. A story had got abroad that the *khedive* had obtained a secret *"fetwah,"* or decree, from the

Sheikh-el-Islam, condemning them to death for high treason. There was no foundation for the story, but it was currently believed. Under these circumstances, all the chief officers signed a declaration of loyalty to the *khedive* and his government. Their next step was to organize the demonstration of the 9th September, 1881.

The immediate origin of the disturbance was the order given by the Minister of War for the removal from Cairo to Alexandria of the regiment of which Arabi was the colonel.

On the 9th September the Minister of War received a communication from Arabi, informing him that the troops in Cairo were going at half-past three in the afternoon to the Palace of Abdin to obtain from the *khedive* the dismissal of the ministry, the convocation of the National Assembly, and the increase of the army to 18,000 men.

When the terms of Arabi's communication were laid before the *khedive* at his palace at Koobah, none of the ministers were present. In the absence of the British Consul-General, Tewfik consulted the British Controller, Mr. (afterwards Sir Auckland) Colvin, who invited the *khedive* to take the initiative himself.

Two regiments were said to be faithful. Colvin advised the *khedive* to summon them to Abdin Square with all the military police available, to place himself at their head, and when Arabi arrived to arrest him.

Colvin accompanied the *khedive* to the Abdin Barracks, where the first regiment of the Guard turned out and made the warmest protestations of loyalty. The same thing occurred with the soldiers at the citadel, though it was ascertained that the troops there had, previously to the *khedive*'s arrival, been signalling to Arabi's regiment at Abbassieh. The *khedive* then announced his intention of driving to the Abbassieh Barracks, some three miles distant. It was already past the time fixed for the demonstration, and Colvin urged him instead to proceed at once to Abdin, taking with him the Citadel regiment. Tewfik, however, wavered. Either he desired to assure himself of the support of more of his soldiers, or more probably he desired to put off the critical moment as long as possible. He persisted in driving to Abbassieh.

It was a long drive, and when he arrived there he found that Arabi had marched with his regiment to Cairo. The opportunity sought of anticipating his movements was, therefore, lost. The carriages were turned round, and on entering Cairo took a long *détour*, and arrived at Abdin Palace by a side door. The *khedive* at first desired to enter the palace, but, on Colvin's entreaty, consented to come out into the square. They went together, followed by half-a-dozen native and European officers. The place was filled with soldiers, some 4,000 in number, with thirty guns placed in position.

The *khedive* advanced firmly towards a little group of officers and men (some of whom were mounted) in the centre. Colvin said to him, "When Arabi presents himself, tell him to give up his sword and follow you. Then go the round of the regiments, address each separately, and give them the 'order to disperse.'" The soldiers all this time were standing in easy attitudes, chatting, laughing, rolling up cigarettes, and eating pistachio nuts, looking, in fact, as little like desperate mutineers as could well be imagined. They apparently were there in obedience only to orders, and, without being either loyal or disloyal, might almost be regarded as disinterested spectators.

Arabi approached on horseback: the *khedive* called out to him to dismount. He did so, and came forward on foot with several others, and a guard with fixed bayonets, and saluted. As he advanced, Colvin said to the *khedive*, "Now is your moment, give the word!"

He replied, "We are between four fires. We shall be killed."

Colvin said, "Have courage!"

Tewfik again wavered, he turned for counsel to a native officer at his side, and repeated, "What can I do? We are between four fires." He then told Arabi to sheathe his sword. Arabi did so at once, his hand trembling so with nervousness that he could scarcely get the weapon back into its scabbard. The moment was lost. Instead of following Colvin's advice, and arresting Arabi on the spot, a step which would at once have put an end to the whole disturbance, the *khedive* then walked towards him and commenced to parley.

He demanded what was the meaning of the demonstration. Arabi replied by enumerating his demands, adding that the army had come there on behalf of the people to enforce them, and would not retire until they were conceded. The *khedive* addressed Colvin, and said, "You hear what he says?" Colvin answered that it was not befitting for the sovereign to discuss questions of this kind with colonels, and suggested his retiring to the palace, leaving others to speak to the military leaders. The *khedive* did so, and Colvin remained for about an hour, explaining to them the gravity of the situation for themselves, and urging them to withdraw the troops whilst there was yet time.

At this moment Mr. (afterwards Sir Charles) Cookson, Acting British Consul-General, arrived, and Colvin left the continuation of the negotiations to Her Majesty's representative. The latter pointed out to

Arabi the risk which he and those with him incurred by the menacing attitude they had assumed. He told him that if they persisted in assuming the government of the country, the army must be prepared to meet the united forces of the Sublime *Porte* and of the European Powers, both of whom were too much interested in the welfare and tranquillity of Egypt to allow the country to descend through a military government to anarchy. Arabi answered that the army was there to secure the liberties of the Egyptian people. Cookson replied that the *khedive* and Europe could not recognize a mere military revolt as the expression of the will of the people, and added that even now, if the troops were withdrawn, any representations presented in the proper manner would be attended to, and he would guarantee Arabi's personal safety and that of his associates.

Arabi, though civil, firmly refused to take the course proposed. He insisted on the adoption of the three points demanded. Cookson then communicated the result of the interview to the *khedive*, adding that he was convinced that the only concession to which any real importance was attached was the dismissal of the ministry. His Highness, after a conference with Riaz Pasha, consented to this, on the understanding that the other points demanded should be in suspense until the *Porte* could be communicated with.

Arabi accepted these terms, insisting only that no member of the *khedive's* family should be included in the new Cabinet, and that the Minister of War should not be a Circassian. On these conditions Arabi promised to withdraw the troops. This, however, was not effected until an order had been signed announcing the dismissal of the ministry and the nomination of Cherif Pasha as the new premier.

After this, Arabi entered the palace and made his submission to the *khedive*, and the soldiers, with their bands playing and amid loud cheers for the "*Effendina*" (Sovereign), retired to their barracks. By eight o'clock all was over, and Cairo, which had been much excited, had relapsed into its ordinary tranquillity.

With regard to the outbreak—the third, it will be remarked, of its kind—it was on a larger scale than any previously organized, and was, as events showed, correspondingly more successful. The rebellious troops were, indeed, quieted, as on former occasions, but only by concessions which went far to place the whole government of the country under irregular military control.

With regard to the attitude assumed by the *khedive* on the occasion, considerable allowance must be made. Tewfik in the life-time of his father had never, or at all events until the latest period of Ismail's reign, been allowed to come to the front. He was, therefore, the less fitted for dealing with a crisis of so formidable a character as that of the 9th September. Born of one of Ismail's female slaves in the year 1853, Tewfik was never a favourite with his father, and when his brothers were sent to Europe to be educated, he himself was kept in Cairo and lived in quiet obscurity. Whilst they were made much of, both at home and abroad, Tewfik remained quietly cultivating his farm at Koobah.[1]

The difference in developing the character and dispositions of the princes was natural enough, and yet the late ruler of Egypt was in many respects in no way inferior to the other members of his family. He possessed a remarkable degree of intelligence, and although a strict Mahomedan he was the husband of only one wife, to whom he was devotedly attached. Determined to avoid, in bringing up his children, the error perpetrated towards himself, he sent his sons to Europe to be educated. In appearance he somewhat resembled his father, being short and inclined to stoutness.

Unlike Ismail, however, Tewfik was wanting in energy and determination. With either Ismail, or his grandfather, Mehemet Ali, the demonstration of the 9th September would have been impossible. With Ismail—supposing such an event could have taken place—the end would not have been far off. The fate of Ismail Pasha Saddyk, Minister of Finance, known as the "*Mofettish*," sufficiently shows the means by which Arabi would have been disposed of.[2]

With Mehemet Ali the procedure would have been yet more summary. The report of a pistol would have been heard, and Arabi would have rolled lifeless on the square of Abdin. A volley of musketry would have dispersed his followers, and the incident would have been closed.

Tewfik, with his genial kindly disposition, was not the man to adopt either of the above expedients, and, as has been seen, Arabi triumphed.

---

1. Tewfik went to Europe in 1870, but was recalled when he had only got as far as Vienna. 2. Saddyk was taken by Ismail in his carriage to the palace at Ghezireh on 14th November, 1876, and was never after seen alive.

Chapter 5

Foreign Intervention

Difficulty was at first experienced in getting Cherif Pasha to undertake the formation of a ministry. His idea was that it was inconsistent with a due regard for his own reputation for him to pose before the world as the accomplice of the mutinous soldiery, and at one time, after an interview with Arabi, Cherif positively declined. Meanwhile, meetings of the officers were held in which the most violent appeared to have the upper hand, and the belief that they had nothing to fear from Turkish intervention emboldened them to reject an ultimatum of Cherif, which was that, on condition of his undertaking the government, and guaranteeing the safety of the leaders, they should withdraw their regiments to certain posts assigned to them.

Public opinion, more particularly amongst the Europeans, became much alarmed, and the *khedive* declared himself ready to yield everything in order to save public security.

On the 13th September, however, things took an unexpected turn for the better. Arabi, at the suggestion of Mahmoud Sami, who hoped to render Cherif impossible, and to get himself nominated in his place, summoned to Cairo the members of the Chamber of Notables. Cherif had acquired a good deal of popularity among the class to which the Notables belonged, and at their first meeting he found arguments to induce them to adopt a tone hostile to Arabi and his friends, whom they told to attend to the army, and mind their own business. The notables went even further, and signed an address to Cherif entreating him to form a ministry, and giving their personal guarantee that if he consented, the army should yield absolute submission to his orders. Arabi, it will be remembered, had all along professed to act on behalf of the Egyptian people, and the attitude of the Notables was a severe check to him, or rather to Mahmoud Sami, who was pulling the wires.

This last individual, seeing that the Notables were playing into the hand of Cherif, at once declared himself the partisan of the latter and of the Chamber, and as a consequence Sami was reappointed Minister of War in the Cabinet which Cherif was eventually persuaded to form.

On the 14th of September the new ministry was gazetted, and steps were taken for the dispersal of the disaffected regiments in the provinces. On the 6th of October Arabi and his regiment left Cairo for the military station of El Ouady, in the Delta. Before he left he was received by the *khedive*, whom he assured of his respect and entire devotion. When one remembers how often Arabi had gone through this ceremony, one can hardly help thinking that Tewfik must, by this time, have begun to get a little tired of it. Before leaving, Arabi made speeches to the troops, in which he exhorted them "to remain united, and to draw even more tightly, if possible, those bonds of fraternity of which they had already given such striking examples." Finally, after pointing out—it must be presumed by way of a joke—that obedience in a soldier was the first of virtues, he declared that as long as he possessed a drop of blood, or a living breath, both should belong to his beloved sovereign.

Meanwhile the elections for the Chamber of Notables, which had been convoked by the *khedive* for the 23rd of December, were proceeding. The chamber was called together under an old law of Ismail's time, made in 1866, under which the notables possessed but very limited functions. They were, in fact, simply a consultative body, with power only to discuss such matters as might be brought before them by the advisers of the government.

There is no doubt that, apart from the military movement, there was a widespread feeling of discontent in the country at this time. Ismail's merciless exactions, and the pressure of foreign money-lenders, had given rise to a desire to limit the power of the *khedive*, and, above all, to abolish the Anglo-French control, which was considered as ruling the country simply for the benefit of the foreign bondholders. The control was further hated by the large landowners, because the law of liquidation (with which the controllers in the minds of the people were associated) had in a measure sacrificed their claims for compensation in respect of the cancelling of a forced loan known as the "*Moukabeleh*," and it was still more detested by the *pashas* and native officials, because it interfered with the reckless squandering of public money, and the many opportunities for corruption by which they had so long benefited.

In addition to this, there was a great deal of irritation at the increasing number of highly paid European officials which the reformed regime inaugurated in the latter days of Ismail involved. The people began to suspect that what was occurring was only part of a plan for handing the country over to Europeans. The examples lately set by England with regard to Cyprus, and by France in Tunis, were, it must be owned, but little calculated to inspire confidence in the political morality of either of these two powers.

The prevailing irritation was kept alive by the native press, which began to indulge in the most violent abuse of Europeans. The army, too, continued to show signs of insubordination in many ways. To add to the difficulties of the situation, the colonels of the regiments which had been expressly sent away into the provinces had acquired the inconvenient habit of coming back to the capital, and joining in the many intrigues on foot.

Next followed a demand by the Minister of War for an augmentation of the War Budget, in order to increase the army to the maximum allowed by the *sultan's firman*.

Under these circumstances the Chamber of Notables assembled on the 25th of December, 1881.

The earliest trouble arose from the demand of the notables that the law under which they were assembled should be modified so as to give them power to vote the budget so far as it related to such of the revenues as were not assigned to the Public Debt.

The claim of the chamber, though plausible enough at first sight, was really, if granted, calculated to infringe all the international arrangements for the Debt. It was obvious that if the chamber had the power and chose to vote an extravagant Budget so far as related to the *unassigned* revenues, the administration of the country could not be carried on, national bankruptcy might ensue, and the collection of the assigned revenues would become impossible.

The chamber, however, not only refused to give way on the question of the budget, but it demanded that the law should be further amended by giving the notables other privileges, namely, the right to control the acts of public functionaries, to initiate legislation, and to hold the ministers responsible to the chamber. By getting the notables to make these demands, which he knew could not be accepted, Mahmoud Sami's object was to bring about a crisis which could only end in the downfall of Cherif's Cabinet. He had already persuaded Cherif to make Arabi Sub-Minister of War, under the pretext of securing him on the side of the ministry, and so neutralizing the influence which the army was exercising over the chamber. In reality the appointment only afforded Mahmoud Sami and Arabi increased facilities for intriguing against Cherif. The result was soon seen.

The amendments to the law giving the chamber increased power were inadmissible on many grounds. Were there no other objection, there was the insurmountable one that the *sultan* had already refused a constitution to other parts of his dominions, and would certainly oppose its being granted to Egypt. To put it shortly, the amendments after being submitted to the English and French Governments were declared unacceptable.

This at once brought about a crisis, and the chamber, on the 2nd February, sent a deputation to the *khedive* to require him to summon a new ministry.

At this period it was reported to the English and French Governments that activity was being displayed in putting all the coast fortifications in an efficient state, and that the strength of the army was being augmented under the provisions of the new War Budget.

These circumstances, taken in conjunction with the political events above recorded, led the English and French Governments to conclude that if the *khedive* was to be maintained in power, the time was coming for them to think about doing something in Egypt. On the 20th of January, 1882, Sir Edward Malet wrote that:

> . . . . . armed intervention had become necessary if the refusal to allow the chamber to vote the budget was to be agreed to, and yet it was impossible to do otherwise, as the measure only formed part of a complete scheme of revolution.

As far back as December, 1881, M. Gambetta, then at the head of the French Ministry, had suggested that England and France should take:

> . . . . . joint action in Egypt to strengthen the authority of the *khedive*, and to cut short intrigues at Constantinople, as well as to make the *Porte* feel that any undue interference on its part would not be tolerated.

This proposal shortly after resulted in the famous Joint Note communicated by the English and the French representatives to the *khedive* in Cairo, on the 8th January, 1882. The document was to the effect that the English and French Governments considered the maintenance of His Highness upon the throne in the terms laid down by the *sultan's firmans*, and officially recognized by the two governments, as alone able to guarantee for the present and the future good order and prosperity in Egypt, in which England and France were equally interested. It continued to say that:

> The two governments, being closely associated in the resolve to guard by their united efforts against all cause of complication, internal or external, which might menace the order of things established in Egypt, did not doubt that the assurance publicly given of their intention in this respect would tend to divert the dangers to which the government of the *khedive* might be exposed, and which would certainly find England and France united to oppose them.

The parentage of the Joint Note is attributable to the French Government, which, up to this time, seemed bent on retaining the lead which it had from the first taken in regard to Egyptian affairs. The wording of the document had been altered more than once to suit the late Lord Granville, then foreign secretary, who appears to have been not quite sure how far he was getting out of his depth in regard to Egyptian matters.

It was under the influence of some such misgiving that Lord Lyons, the British ambassador in Paris, was instructed on the 6th January, 1882, in communicating to the French Government England's assent to the note, to make the reservation that she must not be considered as thereby committing herself to *any particular mode of action*, if action should be found necessary. In reply, M. Gambetta, by a despatch dated the following day, stated that he observed with pleasure "that the only reservation of the Government of the Queen was as to the *mode of action* to be employed, and that this was a reservation in which he participated."

When one sees how, later on, when action became necessary, the attitude of the two countries became reversed, the extreme reluctance of the English Government to move at this time seems curious enough, especially when it is contrasted with the continued readiness of France to come forward in the interval. The explanation is that M. Gambetta, with his clear statesman-like intellect, foreseeing that some sort of intervention would become necessary, was determined that it should be limited to that of England and France to the exclusion of

Turkey, and so long as he remained in power boldly shaped his policy with that object. The English Government, on the other hand, had throughout no real settled policy with regard to Egypt. Their first idea was to have no intervention at all; they hoped that things would mend of themselves.

When they found that this was not likely to be the case, the idea of a Turkish intervention found favour. France, however, was resolutely opposed to this, and to allow the latter power to take isolated action, as indeed she appeared disposed to do if thwarted, was open to serious objections. To avoid such a catastrophe the English Government found themselves under the necessity of following, for the time being, the masterly lead of M. Gambetta. However this may have been, England, by taking part in the Joint Note, assumed a definite position relative to Egypt, and, throwing off all hesitation as to "interference with the internal affairs of the country," pledged herself jointly with France to support the *khedive* against all enemies from within or without.

The first to take offence at the Joint Note was naturally enough the *sultan*, who caused Lord Granville to be informed that the *Porte* considered that sending the *khedive* any such communication except through itself was highly improper.

The *sultan* added that, "To protect the immunities granted to Egypt, and to preserve the order and prosperity of that province, was the sincere wish and interest of the *Porte*, whose efforts had till then always been directed to that end, and that there were no circumstances in Egypt which could serve as a motive for any foreign assurances of the kind made." Finally, the Turkish ambassador requested that the two powers would give an explanation of what they meant. At the same time the *sultan* sent a circular to the other powers, protesting against the action of England and France.

Lord Granville now began to doubt whether he had not gone a little too far, and drafted an answer to the *Porte* of an apologetic character. The tone of the proposed reply was somewhat of the kind that a schoolboy taken to task for an act of impertinence towards his master might be expected to give. Substantially, it was that the two powers did not mean anything at all.

The despatch, as originally drafted, began by disclaiming any doubt whatever as to the sovereignty of the *sultan* over Egypt. It proceeded to declare that there was no change in the policy of Her Majesty's Government, which was as anxious as ever for the continuance of the sovereignty of the *Porte*, and for the maintenance of the liberties and administrative independence secured to Egypt by the *sultan's firmans*. Having paid the *Porte* these little compliments, the despatch disclaimed all ambitious views with regard to the country (of which, by the way, the Sultan had been careful never to accuse the two powers), but said that they could never be indifferent to events which might plunge Egypt into anarchy, and that it was only with a view to warding off such a catastrophe that Her Majesty's Government thought it advisable, in conjunction with the French Government, to forward a declaration showing the accord of the two in carrying out the policy described. The despatch finally pointed out that the form of the Note was not a new one, and that similar declarations had been on special occasions made to the *khedive* without calling forth any remonstrance from the *Porte*.

Gambetta, however, viewed the matter in a different spirit. Having once gone forward he was not disposed to draw back. He had, moreover, the interests of the large body of French bondholders to protect. He at first objected that no explanation of the Joint Note at all was necessary, and that any attempt to explain it would only tend to encourage the military party. Seeing, however, that Lord Granville was determined to send some reply, Gambetta insisted on certain modifications in the despatch. Amongst them he suggested that the assertion of the *Porte*, that there were no circumstances that could justify the steps taken by England and France, should be answered, and proposed that it should be pointed out, first, that the authority of the *khedive* had been modified and diminished; second, that the Chamber of Notables had arrogated to itself the right of interfering with matters expressly exempted from its jurisdiction by the *khedive*'s decree; and third, that the chamber had aimed at setting aside arrangements to which Egypt was bound by international engagements with England and France.

Lord Granville once more yielded to what he had begun to recognize as the superior mind of the French statesman, and Gambetta's amendments were agreed to.

It was not until the 2nd February, however, that the reply to the *Porte*'s remonstrance was actually sent off.

In the meantime the Gambetta Ministry had fallen, and from this moment dates a marked change in the attitude of the French Republic with regard to Egypt. M. de Freycinet, the successor to Gambetta, though agreeing to the amended reply to the *Porte*, cautiously inquired what meaning was to be attached to the reservation as to "taking action" made by Her Majesty's Government in assenting to the original note.

Lord Granville, no longer under the influence of Gambetta, and apparently anxious to recede as far as possible from the somewhat bold position which he had been induced to adopt, answered, contrary to the plain words in which the reservation had been expressed, that Her Majesty's Government reserved to themselves the right to determine, not merely the *particular mode of action* to be adopted in Egypt, but whether any action at all was necessary.

De Freycinet, who, it must be admitted, was equally glad to back out, then plainly declared that he was disinclined to any armed intervention in Egypt, whether by France and England together, or by either separately. This announcement must have been a surprise to the British Government, which, after being led by France into sending the Joint Note, now began to discover that in the event of its becoming necessary to take any steps to carry it into effect, England could no longer count on her as an ally.

Under these circumstances, and feeling that the time when action would have to be taken might not be far off, Lord Granville addressed a Circular to the other Powers, requesting them to enter upon an exchange of views as to the best mode of dealing with the Egyptian Question.

The effect of the Joint Note upon the *Porte* has been stated. It only remains to consider its effect upon the *khedive* and the Notables. The *khedive* received the assurances of protection given by England and France gratefully enough. It was not so, however, with his ministers, who, on the note being communicated on the 8th January, wanted, like the *sultan*, to know what it meant. Sir Edward Malet, in reply, assured them that the note was merely intended to convey to the *khedive* the assurance of the friendship of the powers, and that in point of fact it did not really mean much.

It is obvious that to produce any good effect on the chamber and the National Party it was necessary that the note should have been backed by the display of force, and this unfortunately was just what was wanting. In short, England and France launched their threat without being prepared to follow it up by immediate action. It created great indignation on the part of the military leaders and in the chamber; Arabi declared point-blank that any intervention on the part of England and France was inadmissible. Later on, when it was seen that the two powers were not really to act, but, on the contrary, were busy doing all they could to attenuate the step they had taken, the feeling of indignation gave way to one of contempt, very natural under the circumstances.

Amongst those who misled the chiefs of the National Party none were so conspicuous as two Englishmen, namely, the late Sir William Gregory, an ex-colonial governor, and Mr. Wilfred S. Blunt. Both these gentlemen had, whilst spending some months in Egypt, conceived a violent sympathy for the National movement. They had witnessed during their stay in the country numerous instances of misrule and oppression, and they regarded Arabi and his friends as the leaders of a genuine popular effort to secure political liberty and good government.

In addition to the assurances which they received from Sir William Gregory and Mr. Blunt, the leaders of the National Party were led to believe, and as has been seen not without reason, that England and France were not really agreed to do anything, much less to take any decisive step in the way of intervention; that the two powers were jealous of each other, and that the Joint Note might be safely disregarded. The Arabists further clung to the hope that even were France and England allied, the other powers would prevent their interference, and the protests which four of them, namely, Germany, Austria, Russia, and Italy, made at the time against any foreign interference in Egypt without their consent, certainly tended to confirm this view.

This was the condition of affairs on the 2nd February, when, as already stated, the deputation from the Chamber requested the *khedive* to summon a new ministry. Tewfik had by this time become thoroughly alarmed. The tonic effect produced by the Joint Note had quite gone off, and he was beginning to doubt how far he could rely on support from England and France. He realized that by placing himself under the tutelage of the Western Powers he was injuring himself with the *Porte*, and he had daily proofs afforded him of his growing unpopularity with his subjects. Under these circumstances he saw nothing for it but to yield. At the suggestion of the chamber, the intriguer Mahmoud Sami was directed to form a new ministry, which he lost no time in doing, in conjunction with his confederate Arabi, who now filled the important post of Minister of War.

CHAPTER 6

Critical Position

Although the Ministry of Mahmoud Sami was forced upon the *khedive*, the position of the latter was at the time so hopeless that one must not be surprised at his endeavouring to make the best of it and put a good face upon the matter. Accordingly, on the 4th of February, 1882, Tewfik, in true Oriental style, wrote to his new premier that, in accepting the task of forming a Cabinet, he had given a fresh proof of his devotion and patriotism, and the letter ended by approving of the programme which the new premier had drawn up.

The programme in question referred to the arrangements for the Public Debt, including the control. It spoke of the necessity for judicial and other reforms, and then passed on to the burning question of the Chamber of Notables, and stated that the first act of the ministry would be to obtain sanction for the proposed law for the chamber. This law, it was stated, would respect all rights and obligations, whether private or international, and would wisely determine the responsibility of ministers towards the chamber as well as the discussion of laws.

Mahmoud Sami's programme elicited from the English and French controllers a memorandum, in which they very sensibly observed that it mattered very little whether or not the intention of attacking the control was asserted, as by the very force of circumstances it became ineffectual when the controllers found no longer in the presence of the *khedive* and of ministers freely appointed by him, but of a chamber and an army. It added that the Chamber, under the influence of certain military chiefs, did not hesitate to claim rights incompatible with the social condition of the country; it had gone so far as to compel the *khedive* to change the ministry which had his confidence, and, under pressure of certain officers, to impose on him the late Minister of War as Prime Minister, and concluded with the significant words: "The *khedive's* power no longer exists."

After this it is not surprising that the controllers resigned office. Sir Auckland Colvin was requested by the British Government to remain at his post and maintain "an attitude of passive observation." His French colleague was replaced by M. Brédif. There is no doubt that the controllers' view of the situation was only too just. With Arabi as Minister of War, and his co-conspirator, Mahmoud Sami, President of the Council the country was simply under a military dictatorship.

Meanwhile, the reserves of the artillery were called in and distributed amongst the coast fortifications, recruiting in the provinces was being actively carried on, ninety Krupp guns were ordered from Europe, and Arabi was created a *pasha* by the *sultan*.

The National Party had now become complete masters of the situation. Notwithstanding this, a collision might for some little time have been averted but for an incident which occurred shortly after.

The differences between the Circassians and the native-born Egyptians in the army have been already touched upon. One peculiarity of the Arab race is a revengeful disposition. Arabi and his friends had, as already stated, met with rough usage at the hands of the Circassian party. Hence it followed that the first idea of the former on getting into power was to avenge themselves on their old enemies. This was carried out by the wholesale arrest of fifty Circassian officers, and of Osman Pasha Rifki, former Minister of War, on a charge of conspiracy to assassinate Arabi. It was also alleged that the plot comprised the deposition of the *khedive* and the restoration of Ismail Pasha.

The prisoners were tried in secret by a court martial appointed by the military leaders, and, of course, found guilty. They were, it is said, subjected to torture to induce them to confess, and persons of respectability testified that they heard at night shrieks of pain coming from the place where the prisoners were confined. The sentence passed on forty of them, including Osman, was that of exile for life to the remotest limits of the Soudan. This was equivalent to a sentence of death as regards most of the prisoners.

It was necessary that the sentences should be confirmed by decree of the *khedive*, and he consulted Sir Edward Malet as to the course to be taken. The story of the plot was, there is reason to believe, purely imaginary.

With some little hesitation, and after conferring with the diplomatic agents of the powers, the *khedive* boldly determined to exercise his prerogative without reference to his ministers, and signed a decree commuting the sentences to simple banishment from Egypt, without loss of rank and honours.

This was a defiance of Mahmoud Sami, to which he was not disposed to submit. On the 10th May, the *khedive* summoned the consuls-general, and informed them that the President of the Council had insisted that this decree should be changed by condemning the prisoners to be struck off the strength of the army, and had threatened that his refusal would be followed by a general massacre of foreigners. The significance of this threat coming from Mahmoud Sami, the minister who was in power when just a month later—namely, on the 11th June—a massacre of foreigners *did* take place in Alexandria, will probably be remarked.

The Chamber of Notables had ceased to sit on the 26th March, when the session closed; but Mahmoud Sami now announced that since the *khedive* and his ministers could not agree, and as it was impossible for the ministry to resign, they had determined themselves to convoke the chamber, and to lay the case before it, and that he did not intend to hold any further communication with the *khedive* until the difference between them had been decided by the chamber. He added that in the meantime the ministry would answer for the public safety.

The alarm in Cairo now began to be general. It was open warfare between the *khedive*, and his ministry supported by the army. The National Party made no secret of their intention to depose the *khedive* as soon as the chamber assembled.

The notables, when the day for assembly arrived, began to show a disinclination to support the National Party. They had commenced to realize that they had already gone further than they had intended, and also that they were being merely used as tools by Arabi and his colleagues.

At first they refused to meet at all, on the ground that they had not been convoked by the *khedive*, but only by the ministry. They were, however, induced to assemble, and on the 13th May they met at the house of Sultan Pasha, the President of the Chamber. Here Mahmoud Sami read an indictment against the *khedive*, charging him principally with not governing through his ministers, and with compromising the liberties of Egypt. On the 14th the ministers were so little sure of the support of the notables, that Mahmoud Sami and Arabi went to the palace, and, in the names of themselves and their colleagues, offered to resign if the *khedive* would guarantee public order. His Highness answered, that such a condition was a most unusual one, and that it would be the business of the ministry to see that public order was not troubled; he added that the only persons likely to cause trouble were Arabi and his associates. On the 15th, the English and French consuls-general gave notice to Arabi that if there was a disturbance of public order, he would find Europe and Turkey, as well as England and France, against him, but that if, on the other hand, he remained loyal to the *khedive*, his acts and person would be favourably regarded.

Arabi, in reply, stated that he would guarantee order only as long as he remained minister, except that in the event of a fleet arriving he could not answer for the public safety. The same day the two consuls-general announced to the *khedive* that an Anglo-French fleet was hourly expected at Alexandria. This was followed by the ministers going in a body to the palace and making a complete submission to the *khedive*.

A reconciliation of the *khedive* with his ministers was accepted by the former only on the earnest representations of the notables and the consuls-general, in order that tranquillity might not be disturbed, the idea was to keep the ministry in office as a temporary measure, in order that there might be someone to treat with when the fleets should arrive.

Notwithstanding the improved aspect of affairs, the alarm in Cairo continued, and crowds of people daily left the city. To allay the panic, Mahmoud Sami and Arabi declared that they would guarantee the preservation of order on the arrival of the fleets.

On the 19th and 20th of May the much-talked-of "fleets" arrived at Alexandria. They consisted only of the British ironclad *Invincible* with two gunboats, and the French ironclad *La Gallisonière*, also accompanied by two gun-vessels. The remainder of the allied squadron was left at Suda Bay, in the island of Crete.

The despatch of the English and French ships to Alexandria by two Powers, each professing to be "disinclined to armed intervention in Egypt," was so important a step that it may be interesting to go back a little to consider the means by which it was brought about. Lord Granville, immediately after the Abdin demonstration of the 9th September, had intimated to the French Government as his idea of a remedy for the military insubordination prevailing the sending of a Turkish General to Egypt. M. Barthélemy St. Hilaire, Minister for Foreign Affairs, objected that this might lead to further steps, and possibly to the permanent occupation of the country by Turkish troops. The French minister expressed himself in favour of a "joint military control," consisting of an English and a French general, to restore discipline in the Egyptian Army. Nothing was done to carry out either suggestion.

In March, 1882, when the struggle between the *khedive* and the Chamber was at its height, Lord Granville suggested that England and France should send two "technical advisers" to assist the representatives of the two powers in settling the details of the financial matters then pending. The proposal was so ludicrously absurd under existing circumstances, that it says much for the politeness of the French minister that he took the trouble to give a serious reply. He objected that the measure would give offence to the other powers, as an attempt on the part of England and France to effect a separate settlement of Egyptian affairs, and also that it would tend to lower the consuls-general in their own eyes and in those of the Egyptians.

Again baffled, Lord Granville, in April, 1882, could think of nothing better than that the *sultan* should be asked "to send a general with full powers to restore discipline in the Egyptian Army, with the understanding that he was not to exercise those powers in any way without the concurrence of an English and a French general, who would be associated with him."

This proposal also fell through, the French Government objecting that the sending of a Turkish general at all would tend sooner or later to the sending of Turkish troops, which was not desirable.

The despatch of a Turkish commissioner of some kind continued to be talked about, when, on the 7th May, 1882, Sir Edward Malet wrote to the Foreign Office that the *khedive*'s ministers would certainly resist by force the arrival of any commissioner from Turkey. After this, Lord Granville was for a time forced to abandon his favourite hobby of Turkish intervention. Sir Edward Malet's despatch contained the following significant passage:—

> I believe that some complication of an acute nature must supervene before any satisfactory solution of the Egyptian question can be attained, and that it would be wiser to hasten it than to endeavour to retard it, because the longer misgovernment lasts the more difficult it is to remedy the evils which it has caused.

This very sensible opinion had its effect, for, on the 11th May, Lord Granville was so far able to make up his mind as to say that the English Government were willing to send two ironclads to Alexandria to protect European residents. This announcement, however, was only made after the idea had been suggested by the French minister. Even at this period, Lord Granville could not help referring regretfully to his original idea of sending the three generals (an expedient about as hopeful as sending three flowerpots with water to extinguish a fire), and in reply to M. de Freycinet, his Lordship said that he could still think of nothing better.

The French Government, in agreeing to the despatch of the Anglo-French fleet, appeared resolved to abandon the cautious attitude which it had assumed on M. de Freycinet taking office. The French premier, on the 11th May, informed the Chamber of Deputies that in its Egyptian policy the ministry had two objects, first, to preserve "the preponderating influence of France in Egypt;" and, second, to maintain the independence of Egypt, as established by the *firmans*; and added that the means which would be employed to carry out this policy would be an intimate alliance with England.

M. de Freycinet, on the 12th May, informed Her Majesty's Ambassador in Paris, that as the *khedive* had been acting under the advice of England and France, the French Government considered it the bounden duty of the two Powers to support His Highness *as far as circumstances would allow*, and that France would co-operate loyally and without *arrière pensée* with England in that sense. M. de Freycinet, with some sense of humour, added that sending the three generals would be inopportune.

On the 13th the English Government notified their concurrence in the views of France with regard to the *khedive*, and welcomed the co-operation of the French Government. Lord Granville, at the same time, expressed the readiness of himself and his colleagues to defer to the objections raised to the mission of the three generals.

It now became known that the Notables were assembling in Cairo, and that the Ministry of Mahmoud Sami was about to propose the deposition of the *khedive*. It was also reported that Mahmoud Sami proposed to declare himself "Governor-General of Egypt by the national will."

These alarming reports caused the preparations for the departure of the ships to be hastened, and, at the same time, with a view to keep the ground clear, the two Western Powers sent an intimation to the *Porte* desiring it to abstain for the moment from all intervention in Egypt.

The instructions to the British admiral were as follows:—

Communicate with the British Consul-General on arrival at Alexandria, and in concert with him propose to co-operate with naval forces of France to support the *khedive* and protect British subjects and Europeans, *landing a force, if required,* for latter object, such force not to leave protection of ships' guns without instructions from home.

The French admiral's instructions were somewhat different, and tend to show that the two powers were not completely agreed as to the means to be employed to support Tewfik. His instructions were in these words:—

On arrival at Alexandria communicate with the consul-general, who will, if necessary, indicate to you what you will have to do to give a *moral* support to the *khedive*. You will abstain, until you have contrary instructions, from any material act of war, unless you are attacked or have to protect the safety of Europeans.

The British and French consuls-general, on the arrival of the fleets, advised the *khedive* to take advantage of the favourable opportunity to dismiss the existing ministry, and to form a new Cabinet under Cherif Pasha, or any other person inspiring confidence. Negotiations were simultaneously opened with Arabi in order to induce him, with the other rebel leaders, to retire from the country, in return for which they were to be guaranteed their property, rank, and pay.

None of these plans succeeded. The *khedive* recognized the futility of dismissing a ministry that insisted on remaining in power. Mahmoud Sami replied that the ministry would not retire so long as the squadrons were kept at Alexandria, and Arabi declared that he must refuse either to retire from his position, or to leave the country.

On the 25th May, the representatives of England and France handed to Mahmoud Sami, as President of the Council of Ministers, an ultimatum in the form of a Dual Note, demanding the retirement of Arabi from the country, the withdrawal of "the Colonels" into the interior, and the resignation of Sami's Ministry. The note added that the two governments would, if necessary, insist on the fulfilment of these conditions.

The ministers, on receipt of the "Dual Note," waited on the *khedive* to ask his opinion as to the answer that should be given, and His Highness distinctly told them that he accepted its conditions. They urged a reference to the *Porte*, on which the *khedive* told them that it was an internal question, and that it was strange that they, who had complained that he had failed to uphold the privileges of Egypt, should suggest such a course. On the 26th the ministers resigned, alleging as a reason that the *khedive*, in accepting the conditions of England and France, had acquiesced in foreign interference in Egypt.

The *khedive* promptly accepted the resignation of the ministry, and sent for Cherif Pasha to form a new Cabinet. Cherif refused on the ground that no government was possible while the military chiefs remained.

On the 27th an event occurred in Alexandria which tended to bring matters still more to a crisis. The officers of the regiments and the police force in that city held a secret meeting, and telegraphed to the *khedive* direct that they would not accept the resignation of Arabi, and gave the *khedive* twelve hours to reply, after which the officers declared that they would not be responsible for public tranquillity.

On receipt of this message, the *khedive* summoned to his presence the chief personages of State, the principal members of the chamber, and the head officers of the Cairo garrison, and placed the situation before them.

Toulba Pasha, one of Arabi's strongest supporters, interrupted the *khedive* in his speech, and stated that the army absolutely rejected the Dual Note, and awaited the decision of the *Porte*, which was the only authority they recognized. On the same day Arabi, at the head of a hundred officers, met the chief persons of Cairo and the notables, and demanded the deposition of the *khedive*, threatening death to the recalcitrant. Nevertheless almost all present, excepting the officers, persisted in supporting their sovereign. Arabi and the officers demanded of the *khedive* a decree reinstating Arabi as Minister of War. Amongst those present, Sultan Pasha and some of the notables warned the *khedive* of what had taken place, and told him his life was not safe unless he reinstated Arabi. The *khedive* consulted the English and French consuls-general, who advised him not to comply.

In the afternoon of the same day, a deputation consisting of the Coptic Patriarch, the Chief *rabbi*, the notables, and others, waited on the *khedive*, begging him to reinstate Arabi, adding, that though he might be ready to sacrifice his own life, he ought not to sacrifice theirs, and that Arabi had threatened them all with death if they did not obtain the *khedive*'s assent to his reappointment. In his perplexity, the *khedive*, in order to prevent bloodshed, yielded, and issued a memorandum stating that at the repeated requests of the population, and with the desire of maintaining order and the tranquillity of the country, he reinstated Arabi.

Although one may be disposed to blame Tewfik for his conduct on this occasion, it must be owned that his position at the moment was a critical one. The despatch of the fleets on which he had been led to rely had turned out a ridiculous fiasco. Instead of ten vessels, there were only two accompanied by four gunboats, and no troops for landing. The lamentable weakness of the demonstration only excited the ridicule of the military party. It was beyond doubt that the guard at the palace had been doubled, and that orders had been given to the sentries not to allow Tewfik to leave the palace unless the deputation received a favourable reply, and to fire on him if he insisted on going out. All the outlets of the palace were carefully watched, and a mob was collected for the purpose of rushing into the palace and ill-treating him, if the prayer of the deputation were refused. It was also announced that there was to be a military demonstration at five in the afternoon, and that it was the intention of the army to depose the *khedive*. Under these circumstances, and seeing how little material aid he had from England and France, it is not surprising that he yielded.

One of the first acts of Arabi on resuming office was to publish a declaration that now he had been reinstated, he guaranteed the security of the life and property of all the inhabitants of Egypt irrespective of nationality or religion. This assurance was not made before it was required.

For several days past a feeling of uneasiness had prevailed, especially in Alexandria; when the military and police in that city made their demand for Arabi's reinstatement, Mr. Cookson, the British consul, asked the governor, Omar Pasha Loutfi, if he could answer for the safety of Europeans. He replied that he had exhausted every effort to calm the officers and soldiers, but had entirely failed, and that he could not answer for their conduct, although he saw no reason to apprehend any disturbance.

In the prevailing state of things, the consul thought it his duty to confer with Admiral Seymour as to the best means of protecting British subjects in case of a general attack upon Europeans, and was informed that the admiral was not prepared to land any force, although he would protect the embarkation of women and children and others who might seek refuge on board ships in the harbour. The admiral sent an officer with the consul, and a spot for embarkation was selected.

This arrangement was communicated to the British residents at a meeting held at the Consulate the same day (the 28th).

The European population now became seriously alarmed, and on the 29th a memorial was drawn up by the British residents, calling upon Her Majesty's Government to provide efficient means for the protection of their lives. It pointed out that—

> During the twenty-four hours, from the 26th to the 27th, Alexandria was in continual danger of being stormed by the soldiery, who, it was reported, actually had cartridges served out to them to be used against Europeans.
>
> There was every reason to believe that the perils which had come without warning would recur again, and against them, Europeans were absolutely defenceless. They had not even the means of flight, as in order to reach the ships in harbour they would have to run the gauntlet through the streets. The small squadron in port could only silence the forts, and when these forts were disabled, then would commence a period of great danger for Europeans, who would be at the mercy of soldiers exasperated by defeat, whilst the English admiral could not risk his men ashore, as his whole available force for those operations did not exceed 300 men. The memorial concluded by stating that every day's delay increased the dangerous temper of the soldiery and their growing defiance of discipline.

Mr. Cookson at once telegraphed the contents of the memorial to the Foreign Office, where it was carefully placed amongst the archives.

The history of events has now been brought down to the 29th May, on which date Admiral Seymour reported that the Egyptians were raising earthworks opposite his flagship, the *Invincible*, then lying in the inner harbour at Alexandria, and suggested that his squadron should be strengthened by the despatch of three of the ships of war which had been left at Suda Bay.

In a later telegram he added that when the earthworks were armed, the position of the unarmoured vessels of his squadron would be untenable, if fired on without warning. In reply, the admiral was directed to arrange with the French admiral to dispose the ironclads so as to silence the batteries if they opened fire.

On the 30th May, the British ironclad *Monarch*, and two gun-vessels, the *Cygnet* and the *Coquette*, as well as three French vessels of war— the *Alma*, the *Thétis* and the *Hirondelle*—were ordered from Suda Bay to Alexandria, where they arrived between the 2nd and 5th June.

The rest of the British Squadron in Suda Bay were directed to cruise off the coast of Egypt, and to communicate with Alexandria for orders from time to time.

Arabi, on being applied to on the subject of the earthworks, answered that repairs only were being effected, and refused to order them to be discontinued. It was useless to remonstrate with the *khedive*, whose orders that all warlike preparations should be stopped had already been disregarded. The *sultan* was therefore appealed to, and he sent an order to Arabi to desist from further armament. Arabi gave the necessary instructions, and the new works, on which two guns were already mounted, were discontinued.

The *khedive*, on his part, applied to the *sultan*, and requested that an Imperial commissioner should be sent to Egypt. On the 3rd June it was known that Dervish Pasha, a Marshal of the Ottoman Empire, had left Constantinople for Alexandria as special envoy from the *sultan*, and his arrival was awaited with anxiety by both the *khedive* and the Arabists.

The following observations, taken from one of the highest authorities on Egyptian matters,[1] throw a light on Dervish Pasha's mission.

> The *sultan's* aim naturally was not to reinforce, but to counteract Anglo-French influence in Egypt. By accepting his intervention England and France confessed themselves worsted, and opened the door for a host of intrigues. His Majesty was not slow to take advantage of the opportunity and tried to play a complicated double game. Dervish Pasha, the first commissioner, was instructed to support the *khedive*, and if possible intimidate the leaders of the military party, while Ahmet Essad, the second commissioner, was instructed to conciliate Arabi and his friends, and assure them that they had in the *sultan* a sure friend and ally. The third commissioner's duty was to act as a spy on his two colleagues, and he in his turn was closely watched by a secretary, who sent secret reports direct to Constantinople.

On Dervish's arrival in Cairo, on the 7th of June, he was greeted by the acclamations of a mob of the lowest class of natives, who shouted before his carriage the praises of Arabi, and denounced the Christians.

---

1. *Egypt and the Egyptian Question*, by D. Mackenzie Wallace.

Dervish was known before his arrival to be accessible to Egyptian arguments, and there can be no doubt that they were boldly asked for and liberally given. Upon his arrival he showed marked favour to the Arabi party. Then he had a long interview with the *khedive*, and then his conduct suddenly became very satisfactory to the palace. Mahmoud Sami had arranged that the petitions from all the provinces should be brought to the Commissioner by deputation. Dervish received them graciously, placed the petitions in a pile on the divan, begged the deputation to consider all grievances settled by his arrival, and dismissed them.

The ministers came next. Mahmoud Sami entered with effusion, and introduced his colleagues. Dervish remained seated, continued his conversation with his secretary, and then made a casual remark to Sami on the beautiful situation of the Palace of Ghezireh. The ministers looked dumfounded, but Dervish, continuing his conversation, begged his secretary to repeat to him the story of the massacre of the Mamelukes by Mehemet Ali at the citadel,[2] which he could see from the window where he sat. When the suggestive story was completed, the envoy, with one of his pleasantest smiles, remarked to Arabi, 'The one man who escaped was a lucky dog,' and with a remark on the weather dismissed them.[3]

After this slap in the face the ministers left, feeling that there was no alternative between complete submission to the *khedive* and absolute defiance of the *sultan*.

Before two days elapsed, events occurred at Alexandria which demonstrated that Arabi was the only power in Egypt, and brought Dervish to his feet as a suppliant.

What those events were, will be recorded in the next chapter.

---

2. Every reader of Egyptian history will remember that the Mamelukes being in revolt against Mehemet Ali, were by a device induced to meet at the Citadel, where, with the exception of one who escaped by a perilous leap on horseback, they were all put to death.

3. *Khedives and Pashas*.

Chapter 7

The Riots at Alexandria

For some days previous to Sunday, the 11th June, 1882, the demeanour of the natives towards the European population of Alexandria had been growing more and more unfriendly; and there were many indications that some disturbance, the precise nature of which no one was able to discover, was impending. The forenoon of the 11th passed off quietly enough and without any unaccustomed incident, and the European population attended the churches and places of worship as usual.

Between two and three in the afternoon the tranquillity of the town was disturbed by shouts and yells from some two thousand natives, who were suddenly seen swarming up the Rue des Sœurs, the Rue Mahmoudieh, and the adjacent streets, crying, "Death to the Christians!" Others came soon after from the Attarin and the Ras-el-Tin quarters; and the riot, which appears to have broken out in three places almost at the same time, became general.

The crowd rushed on, striking with their "*naboots*" all the Europeans whom they could meet, knocking them down and trampling them under foot. Shots were fired; the soldiers and police interfered; but, in most instances, only with the object of making the butchery more complete. Many Europeans, flying for refuge to the police stations, were there slaughtered in cold blood. Shops and houses were broken into and pillaged, and for four and a half hours, until the soldiers arrived on the scene, the usually quiet and prosperous city of Alexandria experienced a fair share of the horrors of war.

The signal for the massacre was a feigned Arab funeral procession, in which natives marched wearing green turbans, and which passed between 10 a.m. and noon through the main streets of Alexandria.[1]

---
1. Parliamentary Papers, Egypt, No. 4, 1883.

The next thing which occurred was a disturbance which broke out about 1 p.m. between Europeans and natives in the neighbourhood of a coffee-house called the "*Café Crystal,*" in the Rue des Sœurs.

Of the precise origin of the riot it is difficult to speak with certainty. It has been stated that it originated in a dispute between a Maltese and a native coachman or donkey-boy, in which the Maltese, being beaten with a stick, retaliated with his knife, and, according to one account, killed his adversary. Another version is that two natives attempted to break into the shop of a Maltese with whom they had previously quarrelled, and were violently resisted by the owner. Both accounts are involved in doubt, and the better opinion is that whatever may have been the origin of the alleged quarrel, it was only a pretext for what was to ensue. Anyhow, about the time last mentioned, Mr. Cookson, the British Consul, was summoned by the local police to assist in quelling a disturbance between Maltese and natives in the quarter of the Caracol Labban, a police-station in the Rue des Sœurs. He found there the governor and sub-prefect of police, and, after waiting more than an hour, under the impression that they had succeeded in calming the excitement, Mr. Cookson returned to the consulate. This was not, however, until he had been struck by one of the stones which were flying about.

About 3 p.m. he found a messenger, purporting to come from the governor, to summon him with all the other consuls to a meeting at the same *caracol* as before.

There is good reason to believe that no such request was ever made by Omar Pasha Loutfi, and that the messages sent were part of a preconceived scheme to decoy the consuls into the streets, where they would be in the power of the mob. It is a singular thing that there were considerable intervals of time between the delivery of the messages, not warranted by the positions of the different consulates, as if the intention was for the consuls to arrive separately. Mr. Cookson, accompanied only by a *janissary* in uniform, drove immediately towards the *caracol*. He found marks of recent conflict in the streets and groups of excited natives moving about.

On approaching within about ninety yards of the *caracol*, at a place where four roads met, he was first assailed with stones and then felled to the ground with a blow from a "*naboot.*" When the consul recovered consciousness, he was lying in the street surrounded by a crowd, one or two members of which, including a native officer, were trying to protect him, whilst others were striking at him. Fortunately he was able to escape with his life to the *caracol*, where he remained till about 4 p.m., when he was brought by a circuitous route to the consulate.[2]

It has been stated that the inaction of the police at the different *caracols* was due to the fact that the day previous all the officers and sub-officers in charge had been convoked, and told that the men were to remain at their posts under any circumstances, without interfering even in the event of an outbreak happening.

Almost at the same time and place, the other members of the consular body, as they arrived on the scene, were similarly attacked.

All this time the governor was at the door of the *caracol*, giving orders to the *mustaphazin* (military police) to disperse the mob, though his orders were never executed. In fact, the *mustaphazin* were quite beyond his control, and at times openly cursed and reviled him when he tried to interfere on behalf of the Europeans.

Whilst the fighting went on, the Arabs, the police, and the soldiers occupied their time in breaking open and plundering the shops and houses on the line of route, tearing down doors and shutters, and using the materials as well as the legs of tables and chairs as weapons of offence.

The rioting gradually extended up the Rue des Sœurs, towards the Place Mehemet Ali (the great square), the Europeans here and there firing at times from the terraces and balconies of the houses, and the soldiers and the mob replying with firearms and stones.

At an early period of the fray, one of the *mustaphazin* was killed by a shot from a house, and his body being taken to an adjoining *caracol*, his comrades became so exasperated, that they butchered every European who sought refuge there.

In the streets, the conduct of the *mustaphazin* was almost equally bad. When they did interfere, they did so in a half-hearted, indifferent manner. In the great majority of cases, where they did not join in the killing themselves, they encouraged their countrymen to do so. There is reason to believe that the *mustaphazin* did a large proportion of the killing, as they were armed with sword-bayonets. The natives, on the other hand, had in most cases only heavy sticks, with which they stunned and bruised their victims.

A considerable number of Bedouins were observed amongst the mob, which emerged from the Rue des Sœurs by the side streets lead-

---

2. It is gratifying to be able to add that, as an acknowledgment of Mr. Cookson's services on this occasion, he received by telegraph an expression of sympathy from Her Majesty's Government.

ing into the adjoining quarters. The Bedouins were armed with their long guns, with which they shot down passing Europeans. One of a group of Bedouins, stationed opposite the European hospital to intercept the fugitives, was seen to shoot a man who was running past, and crouching down, in the hope of escaping observation.

About 4 p.m. a second mob came down from a different part of the town known as the Attarin quarter, and similar fighting went on, the natives attacking every European who came in their path. Amongst other victims was a little boy five years old, apparently a Maltese, who was killed with a *naboot* in front of the Austrian post office.

At half-past five, the portion of the Rue des Sœurs where the disturbance began was almost deserted, the ground being strewn with *débris* of wood and glass, and the windows shattered, many of them by bullets. Further up, and opposite the Lazarist College, in the same street, but nearer the Place Mehemet Ali, the crowd from the Attarin quarter mingled with the other mob were continuing the work of destruction. They hunted down every European they saw; one they fell upon and killed with sticks and pieces of wood at the very door of the college itself. All this while the *mustaphazin*, some thirty or forty in number, in front of the college, were observed firing off their rifles without any apparent motive. The street at this part was now filled with rioters. A number of Europeans found refuge at the college, the doors of which were bolted and barred by the inmates. From the terrace above these were able to look down on the work of destruction.

About 5.30 a European in black clothes, and apparently of good social position, covered with blood and with his trousers torn to rags, was seen running backwards and forwards, as if distracted. Just as he reached the corner of the Rue des Sœurs, a point guarded by two *mustaphazin*, a band of natives armed with sticks emerged from the street, rushed at once on him and beat him on the head. The two *mustaphazin* not only did not prevent the Arabs from ill-treating their victim, but, on the contrary, were seen to seize the wretched man by the arm, and laughing, thrust him into the midst of the band which was assailing him. Whether he subsequently escaped or not is unknown. One of these *mustaphazin* being remonstrated with, candidly replied, "We are ordered to do it."

In one spot in the Rue des Sœurs the bodies of three Europeans were found lying in a heap. One had a bullet-hole in the head, another was stabbed through the chest, and another with his skull fractured was lying on his face with his shoes and stockings stripped off.

The mob now turned their attention to indiscriminate pillage. The shops in the square itself were broken into and the kiosks wrecked. Next, crowds of looters were observed going back in the direction of Gabari, laden with goods from the neighbouring shops. These the *mustaphazin* allowed to pass without opposition; indeed, several of their own number were themselves carrying the stolen goods. Soldiers were seen to take from Europeans, whose lives they spared, their watches and such valuables as they had about them.

In the Strada Nuova both police and soldiers were observed encouraging the mob to break open shops, and each time this was done the police and soldiers entered first, and had the first choice.

In another quarter two native policemen were observed attacking even a native, who was carrying gold articles and a quantity of money, when a mounted soldier appeared on the scene, and he and the policemen shared the plunder between them, leaving the thief to go empty away. In their selection of objects of plunder the mob were far from particular. One soldier was seen walking down the street with a glass chandelier on his head. Another was seen riding down the street on a toy horse. The tobacco shops suffered more severely than any others; wherever one of these was seen, it was invariably broken into and the contents distributed among the crowd.

Wearing apparel, also, was in great request, and one of the native officers was observed sitting on the pavement exchanging the trousers he was wearing for a new pair stolen from a neighbouring shop. In the few cases where a native had not succeeded in obtaining any plunder for himself, he invariably turned to one of his more fortunate comrades and helped himself to his stock. One man who was carrying off some dozens of slippers was stopped by no less than three of his fellow-countrymen, who made him wait whilst they selected those which fitted them best.

Whilst this was occurring similar scenes of violence were being perpetrated in another part of the town, namely, in the streets leading from the Place Mehemet Ali to the Marina and to Ras-el-Tin.

On that Sunday a considerable number of Europeans had been to visit the ships in the harbour. On their return, between 4 and 5 p.m., they found the Marina Street, Frank Street, and the adjoining thoroughfares in the possession of a mob armed with *naboots*. What happened may be learned from the case of an English missionary, Mr. H. P. Ribton, one of the victims. Ribton, accompanied by his little daughter and two friends, was amongst those who had been afloat in the afternoon. On landing from the ships they found the city gate, leading from the Marina into the town, closed; but they were allowed to pass through by a door in the police-office. The shops were shut, and the streets were filled with soldiers. Ribton and party were in the rear of some other Europeans who had landed with them. Suddenly the police called out in Arabic, "Quick! quick!" and all the Europeans commenced running. In a moment or two those in front wheeled round, crying that the mob were coming. Mr. Ribton and his friends turned at the same time, but the police with fixed bayonets drove them back, and in an instant they found themselves face to face with the mob, who had already overwhelmed the Europeans in front.

The mob consisted of the lowest class of Arabs in the city; they were armed, like the rest, with clubs, with which they beat their victims to death. As soon as the latter fell the Arabs dragged them out to the back streets, stripped their bodies and flung them into the sea.

The missionary and his two male companions in vain attempted to shield his daughter from the blows. Though Ribton himself was twice felled to the ground he again staggered to his feet, attempting to save his daughter. The third time he fell he rose no more, and when afterwards his body was found his head was so battered as to be unrecognizable.[3] Ribton's two friends were killed by his side. His daughter was seized by a native soldier, who, throwing her across his shoulders, carried her off to the Arab quarter. Here she was rescued by a friendly *sheikh*, who had heard her screams, and who kept her in his house till nightfall, when he sent her home disguised in native clothes.

Some of the most atrocious acts of violence were perpetrated in immediate proximity to the *Zaptieh*, where is situated the prefecture of police. Here soldiers and mob, mixed together, pursued the Europeans who were passing on their way to the Marina in the hope of escaping to the ships. Whenever a European appeared in sight the mob cried out in Arabic, "Oh, Moslems! Kill him! Kill the Christian!"

The master of a Greek merchant ship was forced by the police to descend from his carriage, and bayoneted on the spot. A French subject, who was being pursued by the mob, applied to a soldier for protection. The latter responded by taking deliberate aim at him with his rifle and bringing him to the ground. A *mustaphazin* was seen holding a young man from behind, whilst a soldier shot him dead; his body was then maltreated and thrown into the sea.

---

3. The actual murderer of Mr. Ribton was Hag Mahomed Ismail, who was subsequently convicted and hanged.

A man on guard at the *Zaptieh*, or chief police office, was seen to shoot down a European who was running away from the mob, who speedily battered him to death.

Some officers of H.M.S. *Superb*, Lieutenants Saule and Dyrssen, Dr. Joyce and Mr. Pibworth, engineer, about 6 p.m., seeing the mob rushing towards them, attempted to obtain shelter at the Caracol Midan. The man on duty refused to admit them. They then ran to the Danish Consulate close by, where they were offered an asylum by the consul. As their ship was going to sea at 7 p.m., the officers were unwilling to stop, and, taking advantage of a carriage which had been secured, they proceeded towards the marina by Frank Street. When about halfway down they found themselves in the centre of the mob, who, howling and shouting, seized the horses' heads and commenced striking the officers with their sticks; several brandished knives, and one of them stabbed Mr. Pibworth, wounding him mortally, and attempted to stab the others. They then jumped from the carriage and managed to run through the crowd, receiving several blows in doing so. Mr. Pibworth was removed to the police station, where he died half-an-hour afterwards.

A fireman of the S.S. *Tanjore*, who was in a carriage with five of his companions, also on his way to the harbour, was stopped about 4 p.m. by the mob in the open piece of ground near the *Zaptieh*, and ordered to alight. They were then surrounded and beaten by the natives, some of the party receiving wounds from the swords of the *mustaphazin* drawn up there. The party tried their best to escape, but the fireman was dragged by the arm into the *Zaptieh*. Two minutes later he saw one of his companions brought in by a soldier. Almost at the same moment the guard on duty at the gate drew his sword and struck the man twice, splitting his skull with the first stroke, and severing his head from his body with the second. The fireman was detained for three hours, and, according to his statement, all who were brought in during that time were slaughtered.

Witnesses living near the *Zaptieh* spoke of the cries and groans which came from the building at this period, and another witness has stated that from a window opposite he counted no less than thirteen bodies of Europeans being dragged out and taken down a side street towards the sea.[4]

The rioting in the Rue des Sœurs, near the *caracol*, was at its height at 4.30 p.m., and that in Frank Street about 5.30 or 6, when the two mobs of rioters marched on until they united in the great square or

---
4. Parliamentary Blue Book, Egypt, No. 16, 1882, page 17.

Place Mehemet Ali.

The brutality of the mob extended even to the Arab children. One of them was seen to go up to the dead body of a European and fire off a toy-gun at his head, and the shoe-blacking boys in the Place Mehemet Ali were observed to beat out the brains of the wounded who lay groaning on the pavement.

Whilst this was going on, the troops, to the number of about 7,000, remained at the different barracks under arms, waiting instructions to act. The governor, about four in the afternoon, had asked the military commandant of the town to place at his disposal a battalion of the regiment at Ras-el-Tin; but the messenger returned, saying the colonel required an order in writing before he could move. The governor then sent the written order demanded, and also despatched an order to the colonel of the regiment at Rosetta Gate to send a battalion of his troops into the town without delay. He also, to prevent the disorder spreading to the Place Mehemet Ali and the Place de l'Eglise, ordered a company of *mustaphazin* to each of those places.

The *mustaphazin*, this time, obeyed, but the soldiers still remained drawn up at the barracks. In spite of the governor's request, they refused to march without an order from the Minister of War. Much valuable time was thus wasted.

Now came Arabi's opportunity. Arabi, it will be remembered, had, a few days before, been treated by Dervish Pasha as an ignoble rebel against the *sultan*, and made to feel his inferiority. When the news of the riot was telegraphed to Cairo the great envoy himself was sent to fetch Arabi, and had, almost on his knees, to beg him to intervene. Arabi consented, and the desired despatch was sent by telegraph from Cairo, and a little after 6 p.m. the soldiers began to march. As they advanced, the mob gradually fell back, and then dispersed as if by magic; and the tramping, shouting, and yelling suddenly ceased, and there was silence in the streets save for the groans of the wounded.

The behaviour of the troops was strictly in accordance with discipline. They had their orders to put an end to the disturbance, and they did so. One of them being asked if the massacre was finished, naively replied, "Yes; the order has come to cease striking."

In the course of the afternoon, hundreds of Europeans rushed for protection to the different consulates, where they remained with the gates closed and guarded. Every moment increased the number of fugitives. The British Consulate was literally crammed with officers, civilians, ladies and children.

Telephonic communication was open with Admiral Seymour on board the *Helicon*. The admiral had himself been on shore that afternoon, and narrowly escaped the rioters. His movements at this critical moment were marked by great indecision. His first idea appears to have been to land an armed force for the protection of the Europeans, for at 5.32 p.m. the *Helicon* made the general signal to the fleet, "Prepare to land armed boats." This order, however, was annulled five minutes later. The captains of the English men-of-war were then signalled to assemble on board the flag-ship, when, after consultation, it was decided, as the only course open, to send boats round to the Eastern Harbour under cover of the guns of H.M.S. *Superb*, to be in readiness to embark those who had taken refuge in the consulate; and boats were sent to the arsenal and other landing-places to bring off the officers who remained on shore.

It had been arranged that the *Superb* was to take up a position off the Eastern Harbour, near the European quarter, and to have a force of seamen and marines ready for immediate service on shore, sending her boats as near as possible to the beach, with a view to the removal from the town of all the women and children whom they might be able to find. The landing party, to be used only in case of need, was, on a signal being made, to clear the streets leading to the English Consulate.

Between 8 and 9 p.m. the governor, to whom the arrangements were communicated, begged that the boats might not be sent, as their appearance would, in his opinion, excite the troops beyond control. He also stated that the disturbance had now been suppressed, and that he could guarantee the safety of everybody. Under these circumstances, it was decided that the instructions to the *Superb* should be countermanded. This, however, appears not to have been communicated to that vessel.

The night passed off badly enough at the consulate, which was crowded with terrified fugitives. There were, however, no serious alarms until about 11.30, when an event happened which might have brought about a catastrophe.

One of the *Superb's* armed boats, mistaking a bright light on the shore for the signal arranged in the event of the boats being required to land, answered the supposed signal with a blue light, and thus disclosed her position near the shore, hitherto concealed by the darkness. In an instant the bugles sounded the alarm, there was a call to arms all over the town, and a rush made by the troops towards the beach, showing that the governor's fears were well founded, and that had the boats touched the shore, the troops, already much excited, would have been quite beyond the control of their officers. There was not a moment to be lost. A peremptory order was sent from the consulate to the officer in charge of the boats to withdraw out of sight, and the soldiers, seeing no signs of a landing, retired to their posts.

The rest of the night passed quietly and without incident. The population mostly remained indoors, and detachments of soldiers with fixed bayonets guarded the various consulates and stationed themselves at the corners of all the principal streets. But for these circumstances, and for the broken *débris* from the wrecked shops and houses, there was little to indicate that anything unusual had taken place.

There are no means of arriving accurately at the numbers killed on the 11th June, but they have been estimated, by competent persons, at one hundred and fifty Europeans, besides natives.[5] Many of the latter are known to have been off to the houses at nightfall and then secretly buried. The European doctors who visited the hospitals on the following day found forty-nine bodies—forty-four of which were Europeans. Thirty-seven were so battered as to be unrecognizable. Seventy-one persons were also found wounded; of these, thirty-six were Europeans, two Turks, and thirty-three natives. Of those killed or wounded, some had received stabs on their bodies, but the majority had their injuries inflicted by *naboots*. One witness speaks to having seen several cartloads of bodies thrown, at night, into the sea near the Western Harbour, and it is quite possible that many were so disposed of. In a fluctuating population, such as that of Alexandria, it is obvious that many persons might disappear and never be inquired for.

The governor, on the 12th, visited the sacked and looted quarters of the town, and took note of the houses injured. He also arrested and imprisoned between two and three hundred natives who had taken part in the riot of the previous day.

On the same day, the women and children, who had taken refuge at the British Consulate, embarked under an escort provided by the governor. Thousands of other Europeans of all nationalities also went afloat, and during the whole day the streets were blocked with fugitives. At first these were cursed and spat upon by the natives as they passed, but later on they were allowed to go by unmolested.

In Cairo a meeting was held at which the *khedive*, Dervish Pasha,

---

5. It is only right to mention that the authenticated cases are less than half the number above given.

the ministers, and the consuls-general were present. This was to obtain a reply to a demand of the consular body that measures should be taken to insure the safety of Europeans. Arabi promptly undertook to stop all inflammatory preaching, and to obey all orders given him by the *khedive*. The *khedive* engaged himself to issue orders immediately with the object of restoring public tranquillity. Dervish Pasha, on his part, consented to accept joint responsibility with Arabi for the execution of the orders of the *khedive*.

It was then decided to increase the number of patrols and to reinforce the police stations by troops. Yacoub Pasha Sami, Under-Secretary of War, was sent from Cairo with two regiments of infantry and some artillery. Guards with their arms were placed at the corners of the streets, and at night they lay down on the ground in the Place Mehemet Ali and other open spaces. In the course of the day a proclamation was issued by the consular body to the Europeans, pointing out that the disorder had been suppressed by the army, and that its chiefs guaranteed public tranquillity. It further called upon the European population to remain in their dwellings, and to abstain from carrying firearms. The effect of the proclamation in reassuring the inhabitants was simply nil, and many persons who might otherwise have remained on shore betook themselves to the ships.

On the 13th the *khedive* and Dervish Pasha arrived from Cairo. Their reception was anything but enthusiastic.

Alexandria remained quiet, the streets being still patrolled by soldiers night and day. The general flight of Europeans continued. The number seeking refuge on board the ironclads was so great that the ships would have been useless in the event of their having to act. Three hundred were on board the *Invincible*, the same number on board the *Monarch*, and all the smaller men-of-war were similarly crowded. On the admiral's representation, merchant-steamers were chartered by the British Government, and employed to take the refugees to Malta; one of the *Poste-khedive* steamers was, subsequently, taken up as a temporary refuge, and some hundreds of persons were placed on board. Other steamers were thronged with passengers leaving for Cyprus, Constantinople, and other places; fabulous prices were charged the fugitives by the boatmen who took them off to the various vessels.

A Commission of Inquiry was next instituted by the Egyptian Government, with a view to discover the authors of the events of the 11th June. The president of the commission, oddly enough, was Omar Pasha Loutfi, Governor of Alexandria, the official who was responsible for the maintenance of order on the day in question, and who was therefore himself, to some extent, on his trial. The commission assembled, and evidence was taken from the wounded and others. An English barrister attended as the delegate of the British Consulate. Before the inquiry had proceeded far it developed into mutual recriminations, and a pretext was afforded to the Egyptian Government for bringing counter charges against Europeans. Eventually such determined opposition was raised by the Egyptian members to the institution of a satisfactory inquiry that the British delegate had to be withdrawn, and the Commission collapsed.

On the 20th of June a new ministry under Ragheb Pasha, an old and infirm statesman, was formed. In this, as before, Arabi figured as Minister of War. The men forming the cabinet were not such, however, as to inspire confidence. Many of them were pronounced Arabists, and the rest were about fair specimens of the usual Egyptian minister.

Arabi, who had come to Alexandria at this time, now made a point of showing himself a good deal in public, driving out every evening, sometimes in the same carriage with the *khedive*, and always attended by a cavalry escort. On these occasions great crowds of natives assembled, and showed unmistakably the interest they took in the *de facto* ruler of Egypt.

That Arabi and the *sultan* were in accord at this time is unquestionable. But if any doubt existed it was removed by the fact that on the 25th June the *sultan* decorated with the Grand Cordon of the Medjidieh the man who had plunged his country into anarchy. The order was presented by the *khedive* personally, who (Arabi declares) expressed his satisfaction and gratitude for his faithful services and attention to duty.

The attitude of Tewfik, on this as on other occasions, appears at first sight inexplicable. It is only to be accounted for on the hypothesis that His Highness, having just reason to doubt how far he could calculate on the sincerity of England and France, or on receiving help from them, was unwilling to cut himself altogether adrift from the National Party.

It is due to Arabi to say that during the period which elapsed between the day of the massacre and the subsequent bombardment perfect order was maintained in Alexandria. It was not so in the interior, however, and on the 26th June it was reported that ten Greeks and three Jews were massacred at Benha, an important town in the Delta. In other provincial towns, Europeans were openly insulted by the natives, and soon began to join the fugitives to Europe. At Rosetta and Damietta, things grew so threatening that even the European lighthouse-keepers had to be withdrawn, and their duties confided to natives.

At Alexandria, the British Consul, disabled by the wounds which he received on the 11th June, had to leave for Europe. The vice-consul, incapacitated by age, and suffering from the shock brought about by recent events, had also to depart. Most of the consular clerks and *employés* likewise found it necessary to quit their posts, and Sir Edward Malet, overtaken at a critical moment by severe illness, had to betake himself to Europe. In this emergency, Mr. Cartwright was called upon to discharge the duties of consul-general, assisted by the knowledge and local experience of Sir Auckland Colvin.

On the 29th June, Mr. Cartwright wrote to Lord Granville as follows:—

> The exodus of Europeans and the preparations for flight, after seeming temporarily to have abated, continue with increased vigour. The hotels are closing; the shipping agents have transferred their offices to the neighbourhood of the port; and the banks which still remain open are preparing to transfer their staff to the ships. It is impossible to describe the collapse and ruin which have overtaken the country. . . . A large number of respectable natives are leaving. The departure of Turkish families is taking larger proportions, while 200 destitute Jews and Rayahs have been sent away at the expense of the government itself.

Thrown out of employment by the exodus of Europeans, the greatest distress prevailed, and it was estimated that nearly 30,000 persons were left destitute in Alexandria alone.

Thus matters went on, until the measures taken by the government in adding to the armament of the forts led to actual hostilities. On the part of the Europeans, a sort of stunned feeling prevailed; there was, with a few exceptions, absolute panic. On the side of the natives, there was a vague feeling of disquietude. They realized that they had irretrievably committed themselves, and imagined that the day of retribution was drawing nigh.

Ships of war continued to arrive from all parts, until a squadron of twenty-six vessels belonging to the navies of England, France, Italy, Austria, Russia, the United States, Spain, Greece, and Turkey, lay off

Alexandria.

Meanwhile, the crowd of fugitives continued to embark. The French and Greek Governments sent transports to remove their subjects *en masse*, and ships laden with British refugees left for Malta as fast as the vessels could fill up. Europeans arrived from Cairo and the interior, and the trains were thronged with passengers, many of whom rode on the roofs and steps of the railway carriages. As many as 4,000 arrived on one day, the 15th.

Alexandria, at this period, presented a curious spectacle. Beyond the business of transporting the fugitives, there was nothing else done. The shops were shut, and the doors barred and padlocked. The banks were occupied in putting up iron shutters, and blocking up their windows. The few business firms which remained hired steamers in the harbour and removed their books and effects on board, so as to be ready for any eventuality. The streets in the European quarter presented a deserted appearance, the Arab soldiers being almost the only persons seen about.

In Cairo things were but little better, the whole of the foreign population had taken flight, together with most of the well-to-do natives.[6]

The events of the 11th June created a profound sensation in England. That a large number of unoffending Europeans, living in a civilized or quasi-civilized country, should have been without provocation suddenly attacked and slaughtered, was bad enough. But that this should have occurred at a moment when eight British ships of war, and nine others belonging to other powers, were there, for the avowed purpose of protecting European life and property, was worse still.

The opportunity was not lost upon the Opposition. Indignation meetings were held throughout the United Kingdom, in which the conduct of Mr. Gladstone's Administration was denounced in the strongest terms. Lord Salisbury, as the leader of the Opposition in the House of Lords, was particularly vehement in his condemnation of a policy which had resulted in British subjects being "butchered under the very guns of the fleet, which had never budged an inch to save them."

---

6. Mr. Simon Wolff, the United States Consul-General, was invited by one of his colleagues to flee with the rest, as "there was to be a massacre of all the Europeans and Christians." Mr. Wolff, who was a member of the Hebrew community, remarked that he did not see how that would affect him, as he was neither one nor the other, and he remained at his post.

On board the vessels of the British fleet, a similar feeling of indignation prevailed. When the bodies of the officer and seamen massacred were on the 13th June taken out to sea for burial, officers and men alike clamoured for revenge. It was felt that an insult had been offered to the British flag, which ought to be avenged.

Public feeling at home became fully aroused, and Her Majesty's Government caused it to be intimated that it was their intention to demand reparation for the loss of life and property which had occurred. To strengthen the Mediterranean fleet, the Channel Squadron, consisting of the *Minotaur, Achilles, Agincourt, Northumberland* and *Sultan*, was despatched to Malta on the 15th, and placed under the temporary command of Admiral Seymour. More energetic measures still were in contemplation, but it was deemed unwise to decide upon them until the great body of Europeans should have had time to clear out of Egypt.

Chapter 8

The Alexandria Bombardment

On the 1st of July, 1882, matters had become so threatening that the consular archives and such of the staff as remained were removed on board a Peninsular and Oriental steamer, chartered as a place of refuge for the British subjects whose duties compelled them to remain in Egypt.

The same day Admiral Seymour telegraphed that there were upwards of 10,000 men in the forts and barracks of Alexandria, and that Arabi hoped to get the allied fleets into a trap by sinking stone barges at the harbour mouth.

On the 3rd, Seymour received the following instructions:—

> Prevent any attempt to bar channel into port. If work is resumed on earthworks or fresh guns mounted, inform military commander that you have orders to prevent it; and if not immediately discontinued destroy earthworks and silence batteries if they open fire.

On the 4th, Dervish *pasha* made a final attempt to get rid of Arabi and his party by diplomacy. The Turkish Envoy invited the Minister of War to go to Constantinople "to live with the *sultan* and other friends." Arabi, to his credit, refused to desert his followers, and replied that the people would not suffer him to leave, and that as they were attached to him he could not abandon them.

The same day a telegram was sent to the admiral as follows:—

> Acquaint Military Governor that any attempt to bar the channel will be considered as a hostile act, which will be treated accordingly. Concert with consul-general as to notice to Europeans if occasion arises. Before taking any hostile step, invite

co-operation of French admiral; but you are not to postpone acting on your instructions because French decline to join.

The admiral replied:—

> Two additional guns placed in Pharos Castle last night. Parapet facing sea-wall was also strengthened. Consul-general would prefer I postponed operations until Thursday morning to allow time for people to quit Cairo. No change in the works bearing on the harbour. French admiral has asked for orders.

Seymour had now taken steps for strengthening the fleet, by ordering the ironclad *Sultan* from Malta. He had also received intelligence that two battalions had been ordered to Cyprus from Malta in ships of the Channel squadron. He had, moreover, in concert with the acting consul-general, succeeded in getting nearly the whole of the European residents out of the country. It only remained to see how far, in the event of action becoming necessary, he could count on the support of the Power which had joined England in presenting the celebrated Joint Note.

On the question being put to M. de Freycinet by Lord Lyons, the French foreign minister replied that his government had decided "not to instruct Admiral Conrad to associate himself with the English admiral in stopping by force the erection of batteries or the placing of guns at Alexandria." The reasons given were, that such a step would be an act of war, which could not be resorted to without the consent of the legislature, and that if the government applied to the Chamber for sanction, they did not feel sure of obtaining it.

On the 6th, the French ambassador called on Lord Granville and informed him, that in the event of a bombardment taking place, the French ships would go to Port Saïd.

On the same day, Admiral Seymour, finding that the warlike preparations on shore were continuing, wrote to the military commandant of Alexandria, that unless such proceedings were discontinued, it would become his duty to open fire on the works in course of construction.

The following reply was received:—

> To the Admiral of the British Fleet.
> My Friend English Admiral,
> I had the honour to receive your letter of the 6th July, in which you state that you had been informed that two guns had been

THE BOMBARDME

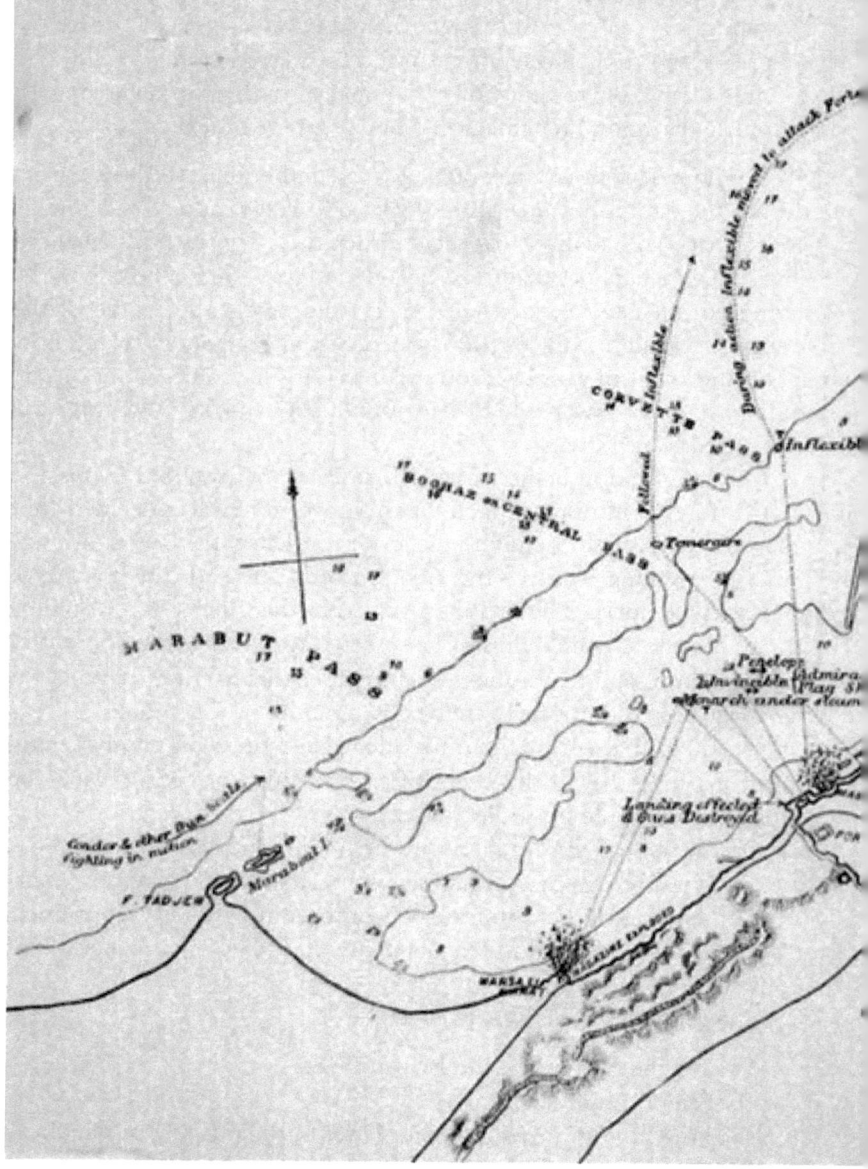

OF ALEXANDRIA.

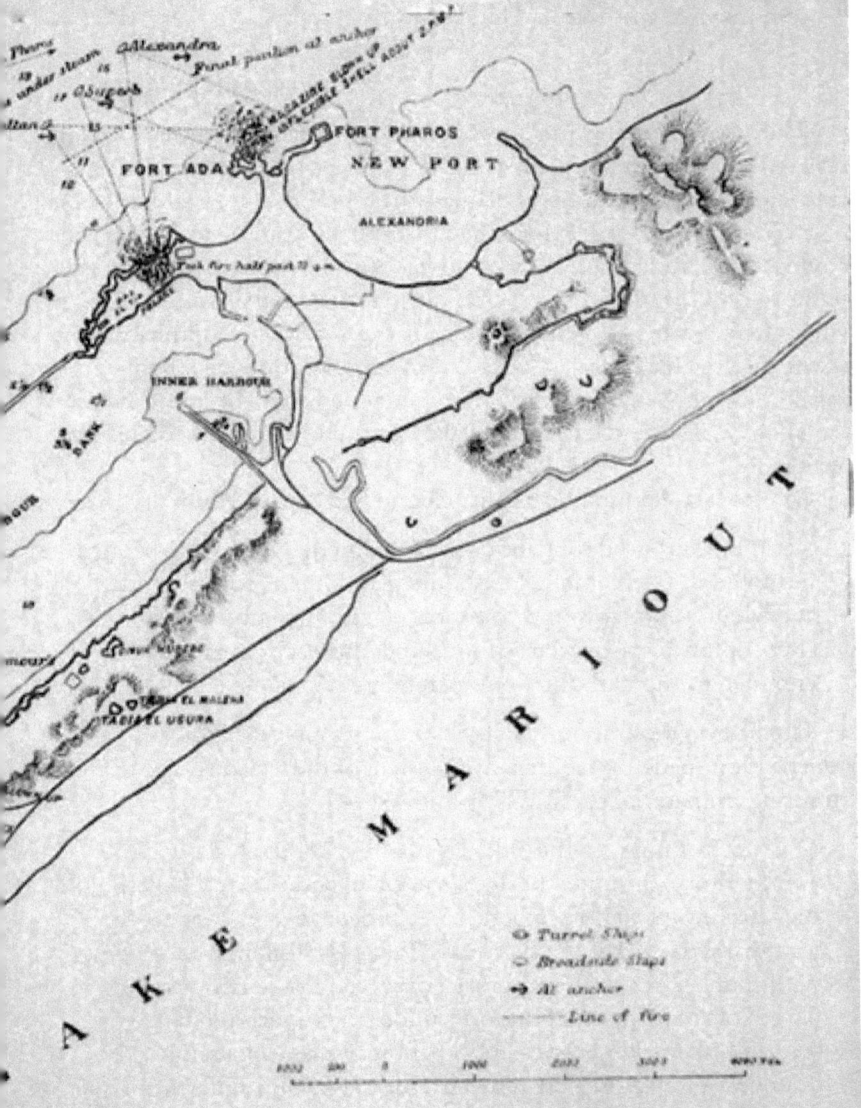

mounted and that other works are going on on the sea-shore, and in reply I assure you that these assertions are unfounded, and that this information is like the intimation given to you about the blocking up of the entrance to the harbour, of the falseness of which you were convinced. I rely on your feelings of humanity, and beg you to accept my respects.

(Signed) Toulba,
Commandant of Forces.

The *khedive* during this period retained great self-possession. He realized perfectly the difficulties of his position, and sent for Sir Auckland Colvin, to whom he explained that should a bombardment be resolved upon he was determined to remain faithful to Egypt. He could not, he said, desert those who had stood by him during the crisis, nor could he, merely to secure his personal safety, abandon Egypt when attacked by a foreign power. In the event of a bombardment taking place, His Highness announced his intention of retiring to a palace on the Mahmoudieh Canal, and added that the more rapidly the affair was conducted, the less danger there would be for himself personally.

On the 9th, Admiral Seymour telegraphed to the Admiralty that:

.... there was no doubt about the armament. Guns were being mounted in Fort Silsileh. He should give foreign consuls notice at daylight tomorrow, and commence action twenty-four hours after, unless forts on the isthmus and those commanding the entrance to the harbour were surrendered.

The information upon which Seymour proposed to act was partly a declaration made by Lieutenant Dorrien, of the *Invincible*, and which (omitting immaterial parts) was as follows:—

On the morning of the 9th day of July, 1882, at about 7.30 a.m., I drove through the Rosetta Gate, and . . . reached the old quarantine station, where I . . . proceeded on foot to the fort marked on Admiralty Chart 'Tabia-el-Silsileh,' and when within fifty yards of the said fort I observed inside two working parties of Arabs about 200 strong, under the superintendence of soldiers, parbuckling two smooth-bore guns—apparently 32-pounders—towards their respective carriages and slides, which were facing in the direction of the harbour, and which seemed to have been lately placed ready for their reception.

On the 10th, the Admiralty telegraphed to the admiral directing him to substitute for the word "surrendered" the words "temporarily surrendered for the purposes of disarmament."

The same day, the admiral sent his ultimatum to the military commandant, in the terms following:—

> I have the honour to inform your Excellency that as hostile preparations, evidently directed against the squadron under my command, were in progress during yesterday at Forts Pharos and Silsileh, I shall carry out the intention expressed to you in my letter of the 6th instant, at sunrise tomorrow, the 11th instant, unless previous to that hour you shall have temporarily surrendered to me, for the purpose of disarming, the batteries on the isthmus of Ras-el-Tin and the southern shore of the harbour of Alexandria.

The actual danger to Admiral Seymour's ships from the Egyptian preparations was at this time simply nil, and even were it otherwise he had only to make a slight change in the position of his vessels to place them completely out of harm's way. At the same time, the bombardment which he threatened, had, after the events of the 11th of June, become, in a certain sense, a necessity, if only to restore European prestige in Egypt: moreover, it formed the first step towards shattering the power of Arabi and his army, which was now, to a great extent, concentrated in Alexandria.

In hurrying on the bombardment, the admiral was probably influenced not a little by the desire to allay the growing impatience of the officers and men under his command. Ever since the murder of an officer and two men of the fleet, on the day of the riot, a good deal of dissatisfaction was expressed at the continued inaction of the naval force, not only by the seamen, but by the officers as well.

It was foreseen that the arrival of British troops was only a question of days, and the bluejackets naturally desired that, as what had taken place was an insult to the fleet, to the fleet should be given the work of avenging it. They were unwilling, as they put it, that they should be employed merely "to carry Sir Garnet Wolseley's baggage on shore."

The admiral himself, whilst sharing these sentiments, may not unnaturally have had in his mind the fact that the Channel squadron, under Admiral Dowell, was on its way to share in the honours of the day.

On the receipt of Admiral Seymour's ultimatum, a Cabinet Council was held at Ras-el-Tin, presided over by the *khedive* in person. It was decided to send a deputation to the admiral, to inform him that no new guns were being mounted in the forts, and to tell him that he was at liberty to send one of his officers, if he desired to test the truth of this statement. The deputation came back with the answer that the admiral insisted on the disarmament of the forts.

The council again met in the afternoon, and decided that the Silsileh Fort and Fort Pharos, and the guns placed in them on the Eastern Harbour, could not constitute any threat towards the vessels which were in the Western Harbour, and that the president of the council should write to the admiral in the terms of the despatch mentioned below. It was at the same time resolved that in the event of the admiral persisting in opening fire, the forts should not answer until the fifth shot, when they were to reply.

Alexandria, July 10th, 1882.

Admiral,

As I had the honour to promise in the conversation I had with you this morning, I have submitted to His Highness the *khedive*, in a meeting of the ministers and principal dignitaries of the State, the conditions contained in the letter you were good enough to address this morning to the commandant of the place, according to the terms of which you will put into execution tomorrow, the 11th instant, at daybreak, the intentions expressed in your letter of the 6th instant to the commandant of the place, if before that time the batteries on the isthmus of Ras-el-Tin and the southern shore of the port of Alexandria are not temporarily surrendered to you, to be disarmed.

I regret to announce to you that the government of His Highness does not consider this proposition as acceptable. It does not in the least desire to alter its good relations with Great Britain, but it cannot perceive that it has taken any measures which can be regarded as a menace to the English fleet by works, by the mounting of new guns, or by other military preparations.

Nevertheless, as a proof of our spirit of conciliation, and of our desire, to a certain extent, to accede to your demands, we are disposed to dismount three guns in the batteries you have mentioned, either separated or together.

If in spite of this offer you persist in opening fire, the government reserves its freedom of action and leaves with you the responsibility of this act of aggression.[1]

The previous day the Acting British Consul-General visited the *khedive* and urged his removal to Ramleh, a suburb about four miles to the east of Alexandria. On the 10th Sir Auckland Colvin called to say farewell to His Highness, and used every argument to induce him to embark in one of the British vessels, but in vain. Tewfik remained firm, and announced his intention of standing by his country.

At seven in the evening all the consuls-general were warned to withdraw their subjects. The acting British Consul-General and Sir Auckland Colvin embarked on board the *Monarch*, and the few remaining British residents betook themselves to the P. & O. s.s. *Tanjore*.[2]

In the course of the day all the merchant vessels in the harbour left, and these were followed by the foreign men-of-war. One by one the latter steamed slowly out, and as they passed the British flag-ship her band struck up the different national airs. The last ship to leave was the Austrian frigate *Landon*, and when darkness closed in, the English ships of war were alone in the harbour of Alexandria.

At 9.20 p.m. the admiral, in the *Invincible*, with the *Monarch* in company, weighed anchor, and steamed to a position outside the harbour. All lights were extinguished, and perfect silence was maintained as the ships cautiously felt their way through the water. At 10.10 both vessels came to an anchor off Mex, where their consort, the *Penelope*, was already lying.

In the meantime, all the ships, including the larger ironclads *Sultan*, *Superb*, *Temeraire*, *Alexandra*, and *Inflexible*, which were lying in the offing, had struck their upper masts, sent down top-gallant and royal yards, and got everything ready for action. In this state they remained for the night.

In order to give the reader an idea of the comparative strength of the opposing forces, it is necessary, in the first place, to give a short description of the fortifications of Alexandria and their armaments.

---

1. This despatch was not delivered to the admiral till the following day.
2. There were, however, two exceptions which deserve to be mentioned. One was Mr. J. Easton Cornish, the English manager of the Alexandria Water Works, who resolutely refused to desert his post. The other was the Director-General of the Egyptian Postal Administration, the late Halton Pasha, likewise an Englishman, who, having a large number of European *employés* under his care, determined not to forsake them, and embarked at the last moment with them in a small steamer which remained moored alongside the breakwater during the bombardment.

Alexandria is situated on a strip of land between the Mediterranean and Lake Mareotis; a considerable portion of the town stands on a promontory, which, jutting out from the rest towards the north-west, is bounded on the north-east by the new or Eastern Harbour, and on the south-west by the old or Western Harbour.

The fortifications, which were intended to protect the city from an attack, not only by sea, but also from the direction of Lake Mareotis, are said to have been planned in Paris, and executed under the direction of French engineers. The whole of the works were originally well built, but had fallen much out of repair.

The material used was a soft limestone but little calculated to withstand modern artillery. The parapets were of sand, covered with a thin coating of cement. The scarps and counterscarps were riveted with stonework. The rifled guns, without exception, fired through embrasures, and nearly all the smooth-bore guns fired over parapets.

The buildings were none of them bomb-proof; nor, except in the case of Fort Pharos, were there any casemated or covered batteries. The forts on the sea face of Alexandria may be summed up as follows:—

West of Alexandria—Forts Marabout, Adjemi, and Marza-el-Kanat.

South-west of Alexandria—Citadel of Mex, Old Fort of Mex, and Mex Lines.

South of Alexandria—Forts Kamaria, Omuk Kubebe, Saleh Aga, and a small battery between the two last named works.

North of Alexandria—Lighthouse or Ras-el-Tin Fort, Lines of Ras-el-Tin (including the Hospital Battery), Fort Adda, Fort Pharos, and Fort Silsileh.

Of the above, Fort Adjemi took no part in the subsequent bombardment.

The British squadron consisted of the ironclads *Alexandra, Superb, Sultan, Temeraire, Inflexible, Monarch, Invincible,* and Penelope, the torpedo-vessel *Hecla*, the despatch boat *Helicon*, the gun-vessels *Condor* and *Bittern*, and the gunboats *Beacon, Cygnet,* and *Decoy.* The battleships, with the exception of the *Invincible* and *Penelope*, were the most powerful then in the British navy. Their size and armament may be briefly summarized:—

The *Alexandra*, Captain C. F. Hotham, 9,490 tons, 8,610 h.p.,

674 men, 2 11-inch 25-ton and 10 10-inch 18-ton guns.

The *Superb*, Captain Thomas Le Hunt-Ward, 9,170 tons, 6,580 h.p., 620 men, 8 18-ton and 4 12-1/2-ton guns.

The *Sultan*, Captain W. J. Hunt Grubbe, 9,290 tons, 7,720 h.p., 620 men, 8 18-ton and 4 12-1/2-ton guns.

The *Temeraire*, Captain H. F. Nicholson, 8,450 tons, 7,520 h.p., 530 men, 4 25-ton and 4 18-ton guns.

The *Inflexible*, Captain John Fisher, 11,407 tons, 8,010 h.p., 440 men, 4 80-ton guns (in two turrets).

The *Monarch*, Captain Henry Fairfax, 8,320 tons, 7,840 h.p., 530 men, 4 25-ton, 2 9-inch 12-ton and 1 7-inch 6-1/2-ton guns.

The *Invincible*, Captain R. H. Molyneux, 6,010 tons, 4,830 h.p., 480 men, 10 9-inch 12-ton and 4 64-pounder guns.

The *Penelope*, Captain St. G. D. A. Irvine, 4,390 tons, 4,700 h.p., 230 men, 8 8-inch 9-ton and 3 40-pounder guns.

The *Hecla*, torpedo vessel, 6,400 tons, 1,760 h.p., 251 men, and 6 guns.

The *Helicon*, despatch vessel, 1,000 tons, carrying 2 20-pounder guns.

The *Condor* and *Bittern*, gun-vessels, 805 tons, 100 men, 1 7-inch and 2 40-pounder guns each.

The *Beacon*, gunboat, 603 tons, 80 men, 1 7-inch and 1 64-pounder gun.

The *Cygnet* and *Decoy*, gunboats, 455 and 430 tons, 60 men, 2 64-pounder and 2 20-pounder guns each.

In addition to the armament above given, the eight ironclads each carried from six to eight 20-pounder rifled breech-loading guns, and, with the exception of the *Penelope*, from eight to twelve machine guns.

There were also 880 supernumerary seamen and marines on board the fleet, making the total force 5,728 men.

The relative strength of the opposing forces may be seen from the following tables:—

The ordnance *mounted* in the forts was as follows:—

Fort or Battery.	R. Guns.	S. B. Guns.	Mortars.	Total.
Fort Silsileh	2	3	1	6
„ Pharos	8	37	4	49
„ Adda	5	14	5	24
Ras-el-Tin Lines	9	30	10	49
Lighthouse Fort, or Ras-el-Tin	6	28	3	37
Fort Saleh Aga	...	12	...	12
Battery	...	4	...	4
Fort Omuk Kubebe	2	16	2	20
„ Kamaria	...	5	1	6
Mex Sea Lines	...	24	...	24
„ Fort	5	9	5	19
Fort Marabout	3	8	...	11
TOTAL...	40	190	31	261

The guns on board the ironclads are shewn in the following table:—

SHIPS.	Rifled Guns.									Total
	in. 16	in. 12	in. 11	in. 10	in. 9	in. 8	in. 7	pr. 64	pr. 40	
Alexandra	...	...	2	10	...	...	...	...	...	12
Inflexible	4	...	...	...	...	...	...	...	...	4
Superb	...	...	...	16	...	...	...	...	...	16
Sultan	...	...	...	8	4	...	...	...	...	12
Temeraire	...	...	4	4	...	...	...	...	...	8
Invincible	...	...	...	...	10	...	...	4	...	14
Monarch	...	4	...	...	2	...	1	...	...	7
Penelope	...	...	...	...	...	8	...	...	3	11
TOTAL...	4	4	6	38	16	8	1	4	3	84

This does not include the six to eight 20-pounder guns and eight to twelve machine guns carried by each vessel.

Admiral Seymour's plan for the bombardment comprised two separate attacks: one by the *Sultan, Superb, Alexandra, Inflexible,* and *Temeraire* from outside the breakwater, the other by the *Invincible, Monarch,* and *Penelope* inside the reefs.

The three first-mentioned vessels, supported by the fire from the after turret of the *Inflexible,* which was anchored off the Corvette Pass, were directed to destroy the batteries on the Ras-el-Tin peninsula, and then to move to the eastward and attack Forts Pharos and Silsileh. The *Invincible, Monarch,* and *Penelope,* aided by the fire from the *Inflexible's* forward turret and by the *Temeraire,* which took up a position off the Boghas Pass, were ordered to open fire on the guns in the Mex Lines.

The gun-vessels and gunboats were directed to remain outside until a favourable opportunity should offer for moving in to the attack on Mex.

At 7 a.m. the admiral, whose flag was flying from the *Invincible*, signalled to the *Alexandra* to fire a shell into the recently armed works on Ras-el-Tin, known as the Hospital Battery, and followed this by a general signal to the fleet, "Attack the enemy's batteries." Upon this immediate action began between all the ships, in the positions assigned to them, and the whole of the forts commanding the entrance to the harbour.

A steady cannonade was maintained both by the attacking and defending forces, and for the next few hours the roar of the guns and the shrieks of passing shot and shell were alone audible. The spectacle as seen from the offing was imposing in the extreme. On the one side were the most powerful ships of modern times, all in fighting trim, with upper masts and yards struck, some slowly steaming ahead, others at anchor, but all pouring deadly broadsides into the Egyptian batteries. On the other were the forts, standing out bright and clear in the sunshine, vomiting forth volleys of fire and smoke in the direction of the attacking squadron.

The weather was fine and the sea smooth, both of which circumstances were to the advantage of the attacking force. On the other hand, the wind and sun were in the enemy's favour, and the smoke, which rose like a thick wall, at times prevented those on board the ships seeing the result of their fire.

At 9.40 the *Sultan*, *Superb*, and *Alexandra*, of the outside squadron, which had previously been under way and turning in succession at a range of about 1,500 yards, came to an anchor off the Lighthouse Fort. The batteries had proved stronger than had been anticipated, and the Egyptian gunners were making very good practice. The firing of the ships at the same time was less effective than could be wished. Under these circumstances, and to obtain the exact range, the three ships adopted a stationary position, and from this moment their fire steadily improved.

A little after 10 o'clock the *harem* buildings of Ras-el-Tin Palace were set on fire and partly destroyed by a shell.

At 10.30 the *Alexandra* had one of her heavy guns dismounted and rendered unserviceable. Shortly after the *Inflexible* weighed anchor and joined the *Sultan*, *Superb*, and *Alexandra*, and by 12.30 p.m. the combined fire of the four ships had nearly silenced all the guns in the Ras-el-Tin Forts. It should be mentioned that, in addition to helping these three vessels, the *Inflexible* had at the same time been engaging the Mex Forts, and doing great execution with her 80-ton guns.

The remaining vessel of the outside squadron, the *Temeraire*, was meanwhile supporting the attack of the inside squadron on the Mex batteries at a range of from 3,500 to 4,000 yards, and making great havoc with her guns. Unfortunately, in taking up her position, she had got too close to the shoal water of the Boghas Pass, and in swinging round had grounded on the reef. The gunboat *Condor* promptly went to the assistance of the huge ironclad, and eventually the ship was got off without injury.

Although the batteries at Ras-el-Tin had, as above stated, practically ceased firing, some heavy guns in Fort Adda still kept up a desultory cannonade.

At 12.30 p.m. the *Sultan* signalled to the *Inflexible*, whose work was now finished both at Ras-el-Tin and Mex, "Adda and Pharos are the only ones not silenced, all our filled shell are expended, and if you are going that way, one or two shells from your heavy guns would do much good, if you don't mind." At 12.35 the *Sultan* added, "Please silence Adda as well." The *Inflexible* then stood across to Fort Adda, and at 12.40 opened fire. Shortly after, the *Temeraire* was signalled, "Assist *Inflexible* in destroying Pharos and Silsileh." The *Temeraire* then weighed and steamed over to the position indicated, and assisted in shelling both forts.

About 1.30 p.m. a lucky shell from the *Superb*, whose practice was very good, blew up the magazine of Fort Adda. The explosion was terrific, and huge pieces of *débris* were thrown into the air, whilst a dense cloud of smoke for some seconds hid the works from view. The fort at once ceased firing, and when the smoke cleared away it was seen that the garrison had retreated from the blackened ruins.

As early as 1.30, the ships were beginning to run short of ammunition, and the *Sultan* signalled to the *Alexandra*, "How many filled shell have you?" and received the answer "Twenty." At one o'clock the *Alexandra* signalled that she had only thirty common shell left, and was answered by the *Sultan* that she had none at all, and that the *Alexandra* had better use common shell as the *Sultan* was doing.

At 1.35, with the exception of the Hospital Fort, where one rifled gun continued firing, all the batteries from Fort Adda westward being silenced, the *Superb* signalled the fact to the *Sultan*, and suggested getting under way. The *Sultan* replied in the affirmative, adding, "Can you touch up Pharos? *Temeraire* now on her way to assist *Inflexible* at Pharos. I have no shell filled, nor has *Alexandra*." The *Superb* accordingly proceeded towards Fort Pharos and opened fire.

At 2.0 the *Sultan* signalled to the *Inflexible*, which was engaging the Hospital Battery and Fort Pharos, "Proceed to Pharillon" (Silsileh).

At 2.55 a shot from the Hospital Battery struck the *Inflexible* aloft, carrying away the slings of the mainyard.

At 5 the Hospital Battery fired its last shot.

At 5.10 the *Inflexible* proceeded across to engage Fort Silsileh, all the other forts from Ras-el-Tin eastward having been silenced.

At 5.15 the general signal, "Cease firing," was made, followed at 6.5 by, "Anchor in same position as last night."

While the off-shore squadron was thus occupied, the other division of the fleet under the admiral's immediate command was not idle. The *Invincible* at anchor, with the *Monarch* and *Penelope* under weigh inside the reefs, assisted by the *Inflexible* and *Temeraire*, in the Corvette and Boghas Channels, were engaging from a distance of 1,300 to 1,500 yards the batteries and lines of Mex, also the forts of Marza-el-Kanat and Omuk Kubebe at various ranges. The enemy replied briskly both from rifled and smooth bore guns. At 8.45 one of the *Monarch's* shells exploded the powder magazine at Marza-el-Kanat. At 8.27 the admiral signalled to her, "Close nearer the forts, keeping as close to them as possible." By 9 a.m. the enemy's guns, except four at Fort Mex, were silenced. These four nevertheless gave considerable trouble to the ships, for it was difficult to hit upon their exact position, placed as they were almost on a level with the water, and only dimly and occasionally seen through the smoke.

About an hour before this Lord Charles Beresford, in the *Condor*, stationed as repeating ship, saw that the 10-inch rifled guns in Fort Marabout were playing with great accuracy, at a range of 4,200 yards, upon the ships engaged off Fort Mex, the shots falling only from 10 to 30 yards short. Steaming within range of his 7-inch gun, he chose with great skill a position, 1,200 yards off, upon which the enemy's guns could not be brought to bear, and engaged the fort single-handed for two hours. The *Condor's* excellent practice soon checked the fire from Fort Marabout, and elicited from the Admiral, who sent the other gunboats to his aid, the signal, "Well done, *Condor*." It is satisfactory to be able to add that during his operation no casualties occurred on any of the vessels engaged.[3]

---

3. Although the fact in no way detracts from the gallant conduct of Lord Charles Beresford's exploit, it is necessary to add that the only real (continued next page)

At 10.35 the flag-ship signalled to the *Monarch*, "Steam close in to the batteries we have silenced and drop a few shells into them at close range." This was followed by, "Go as close to forts as water will permit." The *Monarch* then steamed in shore and poured in a tremendous fire from all her guns. At 11.30, there being no return fire, she, as well as the *Invincible*, ceased firing.

At 11.40, the gunboats having returned from Marabout, the *Monarch*, which remained under way, was signalled to support them in an attempt to destroy the Mex works, but ordered not to fire unless fired upon. All the gunboats were at the same time signalled to close in to the batteries, and, remaining under way, to destroy their rifled guns. The *Condor*, ten minutes after, signalled that she had only twenty-one shells for each gun left, and received the order to cease firing. The gunboats, supported by the *Monarch*, continued to fire on the works.

At 11.58, the *Monarch* observing soldiers running back into the batteries, permission was given her to reopen fire.

Permission was also given to the *Penelope* to fire at the rifled guns in the batteries with her 40-pounders. At 12.20 p.m. the *Monarch* ceased firing, signalling that she had driven about 200 soldiers out of the works. At 12.50 p.m. the *Penelope* was ordered to get under way, and taking advantage of her light draught, to try to dismount the guns at Mex. She then weighed and proceeded in towards Mex Fort, firing at intervals. At 1.10 the windmills in the neighbourhood of the forts were seen to be full of soldiers, and the *Monarch* was ordered to open fire on them with her light guns.

About 2 p.m. the Admiral, seeing that the gunners of the western battery of Mex had abandoned their guns, and that the supports had probably retired also, landed a party, under cover of the gun-vessels and gunboats, who destroyed with gun-cotton two 10-inch rifled guns, and spiked six smooth-bore guns in the right hand battery. The party returned without a casualty beyond the loss of one of their boats, which got capsized on the rocks, on an alarm (happily unfounded) being raised that some soldiers were approaching to attack the little force.

At 3.25 the *Penelope* signalled to the admiral that Fort Kamaria had its guns manned, though, from her inshore position, the ship's guns would not bear on them. The Admiral, in consequence, directed the *Penelope* to change her position and open fire on the fort. About the

---

injury sustained by the fort was the burning of a small store. There were several hits on the scarp, but none of the guns were touched.

same time soldiers were observed transporting light guns into one of the Mex batteries, and the *Monarch* was signalled to attack again. Both vessels promptly responded, and, steaming into position, poured in a devastating fire on the points indicated. At 5.30, there being no reply from the enemy, the inside squadron ceased firing. This concluded the operations of the day.

The casualties on board the ships were but slight, amounting only to five killed and twenty-eight wounded—a fact to be attributed partly to the protection afforded by the armour plating of the ships principally engaged, and partly to the inaccurate fire of the enemy's batteries.[4]

A courageous act was reported from the *Alexandra*. In the course of the bombardment a lighted shell from one of the Egyptian batteries fell on the main deck of the vessel. Mr. Israel Harding, gunner, rushed for the missile all burning as it was, and immersed it in a bucket of water.[5]

The Egyptians, it must be allowed, were overmatched both in the size and number of the guns brought into action, but the way in which they responded to the heavy fire was marvellous. When the *Inflexible's* 1,700 lb. projectiles struck the scarp of the Lighthouse Fort immediately underneath an embrasure they threw up a cloud of dust and fragments of stone as high as the lighthouse itself. To the looker-on, it seemed impossible to live under such a fire, yet after a few minutes the dust would clear away, and the gun's crew would pluckily send another shell back at their huge opponent.

The Egyptian forces were under the immediate command of Toulba Pasha. From the best sources of information accessible, it is gathered that the defences contained no less than 2,000 artillerymen, and of infantry and civilian volunteers there was no lack.

The disposition of these troops has not been accurately ascertained, but it is known that Mex was commanded by an adjutant-major, who had with him one captain, three lieutenants, and 150 men. Of this small number one lieutenant was mortally wounded, 50 men were killed, and 48 wounded.

Fort Omuk Kubebe, as already mentioned, was subjected to the *Inflexible's* fire during the forenoon. Its garrison consisted of 75 artillerymen, aided by a considerable number of native volunteers. Eight-

---

4. At the bombardment of Algiers, by Lord Exmouth, the British loss was no less than 128 killed and 690 wounded.
5. For his conduct on this occasion Mr. Harding received the Victoria Cross.

een of these were wounded. In all, along the southern or inside line, from Saleh Aga to Marabout, 65 men were killed, and from 150 to 200 wounded.

In the northern line of defences at Ras-el-Tin, and also in Fort Adda, at least 50 men are believed to have been killed and 150 wounded, but the record is very vague. Stray pieces of shell are reported by the chief of police to have killed and wounded between 150 and 200 citizens, but this statement must be accepted for what it is worth.[6]

It is only fair to the other side to give the Egyptian narrative of the bombardment. The account published in the Arab paper *El Taif*, in Cairo, was as follows:

> War News.—On Tuesday, 25 Shaban, 1299, at twelve o'clock in the morning (July 11th, 7 a.m.). The English opened fire on the forts of Alexandria, and we returned the fire. At 10 a.m. an ironclad foundered off Fort Adda. At noon two vessels were sunk between Fort Pharos and Fort Adjemi. At 1.30 p.m. a wooden man-of-war of eight guns was sunk.
>
> At 5 p.m. the large ironclad was struck by a shell from Fort Pharos, the battery was injured, and a white flag was immediately hoisted by her as a signal to cease firing at her, whereupon the firing ceased on both sides, having lasted for ten hours without cessation. Some of the walls of the forts were destroyed, but they were repaired during the night. The shots and shells discharged from the two sides amounted to about 6,000, and this is the first time that so large a number of missiles has been discharged in so short a time.
>
> At 11 a.m. on Wednesday the English ships again opened fire and were replied to by the forts, but after a short time the firing ceased on both sides, and a deputation came from Admiral Seymour and made propositions to Toulba Pasha, which he could not accept.

★★★★★

No soldiers ever stood so firmly to their posts under a heavy fire as did the Egyptians under the fire of twenty-eight ships during ten hours.

★★★★★

---

6. Mr. John Ninet, in his work, *Arabi Pasha*, puts the number of Egyptians killed during the bombardment at 680. General Stone, an American officer, serving as the *khedive's* chief of the staff, estimates them at 700.

At 9 a.m. on Thursday an English man-of-war was seen to put a small screw in place of the larger one which she had been using, and it was then known that her screw had been carried away by a shot from the forts. On examining other ships it was observed that eight had been severely battered on their sides, and that one had lost her funnel.

CHAPTER 9

Observations on the Bombardment

The bombardment of the forts of Alexandria was an occurrence of such importance, and so rare are bombardments in recent naval annals, that a few general observations will probably not be without interest.

The most obvious mode of attack on fortifications would be for the ships to form in line ahead and steam past the batteries, each ship delivering her fire in succession as her guns would bear. Having thus passed the line of defence, the ships would turn and repeat the process with the other broadside. By manoeuvring in this manner, the forts (which have the advantage of a fixed gun-carriage), would labour under the disadvantage of having a moving target to fire at.

On this principle for two and a-half hours the bombardment of the forts from Ras-el-Tin to Pharos was conducted by the *Sultan*, *Superb*, and *Alexandra*. From the fact that at 9.40 a.m. this mode of attack was changed for one which consisted in the systematic concentration of fire on individual forts, from ships more or less stationary, it may be concluded that the former plan was found faulty.

It is submitted that the best principle in practice is the consecutive silencing of individual batteries, and not a general, and so to speak collective, bombardment. In support of this principle it may be mentioned that from the time of the adoption of the second plan the fire of the ships improved very much in accuracy. This also had the further advantage of being accompanied by a simultaneous diminution in the accuracy of the fire of the enemy: as is shown by the circumstance that the majority of the hits received by the *Sultan*, *Superb*, and *Alexandra* were[76]sustained before 9.40—the time when these vessels came to an anchor and adopted the concentration principle.

That the fire of the ships would improve as soon as the vessels became stationary is intelligible enough, and is accounted for by the

88

exact range being then attainable, but that the enemy should have made worse practice against a fixed than against a moving target appears a little difficult to understand. The naval officers engaged have, with some sense of humour, suggested that the vessels in manoeuvring from time to time steamed across the line of the Egyptian fire and so got struck. The explanation, however, is probably to be found in the increased state of demoralization of the artillerymen as soon as the ships anchored and made more accurate practice.

In the inshore squadron the flag-ship *Invincible* was anchored for the most part 1,300 yards from Mex, and was kept broadside to the wind on one side, and to the batteries on the other, by a kedge carried out to windward. The *Monarch* and *Penelope* remained under way, passing and repassing the forts. The *Penelope* adopted the plan of steaming out three-quarters of a mile towards the reef, and then drifting towards the shore broadside on until within about 700 yards, whilst the *Monarch* kept more way on, moving in a line parallel with the shore. The fire from these two ships was throughout less effective than that from the *Invincible*, which was at anchor.

The range at which the fleet generally engaged seems to have been needlessly great. The outside squadron could have got to within 1,000 yards of the Lighthouse Fort and 800 yards abreast of the Ras-el-Tin lines, to within 500 yards of Fort Adda and 200 yards of Fort Pharos, whilst the inshore division could easily have got within 400 yards of all the batteries in the neighbourhood of Mex. It can hardly be doubted that the boldness of this move would have been rewarded by the more speedy and extensive dismounting of the guns, which was confessedly the chief object of the attack, and would have allowed the machine guns in the vessels' tops to be used with greater effect.

It must be remembered that the target in each case was the muzzle of a gun, a mere pin's head at the distance at which the ships were engaged, and that a successful hit meant either good luck or phenomenally good shooting. This hammering away at long range was tolerably successful, but the length of the action was a disappointment to those who expected short work to be made of the Egyptians, while, as has been seen, it drained the stock of ammunition to a dangerously low ebb.

The enormous disproportion between the damage sustained by the ships and batteries respectively may be accounted for, partly by the inferior construction of the works, and partly also by the inferior practice of the gunners by whom they were manned. There were other faults in the defence. For example: the batteries were so placed as to be unable, except at Fort Pharos, to support one another; there was no bomb-proof cover; there was too small a stock of ammunition in readiness; and the men who should have been employed as reliefs for manning the rifled guns wasted their efforts with the smooth bores, which were practically useless.

With regard to the fire of the fleet generally, a variety of opinions has been expressed. One authority states that, with the exception of the *Inflexible* and *Temeraire*, the English gunners did not greatly distinguish themselves. Many of the shells of the *Monarch*, *Inflexible*, and *Superb* fell short.[1]

The fire also was said to have been too slow, thus giving the enemy's artillerists time to recover themselves. The fire of the *Inflexible* was stated to have been particularly disappointing in this respect. That of the *Alexandra* was much more rapid than that of the others, as her much greater expenditure of ammunition shows.

A naval officer of experience has expressed the opinion that, considering the nature of the works attacked, an old line-of-battle ship, with her numerous though much smaller guns, would have been more effective than the modern ships which took part in the bombardment. If one considers the great size and weight of the majority of the projectiles used, as well as the capacity of the shell and the consequent amount of their bursting charges, one can hardly fail to be astonished at the small effect produced on the sand parapets, especially when it is remembered that the latter were in many cases, according to modern theory, too weak to afford any real protection.

It is a fact, and one on which too much stress cannot be laid, that in only one instance was any one of the parapets pierced by a shell from the fleet, and that Fort Mex was the only battery which could not have been sufficiently repaired during the night to resume the action on the following day. One remarkable feature of the fire from the fleet was the enormous number of shells which failed to explode, and this has never been satisfactorily accounted for.

The expenditure of ammunition by the squadron appears from the

---

1. The uncertainty attending the fire of war-ships in action was recently illustrated, though under totally different circumstances, in the engagement between the American and Spanish fleets at Santiago. On that occasion, out of a total of 8,060 rounds fired from the United States vessels, only 123, or 1·4 *per cent.*, struck the enemy; whilst out of 47 rounds fired by the 13-inch guns there was not a single hit. The American loss was one man killed and one wounded, against 350 killed and 160 wounded on the Spanish side.

following table:—[2]

SHIP.	Common.	Palliser.	Shrapnel.	Segment.	Empty Shell.	Shot.	Case.	TOTAL.*	Martini-Henry.	Nordenfeldt.	Gatling.	Rockets.
Alexandra	379	23	1	...	...	4	...	407	...	4000	340	...
Superb	257	83	25	34	...	12	...	411	...	1161	880	...
Sultan	247	24	3	44	10	10	...	338	...	1800	2000	...
Penelope	241	...	45	32	...	62	...	380	5000	1672	...	...
Monarch	227	5	129	...	...	6	...	367	1800	3440	2680	21
Temeraire	139	70	13	6	...	...	...	228	...	160	...	...
Invincible	221	...	25	...	2	2	...	250	2000	2000	1000	...
Inflexible	139	21	11	37	...	...	...	208	...	2000	...	...
Beacon	21	...	...	1	61	18	...	101	320	...	...	3
Condor	162	...	8	...	31	...	...	201	1000	...	200	13
Bittern	66	7	1	...	...	12	3	89	...	...	...	...
Cygnet	72	...	...	...	71	...	...	143	...	...	...	...
Decoy	69	...	...	...	...	...	...	69	40	...	...	...
Helicon	6	...	...	...	...	...	...	6	...	...	...	...
TOTAL	2246	233	261	154	175	126	3	3198	10,160	16,233	7100	37

The hits received by the fleet were as follows:—

Alexandra. Twenty-four shot and shell penetrated the ship above the armour-plating. Several shot and shell struck the armour; of these, some made indentations on the plates from five inches to one inch in depth. The foremost funnel was struck in three places. The total number of hits was about sixty.

Sultan. Number of hits, twenty-seven, of which two struck the armour, denting two plates, and starting one. One shot went through the after funnel. The holes made in the side were as follows:—One sixteen inches by twelve inches; another fifteen inches in diameter; and a third fourteen inches in diameter. A hole sixteen inches by ten was made through the mainmast.

Superb. Fourteen hits, of which seven were on the hull, and seven on the upper works and spars. A 10-inch shell struck the port side, and, bursting, tore a hole in the side ten feet by four feet, within three feet of the water-line. The armour-plating on the port side was struck

---

2. There were 1,731 shot and shell fired from the heavy guns. Of these, 88 were fired from the *Inflexible's* 80-ton guns. The average number of rounds for the heavy guns of the fleet was a little over 20 for each gun. At the bombardment of Algiers one ship, H.M.S. *Queen Charlotte*, alone fired 4,462 round shot.

by two shells, of which one indented the armour three inches, and the other burst, starting a plate, and breaking fourteen rivet-heads. Some of the rigging was shot away, and a hole twelve inches in diameter was made in the foremast. Two other holes in the side were as follows:—One ten inches in diameter, four feet above the water-line; the other twelve inches in diameter (made by a 10-inch shot), five feet above the water-line.

Penelope. Eight hits, of which three were on the armour, making little or no indentation. Of the others, one passed through the after embrasure on the starboard side; another hit the starboard quarter gallery; the third struck a 9-pounder gun, carried off the sight and damaged the carriage; the fourth hit the mainyard, port side; and the fifth struck the muzzle of one of the 8-inch guns, then broke up and destroyed the transom plate of the carriage. The gun and carriage were put out of action.

Invincible. Eleven hits, six of which passed through the side. A large dent was made in the armour by a shot which also started a plate.

Inflexible. About six hits altogether. One shot struck the unarmoured part of the hull, and, penetrating, damaged the bollards and did other injury. Other shots damaged the upper-works, but the armour-plating was not struck.

The *Monarch, Temeraire, Hecla,* and gunboats received no hits at all.

With regard to the effects of the bombardment on the various forts, it is proposed to give a short account, taking them in the same order in which they were first presented to the reader.[3]

1. *Fort Marabout.*—A small store was burnt. There were several hits on the scarp, but none of the guns were in any way injured.

2. *Fort Adjemi.*—Uninjured.

3. *Marza-el-Kanat.*—No injury was done to the fort, but a store of gun-cotton was exploded.

4. The citadel of Mex had several breaches made in the works, but no guns were dismounted.

5. *Old Fort of Mex.*—Parapets were uninjured, but the buildings in the rear were almost swept away. A small store in front of magazine was levelled to the ground. The large store was riddled with shot, but the magazine was untouched. The barracks were much damaged.

---

3. The writer is indebted for much of the following information to the able report of Captain N. L. Walford, R.A.

The fort was found to contain many fragments of shell, and the loss of life among the defenders was probably considerable. The damage to the guns was as follows:—A 10-inch Armstrong gun was struck in the second coil by a shell which cut a groove of an oval shape in the metal; the coil was shaken out of place and cracked, but the gun was left serviceable. A 9-inch Armstrong gun was struck by a shell, and received an oval graze 1·25 inch in depth. In the right portion of the battery, a 10-inch S.B. and two 8-inch Armstrong guns were struck by shrapnel bullets, and the fifth gun from the left, an 8-inch Armstrong, was struck on the coil by a shell. The blow dismounted gun, carriage and slide. The metal of the gun was ripped off for eighteen inches, and the trunnion ring was also started by the force of the blow. The remaining guns (36-pounders) were uninjured.

Left Flank Battery.—Left gun(10-inch S.B.). This gun was hit on the right of the carriage by a splinter, the gun was uninjured. No.3 gun (10-inch S.B.).—This was hit by a shell on the muzzle, gun uninjured.

6. The Mex Lines, armed with S.B. guns, were not fought, and the works escaped injury.

7. *Fort Kamaria* was not much injured. A 10-inch S.B. gun was dismounted by a shell.

In view of the tremendous fire to which Fort Mex was subjected, and the comparatively short range at which all the ships except the *Temeraire* engaged it, it is almost impossible to believe that not a single gun here was disabled or dismounted during the action proper. The 8-inch gun which was dismounted was bowled over by the *Penelope* long after the fort had ceased firing, and from a distance stated to be about 300 yards. The successful shot was the thirtieth of this series, and was aimed by the gunnery lieutenant.

> This fort was the only one which could not have resumed action on the following day, in consequence of the injury done by the landing-party by exploding gun-cotton and spiking the guns.[4]

8. *Omuk Kubebe.*—The effects of the bombardment were considerable, though they were due less to the number of hits than to the size and weight of the 16-inch shells which caused most of the injuries. The effect of three of these shells from the *Inflexible* was worthy

---

4. Report of Lieutenant-Commander Goodrich, U.S.N.

of note. One shell having burst on the top of the scarp made an almost practicable breach. Two others, within a few feet of each other, hit the parapet, 24 feet thick, and almost pierced it. They appear to have struck the exterior slope, and having cut a trough in the parapet about 11 feet in width, burst after penetrating 17 feet, and formed craters 16 feet in diameter, and 5 feet and 4 feet 6 inches in depth, respectively. With regard to the ordnance, the only damage was the destruction of a 36-pounder S.B. gun.

9. *Saleh Aga.*—One 10-inch and one 6·5 S.B. gun were dismounted, and one of the 6·5-inch S.B. guns was destroyed, though not dismounted.

10. The adjoining battery received only slight injuries.

11. *Lighthouse Fort, or Fort Ras-el-Tin.*—The barracks to the north of the fort were riddled with shell, and in many parts left in ruins. The parapets on the west side were so scored with shell that it was difficult to estimate the number of hits, but at no point had they been pierced. The scarp also suffered severely, both at the bastions and on the curtain; and the right face of the bastion was much marked by shrapnel bullets. On the west front the parapet showed about twenty-three hits, and the scarp twenty-four; two stores were burnt, and the rifled-shell store was riddled with shell. The lighthouse itself was hit by several shells, and the buildings round its base were reduced to ruins.

Right gun (9-inch).—This gun was sent back to the end of the slide, and breaking the ties was tilted up on its breech with the muzzle in the air. Left gun (9-inch).—This was struck by two shells, and gun and carriage were both destroyed. The former was hit on the trunnion ring, which had been partially carried away, the carriage was in pieces, and the brackets were torn off and broken. The gun was thrown about twelve feet to the rear and crushed several of the gunners, ten bodies having been found beneath it. In the left bastion, a 10-inch Armstrong gun was hit on the muzzle, but the tube was not damaged.

The sockets of the levers were broken by use, the tackle shot away, and the shot-crane broken and useless. A 9-inch gun was run back and tilted up on the breech in the same manner as the 9-inch gun in the right bastion. An 8-inch gun was struck in reverse by shells. The gun and carriage were capsized on the left side, but uninjured. One truck of the slide was cut away. The Lighthouse Fort suffered more severely than either Pharos or Adda, since there was not one of the rifled guns which could bear on the fleet left fit for service.

12. *The Lines of Ras-el-Tin.*—(Left or Harem Battery.) The effects of the bombardment on the fort were small, but the loss of life must have been considerable, as many shells burst in it. The rear face of the tower was in ruins. Right gun (8-inch Armstrong).—A 9-inch Palliser shell struck the lower side of the gun and burst on the breast of the carriage with the following results: the gun beyond being indented for a distance of 8 inches in length was uninjured, but had been thrown about 10 feet from its original position. Both brackets of the carriage were torn away. The entire carriage was a wreck. Centre gun (8-inch Armstrong).—The right-front truck of the carriage was broken, and the gun was struck by a splinter on the chase. The gun and the carriage, however, suffered no serious injury, though the left bracket of the latter was pierced by a splinter.

The centre battery in the interior was almost uninjured, though the parapet was deeply scored in all directions by shells. The embrasure of the left gun (9-inch) was choked up by the ruins of the cheeks, whilst the revetment on each side of the neck was swept away. The condition of the guns was as follows:—10-inch Armstrong gun.—The right-front truck of the carriage was carried away, and the buffers of the slide were much damaged by the recoil of the gun. 9-inch Armstrong gun.—The gun and carriage were uninjured except that the lever of the elevating gear was bent, and the holdfast was rising off the pin. 9-inch left gun.—This was hit on the left trunnion by a shell which tore off the cap square, and also by a second shell, on the right bracket six inches in the rear of the trunnion.

The gun and carriage were, however, practically uninjured. This battery in the early reports of the bombardment was miscalled the Moncrieff Battery, but there was in it no gun mounted on that system. The Moncrieff gun, 180 yards to the westward, was hit on the left side by a splinter of a shell, and a bolt in the rear of the left bracket was also cut out by a Nordenfeldt bullet. Beyond this it was unhurt, and remained perfectly serviceable.

The Hospital Battery.—The effects of the bombardment here were overwhelming. The entire gun portions were so entirely destroyed that it was difficult to discover where the original crest had been. The injuries to the guns were as follows:—Right gun (7-inch Armstrong).—The cheeks of the embrasure were driven in on the gun, and the trucks were jammed, otherwise the gun and carriage were uninjured. The former was, however, scored with forty-nine hits from a 10-inch shrapnel shell, the greatest depth of any hit being 5 inches. Left gun

(7-inch Armstrong).—A shell burst under the front racer on the left side of this gun, tore it up and bent it into a vertical plane, twisting the truck and forcing it off the racer. The slide was also jammed by the ruins of the revetment. The gun-carriage and slide were otherwise uninjured, and were left fit for service.[5]

13. *Fort Adda.*—The barracks and stores, especially on the east side of the fort, were very much injured, but the batteries were not materially damaged. The only shell which entered, that on the southern half of the western side, blew up the magazine. The loss of life from the explosion was probably very great, and the entire space between the magazine and the gate was covered with stones, timber, and broken shell. The injury to the guns was as follows:—A 10-inch S.B. gun was dismounted by a shell which threw the gun and carriage to a distance of about 15 feet from the slide. Another 10-inch S.B. gun was similarly dismounted, whilst a third was struck on the left side of the platform by a shell which had previously cut off the cascabel of the second gun to the left; the beams of the platform were completely shattered, and the gun with its carriage was overturned and wrecked.

14. *Fort Pharos.*—The west tower and front were breached in many places; the minaret was partly knocked down, and the whole of the west front of the keep, with its two turrets, were in ruins. The southeast corners of the fort were also much shattered by the shells which passed over the west front. The stores and barracks suffered severely, and the destruction of so much masonry must have added considerably to the moral effect of the fire of the ships. With regard to the sea front, the parapet was hit in several places (seven in all), but only in three cases did a shell enter the battery. The corners of the traverse to the right of the 8-inch Armstrong guns were carried away by two shells; a third shell pierced the sole of the embrasure of the 10-inch Armstrong gun, and threw the large granite block which formed the sill on to the platform of the gun, so the gun might be said to be out of action. Of the S.B. guns, one heavy 10-inch on the west tower was dismounted, by a 16-inch shell from the *Inflexible*, one 10-inch gun on the west front was capsized and put out of action, and it is not unlikely that another, with its carriage, fell into the crater formed by a shell.

On the rear face, a 36-pounder, having been hit on the cascabel by a chance shell, was thrown completely over the parapet, and left stand-

---

5. In August, 1882, these two guns were removed to Ramleh for the purpose of firing on the enemy's lines.

ing on its muzzle at a distance of 30 feet from its original position. Another gun was also unserviceable, owing to the partial destruction of its carriage by a shell. But it was in the casemates below that the fire of the ships inflicted the greatest injury.

The front wall of the casemates, which is faced with masonry two feet in thickness, was in many places torn away under the stress of fire, leaving only six feet of rubble as a protection to the guns. Through the latter the heavy shells pierced with ease. The results were as follows:— Under west tower, casemate penetrated, gun not disabled. In casemates Nos. 1 to 12, just one half of the guns were disabled. Of the casemates on the right sea front, No. 17 was the only one in which there was no gun hit. The loss of life in the casemates must have been out of all proportion to the effect produced by the feeble guns (six 5-inch S.B.) mounted within.

On the scarp of casemates Nos. 1 to 12 there were about 13 hits, of which seven pierced the wall.

15. *Fort Silsileh.*—The fire does not appear to have in any way injured the guns or stores of this fort, though fragments of at least two shells lay around the rifled guns.

The total number of guns dismounted was, four M.L.R. guns, sixteen S.B. guns, and one mortar.

The forts at Alexandria generally were badly knocked about, but the more modern parapets were not seriously injured. If the bombardment were directed against the forts in their defensive capacity, it must be pronounced a failure. If its object were the dismounting of the rifled guns, it must be conceded that such results as attended the work of either the inside squadron (where only one gun of this type was seriously affected), or even of the outside squadron (where less than half of the guns were permanently disabled), do not justify the verdict of success.

In the wider sense, however, of having driven the Egyptian gunners from their batteries and having silenced the forts, the fleet was unquestionably victorious.

CHAPTER 10

The Day After the Bombardment

The following day, the 12th July, when it was proposed to renew the bombardment, there was dull gloomy weather off Alexandria, with a haze hanging over the city. There had been a strong breeze from the sea during the previous night, and it was still blowing fresh from the N.N.W., causing the ironclads forming the outside squadron to roll somewhat.

The gunboat *Beacon* at daylight collected the bodies of the men belonging to the fleet, killed the previous day, and buried them at sea.

The *Humber* storeship appeared in sight, and working parties were sent to her for ammunition.

At 9 a.m. the *Inflexible* and *Temeraire* were sent to reconnoitre the batteries from Eunostos Point on Ras-el-Tin, to Fort Pharos.

At 10.15 the *Temeraire* reported that the Hospital Battery was prepared, that two large rifled guns were ready with guns' crews about them, and that numbers of men under arms were in the barracks and covered way. The *Inflexible* at the same time signalled that a large body of men, armed with rifles, was in the rear of the Hospital earthworks. In reply, the *Sultan* signalled to the *Inflexible* and *Temeraire*, "Close, and open fire with shell." At 10.40 the two ships, having taken up position, fired twelve shells, to which there was no reply, and the men were observed leaving the batteries.

At 10.48 flags of truce were displayed at the Lighthouse Battery and at Fort Adda. At the same time, a boat bearing a white flag came out towards the *Inflexible*. This being noticed, the vessels were ordered to cease firing. The boat then returned to the shore without communicating.

At 11 the admiral signalled to the *Penelope* and *Sultan*, "Weather having moderated, Admiral intends to attack Marabout and Adjemi; approach with *Sultan, Alexandra, Temeraire,* and *Superb*. I will send gunboat to summon enemy to surrender."

At 11.10 the *Bittern* was sent with a flag of truce to communicate with the Egyptian authorities.

At 11.30 the squadron was reinforced by the arrival of the ironclad *Achilles*, belonging to the Channel Fleet.

At 2.50 p.m. the *Bittern* returned, and signalled, "Negotiations have failed, have informed authorities you will engage batteries at 3.30 precisely." At 3.40 the *Bittern* hauled down her flag of truce, and it was reported that the flag of truce at Ras-el-Tin was also taken down, though this was subsequently found not to have been the case.

At 3.50, the Egyptian flag at Marabout having been hauled down, the vessels there were recalled, and the Admiral signalled to the *Sultan*, "Engage batteries off Pharos and Ras-el-Tin with your squadron." At the same time the *Invincible* fired a shot into the Mex Forts, but got no reply.

At 4.40 a general signal was made to the ships to "take up position for engaging batteries, anchoring as convenient;" and at 5 the *Alexandra, Temeraire, Achilles, Superb,* and *Sultan* weighed anchor, and proceeded in line towards Fort Pharos. None of the ships, however, opened fire, as the flag of truce at Ras-el-Tin was seen to be still flying.

At 5.40 the *Helicon* was sent into harbour with a flag of truce. The instructions of the officer in command were to inform the authorities that if they wished to treat with the Admiral they could do so by returning in the *Helicon*, and that if they did not do so, no more flags of truce would be respected.

At 5.50 the signal was made for the squadron to anchor for the night.

The *Helicon*, pursuant to orders, steamed up the harbour and lay off the Arsenal wall, whilst the officer in command went on board the khedive's yacht *Maharoussa*, expecting to find someone to treat with, but not a person was on board. After waiting half an hour, he signalled that he had been unable to find any of the authorities to communicate with, and returned at 8.20 p.m.

As early as four in the afternoon a part of the town had been observed to be on fire, and the conflagration soon after was seen to spread rapidly.

During the night the fires on shore continued to extend, and it became evident that it was the richest part of Alexandria, the European quarter, which was in flames.

The spectacle as viewed from the ships was grand, but awful in character. The sky on the land side was lighted up with a fierce red glare, and columns of smoke covered the city and surrounding country.

The admiral's first idea was to send a landing-party to save the town. He, however, hesitated on account of the risk to his men. Eventually, to discover the state of things on shore, he landed a party of fifteen men from the *Invincible*. The streets were found completely deserted, and all was silent save for the roar and crackle of the flames and the sound of falling beams and walls. The party returned at three a.m. on the 13th.

Daylight revealed the town still wrapped in flames, and an immense cloud of smoke hung over its whole extent.

At 5.40 a.m. the *Invincible*, *Monarch*, and *Penelope* left their anchorage off Mex, and steamed into the outer harbour, with the *Beacon* and *Bittern* in company. At 5.50 the *Helicon*, which had again gone in to pick up refugees, embarked and brought 170 of them for distribution amongst the ships outside. They were of all classes and nationalities, and included several women and children. They had passed through the streets unmolested, and reported Alexandria deserted, and that all the troops had left the previous day, after setting fire to the town. It was believed that part of the soldiers had gone to Rosetta, and part to Damanhour. The *Helicon* reported that there were a great many more refugees, women and children, inside the mole waiting for an opportunity to come off.

In the meantime the admiral held a consultation with some of the captains and officers under his command as to what was best to be done. On the one hand, there was the certainty that unless some step should be taken, a great part, if not the whole, of Alexandria would be destroyed. On the other, it was uncertain how far Arabi's troops had retired, and one report was that they were massed to the number of 9,000 outside the town, no further off than Moharrem Bey Gate. The number of men that could be landed without disabling the ships was not large. The admiral found it difficult to decide.

Already he must have begun to realize the error he had committed in opening fire with such precipitation. The Channel Fleet (of which, as already stated, the *Achilles* had arrived) were known to be on their way from Malta, as well as the *Orontes*, troop-ship, with troops from Gibraltar. The *Tamar*, too, with 1,000 marines, was at Malta. The ships of the Channel Fleet alone could have furnished a contingent of 1,800 men in addition to those whom Admiral Seymour could have disembarked from his own squadron.

The bombardment, so long delayed, might well have been retarded for the short period necessary to enable the reinforcements to arrive. What had occurred was not altogether unforeseen. Arabi had, before the bombardment, declared that if the ships opened fire he would burn the European quarter; and the fulfilment of his threat would have not only gratified his thirst for revenge, but would have also covered the retreat of his forces.

At last a landing was resolved on, and at 8.35 a.m. the general signal was made, "Prepare to land marines," followed ten minutes later by the order, "Prepare to land brigade of seamen." The *Helicon*, *Bittern* and *Beacon* were despatched to the outside squadron to bring in as many men as possible, whilst the *Condor* and *Cygnet* were told off to take the seamen and marines from the inshore vessels. At 9.5 the *Alexandra* was detached to reconnoitre off Rosetta Gate, and the remaining vessels of the outside squadron were directed to take stations for bombarding, in case the landing should be resisted.

At 10.30 the landing-party left the ships. The force consisted of four hundred men, including all the marines of the squadron; it was led by Commander Hammill, of the *Monarch*, and had with it a Gatling gun.

The *Invincible*, at the same time, sent ashore and spiked the guns at Fort Saleh Aga, and the other vessels landed men to destroy the guns in the Lighthouse Fort at Ras-el-Tin.

Whilst Commander Hammill's force was disembarking, large bodies of soldiers were seen moving towards Fort Silsileh, apparently accompanied by field-pieces, and the *Sultan*, *Temeraire*, and *Achilles* were ordered to watch that point, and to bombard if necessary.

In the intervals between carrying out the above-mentioned operations, the larger ships were engaged in recruiting their exhausted stock of ammunition from the store-ship *Humber*. In this matter a most unexpected difficulty arose. Through some unpardonable blunder the ship had been despatched from Malta without a single filled common shell on board, and actually without powder to fill the empty shells she had brought with her. Further than this, she had brought no fuses, and as the vessels of war had no reserves of powder, they would, had hostilities been resumed, have been speedily reduced to a state of comparative impotence.

In the course of the day, anxiety being felt for the safety of the *khedive*, the *Condor* was sent to cruise off the palace at Ramleh.

Further parties of men were landed in the town, making the total force disembarked about 800 men. They took with them a day's provisions, Gatling guns, and ammunition.

At 3.25 p.m. the *Temeraire* signalled that great activity was observed about Ramleh Palace, and that Dervish Pasha was supposed to be there.

At 4.43 the *Temeraire*, having reported that Fort Pharos did not appear to be entirely deserted, had permission given her to send a party to spike the guns there.

At 5 the *Bittern* was directed to take a guard of fifty marines to the Palace of Ras-el-Tin, for the protection of the *khedive*, who was expected from Ramleh.

What had been taking place on shore in the meantime is reserved for another chapter.

CHAPTER 11

Alexandria During the Bombardment

After the preceding narrative of events from a naval point of view, it may be convenient to relate what was taking place at the time in Alexandria itself.

During the whole of the night preceding the 11th July, the native population had been leaving the town in crowds, some in carts and others on foot, the women crying and uttering loud lamentations. Towards daylight the movement slackened. From three a.m. troops were marching through on their way to Ras-el-Tin; at five the last detachment passed.

The morning dawned on the city without a cloud in the heavens. There was a gentle breeze from the north-west, all was quiet as the early sun gilded the tops of the domes and minarets of the various mosques, and lighted up the acacia trees of the Place Mehemet Ali and the Place de l'Eglise. In the streets the soldiers, who had passed the night on the door-steps of the houses, on the marble benches of the square, or on the ground, slowly roused themselves, and, yawning, looked about them in a somnolent way. The streets were being watered as usual, the "*bowabs*," or door-keepers, were tranquilly smoking their cigarettes at the house-doors, and the Arab women were going about selling milk as if nothing unusual were about to happen. With the exception of these few indications of life, the streets were deserted. The military posts were relieved at six o'clock, as usual each soldier carrying a linen pouch full of cartridges.

The clock of the church of St. Catherine struck seven, and before the sound had died away, the thundering boom of the first gun from the fleet startled the city, and the few civilians who were about sought refuge in their dwellings. The Egyptian soldiers remained at their posts.

Then came a solemn silence which lasted some minutes, after which the bombardment, with all its horrors, began. The English ships were seen in the distance vomiting volumes of fire and smoke, whilst the forts in their turn thundered forth a reply. The scene was of the grandest description, and a few seconds later the shrieks of the projectiles as they flew overhead mingled with the boom of the cannon, which echoed and re-echoed on all sides. The report from the huge 80-ton guns of the *Inflexible* was easily distinguishable above the general roar.

At a little before eight a shell fell in the Arab quarter, behind the Ramleh railway station, causing a panic, which forced many of the inhabitants into the forts close by.

Arabi, who had from an early hour stationed himself at the Ministry of Marine in the Arsenal, finding the missiles from the fleet falling thickly there, left with Toulba Pasha and an escort of cavalry, and at eight o'clock drove to the fortifications behind Fort Kom-el-Dyk, where he remained till four p.m.

By nine o'clock the streets were totally deserted except by the soldiers. The cannonade slackened, and sounds of rejoicing came from some of the native *cafés*, where it was reported that two ironclads were sunk and five were disabled.

At about the same time a shell fell on the terrace of a house alongside the Palace Menasce in the Rosetta Road, and another burst over the German Consulate. The discharges averaged about two per minute. The soldiers now commenced to send patrols to the houses of such Europeans as were ashore, to prevent any attempt at signalling to the English squadron.

The number of Europeans ashore at this period amounted to about 1,500. Of these some 100 were at the College of the Frères, a great number in the Greek Church, and in the Greek and European Hospitals. The German Hospital at Moharrem Bey also sheltered a large number of nurses, invalids, and refugees. The Anglo-Egyptian Bank, in the Rue Cherif Pasha, was held by a determined party of about twenty (subsequently increased to eighty-two). The Danish Consul-General had fortified the Danish Consulate, where a large number of people, including many women and children, found a refuge.

There were other Europeans, mostly of the poorest class, hidden away in their dwellings in various parts of the town, and to all these the movements of the patrols naturally occasioned serious disquietude.

Early in the forenoon, an Egyptian officer mounted the roof of the Crédit Lyonnais Bank, and commenced cutting away the telephone wires. Shortly afterwards a gang of native boys in the same street began pulling down all the wires they could reach, raising at the same time the wildest shouts.

At nine, a shell fell in some stables in the Rue Copt, and for a quarter of an hour the neighbourhood was enveloped in a cloud of dust. At ten, a shell fell in the Franciscan Convent, where a number of persons were assembled, but, as it did not burst, did no injury beyond destroying one or two of the walls.

Shortly afterwards a shell fell into a house in the Rue Cherif Pasha, making a large hole. Another pierced the wall of the Jewish Synagogue. Another hit the *Zaptieh*, and a fourth struck a house in Frank Street. As the missiles fell, the soldiers sought shelter in the doorways of the houses, but did not entirely desert their posts. At eleven o'clock, the natives spread a report that only three ironclads remained afloat, and great rejoicings took place in the Arab *cafés*.

Half-an-hour later, an officer and a detachment of soldiers stationed themselves opposite the Anglo-Egyptian Bank, and insisted on mounting to the roof to satisfy themselves that there was no signalling going on. They also went to the central Telephone Office and to the Telegraph Offices and cut the wires. At the office of the Eastern Telegraph Company, they found one of the *employés*, a French subject, who had refused to go afloat, and murdered him on the spot. At this period, isolated firing from a westerly direction was all that was heard; otherwise the silence of death prevailed throughout the town.

At half-past twelve, two shells, one following the other in quick succession, struck the Khedivial Schools, in the Rosetta Road, and, bursting, destroyed the south-western angle of the building.

Soon after the cannonading commenced, a number of empty carts and drays was seen going towards the Marina. During the forenoon, these began to return laden with dead artillerymen. The first load passed up soon after ten in the morning, the bodies being stripped and tied in with ropes. A little later, the wounded began to arrive in great numbers, some in carriages and some in carts, many of the men showing ghastly wounds. Crowds of women followed them, uttering cries of distress and lamentations.[1]

---

1. The dead were taken along the Boulevard de Rosette to the native hospital, where the bodies were at once interred.

At one p.m. a crowd of native children carrying a green flag passed down the Rue Cherif Pasha beating petroleum tins and calling on God and the Prophet. During the day many of the houses in which Europeans were seen on the terraces or roofs, watching the bombardment, were surrounded by soldiers, who, under the pretext that the inmates were signalling to the fleet, forced them to descend and accompany them to the police-stations. Eight or ten Europeans were dragged from their dwellings and set upon in the streets by the mob. As soon as they fell into the power of the latter, they were forced along by soldiers towards the Moharrem Bey Gate, and struck with the butt ends of rifles, and received blows from *naboots*. As they passed along they were subjected to every species of ill-usage. On their arrival, covered with blood and in a wretched condition, fresh troubles awaited them. They were cast indiscriminately into cells with natives, and endured the vilest usage.

A mob of natives in the course of the day broke into the German Hospital, where there were many European refugees as well as the patients. The inmates ran for the cellars, where the invalids had already been placed for safety. The Secretary of the German Consulate was the last to flee, and as a final effort he fired a shot from his revolver. The effect on the crowd was magical. They drew back, and contented themselves with demanding that the flag which was flying over the hospital, and which they imagined was being used for signalling to the fleet, should be given up to them. This was acceded to, and they then dispersed.

The Danish Consulate was surrounded by soldiers and a mob of Arabs, who required the consul to haul down the flag flying over the house. This he courageously refused to do, and whilst the dispute was at its height, three Arabs were killed by shells almost at his door, and the rest fled.

At three, the fire of the ships, which had in the meantime slackened, was resumed with great vigour. One shell burst at Moharrem Bey Gate, and killed two officers and six men of the police.

According to Arabi's statement, he received during the day several messages from the *khedive*, congratulating him on the behaviour of the troops. Shortly after four o'clock Arabi left the town in a carriage with an escort of soldiers, taking the route by the Rosetta Gate.

About this time the *Inflexible* and *Temeraire* were observed to approach Fort Pharos and reopen fire on the batteries there, and a great number of their shells were seen to strike the rocks, raising clouds of *débris*, and bounding in repeated ricochets over the face of the water. Towards five o'clock the picturesque mosque in the fort fell, burying in its ruins a number of the wounded who had taken refuge behind the walls. The two ships at the same time pitched a few shells at Fort Silsileh. The firing continued, at intervals, until past five o'clock, when it ceased altogether.

As soon as the cannonade was over, the exodus of natives from the town recommenced, and the streets were again filled. The desire of all was to escape from the town as soon as possible. Along the banks of the Mahmoudieh Canal, and the line of the railway to Cairo, was one vast stream of fugitives, which only ceased as night fell.

Then a great stillness came over Alexandria.

The night was calm. The gas was not lighted, and the city, plunged in darkness, resembled a vast necropolis. The only sounds heard from time to time were the plaintive howlings of forsaken dogs. A few fugitives ventured into the streets, and encountered only the sentries and patrols.

On the morning of the 12th, the movement of the natives recommenced. All those who had remained in the Ras-el-Tin and other quarters endeavoured to get out of the town with their luggage and effects. It was rumoured that the bombardment was to recommence, and the terror of the people was indescribable. The trains from Moharrem Bey Station were thronged with fugitives, who not only rode inside, but on the roof, the steps, and even the buffers of the carriages.

In the Place Mehemet Ali a regiment of infantry were scattered about, the men, with arms piled, seated or lying on the ground, tranquilly smoking their cigarettes. A few of the *bowabs* were seen going to the bazaars and returning to the houses with small stores of meat and other provisions. Amongst the Europeans, the greatest anxiety prevailed, and everyone was asking when the disembarkation would begin. The soldiers on duty became more and more threatening, and the supplies of provisions began to run short. Gangs of disorderly natives from time to time appeared and made violent demonstrations in front of such houses as were known to shelter Europeans.

From early morning, bands of natives ran through the streets with soldiers at their head, looking for any Europeans who might be concealed. At a little before eleven the cannonade recommenced, and a dozen reports were heard coming from the westward. There was then a silence, and all wondered what next would happen.

As soon as the cannonade ceased, the troops at Moharrem Bey and Rosetta Gates precipitated themselves into the streets, calling on the natives to flee, as the dogs of Christians were going to disembark and massacre the Mussulmans. The news soon after spread that the convicts in the Arsenal had been let loose, and were going to pillage and fire the town.

An hour later, part of the garrison left the town by the Rosetta Gate, taking the road to Ramleh. The first of them marched in fours in fairly good order, and were followed by 1,500 more who passed in gradually increasing disorder, until they became confused with the rabble of fugitives who crowded the roads.

At one o'clock the soldiers in the street received the order to eat their midday meal, and, each opening his haversack, set to work with an appetite indicating hours of abstinence. When the men had finished their repast, mounted *mustaphazin* and officers, amongst whom was Soleyman Sami, appeared, and gave hurried orders to the soldiers at the various posts. It appears that these orders were for them to abandon the town, and retire outside. The military at once formed at certain given points, such as the Place Mehemet Ali, the Place de l'Eglise, and the Place de la Mosque d'Attarin, and shortly after the evacuation commenced the greater part of the soldiers proceeded to the Mahmoudieh Canal.[2]

Then arose a general cry of "Death to the Christians!" People were heard hammering at the doors and windows of the houses. This was followed by the sound of falling shutters, and the crash of broken glass. Infuriated crowds appeared on the scene, armed with heavy sticks, with which they carried on the work of destroying and plundering the shops and dwellings. The soldiers, too, broke from the ranks and joined in the looting, and with the butt-ends of their rifles assisted in forcing open doors and windows.

Continuous lines of soldiers and civilians staggered past laden with plunder. In a short time the streets were literally blocked by the mob.

The order was given to the natives to quit the town, and from two p.m. a constant stream of fugitives flowed out of the Rosetta and Moharrem Bey Gates. When outside the town, they were met by Bedouins, who, in many cases, fought with them for the spoil.

---

2. On the 13th the troops removed to Esbet Horshid, 5,000 metres south of Millaha junction on the Cairo railway, so as not to be exposed to the fire of the ships. On the 14th they moved to Kingi Osman and Kafr Dowar, where they entrenched themselves.

One eye-witness stated that a common handkerchief changed hands in this way no less than three times whilst he was looking on. Not only furniture, looking-glasses, and such things, were carried off, but horses and carriages as well. The soldiers, in many instances, undressed themselves and wrapped round their bodies all sorts of rich stuffs, such as silks and satins. Some brought gilt chairs and sofas with them, but, finding the articles too cumbersome, broke them to pieces, and tore off the velvet coverings, leaving the remainder in the road.

The large open space between the water-works and the European cemeteries was crowded by a huge mob of pillagers, fighting and struggling amongst themselves for the plunder. Those who could get away with their spoils took them either by the road to Ramleh, or by that leading to the Mahmoudieh Canal.

The wildest disorder prevailed, and amongst the fugitives were Turkish women and children of good position from the different *harems*. On arriving at the gates of the town the women were attacked by the mob and outraged. The marauders, in their haste to get possession of the jewellery which the women were wearing, even cut their ears and wrists, and to silence their cries stunned them with blows from their sticks. Soon afterwards several soldiers were seen returning to the town, apparently to share in the pillage, and struggling to force their way through the gates against the stream of pillagers and fugitives going the other way. Many of those coming out encumbered with heavy loads were upset in the *mêlée*, and several of the soldiers, finding it impossible to re-enter the town, contented themselves with joining the Bedouins in seizing the loot of the fugitives.

About four p.m. volumes of smoke, accompanied by the crackling of flames, were observed in the neighbourhood of the British Consulate. These indications increased every instant, and as the sun went down the whole sky became lighted up with a lurid glare. This was accompanied by the shouts and cries of Europeans, who were either burned out or dragged from their dwellings by natives, who, with sticks and knives in their hands, spared few whom they met. A small number found refuge in the houses as yet untouched by the fire and guarded by Europeans, but most of the rest fell victims. Amongst those who humanely opened their doors to the fugitives was the Danish Consul, who sheltered no less than 150.

It was a night to be remembered. From the terraces of the houses the flames were observed extending in the direction of the Rue Cherif Pasha. The French Consulate, the Okella Nuova, and other parts of the

Place Mehemet Ali, were already wrapped in flames.

During the night nothing was heard but the crackling of the flames, mingled with the cries of the incendiaries and the occasional fall of a heavy building. The volumes of smoke filled the air with the most nauseating vapours. In some cases, cotton soaked in petroleum and set on fire was thrown into the houses, whilst in others tins of paraffin were poured over the furniture and ignited. Where ingress to the dwellings could not be obtained, bedding soaked with petroleum was piled up on the outside and fired. On every side the smell of petroleum was distinguishable.

The night passed without slumber for those on shore, and on the morning of the 13th Alexandria presented the appearance of a vast bonfire. The Europeans who remained on shore saw the flames gradually closing in on them. The pillagers and assassins had disappeared, but the atmosphere had become unbearable. There was further a fear that the Arabs, seeing that no force was being landed, might return to complete the work of massacre.

All hope of a disembarkation appeared as remote as ever. Two of the ironclads had indeed been seen to approach Fort Pharos and send their boats ashore, and for a moment it was thought help was coming. The idea was a vain one. The landing was only for the purpose of spiking the Egyptian cannon, and this having been accomplished, the ships steamed away.

The courageous garrison of the Anglo-Egyptian Bank, seeing there was no help to be expected, resolved to make a sortie, and early in the morning they all sallied forth together, the women and children were put in the middle of the troop, and thus they marched towards the Marina. On their way they were joined by others in the same condition as themselves. They passed, without encountering any opposition, over masses of burning and smouldering ruins. They broke open the gates at the Marina, and seizing some native boats rowed out to H.M.S. *Helicon*.

The Danish Consul and his party still held out, but the situation becoming worse and worse, at three in the afternoon, they, too, quitted their stronghold, and having secured the attendance of a European police officer, marched to the shore, having more than once to go out of their course to avoid the falling houses. On reaching the Custom-House Quay, they met the landing party under Commander Hammill. The fugitives passed the night in safety on board an Egyptian steamer in the harbour, and were next day taken off to the vessels outside.

CHAPTER 12

Events on Shore

On the day of the bombardment the *khedive* was at his Palace at Ramleh, abandoned by all but a few faithful followers.

His Highness was kept badly posted up as to the progress of the bombardment, and amongst those who came and went with despatches were a number of spies, who, from time to time, went off to Arabi to inform him of what was passing at the palace.

At 8.30 a.m. an *aide-de-camp* arrived with the news that a considerable number of the Egyptian gunners were killed, and that several guns had been dismounted. On the part of the commandant he begged the *khedive* to order reinforcements to be sent. The greatest excitement reigned. There were no artillerymen available, so the Minister of War was directed to despatch a force of infantry.

In the course of the forenoon news was brought that the forts were offering a stout resistance, and that serious damage was being inflicted on the English fleet. But later, in the afternoon, it became known that the forts were destroyed, and incapable of offering further opposition.

No further accounts arriving, the *khedive* sent for Arabi, about seven o'clock in the evening. Arabi came from Alexandria, where he had been during the bombardment, and on his arrival told the *khedive* that the forts were destroyed, and that it was no longer possible to defend them. "We must," he added, "either have recourse to other measures, or else come to terms with the admiral." After some consultation, and more or less vehement discussion, it was decided that Toulba Pasha should be sent to the admiral to confer.

On the morning of the 12th July about 500 Bedouin Arabs appeared before the Palace with the intention (as they said) of assuring the *khedive* of their fidelity, and with offers of assistance in case of need; but after a slight demonstration of loyalty they retired.

Shortly after mid-day Toulba returned and announced that the Admiral had said that, unless he was allowed peaceably to land his men at three points on the coast, he would recommence the bombardment at two o'clock.

To this demand Toulba said he had objected, as it gave him no time to obtain instructions, but that the admiral had refused to allow further delay. A hurried consultation took place, and it was decided to send Toulba Pasha to the admiral to tell him that Egypt had no power to authorize the landing of foreign troops on her shores without the consent of the *Porte*.

Toulba proceeded as far as the Arsenal, and, it being after two o'clock, the time fixed for recommencing the bombardment, he became alarmed at the signs of pillage and destruction he saw around him and refused to go any farther.

Shortly after his departure the Ramleh Palace was surrounded by cavalry and infantry, about 400 men in all; the first thought was of the loyal Bedouins, who had been there in the morning and declared their fidelity; but it was soon discovered that Arabi's people had distributed £2,000 amongst these and other loyalists to secure their absence; that the force was a hostile one, and that the *khedive* was left helpless with his handful of attendants. Panic spread in the palace, and the numerous domestics were beside themselves with fear. The *khedive* showed complete calmness and self-possession, and, sending to the commander of the troops, inquired what he wanted. He replied that his orders were to guard the palace. The *khedive* then sent Sultan Pasha to Arabi to ask the meaning of this proceeding. Arabi was at Rosetta Gate when Sultan Pasha arrived with the message from the *khedive*.

After some time Toulba Pasha reappeared at the palace with some of the ministers, who endeavoured to explain that the surrounding of the palace was a mistake, and that the officer in command should be punished. The situation remained unchanged until seven o'clock, when it was observed that the cavalry were preparing to depart—orders, it appeared, having been given that all troops should follow Arabi. One officer, however, remained behind with about 250 men.

A General Council was called at the palace, and it was determined to inform Admiral Seymour of the situation, and, if possible, get the *khedive* within reach of the fleet. This state of uncertainty and anxiety continued till the next morning, when the officer left in charge of the 250 men came to His Highness and declared himself to be loyal to the *khedive*. The *khedive* made him a firm and impressive speech. The other officers of his company were called up, and all swore loyalty and devotion, and kissed His Highness's hand. A distribution of decorations followed, and confidence was restored.

Zohrab Bey[1] was then sent to inform the Admiral that the *khedive* wished to return to Ras-el-Tin, and at once returned with the news that the admiral had sent a guard to assist him.

Tewfik then started for Ras-el-Tin Palace, and in driving into the town had to make a *détour* so as to enter by the Moharrem Bey Gate. He was escorted by sixty or seventy cavalry, and preceded by a group of outriders carrying white flags on the points of their sabres. He had to pass *en route* numerous bands of pillagers and incendiaries, and on reaching the palace was received by Admiral Seymour and a force of marines.

In the meantime Commander Hammill's party of 250 bluejackets and 150 marines had landed without opposition. They reached the palace of Ras-el-Tin at 10 30 a.m., seized the western end of the Peninsula, occupied the Arsenal, and threw out a line of sentries north and south extending from shore to shore. At 12.30 p.m. a small party of marines and a Gatling's crew from the *Monarch* pushed on towards the town and guarded the streets in the immediate neighbourhood, making prisoners of natives who were seen looting inside the gates, and firing upon those more remote. In Frank Street they found every shop looted and burnt. The looters retreated before them, and dropped their plunder.[2]

The streets were strewn with the most miscellaneous articles—broken clock-cases, empty jewel-boxes, and fragments of all kinds. Every now and then the party had to run up a side street to avoid the fall of a house or wall. Bodies of Europeans, stripped and mutilated, were seen in the Place Mehemet Ali, in an advanced state of putrefaction.[3]

The work of incendiarism was still going on, and even the women were seen setting fire to houses with petroleum. The fires had occasioned enormous damage in the European quarter, where not a street was passable for any distance, all being more or less blocked by the smoking ruins of the fallen houses. Walls were still tumbling down, and the hot air was opaque with lime-dust and smoke.

The scenes on every side were appalling. The parts of Alexandria

---

1. Afterwards Sir Edward Zohrab Pasha K.C.M G.
2. At the time when the town was a mass of smouldering ruins, and such shops as existed had been looted, a youthful midshipman of the fleet, ashore, on being asked what he thought of Alexandria, replied, "Oh, the place is well enough; the only thing is, *jam* is so dear."
3. The commander of the German gunboat *Habicht*, who landed on the 14th, found a dozen bodies of Europeans lying in the streets which he had to pass through on his way to the German Hospital.

which were found to have been destroyed, or which were destroyed in the next two days, included not only the Grand Square, or Place Mehemet Ali, but all the streets leading from it to the sea, the Rue Cherif Pasha and the Rue Tewfik Pasha, with the adjoining streets. In the square itself the kiosques were destroyed; the statue of Mehemet Ali on horseback in the centre alone remained untouched. One side of the Place de l'Eglise, one side of the Rue de la Mosque d'Attarin, a portion of the Boulevards de Ramleh and de Rosette, and the whole of the northern portion of the Rue de la Bourse, were also consumed. In addition to these, most of the houses in the following thoroughfares were destroyed: Rue Osman Pasha, Rue de l'Attarin, Rue des Sœurs, Rue de l'Enchere, and Rue du Prophete Daniel. The French and Austrian post offices were burned, together with the Hôtel d'Europe and the Messageries Hôtel;[4] also the English, French, Greek, Portuguese, and Brazilian Consulates, the Mont de Piété, and one police-station.

Such of the European dwellings as were not burnt were looted from top to bottom; articles of furniture not easily removed were wantonly injured or destroyed. Several of the native houses and shops also suffered in the general looting carried on. Almost the only European dwellings untouched were the few in which Europeans were known to have remained.

The English Church was struck by a shell, but not otherwise injured; the German, the Coptic, the Catholic, and the Israelitish churches were also uninjured, except that the last-named received one shell. The theatres, the banks, and the tribunals escaped injury.[5]

---

4. The Hôtel Abbat, so well known to European visitors, was only saved by a clever ruse on the part of the Berberine "*bowab*," or doorkeeper, who was left in sole charge of the premises. When a mob of native pillagers hammered at the door to obtain admittance, the faithful domestic, from the inside, recollecting some of the choice expressions he had picked up from British tourists, shouted, "You b——b——s; what the b—— h—— do you want?" &c., &c. The effect was magical. The assailants said to each other, "Why, the house is full of *Inglesi!*" and hurriedly made a retreat, leaving the hotel uninjured.

5. Of the pecuniary loss sustained through the pillage and incendiarism some idea may be formed from the statistics subsequently furnished by the International Commission of Indemnities. The total sum awarded was 106,820,236 *francs*, or £4,341,011. Of this sum, 26,750,175 *fr.*, or £1,070,007, was given for house property destroyed, and 34,635,050 *fr.*, or £1,385,402, for furniture, and 43,395,061 *fr.*, or £1,735,806, for merchandise. When one bears in mind that the decree appointing the commission expressly excluded claims for money, jewellery, securities, and works of art, it will be obvious that the total value of property stolen or destroyed must have considerably exceeded the sums above quoted.

It must be borne in mind that all this destruction was the work, not of the ships, but of the native population. The aim of the vessels, directed solely on the forts, had been so true that the damage done to the town by the half-dozen or so shells which struck it was insignificant, and, with the exception of the harem buildings at Ras-el-Tin, the British missiles did not create a single conflagration.

At the same time it is difficult to hold Admiral Seymour quite blameless in the matter. So great was the demoralization of the Egyptians that had the admiral, on his own initiative, landed but a few hundred of the 5,880 men on board his ships on the morning of the 12th, they could easily have occupied the town and averted the catastrophe.

Curiously enough, after the mischief was done, the Admiralty on the 13th sent a telegram directly authorizing "a landing of seamen and marines for police purposes, to restore order."

During the afternoon and evening the marines of the *Superb, Inflexible, Temeraire, Achilles,* and *Sultan* were added to the forces on shore. Captain Fisher, of the *Inflexible,* took command of the whole force, and the patrolling of the city was begun. A company of Royal Marine artillerymen, armed as infantry, marched through the European and the Arab quarters of Alexandria. They shot some natives caught in the act of setting fire to houses, and also three of the native police, who were pillaging a house after having maltreated the Berberine doorkeeper.

The *Inflexible, Temeraire,* and *Achilles* were stationed off Ramleh to command the land approaches to Alexandria from the southward and westward.

On the 14th the *Penelope,* with Admiral Hoskins, left for Port Saïd.

Of the events of the 14th, Admiral Seymour says, "Employed during the whole of the day landing as many men as we could spare from the squadron, and by evening we had occupied the most important positions."

Alexandria being a walled town, the distribution of the force at Captain Fisher's disposal had to be governed by this fact, and was practically as follows:—At the Ramleh station were marines from the *Monarch*. At the Rosetta Gate were marines from the *Temeraire*. At the Moharrem Bey Gate were marines from the *Alexandra*. At Fort Kom-el-Dyk Gate were marines from the *Sultan*. At Pompey's Pillar Gate were marines from the *Superb*. At the Gabari Caracol Gate were marines from the *Achilles*. At the Gabari railway station were marines and bluejackets from the *Alexandra*. At the *Zaptieh* and Arsenal were marines from the *Invincible*. As the streets were gradually explored the bodies of many Europeans were discovered; others were found floating in the harbour. The corpses found in the streets were buried as quickly as possible. During this time the town was still being fired and looted in places.

On the 15th the *Minotaur* arrived with Admiral Dowell, in command of the Channel Squadron, and a brigade of seamen and marines from her was at once disembarked. Fort Napoleon was occupied by gunners from the fleet. Fort Kom-el-Dyk, which it was reported had been mined, was also occupied by bluejackets. A party of men from the *Alexandra* destroyed the guns at Fort Silsileh with gun-cotton.[6]

The German, American, and Greek ships of war landed men to assist in restoring order. Lord Charles Beresford was appointed Chief of Police, and persons found pillaging or setting fire to houses were brought before him and summarily dealt with. Those guilty of pillaging were flogged, and incendiaries were sentenced to be shot. The American marines rendered much service in promptly disposing of incendiaries, and in blowing up houses with gunpowder to check the conflagration.

In consequence of a rumour that Arabi intended to attack the town, a large number of bluejackets and marines, with Gatling guns, were landed, each ship reinforcing its detachment on shore.

As a fact, Arabi was busy entrenching himself at Kafr Dowar, and had no more thought of attacking the British forces than they had of making an onslaught on him. This, however, was not known to the British admiral, who at eleven p.m. telegraphed to the Admiralty as follows:—"Arabi Pasha reported to be advancing on Alexandria. I have telegraphed to Port Saïd to intercept ships from Cyprus, and ordered them to call here on their way back."

On the 15th the *khedive* summoned Arabi to Alexandria, which was a little like "calling up spirits from the vasty deep;" and Arabi telegraphed from Kafr Dowar, by way of response, that "His Highness

---

6. This wanton and useless work of destruction was repeated at all the forts bearing on the sea. The light guns (6-1/2 inch S.B.) were hove off their carriages, and the rifled guns treated with gun-cotton. Hundreds of tons of gunpowder were ruined, and scores of valuable guns rendered useless. The object of this destruction is hardly evident. It is the more incomprehensible as on the 13th July Admiral Seymour had received a despatch from the Admiralty in the following terms: "Opposition having ceased, do not dismantle forts or disable guns."

would be glad to hear that recruits were coming in to assist him to fight the English."

At the *khedive*'s suggestion the admiral, on the 16th, despatched two ships to command Aboukir in case Arabi should attempt to cut the dyke there and let in the sea.

The same day it was found necessary to re-embark the Greek marines who had been landed to restore order, without, however, being very successful. The Americans and the others, excepting the Germans, likewise re-embarked. The Germans remained on shore some days later, and were most useful.

On the 16th fresh fires broke out in the town, and a party of Bedouins, 150 strong, appeared at Gabari Gate, bent upon looting. They succeeded in capturing a donkey, when they were fired on by a midshipman of the *Alexandra* and twelve seamen, and two of their number were killed.

On the 17th further reinforcements arrived. The *Tamar* arrived with 1,000 marines from Cyprus. The *Agincourt* and *Northumberland* (ironclads) arrived from Port Saïd with the 38th (South Staffordshire) Regiment, 860 strong, and a battalion of the 60th Rifles, 1,700 in all. The *Salamis*, with General Sir Archibald Alison and staff, also arrived, and the General assumed the command of the land forces, now numbering 3,686 men.

On the same day, Commander Maude, of the *Temeraire*, rode out to within 300 yards of Arabi's position at Kafr Dowar. At Millaha Junction, Commander Maude found several human bodies lying about in various stages of decomposition. There were signs of loot in all directions, and the bodies were evidently those of looters who had in their turn been robbed by the soldiers.

The rebel camp was reported to consist of 6,000 men, with six batteries of rifled guns, one battery of Gatlings, and 300 marine artillery, besides Bedouins. They were intrenching themselves behind earthworks on the line of railway.

The *khedive* now announced that Arabi had been suspended from his functions as Minister of War. The Ministry of Foreign Affairs, in communicating to the admiral the dismissal of Arabi, stated that "the publication of the decree was deferred for fear of seeing reproduced in Cairo and other towns the disorder which had taken place in Alexandria."

On the 18th, the troopship *Orontes* arrived from Malta, but through some unaccountable blundering of the authorities, she came without a single soldier.

By this time order was beginning to be re-established in Alexandria; the fires, too, had either burnt themselves out or been extinguished. The Egyptian Post Office was reopened in the town, and the work of clearing the streets was proceeded with rapidly. For this purpose many natives and others out of employment were utilized.

The first day's work in street-clearing was marked by the first public execution. A negro, who had been caught setting fire to some houses, was, after a court-martial, tied to a tree in the Place Mehemet Ali, and shot by a party of sailors. The people too began to return to the town. These, however, required to be watched, as they were almost to a man Arabists, and ready to resume the work of incendiarism and plunder on the first opportunity. Looters were still to be found lurking in odd corners, notably in the Minet-el-Bassel quarter, where there were stores containing sugar and grain.

The sanitary condition of the town now began to give rise to apprehension. Disagreeable odours, indicating the presence of dead bodies, were perceived proceeding from many of the houses. These were, no doubt, the victims of the pillagers, left to lie where they fell.

On the 18th the land defence of the city was definitely assumed by the army, assisted at the Rosetta Gate by marines from the ships, and elsewhere by the bluejackets with their Gatling guns.

At this period it was found that the supply of provisions in Alexandria was running short, and steps had to be considered for stopping the return of the European fugitives.

Chapter 13

The Situation

On the 19th July, Dervish Pasha, the *sultan's* envoy, whose pacifying mission to Egypt had so signally failed, left Alexandria for Constantinople.

On the 20th a proclamation was issued by Admiral Seymour, with the permission of the *khedive*. It announced that "Orders had been given to officers commanding patrols to shoot any person taken in the act of incendiarism; that any person taken in the act of pillage would be sent to the Zaptieh to be tried and punished; that any person taken a second time for the same offence would be shot; and that no person would be allowed to enter or leave the town after sunset."

On the 23rd three natives and one Greek were shot for incendiarism.

It may be interesting to know how things were going on in the interior. Omar Pasha Loutfi, Governor of Alexandria, returning from Cairo, reported that he had seen Europeans massacred, and their houses pillaged, at Damanhour, Tantah, and Mehalleh. The governor also stated that he had seen a European and his wife murdered at the Tookh Station, half-an-hour distant by rail from Cairo.

According to an inquiry made by the prefect of police at Tantah, the number of Europeans murdered, and subsequently buried, in that town, amounted to fifty-one, and there were about an equal number massacred and thrown into the canal. At Kafr Zayat, six persons were killed. Ten Greeks and three Jews were murdered at Benha. Disturbances also occurred at Zag-a-zig, but no persons were killed there, although one was wounded. At Galioub, a family was taken out of the railway train, put under the carriages, and crushed by the wheels. The inspector of the "Cadastre" at Mehalleh Kebir reported that fifteen Europeans were killed there. At Kafr Dowar also some Europeans were massacred. The exact number is not known. Five Europeans were killed at Mehalla-Abou-Ali.

In Cairo, Omar Loutfi found that the greatest excitement and panic prevailed. The Prefects of Menoufieh and Garbieh, and the *Mudir* (or Governor) of Galioubieh, were imprisoned in the citadel for obeying the *khedive*.

A general council had been summoned at the Ministry of the Interior to consider the question of continuing the military preparations. It was attended by about a hundred *pashas, ulemas*, and merchants. After a number of violent speeches against the *khedive*, the Coptic Patriarch remarked that the assembly had as yet heard only one side of the question, *viz.*, that of Arabi, and that before coming to any decision it was necessary to hear the *khedive*'s side as well. The views of the Coptic Patriarch were adopted by the majority of the assembly, which proceeded to nominate a delegation.

The delegation consisted of Ali Pasha Moubarek (a former minister) and five others, who were directed to proceed to Alexandria to see the *khedive*, and ask His Highness what truth there was in the charges of the Arabists; they were also directed to ascertain whether all the Ministers were really in prison, as had been stated.

As regards the rebel military preparations, Mahmoud Pasha Sami had been appointed commander-in-chief of the army corps stationed in the neighbourhood of the Suez Canal. Arabi demanded that one-sixth of the male population of every province should be sent to Kafr Dowar. All old soldiers of every description were called upon to serve again, and horses and provisions were everywhere requisitioned for the army.

"Arabi's chief strength," wrote Mr. Cartwright, the Acting British Consul-General, "lay in his unscrupulous and barbarous mode of warfare." At the moment, there was such a terrible dread among the officials at the palace of what might happen to their property in Cairo and elsewhere, that the *khedive*'s action was paralyzed, and His Highness was deterred from denouncing Arabi as a rebel by his unwillingness to incur the consequences of Arabi's retaliation. At an interview with the *khedive*, Mr. Cartwright endeavoured to represent to him the moral effect which such a denunciation would produce, and the encouragement it would afford to those who remained faithful to His Highness.

On the 22nd the *khedive* published a decree dismissing Arabi from his post of Minister of War, and proclaiming him a rebel. Omar Loutfi was appointed in his place. The reasons for Arabi's dismissal as set forth in the decree were the insufficient resistance offered to the British fleet, the loss of 400 guns, allowing the English to land without resistance, the retreat to Kafr Dowar, and his disobedience in not coming to the *khedive* when summoned.

Considering the relations existing between the *khedive* and the British forces at this time, the decree, issued at a period when Tewfik was no longer under any sort of coercion, is as curious a specimen of an Oriental document as generally comes to light. The proclamation itself may be regarded as a reply to one issued by Arabi against the *khedive*, and transmitted to the governors of the various provinces in Egypt.

On the 26th, Arabi telegraphed to the *sultan* protesting his fidelity to the *khalifate*, and saying:

> That being provoked into a war, he was in possession of all that was necessary to overcome his enemies, thanks to the Divine assistance.
> That he did not believe that, as the enemies of his country and religion asserted, he would find Ottoman troops on his path, which would place him under the cruel necessity of treating as enemies his brethren in the faith.

Ali Pasha Moubarek succeeded in reaching Alexandria. He reported that at Kafr Dowar large numbers of soldiers were flocking to Arabi from the villages, arms were being distributed to all comers, and a total force of 30,000 men had been got together. Raouf Pasha, however, who came from the camp a few days later, gave the number of Arabi's men as only 15,000, and related that much sickness prevailed amongst them.

On the 3rd August the official journal of Cairo published the decision of a great National Council of the week before, to the effect that—

> In consequence of the occupation of Alexandria by foreign troops, of the presence of the English squadron in Egyptian waters, and finally of the attitude taken up by Arabi Pasha for the purpose of repulsing the enemy, Arabi Pasha was to be upheld as Minister of War and Marine, intrusted with the general command of the Egyptian army, and full authority in all that concerned military operations, and that the orders of the *khedive* and his ministers would be null and void.

The document bore the signatures of the three Princes Ibrahim,

Ahmed, and Kamil (cousins of the *khedive*), of the Sheikh of the El Azhar Mosque, of the Grand Cadi of Egypt, of the Coptic Patriarch, of the Grand Cadi of Cairo, besides those of the Ulemas and Judges, and in fact all the notabilities left in Cairo.

On the 19th July, at the request of the Foreign Office, additional troops were ordered to Malta and Cyprus to bring up the forces there to 15,000 men; and the next day the British Cabinet had so far realized the gravity of the situation as to decide on the despatch of an English expedition to Egypt, with or without the consent of the Powers.

The vote of credit for the expedition, £2,300,000, was asked in Parliament on the 24th July, Mr. Gladstone carefully explaining that the country *"was not at war."*

The Scots Guards sailed for Alexandria on the 30th July, the head of a column of ships and regiments which from that time until the occupation of the Suez Canal on the 20th August never ceased to stream towards its ultimate point of destination.

The force was originally fixed at 21,200 men, composed as follows:—Cavalry, 2,400; infantry, 13,400; artillery, 1,700; hospital and other non-combatant services, 3,700, with a reserve of 3,100, to sail at a later period. The entire force was to be under the command of General Sir Garnet Wolseley, G.C.B., with General Sir John Adye, K.C.B., as second in command, and Lieutenant-Generals G. H. Willis, C.B., and Sir E. B. Hamley as divisional commanders.

One hundred men of the 24th Middlesex (Post Office) Volunteers were chosen to accompany the forces and take charge of the postal arrangements during the campaign.[1]

---

1. The reinforcements which were prepared after the despatch of the first corps amounted to 280 officers and 10,800 men, so that the total force despatched, or in the act of being despatched, to the end of the war from Great Britain and the Mediterranean stations amounted to 1,290 officers and 32,000 men. The Indian contingent, including a small reserve left at Aden, consisted of 170 officers and 7,100 men. Some of these, consisting of depôts, and drafts, and one infantry battalion, were stopped at the last moment, but on the whole not far short of 40,000 men were sent. The troops despatched from India were the 1st Seaforth Highlanders and the 1st Manchester, two Bengal and one Bombay battalions of Native Infantry, with one 9-pounder field battery and one mountain battery, each of six guns, and three regiments of Bengal Cavalry, with some sappers and miners from Madras. The force was accompanied by about 3,500 followers, including transport drivers, 1,700 horses, 840 ponies, and nearly 5,000 mules, some for regimental and others for general transport purposes. The first battalion left Bombay on the 22nd July. The rest of the force received their orders on the 24th July, and began to leave on August 5th. The government engaged 71 transports in England and 54 in India.

Sir Garnet Wolseley's instructions were to take command of the army ordered for service in Egypt in support of the authority of the *khedive* to suppress a military revolt in that country. He was told that Her Majesty's Government did not wish to fetter his discretion as to the particular military operations which might be necessary, but that the main object of the expedition was to re-establish the power of the *khedive*. He was empowered, after successful operations against Arabi and those in arms against the *khedive*, to enter into any military convention which the circumstances might warrant, but to make no arrangements involving a political settlement.

In despatching the British expedition, Mr. Gladstone's Government made a final plunge in the direction which they had from the first wished to avoid. No one can say that their intervention came too soon.

The *khedive* on the 19th had sent for Sir Auckland Colvin, who was the right-hand man of the Acting British Consul-General, and begged him to urge Her Majesty's Government to take further action without delay. He pointed out that it was most necessary, as Arabi's power had become so great as to spread terror and consternation in the minds of all the natives. His possession of the country, and especially of Cairo, His Highness added, left at his mercy the families and property of all who remained loyal to the *khedive*. His Highness concluded by saying he should be glad to receive an intimation as to the steps which were contemplated. Those steps, as has been seen, culminated in the despatch of the British expedition.

The means by which the British Government was gradually induced to adopt a resolute attitude in regard to Egypt, and the degrees by which it arrived at a decision, will appear later on.

The general feeling of uneasiness at Alexandria was augmented by Omar Loutfi's report. It was further known that Arabi's forces were daily increasing, and scouts ascertained that his outposts had been advanced in the direction of the town. Repeated rumours of intended attacks from time to time prevailed, and scarcely a night passed without an alarm of one kind or another.

The British authorities now began to employ themselves seriously in looking to the defences of the town, and on the 20th Major Ardagh and the engineers proceeded to repair the drawbridges, to mend the walls at Kom-el-Dyk, to mount guns at Rosetta Gate, to secure the railway station, and to place Gatlings in position. Three 9-pounder rifled guns were mounted in Fort Kom-el-Dyk, as part of the permanent defences of the city, and manned by bluejackets from the fleet.

On the 19th, a brisk wind fanned the embers of some of the ruins into flames, which occupied the fire brigade several hours to subdue.

The water supply of Alexandria at this time began to be a source of anxiety. The supply to the town comes from the Mahmoudieh Canal, which joins the Rosetta branch of the Nile at Atfeh, forty-five miles distant. The canal itself adjoins the position taken by Arabi at Kafr Dowar. Throughout the bombardment, and subsequently, the town had been abundantly supplied by the efforts of Mr. J. E. Cornish, the manager. When, previous to the bombardment, all his countrymen, and the great mass of Europeans, sought safety afloat, he refused to desert his post. He contrived an elaborate system of defence for the water-works. It comprised an arrangement for throwing jets of steam at any possible band of assailants, as well as a line of dynamite bombs, capable of being exploded by means of electricity.

The upper part of the engine house was also converted into a kind of arsenal, into which he and his men could retire as a last resort, and where rifles and ammunition were in readiness. During the bombardment, the works happily escaped injury. Subsequently, from the roof of the engine house, Mr. Cornish and his companions (nine Europeans in all) watched the progress of the bombardment, until the shot and shell which whistled overhead from the vessels firing at Fort Pharos compelled them to descend. Meanwhile, the pumps were kept going as in ordinary times.

When, on the afternoon of the 12th, the mob of rioters left the town, the majority of them passed a few yards from the works, and indulged in curses and execrations at the "Christian dogs" within. With humane forethought, two large jars of water were placed in front of the gate and kept supplied from within. Thousands of thirsty natives, coming from the dust and smoke of the town, stopped to drink, and, after cursing the manager heartily, passed on. To whatever cause it may be attributed, no attack was made on the works, and their courageous director survived to receive the congratulations of the *khedive* and of his own countrymen.[2]

Arabi's position at Kafr Dowar placed the water supply of Alexandria at his mercy, and he was not long in taking advantage of the circumstance. On the 21st July, the water in the Mahmoudieh Canal was observed to be rapidly falling. Arabi had made a dam, at a point

---

2. Mr. Cornish had the decoration of the C.M.G. conferred on him for his conduct on this occasion.

called Kinje Osman, between Kafr Dowar and Alexandria, by which all further flow from the Nile was stopped. Assuming that his operations were limited to this, the great quantity of water in the Alexandria end of the canal insured a supply for about twelve days. It was rumoured, however, that he had broken the banks of the canal on the Alexandria side.

This would, of course, have soon cut off the supply altogether, and have caused much suffering among the population, beside forcing the troops to rely on the distilled water from the ships. In view of the emergency, Admiral Seymour appointed a commission to sit every day to consider the measures to be adopted. Steps were taken to stop all the steam-engines and "*sakeah*" (or water-wheels) taking water from the canal for irrigation purposes, arrangements were made for clearing out and filling the old Roman water-cisterns, and H.M.S. *Supply* was ordered from Malta with the necessary apparatus for distilling water in large quantities.

On the 21st, Arabi caused salt water to be let into the Mahmoudieh Canal, by cutting the dam separating it from Lake Mareotis, thereby considerably aggravating the difficulty of the water supply.

A rumour was started that the *khedive*'s palace at Ramleh had been looted by the English soldiery. Major Ardagh was instructed to hold a searching inquiry, the result of which was that the report was found to be utterly without foundation. The soldiers, individually, were searched, and no loot was discovered. The palace had, indeed, been looted to a large extent, as might have been expected from the fact that, from the time of its evacuation till the 24th, it was wholly unguarded.[3]

---

[3]. It is only fair to the British Army to say that but very little looting was ever proved against them during this period. Isolated cases of breaking into houses and carrying off wines and spirits occurred, but these were almost the only instances. The foreign population of Alexandria and Ramleh have frequently borne testimony to this effect, as well as to the perfect impartiality with which British cellars, as well as those of other Europeans, were requisitioned by individual soldiers and sailors in an informal manner.

Chapter 14

Military Operations

On the 21st July Sir Archibald Alison moved two regiments of infantry and a squadron of mounted men out to Ramleh in the direction of Arabi's intrenchments. They went as far as Water-Works Hill, a commanding position from which a good view of the Egyptian lines at Kafr Dowar could be obtained.

On the morning of the 22nd a force of 250 men of the Rifles was pushed forward beyond Millaha Junction, on the Cairo Railway, to blow up the line. They met Arabi's cavalry and exchanged shots with them. The Egyptians fled, leaving two dead on the field. Having finished the work intrusted to them, the Rifles then withdrew. A strong patrol was the same day sent to Ramleh.

On the 24th, the troopship *Malabar* having arrived the previous day from Gibraltar and Malta with the 46th (Duke of Cornwall's Light Infantry) Regiment, a wing of the 35th, and a battery of artillery, in all 1,108 men, Sir Archibald Alison, at 3 a.m., sent mounted infantry to the position intended to be occupied in front of the Ramleh Barracks. The general followed by the train of the Alexandria and Ramleh Railway with the 60th Rifles, two 7-pounder naval guns, and some sappers. On arriving he found the ridge running from the palace to the Mahmoudieh Canal occupied by the mounted infantry, and at once took possession of the water-works tower on the ridge, a strongly defensible building, and established outposts at the railway bridge, and at the front of the canal bend.

Shortly after the British troops were in position a small force of Arabi's cavalry, followed by infantry, advanced towards the railway bridge, across the canal, within 400 yards of the Rifles. After exchanging shots for some time, the cavalry retired rapidly on the Mahmoudieh Canal. The enemy's advance then became more decided. A considerable force of cavalry with two horse-artillery guns pushed on rapidly, the guns coming briskly into action. The infantry followed, and the movements of a considerable body of troops were observed on the high ground behind. A fight ensued which lasted about an hour, several of the enemy being observed to drop. The attack, however, was not pushed home, and the firing gradually ceased. There were no casualties on the English side.

Ramleh was from this day occupied and held by the British forces. The work of fortifying it was begun at once, and prosecuted with vigour, for the force opposed to the English far outnumbered the latter at all times, and the need of the moment was to hold on until the army corps under General Wolseley could be collected and transported to Alexandria.

It may be here mentioned that Ramleh is not a village or town, but a species of summer resort for the European residents of Alexandria, who have built houses and villas upon the sandy neck of land lying between Lakes Mareotis and Aboukir on the one hand, and the Mediterranean on the other. The houses are distributed over a length of some miles, and are mostly surrounded by high walled inclosures, with, in many cases, luxuriant gardens. Between these scattered country villas the sand lay everywhere ankle-deep. There was an occasional pretence of a road, but, generally speaking, communication between any two points was in the straightest possible line, and over the sand. To supply the needed transit to and from the city, a private company has constructed the Alexandria and Ramleh Railway, which has no connection, material or otherwise, with the government lines. An incidental advantage due to the military occupation of Ramleh was the protection enjoyed by the Ramleh Railway, and by the owners of property in this quarter.

The water-works at Ramleh contain the pumping engines which deliver the fresh water for distribution from the Mahmoudieh Canal to the tower and reservoir just behind them on higher ground. These two points, the water-works and the tower, were the centre of the defence. A strong detachment was always maintained at the former, whilst the head-quarters were established at the latter. An elevation immediately in rear of the tower was strengthened, a trench dug, and a number of guns, *viz.*, five breech-loading 40 pounders and two 12-pounders, were mounted on the 26th by seamen from the fleet. A magazine was also sunk, and working parties ran a shelter trench along the crest of the rising ground, and this was gradually converted into a musketry parapet four and a half feet high. In this work places were arranged for the guns, the platforms being of railway sleepers and the parapets riveted with sand-bags and timber.

Small musketry redoubts were thrown up upon the flanks of the position. To the east and west were intrenched infantry camps. Two 9-pounders of the Naval Detachment were mounted in the adjoining earthwork. The extreme eastern picket was placed in a fortified house, a mile and a half distant. Its object was to serve as a feeler in the direction of Aboukir. The Egyptians could advance from Kinje Osman either by the road on the canal bank or by the railway embankment. The outpost on the former line was called "Dead Horse Picket;" on the latter no regular picket was maintained beyond the iron railway bridge over the Mahmoudieh Canal, although vedettes were thrown out in the direction of Millaha Junction.

As a barrier against a movement along the southern branch of the railway (that coming from the Gabari Station), a strong force was established at the Villa Antoniadis on the canal. Inside the entrance to the villa garden was a semi-circular breastwork facing the villa, and reaching across the gateway. Two B.L.R. 40-pounder guns were permanently mounted. These commanded the approach along the railway embankment. Other stockades were built across the road to protect the rear, and temporary bridges were built across the canal. The walls of a deserted Arab village on the other side were loopholed and otherwise defended.

The general defence profited by the presence of the Mahmoudieh Canal, with its high banks, and by the railway embankment, which stretched from the Antoniadis garden towards Ramleh. For night-work an electric light was placed on the roof of a house at Fleming Station, on the Ramleh Railway, so as to illuminate the approaches from Aboukir and Kafr Dowar.

An ingenious device for reconnoitring was at this time adopted, in fitting out an armour-clad train in which to make reconnaissances towards Arabi's lines. One of the government locomotives was armed under the direction of Captain Fisher, of the *Inflexible*, with a 40-pounder gun, and fitted with boiler plates, iron rails, and bags of cotton to protect the vital parts. This, accompanied by two or three open carriages filled with bluejackets, rendered considerable service. It was frequently brought into action, and whilst able to considerably harass the enemy's forces at Kafr Dowar, never sustained any injury in return.

At this time, Mr. Dudley de Chair, midshipman of the *Alexandra*, was captured and taken to Arabi's lines. He had been ordered to proceed with despatches from Alexandria to the British post at Ramleh, following the line of rail. Unfortunately, he went by the wrong line and found himself at Mandara, some miles beyond his destination, where, meeting some natives, he inquired his way, and they undertook to direct him to the British lines, but taking advantage of his ignorance of the locality, they led him to an Arab outpost, where he was made prisoner.[1]

On the 31st July, some Bedouins, who had been pillaging the neighbouring houses, attacked the night pickets at Ramleh with considerable energy, but were beaten off. In one of these skirmishes, what was taken to be the figure of a Bedouin was seen under the palm trees. A whole volley was fired at the supposed enemy, which proved to be only a pump. When examined closely the next morning the pump was found not to have received a single bullet.

On the following night, the Bedouins returned and attacked a picket of the 60th Rifles, posted at the extreme limit of the British position on the Mahmoudieh Canal. The picket, uncertain of the strength of the attacking force, fired a single volley and fell back on the pumping-station, a mile distant. Reinforcements were sent, and the position was reoccupied.[2]

On the 5th August, the first serious engagement of the campaign took place, when Sir Archibald Alison, being desirous of ascertaining the enemy's true position and strength, made a reconnaissance towards Kinje Osman. A half battalion of the Duke of Cornwall's Regiment and a half battalion of the 38th (South Staffordshire) Regiment, 800 in all, with one 9-pounder gun and the mounted infantry, numbering 80, were told off to advance along the east bank of the Mahmoudieh Canal.[3] Six companies of the 60th Rifles, about 500 strong, with one 9-pounder gun, formed the centre, and were to advance along the west bank. These constituted the left attack. They were to follow the

---

1. Mr. de Chair was sent by Arabi to Cairo, where, a report having been circulated that Admiral Seymour was being brought a prisoner to the capital, great crowds of natives assembled. Mr. de Chair was lodged in a building at Abdin used as a school for the sons of officers of the army and well treated, and at the conclusion of hostilities he was released.

2. The picket on this occasion retired with some precipitancy, and the circumstance was taken advantage of by one of the London newspapers to publish a highly coloured account of the affair, which was afterwards officially contradicted.

line of the canal till they reached a house in a grove of trees towards the point where the Cairo Railway approaches nearest to the canal.

Along the line of rail a battalion of marines, 1,000 in number, was to come up by train to Millaha Junction, preceded by the armoured train carrying one 40-pounder, two 9-pounder guns, a Nordenfeldt, and two Gatlings, this formed the right attack. The train was to stop at Millaha Junction. The marines were ordered to descend there and advance by the railway line, accompanied by the two 9-pounders and covered by the fire of the 40-pounder from the train.

The ground beyond Millaha Junction between the canal and railway was occupied by native houses and gardens, and traversed in all directions by small irrigating canals or ditches. Here were the Egyptian outposts, the point of attack. It was a place admitting of very thorough defence, and it gained in practical value by the fact that the attack was divided by the Mahmoudieh Canal into two parts, which could only pass from one side to the other with great difficulty and at considerable risk. An enemy on the alert might have routed the extreme left column before any assistance could have been rendered by the right.

The left column commenced its advance from the Ramleh out-picket station at 4.45 p.m., moving by both banks of the canal. It soon came into action with the enemy, who were strongly posted in a group of palm trees on the eastern side, and a strong defensible house and gardens on the western side, of the canal. The Egyptian fire was very inaccurate, most of their bullets passing harmlessly overhead. Both positions were carried, though not without the loss of Lieutenant Howard Vyse, of the Rifles, who was killed.

The enemy then took up another position half a mile in the rear of the first upon the east bank of the canal, amongst high crops and houses, and behind the irregular banks of the canal. From this position also they were driven back.

General Alison accompanied the right column himself. The marines and 9-pounder guns, dragged by bluejackets, were placed to the

---

3. The Mahmoudieh Canal, connecting Alexandria with the Nile, was one of Mehemet Ali's greatest works. Whilst it was in course of construction a French engineer was asked by the *pasha* what he thought of the plan. The Frenchman replied, "Your Highness must pardon me if I suggest that your canal will be very crooked." "Do your rivers in France run in a straight line?" asked the *pasha*. "Certainly not," said the man of science. "Who made them; was it not *Allah*?" again questioned the *pasha*. "Assuredly," was the reply. "Well then," the *pasha* triumphantly exclaimed, "do you think that either you or I know better than *Allah* how water ought to run?"

west and under cover of the railway embankment, and moved forward as rapidly as possible, and quite out of sight of the enemy engaged with the left column, with a view to cutting off their retreat. After a time this movement was perceived, and the enemy opened fire with artillery on the right column. General Alison pushed on as rapidly as possible to the spot where the railway approaches nearest to the Mahmoudieh Canal. He then opened fire with musketry from the railway embankment upon the enemy lining the banks of the canal. The two 9-pounders were dragged on to the embankment and came into action against the enemy's guns, the 40-pounder from the train firing overhead against the point where the enemy were beginning to appear.

Fixing his right upon both sides of the embankment, Alison then threw forward two companies to carry a house near the canal, and followed up this movement by throwing some four companies still more to his left on the banks of and across the canal. The left column, it appears, had orders to seize a certain white house on the canal, but its commander, Lieutenant-Colonel Thackwell, of the 38th, mistook the first white house reached for the one intended. In consequence, the left of the marines was uncovered and the substantial benefits of the fight lost. Had the two wings joined many prisoners would have been secured, and two guns, if not more, been captured. Signals were made to the left wing to advance, but the smoke of the battle and the failing light prevented their being understood.

As it was, Sir Archibald succeeded in taking up a position forming a diagonal line across both the canal and the railway, the enemy falling back slowly before him. The fire of their 7-pounder and 9-pounder guns was soon got under by the fire of the English bluejackets. Desirous of inducing the Egyptians to develop their full power before withdrawing, the general held his position for about three-quarters of an hour, until dusk was drawing on. The order to retire was then given. The movement was carried out with the most perfect regularity and precision by the marine battalion under Colonel Tuson, and the men fell back by alternate companies with the regularity of a field-day. Every attempt of the enemy to advance was crushed by the excellent practice of the 40-pounder and 9-pounder naval guns under Commander Henderson. The right column was quickly *entrained* at the junction, and slowly steamed back to Alexandria; at the same time the left column withdrew along the banks of the canal to the Ramleh lines unmolested.

The British loss in the engagement was one officer and three men killed and twenty-seven men wounded. The Egyptian loss was given by a deserter who, four days later, made his way from Arabi's camp to Alexandria, as three officers and seventy-six men killed, and a large number wounded. According to the prisoners' statements, which had to be received with some caution, the Egyptian force engaged was 2,000 strong.

The Egyptians next erected earthworks at Mandara, between Ramleh and Aboukir. They, however, overlooked the fact that the place was accessible from the sea, and the *Superb* having been sent round, shelled them out without difficulty.

Chapter 15

The Conference

It is now necessary to go back a little, to consider the diplomatic steps taken by the Powers in view of the crisis in Egypt.

On receiving the news of the bombardment, the Sublime *Porte* was so impressed with the gravity of the situation that a council sat continuously for twenty-four hours at the palace, and separated without arriving at any conclusion.

On the 15th July, however, the *sultan's* advisers had so far recovered themselves that the Turkish Ambassador was instructed to protest, and to demand of the English Government the withdrawal of the forces landed in Egypt.

In reply Lord Dufferin stated that the bombardment was an act of self-defence, and that the seamen and marines were landed for the purpose of restoring order, and with no view to a permanent occupation. "They were, and continued to be, necessary for the defence of the *khedive*," said his Lordship, "in the absence of all steps by the *sultan* to maintain his own authority and that of His Highness." Lord Dufferin concluded by observing that "Her Majesty's Government were desirous to maintain the sovereignty of the *sultan* over Egypt, but that if His Majesty took no steps to vindicate his authority, and objected to the provisional measures taken by England and the other powers, it would be difficult to find arguments for the continuance of the existing arrangement." In order to understand what were "the provisional measures" referred to, it is necessary to consider the proceedings of the Constantinople Conference, which had in the meantime assembled.

When, in May, France and England had at length agreed to send their vessels of war to Alexandria, it was at Lord Granville's suggestion proposed that if it was found advisable that troops should be landed, Turkish troops should be called for, but France objected and the proposal dropped.

When the *khedive* and his ministry became reconciled the *Porte* addressed a circular to its representatives abroad, arguing that the Egyptian Ministry having submitted to the *khedive*, the crisis no longer existed, and the naval demonstration was unnecessary. Lord Dufferin was instructed to calm the apprehensions of the *sultan* as to the character and objects of the naval demonstration. He succeeded so well that Said Pasha stated that His Majesty was willing to discuss with the Western Powers any arrangements that they might suggest for the maintenance of the *status quo* in Egypt, upon the understanding that the presence of the fleets should be restricted to the shortest possible period.

When Admiral Seymour complained of earthworks being thrown up alongside his ships, the French Government on the 30th May proposed an immediate conference on Egyptian affairs. This proposal was accepted by Lord Granville, and invitations to the conference were issued the same day.

Considerable delay ensued in regard to the meeting of the conference, owing to the opposition of Turkey, which refused to join, and persisted in maintaining that the mission of Dervish Pasha having effected a satisfactory settlement, there was really nothing left to discuss.

Eventually the conference met on the 23rd June at Constantinople, without the participation of the *Porte*.

The powers were represented by the different ambassadors at Constantinople, and Lord Granville, in the apparent desire to tie the hands of the British Government as much as possible, irrespective of future eventualities, succeeded in getting all the powers represented to sign a self-denying protocol, by which each engaged "not to seek, in any arrangement which might be made in consequence of the concerted action for the regulation of the affairs of Egypt, any territorial advantage, nor any concession of any exclusive privilege, nor any commercial advantage other than those which any other nation might equally obtain."

On the 27th June, the position of Admiral Seymour with regard to the forts in course of being armed by Arabi being explained to the conference, it was agreed that so long as the conference lasted the powers should abstain from isolated action in Egypt, with the reservation of *force majeure*, such as the necessity for protecting the lives of their subjects.

On the 30th the conference met again, when the critical situation in Egypt was dwelt upon, and the English representative explained that under the words *force majeure* he should include any sudden change or catastrophe which menaced British interests.

Notwithstanding the pressure put upon the *sultan* at this time to induce him to send a force to Egypt, he still hesitated. His anxiety seemed to be to avoid doing anything himself, and at the same time to prevent intervention by anyone else. He reminded the English ambassador that at his request the *Porte* had ordered the Egyptians to discontinue the fortifications at Alexandria, and in return asked that the warlike preparations of the British fleet should be stopped.

On the 6th of July, the Conference met again and agreed on the terms of an "Identic Note" to be addressed to the *Porte*, fixing the conditions on which the *Porte* should be invited to send Turkish troops to Egypt as a provisional measure to restore order.

On the 8th the *sultan's* Minister of Foreign Affairs begged the English ambassador from considerations of humanity to enjoin Admiral Seymour not to do anything precipitate at Alexandria. Lord Dufferin curtly replied that "the Egyptian authorities had the matter completely in their own hands. They had only to do what was required of them, and not a shot would be fired." Lord Dufferin added the question, "Why was the *sultan* not there with his troops to keep them in order?"

On the 9th the *Porte* was so far alarmed at what was going on at Alexandria as to send a despatch to Musurus Pasha, in London, pointing out that Admiral Seymour's statements respecting the Alexandria armaments were denied by the Egyptian authorities, and begging that the British admiral might be directed to adopt a line of action more in conformity with the peaceful and conciliatory feelings which animated the Ottoman Government and the Court of St. James.

On the 10th Lord Dufferin intimated to the *Porte* that it was the intention of Admiral Seymour to open fire upon the batteries of Alexandria unless there was a temporary surrender of the forts for the purpose of disarmament. The *sultan* replied that he would send a categorical answer on the following day. At the same time he requested that the bombardment might be delayed.

Said Pasha called on Lord Dufferin in the middle of the night (2 a.m. on the morning of the 11th), urging him to send a telegram to the British Government to order the bombardment to be arrested. The British ambassador transmitted the message. It arrived too late.

The bombardment had already taken place. As Lord Dufferin, in a letter to Said Pasha in the course of the following day, observed, "When such grave issues were at stake, it was unwise to run things so fine."

On the 12th the *sultan's* minister informed His Lordship that the bombardment having added to the gravity of the situation, he was not in a position to make any communication, but that the council were still deliberating as to the course to be pursued. This was the council referred to at the beginning of the present chapter, which sat for twenty-four hours, and decided nothing.

On the 15th Said Pasha asked if an intimation to the powers of the *sultan's* intention to go to Egypt would be well received. Lord Dufferin said in reply that at one time he was certainly of that opinion, and that even then it might not be too late, provided His Majesty would authorize a commissioner to enter the conference.

On the same day all the powers represented at the conference presented the Identic Note to the *Porte*, inviting it to send troops to Egypt to assist the *khedive* to re-establish order.

The *sultan*, on receiving the note, observed that if the Imperial Government had not up to the present decided on its own initiative to send troops, it was because it was convinced that measures of force could be dispensed with. He also announced that his government now consented to take part in the conference.

On the 16th July Lord Lyons was instructed to inform M. de Freycinet that, in view of the uncertainty which prevailed as to the movements of Arabi and his forces, Her Majesty's Government had telegraphed to the British admiral at Port Saïd, authorizing him to concert with the French admiral for the protection of the Suez Canal, and to act in the event of sudden danger. In reply, the French minister stated that the French admiral would be instructed to concert measures with the English admiral for the protection of the Canal, but that the French Government could not, without the sanction of the chambers, authorize him to act.

On the 17th appearances became still more threatening. The Admiralty received a despatch from Admiral Hoskins reporting the arrival at Port Saïd of Ali Pasha Fehmi,[1] whom Arabi had nominated Governor-General of the Suez Canal. This was followed by another, announcing that Arabi had called upon all Mussulmans to rise. Lord Granville thereupon urged the French Government to give their admiral full discretion by telegraph in view of any emergency. In reply,

---

1. One of the three mutinous colonels.

M. de Freycinet informed the British minister that he regretted very much to be unable to comply.

On the 19th the news from Egypt assumed a yet more serious character, and Lord Dufferin was instructed to inform the *sultan* that after the delay which had occurred he could only hope to recover the confidence of Her Majesty's Government by the immediate issue of a proclamation in favour of the *khedive*, and denouncing Arabi as a rebel.

Whatever might have been the Sultan's views with regard to Arabi, he was not at the time disposed to comply with the ambassador's request. Accordingly, His Majesty said that the issue of such a proclamation as was suggested might not be a bad thing, and then turned the conversation to some other subject.

The same day news came of the blocking of the Mahmoudieh Canal, of the issue of proclamations against the *khedive* by Arabi, and of the military preparations being made by him.

At a meeting of the conference, the English and French ambassadors presented proposals relative to the measures to be adopted *for the protection* of the *Suez Canal*, and asked the conference to designate the powers who should be charged, in case of need, to take the measures specially necessary for the purpose. The four other representatives reserved to themselves the right of referring the matter to their respective governments.

On the 20th July Her Majesty's Government ordered the despatch of the expedition to Egypt.

On the 21st the Austrian Government declined to join in giving to other powers the *mandat* proposed for the defence of the Canal.

On the 22nd Lord Granville made the following proposal to the French Government:—

1. Unless the *Porte* sends an acceptance of a kind immediately available, the English and French representatives should be instructed to say to the other ambassadors that England and France can no longer rely upon Turkish intervention; and as they consider immediate action necessary to *prevent further loss of life and continuance of anarchy*, they intend, unless the conference has any other plan, to devise with a third power, if possible, military means for procuring a solution.

2. To ask Italy to be that third power.

3. To consult immediately upon the division of labour.

4. The Suez Canal may be included in the general scheme of allied action.[2]

M. de Freycinet, in reply, cautiously stated that the French Government understood that the measures to be taken by them for the protection of the Canal would not extend to any expedition into the interior of the country, but would be limited to naval operations, and to the occupation of certain points on the Canal itself; *and that although they would not object to an expedition by England into the interior of Egypt*, they could not themselves take part in any such expedition. He added that before giving an official answer he must bring the matter before the Council of Ministers.

The German *Chargé d'Affaires* stated to Lord Dufferin and the French ambassador, in very positive terms, that the northern governments would never agree to a mandate, that it would be better for England to go forward at once by herself, and that every one admitted that the reserve made under the term *force majeure* would cover anything that she might be obliged to do in Egypt.

On the 23rd July the *sultan* determined to allow Said Pasha and Assim Pasha to represent him at the Conference. At the meeting, the following day, the two Ottoman delegates took their seats, and the other delegates having given the Turkish representatives to understand that a formal answer was expected to the Identic Note of the 15th July, the Turkish minister declared that "he accepted in principle the despatch of Ottoman troops to Egypt."

This statement, made at the eleventh hour, was not without its effect on the different great powers. As a fact, with the exception of England, and possibly France, none of them desired to meddle either directly or indirectly in Egyptian matters, and they were glad of the pretext to let England settle Egypt alone.

The Austrian Government notified that, "in case the *sultan* refused to send his troops to Egypt, Austria would be even less disposed to join in asking other governments to act as European *mandataires*, for the general maintenance of order, than to do so for the protection of the Suez Canal."

On the 24th July Italy was invited to co-operate with England and France in the steps to be taken for the protection of the Canal. The

---

2. It will be noticed that Lord Granville's proposal was no longer limited to the protection of the Suez Canal, but pointed to a joint military intervention to put an end to loss of life and anarchy.

Italian minister, M. Mancini, thanked Her Majesty's Government for the proof of confidence and friendship afforded by their invitation to her, but thought that at the moment when Turkey had accepted all the conditions of a note to which England and Italy were parties, it would be a contradiction for those two Powers to enter into engagements as to another form of intervention.

On the 25th M. de Freycinet, being pressed for a formal answer to the proposal made for the joint military intervention, answered that for the moment the French Government could not go beyond the projected co-operation for the protection of the Suez Canal.

On the 24th a bill was brought into the Chamber of Deputies to enable the French Government to carry into effect arrangements with England for a joint protection of the Canal. The amount asked for was 9,410,000 francs. The result was a most stormy debate, which was adjourned amid much excitement.

CHAPTER 16

The Porte and the Powers

On the 26th July Said Pasha formally announced that the Sublime *Porte*, resolved to give effect to its incontestable sovereign rights over Egypt, had decided to send immediately a sufficient number of troops. This was communicated to the Conference at its sitting the same day.

Said Pasha admitted, on being pressed, that the despatch of the troops could only be the result of an understanding arrived at between the powers. The British and French ambassadors then made the following declaration:—

France and England have communicated to the conference their views, which have also been communicated to the different Cabinets, and their proposals having encountered no objections, the two powers are at present agreed that in the present state of affairs they are ready, if necessity arises, to employ themselves *in the protection of the Suez Canal*, either alone, or with the addition of any power which is willing to assist.

At a meeting on the 27th, the representatives of the *Porte* communicated a declaration to the effect that having again informed the members of the conference that the Imperial Government was on the point of sending troops to Egypt, the government earnestly hoped that, in face of this determination, the existing foreign occupation of that country would be abandoned as soon as the Ottoman troops should arrive at Alexandria.

In reply, Lord Dufferin was instructed to say that Her Majesty's Government could neither withdraw their troops, nor relax their preparations; adding that the arrival and co-operation of Turkish forces in Egypt would be accepted by England, provided the character in which they came was satisfactorily defined beforehand.

At this period, it must be borne in mind that the British expeditionary forces had already started, and the ministry of Mr. Gladstone had now no desire to have the Turkish troops, for which they had previously professed so much anxiety. It was, however, necessary to keep up appearances, and to find from time to time plausible pretexts to prevent the *sultan* from carrying out his determination.

In effecting the desired object Lord Dufferin, as will be seen, found means to throw such difficulties in the way as to prevent the despatch of a Turkish army to Egypt.

The views of Germany were also at the same time communicated to Lord Granville, and were stated to him as being that the *sultan* had the first claim to exercise the proposed protection. In the event of his being unwilling or unable to do so, the powers interested in the Canal would be justified in acting themselves. If those Powers had the intention of protecting their own interests in the Canal, Germany could not take upon herself any responsibility for the measures to be taken for this purpose. Finally Austria, Russia, and Italy adopted the same view as Germany.

On the 28th the adjourned debate on the vote of 9,410,000 *francs* for the despatch of French troops to Egypt for the protection of the Canal took place in the French Chamber of Deputies. The force, it was explained, was to be 8,000 men and two gunboats. The ministers pointed out that all that was intended was to occupy one or two points of the Canal. France would be charged with the surveillance of the Canal between Port Saïd and Ismailia, and England of the part between Ismailia and Suez.

The vote was violently opposed, and in the end rejected by a majority of 341 against the government. The debate was wound up by a remarkable speech from M. Clemenceau, who said,—

> *Messieurs, la conclusion de ce qui se passe en ce moment est celle-ci, l'Europe est couverte de soldats, tout le monde attend, toutes les Puissances se réservent leur liberté pour l'avenir; réservez la liberté d'action de la France.*

Lord Granville, seeing that all hope of French co-operation was gone, intimated to M. de Freycinet that, although Her Majesty's Government accepted the co-operation of Turkey, it would nevertheless proceed with its own measures. "That then," said the French minister, "is *intervention à deux*."

On the 1st August Lord Dufferin informed the Turkish minister, in reply to his request that the British expedition should be countermanded, that it was useless for him to base any of his calculations on the supposition either that the troops would be countermanded, or that the British *corps d'armée* would leave Egypt until order had been completely re-established.

The minister said with reference to the proclamation against Arabi, that he thought it would be advisable to defer it until after the Turkish troops were landed.

Lord Dufferin answered that if the proclamation was not previously issued, no Turkish troops would be allowed to land in Egypt. The ambassador said, "If the *sultan* desired to co-operate with England it was necessary he should first clearly define the attitude he intended to assume towards Arabi and the rebellious faction."

On the same day the Ottoman plenipotentiaries delivered to the other members of the conference the reasons for the *Porte* not issuing the desired proclamation declaring Arabi a rebel. The principal passage was as follows:—"It is, therefore, quite natural to suppose that a proclamation which would accuse a subject of His Imperial Majesty the *sultan*, who, at a moment when he showed fidelity and devotion to his sovereign, was the object of distinctions, would derive its force from the immediate presence of the material factor, the absence of which at the time of its publication would render its provisions barren."

Orders were sent to the English admiral that, until the *Porte* should have entered into an agreement with Her Majesty's Government for the issue of a proclamation by the *sultan* in support of Tewfik Pasha, and denouncing Arabi as a rebel, and should have signed a Military Convention for the co-operation of the Turkish troops, no Turkish troops could be allowed to land in Egypt.

On the 5th Lord Dufferin formally notified this to the Ottoman delegates, and Said Pasha intimated that he fully understood the grave nature of the communication.

On the 2nd two large Turkish transports started at night from Constantinople for Salonica with stores, provisions, and details of troops. Two other steamers left the same night, one for Smyrna, the other for the Dardanelles. On the 3rd other transports, with soldiers on board, left also at night, and two more transports commenced taking on board stores, ammunition,&c. On the 5th two transports with men and stores left the Golden Horn for Suda Bay, in Crete. A third was to leave the same evening. It became known that Dervish Pasha was to command the force, taking four other generals with him. They were to leave in the *Izzedin* for Salonica. The fleet was to rendezvous either at Rhodes or Suda Bay.

In consequence of the foregoing, Admiral Seymour was instructed, if any vessel with Turkish troops appeared at Port Saïd, Alexandria, or elsewhere, to request the officer in command, with the utmost courtesy, to proceed to Crete or some other place, and apply to the Turkish Government for further instructions, as Seymour was precluded from inviting them to land in Egypt. He was further instructed to prevent their landing if they declined to comply with his advice.

On the 7th the Ottoman delegates made the following declaration to the conference:

> The Sublime *Porte* accepts the invitation for a military intervention in Egypt made to it by the Identic Note of the 15th July, as well as the clauses and conditions contained therein.

On the 8th Said Pasha informed Lord Dufferin that the Sublime *Porte* was disposed to issue the proclamation against Arabi, and that he, the Minister, was authorized to negotiate the Military Convention.

He also stated that, by reason of the importance of the events in Egypt, the Ottoman troops would leave on the 10th.

Lord Dufferin, on the 9th August, informed the *sultan's* government that before any other step was taken the British Government adhered to the necessity for the issue of a properly-worded proclamation. On the 9th the draft of the proposed proclamation was sent to Lord Dufferin for approval.

On the 15th Sir Garnet Wolseley arrived at Alexandria.

At the meeting of the conference on the 14th of August, the representatives of the powers having expressed their opinion that the moment had come to suspend the labours of the conference, the Ottoman delegates, apparently still anxious to be on the opposition side, stated that they did not share in this opinion, and reserved the right of informing the others of the date of the next meeting.

On the 16th August, Lord Dufferin was informed, with reference to the negotiations for the Military Convention, that Her Majesty's Government would have no objection to a part of the Turkish troops being landed at Damietta or Rosetta, should the Turkish Government desire it.

On the next day the Turkish Government, instead of accepting at once the Military Convention, began to make efforts to get it laid before the conference. These failed, however, thanks to Lord Dufferin, who contended that the engagement was one between England and Turkey alone.

The foregoing brings the narrative of events down to the eve of Sir Garnet Wolseley's sailing for the Canal.

CHAPTER 17

Wolseley's Move to the Canal

On the 7th August the *khedive* issued a proclamation against Arabi and the rebels generally.

The same day the *khedive* addressed a letter to the President of the Council of Ministers, announcing his intention to indemnify the sufferers by the recent events.

At this period the European population was flocking back to Alexandria in such numbers that Mr. Cartwright, the British Consul-General, deemed it necessary to make strong representations on the subject to the representatives in Egypt of the several Powers. A system of examination of passports was now established, and people of suspicious character, or who were unable to show that they had some employment, or other means of subsistence, were forced by the authorities to re-embark.

Alexandria was now fast filling with British troops, and fresh detachments were disembarking daily. On the 10th August, Sir John Adye, chief of the staff, arrived at Alexandria with the Duke of Connaught. The whole of the brigade of Guards arrived two days later, and astonished the people by their size and martial appearance as they marched through the town to Ramleh. The Duke of Connaught rode at their head. Egypt in the present generation had never seen such soldiers before, and loud were the expressions of admiration on all sides. The stalwart pipers particularly impressed the natives.

The brigade consisted of the 2nd battalions of the Grenadier and Coldstream Guards, and the 1st battalion of the Scots Guards. The force was encamped on a piece of desert land at Ramleh, near the sea, between the stations of Bulkeley and Fleming on the Ramleh Railway.

Sir Garnet Wolseley reached Egypt on the 15th in the *Calabria*. He had made the voyage by sea on account of his health.

Major-General Sir Evelyn Wood arrived the same day. Transports were coming in rapidly, and everything pointed to an immediate advance upon Kinje Osman and Kafr Dowar. The following is a list of the principal officers in the expeditionary force:—

> General-Commanding-in-Chief: Sir Garnet J. Wolseley.
> Chief of the Staff: General Sir John Adye.
> Officer Commanding Royal Artillery: Brigadier-General W. H. Goodenough.
> Officer Commanding Royal Engineers: Brigadier-General C. B. P. N. H. Nugent.
> Command of Base and Lines of Communication: Major-General W. Earle.
> 1st Division: Lieutenant-General G. H. S. Willis.
> 1st Brigade: Major-General H.R.H. the Duke of Connaught.
> 2nd Brigade: Major-General G. Graham.
> 2nd Division: Lieutenant-General Sir E. B. Hamley.
> 3rd Brigade: Major-General Sir Archibald Alison.
> 4th Brigade: Major-General Sir H. Evelyn Wood.
> Garrison of Alexandria: Major-General G. B. Harman. Cavalry Division: Major-General Drury-Lowe.

Sir Garnet Wolseley lost but little time after landing. He made a hasty inspection of the position at Ramleh, and gave his orders.

On the 18th August the Guards Division, the Household Cavalry, the 60th Rifles, and the 46th Regiment marched in from Ramleh and commenced embarking, the troops of the Second Division taking their places at Ramleh. The Manchester Regiment landed and took over police duty in the town, relieving the Berkshire Regiment, which joined General Wood's Division at Ramleh.

At 11.15 a.m. the greater part of the British force was embarking. The troops selected were the First Division under General Willis. Several transports the same day steamed out of harbour and anchored off the Boghaz Pass. The following day, the 19th, the transports, escorted by the ironclads *Alexandra, Inflexible, Minotaur, Superb,* and *Temeraire,* steamed away in a stately procession to the eastward. Both Sir Garnet Wolseley and Admiral Seymour accompanied the force.

It was given out that Aboukir was to be the place of attack, and at 3.30 p.m., on arriving off the bay, the ships, with the exception of the *Alexandra, Euphrates, Rhosina,* and *Nerissa,* which pushed on to

Port Saïd, anchored in regular lines according to a prearranged plan, the men-of-war being nearest the shore. The ironclads struck their topmasts, and made other preparations for an attack. Every facility had been given to newspaper correspondents to obtain such details as might prudently be made public without exciting too much suspicion of a *ruse de guerre*. It succeeded perfectly. Not only the Europeans, but the enemy, were completely deceived. The gunners in the forts at Aboukir stood to their guns, expecting every moment the fleet would open fire. After dark the troopships moved off to the east, followed later on by the men-of-war. When day broke the whole fleet had disappeared.

As rapidly as possible the fleet steamed for Port Saïd. The transports *Rhosina* and *Nerissa* had singularly bad luck, the last two breaking down *en route*. The delay was not serious, for their escort the *Alexandra* towed the *Nerissa* at the rate of twelve knots an hour, whilst the *Euphrates* helped the *Rhosina*.

The next morning the whole fleet arrived at Port Saïd, when they found the entire Maritime Canal in the hands of the British Navy.

It may now be convenient to refer to what had in the meantime been taking place on the Canal.

On the 9th July, Mr. J. E. Wallis, the British Consul at Port Saïd, received instructions to warn British subjects to embark. Next morning a large number of Europeans took refuge in vessels in the harbour. A report was spread of troops being ordered from Damietta, and some alarm prevailing, the governor issued a circular assuring everybody that there was no danger.

On the 11th, whilst the bombardment was going on at Alexandria, the Port Saïd refugees remained on board ship. The town was quiet and orderly. The British despatch vessel *Iris* acted as guardship during this period. The Egyptian corvette *Sakha* had arrived from Alexandria a day or two previous to the bombardment. Her captain was an Arabist of the most pronounced type. Immediately after her arrival telegraphic information reached the authorities and the Canal Company's officials that the *Sakha* had a considerable quantity of dynamite on board, intended to be used against vessels entering the Canal. The *Iris*, which had taken up a berth inside the harbour, shifted berth, and her commander, Captain Seymour, moored his ship opposite the *Sakha*, the better to watch her movements. A great noise was observed on board the Egyptian vessel at night, the men moving up and down as if transporting heavy cases.

The next morning Captain Seymour called on her captain, and on inquiring the reason of the commotion, was informed that the men were "practising." Captain Seymour replied that, considering the troubled state of the country, practising at such an unusual hour was calculated to create an alarm on shore, and expressed a hope that it would be discontinued. "I am the only master on board my own ship," was the Egyptian commander's reply.

"In that case," Captain Seymour replied, "I shall be under the painful necessity of either seizing your ship or of sinking her." From that moment no further night exercise was indulged in, and hostilities were avoided, though both ships remained with their guns pointed at each other. The commander of the *Iris* took the further precaution of placing a torpedo in a position which would enable him to blow up the Egyptian vessel at any moment. After this, nothing of importance occurred for some days.

The naval force at Port Saïd was strengthened by the arrival of the *Penelope*—the flagship of Admiral Hoskins—and the *Monarch*, *Agincourt*, and *Achilles*.

On the 13th July the British Government notified that British merchant ships might go through the Canal if clear. On the 14th British gunboats commenced to convoy vessels. On the 15th the French Government authorized their gunboats to be employed on similar service. This was followed by the like arrangements on the part of Germany and Italy.

The English ironclad *Orion*, Captain R. O. B. Fitz-Roy, arrived from Alexandria, *en route* to Ismailia, on the 26th, and at once attempted to enter the Canal. Several objections were made by the Canal Company to her doing so. More than once she got under way, and was stopped under various pretexts. The last objection was that the *Coquette* being already in Lake Timsah, there was no room for another vessel of war. Eventually, having embarked 142 officers and men from the *Agincourt*, the *Orion* entered the Canal, ostensibly bound for Suez, and at 3 p.m. on the 27th she reached Lake Timsah. Captain Fitz-Roy took his ship out of the hands of the pilot, and anchored her about 800 yards from the town of Ismailia.

On the 28th the governor and sub-governor of Port Saïd, fearing that their lives were in danger from the military party, took refuge on board the P. and O. s.s. *Poonah*. The town of Port Saïd was, in consequence, left completely in the hands of the supporters of Arabi. Nevertheless, though considerable anxiety prevailed, no outbreak took place.

On the 29th the German gunboat *Move* was ordered to take part in the patrolling of the Canal.

On the 31st July Admiral Hoskins telegraphed that the French Admiral at Port Saïd was ordered to suspend action, and the French ironclad *Thétis* was to leave Ismailia. Rigid neutrality was to be observed.

On the 3rd August Admiral Hoskins was directed for the present to confine his operations on the Suez Canal to maintaining the *status quo*, and not to land except for the protection of British subjects, or in the event of any attempt being made to block the Canal, as to which he was allowed discretion. This reservation, he was informed, was only temporary, and was contingent upon future military requirements.

On the 5th the ships of war off Port Saïd comprised the *Penelope*, *Agincourt*, *Monarch*, and *Northumberland* armoured ships, the *Tourmaline* and *Carysfort* sloops, and the *Ready* and *Beacon* gun-vessels. The *Don* and *Dee*, river gunboats, arrived a day or two later.

What had been taking place at Suez was reported in a letter from Mr. West, the British Consul, to Lord Granville, from which the following are extracts:—

> The whole of the British residents, with one or two exceptions, had taken refuge afloat, and were living in discomfort on board boats, barges, and lighters in the open roadstead. Her Majesty's ship *Euryalus* arrived on the 29th.
> Admiral Sir William Hewett, who, on the 2nd August, had under his command in the Suez Roads the following ships of Her Majesty's fleet, *viz.*, the *Euryalus*, *Eclipse*, *Ruby*, *Dragon*, *Mosquito*, and *Beacon*, then decided to act, and I went on shore with a proclamation to be delivered to the acting governor, informing him that the place had been occupied by British forces, which occupation was effected without opposition or resistance on the part of the native soldiers. The town was then occupied by the marines and bluejackets, about 500 men in all. The few native soldiers in the place got away in the train that was about to leave Suez with more fugitives. The governor's dwelling and public offices were guarded by marines; the Victoria Hospital, and commanding positions in the environs of Suez, were also held by the British forces.

To return to Ismailia, where, as above stated, the *Orion* had arrived on the 27th July. The place was found perfectly tranquil, but the telegraph being in the hands of Arabi's people, Captain Fitz-Roy could get no news or telegrams. The *Coquette* was anchored, by Captain Fitz-Roy's orders, off the lock-gates of the Fresh Water Canal, with orders to report everything going in and coming out. By this means information was obtained that Arabi was receiving daily several boat-loads of coal. On the 29th H.M.S. *Carysfort* arrived from Port Saïd. Lake Timsah was patrolled at night by a steam-launch with an armed crew, which moved about twice in every watch. The *Orion's* electric light was also used during the first and middle watches of the night, and turned on the Arab guardhouse outside Ismailia.

On the 2nd August Egyptian troops, estimated at about 800, arrived at Nefiché Junction, and encamped outside the railway station. From the 6th, torpedo and picket-boats were employed to keep up communication with Suez and Port Saïd. The guns of the different vessels were cleared for action every night, and the marines and small-arms men kept in readiness to land.

On the 16th the Egyptian force at Nefiché was largely reinforced. Several refugees came off to the ships.

On the 19th, with a view to assist in the contemplated landing, the compass-bearing and distance of the camp at Nefiché were taken during the day from the masthead of the *Carysfort*, and one of the *Orion's* 25-ton guns was laid accordingly. To secure sufficient elevation to carry the projectile over the intervening sand-hills, the vessel's port boilers were emptied and shot removed, so as to give the ship a strong list to starboard. The same night the crews of the vessels were mustered at 8 o'clock in working dress, with ammunition and provisions all ready for landing.

The foregoing narrative brings the history of events down to the eve of the British forces taking possession of the Canal.

CHAPTER 18

De Lesseps and the Canal

The history having now been brought to the period when the Suez Canal was occupied by the British forces, it may be interesting to refer to the attitude assumed by M. Ferdinand de Lesseps, the President of the Canal Company, and to show how his communications with the rebel leaders led the latter to postpone until too late the steps resolved on for the destruction of the Canal.

De Lesseps from the first opposed any interference with the Canal by the British forces. The earliest indication of his views was afforded immediately before the Alexandria bombardment. When that operation was impending, Admiral Seymour warned British ships not to enter the Canal in case of hostilities. In consequence of this warning eleven ships were stopped at Port Saïd and Suez on the 10th July. M. Victor de Lesseps, the Company's agent at Ismailia, thereupon protested against what he termed "this violation of the neutrality of the Canal."

On the same day, M. de Lesseps, then in Paris, communicated to the British ambassador there, and to all the other representatives of the powers, a copy of the telegraphic instructions which had on the 8th July been sent to the agent of the Company at Ismailia. Their effect was that any action or warlike demonstration in the Canal was forbidden, and that "its neutrality had been proclaimed by the *Firman* of Concession, and had been recognized and acted upon during the two last wars between France and Germany and Russia and Turkey."

A very slight examination of the question will suffice to show that the Canal had absolutely nothing of the neutral character so persistently claimed for it by M. de Lesseps at this time and during the subsequent operations.

Its claim to neutrality was based solely on a clause in the concession, in which the Canal was declared by the *sultan* to be "a neutral highway for the ships of all nations." This clause, inserted apparently to indicate the peaceful and industrial character of the enterprise, was an expression of intention no doubt binding upon the parties to the Concession, but upon no one else. This, it is obvious, was a totally different matter from construing it, as De Lesseps sought to do, as laying down for the rest of the world a law under which, for all time and all circumstances, the Canal should be considered as outside the range of belligerent operations.

No one can contend that the ruler of a country, by a mere *à priori* declaration of his own, can confer the quality of neutrality upon any particular part of his territory irrespective of future eventualities. This is a matter where the rights of other States come in. Whether a country is or is not neutral is a matter which, on war breaking out, has to be determined by the application of certain well-known principles of International Law, and does not depend upon the mere declaration of the ruler, unless followed by a strict observance of neutrality.

Assuming that, as was practically the case, England was at war with the *de facto* ruler of Egypt, which was Arabi, any declaration that the *sultan* might choose to make that this or that portion of Egyptian territory should be considered as neutral, and therefore exempt from warlike operations, would clearly be illusory.

The most that could be done towards the so-called neutralization of the Canal was subsequently effected in December, 1888, when, by an agreement between Egypt and the principal powers, it was arranged that (subject to certain reservations made by Great Britain) no hostilities on the part of any of the contracting powers should take place in the Canal, nor, in the event of the territorial power being itself a belligerent, should the ships of that power attack, or be attacked, in the Canal, nor were the entrances to the Canal to be blockaded. This, it will be seen, is "neutralization" only in a limited and vague sense of the term, the employment of which was carefully avoided in the agreement.

The precedents invoked by M. de Lesseps from the Franco-German and the Russo-Turkish wars, in reality, were worth nothing. When France and Germany were at war, Egypt was at peace, and her neutrality had to be respected, neither Turkey nor Egypt being in any way mixed up with the dispute. As regards the Russo-Turkish war, it is incontestable that if Russia, in the exercise of her undoubted rights as a belligerent, had seized on the Canal as a piece of Ottoman territory, no other Power would have had reason to complain. Whether by doing so Russia would have made an enemy of England, and so have caused her to take part against her, was another matter; and, influenced probably by considerations of this kind, Russia was induced to abstain. This, however, in no way affects the principle involved.

But, apart from the general reasoning above mentioned, there were certain special circumstances affecting the matter which made the case of De Lesseps still weaker, and rendered the ordinary rules regarding neutrality inapplicable. By the terms of the concession, although the Canal itself was to be the property of the Company for a term of years, the land through which it ran remained none the less Egyptian territory, and by Article 9 it was expressly declared that the government should have the same right of acting for the maintenance of public security and the enforcement of the law within the limits of the Company's property as might be exercised at any other point of the *khedive*'s dominions.

Arabi at this time was a rebel, and his forces were occupying positions in the immediate neighbourhood of the Canal. This gave the *khedive* an undoubted right to act against him, whether on the Canal or elsewhere. To assert that the ruler of Egypt was not at liberty to suppress a revolt in his own dominions would be too startling a proposition for even M. de Lesseps to bring forward. Whether the *khedive* interfered by himself or by his agent, who in this case was Sir Garnet Wolseley, comes to exactly the same thing. What took place was a simple matter of police, and if, in the course of suppressing Arabi, certain points on the Canal had to be occupied, the case came expressly within the terms of Article 9. This being so, of what had De Lesseps to complain, and where does the question of neutrality arise?

Regarded, then, from any point of view, the fallacy of the claim to neutrality advanced on behalf of the Canal is so clear that it is difficult to imagine how it could ever have been seriously put forward.

Here, too, it may be remarked that not only was the Canal not a "neutral" concern, but it never possessed any of the "international" or "universal" character claimed for it. It was, in fact, no more "international" or "universal" than a tramway or a dry goods store, to which the citizens of all nations could have access on payment for the accommodation or goods supplied. Viewed in this light, the pretensions of the president of the Company appear simply ridiculous, and in any less distinguished individual would only have excited ridicule.

The question of neutrality having now been dealt with, it only remains to relate the steps taken by the President of the Canal Company.

According to his published memoirs:—

On his arrival in Egypt with his son Victor, on the 19th July, he found that everything had been prepared by the French and English commanders for the joint occupation of Port Saïd, with a view to protect the population. De Lesseps hastened to the French admiral's flagship, and was informed by that officer that he had been asked by two of the French residents to land troops for their protection. After some difficulty De Lesseps prevailed on the French commander to confide to him the petition, which was signed by two names he knew very well. As the document was legalized by the French consul, he went straight to his house and got that official to summon the two petitioners. They were soon found, and De Lesseps rated them soundly for what he called their stupidity.

He told them that now he was at Port Saïd they might sleep without fear; that he would be responsible for the safety of everyone; and then, taking the petition, he tore it up in their faces, threw the pieces on the floor, and told the men who had signed it that as it was withdrawn they might go home. They did so, and De Lesseps, returning to the French admiral, informed him that the petition no longer existed, and that, therefore, he had no reason for landing. The French admiral not having yet been informed by his government of their determination not to co-operate with the English, De Lesseps found it no easy matter to persuade him to alter his decision with regard to the projected landing. The fact that the French fleet had withdrawn from Alexandria when it was bombarded by the English aided De Lesseps in prevailing on the French commander to abstain. When at last he had attained that object, it was De Lesseps himself who informed the English commander of the fact.

According to the official journal of the Canal Company ("*Le Canal de Suez*"), which, however, must not always be regarded as an accurate record of events, De Lesseps found both the native and European population of Port Saïd much disturbed at the idea of the projected landing, and he called a meeting of the native Notables and *Sheikhs* to reassure them.

After these incidents he received from Arabi a telegram, of which the following is a translation:—

> Thank you for what you have done to prevent the landing of foreign troops at Port Saïd, and for your efforts to restore tranquillity of mind to the natives and the Europeans.

De Lesseps then went through the Canal to Suez, returning again as far as Ismailia, from which place, on the 26th, he sent a telegram to M. Charles de Lesseps, the Company's agent in Paris, to the effect following:—

> The English admiral having declared to me that he would not disembark without being preceded by the French Navy, and a disembarkation being possibly ruin to Port Saïd, I have had to reassure the numerous Arab population, without whom we should be forced to suspend our works. In the presence of the Ulemas and Notables, I have sworn that not a Frenchman shall disembark whilst I am here, and that I will guarantee public tranquillity and the neutrality of our Universal Canal. The government of my country will not disavow me.

This was followed by another telegram, of which the following is a translation, to the same person:—

> Ismailia, 29th July, 1882.
> To disembark at Ismailia, where there is not a solitary Egyptian soldier, is to determine to take possession of our Canal. The only persons here are a chief of native police and some agents. The inhabitants are our *employés*, their families, and some refugees. The invaders will find us unarmed at the head of our *personnel* to bar their passage with 'protests.'

And by yet another, on the 4th August:—

> The English admiral at Port Saïd writes me that he has decided to take, in spite of my protests, such measures as he judges necessary to occupy the Canal. I have decided to oppose any warlike operation on the Canal.

On the same day, M. de Lesseps went on board H.M.S. *Orion* at Ismailia. He was in evening dress, and wore his Order of the Star of India, and was attended by his son Victor and M. de Rouville, the Canal Company's agent. He demanded the intentions of the English towards the Canal, and protested energetically and with much excitement against any landing as "a violation of international rights."

On the day following, M. de Lesseps telegraphed to Paris as follows:—

> The English admiral having announced the occupation of Ismailia, I went yesterday on board the *Orion* with Victor. We have signified verbally our resolution to resist, to prevent serious disorder and interruption in navigation of the Canal. We have obtained a declaration that a landing should only take place on our demand.

In consequence of this last telegram, Admiral Hoskins was desired to report on the statement that he had promised only to land a force on the Canal upon being asked by De Lesseps. The admiral replied that the statement was "quite unwarranted."

The council of the Canal Company assembled on the 5th August, and passed resolutions supporting their president, and declaring that "the Company could not lend itself to the violation of a neutrality which was the guarantee of the commerce of all nations."

On the 15th the *khedive* issued a proclamation declaring that the commander-in-chief of the British forces was authorized to occupy all points on the Isthmus necessary for the operations against the rebels.

On the 19th Admiral Hoskins gave orders that no ship or boat was to enter the Canal, and announced that he was prepared to resort to force to prevent any attempt to contravene these orders. M. de Lesseps replied that he protested against "this act of violence and spoliation."

On the 20th August Lord Lyons telegraphed Lord Granville as follows, omitting irrelevant passages:—

> We communicated to M. Charles de Lesseps last night a memorandum in the terms of your Lordship's despatch to us of the 14th instant; and we requested, at the same time, that the transports should pay dues at Ismailia, and that the regular traffic through the Suez Canal should be suspended during the short period necessary for the passage of these vessels. M. Charles de Lesseps declined to express any opinion of his own, but it was plain to us that he did not expect that the wishes of Her Majesty's Government would be acceded to by his father.

As the sequel showed, M. de Lesseps' acquiescence was not deemed by the English Government essential to the carrying out of the operations decided on.

M. de Lesseps, ever since his arrival in Egypt, had continued to assure Arabi that if he let the Canal alone the English would also respect it. His theory was, "*Le Canal est la grande route ouverte à tous les pavilions. Y toucher amenerait contre nous l'Europe, le monde entier.*" Towards the end of July, M. de Lesseps, having learned that the blocking of the Canal had been decided at the Egyptian camp, telegraphed to Arabi to do nothing to it, adding the words, "*Jamais les Anglais n'y pénétreraient, jamais, jamais!*" Nevertheless, secret orders were given to Mahmoud Pasha Fehmi to prepare everything for the military occupation of the Canal jointly with Mahmoud Choukri Bey, another engineer of the National Party. This was on the evening of the 17th August.

On the 20th, after a simulated attack by the British on the lines of Kafr Dowar, intended to cover the expedition to Port Saïd, Arabi's look-outs signalled the movement of the English fleet in the direction of the Canal.

The day following, M. de Lesseps having been informed of the presence of thirty-two English ships of war and transports in the waters of Port Saïd, sent to Arabi a telegram, the substance of which was as follows:—

> Make no attempt to intercept *my* Canal. I am there. Not a single English soldier shall disembark without being accompanied by a French soldier. I answer for everything.

On receipt of this message, a Council of War was held, which, with the exception of Arabi, who still hesitated, unanimously decided to act. The answer to M. de Lesseps was as follows:—

> Sincere thanks, assurances consolatory, but not sufficient under existing circumstances. The defence of Egypt requires the temporary destruction of the Canal.

Fortunately the despatch ordering the destruction of the Canal was sent by a roundabout route by way of Cairo, and when men and material were ready to carry out the work, the English were already in occupation, in spite of M. de Lesseps' positive declarations. The fifteen hours' delay caused by M. de Lesseps' communication prevented the execution of the orders of the council.

CHAPTER 19

Seizure of the Suez Canal

The seizure and temporary occupation of the Suez Canal by the British forces became an absolute necessity from the moment that Sir Garnet Wolseley determined to make Ismailia the base of his operations.

Once decided on, the evolution was performed on the night of the 19th-20th of August in a quiet, practical, and business-like manner, reflecting the highest credit on the British Navy.

The work at Port Saïd was carried out by the *Monarch* and the *Iris*, the first-named vessel being so moored off the town that her forward turret guns commanded the main street leading to the quay, whilst the *Iris* was to seaward of the *Monarch*, in a position whence she could shell the beach and the Arab town. The ironclad *Northumberland* lay anchored in the offing off Fort Ghemil, the object being to check an exodus of the coal labourers from Port Saïd, and to create an impression that the fort was to be attacked. At 11 on the night of the 19th the ships' companies of the *Monarch* and *Iris* were called on deck and warned that they would be landed at 3 a.m.

At exactly 3.30 on the 20th the landing began amidst the strictest silence. So quietly was the operation carried out that those on board the French ironclad *La Gallissonière*, moored close astern of the *Monarch*, and to the same buoy, knew nothing of what was going on.

The landing party comprised two companies of seamen and one of marines from the *Monarch*, and a small naval brigade and a company of marines from the *Iris*, with two Gatling guns.

The plan of operations, shortly stated, was to surround the barracks in which the government soldiers were quartered, and then to establish a line of sentries across the narrow neck of land which separates the European from the native town, and to bar escape from the former. In a few minutes the work was completed. The soldiers, who were nearly all asleep, were ordered to surrender, and 160 of them fell in and laid down their arms. They were then permitted to return to their barracks, two officers only being detained in custody. The seamen were then posted right across from Lake Menzaleh to the sea, and some temporary earthworks were thrown up across the neck of land already referred to.

Upon Captain Seymour, of the *Iris*, devolved the delicate duty of securing the Canal Company's offices at Port Saïd, and of preventing any information being telegraphed through it to the Company's other stations.

After Captain Seymour had occupied the office of the principal transit agent of the Canal Company, a midshipman, not more than fifteen years of age, was told off with a party of bluejackets to take possession of the Company's telegraph apparatus. The Company's *employés* stood aghast with solemn faces. Such an act of desecration had never been even dreamt of. Presently the Company's Telegraph Agent arrived, full of dignity and importance, and, apparently unconscious of what had taken place, walked towards his office. He was stopped at the entrance by the small midshipman, who said with a very good French accent, "*On ne passe pas.*" The Frenchman (all the important posts in the Company are filled by Frenchmen) looked at the diminutive object in front of him with dignified astonishment, and demanded, "*Qui êtes-vous? Que voulez-vous ici?*" "*Je suis ici pour empêcher le monde d'entrer,*" answered the midshipman.

The Frenchman, quite bewildered, looked round, and from the long faces of his colleagues was able to guess the truth. His anger and humiliation at first prevented his uttering a word. It was not so much that his office had been seized, but that such an important mission should have been confided to so small a midshipman. This was the bitterest sting of all. Had he been suppressed by a troop of soldiers with fixed bayonets, his dignity at least would have been saved, though the result might have been the same. "*Ces sacrés Anglais veulent se moquer de nous en nous envoyant un gamin comme cela,*" was his remark to his brother officials.

Resistance was, however, in vain, and the Company's staff had to submit to the inevitable.[1]

Of course the vital point to be seized was Ismailia, a task which the

---

1. Port Saïd was held by the ship's marines and bluejackets until 16th September, when they were relieved by 200 Royal Marine Light Infantry and 100 Royal Marine Artillery sent from England.

presence of the Egyptian force at the railway junction at Nefiché, just outside the town, rendered especially perilous.

The force landed by Captain Fitz-Roy, of the *Orion*, consisted of 565 officers and men belonging to that vessel, the *Northumberland*, *Carysfort*, and *Coquette*, with two Gatlings and a 7-pounder gun. The men disembarked in absolute silence at 3 a.m. on the 20th. The silence was so perfect that the Egyptian guard at the Lock Gates was surrounded before the attacking force was discovered. The guard, however, fired their rifles, and so did the sailors. The guard at the governor's house laid down their arms, and no further resistance was experienced in the town. The railway and telegraph stations, the Canal lock bridge, and the governor's house (with the governor) were all taken possession of and held.

There was some slight skirmishing in making the further advance, and in the Arab town some of the enemy were killed. The ships in Lake Timsah at 3.40 a.m. fired five rounds of shell each on the guardhouses in the Arab town. By 4 a.m. the whole place was occupied. By intercepted telegrams it was ascertained that the enemy were arranging to send a large force to Nefiché to attack Ismailia and the ships, and Captain Fitz-Roy determined, if possible, to dislodge the enemy from Nefiché, and to destroy their camp and any of the trains running. The *Orion* and *Carysfort* therefore commenced a slow bombardment at 11 a.m., at a distance of 4,200 yards. By noon the enemy's camp was destroyed, and the troops were retreating towards Cairo. The bombardment was then stopped for a time, but at 4 p.m., as another train was arriving laden with troops, firing was resumed, one shot wrecking the train, overturning the trucks and scattering the soldiers right and left. The fortunate shot was fired from the *Orion* at an unseen enemy, from bearings taken from the masthead of the *Carysfort*.

This concluded the fighting until 10 p.m., after which shells were fired at Nefiché at intervals of half an hour until daylight, to prevent the railway being cleared, and check troops coming from the west by train. At 10.30 General Graham arrived with the advance guard of the army, reinforced the different positions, and took over the military command.

Throughout the operations there was only one European injured. The brother-in-law of the Dutch Consul happened to be walking in the neighbourhood of the lock, and not stopping when challenged, was unfortunately shot in the arm, and subsequently died.[2]

---

2. His relatives received £1,000 by way of compensation from the British Government.

The account given by M. Victor de Lesseps, the Canal Company's local agent, in his official report of the operations at Ismailia, differs somewhat from the foregoing. It is nevertheless not devoid of interest, and for this reason a translation of some of the more important passages is given below.

> During the night of the 19th to 20th all the European population, the *personnel* of the Company, and the principal Egyptian functionaries, were assembled at the house of M. Poilpré, chief agent of the Domain, at one of the gayest of balls, enlivened by the presence of the officers of the Spanish and Austrian ships of war. At two in the morning, everyone went home, and commenced to sleep, when, towards 3 o'clock, in the middle of a very dark night, the streets resounded with warlike cries, mingled with the sound of musketry and of the rolling of gun-carriages dragged at a walking pace.
> It is the English sailors who disembark without having warned the inhabitants that they might be exposed to be killed in the streets. On what are they firing?—on whom?—no enemy is before them. The camp of the Egyptians is at Nefiché, three kilometres from Ismailia. There are in the town only some soldiers of police, very peaceable people, inhabiting Ismailia for a long time, and who have never dreamed of anything but maintaining order.
> Shortly after the embarkation, the cannon thunders. It is the *Orion*—it is the *Carysfort*—which are sending their shells on to Nefiché, or in the desert.
> The musketry fire continues in the streets of Ismailia. At daybreak it ceases in the town, after having happily made only one victim.
> It is a European, a Dutchman, M. Bröens, who, not answering clearly to the challenge of a seaman, received a rifle bullet, which, traversing his body, broke his left arm. M. Bröens lies between life and death. The doctors regard his condition as hopeless.
> The English sailors direct their steps towards our Arab village, inhabited by our native workmen with their families, and where they find no enemies to reply. Nevertheless, they fire on the women and children,[3] who flee into the desert; heartrend-

---

3. This is absolutely untrue.

ing cries from the terrified population reach even us. Some police agents are made prisoners without any of them having tried to defend themselves.

One of them is killed from behind, whilst trying to escape with his family.

Towards eight in the morning the musketry fire ceased. The cannon thunders still, and will thunder until the morning of the 21st.

On landing, the English have cut our telegraph wires to Suez and Port Saïd. Captain Fitz-Roy occupies the Port Office, and our boats are seized. Ismailia is blocked, and we know nothing of what is passing on the rest of the line.

In the afternoon we think of putting the families of our *personnel* in safety. For 300 seamen only occupy the town, and during the night the Egyptians of Nefiché may attack. It is prudent to make the women and children sleep on the lake. As to the *personnel* and M. Ferdinand de Lesseps, they have decided not to quit the town.

The families betake themselves to the landing-place. Captain Fitz-Roy opposes their departure.[4] I then write him a letter. M. Fitz-Roy answers me verbally at seven in the evening, when the night commences, that the families are free, but that M. de Lesseps and all his *personnel* shall pass the night in the town, for he expects to be attacked. There will be a battle in Ismailia, and he wishes that M. de Lesseps and all his *personnel* should be there. 'I am the master, now,' says he.

These odious words were quite gratuitous, since M. de Lesseps and all the *personnel*, chiefs and *employés*, had declared that they would not go out of the town, and there had never been a question except as regards their families.

A part of the families preferred to return to town; the other part was enabled to embark in the boats sent by the ironclad Spanish frigate *Carmen*, and by the Austrian gunboat *Albatross*.

The night, happily, passed without any incident; the silence was broken only by the shells thrown by the *Carysfort* and *Orion* on Nefiché. At daylight Ismailia woke up in the midst of several thousands of English soldiers of the army. The Lake is full of transports and ships of war.

We learn then that in the night of the 19th to the 20th the

---

4. But see letter from the Secretary to the Admiralty on the next page.

English have disembarked at Port Saïd, but peaceably, and that Admiral Hoskins has taken possession of our offices, from whence M. Desavary, Principal Transit Agent at Port Saïd, had been expelled. Ships of war and transports entered the Canal without pilots, and without paying their dues.[5]

During the 20th and 21st the movement without pilots of the English vessels of war gave rise to complete confusion. The greater part got ashore, and several were obliged to disembark their troops on the bank before arriving at Ismailia, being incapable of extricating themselves by their own resources. Admiral Seymour has been forced to recognize this, and the hurry that he was in on the 21st to hand back the working to us is the proof of it.[6]

It is desirable to add that the British naval authorities tried to obtain the services of several of our pilots behind the backs of their superiors, and that all the pilots, without exception, refused to move without the order of the Company.

During all this crisis no *défaillance* has been produced in all the *personnel* from Port Saïd to Suez. The Company may well be proud of it.

The substance of M. Victor de Lesseps' account of the occupation of Ismailia being telegraphed to the *Standard* newspaper, the Lords of the Admiralty thought the matter of sufficient importance to be noticed, and on the 1st September communicated to the Foreign Office as follows:—

From these reports[7] we are able to give the following account of the occurrences of that day: Ismailia was garrisoned by rebel troops; guards were placed at the lock, the governor's house, and the Arab town. The lock was surrounded by a party under Commander Kane, R.N. The guard fired and wounded that officer slightly. Their fire was returned, and it is believed that it was here that a brother of one of the *employés* of the Canal was unfortunately wounded, who died on the 29th ultimo in the British hospital. The guard at the governor's house laid down

---

5. These dues were, with unnecessary liberality, paid subsequently by the British Government.
6. On the contrary, the ships in general were navigated by their own officers and almost without accident.
7. Despatches from the captains of the *Orion* and *Carysfort*.

their arms. The Arab town was occupied by Captain Stephenson; the guard retreated and were fired upon, and two men killed. A few rounds of shell were also fired from the ships at the guardhouses in the Arab town.

Sir Beauchamp Seymour also reports that he saw on the 21st *ultimo* many women on board the Spanish ship *Carmen*; that he was told by the captains that they took refuge on board of her and the Austrian ship *Albatross* on the 20th. It appears that Captain Fitz-Roy permitted two large Canal boats to be used for their embarkation, although he did not consider it consistent with his duty to allow Canal officers to leave Ismailia.

In the southern half of the Canal from Lake Timsah to Suez, the events of the day were on a smaller scale, but none the less interesting. It will be remembered that Suez had been by this time in the possession of the British navy for nearly three weeks, and the advanced guard of the Indian Contingent and the first battalion of the Seaforth Highlanders, under Lieutenant-Colonel Stockwell, had arrived from Aden.

Rear-Admiral Sir William Hewett, commander-in-chief of the naval forces in the East Indies, had charge of the operations at Suez. According to his reports, in the afternoon of the 17th August, the rebels were seen intrenching themselves in front of the British position, and movements of Bedouins on the left flank also called for attention. Under these circumstances, it was decided by the admiral not to send any of the Highlanders away without previously reconnoitring the neighbourhood.

On the night of the 18th, Hewett caused the telegraph wires to be cut between Suez and the first Canal station, and on Saturday morning notices were issued that from that date, the 19th instant, until the prohibition was formally removed, no ships or boats would be allowed to pass into the Canal from the Suez side without special permission. The damage to the wire on the above occasion was soon repaired, but on the following night he caused the poles which conveyed the line across the creek close to the Company's offices to be cut down, and placed a guard over them to prevent their being restored.

On the 20th, at daylight, 400 Highlanders, under Colonel Stockwell, were disembarked from the transport *Bancoora*, and marched eight miles in the direction of Chalouf to make a feint attack in front. At the same time the gun-vessels *Sea Gull* and *Mosquito*, with 200 more of the Highlanders, were also despatched to Chalouf by the Maritime Canal. The party under Colonel Stockwell returned about 4 p.m. without having come in touch with the enemy.

The gun-vessels, meanwhile, had been more successful. The first that they had seen of the enemy along the Canal was a cavalry patrol, about three miles from Chalouf. On the gun-vessels approaching this latter place, some 800 infantry were discovered behind the railway embankment, which thus formed a natural intrenchment. The ships at once opened fire from their tops, to which the enemy replied, but made bad practice. This was followed by the prompt disembarkation of the 200 Highlanders, who, crossing the intervening Fresh-water Canal in boats, or by swimming, climbed up the intrenchment and carried the works with a rush, the enemy, scattered and broken, retreating across the plain. The gun-vessels then returned to Suez.

With the exception of the Serapeum portion between Lake Timsah and the Bitter Lakes, where no annoyance or interruption of traffic was expected, the whole of the Maritime Canal was in possession of the British Navy by nightfall of August the 20th. On the following day the *Tourmaline* and the *Don* moored permanently at Kantara, where a caravan road to Syria crosses the Canal, and there established a strongly defended post; while the gunboats in the southern half completed the link which perfected the chain from Port Saïd to Suez.

Having seized the Canal, the British prepared to protect it. Between Ismailia and Suez this was effected by the *Mosquito* and *Sea Gull*, which patrolled it constantly, no force being permanently landed. In the northern half the *Tourmaline* and *Don* held Kantara and the stations adjoining on either side. Strong detachments of sailors from the fleet at Port Saïd, with Gatlings, were landed at the other stations. Breastworks were thrown up and regular camps established each night. At Port Saïd a camp was pitched between the European and Arab towns, where never less than 500 bluejackets and marines were kept. Intrenchments were thrown up across the Isthmus from Lake Menzaleh to the Mediterranean, and field-pieces mounted. In the Canal itself steam launches, &c., with armed crews were used as patrols, and the fast Thorneycroft torpedo launches of the *Iris* and *Hecla* were employed as despatch boats.

Sunday, August 20th, was a busy day at Port Saïd. The whole of the immense fleet of men-of-war and transports, as well as Sir Beauchamp Seymour in the *Helicon*, arrived early in the forenoon. As was expected, the Canal Company would accept no dues and would provide no pilots. There was some little delay until the way was clear. During this interval, to provide against possible trouble, 300 of the York and Lancaster Regiment were put on board the gun-vessel *Falcon*, and a similar number of the West Kent Regiment was embarked on board the gun-vessel *Beacon*, to form the advance. These vessels arrived at Ismailia in the evening of the same day.

Early in the afternoon the *Nerissa* led the transport fleet into the Canal, followed by the *Rhosina*, the troop-ship *Euphrates*, and the rest, including the *Penelope*, Admiral Hoskins' flagship. Slowly the stately procession passed through the Canal to Ismailia, which the vessels one by one reached either that night or early the next morning. Although the ships were unprovided with pilots, they were so skilfully navigated by their own officers, that very little difficulty arose, almost the only exception being the grounding of the *Catalonia*,[8] with the West Kent Regiment on board. She grounded at a distance of seven miles from Lake Timsah, and caused a temporary block; but did not for long interrupt the passage of the other vessels.

M. Ferdinand de Lesseps, from the steps of the empress's chalet at the entrance to Lake Timsah, watched the long line of British vessels of war and transports arriving from the Canal.[9] So little space was there that the vessels as they entered the lake were moored abreast of each other, bow and stern. The *Penelope* was one of the first to take up her position.

In M. de Lesseps' memoirs, already referred to, it is stated that he had refused to give pilots to the British vessels, under pretext that they were violating the neutrality of the Canal, and that it was doubtful whether he would in the end have consented to give the pilots if he had not perceived that the English were determined to use the Canal at the risk of a vessel or two being stranded. He knew how detrimental the blocking of the Canal would be to his enterprise, so he made a bargain with the English commander, and on receiving a

---

8. This vessel was one of the few which had a pilot (formerly in the Canal Company's service) on board.

9. It is related that the President of the Canal Company subsequently posted himself at the landing-place at Ismailia at the moment when a number of men from the ships were about to disembark, and emphatically declared that "no one should land except over his dead body." This, however, was without effect, for according to the story he was gently pushed aside by a bluejacket with the observation—"We don't want any dead bodies about here, sir; all you've got to do is to step back a bit." Though the anecdote is probably apocryphal, it serves to illustrate exactly the attitude adopted by the British Navy towards the Canal authorities.

cheque on the Bank of England for £100,000 as compensation for the damage done, he placed the whole administration of the Canal at the disposal of the British. Being powerless to prevent the violation of the Canal's neutrality, he thus preserved intact the pecuniary interests of the Company.

It is scarcely necessary to say that the whole of the above statement is "fallacious," as was pointed out by Sir Beauchamp Seymour (then Lord Alcester) in a letter which he wrote to the *Times* as soon as the matter was noticed by the British Press.

At 9 a.m. on the 21st Sir Garnet Wolseley arrived in the despatch vessel *Salamis*, and issued the following proclamation by order of the *khedive*:—

> Proclamation to the Egyptians.
>
> The general in command of the British forces wishes to make known that the object of Her Majesty's Government in sending troops to this country is to re-establish the authority of the *khedive*. The army is therefore only fighting against those who are in arms against His Highness. All peaceable inhabitants will be treated with kindness, and no violence will be offered to them. Their religion, mosques, families, and property will be respected. Any supplies which may be required will be paid for, and the inhabitants are invited to bring them. The general in command will be glad to receive visits from the chiefs who are willing to assist in repressing the rebellion against the *khedive*, the lawful Ruler of Egypt appointed by the *sultan*.
>
> G. J. Wolseley, General,
> Commander-in-Chief of the British Army in Egypt."

CHAPTER 20

Tel-El-Mahuta to Mahsameh

The country between Ismailia and the Delta is so monotonous that a few words only are necessary to give a notion of its character. It is a desert of sand, across which run the Fresh Water Canal and the railway side by side. To the northward of these the ground is, as a rule, somewhat higher, sloping in a southerly direction across the Canal. From these elevations occasional peeps can be obtained of the blue waters of Lake Timsah, and of the violet-tinted hills of Gebel-Attakeh in the distance. The surface is occasionally varied by low hummocks and mounds, and is dotted at intervals by tufts of scrub, called "camel grass." The soil is a deep light shifting sand near Ismailia, but it gradually increases in firmness towards the westward; and at Tel-el-Kebir, especially on the upper crests of the hills, is a fairly compact wind-swept gravel, over which progress is comparatively easy.

The sky is here rarely cloudy, so that the sun beats down with full force during the day, whilst at night the air becomes cool and almost chilly, even in summer. Shelter is needed against the sun in day-time, and at night a blanket is indispensable, both on account of the low temperature and of the dews.

By reason of the absence of rain and the dry temperature, stores of all kinds could be freely piled up uncovered in the open air without fear of injury. The Fresh Water Canal, joining the Nile just below Cairo, furnished the necessary water, of fair quality when once the mud held in suspension was got rid of. The Egyptian flies, the worst of their species, however, made life almost unendurable. They disappeared with the sun, only to be relieved by countless hosts of mosquitoes.

No time was lost after the landing of the troops at Ismailia, the advance commencing the day following the occupation. At 11 a.m. General Graham started from the town with 800 men and a small naval contingent, and marched across the heavy sand, arriving in position at Nefiché at 1.30 p.m.

The Egyptian camp was found completely deserted, the enemy having retired to the westward along the Fresh Water Canal. A few tents were left behind, and about thirty railway trucks full of provisions and ammunition. The remains of the wrecked train which had been struck by the *Orion's* shell were also lying about. The locomotive, however, which was badly wanted, was gone, and the telegraph wires were cut. The entire force under Graham bivouacked here, and the position was at once placed in an efficient state of defence. Shelter trenches were thrown up, and guns were placed in position.

Later in the day a reconnaissance was made to the westward, and the presence of the enemy was discerned about four miles distant.

The troops had carried with them two days' rations, and it was necessary to accumulate a small stock of stores before continuing the advance. In consequence, the next two days were devoted to preparations.

Transports continued to arrive daily in Lake Timsah, and landing went on rapidly. On the 22nd, twenty-six transports, besides vessels of war, were moored off Ismailia. At 4 p.m. all the bluejackets from the fleet re-embarked, except three Gatling guns' crews and a torpedo party, who had advanced with Graham to Nefiché.[1]

On the 23rd there was increased activity in Ismailia, several transports arriving from Suez with portions of the Indian Contingent. The *khedive's* palace was converted into a hospital. Lines of rails were laid down from the landing-place to the station, and stores were disembarked in great quantities and moved up to the front.

On the following day commenced a series of engagements, which, with some intervals, continued until the dispersal of the Egyptian Army at Tel-el-Kebir.

At 4 a.m. on the 24th, Wolseley made an advance with the object of seizing a position on the Fresh Water Canal and railway which would insure the water supply. His force consisted of three squadrons of cavalry, two guns (R.H.A.), and 1,000 infantry (York and Lancaster Regiment and Marines). Following the line of railway, they arrived

---

1. It is related that one of the men-of-wars' men, when in working dress and carrying a huge package of stores, was accosted by a smart commissariat officer, who asked the sailor who he was. Jack stopped in his work, and wiping the perspiration from his brow, replied, "Well, sir, I used to be a British sailor, but now I'm blowed if I don't begin to think I'm a blooming commissariat mule."

at 7.30 a.m. on the north side of the Canal, at a point about midway between El Magfar and the village of Tel-el-Mahuta. At this point the enemy had constructed his first dam across the Canal, and after some skirmishing, in which the Household Cavalry made a successful charge, the dam was taken possession of.

From this point the enemy could be seen in force about a mile-and-a-half further on, holding a line extending across the Canal, at a distance of 2,000 yards from the British front. At Mahuta also a large embankment was seen blocking the railway, and a second dam had been constructed across the Canal. The smoke of locomotives constantly reaching Mahuta indicated that reinforcements were arriving at that point from the direction of Tel-el-Kebir.

Nevertheless, Wolseley, at the risk of being outnumbered—the enemy's force amounting in all to about 7,000 men—decided to hold his ground till evening, by which time the reinforcements sent for to Nefiché and Ismailia would arrive.

The enemy began with a heavy artillery fire from twelve guns, and their infantry advanced to within 1,000 yards of the British line, meeting with a steady and well-directed fire from the York and Lancaster Regiment, which held the captured dam. From 10 to 11 o'clock the enemy continued to develop his attack on the centre and right of Wolseley's position. The Egyptian guns were served well, but, fortunately, the shells used were fitted with percussion fuses, which sank so deeply into the sand before bursting that few splinters flew upwards. The fire was returned by the two guns of the Royal Horse Artillery (which had taken up a position on a sandy hillock near the railway embankment), and the practice from which was very good.

In the meantime, the cavalry, under General Drury-Lowe, manoeuvred on the right of the position to check the enemy's advance on that side; but the horses, just landed after a long sea voyage, and fatigued by their march across a desert deep in sand, were in no condition to charge.

This was the situation at noon, when two Gatling guns, with a party of sailors belonging to H.M.S. *Orion*, arrived and took up a position for action. The manner in which the sailors brought their guns into position excited general admiration.

At 1 p.m. the 2nd battalion of the Duke of Cornwall's Regiment arrived from Nefiché.

The artillery fire of the enemy was now directed more on the right, until about 3.30 p.m. General Lowe, with the cavalry, moved forward, and caused the enemy partially to withdraw his attack in that direction.

At 5.15 p.m. the enemy again advanced, his left pushing forward four guns, some cavalry and infantry, but not coming within effective infantry or Gatling fire.

Reinforcements now began to come up rapidly—Colonel Sir Baker Russell with 350 of the 4th and 7th Dragoon Guards, and at 6 p.m. the Brigade of Guards, under the Duke of Connaught, arrived on the scene. It was by this time too late to begin an offensive movement; the troops were tired by their exertions during the early part of the day, and the Brigade of Guards, which had moved from Ismailia at 1.30 p.m., had suffered much from the heat of the desert march. Shortly after sunset the entire force bivouacked on the field which they had so tenaciously held all day, and the enemy withdrew to his position at Mahuta.

The events of the day may be shortly described as a successful attempt to seize the dam,[2] and the retaining of the position, gained in the face of greatly superior numbers. It is therefore to be regretted that Sir Garnet Wolseley should have thought it necessary to refer to the matter in somewhat bombastic language in his official despatch, in which he expresses himself as follows:

> Although I had but three squadrons of cavalry, two guns, and about 1,000 infantry, I felt it would not be in consonance with the traditions of Her Majesty's Army that we should retire, even temporarily, before Egyptian troops, no matter what their numbers might be.

Had Sir Garnet only been well acquainted with military history, he might have recollected one of the events connected with the British Expedition to Egypt in 1807. In the course of that disastrous campaign 1,000 British infantry, under Colonel Stewart, had to retire before a force, composed of Egyptian and Albanian troops, at El Hamad, on the

---

2. The dam, which by threatening the water supply had necessitated the advance, was found to have been made of bundles of reeds cleverly lashed together with telegraph wire, with sand thrown over each layer. All the next day the bluejackets, assisted by a fatigue party of soldiers, went to work up to their necks in the water trying to cut through the dam. Little or no impression, however, was made upon it. It was then operated on with gun-cotton, which had but little effect on the sand. A large hole was made, but it instantly filled up again. Pickaxes and shovels were then set to work, but it was not until the 27th that the dam was at last cleared away and the Canal opened to navigation.

Nile, and further, were all either killed, wounded, or taken prisoners.[3]

During the night of the 24th August further reinforcements from Ismailia continued to arrive, and the attack on the intrenched post of Tel-el-Mahuta commenced soon after daybreak on the 25th.

As the British force advanced, the infantry in echelon, the Brigade of Guards leading and the cavalry on the right, the enemy was observed abandoning his earthworks at Mahuta, and falling back along the railway line to Mahsameh. His railway trains were all seen moving off in the same direction. At 6.25 a.m. the British artillery came into action with the Egyptian infantry and guns posted on the Canal bank to the west of Mahuta.

As it was of importance to capture some of the enemy's locomotives, the cavalry and eight guns were pushed forward with all speed to cut off the retreating trains. The enemy offered considerable resistance in the neighbourhood of Mahsameh, but nothing could stop the advance of the mounted troops, and Mahsameh, with its extensive camp, was soon in their possession. Seven Krupp guns, great quantities of ammunition, two trains of railway waggons loaded with provisions, and vast supplies of various kinds were captured. The Egyptian soldiers fled along the railway and Canal banks, throwing away their arms and equipment, and showing every sign of demoralization.

The Canal had been filled with dead bodies, and the banks were still strewn with them, probably with the idea of making the water undrinkable. It was here that one of the English artillerymen, having offered to fetch water for a wounded Egyptian, was shot dead by the latter whilst doing so.

The stock of provisions captured was a most welcome addition to the stores in hand, and in particular the grain left on the ground in large quantities was invaluable, for the horses had been for several days on an extremely short allowance of forage.

It will be remarked that the operations of the day hardly attained to the dignity of an engagement, the Egyptians offering practically no resistance, but falling back on Tel-el-Kebir, where a large camp had been established north of the railway, and where extensive intrenchments were begun along the crest of a range of hills running north and south.[4]

---

3. *Egypt in the Nineteenth Century*, by A. D. Cameron.

4. Mahmoud Pasha Fehmi, who was captured, was the Chief of the Staff of the Egyptian Army. He missed the train and was found strolling, apparently unconcerned, about the railway station at Mahsameh. As he was in the ordinary Egyptian dress with a "*tarboosh*" and white umbrella, he would probably have got away unobserved had he not been recognised and denounced by a wounded Egyptian soldier.

The losses on the side of the British were small—only five killed and twenty-five wounded; but the cases of sunstroke were numerous, the 4th Dragoons having sixteen and the York and Lancaster Regiment twenty-five men disabled from this cause.

On August 26th a small force of the dragoons occupied the lock on the Fresh Water Canal at Kassassin without opposition. This was a most important step, because the possession of the lock gave Sir Garnet Wolseley control of the water in the upper reach of the Canal—no small advantage to an army worked like his on strictly temperance principles. That it could have been accomplished so easily is an indication of the ignorance or carelessness of the enemy. Later in the day the Duke of Cornwall's Light Infantry, the 84th York and Lancaster Regiment, as well as two guns of the Royal Horse Artillery, were marched to the lock, where they established themselves, the cavalry withdrawing to Mahsameh. A house on the left bank of the Canal was occupied by General Graham and his staff, who remained in charge of the advanced guard. As it was known that the enemy was not far off, the cavalry scouted by day and night, and strong outposts were established.

CHAPTER 21

Kassassin

The British force had now outrun its commissariat, and for two days the men had lived from hand to mouth. To secure the water supply it had become necessary to push forward a force into the Desert nearly twenty miles from the base of operations at Ismailia. The question arose how the troops were to be supplied with food, and the want of a proper organization for the transport of provisions began to be severely felt. The men, weakened by prolonged exertion under a terrible sun, were forced to live for two or three days on biscuits and muddy water, flavoured only with the dead bodies of Egyptian men and horses. The English horses also were short of forage and showed signs of fatigue and exhaustion. The question of supply became an anxious one. Mules were not forthcoming, the railway had been cut, and no rolling stock was available, and the British force was for days almost without food.

On the third day, owing to the vigorous efforts of the navy, some stores were forwarded to the front by the Fresh Water Canal, but the prospects were, to say the least, gloomy. The men were compelled to live on pigeons, water-melons, &c., looted out of the neighbouring village. On the 27th, however, a foraging party was conducted into the country by the transport officer, and some fourteen head of cattle were driven in, besides some sheep and turkeys. The general ordered them all to be paid for, and this rule was observed on subsequent occasions.

On the 28th the Egyptians made an effort to regain their lost ground by a serious attack upon the advanced force under General Graham, at Kassassin.

The position occupied by the British was not the most favourable for defence. The troops were astride the Canal, and although a bridge existed, the separation of the right and left wings was partial in any case, and complete if the force had either to advance or retire. However, on the right of the position the Desert rose to a ridge some 100 to 160 feet high, which with a force like Graham's, too weak to occupy it, might easily conceal the movements of an outflanking force.

About 9.30 a.m. the Egyptian cavalry appeared in force on the left front on the north side of the Fresh Water Canal. Graham's troops, consisting of 57 cavalry, 70 mounted infantry, 1,728 infantry, and 40 artillery, with two 13-pounder guns, were at once posted under cover, fronting to the north and west, the cavalry being thrown out on the flanks to observe the enemy's movements. About 11 a.m. it was reported that a large force of cavalry, infantry and artillery was being moved round towards the British right behind the ridge already referred to. At noon, the Egyptians opened fire from two heavy guns on the left front of Graham's position. The range being at least 4,000 yards, the shot all fell short. After a time the fire slackened, and about 3 p.m. the enemy were reported to be retiring.

Graham's men, who had been suffering very much from their long exposure to the sun without food, were then ordered back to their camps.

The matter, however, was not destined to end here, for at 4.30 the enemy advanced his infantry in great force, displaying a line of skirmishers at least a mile in length, with which he sought to overlap the left of Graham's front. This movement was supported by a heavy and well-directed artillery fire, which searched the camp and wounded a sick officer in the building occupied as a hospital.

The dispositions to meet the attack were as follows:—On the left the Marine Artillery were directed to take up a position on the south bank of the Canal, whence they could check the enemy's advance by a flank fire. In the centre was the Duke of Cornwall's Regiment, extended in fighting line, about 800 yards to the right rear of the Marine Artillery, and the York and Lancaster extended the fighting line of the Duke of Cornwall's with two and a half companies, keeping the remainder in support and reserve.

The position of the infantry was an irregular echelon, the right thrown back. A troop of the 7th Dragoon Guards was kept on this flank, and the two 13-pounders, now reinforced by two others, took up a position on the ridge, and promptly replied to the Egyptian cannonade. Unfortunately, these guns had only the ammunition contained in their limbers and had soon to cease firing for want of a further supply, though they did good service while it lasted. The reason of the ammunition failing was the heaviness of the road from the base to the front. Efforts were made to get up a proper supply, but the waggons stuck in the sand and so arrived late.

The Mounted Infantry and a dismounted detachment of the 4th Dragoon Guards occupied a portion of the gap between the Marine Artillery and the Duke of Cornwall's Regiment, and although the attacking force made persistent efforts to break through at this point, it failed owing to the steady fire of the Marine Artillery and the little band of dragoons and Mounted Infantry.

The enemy made repeated attempts to overcome this resistance, putting a number of men across the Canal; and three times their guns were kept from advancing by the horses and men being shot when trying to press past.

Feeling secure on his left, Graham turned his attention to the right flank of his position. On the first notice of the attack (4.30 p.m.) he had sent a message to General Drury-Lowe by heliograph, and by a mounted officer to Mahsameh, three or four miles distant, requesting him to move up the cavalry brigade to cover the right flank, and also to send forward the Marine Light Infantry as a reinforcement.

At 5 p.m. Graham sent a further order for the cavalry to advance under cover of the ridge on the right, fall upon the left flank of the enemy's skirmishers and roll up his line. The particulars of the cavalry attack made in pursuance of this order are given later on.

Reinforcements for the enemy being observed arriving by train, still further to protect his exposed right, Graham sent a reserve company of the York and Lancaster in that direction. Near the same point a Krupp gun, taken from the enemy at Mahsameh and mounted on a railway truck, was brought into action, and worked by a detachment of Marine Artillery. This gun was admirably served and did great execution among the attacking force.

Although fired upon by as many as four guns at a time, not a man of the gun detachment was hit, and the gun continued to fire on to the last, expending ninety-three rounds. The immunity enjoyed by the gun's crew was doubtless due to the constant shifting of the gun backwards and forwards on the line of rails. The gun itself was protected by a breastwork of sandbags.

At 6.45 p.m. a general advance was ordered, with the object of closing on the enemy's infantry about the time that Graham reckoned Drury-Lowe's cavalry charge would be taking place.

The advance was made very steadily, the British infantry firing volleys by companies, the reserves following in rear of the railway embankment. The Marine Light Infantry had now come on to the ground on the right and joined in the advance, which was continued for from two to three miles, the enemy falling back and only once attempting to make a stand. This was on the British left, but here the Egyptians broke at the first volley of the marines.

At 8.45 p.m. Graham heard of the cavalry charge from an officer of the 1st Life Guards, who had lost his way. Graham's force had now been marching forward for an hour and a half in the moonlight, and his men had had narrow escapes in mistaking detached bodies of the enemy for British troops. Fearing some mistake might be made, and seeing no further chance of co-operation with the cavalry, Graham ordered the troops back to camp.

To describe the movements of the cavalry under General Drury-Lowe. According to that officer's report, the *aide-de-camp* despatched by Graham reported at 5.30 that the enemy was advancing in force, and the brigade was at once turned out. It consisted of the Household Cavalry, the Dragoon Guards, and four guns of the Royal Horse Artillery. As the troops advanced, the sound of heavy firing was heard, and, *en route*, a galloper from General Graham arrived, and stated that the general desired to say that "he was only just able to hold his own, and that he wished the cavalry to attack the left of the enemy's skirmishers."

The sun had now set, and a bright moon was shining. The light, however, was not good, and the force had to be guided by the flash of the guns and musketry.

General Drury-Lowe made a wide circuit, so as to turn the enemy's left, and the brigade arrived close to this portion of their line without being noticed.

As the cavalry advanced, it was received by a fire of shells and musketry, which, being aimed too high, was practically harmless. When within 500 or 600 yards of the enemy, the guns of the Horse Artillery, then in the rear of the Household Cavalry and dragoons, were unmasked by the retirement of the first line, and brought into action. After a few rounds had been fired, Sir Baker Russell led a charge of the Household Cavalry against the enemy's infantry, which had commenced to advance. Moving steadily towards the flash of the rifles, the charge was gallantly led and executed. The British cavalry carried all before them. The enemy's infantry was completely scattered, and, according to the official report, the cavalry swept through a battery of nine guns. In daylight these must have been captured, but, unfortunately, their exact position could not be found afterwards, and it is supposed that they were subsequently removed during the night.

This moonlight charge was the most dramatic, as it was one of the most dashing, episodes of the campaign. Whether the charge, brilliant as it was, occurring so late in the engagement, had any real effect upon the fortunes of the day may well be doubted. The general opinion of military men appears to be that its importance has been much exaggerated. The non-capture of the Egyptian guns is especially to be regretted, and has indeed led to the expression of a serious doubt as to their existence.

The message referred to by General Drury-Lowe, to the effect that General Graham wished to say that "he was only just able to hold his own," was, it appears, not sent by the general, but was merely the appreciation of the person who brought the message. There is no doubt, however, that it correctly represented the situation at the time.

The British loss was a total of killed or dangerously wounded, 11; wounded, 67. The enemy's loss is unknown, but was believed to have been heavy, the ground being thickly strewn with their killed, more especially in the spot where the cavalry charge took place. The burying parties next morning found that many of the bodies had been shockingly mutilated during the night. The circumcised had all been left untouched. The persons committing these outrages followed a fixed plan, which they applied to the uncircumcised corpses of both armies. They lopped off the feet, hands, and other members, and deeply gashed the abdomen and the upper part of the forehead. General Graham's estimate of the Egyptian forces engaged was 1,000 cavalry, 8,000 infantry, and 12 guns.

It may be remarked that, small as was the British force employed, the results of the engagement were of the greatest importance. It showed, in the first place, that Arabi felt himself strong enough to attack and act on the offensive, with a view to regain the prestige which his troops had lost in the previous encounters. In the second place, it showed that the campaign was likely to be something more than a parade across the desert, and that the enemy was willing to come within range and hold his own for hours together. It showed also that he would not stand an attack at close quarters, and that, unless in greatly superior numbers, he might be expected to give way if resolutely assailed.

The British left being well supported by the Canal and its banks, the most obvious move on the part of the attack was to double up their right and force them into the Canal, cutting off communication with their rear. The Egyptians had no commander capable of realizing the importance of this object, and, in consequence, the main attack was made in front, the strongest part of the British position, and the flanking movement was only half-hearted and unsuccessful.

With this fight ended the first part of the campaign. There was then necessarily a pause in the military operations. A further advance was beset with many difficulties. The railway was damaged in many places, and blocked in others. There were no locomotives to haul the trucks containing stores from the base to the front, and the army transport had in great measure broken down. The draught animals were few and in poor condition; pack-mules in sufficient numbers were lacking, and camels were almost entirely wanting. The strong regulation carts, suitable for use on European roads, were so heavy as to stick hopelessly in the sand. A waggon designed for two horses required not less than six to move it under existing conditions. The navy, it is true, was doing its best to make up for the defects of the army transport. The boat service on the Canal had been definitely organized under Commander Moore, of the *Orion*, and rendered most valuable service in getting provisions and stores to the front.

Notwithstanding all that the boats could do, it became doubtful whether even the few troops at the front could be maintained, and every effort had to be made to keep them supplied with the food requisite to enable them to exist. The men bore their privations and discomforts cheerfully until the arrival of locomotives from Suez made it possible to supply the army properly. The water, too, was the reverse of good, the only supply practically being from the Canal, and this at times was simply loathsome.

In addition to this discomfort, there was always the possibility of the railway or Canal being intercepted by marauding parties of the enemy. Either of these contingencies would have seriously imperilled the troops at the front.

In the meantime, the 3rd Brigade, 2nd Division, composed of Highlanders, under the command of Sir Edward Hamley arrived at Ismailia from Alexandria.

Three more transports with Indian troops also turned up, making the total number of transports in Lake Timsah no less than 93, besides men-of-war. The 3rd Brigade was not landed at once, but remained on board the troopships, pending the solution of the transport problem.

The state of affairs at this period appears from a telegram from Sir Garnet Wolseley to the Secretary of State for War, and which was as follows:—

> Ismailia, September 1, 1882.
> In reply to your inquiry of 29th *ultimo*, circumstances have forced me ahead of transport, but it is rapidly becoming efficient. The necessity of securing a sufficient supply of fresh water in the Canal rendered it imperative to push on as quickly as possible. My successes on the 24th and 25th, and retreat of the enemy, have enabled me to seize (the) two important positions on the Canal of El Magfar and Kassassin Lock, the latter about twenty miles from this place. I am, therefore, in a more forward and favourable position generally than I had anticipated, and am only now waiting till my transport arrangements are more complete to enable me to make a further movement.
>
> In the absence of roads, I had always calculated on partially using the Canal and railway in sending supplies to the front, but the enemy having blocked the former by two large dams, and the latter by an embankment, and the partial removal of rails, it has been necessary to get these obstructions removed. I have one engine on the line, and expect a second from Suez tonight, and am preparing the land transport companies, some of which are now landing, to supplement the other means above indicated.
>
> A supply of mules has arrived at Cyprus. I expect 400 more from Malta and Italy tomorrow; and the large supply collected at Smyrna and Beyrout at last released by the Ottoman Government are on their way. In a desert country, like this part of Egypt, it takes time to organize the lines of communication.

By the 2nd September the whole of the Indian Contingent, except the 6th Bengal Cavalry, had reached Suez, and many of its troops had gone to the front.

Except for an occasional reconnaissance, bringing about an interchange of shots and one real attack, the period now entered upon was one merely of preparation for a further advance. With this object, stores first, and then men, were gradually being accumulated at Kassassin.

On the 9th September the Egyptian leaders apparently began to realize the fact that Sir Garnet Wolseley's force was daily increasing in size and importance, and that if any attempt was to be made to crush him there was no time to be lost. Accordingly an attack was made that day on Kassassin.

On this occasion Arabi himself was on the ground, though the attacking forces were commanded by Ali Pasha Fehmi. The Egyptian force turned out in great strength, comprising seventeen battalions of infantry, several squadrons of cavalry, thirty guns, and some thousands of Bedouins.

The Egyptian attack was meant to be from two sides: on the west by an advance of the garrison of Tel-el-Kebir, and on the north by a body, variously estimated at from 1,500 to 5,000 men, from Salahieh.

There is very little doubt that the British force came very near being surprised. Early in the morning Colonel Pennington, of the 13th Bengal Lancers, going out to the westward to post vedettes, found the Egyptians advancing in force. Although he had but fifty men with him he dismounted them behind a ridge, and opened fire on the advancing enemy, and when hard pushed charged some squadrons of cavalry, killing ten men and capturing five horses. Warning of the impending danger was thus given to the camp, enabling a line of battle to be formed.

By 7 a.m. Arabi had succeeded in posting most of his guns on an eminence described in Wolseley's despatches as "Ninth Hill," 2,000 yards to the British right front, whilst his infantry deployed for attack, with the right resting on the Canal, and then advanced to within 1,200 yards. A few of his troops got south of the Canal, with a view to a flank movement.

No sooner were the Egyptian guns posted than they opened fire. The practice was very accurate, shot after shot falling admirably into the British camp and lines. The shells, however, burst so rarely as to neutralize the excellence of the aim.

The British artillery batteries and the guns on the railway replied vigorously with shell and shrapnel. The 25-pounders did excellent work on the enemy's right on both sides of the Canal, sending their projectiles over the heads of the British infantry until the advance was begun. The Horse Artillery batteries shot down the men working two of the guns, and these were seized by the infantry as they advanced; two others were captured by the marines in their forward march. Their battalion, in regular formation for attack, came upon a battery of four guns which was playing briskly upon the marines at a distance of 1,400 yards. Without returning the fire they kept on their way until within 400 yards, when they began firing volleys by half companies, still continuing the march. This steady work proved too severe for the Egyptian gunners, who broke and ran, leaving two of the four guns behind.

The infantry also engaged, holding its ground for an hour and a half, no forward movement being permitted until it was ascertained that no danger was to be apprehended from the direction of Salahieh.

At 8.30 it was deemed prudent to assume the offensive, and the line was ordered to advance, the right being always kept in reserve. The 46th (Duke of Cornwall's), 84th (York and Lancaster), and 50th (West Kent) Regiments, which had been stationed on the south bank of the Canal to check any flank movement of the enemy, were ordered to retire across the Canal bridge, and, crossing the plain in front of the camp, to form up with the rest. The infantry, with the four batteries of artillery on its right, moved forward about 1,000 yards and re-engaged the enemy, who by this time had retired.

To prevent any attempt to overlap the right of the position, the 46th was advanced in this direction over the hills. The attack in this quarter, however, resolved itself into nothing. At 9.30 the general advance was resumed amid a smart musketry fire, and the enemy broke and retired with precipitation upon Tel-el-Kebir. The cavalry and Royal Horse Artillery ran them very close, the fortifications being approached as near as 6,000 yards.

CHAPTER 22

Tel-El-Kebir

On the 9th September, Sir Garnet Wolseley, who had been to the front during the engagement of that day and had made a reconnaissance towards the enemy's lines at Tel-el-Kebir, established his headquarters at Kassassin.

The same day the Highland Brigade, under Sir Archibald Alison, commenced its march from Ismailia to the front. The Guards were also brought up. The 10th, 11th, and 12th were occupied in bringing forward troops and stores, and in making preparations for a general advance.

At 2 p.m. on the 12th, the army was concentrated at Kassassin, the Royal Irish Fusiliers being the last battalion to arrive.

To remain behind and guard the line of communication, 800 of the Manchester Regiment and 500 of the native infantry were left at Ismailia. At Nefiché, Mahuta, and Mahsameh, small detachments were also stationed, whilst at Kassassin 200 of the West Kent Regiment and two companies of the Royal Engineers were told off to form a garrison for the time being. This left available for the forward movement 11,000 infantry, 2,000 cavalry and 60 guns.

Tel-el-Kebir, properly written "El-Tel-el-Kebir," "The Great Hill," is the name of a peaceful Arab village on the south side of the railway leading from Ismailia to Cairo, and on the banks of the Fresh Water Canal. On the opposite side of the railway and Canal stands the "hill," an elevation of considerable height, near which Arabi had for some weeks past been intrenching his forces.

Tel-el-Kebir had for many years past been used as a military station and camp, and it was here that Arabi had been exiled with his mutinous regiment in the autumn of 1881.

The position selected by the Egyptians for a final stand was by

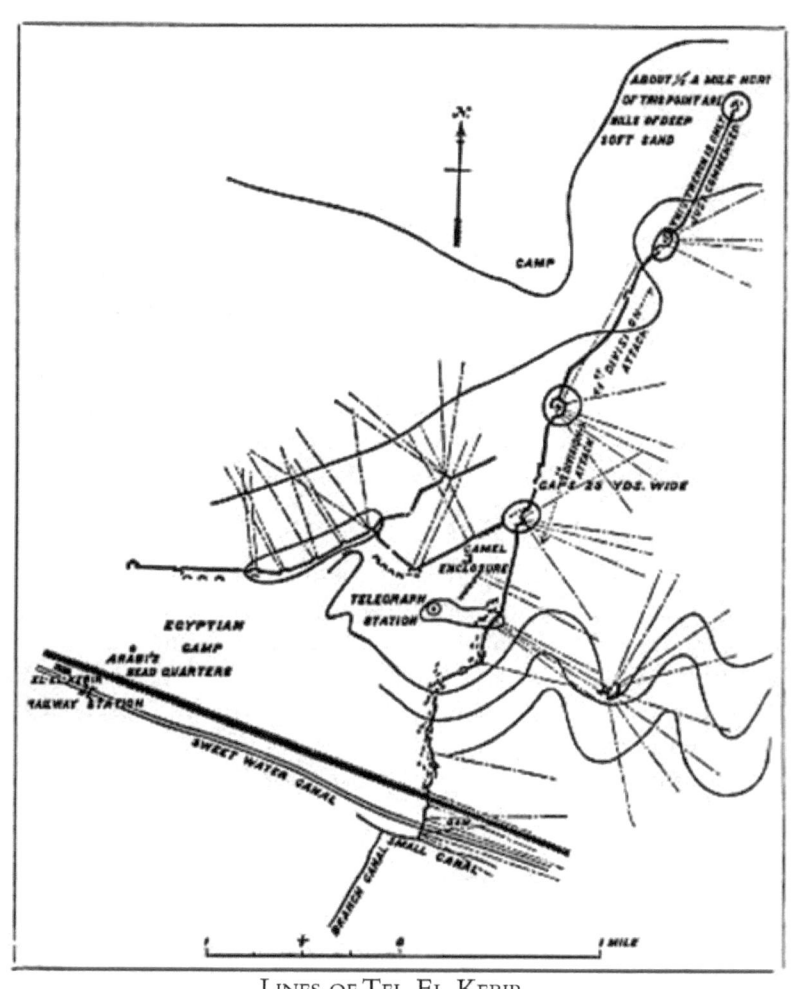

LINES OF TEL-EL-KEBIR.

nature the strongest it was possible to find in that flat section of country.[1] Near the station of Tel-el-Kebir there is a general and gradual rise of the ground towards the west, culminating in a range of hills that stretch from a point on the railway about a mile and a half east of the station, northward to Salahieh. Roughly parallel to the Fresh Water Canal is a second series of hills intersecting the first about two miles distant from the railway. Viewed from the railway, this east and west range appears as a moderate hill.

Its real character, however, is that of a table-land sloping away to the northward with a rather steep descent towards the south. The ground is generally even, and barren almost to desolation, the soil consisting of sand and rock, producing only a small scrub. The Egyptian intrenchments were laid out along the crests of these hills, the lines running north and south, starting from the railway and canal (see plan), and running in a northerly direction for over two miles beyond the intersection, making a total frontage to the eastward of nearly four miles. The plan included a dry ditch from eight to twelve feet wide, and from five to nine feet deep, in front of a breastwork from four to six feet high with a "*banquette*" in rear. The trace was broken by occasional salients, where were placed well-designed redoubts, possessing a wide command on either flank.

In the rear were frequent shelter trenches. Passages through the parapet were provided for field-pieces and vehicles in various places, and were guarded by traverses and breastworks. The revetment differed mainly in the care which had been bestowed upon it, and consisted mostly of reeds, grass, &c. The interior slopes were the only ones thus treated.

The southern portion of the defences was practically completed at the time of the battle. Here the revetment was neatly finished. Work was in progress on the northern and western lines, their extremities being scarcely more than laid out. The extent of these defensive works, which was enormous in comparison with the number of troops at Arabi's disposal, would seem to imply an inordinate reliance upon mere ditches and breastworks to keep out an enemy however vigorous. It led as a necessary consequence to the excessive spreading out of the defenders, and the fatal weakening of the force which could be gathered at any given point. Had the same amount of labour been expended in several concentric lines, it would have resulted in a position

---

1. Tel-el-Kebir and Kafr Dowar are the two great strategical points to be held in defending Lower Egypt. This will at once be seen on referring to a map of the Delta.

of great strength, permitting the retiring, if necessary, from one line to the next, and an almost indefinite prolongation of the fight.

The batteries were along the front, and were thus distributed. At the southern end of the line there were two well-built redoubts, mounting each three guns, on either bank of the Canal. Connecting the two, and stopping the flow of water in the Fresh Water Canal, was a stout dam. On each side of the railway was one gun, in a small earthwork.

In front of the lines running north and south, and distant about 1,100 yards, was a formidable outwork standing on rising ground. This was a polygonal redoubt, and mounted six guns. In the rear of this redoubt and on the lines was a 4-gun battery, behind which was a look-out and telegraph station, the wire running back to Arabi's headquarters near the railway station, and in the midst of a large camp. The diminished size of the ditch from this point northwards is very noticeable. The attack was evidently hoped for at and near the railway.

Following the lines in a northerly direction, the next battery was at the intersection of the two lines of intrenchments. This was the most elaborately finished of all the redoubts, and mounted five guns. Still further in the same direction was another formidable battery of five guns.[2] Beyond this there were two other incomplete redoubts, further still to the northward, but this part of the line was hardly begun.

As regards the east and west line, intersecting the lines running north and south, its object was to afford a defence in the event of the enemy succeeding in breaking through those lines at the northern end, their weakest part.[3]

To the eastward of the lines and in the direction of Kassassin was a tolerably level desert with smooth sand and pebble.

The information, received from spies and prisoners, was to the effect that the enemy's force at Tel-el-Kebir consisted of from 60 to 70 guns, twenty-four battalions of infantry (18,000 men), and three regiments of cavalry, together with about 6,000 Bedouins, besides a force of 5,000 men with 24 guns at Salahieh,[4] all under the immediate command of Arabi himself.

The general character of the ground lying between the two armies

---

2. This was turned by the Highlanders, who passed to the south
3. This work was absolutely useless in the battle, being taken by the Highlanders in the rear and by the 2nd Brigade in the flanks.
4. As a fact 25,000 rations were served out to the Egyptian force at Tel-el-Kebir on the 12th September.

was that of gently undulating, pebbly slopes, rising gradually to an open plateau from ninety to a hundred feet above the valley through which the railway and canal ran. To have marched over this plateau upon the enemy's position by daylight, the British troops would have had to advance over a glacis-like slope, absolutely without cover, in full view of the enemy, and under the fire of his artillery, for about five miles. Such an operation would have entailed heavy loss from an enemy with men and guns protected by intrenchments from any artillery fire which the attacking force could have brought to bear upon them.

To have turned the Egyptian position, either by the right or left, was an operation which would have entailed a wide turning movement, and, therefore, a long, difficult and fatiguing march, and moreover would not have accomplished the object Wolseley had in view, namely, that of grappling with the enemy at such close quarters that he would be unable to shake himself free, except by a general fight of all his army. The object was to make the battle a final one, whereas a wide turning movement would probably only have forced Arabi to retreat upon the cultivated country in his rear, where, the land being irrigated and cut up in every direction by deep canals, it would have been difficult for a regular army to follow him. Influenced by these considerations, and also by the information that the enemy did not push his outposts far beyond his works at night, Wolseley determined upon the difficult operation of a night march, to be followed by an attack on the Egyptian position before daylight.

As soon as it was dark on the evening of the 12th September, the camp at Kassassin was struck, and all the tents and baggage were stacked alongside the railway. The camp fires were left burning. The troops then moved into position near a spot described as "Ninth Hill." There they formed in order of battle and bivouacked—no fires were allowed, even smoking was prohibited, and all were ordered to maintain the utmost silence.[5]

The formation of the troops was as follows:—

On the right, the 1st Division, commanded by Lieutenant-General Willis, and consisting of two brigades, *viz.*, the 2nd, under Major-General Graham, in front, and the 1st, or Guards Brigade, under the Duke of Connaught, in the rear; on the left, the 2nd Division, com-

---

5. This order being disobeyed by a drunken soldier, who by his shouting might have betrayed the presence of the force to the enemy, he was promptly seized, bound, and chloroformed into a quiescent state.

manded by Lieutenant-General Sir Edward Hamley, and consisting of two brigades, *viz*., the 3rd, or Highland Brigade, under Major-General Sir Archibald Alison, in front, and the 4th, under Lieutenant-Colonel Ashburnham, in the rear. Between the two divisions was placed the artillery brigade under Brigadier-General Goodenough. On the extreme right was the cavalry division under Major-General Drury-Lowe, and on the extreme left, under Major-General Sir Herbert Macpherson, were the Indian Contingent and the Naval Brigade.

At 1.30 on the morning of the 13th, the order was given for the advance of the 1st and 2nd Divisions simultaneously, and the celebrated march on Tel-el-Kebir began. The Indian Contingent and the Naval Brigade did not move until an hour later, to avoid giving the alarm to the enemy, by the passing of the force through the numerous villages in the cultivated land south of the Canal.

The night was dark, and it was very difficult to maintain the desired formation. More than once the advancing lines, guided only by the light of the stars, formed somewhat of a crescent shape, and there was danger of the advancing force mistaking their comrades for parties of the enemy. Several halts had to be made, as well for the purpose of resting the men as for that of correcting the formation. The final halt was made at 3 a.m., and lasted nearly an hour. Daybreak was the time fixed for the arrival at the enemy's lines, and it would have been as undesirable to have reached them too early as too late.

There were practically three separate but nearly simultaneous infantry attacks, by the 1st Division under General Willis; by the 2nd Division under General Hamley, and away on the extreme left, south of the Canal, by the Indian Contingent, under General Macpherson. In point of time, General Hamley's was somewhat earlier than the others, and General Macpherson's the last of the three.

The action began at early dawn. Willis's leading brigade,[6] commanded by General Graham, was about 900 yards from the intrenchments. Partly owing to the difficulty of keeping a proper alignment during the night march, partly to the fact that the line of march was oblique to the line of the earthworks, and partly to the confusion created by an Egyptian scout who galloped into the lines, Willis was obliged to form again under fire, changing front forward on the left company, before assaulting. Adopting the regular attack formation at 300 yards distance, his men fired a volley, after which they rushed up to 150

---

6. 2nd Battalion Royal Irish Regiment, Royal Marine Light Infantry, 2nd Battalion York and Lancaster Regiment, 1st Battalion Royal Irish Fusiliers.

yards distance, fired a second volley, and then reached the ditch.[7] Here the fighting line was joined by the supports (the 1st Battalion of the Grenadiers, the Scots and Coldstreams), a last volley delivered, the ditch jumped, and amid the cheers of the soldiers the works cleared at the point of the bayonet.

As soon as the brigade reached the parapet, the Egyptians broke and ran, some stopping occasionally to fire back on their pursuers, who chased them until the artillery had got inside the works and had begun shelling the fugitives.

This brigade struck the trenches not 100 yards from the point aimed at. It was longer exposed to the Egyptian fire than were the Highlanders, whose attack had begun a few minutes before and had fully aroused the whole line of the defence, which had been sleeping on their arms behind the parapets.

To the Highland Brigade,[8] under General Alison, fell the task of carrying the lines to the left. The first shots were fired at them at 4.55 a.m. from an Egyptian picket posted about 150 yards in front of the intrenchments, then visible 300 yards distant from the Highlanders. Immediately afterwards the enemy opened with artillery and then with musketry. Without returning this fire, the brigade advanced steadily for about 100 yards further, when the fire became a perfect blaze. At 150 yards bayonets were ordered to be fixed, and the bugle sounded the advance, when with a yell the Scotchmen charged in the dim light through the smoke, carrying the lines in splendid style in the face of determined opposition. So stoutly was the position defended that in many places the assailants, after mounting the parapets, were forced back into the trenches below, only, however, to return and renew the assault.

The left battalion, composed of the Highland Light Infantry, struck the battery already described as situated at the intersection of the two lines of intrenchments. This redoubt had a high scarp, which held the centre companies for some moments till the flank companies got round it and took it. The enemy did not run far, but halted about 60 yards in the rear of the works and delivered a heavy cross fire. The rest

---
7. This firing, which is recorded in the Report of Commander Goodrich, page 153, is in partial contradiction to Wolseley's despatch.
8. 1st Battalion Royal Highlanders, 1st Battalion Gordon Highlanders, 1st Battalion Cameron Highlanders, 2nd Battalion Highland Light Infantry. This brigade was supported by Colonel Ashburnham's, consisting of the King's Royal Rifles and the Duke of Cornwall's Light Infantry.

of the brigade pushed steadily on, driving the enemy before it and capturing three batteries of field guns. The advance was continued, and Arabi's headquarters and the Canal bridge were seized at 6.45 a.m. The Highland Light Infantry, which had suffered severely, soon after joined the rest of the brigade. The gallant Highlanders' attack was made entirely with the bayonet, not a shot being fired until the men were within the enemy's lines.

In the centre, between the two infantry attacks, marched the seven batteries of artillery, under General Goodenough—and after the capture of the enemy's works did good service and inflicted considerable loss upon the enemy, in some instances firing canister at short ranges.

On the extreme left the Indian Contingent[9] and the Naval Brigade, under General Macpherson, advanced steadily and in silence, the Seaforth Highlanders leading, until an advanced battery of the enemy was reached. From this the Egyptian artillery had opened fire down the line of the Canal, although it was still too dark for them to see the approaching troops clearly, whilst the infantry lost no time in opening a heavy fusillade. The Highlanders deployed for attack, and then gallantly stormed the battery with a rush at the point of the bayonet. The Egyptians retreated upon some villages close by, where they were pursued by a squadron of the Bengal Cavalry across the cultivated ground.[10]

The Indian Contingent scarcely lost a man—a happy circumstance, due to the excellent arrangements made by General Macpherson, and to the fact that, starting one hour later than the 1st and 2nd Divisions, the resistance of the enemy was so shaken by the earlier attacks north of the Canal, that they soon gave way before the impetuous onslaught of the Seaforth Highlanders.

On the extreme right the cavalry division,[11] under General Drury-Lowe, was designedly late in arriving, being fully two miles distant when the first shot was fired at the Highlanders. Hearing the sound, the division quickened its pace, reaching the intrenchments in time to permit its two horse batteries to take in reverse and enfilade the lines north of General Graham's assault, while the cavalry took up the

---

9. 7—1 Royal Artillery (mountain battery), 1st Battalion Seaforth Highlanders, 3rd Battalion Native Infantry, made up of detachments of 7th Bengal Native Infantry, 20th Punjaub Infantry, and 29th Beloochees.
10. Meanwhile, on the other side of the Canal, the Naval Gatlings were busily employed firing on the Egyptian lines in front and on either hand.
11. Household Cavalry, 4th Dragoon Guards, 7th Dragoon Guards, Mounted Infantry, Royal Horse Artillery, Bengal Cavalry, Bengal Lancers.

pursuit of the runaways, most of whom threw away their arms, and, begging for mercy, were left unmolested. To have made them prisoners would have taken up too much time, the cavalry being required for the more important work of pushing on to Cairo. The whole division, cavalry and horse artillery, united shortly after near the bridge over the Canal, prior to advancing towards the capital.

The British losses in the engagement were:—

Total—Nine officers and 48 non-commissioned officers and men killed, 27 officers and 353 non-commissioned officers and men wounded, 22 non-commissioned officers and men missing. Grand total of casualties, all ranks, 459.

The officers killed were as follows:—

2nd Battalion Connaught Rangers (attached to 2nd Battalion Royal Irish Regiment)—Captain C. N. Jones. Royal Marine Light Infantry—Major H. H. Strong, Captain C. J. Wardell. 1st Battalion Royal Highlanders—Lieutenant Graham Stirling, Lieutenant J. G. McNeill. 1st Battalion Gordon Highlanders—Lieutenant H. G. Brooks. 2nd Battalion Highland Light Infantry—Major Colville, Lieutenant D. S. Kays, Lieutenant L. Somervelle.

Such is the general outline of the battle of Tel-el-Kebir.

The Egyptians had been sleeping in their trenches when the attack was made, and although in one sense surprised, were nevertheless quite ready.[12]

Probably they never expected a night attack.[13] At the same time there is no doubt that they knew the British Army was in their immediate vicinity and might come on at any moment, and took precautions accordingly.

The best proof of this is the blaze of fire with which both the 2nd Brigade and the Highland Brigade were received. Prisoners taken afterwards stated that the striking of the tents at sunset was observed, and that pickets were on the watch ever since. Anyhow, the English forces, before they closed with the enemy, were subjected to a perfect hail of bullets.

Sir Edward Hamley, relating the attack of the 2nd Division, writes as follows:—

---

12. Sir Edward Hamley was of opinion that the alarm was given by mounted scouts who were met on the march.

13. Arabi subsequently told the late Morice Bey (who conducted him a prisoner to Ceylon) that at the time of the attack he was in bed, and the English did not leave him time enough to get his boots on.

Yet a minute or two elapsed after the Egyptian bugle was blown, and then the whole extent of intrenchment in our front, hitherto unseen and unknown, poured forth a stream of rifle-fire.

One witness writes:

> The Egyptian infantry clustered thickly in the parapets of the redoubts, and fired down the slopes into the trenches. Hundreds of them, lying down, plied the heads of the advancing brigades with fire.

A curious circumstance occurred with regard to the polygonal redoubt already described as standing 1,100 yards in advance of the lines. This was missed by the attacking forces, who must have passed within 200 yards of the work. It is partly accounted for, however, by the prevailing darkness, and partly by the fact that the gunners in the redoubt, either asleep or unprepared, let the Highland Brigade march past them to the lines without firing a shot. It was only when day broke that the Egyptian artillerymen called attention to the existence of the redoubt by aiming their guns and firing at the spot where Sir Garnet Wolseley and his staff were assembled. This was too much, and the British artillery had to be sent for. After being under case and shrapnel fire for a short time, what was left of the garrison threw down arms and formed a stream of fugitives who, with ghastly wounds, poured out from the redoubt, and scattered over the country.[14]

The missing of this redoubt was one of the lucky incidents of the fight. Had the advancing column been aware of its existence they must have paused to take it before storming the lines. In attacking the redoubt the position of the advancing force would have been at once revealed to the enemy, and the fire which was reserved for some minutes later would have at once opened.

The Egyptian guns were 8-centimetre and 6-centimetre Krupp steel B.L.R. of the old pattern (1868), mounted on field-carriages. The small-arms were all Remington breechloaders. The supply of ammunition was practically inexhaustible. At intervals of every three or four yards were found open boxes, each containing 1,050 cartridges.

The trenches, after the battle, were found to be filled with dead, mostly bayoneted, and the ground in rear as far as the railway station was dotted with the bodies of those shot down in retreat. The British cavalry, sweeping around the northern end of the intrenchments, cut

---

14. A naval officer who visited the redoubt the following day described it as a perfect "charnel-house."

down the fugitives by scores, until it became evident that the rout was complete. Most of the bodies were observed to be lying on their backs, as if the men had stopped to have a parting shot at their pursuers.

The Egyptian loss in killed was not far from 2,000. There was no return of their wounded, the army organization having disappeared; but 534 were treated at Tel-el-Kebir, during the four days succeeding the battle, twenty-seven capital operations being performed. Of the wounded, 202 were soon able to go to their homes, whilst the remainder were sent to Cairo in charge of Egyptian surgeons. The British medical authorities did all in their power to alleviate the sufferings of these poor creatures, and furnished tins of meat, bottles of brandy, and skins of water to those being conveyed away in the railway trucks. The greater number, who were slightly wounded, managed to get to the neighbouring villages, and therefore are not counted in the figures above given.[15]

It is stated—and the statement appears credible—that very few superior officers were killed or wounded; and Arabi and his second in command were undoubtedly the first to escape. Arabi himself mounted his horse and rode rapidly towards Belbeis. There appears to be no doubt that proper leaders, in every sense of the word, were wanting in the Egyptian army. It has been both humorously and truthfully remarked that each officer knew that *he* would run, but hoped his *neighbour* would stay.

The Egyptian soldiers, on the other hand, displayed real courage, as the struggles in the trenches and their heavy loss in killed abundantly prove. The black regiments, composed of negroes from the Soudan, were especially noticeable for their pluck, fighting bravely hand to hand with their assailants. It has been well observed that more intelligence and less downright cowardice on the part of their officers might have converted these men into a formidable army.

In the previous encounters between the English and the Egyptians, the artillery and cavalry had borne the brunt of the fighting, and had carried off the honours, but the battle of Tel-el-Kebir was almost entirely an infantry action. The tactics employed, a direct assault without flank movements of any kind, were of the simplest description. The object, to get to close quarters with the enemy, and to crush him, was

---

15. Dr. Shaw, of the Royal Marines, whilst attending one of the Egyptian wounded, happening to turn aside for a moment, was shot at by his patient. This ingratitude was too much for the doctor's orderly, who, with a bayonet, at once despatched the assailant.

accomplished.

After the attack, Arabi's army ceased to exist. In scattered groups it might be found all over Egypt, but as an organization it may be said to have been annihilated.

In view of the complete success of Sir Garnet Wolseley's tactics, comment is superfluous. It has been said by competent critics that the mode of attack adopted was rash to the degree of imprudence; that no commander would dare to employ such tactics against a European foe, and that a night march of nine miles could only be followed by an immediate and successful assault under circumstances so exceptional as to be providential. He has been blamed for having left his camp with his forces so early in the evening on the 12th, and having halted halfway from Tel-el-Kebir, and then only after midnight having set out again, a manoeuvre which might have endangered the whole result of the movement, and which, perhaps, may account for the surprise of the enemy's position not being so successful as it might have been.

Again, it has been said that besides a front attack, there should also have been a flank one, in conformity with ordinary military tactics.

In reply to these and other criticisms, it may be sufficient to observe that the English commander-in-chief formed a just appreciation of his enemy, had a strong conviction as to the proper manner of engaging him, and had unbounded confidence in the officers and men under his own command. What Sir Garnet Wolseley would have done had the enemy been of a different character is another question, the consideration of which does not come within the scope of the present work. The means adopted were exactly adjusted to the end to be attained, and the justification (if any were needed) for the risks run lies in the success which attended them.

Chapter 23

Capture of Cairo and Collapse of the Rebellion

When the Egyptian regiments, mingled together in one wild and disorderly mass, once commenced their retreat, no chance of rallying was for a moment given them. The cannon in the redoubts were turned against their former occupants, and the guns of the Royal Horse Artillery rained shrapnel shell on the fugitives. The cavalry, sweeping round from the north and charging in amongst them, completed the rout. The Egyptians threw down their arms and scattered themselves across the country. Arabi himself, with a few of his chief officers, caught the train at Belbeis and got to Cairo the same day, where it is said he began preparations for the destruction of the city.[1]

The enemy were pursued to Zag-a-zig by the Indian Contingent, the leading detachment of which reached that place a little after 4 p.m., and by the cavalry division to Belbeis, which was occupied in the evening.

The seizure of Zag-a-zig was effected in the dashing manner peculiar to all the incidents of the day, and shows what may be done by a few bold men. The squadron of the 6th Bengal Cavalry left with the

---

1. An elaborate plan was devised for the repetition of the Alexandria outrages. According to this scheme Cairo was divided into a number of districts, and fire was to be applied simultaneously to certain houses indicated. This was to take place after the morning prayer on the 15th, the very day after the city was taken by General Drury-Lowe's force.

No time was lost in reaping the fruits of the morning's work. Advances were at once ordered in two directions, the one along the railway to the important railway centre of Zag-a-zig, whence a double line of railway proceeds to Cairo *viâ* Benha, and a single line *viâ* Belbeis; the other road was along the Ismailieh, or Sweet Water Canal, to Cairo.

Indian Contingent led the way, and when within about five miles of the town broke into a gallop. The horses being somewhat fatigued by the hard work of the preceding twenty hours, were not in a condition to keep together, and, as a consequence, the best got to the front and the others dropped to the rear. The advanced part of the squadron was composed of Major R. M. Jennings, Lieutenant Burn-Murdoch, R.E., and not above half-a-dozen troopers. These pushed right into the railway station, where were five trains filled with soldiers, and seven locomotives.

At the sight of this handful of men, the engine-drivers either surrendered or ran away, except one, who began opening the throttle valve of his engine and was shot by Lieutenant Burn-Murdoch, while the Egyptian soldiers, hundreds in number, and too demoralized to think of resistance, threw away their arms, left the cars, and ran off as rapidly as possible.

By nine p.m. the entire force under General Macpherson had reached Zag-a-zig, not a man having fallen out by the way.

The cavalry division was ordered to push on with all possible speed to Cairo, Wolseley being most anxious to save the city from the fate which befell Alexandria. The division, making an early start from Belbeis on the 14th, and striking across the intervening desert, reached Cairo at 4.45 p.m.

The sun was setting as the cavalry arrived at the suburb of Abbassieh. The men had been in the saddle since daybreak, at which time they had left Belbeis. The men and horses were thoroughly exhausted after their long march under a blazing sun. But suffering from hunger, parched with thirst, and covered with dust as they were, they yet remained equal to the fulfilment of their task.[2]

The garrison of Cairo was divided into two parts; one from 6,000 to 7,000 strong at Abbassieh; the other, of from 3,000 to 4,000 men, at the Citadel of Mehemet Ali, situated on a lofty eminence in the city, and strongly fortified. The former, on being summoned by Colonel Stewart, attached to General Drury-Lowe's force, to surrender unconditionally, at once complied. Captain Watson, R.E., was immediately sent on with two squadrons of the 4th Dragoon Guards, and a detachment of the Mounted Infantry, to demand a surrender of the Citadel. No guides were available, but two Egyptian officers, taken prisoners at Abbassieh, were made to show the way, orderlies being told off to shoot them at once in case of treachery. The route taken was round by

---

2. The cavalry had marched sixty-five miles in two days.

the Tombs of the Khalifs, outside the walls of Cairo. The city was entered, without opposition, by the gate at the foot of the hill on which the citadel stands; by this means only a few hundred yards of the native quarter had to be traversed.

It was now dark, such of the inhabitants as were met were perfectly tranquil, and only looked with curiosity at Captain Watson's party. Arrived at the entrance to the citadel, the Egyptian officer in command was sent for, and he at once agreed to give up possession of the place. The small British force marched in and took up position in fours between the outer and inner gates. The Egyptian infantry, nearly 4,000 in number, with their arms, paraded by regiments in front of the great Mosque of Mehemet Ali, inside the inner gate. They were then ordered to lay down their arms and march down to the Kasr-el-Nil Barracks. This they proceeded to do quite quietly, and as they marched out they passed within a few yards of the English force, whose numbers were concealed by the darkness.

As soon as the Egyptian troops had all left the citadel, the various gates were handed over to Captain Watson's force. The gates were then closed and guards posted. It was now ten o'clock. The troopers were literally dead-beat. But there yet remained the task of taking possession of the fort on the Mokattam Hill, which was occupied by Egyptian troops, and which commanded the citadel. Watson, anxious to save his men as much as possible, sent one of the Egyptian officers who had acted as a guide, and told him to order the garrison to march down towards Kasr-el-Nil Barracks, and there pile their arms. The officer returned in a couple of hours with the keys of the fort, and informed Watson that his orders had been carried out.

In the dungeons of the citadel many unfortunate wretches were found in confinement. Some of them were convicts, but several were political prisoners. They cried out in piteous terms to be set free. Some actually managed to break loose, and fled with their chains clanking round their ankles. They were, however, retaken, and assured that as soon as it was light their cases should be inquired into, and such as were not convicts should be set free. A sentry was posted over the gate, with orders to shoot anyone attempting to escape. One man did make the attempt, and was shot.

It only remains to refer to the combination of courage, energy, and tact displayed by Captain Watson in thus, with a handful of men, taking possession of the strongest fortified work in Cairo, held by a force more than a hundred times that of his own. It should be added that the Egyptian officer who gave up the keys of the Mokattam Fort subsequently put in a claim for the war medal!

The citadel being secured, the next step was to send a message to Arabi Pasha, through the prefect of police of the city, calling upon him to surrender, which he did unconditionally, accompanied by Toulba Pasha.

The vigour shown by General Drury-Lowe in his march on Cairo, and the inestimable results of that movement, together make it one of the most brilliant achievements of the whole campaign.

By the successful attack on Tel-el-Kebir, Sir Garnet Wolseley, at one blow, crushed the armed rebellion against the authority of the *khedive*.

By General Drury-Lowe's successful march, the most beautiful of Oriental cities was saved from destruction, and its European inhabitants from massacre.

So well had Sir Garnet Wolseley matured his plans before entering on the campaign, that he had predicted his arrival in Cairo on the 16th September. As a fact, he arrived a day earlier, that is to say, on the morning of the 15th, when the railway brought him and the Guards to Cairo at the same time.

Arabis' account of Tel-el-Kebir and the subsequent events is as follows:—

> Before our trenches, &c., were completed, the British forces attacked us suddenly at sunrise, the firing lasting for some time, when suddenly in our rear appeared a division of cavalry and artillery, which caused the flight of the Egyptian troops on Wednesday, the 13th September.
>
> After the flight of the troops I left for Belbeis, the English artillery following close behind me. When I arrived there I met Ali Pasha El Roby, with whom I went to Insbuz, and thence by train to Cairo.
>
> In Cairo we found a Council at the Ministry of War, all the Princes being present. After a long discussion, all being confident that England had no intention of annexing Egypt, it was decided to offer no more resistance, more especially as England was renowned for dealing always towards others with equity and humanity; and we were confident that if the necessary inquiries were instituted, and the feeling of the people generally understood, England would do her utmost to put a stop to all

injustice and give back freedom to them.

For this purpose I sent a telegram on the 14th September to the commander of the Abbassieh troops, ordering him to hoist a flag of truce, and to proceed and meet the commander of the British troops, informing him at the same time that the war was altogether at an end, it being understood that the intention of the British Government was to preserve the country from ruin.[3]

The English troops arrived in Cairo at sunset, and were met by Riza Pasha and Ibrahim Bey Fawzi, the Prefect of Police. At 1.30 a.m. Ibrahim Bey Fawzi came and informed me that General Lowe desired to have an interview with me at Abbassieh. The same day the officer in charge at Kafr Dowar (Toulba Pasha) came up to Cairo and was summoned with myself to this interview. We thereupon went to General Lowe. When Toulba Pasha met General Lowe he asked us whether we were willing to give ourselves up as prisoners to the English Government. We thereupon took off our swords and delivered them to General Lowe, who was acting on behalf of the commander-in-chief, telling him at the same time that we only gave ourselves up to the English Government because we were confident England would deal with us justly, and for the safety and peace of our country we had abandoned all idea of resistance, and had surrendered ourselves, being confident that England had no wish to annex the country. The general agreed with this statement, and we remained with him three days, and then were sent to Abdin, and were treated kindly and well.

In the following telegram to Abdel-el-Al, in command at Damietta, the defeat at Tel-el-Kebir was thus described by Yacoub Pasha, the Under Secretary of State for War, who had been with Arabi in the insurgent camp:—

> At half-past ten (Turkish time) the enemy attacked the line of intrenchments, and firing commenced on both sides. We caused a large number of the enemy to perish beside the intrenchments. I found a train about to leave Tel-el-Kebir, and got in

---

3. According to *Arabi Pasha*, by Mr. John Ninet, already quoted, the majority of the council were in favour of defending Cairo. The citadel, it was pointed out, was in good repair, and it would be easy to act as the French did at the beginning of the century to put an end to any revolt. Arabi, however, opposed.

with a few wounded. I know nothing after that, except that on leaving Tel-el-Kebir I saw that a train had been smashed.

The manner in which the news of the fight reached the agricultural population may be gathered from the following extract from the work of one of the native historians of the British occupation of Egypt:—

> The peasants were relating to each other one morning the news of a great victory by which the land forces of the invading foreigner had received a blow, when suddenly a peasant rode into the village on a cavalry horse, without his coat, belt, or arms, and announced that the English were coming! He related how he had been in the camp of Tel-el-Kebir, how he and his comrades had been aroused before daybreak by a dreadful fire of musketry and artillery, and how, before they had time to prepare themselves for defence, the nimble foreigners came scampering over the intrenchments and right into the very heart of the camp. Satan must have aided them, for there was no possibility of resistance, and even Arabi fled! By this time, he thought, the English must be in Cairo, for they were nimble, cunning dogs and sons of dogs, and nobody could resist them.

The submission of the Egyptian Army in Cairo was speedily followed by surrenders in other places—Kafr Dowar, Aboukir, and Rosetta yielded without a struggle. Fort Ghemil, near Port Saïd, was occupied on the 21st September by the British.

Damietta was the last to hold out. A British force, consisting of the Berkshire, Shropshire, South Staffordshire, and Sussex Regiments, under Sir Evelyn Wood, was despatched against it on the 22nd September, after negotiations with the Commandant Abdel-el-Al had failed. A portion of the fleet under Admiral Dowell was ordered to co-operate. However, on the 23rd, Abdel-el-Al, hearing of these preparations, capitulated with all his forces.

The surrender of the Egyptian Army at Kafr Dowar was an event of importance. But to render what follows intelligible, as well as for the sake of completeness, it is necessary to preface the history of that event with an account of occurrences at Alexandria subsequent to the departure of Sir Garnet Wolseley for the Canal.

On the 21st August, the *khedive* relieved Ragheb Pasha and his colleagues of their duties, and named Cherif Pasha President of the Council of Ministers. With him was associated Riaz Pasha, who had in the meantime returned from Europe.

After the departure of Wolseley for Port Saïd and Ismailia, General Hamley took the local command, and the fresh transports constantly arriving at Alexandria were very welcome to reinforce the garrison, which had been considerably weakened by the departure of the main body of the army. Only two ships of war were left in harbour, the *Invincible* and *Inconstant*, which latter vessel had lately arrived from England.

The military operations dwindled into insignificance. Both sides confined themselves to strengthening their positions and to making small reconnaissances. Round Mex the Bedouins kept the troops well on the alert, and several minor skirmishes took place. About August 20th, the defences of Ramleh were strengthened by the mounting of three additional guns. Two were taken from the Hospital battery at Ras-el-Tin, and the third was found unmounted near Mex Fort.

On the 31st of August a party of bluejackets from the *Minotaur* landed at night and demolished, by gun-cotton, a house near the British advanced posts on the Mahmoudieh Canal, which afforded cover to the enemy. Some native houses opposite the Villa Antoniades, which had been used by the Bedouins as a place whence to take shots at our posts there, had for the same reason to be destroyed.

On the 1st September, Generals Hamley and Alison and the Highland Brigade sailed for Port Saïd and Ismailia, General Sir Evelyn Wood being left in command.

Anxious to make the rebel leader believe that the chief attack would be on Kafr Dowar, and to prevent him from sending away his troops to strengthen other positions, the British troops contrived daily to harass the Egyptian lines. Generally the reconnaissances took place at dusk, as the Egyptians seemed to prefer withdrawing their troops under the cover of the darkness. Grown wary by experience, they refused to be drawn out in force, but limited themselves to a brisk artillery fire.

It was at this time that an attempt was made to cut the dyke at Mex, in order to flood Lake Mareotis, the level of which at this season was some feet lower than that of the sea. Although it was reckoned that it would take some weeks in this way to raise the water of the lake to its proper level, the stratagem was not devoid of merit. One of its objects was to enable steam launches with guns to harass the flank of the enemy's position at Kafr Dowar.

Early in September, Mahmoud Fehmi, already referred to as having been made prisoner by Sir Garnet Wolseley's force, was brought to Alexandria, and, in return for a promise to spare his life, furnished full details of Arabi's plans and position.

On the 13th September, Alexandria received the news of the victory of Tel-el-Kebir with the wildest delight. Early in the morning it was known that the fight had begun, and great excitement was manifested by all classes. About eleven in the forenoon, when the facts were published, this feeling increased perceptibly. All business was suspended. Processions of Europeans were formed, and, preceded by bands of music, paraded amid the ruins of the town. Hats and helmets were thrown into the air, and cheers and cries of "*Viva Inghilterra!*" resounded on all sides. The bands played "God Save the Queen" and the Khedivial Hymn by turns. Crowds rushed for the English soldiers on guard at the Tribunals, and embraced them frantically. Sir Edward Malet, the English Consul-General, called to congratulate the *khedive*, who also received a congratulatory message from the queen. Never before had the English been so popular in Alexandria. It took some days before the excitement cooled down and things resumed their ordinary course.

Kafr Dowar was given up to Sir Evelyn Wood on the 16th September. Yacoub Sami, Arabi's sub-Minister of War, represented him on this occasion. Some 6,000 men in all laid down their arms. There were 700 captured horses, 50 field-guns with their equipments, and 15,000 Remington rifles. The captured men were allowed to disband, and the officers were lodged as prisoners in the palace at Ramleh.

General Wood and his staff went out by rail, preceded, as a measure of precaution, by the armour-clad train. The 49th Regiment had been previously sent forward as an escort. Arrived at the bridge crossing the Mahmoudieh Canal, the party proceeded on horseback to Fort Aslam, as the most advanced of the earthworks of Kafr Dowar was called. This formed a part of three long lines of redoubts, flanked on both sides by swampy and impassable ground, and running at right angles across the railway and Canal. These defences were supplemented by shelter-trenches and rifle-pits. The position was one of great strength, and if held by good soldiers could only have been taken, if at all, at a great sacrifice of life. Each line of redoubts had a ditch of 15 feet in width in front of it.

The distance between the first and second lines was 4,000 metres, and between the second and third 5,000 metres. Fort Aslam was the strongest of the redoubts, and was pierced with embrasures for guns. The passage for the railway trains was blocked by a large mass of masonry, which Sir Evelyn Wood at once caused to be blown up with dynamite. Fort Aslam was capable of being easily defended by 250 good soldiers. The garrison, however, had disappeared, leaving only a dozen or so of officers, including Yacoub Sami, who came forward to meet the English commander. In the fort, which appeared to have suffered but slightly, were found 150 horses, besides quantities of arms and ammunition abandoned by the soldiers. Amongst the cannon were some mounted Krupp guns. Between the first and second lines the remains of one camp for about 2,500 men were found, and between the second and third lines, of another camp for the rest of the army. On all sides were found horses and mules, mixed pell-mell with carriages, still loaded with silks, clothes, calico, &c., from the shops and houses pillaged in Alexandria.

The third line of defence, that situated at Kinje Osman, the nearest point to Kafr Dowar, was inferior to other parts of the defence, being provided only with two insignificant bastions, armed with old cannons and a long line of rifle-pits extending across the railway. Behind it, in the camp of Kafr Dowar, stood 6,000 soldiers, armed with Remington rifles, waiting to surrender to the British Army. There were also several batteries of artillery and two squadrons of cavalry. The men were anything but warlike in appearance. Many of them had already thrown away their uniforms, and the greater part wore only the dress of the ordinary *fellah*.

The natives met with along the line showed not the slightest sign of hostility. On the contrary, they tried to conceal their evident uneasiness at the sight of the British force by assuming a pleased air, and waving white rags as a substitute for flags of truce. At Kafr Dowar itself, crowds of Arabs, mostly refugees from Alexandria, were congregated. Many of these were pillagers and incendiaries of the worst class, and strict orders had to be given to prevent their returning to the scene of their former exploits.

Yacoub Sami, on giving up his sword to General Wood, assured him that no one had been throughout more loyal to the *khedive* than he, Yacoub Sami, had been; and as for Arabi, he was simply a scoundrel and a monster who had refused to listen to Yacoub's loyal counsels.

One of the first questions put by General Wood was as to what had become of a lieutenant named Paolucci, who had deserted some weeks before from the Italian ironclad *Castelfidardo* to join Arabi. This officer, in his endeavour to reach the rebels' lines, had the misfortune to fall into the hands of Bedouins, who used him in the most brutal manner. Eventually, after five days' wandering, he succeeded in finding his way to the camp at Kafr Dowar, but in a pitiable condition. He was destitute of every rag of clothing, and so exhausted as to be barely able to stand on his legs. Arabi, on hearing him say that his wish was to serve the cause of liberty, allowed him to be removed to the camp ambulance, where he remained till the surrender.

In reply to General Wood, M. Paolucci himself was produced. He was now dressed in an Egyptian officer's uniform much too large for him, and was still suffering acutely. The general, without making any observation, handed M. Paolucci over to two marines, with instructions to conduct him to the Italian Consul at Alexandria.[4] M. Ninet, who had been in the enemy's lines ever since the bombardment and subsequent destruction of Alexandria, had, it was ascertained, left for Cairo on receipt of the news of the taking of Tel-el-Kebir.

General Wood at once gave orders for clearing the railway. Civilians were requisitioned for the work, and so well was this carried out that the following day, which was fixed for the surrender of the arms, the trains were running freely between Kafr Dowar and Alexandria.

Two British battalions were despatched on the 17th, to encamp at Kafr Dowar, and to take delivery of the Egyptian arms. The army which was to surrender had then practically disappeared. The rifles were piled, the officers were in charge, but their men, they said, "had gone off to the fields."[5]

General Wood received the same day the submission of about 1,000 men from Aboukir and 4,000 from Mex. On the 17th, the *khe-*

---

4. This officer was subsequently tried by court-martial and sentenced to two years' imprisonment.
5. Whilst the Egyptian arms were being handed over, a somewhat amusing incident occurred at a *café* in the village, where some Europeans and natives were sitting. As they were taking their coffee a respectable-looking old Arab Sheikh rushed in and very excitedly asked if there was any one present who spoke "*Inglesi*." One of the party replied in the affirmative, and asked what the man wanted. He declared that the soldiers were breaking into his *harem*, and he wanted someone to go off with him to the general at once. The person addressed then assured him that he ought not to mind, as it was always like that in war time, and asked the old man to sit down and take a cup of coffee. The man refused, and begged his would-be host to come at once, or it would be too late. The latter again assured him that the proceeding complained of was perfectly regular in a state of belligerency, and once more pressed the man to take the coffee. The latter again asked if the other was "quite sure," and receiving a reply in the affirmative he allowed himself to be convinced, and then sitting down said, "In that case I will take the coffee."

dive signed a decree disbanding the Egyptian Army.

One of the most remarkable features of the campaign was the rapidity with which it was conducted. From the firing of the first gun at the bombardment on the 11th July until the occupation of Cairo, but sixty-six days elapsed, the campaign proper occupying only twenty-five in all. It served also to illustrate the power of moving large bodies of troops by sea with a rapidity and certainty of concentration impossible on land.

The difference between the power of steam and sails in connection with military operations may be seen from the following examples:—

On the 19th May, 1798, Napoleon sailed for Egypt from Toulon with favouring winds; nevertheless, it was not until the 10th June (according to some reports the 15th) that he reached even his first port of call, Malta, thus occupying no less than twenty-three days on this short voyage, and it was not till the 1st July that he arrived off Alexandria.

In 1800, when Indian troops were despatched to assist in expelling the French from Egypt, the first detachment sailed from Bombay on the 28th December, but did not get to Suez till the end of April, 1801, and the remainder, following some days later, only arrived at Kosseir, on the Red Sea, *en route* to Keneh, on the Nile, on the 8th June, nearly six months later. As a contrast to the above, the head of the column of British transports left England on the 30th July, 1882, and arrived at Alexandria on the 10th August, thus completing the voyage in only eleven days.

Much has been made of the rapidity of the French invasion of Egypt, but, after all, Napoleon only entered Cairo on the 23rd July, that is, sixty-five days after leaving France, whereas Wolseley left England on the 2nd August, made the long sea-voyage by way of Gibraltar, and arrived in Cairo forty-five days after, *viz.*, on the 15th September.

With regard to Tel-el-Kebir, the shortness of the time occupied in storming the intrenchments has been made use of, more especially by foreign critics, to lessen the credit of the victory. Without pretending that the battle was more than, comparatively speaking, a small affair, exceedingly well-managed, the number of casualties relatively to the number of the attacking force shows that there was a real resistance, and that the fighting on both sides was more serious than is generally supposed.

The news of the victory of Tel-el-Kebir, the capture of Cairo, and the close of the war, produced a profound sensation in Europe. In England the greatest enthusiasm was manifested, and to the events of the campaign was given an importance perhaps in excess of their actual merits.[6]

On the Continent, however, the opposite was the case. The very journals which only a week before had declared that, in undertaking to subdue Arabi, England had assumed a task the difficulties of which she had scarcely calculated, now went to the other extreme, and described Tel-el-Kebir as a mere military promenade. In the *Débats*, M. Gabriel Channes wrote that the fears that an Egyptian campaign would prove hazardous were groundless. The only difficulties which the English army had to encounter were due to the vast amount of baggage it had to transport, owing to the men carrying nothing but their arms. According to the same article an army less burdened would have beaten Arabi and reached Cairo in a few days; and if the campaign had lasted some weeks, this was only due to the slowness of the attack.

The *Avenir Militaire* maintained that Sir Garnet Wolseley did not shorten the campaign by transferring his base to Ismailia, and that the qualities of the English troops were not exposed to a very severe ordeal.

> The attack on Tel-el-Kebir against troops ill on the watch, succeeded with a promptitude which rendered a portion of those qualities useless.

Many of the continental journals went further, and unable in any other way to explain the dashing fight which in twenty minutes placed all Egypt at England's feet, boldly asserted that the victory was bought and paid for by English gold. They even named the exact sum, *viz.*, £E32,000. It was, perhaps, unfortunate that the late Professor Palmer's ill-fated expedition into the Sinaitic Desert to secure the neutrality of the Bedouins, at a price of £5,000, should have given an apparent colour to these reports.[7]

One author,[8] whose writings, however, are not always to be accepted as accurate, states that Sultan Pasha (already referred to as the

---

6. This sentiment, however, subsided very quickly, and when, on a vote of thanks being proposed in the House of Commons to the British army, Sir Wilfrid Lawson moved as an amendment that "a vote of thanks should be given to the Egyptian Army for running away," his observations were received with good-humoured laughter, if not with approval.
7. Professor Palmer was murdered in the desert after the money was taken from him.
8. Mr. John Ninet.

President of the Chamber of Notables) was attached to Wolseley's force with the object of securing by large bribes the fidelity of the Bedouins in the district between Ismailia and Zag-a-zig. According to the same authority, the Bedouins received from £3 to £2 a head, and much of the money found its way into the pockets of officers of the Egyptian Army from the rank of lieutenant to that of colonel.

The events of Tel-el-Kebir are thus referred to by the same writer:—

> On the 12th September, Arabi learned towards twelve o'clock, from a Bedouin *sheikh*, that the English would attack *en masse* the lines of Tel-el-Kebir towards two o'clock in the morning on the 13th, throwing themselves on Belbeis to open the road to Cairo. It was then necessary to guard this point, formerly fortified by the French. Arabi consequently telegraphed to Toulba Pasha at Kafr Dowar to send at once one of his best battalions, the last, or nearly the last, which remained to him, with orders to be in line of battle at Tel-el-Kebir at daybreak on the 13th. At one a.m. the train brought this detachment, which only arrived at Zag-a-zig long after everything was finished. The battalion then returned on its steps in company with the fugitives from the battlefield.
>
> At Tel-el-Kebir, during the night, between two and three a.m., at the first rifle shots, the Bedouins, *en masse*, threw themselves on the Egyptian lines, shouting like demons, and causing the wildest confusion. The native troops knew not who was with them or against them. Whole regiments ran like hares without striking a blow (*sic*), and the English, astonished to encounter so little resistance, massacred the fugitives as if at a shooting-party; 3,000 trained men belonging to the infantry, all that the army of the East possessed, faced the enemy, and with the last vestiges of the artillery, fired valiantly as long as they were able. More than half of them perished.
>
> It is confidently asserted that several of the Egyptian officers, hindered in their flight by the gold which they had in their pockets, seeking to lighten themselves, were arrested and pillaged by the soldiers of one of the black regiments. As to the Bedouins, their treason was so well arranged by agreement with Sultan Pasha, that they, with the speed of the wind, quitted their cantonments without molestation.

In considering M. Ninet's narrative, it must be remembered that he was, from first to last, an avowed ally of the Arabist party, and also that his sentiments towards England had always been of the most unfriendly character. That, under these circumstances, he should seek to explain Sir Garnet Wolseley's success by suggesting treachery and corruption is not altogether unnatural.

It is quite possible that, as regards the corruption of the Bedouins, Sultan Pasha, as an Egyptian official, may have acted in the manner described. But that, as suggested by the Continental Press, English gold was employed by Sir Garnet Wolseley to secure his victory is too ridiculous for serious consideration. Had it been the desire of the British Government to purchase Tel-el-Kebir in the manner stated, it is incredible that by the expenditure of a little additional capital an entirely bloodless victory should not have been obtained.

Further than this, Arabi himself, in all the explanations which he gave of the war, never once hinted at the means alleged by his apologists as having brought about his defeat. The story of the Egyptian officers being so heavily weighted with gold as to be unable to make good their retreat reads more like an Oriental fable than anything else.

The conclusion is that gold had as much to do with the taking of Tel-el-Kebir as the blasts of Joshua's trumpets had to do with bringing down the walls of Jericho.

CHAPTER 24

England and the Porte

As already stated, on the 18th August Sir Garnet Wolseley started from Alexandria with the British force, and two days later Port Saïd, Ismailia, and Kantara were occupied.

Notwithstanding this, the negotiations with the *Porte* for the despatch of the Turkish troops were being, outwardly at least, pressed on by Lord Dufferin. The Turkish ministers continued to make objections to the terms of the proposed Military Convention referred to in Chapter XV.

Meanwhile the export of mules, purchased in Asia Minor for the use of the British force, was stopped, and the drivers were imprisoned. The unfriendly conduct of the Turkish Government in delaying the removal of this prohibition led to remonstrances on the part of Lord Dufferin. It was not until the 23rd August that the *sultan* ordered that the mules and drivers were to be allowed to be embarked.

He, at the same time, sent Lord Dufferin a personal message urging that Alexandria should be the port of disembarkation for the Turkish troops. After an interview with the Turkish ministers, Lord Dufferin agreed to submit the Sultan's request to the British Government, and the *sultan's* ministers finally accepted all the other clauses of the Military Convention, with certain amendments. When, however, the issue of the proclamation against Arabi was demanded, the ministers changed round, and proposed to throw aside the proclamation which had been agreed upon, by which Arabi was declared to be a rebel, and to issue a mere appeal to his loyalty. Lord Dufferin, assuming an air of surprise at this breach of faith, refused indignantly to listen to any such suggestion, and informed the ministers that he would not sign the convention until the proclamation had been officially communicated.

On the 24th Lord Dufferin was instructed that Her Majesty's Government could not accept the amendments made in the convention. Again the Turkish ministers sought out Lord Dufferin with messages from the *sultan*, pressing that the landing might be at Alexandria, and assuring the ambassador that the proclamation should be communicated the moment that the heads of the convention were agreed to.

Things began to look as if they were in a way to be arranged, when it was discovered, on the 25th, that the instructions given for the despatch of the mules and the release of the drivers had been cancelled by an order from the palace. Lord Dufferin was at once instructed that if this information was correct it was no longer possible for him to continue the negotiations.

On the 27th the Turkish ministers accepted Aboukir as the place of disembarkation, and promised that before the convention was signed they would communicate the proclamation officially, and order its publication in Egypt. Lord Dufferin was instructed that he might sign the convention on the preliminary condition that the mules and drivers should be released, and a promise given by the *Porte* to assist in sending them to Egypt, and that the proclamation should be issued at once.

On the 29th Lord Dufferin reported that he had settled the text of the convention with the *sultan's* ministers.

The 30th passed without any further communication from the *Porte*; but in the middle of the night Said Pasha called upon Lord Dufferin at Therapia, with a further message from the *sultan*, urging that the troops should go to Aboukir *viâ* Alexandria; and in the morning the *pasha* came again with the *sultan's* private secretary, and stated that His Majesty was ready to take any step to remove Lord Granville's misgivings if he were only allowed to land his troops at Alexandria. He was willing to reduce their number from that originally proposed to 2,000, or even 1,000. Baker Pasha might go second in command, and take with him as many English officers as he pleased, and the Turkish troops should be as much under English control as they were in the Crimea.

The extraordinary anxiety of the *sultan* to show his troops in Egypt at this period is to be accounted for on the supposition that he foresaw the impending collapse of the Arabi revolt, and was desirous that it should not be accomplished without his appearing, at all events, to have taken part in its suppression. The presence of but a single Turkish battalion in Alexandria would have sufficed to enable him to claim the credit of overthrowing Arabi and his followers. It was, however, not to be. The *sultan's* views were now diametrically at variance with those of the British Cabinet. Sir Garnet Wolseley was, at this time, well to the front, and there was little doubt that he would soon bring the war to a close.

Under these circumstances, the presence of a Turkish force in Egypt would only be a source of embarrassment. Accordingly it was necessary to finesse and to play off upon the *Porte* its own tricks of delay and dissimulation. Lord Dufferin was therefore instructed to inform the *Porte* that Her Majesty's Government were willing to meet its proposals, and to receive 2,000, or even 3,000 troops; but that, in view of the strong objections to Alexandria, it would be preferable that the landing should take place in the Suez Canal.

On the 3rd September the Turkish ministers were willing that the troops should go to Port Saïd, promising at the same time that the proclamation should be issued immediately.

On the 24th August Lord Granville had authorized the Ambassador to conclude the convention as soon as the proclamation should be published, the words "such point or points on the Canal as may be previously arranged with the British commander-in-chief" being substituted for Aboukir.

On Lord Dufferin proceeding to the *Porte* on the 6th September to sign the convention, he found that the proclamation had that morning appeared in the newspapers in a changed form. Lord Dufferin thereupon declined to sign. Said Pasha said that the publication, as it stood, was an act of heedlessness, and he undertook that a correction should be published in the official journal. A further discussion ensued as to the form of the stipulation respecting the landing of the Turkish troops in the Canal, Said Pasha objecting to the words proposed by Lord Granville, and pressing for the mention of Port Saïd.

Lord Dufferin accepted, *ad referendum*, an amended paragraph to the effect that the Turkish forces should proceed to Port Saïd, and from thence to whatever point or points might be agreed upon between the two commanders-in-chief. The British Government, however, insisted that the clause should state that the Turkish troops would "enter the Canal at Port Saïd and proceed from thence," whilst the *sultan* wished to substitute the word "*débarqueront*" for "*se rendront à Port Saïd.*"

On the 10th September the Ottoman plenipotentiaries, who seemed unconscious that they were being played with all the time, came to the embassy with copies of the conventions and memorandum for signature. They were authorized to accept the words *"se rendront à Port Saïd."* Lord Dufferin, however, having in the meantime been informed of the views of Her Majesty's Government, stated that he could not accept them. His Lordship would agree to the retention of the words on the understanding that a paragraph should be inserted in the memorandum, explaining the meaning of the words to be that the troops should "direct their course to Port Saïd in order to enter the Canal."

It was now the eve of Tel-el-Kebir, and Lord Dufferin suddenly discovered that it was necessary to suspend negotiations on account of the arrest by the Turkish authorities of a number of porters who had been engaged at Sir Garnet Wolseley's request for service in Egypt. The men were released the same day with a promise that such proceedings should not be repeated. The signature of the convention, as further amended, was authorized by telegram from Lord Granville, on the 13th, on the condition that the proclamation should be issued with the amendment required by Her Majesty's Government.

On the 13th the battle of Tel-el-Kebir took place. On the 15th Lord Granville instructed Lord Dufferin, that, in view of the defeat and submission of the Egyptian insurgents, the British Government contemplated shortly commencing the withdrawal of the British troops from Egypt, and presumed that, the emergency having passed, the *sultan* would not consider it necessary to send troops; and on the 18th His Lordship was authorized to convey to the *sultan*, in the most courteous terms, the permission given to His Lordship to drop the negotiation of the Military Convention. He was at the same time to express to His Majesty that the British Government conceived this step to be most consistent with the dignity of the two countries, and that it was not intended or calculated to alter the good and friendly relations between them.

The *sultan* now began to realize how completely befooled he had been. It was necessary, however, to put a good face on the matter. The Turkish Foreign Minister accordingly answered by expressing the deep satisfaction of the *sultan* and his government at the sentiments expressed on behalf of the British Government. He declared that the wish of Turkey was to maintain unaltered the old friendship between the two countries. Finally, the minister asked, a little anxiously, what date had been fixed on for the evacuation by the British troops.

This last question was met by Lord Dufferin reminding the *sultan* of the sacrifices made by England in order to restore order in Egypt; and stating that whilst those sacrifices had given England power, that power had thrown upon her great responsibility; that the Egyptian army being disbanded, until the *khedive* had organized the means of securely maintaining his authority it was impossible for England to withdraw her troops, although she had already greatly diminished their number, and had no wish to keep any in Egypt longer than was justified by the circumstances.

With regard to the overtures for a closer alliance, Lord Dufferin pointed out that the *sultan* would remember that the like offer had been made by him on several occasions, without any practical results, owing to the apparent change of His Majesty's views. His Lordship concluded by giving the *Porte* a little lecture, pointing out that offers of friendship were unsatisfactory without some tangible proof of the willingness of the Ottoman Government to adopt that line of conduct which could alone render their friendship acceptable to English public opinion; and suggested that that proof might be given by inaugurating those internal reforms which were indispensable to the existence of the empire and to the maintenance of a really good understanding with England.

No better way can be found of concluding the present chapter than by giving an extract from His Lordship's despatch of the 18th September, 1882, to Lord Granville, which runs as follows:—

> In fact, I can only reiterate that from first to last I have used every means at my disposal to induce the Turkish Government to move quickly and to settle the matter out of hand. I told them at the commencement that I had Your Lordship's instructions to press forward the cnvention with all despatch; that your private letters, as well as your public despatches, evinced your desire to see that instrument executed; that in asking me to telegraph to Your Lordship these repeated references, they were playing into our hands, and that their conduct was so obviously contrary to their interests, that Europe had begun to misjudge the situation. While ruining my reputation as an honest man, they were enhancing it as a diplomatist, for it had begun to be believed that the delay in signing the Convention could not possibly result from their own incomprehensible shortsightedness, but must have been artificially created by the Machiavellian astuteness of the English ambassador.

CHAPTER 25

Restoration of Tewfik and Exile of Arabi

On the 25th September the *khedive* was able to return to Cairo, where a great portion of Sir Garnet Wolseley's forces had assembled. He entered the capital at 3.30 in the afternoon, and was received with great apparent enthusiasm. His Highness drove from the railway station in an open carriage with the Duke of Connaught, Sir Garnet Wolseley, and Sir Edward Malet. The streets through which he passed were lined the whole way by soldiers of the British Army.

Next followed a series of complimentary banquets and a distribution of honours and rewards to the officers of the British forces. The Order of the First Class of the Osmanieh was conferred by the *sultan* upon Sir Beauchamp Seymour and Sir Garnet Wolseley.[1] Other officers also received decorations dealt out with a liberal hand. Later on, an Egyptian medal, in the shape of a bronze star, was struck, and presented by the *khedive* to the whole of the British forces who took part in the campaign. By the British Government both Sir Garnet Wolseley and Sir Beauchamp Seymour were created Peers of the United Kingdom, and a sum of £20,000 was voted by Parliament for each of them. An English war medal for Egypt was also issued to the forces engaged.

With the exception of a small force left at Alexandria, Port Saïd, and Ismailia, the whole of the British Army was concentrated in Cairo, to be reviewed by the *khedive*, in the square in front of the palace of Abdin. The review, which was preceded by a march through the native

---

1. About the same period the *sultan* bestowed a similar order on his bootmaker at Constantinople. Upon the writer remarking to an Egyptian official on the singularity of the circumstance, the latter replied, "Yes; but he is a very good bootmaker, you know."

quarter of the city, took place on the very spot where Arabi and his mutinous troops had defied the *khedive* just a twelvemonth before.

The British soldiers, in spite of the hardships of the campaign, presented an imposing appearance, the Indian regiments especially attracting attention.

As soon as the effervescence which followed the restoration had a little subsided, the Egyptian Government and its English advisers began to take thought for the morrow. A decision was arrived at to reduce the British forces to 12,000 men, which henceforth constituted the Army of Occupation. The Egyptian army having been disbanded, and there being no other native force available to maintain order, it became absolutely necessary, apart from any political considerations, to retain this number of Sir Garnet Wolseley's soldiers.

In announcing their intentions, the British Government informed the Egyptian Ministry that England was prepared to defray all expenditure incurred in the suppression of the rebellion, the date of the conclusion of which was fixed at the 30th September. It was also intimated that from that date Egypt would be expected to repay all extraordinary expenses which the retention of the Queen's troops in Egypt would entail on the Exchequer of the United Kingdom. The contribution for the 12,000 men to be retained was fixed at £4 a month per man, making a maximum monthly charge of £48,000. The Egyptian Government was at the same time informed that it was desired to withdraw the troops from Egypt as soon as circumstances would permit, and that such withdrawal would be effected from time to time as the security of the country would allow.

Pursuant to the intention above indicated, arrangements were at once made for a considerable reduction in the strength of the Army of Occupation. The Indian Contingent embarked, and Sir Garnet Wolseley, as well as a great portion of the army under his command, left for England, Major-General Sir Archibald Alison assuming the command.

The importance attached by Her Majesty's Government to Egyptian affairs at this time was shown by the appointment, early in November, of Lord Dufferin to proceed thither on a special mission. His Lordship, who had filled successively the posts of Under-Secretary of State for India, Governor-General of Canada, Ambassador at St. Petersburg, and Ambassador at Constantinople, was undoubtedly the most capable man at the disposal of the British Government, and his mission was everywhere hailed with satisfaction as preliminary to a satisfactory settlement of the affairs of that country.

Lord Dufferin's instructions were:

> ..... to advise the government of the *khedive* in the arrangements which would have to be made for re-establishing His Highness's authority and providing for the future well-being of all classes of the population.

Lord Dufferin arrived at Alexandria on the 7th November, and was received with all the honours due to his rank. He left for Cairo the same day, the *khedive* placing a palace at his disposal.

It is greatly to Lord Dufferin's credit that one of the first matters to which he directed his attention was a question of humanity, *viz.*, the lot of the many unfortunates whom the late events had relegated to Egyptian prisons.

It was not to be expected that the *khedivial* party should triumph without seeking to wreak vengeance on the heads of their conquered adversaries. Consequently arrests were made wholesale, and the Egyptian prisons were overcrowded. The object of the *khedive*'s advisers seemed to be to make what in sporting language would be called a "big bag." Of the leaders of the Rebellion, as already stated, Mahmoud Fehmi had been captured at Kassassin, and Arabi and Toulba had surrendered at Abbassieh. In addition to these, Mahmoud Sami had been arrested by the police in Cairo. Yacoub Sami had given himself up at Kafr Dowar, and Abdel-el-Al at Damietta. Besides these, there were about 1,200 other political prisoners in the various gaols of Upper and Lower Egypt. These individuals comprised all classes of the population, sheikhs from the mosques, officers and privates of the army, members of the civil service, police officials, merchants and land-owners.

The charges against many of these people were of the vaguest character, such as "stirring up public feeling against the *khedive*," "assisting the rebels," &c.; some of them were absolutely ludicrous, and comprised such offences as "dressing up dogs to imitate Sir Garnet Wolseley, and then shooting at them."

There was reason to believe that a considerable number of the persons arrested were denounced by their neighbours to gratify private malice or revenge. Many others were arrested simply as a matter of precaution, or because they were adherents of Halim or Ismail Pasha.

As may be supposed, the prisoners necessarily suffered considerable hardships from overcrowding. But besides this, instances of ill-usage, and occasionally of torture, were brought to the notice of the British authorities. To remedy these evils inspectors were appointed to visit the prisons, and the agents of the British Government made strong representations to the Egyptian authorities to obtain a speedy gaol delivery.

Their remonstrances took effect. A decree was issued amnestying all sub-lieutenants, lieutenants, and captains in the army (except those who took part in the demonstrations of the 1st February and the 9th September, 1881), those who were under arms on the 11th July, and those who voluntarily enrolled themselves since that date, such persons being, nevertheless, degraded and deprived of their rank and pensions.

Special Commissions were also instituted at Cairo, Alexandria, and Tantah, for the purpose of investigating charges against political offenders. The most important of these were Arabi and the other rebel leaders.

The trial of the ringleaders of the rebellion was naturally one of the first things to be taken in hand after the suppression of the rebellion itself. As was only to be expected under the circumstances, the *khedive* and his advisers were in favour of treating Arabi and his associates with the utmost severity. In this the government met with general support.

Public opinion in Egypt, especially amongst Europeans, was from the first naturally hostile to Arabi. Those who had suffered by the rebellion were not likely to be over-lenient in their views towards the rebels, and the local European press clamoured loudly for their condign punishment.

Opinion in Europe was divided on the question. In France and Italy, especially, it became the fashion to extol Arabi as a sort of African Garibaldi, whose only fault was his want of success. The same view prevailed to some extent in England also, thanks to the agitation got up by Sir William Gregory, Mr. Wilfred Blunt, and others. Even amongst those who did not believe in either Arabi or the movement of which he was the head, there was a suspicion that he was not more guilty than the *sultan* and the *khedive*, and a feeling that it would be unjust to punish him whilst they were allowed to go free.

The Egyptian Government, in dealing with the rebels, had not, however, altogether a free hand. Sir Garnet Wolseley, in August, had proposed that prisoners taken in the course of the military operations in Egypt should be handed over to the *khedive*. This was approved by the British Government, but subject to the important condition that none of the prisoners should be put to death without the previous consent of the British authorities. This condition the Egyptian Government accepted.

The necessity of some means being found of speedily proceeding with the trial of Arabi was more than once pressed by Sir Edward Malet upon the *khedive*. Public feeling in Egypt among the natives was much excited, and all manner of absurd stories were told about Arabi and his relations with the British Government. These circulated freely in the bazaars, and were readily believed by the more ignorant and fanatical of the population.

Early in October, two English barristers, Mr. A. M. Broadley and the Honourable Mark Napier, arrived in Cairo to conduct the defence of the rebel leaders. The Egyptian Government objected that, by the code under which the proposed court martial was to be convened, prisoners were not allowed counsel. Sir Edward Malet, however, insisted, and the Egyptian authorities yielded the point. Next, the government put every difficulty in the way. At first they refused permission to Mr. Broadley and his colleague to see their clients, and then they were told that they could not be permitted to be present at the preliminary investigation. Thanks to the firmness of Sir Edward Malet, who was determined that Arabi should have a fair trial, these troubles were surmounted, and an agreement as to the procedure to be adopted was come to by Borelli Bey, a French advocate who acted for the Egyptian Government, and Arabi's legal advisers.

The *Acte d'Accusation*, or indictment, was to the following effect:—

1. Arabi, Toulba, Mahmoud Sami, Mahmoud Fehmi, and Omar Ráhmi[2] were charged with having abused the flag of truce on the 12th of July, by withdrawing the troops and pillaging and burning Alexandria, whilst the flag was flying.

2. Arabi, Toulba, Mahmoud Sami, Mahmoud Fehmi, Omar Ráhmi, and Ali Fehmi were charged with having incited the Egyptians to arm against the government of the *khedive*.[3]

3. All six prisoners were charged with having incited the people

---

2. Omar Ráhmi was Arabi's Private Secretary.
3. This crime comes under Article 55 of the Ottoman Penal Code, which lays down that everyone who directly or indirectly incites subjects of the Ottoman Empire to arm against the Imperial Government shall suffer death.

to civil war, and with having committed acts of destruction, massacre, and pillage on Egyptian territory.

4. Arabi, Mahmoud Fehmi, Toulba, and Mahmoud Sami were charged with having continued the war after they had heard that peace was concluded.[4]

The counsel for the accused first appeared before the commission appointed to conduct the preliminary inquiry on the 31st October. In the meantime, the commission had collected a mass of hearsay evidence, none of it on oath, and consisting mainly of letters and memoranda and of depositions taken, according to the Egyptian procedure, *ex parte* in the absence of the prisoners and their counsel. It is noteworthy that the president of the commission, Ismail Pasha Eyoub, had been himself a prominent member of the Council of National Defence, and had actually been with Arabi in the camp at Kafr Dowar.

The contention of Mr. Broadley was that, from first to last, the Sublime *Porte* approved the action of his clients, also that the *khedive* for a long period prior to the commencement of hostilities wavered systematically between the two parties, and that after the arrival of Dervish Pasha he acquiesced at three Cabinet Councils in the early phases of resistance to the English (an assertion in great measure borne out by the ambiguous terms of the subsequent proclamations). In addition to the foregoing, Mr. Broadley relied on the fact that Arabi, rightly or wrongly, really headed a great national movement, that he received the moral and material support of nearly the whole of Egypt, and that he was only deserted when he failed to secure success. It must be admitted that the documents in the possession of the accused went a long way to bear out these contentions.

It soon became evident that the principal part of the charges against Arabi and his associates could not be sustained, and Sir Charles Wilson (formerly Consul-General in Anatolia), who attended the proceedings as delegate of the British Government, reported to Lord Dufferin as follows:—

The only direct evidence incriminating Arabi was that of Suleiman Sami,[5] who stated that Arabi had not only ordered him to

---

4. This crime comes under Article 111 of the Ottoman Military Penal Code, *viz*.:— "Every commander who, without motive, continues hostilities after he has been officially informed of the conclusion of peace, or of an armistice, shall suffer death."

5. Suleiman Sami was subsequently convicted and hanged at Alexandria on 9th June, 1883.

burn Alexandria, but to kill the *khedive*. The evidence of this man was open to grave suspicion. He was arrested at Crete and brought to Alexandria, where he was received by the governor and the *préfet de police*, one of whom accompanied him some distance in the train. Immediately on his arrival at Cairo he was brought before an extraordinary sitting of the commission, which lasted till between eight and nine p.m.

No notice was sent to me of the prisoner's arrival, or of the intention of the commission to examine him, though I live close to the building in which the commission sits. The next morning, when Suleiman Sami's examination was continued, he was confronted with two other prisoners, who at once contradicted his statements on important points. His bearing before the commission produced an unfavourable impression, as he was the only prisoner who showed want of dignity, and weakness when questioned. He was also so deeply implicated himself in the burning and looting of Alexandria, that it was only natural he should try to incriminate others. As regards the specific charges against Arabi Pasha it appeared to me—

1. That if there were any abuse of the white flag on the 12th July, a fact in itself not easy to prove, it was through ignorance and not through design. I may mention that white flags were flying on the Aboukir forts throughout the whole of the military operations.

2. That there was no evidence to connect Arabi with the massacre at Alexandria on the 11th June, and that it is doubtful whether a deliberate massacre of Europeans was ever intended. That the massacres at Tantah and other places after the bombardment were caused by the low-class refugees from Alexandria, and that they ceased as soon as the troops were sent down. That, after the first excitement had passed, order was preserved, and that there are instances of orders having been sent by Arabi to the Governors of towns, &c., to preserve order and protect Europeans.

3. That the evidence which connects Arabi Pasha with the burning of Alexandria is conflicting, and that there is no sufficient proof that he ordered the town to be destroyed. The portion of the town actually burned by the troops seems to have been small. The fire appears to have broken out about four p.m.

on the 12th, and the troops evacuated the town on the same evening. It then became the duty of the civil governor to preserve order, as far as he could, until the English occupation of the 14th. It is difficult to say where Arabi's responsibility ended and that of the civil governor commenced. It is also probable that some of the fires were lighted by the Bedouins, who had assembled contrary to the wish of Arabi, and had entered the town on the 12th, and possibly also by British shells.

It is certain, however, that the houses in the Place Mehemet Ali were burned by Suleiman Sami and his regiment. Suleiman Sami asserted that he acted under orders from Arabi. On this point he was contradicted by Arabi and others, and some prisoners stated that Arabi sent messengers to prevent the burning of the houses. It must be remembered that no evidence was taken for the defence, and that no witnesses were cross-examined.

Under these circumstances it became necessary to consider what was best to be done. On the 18th November Lord Dufferin wrote to Lord Granville as follows:—

I have the honour to inform Your Lordship that I saw the *khedive* today, and gave His Highness to understand that I thought it very unlikely that sufficient proof would be forthcoming to authorize the execution of Arabi and the political prisoners, and I suggested the alternative of deportation. I was glad to find that His Highness was prepared, if required, to accept this result, provided Arabi and his family were removed from the country *en bloc*, and his property forfeited; in which event the Egyptian Government would allow a maintenance for his women and children, who, the *khedive* observed, ought not to be punished for another's fault.

Towards the latter part of November all parties interested became more or less disposed to accept a reasonable compromise, somewhat on the lines indicated in Lord Dufferin's letter.

The English Government was aware of the block caused in Egyptian affairs and in the projected reforms by the trial, the proceedings of which Mr. Broadley spoke of extending over some months.

The Egyptian Government, after being informed of the inconclusive character of the evidence, and being given to understand that no capital punishment would be allowed, lost all heart in the business, and only longed to get the rebels out of the country. Mr. Broadley, on behalf of the accused, was equally willing to accept a compromise. With a tribunal such as that before which he was to plead, he felt that his chances of success were small. He might, indeed, drag on the proceedings for an indefinite period, but in the end the solution would probably be less satisfactory to his clients than would result from a well-considered arrangement "out of court."

The details of the compromise arrived at were that all charges except that of simple rebellion were to be withdrawn, and that as regards this the prisoners should plead guilty. A sentence of death was to be recorded on this plea, but a decree should be signed commuting the sentence to exile from Egypt. The prisoners were to forfeit their rank and property, and to give their *parole* to proceed to any British possession indicated, and to remain there until permitted to leave.

Only a very few persons in Cairo were informed on the evening of 3rd December that Arabi and his confederates were to be brought before the court-martial the following morning.

The proceedings were exceedingly simple, everything having been arranged beforehand. A room had been fitted up as a court house in the old Daïra Sanieh, where Arabi was confined, and the proceedings were public. At nine o'clock on the 4th, Raouf Pasha, the president, and the other members of the court-martial, took their seats. General Sir Archibald Alison sat at a desk to the right of the President, and Sir Charles Wilson on the left. Arabi was on Sir Charles Wilson's left, his counsel sitting just beneath him. He wore a dark greatcoat with a white cachemire scarf round his neck. He looked somewhat thinner than he was previous to the bombardment of the forts of Alexandria. He had grown a short beard, which was partly grey.

The report of the Commission of Inquiry to the court-martial was then handed in. The following is a translation of this document:—

> We have the honour to inform you that, having terminated the inquiry concerning Arabi, the commission considers that there are grounds for sending him before the court-martial charged with the crime of rebellion as provided for by Article 92 of the Ottoman Military Code, and Article 59 of the Ottoman Penal Code. It therefore sends the said Ahmed Arabi before the court for trial charged with the said crime. We send you at the same time the complete *dossier* containing the results of our inquiry into this affair.

The president of the court asked the prisoner if he acknowledged himself guilty of rebellion against His Highness the *khedive* in the following terms:—

> Arabi Pasha, you are charged before this court, after due inquiry by the Commission of Inquiry, with the crime of rebellion against His Highness the *khedive*. Are you guilty, or are you not guilty, of the crime with which you stand charged?

Mr. Broadley then handed in a paper to the effect that, acting under the advice of his counsel, Arabi pleaded guilty to the charge.

The court then rose, the president remarking that judgment would be delivered that afternoon at three p.m.

At the time named the court was densely crowded, several ladies being present, and there was a gathering of natives outside the prison. The president, first of all, handed in an official document condemning Arabi to death, which was read, and of which the following is a translation:—

> Considering that Ahmed Arabi Pasha has pleaded guilty to the crime of rebellion, a crime provided for by Article 92 of the Ottoman Military Code and Article 59 of the Ottoman Penal Code. Considering that in consequence of this plea, no other course is open to the court but to apply Article 92 of the Ottoman Military Code and Article 59 of the Ottoman Penal Code, already quoted, which punish with death the crime of rebellion. For these reasons, the court unanimously condemns Ahmed Arabi to death for the crime of rebellion against His Highness the *khedive*, in accordance with the terms of Articles 92 of the Ottoman Military Code and 59 of the Ottoman Penal Code. This sentence is to be submitted for the sanction of His Highness the *khedive*.

Immediately afterwards the decree commuting the sentence to exile for life was read.

Arabi saluted the court and sat down, and the members of the court prepared to retire, the sitting having lasted only six minutes. At this moment, Mrs. Napier, wife of the junior counsel for Arabi, had brought into court a bouquet of white roses for the accused, which, immediately after the reading of the decree, was presented to Arabi in open court. This was a little too much for the audience, who had restrained their feelings during the reading of the decree, and loud hisses arose. After this manifestation the crowd gradually dispersed.

On the 7th December, Mahmoud Sami, Abdel-el-Al, Toulba, and Ali Fehmi were arraigned before the court-martial on the charge of rebellion, and on being called on to plead, they all pleaded guilty. The prisoners were again brought up in the afternoon for sentence to be passed on them. They were all sentenced to death, and immediately after the *khedive*'s decree commuting their sentence to banishment for life was read.

On the 10th December the same formality was gone through with regard to Yacoub Sami and Mahmoud Fehmi.

A day or two later Ceylon was announced as the prisoners' place of exile, and on the 26th December the seven principal rebels left Cairo by special train at 11 p.m. for Suez, there to join the British steamship *Mareotis*. They were accompanied by a guard of thirty men of the 60th Rifles, and a suite of sixty persons, male and female. Morice Bey, an English officer in the Egyptian service, was appointed to take charge of the exiles. The satisfaction of Arabi, who had all along suspected treachery, at finding that he was to make the voyage in a British steamer, and accompanied by British soldiers, with an Englishman in charge, was unbounded, and he more than once expressed his acknowledgments.[6]

It was, of course, impossible, after the lenient sentences passed on Arabi and the other leaders of the National Party, to attempt to inflict capital punishment on any of those who simply followed their lead.

On the 29th December a Decree was issued exiling a large number of the chief prisoners remaining for various periods to Massowah, Souakim, and other places. Others were released either with or without bail, on their undertaking to live quietly on their country estates.

The result of the trial of the rebel leaders produced, at first, a feeling of stupefaction on the European colony in Egypt. When the nature of the judicial farce which had been enacted began to be understood, the sentiment above mentioned gave place to one of profound indignation against the Egyptian Government and its advisers. In passing upon Arabi and his associates a sentence which was regarded as merely nominal, it was said a premium was put upon rebellion, massacre, and pillage.

Such was the view universally entertained. Amongst the foreign

---

6. Toulba, being in ill health, was permitted to return to Egypt early in the present year (1899), and died in Cairo on the 16th July, 1899. On the 18th July, 1899, a decree was issued allowing Mahmoud Sami also to return.

population, England lost in one day all the popularity she had gained at Tel-el-Kebir. "*On ne plaisante pas avec la justice,*" remarked an eminent foreign advocate to the writer. With the natives the worst impression was created. The idea of a compact having been made by England with Arabi was strengthened and confirmed. With many the belief in Arabi's Divine mission was raised to a certainty. The action of England was by a great class of the population attributed to fear. It was given out that Arabi was never really going to Ceylon, and that if he did he would return to raise an overwhelming army and expel the unbelievers. The most moderate charged England with having bribed Arabi, or, at the very least, with having held out, as a reward for his surrender, the promise of immunity for his past misdeeds.

However much the result of the trial of the rebel leaders may be deplored, it was, perhaps, the best solution of the question. After a painstaking examination Sir Charles Wilson came to the conclusion that there was no evidence forthcoming on which Arabi could be convicted of complicity with the riots of June 11th; neither was the evidence adduced as to Arabi's complicity with regard to the incendiarism of Alexandria of a satisfactory nature, and it did not appear possible to connect him with the other massacres. The only evidence against Arabi was of a negative character; that he could have prevented the massacres and other atrocities appears to be freely admitted by his best friends, but this was not sufficient ground for hanging him.

Such being the state of the case, it became necessary to consider what steps should be taken to rid the country of Arabi and his accomplices. The preliminary proceedings had already occupied upwards of two months, fifty-two days alone having been spent in the examination of the witnesses for the prosecution; the defence would probably have required as much time; thus it would have been at least three months before a verdict could have been arrived at. This delay was intolerable, the current business of the ministries and administrations was seriously interfered with in consequence of the great attention being paid to these rebels. Even the consideration of the Alexandria Indemnity Question was in abeyance.

It was determined that if Arabi could be induced to plead guilty of rebellion, an easy way out of the difficulty could be found. As has been stated, he was accordingly arraigned on the charge of simple rebellion, and pleaded guilty. The trial, it is true, was generally looked upon as a farce, and it appeared to be so, but in the face of so many complications, it was about the only course to be adopted.

CHAPTER 26

The Soudan and the Mahdi

Scarcely had the Arabi revolt been suppressed, than troubles which had arisen in another quarter called for attention. Towards the end of October, 1882, Abdel Kader Pasha, Governor-General of the Soudan, telegraphed from Khartoum that the troops which he had sent against the *Mahdi* had been cut off, and that a force of 10,000 men should be sent as a reinforcement, otherwise he would be unable to defend the town. He stated that, without a large force at his disposal, the insurrection would spread through all parts of the Soudan, in which case the pacification of the country would require an army of at least four times the number asked for.

The Soudan is a vast tract of Africa, stretching from Egypt on the north to the Nyanza Lakes on the south, and from the Red Sea on the east to the farthest boundary of Darfur on the west. Khartoum, at the junction of the Blue and White Niles, is about equally distant from the northern boundary of Egypt (the Mediterranean) and from the southern limit of the *khedive*'s Equatorial dominions, Lake Victoria Nyanza, and Uganda. From Khartoum to the ports of Souakim and Massowah, on the Red Sea, the eastern limit of the Soudan, the distance is about 480 miles, and to the westward limit, which is the most indefinite of all, but is generally fixed at the western boundary of Darfur, it is nearly 800 miles. This country is as large as India. It extends 1,600 miles in one direction and 1,300 in another. There were at this time neither railways, canals, nor, except the Nile at some periods of the year, navigable rivers, and the only roads were camel tracks.

The sovereignty of the Soudan was first seized by Egypt in the year 1819, when Mehemet Ali, hearing of the anarchy prevailing there, and wishing to introduce the benefits of a regular government and of civilization, and at the same time to occupy his troops, ordered his

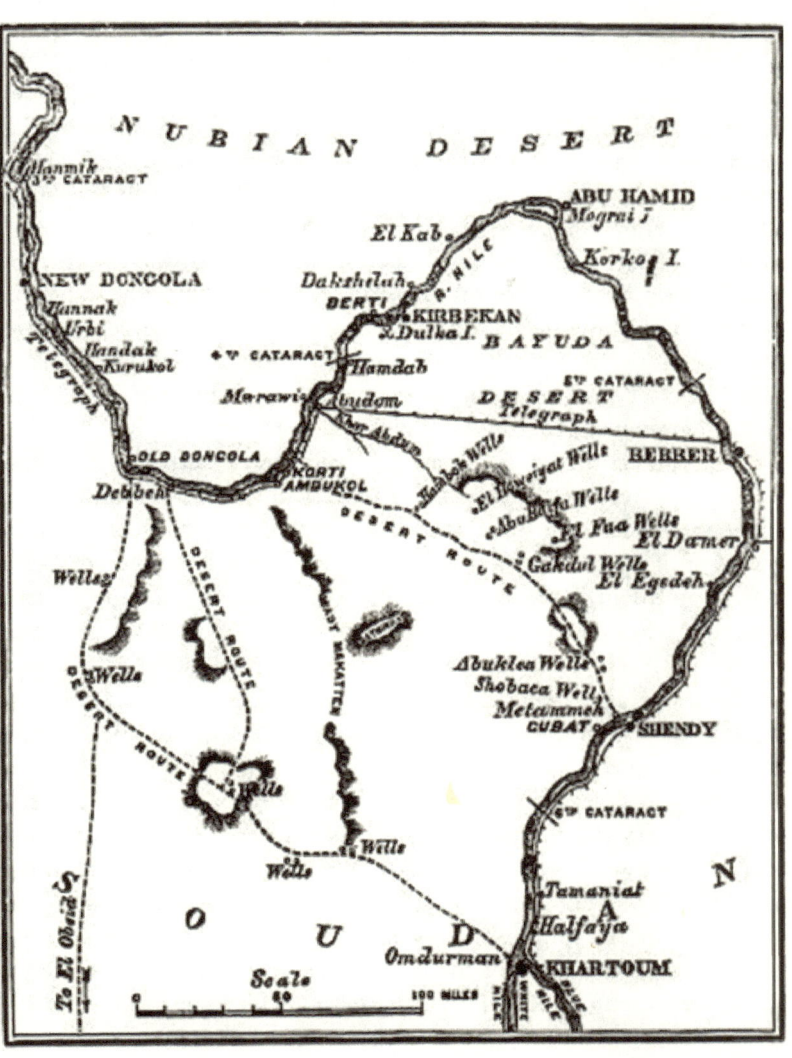

son Ismail, with a large army of regulars and irregulars, to invade the country. Ismail reached Khartoum, and for a time governed the Soudan, but he and all his followers were burnt alive by a native ruler, who first made them drunk at his own table and then burned the house over their heads. For this a terrible vengeance was taken, and Egyptian sovereignty was established over Sennar and Kordofan.

In 1856 the viceroy, Said Pasha, visited the Soudan, and almost decided to abandon the country, but desisted in deference to the representation of the *sheikhs* and notables, who laid great stress upon the anarchy which would result from such an abandonment. He decreed reforms, most of which appear to have been punctually neglected. One governor-general succeeded another, their chief duties being border-warfare with Abyssinia and the suppression of the rebellions which periodically broke out. In 1866 Massowah and Souakim were given to Egypt by the Sultan of Turkey. In 1870 Sir Samuel Baker set out to conquer the Equatorial Provinces, returning in 1873. Colonel Gordon, afterwards Gordon Pasha, was appointed Governor-General of the Equatorial Provinces in the following year.

When, by authority of Ismail Pasha, Gordon became absolute ruler of the Soudan, he established a system of just and equitable government, which led, after his departure, to the revolt against the misgovernment of Egyptian officials. Gordon had warned the *khedive*, before his appointment, that he would render it impossible for the Turks to govern the Soudan again. He was as good as his word. By treating the people justly, by listening to their grievances, and mercilessly punishing all those who defied the law, he accustomed the Soudanese to a higher standard of government than any which had prevailed in those regions before.

After Gordon's departure a horde of Turks were once more let loose to harry the Soudanese. All his old officials were marked men, and his policy was reversed. Ilias, one of the greatest slave-owners of Obeid, was allowed to return to Khartoum; and this man, in concert with Zubehr, the king of the slave dealers (afterwards interned at Gibraltar), took advantage of the wide-spread discontent occasioned by mis-government to foment the rebellion which, under the *Mahdi's* leadership, assumed such serious proportions.

The chief causes of the rebellion were: the venality and oppression of the officials; the suppression of the slave-trade, and military weakness. Of the first it is unnecessary to say much. The same kind of oppression that goes on in Turkey prevailed in the Soudan, though, perhaps, not to the same extent. Here, as there, all over the country there was a class of small officials on salaries of from £2 to £4 a month, who had the responsible duty of collecting the taxes. The officials were mostly *bashi-bazouks*, irregular soldiers of Turkish descent. As there could be but little supervision over such an immense area, these men had it much their own way and squeezed the people to their hearts' content. There were instances where a *bashi-bazouk* on his salary maintained twelve horses, twenty servants, and a number of women, and this in places where the payment for water for his cattle alone would have cost more than three times his salary. It was no uncommon thing for a peasant to have to pay his taxes to the collector four or five times over without the Treasury being any the richer.

That the suppression of the slave trade, or rather the difficulties thrown in its way, was also a potent cause is evident from the list of the tribes who followed the *Mahdi*. Many, if not the majority, of these tribes were Baggara, or owners of cattle. These tribes were all of Arab descent, and from time immemorial had been inveterate slave-hunters. The Gallabahs were, also, to a man, against the government, slave-trading being both their principal and by far most profitable business.

As to the military weakness, there can be no doubt that the Arabi revolt also had its effect on the Soudan population. Telegrams were actually sent them by Arabi, ordering them not to recognize the authority of the *khedive*. At the same time all the available troops were withdrawn, and the revolt followed almost as a matter of course.

Mahomet Ahmed, the *Mahdi*, was a native of the province of Dongola. His father was Abdullahi, by trade a carpenter. In 1852 this man left and went to Shendy, a town on the Nile south of Berber. As a boy, Mahomet Ahmed was apprenticed to his uncle, a boatman, residing at Shakabeh, an island opposite Sennar. Having one day received a beating from his uncle, he ran away to Khartoum and joined the free school of a *fakir*, the head of a sect of dervishes, who lived at a village close by. This school was attached to the tomb of the patron saint of Khartoum, who was greatly revered by the inhabitants of that town and district. Here Mahomet Ahmed remained for some time, studying religion, but did not make much progress in the more worldly accomplishments of reading and writing.

After a time he left and went to Berber, where he joined another free school. This school was also attached to a shrine much venerated by the natives. Here Mahomet Ahmed remained six months, completing his religious education. Thence he went to a village south of Kana, on the White Nile, where, in 1870, he became a disciple of another *fakir*, who subsequently ordained him *fakir*, and he then left to take up his home in the island of Abba, near Kana. Here he began by making a subterranean excavation into which he made a practice of retiring to repeat for hours one of the many names of the Deity, and accompanied this by fasting, incense-burning, and prayers. His fame and sanctity by degrees spread far and wide, and Mahomet Ahmed became wealthy, collected disciples, and married several wives, all of whom he was careful to select from among the daughters of the most influential Baggara *sheikhs* and other notables. To keep within the lawful number (four) he was in the habit of divorcing the surplus and taking them on again according to his fancy.

About the end of May, 1881, he began to write to his brother *fakirs*, and to teach that he was the "*Mahdi*" foretold by Mahomet, and that he had a Divine mission to reform Islam, to establish a universal equality, a universal law, a universal religion, and a community of goods; also that all who did not believe in him would be destroyed, were they Christian, Mahommedan, or Pagan. Among others he wrote to Mahomet Saleh, a very learned and influential *fakir* of Dongola, directing him to collect his dervishes, followers, and friends, and to join him at Abba. This *sheikh*, instead of complying with his request, informed the government, declaring the man to be mad.

In the beginning of *Ramadan*, 1298 (2nd July, 1881), the Governor-General of the Soudan, Reouf Pasha, heard that on the island of Abba, on the White Nile, in the Fashoda district, there was a certain religious *sheikh*, Mahomet Ahmed, who had publicly declared that he was the *Mahdi*; further, that this *sheikh* had been for some time very busy in extending his influence among the tribes by means of emissaries and letters. Reouf became somewhat alarmed, fearing the consequences which might result from such teaching among the credulous and superstitious people of the Soudan, and sent a party of notables and learned men, with a government official and a small military escort, to interview Mahomet Ahmed, and request him to give up agitating and come to Khartoum. Mahomet declined to do either, and boldly declared that he was the *Mahdi*, by which name he will be hereinafter referred to.

On the failure of his first attempt, the *pasha*, on the 11th August, despatched by steamer an expedition of 200 regular soldiers, with orders to use force, if necessary, in bringing the pretender to reason. At 3 a.m. on the following day the party reached Abba, where a discussion arose between two of the officers, each of whom claimed to be in command. Before the difficulty could be settled, the *Mahdi* and his followers turned out, some 4,000 strong, attacked the force and drove them back to the river, killing no less than 120 of their number. The rest of the expedition succeeded in reaching their steamer, and returned to Khartoum. After this further failure, Reouf Pasha organized a new expedition. The officer in command was Mahomet Pasha Said, from the regular army. Not finding the *Mahdi* at Abba, the pasha followed him leisurely on to Talka. On arriving there it was discovered that the *Mahdi* had retreated into the hills of Jeb el Nuba, and the Pasha, deeming it useless to follow him further, withdrew to Kordofan, and the enterprise was abandoned.

In December, 1881, the Governor of Fashoda heard that the chief of the Tajalle (a district of the Jeb el Nuba), who was friendly to the government, had driven out the *Mahdi*, and that the latter had taken refuge in the mountains of Gheddeer. The governor decided to follow up this advantage and attack the *Mahdi* in his new position. Taking with him a force of 400 men, the governor left Fashoda on the 4th December. On the morning of the 9th he reached Gheddeer after marching all night. The troops, fatigued by the march, following their usual custom, on nearing the wells broke their ranks and rushed to the water. At this moment they were attacked by the Mahdists and nearly all killed, including the governor.

The *Mahdi*, seeing that he could defy the government with impunity, was encouraged to believe in his mission, and the various sects of dervishes throughout the country began to think that Mahomet Ahmed might really be the true *Mahdi*. The *Mahdi* himself, though he did not venture to leave the shelter of the Gheddeer hills, occupied himself in fomenting the rebellion by his emissaries and adherents.

On the 4th March, 1882, Abdel Kader Pasha was appointed Governor-General of the Soudan, in place of Reouf Pasha.

During the interval between the departure of Reouf and the arrival of his successor, Giegler Pasha, a German, acted as the latter's deputy. This official formed a new expedition of 3,500 men, starting from three points, namely, from Khartoum, Kordofan, and Sennar. By the 22nd of April the entire force, Nubir Yussef Pasha, a Berberine, being in command, was concentrated at Kaha, for the purpose of attacking Gheddeer, where, as was above stated, the *Mahdi* had taken refuge.

In consequence of these movements, the garrisons all over the country were left very weak, and at Sennar there were but 100 soldiers remaining. Amr-el-Makashef, a prominent agent of the *Mahdi*, collecting a force of disaffected natives and dervishes, attacked and burnt a part of the town, killed most of the small garrison, and besieged the remainder in the Government House. Fortunately, Saleh Aga, an irregular officer sent by Giegler Pasha, arrived on the 13th with 300 men, and after a hard fight defeated Amr-el-Makashef and compelled him to raise the siege.

On the 15th of April Giegler Pasha started south from Khartoum by steamer with 300 irregulars. On reaching the neighbourhood of Mesalamieh, on the Blue Nile, he learned that a notable *sheikh*, called Ahmed Saha, was raising men for the *Mahdi* at a village close by. He sent a detachment of fifty of his men to attack the place, with the result that the expedition was repulsed and most of the men killed. Giegler then telegraphed for reinforcements of six companies of regulars from Galabat, on the Abyssinian frontier, and while awaiting their arrival, having received some small reinforcements, renewed his attack on Ahmed Saha, but was once more defeated, with a further loss of 200 men.

On the 5th of May, however, Giegler was joined by the six companies of regulars from Galabat, and no less than 2,500 of the great Shukuri tribe, headed by their *emir*, Awad-el-Kerim, and a number of chiefs, clad in coats of mail and steel helmets, as in the days of the Crusaders, and riding thoroughbred Arab horses. This was a grateful sight for Giegler, as the *emir* was a personal friend of his own, and had, moreover, taken sides with the government. Encouraged by this accession of strength, the *pasha* renewed the attack on the 6th—this time with success—and Ahmed Saha was defeated with great slaughter.

After the victory the troops were directed on Sennar, where, on the 24th of May, they joined hands with the forces of Saleh Agha. Giegler at once attacked the rebels at a village in the neighbourhood of the town, and succeeded in driving them into the river, with a loss of 800 men. Giegler then returned to Khartoum in triumph, leaving Saleh Agha in command. On the 3rd June the latter, with four companies of regulars, attacked Amr-el-Makashef at Tegu, whither he had retired after his defeat. The rebels were again defeated and dispersed, and Amr-el-Makashef fled across the White Nile by the ford of Aboo Zed and joined the *Mahdi*.

Shortly after these events the rebels again collected—it is said to the number of 10,000 (probably an exaggeration)—at a place called Eddi Binat, on the White Nile. Abdel Kader (who had by this time taken up his command) got together a body of troops from Duem, Kana, and Marabieh, on the White Nile, and despatched them, under the command of Zeyd Bey, against the rebels. About October 5th these troops reached the neighbourhood of Eddi Binat, where they were attacked by Sedi Habbi and his men. The Egyptians formed a hollow square, three sides of regulars and the fourth of Aburoff Arabs. The regulars repulsed the attack, but some 40 or 50 rebels got in on the fourth side, and the result was a defeat, with the loss of 800 men. Although successful, Sedi Habbi was unable to follow up his victory, owing to his heavy losses.

This disaster was followed by an almost unbroken series of defeats for the Egyptian forces at Shaha Fozia, Shatt, and other places.

In April, as already stated, the Gheddeer field force of 3,500 men was concentrated at Kaha, under Nubir Yussef Pasha. His original intention was to march at once to attack the *Mahdi* at Gheddeer. Finding, however, that the direct route was difficult and water scarce, he brought his force to Fashoda on the 22nd of April. Here they halted till the 20th of May, thereby allowing themselves to be overtaken by the rainy season, which much increased the difficulty of advancing through the marshy and thickly wooded country which lay between them and their destination. On the 7th of June the force came in contact with the enemy. The Egyptian troops formed a square, which was assailed by the *Mahdi's* followers. It was broken, and the whole force annihilated.

The situation throughout the Soudan was now very critical, but fortunately the *Mahdi*, instead of following up his success and marching on Obeid or Khartoum, remained at Gheddeer, thus giving Abdel Kader, who had by this time taken charge at Khartoum, a chance of organizing new means of resistance.

Abdel Kader, by drawing upon the garrisons at a distance from the scene of operations, by forming battalions of black slaves, and other like measures, managed, though with the greatest difficulty, to get together a fairly respectable force. This, as soon as it was somewhat organized, was applied in strengthening the various garrisons at the more exposed places, and in preparing for eventualities in general.

For a short time the government forces had a fair share of good fortune, and in various engagements, of no great importance, came off victorious over the Mahdists. This, however, did not last long. On the 17th of July a force sent to attack the Hamar Arabs, on the Darfur frontier, had, although victorious, to be recalled to Obeid to strengthen the garrison, news having come in that the *Mahdi* had broken up his camp at Gheddeer and was marching to attack that important town. The *Mahdi* reached Obeid on the 3rd of September with an enormous force, and at once summoned the garrison of about 6,000 soldiers to surrender.

Many of the inhabitants flocked to his standard, believing the defence to be hopeless; but the garrison resolved to hold out, and intrenched themselves in the government buildings. Here they were attacked on the morning of the 14th, the assault lasting from 6 a.m. to 11 p.m. Though repulsed, the attack was renewed on each of the two succeeding days, with the same result. Eventually the *Mahdi*, after having sustained heavy losses, withdrew, and devoted his energies to the blockade of both Obeid and Bara.

The success of the government troops at Obeid was, however, doomed to be followed by disasters in other directions. When Obeid and Bara were known to be in peril, a relief expedition of two regular battalions[1] and some *bashi-bazouks* started on the 24th of September from Duem, on the White Nile, for Bara. After two days' march they were attacked, but defeated the enemy with heavy loss. On the 6th October the expedition reached a place called Kan, where there was a well, situated in the midst of a thick forest. The soldiers, after making a weak "*zeriba*," or breastwork of bushes, rushed, according to their custom, to the well for water. They were at once attacked, and over a thousand of them killed, the remainder escaping to Bara. On the 9th Bara was attacked, but the enemy were repulsed, and the same thing happened the following day; after which the assault was not renewed.

The *Mahdi* then, to prevent assistance being sent to Obeid, despatched emissaries to cross the White Nile, to stir up the embers of rebellion and secure more adherents to his cause.

The foregoing brings the narrative down to the time of Abdel Kader's pressing demand for reinforcements. At this period the relief expedition had been all but annihilated. Obeid was held by 3,500 men and Bara by 2,000. Both garrisons were short of food and in a depressed condition. Many of the officers and men had deserted to the enemy. The *Mahdi*, with the bulk of his forces, had encamped round Bara, and Amr-el-Makashef was at the same time operating on the Nile.

The latest reports from Darfur were six months old, and the governor reported that the province was disaffected, and that he could not maintain order without the aid of additional troops.

---

1. The strength of a battalion varies from 700 to 750 men.

CHAPTER 27

Arrangements for the Future

The attitude of the European Powers towards the English occupation of Egypt was, at the opening of the year 1883, one of acquiescence tempered by expediency.

On the 3rd of January, 1883, Lord Granville issued a circular note to the powers on the Egyptian question. In it he recalled the fact that events had compelled Her Majesty's Government to undertake the task of repressing the Egyptian rebellion, a task which England would have willingly shared with other powers. His Lordship added that, although for the present a British force remained in Egypt for the preservation of public tranquillity, the British Government wished to withdraw its troops as soon as a system capable of protecting the authority of the *khedive* should be organized. In the meantime, they considered it a duty to give the *khedive* advice, with the object of securing that the order of things to be established should be of a satisfactory character and possess the elements of stability and progress.

Lord Granville further declared that the danger which threatened the Suez Canal during Arabi's revolt, its occupation by British troops in the name of the *khedive*, its employment as a base of operations against the rebels, as well as the attitude of the Canal Company at a critical moment in the campaign, constituted strong reasons for seeking an international settlement of this question in order to avoid similar dangers in the future. Her Majesty's Government thought that free navigation on the Canal, and its protection against damage and obstruction resulting from military operations, were questions of general interest. His Lordship, in consequence, proposed to the powers to come to a common understanding to insure the freedom of passage through the Canal for every description of vessel, under all circumstances, with this reserve in the event of war, that the ships of war belonging to one of the belligerent nations which might be in the Canal while hostilities were proceeding could disembark neither troops nor warlike munitions.

As regards financial arrangements, Her Majesty's Government thought it possible to arrange for greater economy and greater simplicity in the administration by modifications which would not in any way diminish the guarantees of the creditors. His Lordship hoped that he would soon be able to submit definite proposals on this subject to the powers. The government relied on the co-operation of the powers to place foreigners on the same footing as natives as regards taxation.

The public papers contain no reply or acknowledgment of the communication on the part of the French Government.

The first of the other powers to express any opinion on the despatch was Austria. Sir Henry Elliot called on Count Kalnoky on the 16th of January to ask what impression had been made upon him by the document; and his reply was to the effect that, though he could not be expected to pronounce upon it off-hand, he would repeat assurances already given that his government continued to be animated by the most sincere wish not to embarrass Her Majesty's Government in the reorganization of the administration of Egypt. A week later the Austrian Foreign Minister had another interview with the British ambassador, and the conversation left on Sir Henry Elliot's mind the impression that Count Kalnoky would make no observations upon the circular except with reference to the proposal to subject Europeans to the same taxation as natives. He admitted the justice of this proposal, and Sir Henry believed he would not object to it; but it was, he said, a subject that required full examination before it was decided. The suggestions of Her Majesty's Government about the Suez Canal appeared quite to satisfy him.

On the 25th, Count Herbert Bismarck, the German *chargé d'affaires* in London, called on Lord Granville, and stated that his government accepted generally the arrangement regarding Egypt and the Suez Canal proposed in the despatch, and was prepared to await the further information promised respecting the internal reorganization of Egypt. He went on to say that the German Government would continue to preserve the same friendly attitude towards Her Majesty's Government in regard to Egyptian affairs which they had maintained during the summer.

On the 24th January, Count Hatzfeldt informed Lord Ampthill that he was about to instruct Count Herbert Bismarck to inform

Lord Granville that the German Government accepted and agreed in principle to the policy laid down in the circular of the 3rd respecting the reorganization of Egypt.

The Italian Government took much longer time before giving any answer. It was not till the 7th February that Count Nigra called on Lord Granville to state their opinion. It was to the effect that they wished to reserve any detailed expression of their views till the English proposals were communicated in a more definite shape; but he was able to say at once that they concurred generally in those proposals.

The Russian reply was yet later and very indefinite. Sir Edward Thornton asked M. de Giers on the 7th February what he had to say, and the reply was that the Imperial Government considered the views expressed in the circular despatch as "generally satisfactory," and "they had not for the present any objection to make to them."

The minor powers were addressed in a circular dated the 24th January, and enclosing Lord Granville's despatch of the 3rd. The respective foreign ministers were informed that, as their governments were interested in the condition of Egypt, and in the questions relating to the Suez Canal, Her Majesty's Government had thought that it might be agreeable to them "to have cognizance of the communication which has been made by Great Britain on these subjects to the *Porte* and the other Powers represented in the recent Conference at Constantinople."

The Spanish Government were somewhat effusive in their thanks. The Minister for Foreign Affairs promised to lose no time in expressing the opinion of his colleagues, and in the meantime desired to say how much gratified was King Alfonso's Government at the courtesy and consideration shown towards Spain.

The Portuguese Government simply expressed their thanks.

In a despatch to Mr. Wyndham, requesting him to lay the circular before the *Porte*, Lord Granville wrote as follows:—

> Having regard to the exceptional position occupied by Turkey in relation to this important question, and to the special interests of His Majesty the *sultan* which are involved in its solution, Her Majesty's Government desire, in the first place, to address the Sublime *Porte* separately on the subject: and they conceive that they could hardly adopt a more convenient and satisfactory mode of placing their views before the *sultan* than by communicating to His Majesty a copy of the circular which they

propose to address to the Powers, and which resumes all that they have to state on the subject at the present time.

You will accordingly deliver a copy of this despatch and of its inclosure to the *Porte*, and, in doing so, you will express the hope of Her Majesty's Government that His Majesty the *Sultan* will recognize the friendly sentiments which have prompted them to submit separately to the appreciation of the *Porte* their proposals with reference to Egypt, and that these proposals will commend themselves to the favourable opinion of His Majesty, as the result of the most anxious consideration on the part of Her Majesty's Government, and as embodying a system of re-organization in Egypt which, in their opinion, is best calculated to insure the stability of its institutions, the prosperity and happiness of its people, and the peace of Europe in the East, and of the Ottoman Dominions.

On the 17th October Said Pasha had proposed to Lord Dufferin to open negotiations with regard to Egypt with a view to the maintenance of what he termed the *status quo ante*, and expressed the gratitude of the Turkish Government for the assurance of England's intention not to leave the English troops long in Egypt.

Lord Dufferin was instructed to say in reply that as the affairs of Egypt had advanced only partially towards their final settlement, any negotiation would be premature.

On the 23rd December Musurus Pasha asked Lord Granville for a reply as to the period of the occupation by the British troops. Lord Granville answered that he could not fix the exact date, but hoped to be in a short time able to make a communication to the *Porte* on the whole Egyptian question. The communication was the Circular Note of the 3rd January, 1883.

On the 25th January, Mr. Wyndham asked the Turkish Minister for Foreign Affairs if he could tell him what impression the proposals of Her Majesty's Government with regard to Egypt had made upon the Ottoman Government. Aarifi Pasha said that the different points presented had been examined by the ministers, but that they had not yet come to a final decision as to what answer they should return.

One of the first results of the new position adopted by England in Egypt was the abolition of the Dual Control.

As has been already shown, the institution had rendered great services to Egypt, and tended to protect the humbler classes of natives from exaction and injustice. That it should have been so successful in its mission was due to the high character and administrative ability of the gentlemen selected for the duties of Controller-General. Major Baring[1] found a capable successor in Sir Auckland Colvin, and both in turn worked in the utmost harmony with their French colleague, M. de Blignières, afterwards succeeded by M. Brédif, who displayed the same courtesy in his relations with his English colleague.

The objections to the control were summarized in a note addressed by the Egyptian Government to the two Western Powers on the 7th November, 1882. But apart from any other objection to the control, there was also a fear that circumstances might occur which would render that institution a danger to the maintenance of cordial relations between England and France. Its maintenance, moreover, was obviously incompatible with the exclusive predominance of England in Egypt.

Lord Dufferin, on the 28th December, was accordingly instructed to reply, on behalf of England:

> .... that Her Majesty's Government were not prepared, in opposition to the wishes of the Egyptian Government, and in face of the many objections which had been raised to the continuance of the control, to insist on the maintenance of an arrangement which, in its last form, was only provisionally accorded. They thought, however, that for the present it would not be wise on the part of the Egyptian Government to deprive themselves of all European assistance in securing the good administration of the finances, on which must depend the prosperity and credit of the country, and its power to fulfil its international engagements without undue pressure on the Egyptian people. Her Majesty's Government would recommend that, in place of the control, His Highness the *khedive* should appoint a single European financial adviser. This officer would attend Cabinet Councils, exercise powers of inquiry, and give advice on financial questions, but without authority to interfere in the direct administration of the country.
>
> Her Majesty's Government were aware of the great value which the French Government had attached in the past to the Dual Control. They did not deny the practical advantages which for a time attended the system—advantages which were owing to

---

1. Afterwards Sir Evelyn Baring.

the common wish of this country and of France to promote the prosperity of Egypt; but they were convinced that this feeling on the part of France would not extend to thinking it possible that an arrangement of a temporary character should be continued after two of the three parties to it had become desirous to be freed from the obligation for reasons which they considered to be of grave importance.

It was scarcely to be expected that France would accept the arrangement, at all events, without a struggle, and M. Raindre, the French Consul-General in Cairo, was instructed to deny the right of the Egyptian Government to annul the existing arrangement. This in no way altered the programme of Cherif Pasha, who, assured of the support of England, proceeded with the measure; and on the 18th of January, 1883, a decree was issued, stating that the dispositions of the various decrees relating to the control were repealed. The next day the decree was published in the *Moniteur Egyptien*, and the control became a thing of the past.

On the decree appearing in print, the French Consul-General addressed a despatch to Cherif Pasha, in which the former stated that his government declined to recognize the right of the Egyptian Government to upset an arrangement which he maintained was part of an agreement between the French and the Egyptian Governments, and which, he said, formed an essential security for French interests. The despatch concluded with a formal reservation of the rights of the French Government. The abolition of the control excited a burst of indignation from the French Press; the action of the Egyptian Government was loudly condemned, and there the matter ended.

M. Brédif, the French controller, obtained leave of absence; and on the 5th February, Sir Auckland Colvin, who, in the meantime, had resigned his post as English controller, was appointed to the post of "Financial Adviser," created as a substitute for the defunct control.

One of the first measures which had to be considered by Lord Dufferin was the reorganization of the Egyptian Army. The rebellion and the measures taken in consequence had left Egypt absolutely without any army either to defend her frontiers or to maintain order in the interior. If, as was then contemplated, the British forces were ever to be withdrawn, it was necessary to provide others to take their place.

Lord Dufferin, in a despatch to the Foreign Office on the 18th November, 1882, combated the oft-repeated statement that Egypt required no army. According to him:

.... this was a mistake, for although an efficient *gendarmerie* might be able in ordinary times to prevent the Bedouins causing trouble along the desert border and the banks of the Suez Canal, it was essential that these unruly Arab communities should know that the government held in reserve a military force capable of checking any serious attempt on their part to disturb the peace of the country; otherwise they would not hesitate to break through the necessarily sparse and feeble frontier guards in the hope of plundering Cairo.

Lord Dufferin estimated that the strength of the army ought not to exceed from 5,000 to 6,000 men.

On the question of officering the new force, he observed that the officering of the native army had always been its weak point. The *fellah* subaltern, captain, or colonel had seldom been able to acquire the prestige or authority necessary for maintaining discipline during peace and for effective leading in the presence of the enemy. To meet the difficulty, Lord Dufferin approved a proposal which he found under consideration for introducing into the Egyptian Army a certain proportion of British officers. It was also suggested that an English general should be appointed to the chief command.

Both schemes were approved, a number of officers were selected from the English army to fill certain grades in the Egyptian forces, and on the 13th December, Sir Evelyn Wood left England to take the command with the title of "*Sirdar*" (Commander-in-Chief).

The reorganisation of the *gendarmerie* and police was at the same time proceeded with. In a despatch, dated the 1st January, 1883, Lord Dufferin said on the subject of the *gendarmerie* that, "in consequence of the proximity of the desert and the necessity of controlling the wild Arab tribes which infest its borders, it was desirable that this arm of the service should be in a great measure a mounted force, and impressed with a semi-military character. At the same time, for economical and other reasons, it should be also trained to discharge the civil duties of a rural police. Under certain aspects, therefore, it would possess the characteristics and qualifications of mounted infantry, and under others those of simple constabulary."

The administration of the *gendarmerie*, to the number of 4,400 men, was to be placed under the Minister of the Interior, and its chief was to be General Baker, with the title of Inspector-General. Lord Dufferin in the same despatch dealt with the question of the reorganization of the Urban Police, and whilst pointing out the errors committed in the past, showed how they might be avoided in the future.

Lord Dufferin next took in hand the question of the reform of Egyptian institutions generally. On the 6th of February, His Lordship made his report in the form of a lengthy despatch to Lord Granville, in which he dealt with the occupation of Egypt, and the responsibilities thereby devolving on England; the establishment of a Legislative Council, and a Chamber of Notables elected by the people; the Tribunals, canalization and irrigation, the cadastral survey of Egypt, the indebtedness of the fellah, the assessment of the land revenue, agricultural taxes, national education and the Soudan, as to which last His Lordship observed that some persons were inclined to advise Egypt to withdraw altogether from the Soudan and her other acquisitions in that region; but she could hardly be expected to acquiesce in such a policy.

Possessing the lower ranges of the Nile, she was naturally inclined to claim dominion along its entire course; and when it was remembered that the territories in question, if properly developed, were capable of producing inexhaustible supplies of sugar and cotton, we could not be surprised at her unwillingness to abandon them. Unhappily, Egyptian administration in the Soudan had been almost uniformly unfortunate. The success of the present *Mahdi* in raising the tribes and in extending his influence over great tracts of country, was a sufficient proof of the government's inability either to reconcile the inhabitants to its rule, or to maintain order. The consequences had been most disastrous. Within a year and a half the Egyptians lost something like 9,000 men, while it was estimated that 40,000 of their opponents had perished.

His Lordship stated that, in the expectation that the fresh efforts then about to be made would result in the restoration of tranquillity, a plan should be carefully considered for the future administration of the country. Hitherto, it had caused a continual drain on the resources of the Egyptian Exchequer. The first step necessary was the construction of a railway from Souakim to Berber, or what, perhaps, would be still more advisable, to Shendy, on the Nile. The completion of this enterprise would at once change all the elements of the problem. Instead of being a burden on the Egyptian Exchequer, these Equatorial provinces ought to become, with anything like good management, a source of wealth to the government.

Lord Dufferin then referred to the slave trade, the International Tribunals, the right of Egypt to make commercial conventions, and the exemption of Europeans from taxation. He then gave a retrospect of reforms accomplished and made observations on the Egyptian Budget and the Public Debt.

The report concluded as follows:—

> Having thus given a *résumé* of the steps already taken towards the reorganization of Egypt, and of the further measures in progress or in contemplation, it remains for me to consider how far we can depend upon the continued, steady, and frictionless operation of the machinery we shall have set up. A great part of what we are about to inaugurate will be of necessity tentative and experimental. This is especially true as regards the indigenous Courts of Justice and the new political institutions, both of which will have to be worked by persons, the majority of whom will be without experience or instruction. Had I been commissioned to place affairs in Egypt on the footing of an Indian subject State, the outlook would have been different.
>
> The masterful hand of a Resident would have quickly bent everything to his will, and in the space of five years we should have greatly added to the material wealth and well-being of the country by the extension of its cultivated area and the consequent expansion of its revenue; by the partial, if not the total, abolition of the *corvée* and slavery; the establishment of justice, and other beneficent reforms. But the Egyptians would have justly considered these advantages as dearly purchased at the expense of their domestic independence. Moreover, Her Majesty's Government and the public opinion of England have pronounced against such an alternative.
>
> But though it be our fixed determination that the new *régime* shall not surcharge us with the responsibility of permanently administering the country, whether directly or indirectly, it is absolutely necessary to prevent the fabric we have raised from tumbling to the ground the moment our sustaining hand is withdrawn. Such a catastrophe would be the signal for the return of confusion to this country and renewed discord in Europe. At the present moment we are labouring in the interests of the world at large.
>
> The desideratum of everyone is an Egypt peaceful, prosperous, and contented, able to pay its debts, capable of maintaining order along the Canal, and offering no excuse in the troubled condition of its affairs for interference from outside. France,

Turkey, every European Power, must be as anxious as ourselves for the attainment of these results, nor can they be jealous of the means we take to secure them.

The very fact of our having endowed the country with representative institutions is a proof of our disinterestedness. It is the last thing we should have done had we desired to retain its government in leading-strings; for however irresistible may be the control of a protecting power when brought to bear upon a feeble autocracy, its imperative character disappears in the presence of a popular assembly. The behests of 'the Agent' are at once confronted by the *non possumus* of 'the Minister.' But before such a guarantee for Egypt's independence can be said to exist, the administrative system of which it is the leading characteristic must have time to consolidate, in order to resist disintegrating influences from within and without, and to acquire the use and knowledge of its own capacities.

If the multiform and balanced organization we have contrived is to have a chance of success it must be allowed to operate *in vacuo*. Above all, the persons who have staked their future on its existence must have some guarantee that it will endure. How can we expect men born under a ruthless despotism to embark on the duties of an Opposition—which is the vital spark of constitutional government—to criticise, condemn, and countervail the powers that be, if tomorrow the ark of the constitution to which they trusted is to break into fragments beneath their feet? Amidst the applause of the liberal world a Parliament was called into existence at Constantinople; a few months later it disappeared, and its champion and fugleman is now languishing in the dungeons of Taif.

Unless they are convinced that we intend to shield and foster the system we have established it will be in vain to expect the timid politicians of the East to identify themselves with its existence. But even this will not be enough. We must also provide that the tasks intrusted to the new political apparatus do not overtax its untried strength. The situation of the country is too critical, the problems immediately pressing on the attention of its rulers are too vital to be tampered with, even in the interests of political philosophy. Various circumstances have combined to render the actual condition of the Egyptian *fellah* extremely precarious.

His relations with his European creditors are becoming dangerously strained. The agriculture of the country is rapidly deteriorating, the soil having become exhausted by overcropping and other causes. The labour of the *corvée* is no longer equal to the cleansing of the canals. As a consequence the desert is encroaching on the cultivated land, and, unless some remedy be quickly found, the finances of the country will be compromised.

With such an accumulation of difficulties, native statesmanship, even though supplemented by the new-born institutions, will hardly be able to cope unless assisted for a time by our sympathy and guidance. Under these circumstances, I would venture to submit that we can hardly consider the work of reorganization complete, or the responsibilities imposed upon us by circumstances adequately discharged, until we have seen Egypt shake herself from the initial embarrassments which I have enumerated.

This point of departure once attained we can bid her Godspeed with a clear conscience, and may fairly claim the approbation of Europe for having completed a labour which every one desired to see accomplished, though no one was willing to undertake it but ourselves. Even then the stability of our handiwork will not be assured unless it is clearly understood by all concerned that no subversive influence will intervene between England and the Egypt she has recreated.

The projects of Lord Dufferin were theoretically complete, and, taken together, formed a constitution which, on paper, was nearly perfect. An army duly subordinate to the Executive was to form the ultimate guarantee for order. An efficient police, carrying out the decrees of independent and unbribed tribunals, was to offer complete security for personal rights and liberty. A *khedive* checked by a Council of Ministers, which in turn was to be checked by a Legislative Council of twenty-six, while all three were to learn from an assembly of forty-six Notables what were the real wishes of the Egyptian people, was a triumph of constitutional mechanics. A financial councillor at once the servant and the monitor of the *khedive*, and always ready when requested to bring the light of Western science to bear upon the lax ideas of Oriental finance, lent to the whole structure of government a rigidity and stability which could not be too greatly admired. In short, looking at the whole ingenious apparatus, one could not but feel that nothing was wanted to make it perfect except an Egyptian nation.

The machine was beautifully constructed and finished, but one looked in vain for the motive power. In 1883 the Egypt of Lord Dufferin existed only in imagination. For the most part it was a dream, and far off in the haze of a remote future. The constitution was excellent as a model, but where did the strength reside that alone could make it work? One might search through all its parts, from the *khedive* to the policeman, without finding a single trace of the vital force that was to work the whole. It had no organic connection with the people of Egypt; it had not sprung out of their wants or their aptitudes; it did not express their history or embody their aspirations. The ministers were responsible to the *khedive*, and the army was to obey him. On what was the authority to rest which was to enable him to cope with intrigues in his Cabinet or conspiracy among his troops? There could at that time be only one answer, *viz.*, the presence of the British Army of Occupation, and this was the very institution which the project was intended to supersede.

The British forces in Egypt on the 31st of December, 1882, had been reduced to 12,000 men.

At the opening of Parliament on the 15th February, 1883, Egyptian affairs were referred to in the Queen's Speech in the following terms:—

> I continue to maintain relations of friendship with all the powers; order is now re-established in Egypt, and the British troops will be withdrawn as promptly as may be permitted by a prudent examination of the country.

The repeated declarations by the British Government of their intention to withdraw the Army of Occupation excited the utmost alarm amongst the European inhabitants of Egypt. These last, driven from their homes by the events to a great extent brought about by England's intervention in 1882, had now, trusting to the protection of the British force, returned to the country and resumed their former avocations. Upon this class the ministerial utterances produced the worst possible effect. Owing to the feeling of uncertainty which in consequence prevailed, all large operations were at a standstill. No one was disposed to lay out his money in a country which might at any moment be handed back to the care of a native administration, and at Alexandria miles of blackened ruins still marked the results of British interference.

Whether the feeling of alarm was justified or not, there is no doubt that at this time the sentiments of the natives were not friendly towards Europeans. In the provinces Europeans were openly insulted and threatened by the natives, and in many of the villages acts of brigandage were of frequent occurrence.

The repeated ministerial declarations of an impending withdrawal from Egypt not only created anxiety amongst the European population, and to a great extent paralyzed commerce and prevented the inflow of capital, but they exercised a most injurious effect upon the reforms which the British Government professed such anxiety to push forward. On every side the same story was told. The natives, daily given to understand that the rule of the English was shortly coming to an end, opposed a passive obstructiveness, in those cases where they did not offer active opposition, to the intended changes. "What is the use of your making all these alterations," reasoned the Egyptian official, "if they are not to last?" That they *could* last after the departure of the English was an idea which never appeared worthy of a moment's consideration by him.

This was the condition of things when, early in the month of March, a petition in English, French, Italian, and Greek was drawn up and addressed to Lord Dufferin. The document pointed out that whilst recognizing that it was by the British forces that the disturbances of 1882 had been suppressed, the state of affairs in Egypt was such as to show that the permanent retention of a European force was the only means by which order could be maintained, and the security of the European population assured. The petition bore 2,600 signatures, mostly of influential persons of all nationalities. It was presented to Lord Dufferin by a deputation, and by him transmitted to the Foreign Office. From that date nothing more was heard of it, and it was probably placed in the same pigeonhole as the memorial for protection sent by the British residents just previous to the riots of the 11th June.

On the 29th April, Lieutenant-General F. C. A. Stephenson was appointed to the command of the Army of Occupation, in succession to Sir Archibald Alison.

Lord Dufferin left the carrying out of his scheme of Egyptian reform in the able hands of Sir Evelyn Baring, and returned to Constantinople on the 3rd May.[3]

---

3. Two days before Lord Dufferin said farewell to Egypt, that is, on the 1st May, 1883, he had the satisfaction of seeing established by Khedivial Decree: 1st, Provincial Councils, for the purpose of fixing the contributions to be levied for extraordinary local expenditure on works of public utility; 2nd, a Legislative Council, to whom all new laws have to be submitted for discussion; 3rd, a Chamber of Notables or General Assembly, without whose consent no new tax can be levied.

CHAPTER 28

Operations Against the Mahdi

The situation in the Soudan at the period referred to at the close of Chapter 26 was, it must be confessed, critical enough, and it is not surprising that, on the 7th November, 1882, Lord Granville caused the *khedive* to be informed that the British Government were unwilling to take any responsibility in regard to it. Left to their own resources, the Egyptian Government had no alternative but to re-enlist about 10,000 of Arabi's old officers and men for service in the South.

Early in November the collection of these soldiers and their concentration at the Barrage, near Cairo, began. Most of them had to be brought in chains, and desertions were frequent. They were transported by detachments to Berber, *viâ* Souakim, their arms and ammunition being sent separately. Altogether, 9,500 were collected and despatched.

Most of these troops were deplorably ignorant of all notions of drill, and were little more than an armed mob. Their officers were no better. Many of them had been engaged in the recent operations in Lower Egypt, which did not tend to increase their military spirit. Others looked on service in the Soudan as a sentence of death, and deemed that the *khedive*'s purpose in sending them was to get rid of them. Considering, also, the superstitious notions which many of them had of the power and invincibility of the *Mahdi*, and of the valour of his savage followers, it can hardly be supposed that the new levies were such as to inspire confidence, or that to advance with such a rabble was to court anything else but defeat.

The first thing to be done was to try to teach them something. They were, for this purpose, isolated from the town in a camp on the western bank of the Nile. Here Abdel Kader devoted himself personally to giving them instruction in drill, teaching them to fire and lecturing their officers.

Meanwhile, on the 11th November, the *Mahdi* sent Amr-el-Makashef to attack Duem, on the west bank of the White Nile. After some delay, the Mahdist forces arrived before the town. The garrison telegraphed for assistance, and a battalion of the newly arrived levies was sent to their relief, but, owing to a dispute amongst the native officers in command, it effected nothing, and Duem was left to take its chance.

After this failure, it is not surprising that Abdel Kader telegraphed to the Egyptian Government, requesting that some European officers might be placed at his disposal, and on 16th December, Colonel Stewart and two other British officers arrived at Khartoum. They found that place quiet, but Obeid and Bara were still unrelieved, and Abdel Kader was standing out for seven additional battalions before he would advance to their assistance.

At the end of December, news was received that Bara was still holding out, though greatly in want of provisions, and that the *Mahdi* was marching in that direction with the bulk of his forces; also, that a second *Mahdi* had appeared on the scene, but had been promptly hung by order of the first.

Abdel Kader, on 11th January, 1883, left Khartoum to take command of the troops operating between the White and Blue Niles. His intention was to clear the province of Sennar. As the force advanced, the country was found deserted, the inhabitants having gone to join the *Mahdi*. At Abut he determined to await the arrival of another battalion before advancing further.

Whilst halting at this spot it became necessary to despatch the 1st battalion of the 2nd Regiment of the Line from Khartoum to suppress troubles which had arisen amongst the Hassaniyeh nomads on the White Nile. The troops left in two steamers. When near the village where operations were to commence, one steamer ran aground. The other went on, landed three companies and opened fire on the rebels. At this moment a handful of the latter falling on two of the companies which had not yet formed up was the signal for a general flight of the troops to the river, with heavy loss, including the *bimbashi* (or major) in command, who was killed by his own men in the confusion. When the other steamer arrived a council of war was held, and it was decided to make no further attack upon the enemy, although they were only 400 strong.

On the 26th, another *bimbashi* arrived to replace the one who had been killed. He took the field at once, and ordered an advance on the village before daybreak. The other officers remonstrated, saying that, if they marched in the dark through an unknown country, they would all be killed, and on the *bimbashi* remaining firm, five of them went at once on the sick list. The advance was made in square formation, preceded by a guard and scouts, up to a narrow strip of forest, which lay between the Egyptian force and the village. Two companies were ordered into the forest to reconnoitre the road, but the officers refused to advance, saying that they and their men would certainly be killed. Some of the soldiers at this time, firing off their rifles contrary to orders, gave the alarm to the rebels, who advanced through the wood, and the Egyptian force fled back to their boats.

The above episode gives a fair idea of the fighting capacity of the Egyptian officers and men, and the truth of the matter seems at this period to have dawned upon the authorities at Cairo; for on the 23rd of January a telegram from the *khedive* to Hussein Pasha Serri, the senior military officer in charge at Khartoum, ordered all operations to be suspended, and all the troops to be concentrated there, pending the arrival of English staff officers from Cairo.

The orders of the *khedive* were communicated to Abdel Kader, who, nevertheless, declined to obey. The reason he gave was that, by the withdrawal of the troops, the rebellion would be allowed to extend in the eastern provinces, and that if the expedition did not leave promptly for Kordofan, that province, as well as Darfur, would be lost to Egypt. It is quite possible, also, that Abdel Kader, who was undoubtedly an able leader, was disinclined to allow the work to be taken out of his hands. In any case, he did not for a moment relax his efforts. On the 27th he defeated the rebels at Maatuk, with a loss of 600 killed and wounded; directed a successful engagement at Baatuk; and on February 1st reached Kawa, where he was joined by three battalions ordered up from Shawal and Karash. He then left for Khartoum, after giving directions for the disposal of the force in his absence.

On the 11th of February a messenger brought the news to Khartoum that Bara had surrendered to the *Mahdi* on the 5th January. Four days later intelligence was received of the capitulation of El Obeid on January 17th. According to the details received from this last place, it would appear that on the 16th or 17th negotiations were opened, and a meeting of delegates on either side was appointed for the next day. On this becoming known, many of the troops at once left and joined the rebels, who made an attack in force on the following day. The *bey* in command ordered the soldiers to resist, but they refused and went over to the enemy; the artillery fired in the air, and the commandant, taking this as a sign of collusion with the rebels, made an unconditional surrender. The capture of these two strongholds placed the whole of Kordofan in the hands of the *Mahdi*, who also obtained possession of 5,500 prisoners, 600 Remington rifles and five guns.

On the 13th February Abdel Kader rejoined his troops and proceeded towards Sennar with three battalions and about 600 Bashi-Bazouks. The *Mahdi*, on his approach, advanced from Sennar to meet him with a force estimated at from 10,000 to 12,000 men. These, under the command of Amr-el-Makashef, attacked the Egyptians on the 24th, but after a fight lasting three hours were repulsed with a loss stated at 2,000 in killed alone. After this success, Sennar was occupied without resistance, and communications were re-established between that place and Khartoum.

On the 20th February, Al-ed Din Pasha, a Turkish cavalry officer, who was sent to supersede Abdel Kader, arrived at Khartoum, and was on the 26th March proclaimed Governor-General of the Soudan.

It now becomes necessary to go back a little to the period of the appointment of the European officers applied for by Abdel Kader.

In January, 1883, Colonel W. Hicks, subsequently known as Hicks Pasha, was appointed by the *khedive* Chief of the Staff of the Army of the Soudan, with the local rank of Major-General. Though not named Commander-in-Chief till the August following, it was intended that he should direct and be responsible for all the operations, whilst nominally holding a subordinate post.

Hicks was a retired officer of the Indian army, which he had entered in 1849. He had taken part in the suppression of the Indian Mutiny, under Lord Clyde, and had accompanied Lord Napier's expedition to Abyssinia, being present at the taking of Magdala. In 1882, when holding the retired rank of Colonel, he went to Egypt, and joined the Egyptian service in the following year. Though a popular and attractive officer, he is said to have had little or no experience in handling troops in the field. His appointment was made by the Egyptian, without reference to the English, Government. With him were associated the following British officers, all nominated in the same manner, *viz*.: Colonels Colborne and De Cöetlogon, Majors Farquhar and Martin, and Captains Warner, Massey, and Forrestier-Walker.

Hicks and his staff left Cairo on the 7th of February for Souakim, and started thence for Berber by the desert route on the 11th. The caravan, which consisted of 145 camels, besides horses, and was accompanied by 350 Bashi-Bazouks and over 100 Egyptian soldiers, reached Berber on the 1st of March. Here the news of the fall of Bara and Obeid was received.

Hicks proceeded to Khartoum on the 4th of March, and the next few weeks were spent in the necessary training of his men.

On April 6th, Hicks and Colborne, bringing reinforcements, joined the Egyptian force encamped at Kawa, to lead it against a body of about 6,000 Mahdists, reported to be assembling at Marabieh and Abu Djumal, on the White Nile, south of Khartoum. On the 21st, Hicks started to reconnoitre the enemy, and on the 23rd the Egyptian army, numbering about 5,000 men with four Nordenfeldt guns, under the nominal command of Suleiman Pasha,[1] marched against the enemy. On the 25th, Hicks rejoined the camp with the intelligence that the rebels had left Geb-el-Ain and were moving to attack the "Turks," as the Egyptian force was termed, on their march from Kawa.

On the following day the enemy threatened an attack, but, finding the Egyptians on the alert, retired. Two days' more marching brought the force close to the village of Marabieh. On the 28th, when about an hour from this place, Colonel Farquhar, who had been scouting in company with four Bashi-Bazouks, raced in to report the enemy's advance. So rapid was this that in a quarter of an hour they were seen coming on in a cloud, consisting of both cavalry and spearmen, led by their chiefs carrying gaily-coloured banners. They emerged in thousands through openings in a wood in front. Fortunately Hicks had his men formed in a solid square and ready to receive the attack.

As usual, all baggage, camels, and camp followers were in the centre. Along each face bristled a thousand rifles and at each corner were placed Nordenfeldt guns and rocket tubes. "Crows' feet," or little iron spikes joined four together, were thrown out so as to make the ground difficult for bare-footed men or unshod horses. As the enemy came on they spread out towards the flanks, as if with the intention of attacking the angles of the square. A couple of rockets were discharged from the Egyptian force, but the missiles burst amongst Hicks' own men. This was followed by the fire of the howitzers, and no sooner had the first few shells fallen amongst the advancing horsemen than they broke and moved off the field.

---

1. The reason for giving the nominal command to Suleiman was that the Mahdist movement being a religious one, it was undesirable to increase the fanaticism of its supporters by placing a Christian at the head of the Egyptian troops.

The infantry still came on boldly, sweeping with an inward curve right and left, the extreme flanks converging towards the opposing corners of the position. File firing commenced from the front of the Egyptian force, which was directly assailed. The men were formed in ranks four deep, and used their Remingtons with deadly effect. Nevertheless, though shot down in numbers many of the enemy continued their onward rush, and succeeded in getting close enough to the square to throw their spears into it. Encouraged by the presence of their English officers, the Egyptians stood their ground and poured volley after volley into the attacking force, whilst the Nordenfeldts, when got to work, did much execution.

After half an hour's fighting, in which Amr-el-Makashef, who was in command, and other chiefs were killed, the force was entirely broken up and fled in confusion. A few of the rebels continued to come up singly after the rest had retired, and brandished their spears in defiance. One after another these courageous fanatics were knocked over, and when the smoke had rolled away the ground was seen strewn with corpses, most of them within 400 yards of the square.

When victory was assured, the enthusiasm of the soldiers knew no bounds, and unaccustomed to find themselves on the winning side, they indulged in the wildest demonstrations, whilst the Egyptian officers rushed to shake hands with their English comrades.

The number of Amr-el-Makashef's forces engaged was estimated at from 4,000 to 5,000 (though they may have been less), and their losses at 500. The Egyptian loss was merely nominal, only two men being killed and five wounded. This may be accounted for by the fact that, so far as appears, the enemy were unprovided with firearms, and that no hand-to-hand fight took place.

After Suleiman's men had rested sufficiently, there being no indications of the attack being renewed, the bugles sounded the advance, and the troops were again on the march. Halting every night, a few days only witnessed their arrival at Geb-el-Ain, whence after a short stay Hicks and the whole force returned to Khartoum, leaving only a few men to garrison Kawa and Duem.

Hicks, as has been seen, began well, and the immediate result of his victory was that the province of Sennar, the capital of which had been threatened, was entirely pacified, whilst the population of Khartoum was reassured.

The rebel chiefs in great numbers came in, made their submission, and returned to peaceful occupations.

The reconquest of Kordofan was now decided on by the Egyptian Government, the annihilation of the *Mahdi* having become a matter of vital importance from the fact of his emissaries being discovered engaged in fomenting a revolt in Khartoum itself.

On the 13th of May, Hicks telegraphed to Cairo requesting that he might be put in undisputed command of the troops, as otherwise he could not be responsible for the proposed expedition. He was fully alive to the difficulties of the task before him. A council of war was held at Khartoum on the 6th of June, when the measures to be adopted in the coming Kordofan campaign were discussed, and it was unanimously decided to ask for reinforcements from Cairo, the available force at Hicks' disposal being quite inadequate for the undertaking. Hicks' application was for 6,000 men, who, he begged, should be sent in time to enable him to commence operations as soon as the rainy season should be over.

The Egyptian Government, on the 11th of June, decided to despatch 3,000 men as reinforcements; 600 of these were *Bashi-Bazouks,* and 1,800 were old soldiers who had been rejected by General Baker as unfit for the reorganized army.

Hicks was evidently at this time in doubt as to how far he was to exercise real authority over the expedition, and asked that distinct orders should be sent that all directions he might give during the campaign should be obeyed. On the 23rd of July Hicks telegraphed his resignation in the following terms:—

> I have today sent to the War Office my resignation of my appointment with the Soudan Army. I have done so with regret, but I cannot undertake another campaign under the same circumstances as the last. Suleiman Pasha tells me that he does not understand from the telegram of the President of the Council, dated the 14th July, that he is bound to carry out my views with regard to the order or mode of advance or attack of the army now preparing for Kordofan, unless he approves of them. In fact, he says he should be acting contrary to instructions if he carried out my views, and did not agree with them. As my views and his were so opposed in the last campaign, and would be more so in the Kordofan campaign, I can only resign. Within the last few days, on two important occasions my views have been disregarded.

On the 31st of July Hicks withdrew his resignation and was appointed to the chief command, Suleiman being recalled and nominated governor of the Red Sea Provinces.

Great efforts had to be made to supply the means of transport for the Kordofan column, and Al-ed Din Pasha himself had to go off to the country east of the Blue Nile for camels, at least 5,000 of which were required. Early in August he returned, having succeeded in getting together some 4,000.

The *Mahdi* seems, at this time, to have also been giving his attention to the question of transport. According to one report he had sent some Dervishes to the Kabbabish tribes to requisition camels. At first the tribesmen thought of refusing to obey this order, but on second thoughts they resolved to dissemble. The *sheikh* accordingly wrote to say, "Send your men down and we will give you camels." When, however, the emissaries of the *Mahdi* came to fetch them they were greeted in the following logical manner, "Your master is a lost man. If he is the Prophet he can have no need of camels. If he is not we are not bound to give him any," and in order that there might be no mistake as to their views, the Kabbabishes promptly fell upon the Dervishes and killed them.

In the months of July and August the reinforcements from Cairo began to arrive, and as they came up were concentrated with the rest of the force at Omdurman, opposite Khartoum where a regular camp had been formed.

On the 9th of September, 1883, Hicks' army marched out from the camp at Omdurman on its way to Duem, 110 miles distant. The force then consisted of 10,000 men (including camel-men and camp followers) with four Krupp field guns, ten mountain guns, and six Nordenfeldts. The undermentioned Europeans accompanied the force, which Hicks subsequently joined at Duem:—Colonel Farquhar, chief of the staff; Majors Seckendorff, Warner, Massy, and Evans; Captains Herlth and Matyuga; Lieutenant Morris Brody; Surgeon-General Georges Bey and Surgeon-Major Rosenberg; Mr. O'Donovan, correspondent of the *Daily News*," and Mr. Vizetelly, artist of the *Graphic*.

On the march to Duem no hostility was encountered. Most of the natives had fled at the approach of the troops. The heat was intense, the thermometer ranging from 105 to 115 degrees Fahrenheit in the shade. Four men and 200 camels died on the way. The expedition reached Duem on the 20th, where it was met by Al-ed Din Pasha.

Hicks on the 6th of September had telegraphed to Cairo that he was starting for Kordofan; he added that he expected to encounter great difficulties in supplying his force with water. Kordofan, it may be observed, is the driest province in the Soudan. The wells contained but little water except immediately after the rains, and even then they were insufficient for a large force with camels, horses, &c.

His original plan was to march to Bara and Obeid by the northern and more direct route. By this road the distance would be about 136 miles. Posts were to have been established along the line to keep up communication with the river at Duem, where a *depôt* was to have been formed. Both Bara and Obeid were to have been retaken and garrisoned. The former, being thirty-five miles to the north of the latter, and situated in a fertile country, was to have been first attacked. Here it was proposed the army should remain for a few days to rest and replenish its stores.

On Hicks joining the army at Duem, these arrangements had to be entirely changed. According to Al-ed Din Pasha, the information he had obtained led him to believe that the best supply of water would be found on the southern route by Shatt, Norabi, and the Khor-Abu-Hable to Rahad, some forty-five miles east of Obeid. The distance by this route, however, was fully 250 miles, being more than 100 miles greater than by the northern road—a very grave objection. It had been all along known that on striking the Khor-Abu-Hable, which is a torrent taking its rise in Ghebel-Kulfan, a mountain some fifty miles south of Obeid, the army could follow its course for 100 miles, thus making sure of an ample supply of water for that distance.

But the difficulty consisted in reaching Norabi, ninety miles distant from Duem, and it was this consideration which had induced Hicks to reject this route. Now Al-ed Din represented that water could be found between the two places, and the question of water supply being paramount, Hicks was induced to change his decision and proceed by the southern route, notwithstanding the increased distance.

On the 24th of September an advance party of 2,400 infantry, one squadron of *Bashi-Bazouks*, two Krupp and four mountain guns, seized the wells at the village of Shatt, sixteen miles distant. Here the first post was established.

On the 27th, Hicks telegraphed to the Minister of War from Shatt that the main body of the army would march forward that day, and added, "The difficulty of getting over the increased distance is nothing when the facilities for obtaining water on the march by this route are taken into consideration."

On the same day the army marched forth to its fate. Taking a south-westerly direction, on the 30th it encamped at Zeraiga, a village thirty miles south-west of Duem. The heat continued to be overpowering, and the camels were dying in numbers. During the march a difference of opinion arose between Hicks and Al-ed Din, the latter, in view of the change of route, wishing to give up the proposed series of posts connecting the army with its base. Hicks, on the other hand, was most unwilling, for obvious reasons, to take any such step. In a despatch, without date, in the general's writing, purporting to be written from a spot twenty-eight miles from Serakna, Hicks thus expresses himself:—

> The army has arrived within twenty-eight miles of Serakna, which place is twenty-two miles from Norabi. We have depended upon pools of rainwater for supply, which we have fortunately found. A reconnaissance made today insures us water as far as Serakna, guides' information is vague. I regret that I have to abandon my intention of establishing military posts and line of communication with base at Duem. Al-ed Din assures me that the Arabs will close in on my route after the army has passed in sufficient force to prevent posts forwarding supplies. Besides, the pools of rain-water, the only supply, will dry up. Water not to be obtained by digging wells. I have no information regarding water between Serakna and Norabi, nor reliable information of the supply there. This causes me great anxiety.

The determination to abandon the posts was not come to without a council of war being summoned; and Hicks on the 3rd of October, on the army reaching a place near Serakna, wrote a report (the last communication ever received from him) giving the opinions of the members of the council in favour of abandoning the series of posts which he had wished to establish, and the reasons which induced him, against his better judgment, to bow to their decision.

After this the army appears to have arrived on the 7th of October at Sanga Hamferid, forty-five miles south-west of Duem. A letter from Mr. O'Donovan from that position, and dated the 10th of October, says:

> We have halted for the past three days owing to the uncertainty of the water supply in front. Here we are entirely dependent on surface pools. A reconnaissance of thirty miles forward yesterday by Colonel Farquhar ascertained that the pools were barely sufficient for a rapid march to the village of Serakna, now deserted, where there are a few wells. The enemy is still retiring and sweeping the country bare of cattle.

Chapter 29

The Destruction of Hicks' Army

Then came a long period of silence, and great anxiety began to be felt. From its outset Hicks' army had been beset with spies, who informed the *Mahdi* of every movement. Hicks, on the other hand, had to trust to treacherous guides, and possibly false reports. It was, moreover, no secret that there was dissension in the Egyptian force, for Al-ed Din Pasha was jealous at not having been intrusted with the chief command, and some of the Egyptian officers were suspected of treachery.[1] Here, then, were all the elements of failure.

Military critics had from the first condemned the decision forced upon Hicks to give up the proposed series of posts connecting the army with its base. Sir Samuel Baker, a high authority on the Soudan, as well as General Stone, an American officer of experience, formerly chief of the staff, stated that the force despatched was wholly inadequate, and that they anticipated nothing but disaster. As week after week passed on without intelligence, the public anxiety increased. Daily telegrams were sent by the government to Khartoum, demanding news, and a steamer was despatched from there to patrol the White Nile, but in vain. Attempts to send messengers to communicate with the army failed. One messenger, who had been captured by the rebels, was put alive into an ant-hill, and this naturally tended to discourage others who might have been induced to make the attempt.

At last three soldiers returned to Khartoum from Duem, and reported that Hicks had been attacked by from 25,000 to 30,000 Mahdists at a place three leagues from Obeid, had repulsed the attack, inflicting a loss of 8,000 men on the enemy, had laid siege to Obeid, and

---

1. A German servant named Klein, attached to the expedition, subsequently related that he remembered Colonel Farquhar coming into his master's tent and saying, "We find the *Mahdi* has many friends among the Egyptian officers."

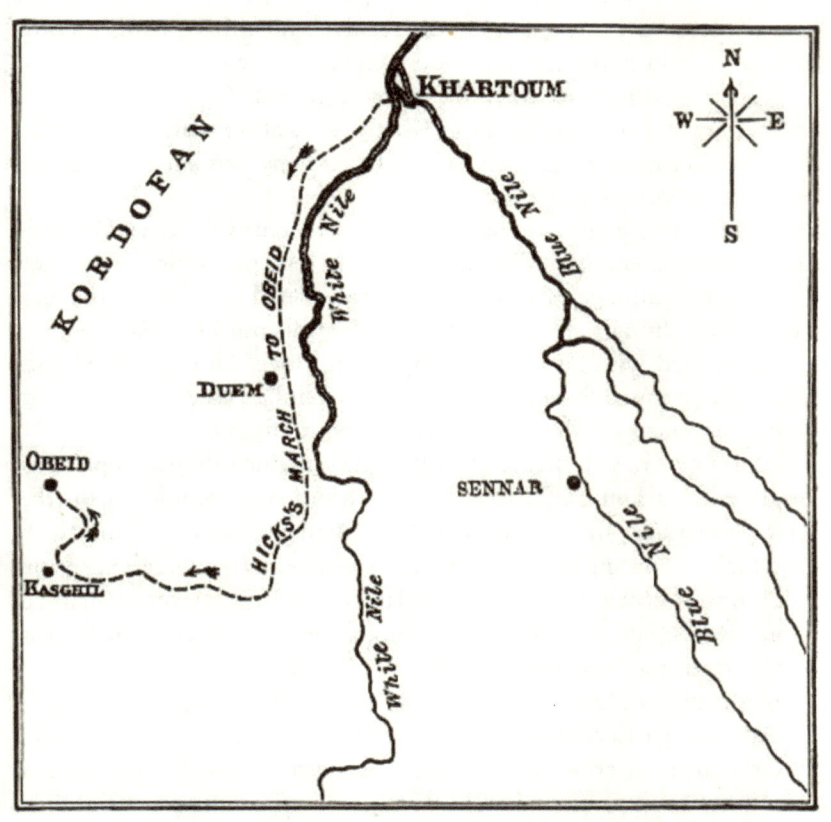

Route of Hicks' Army.

captured it on the 4th of November, the Egyptian losses being nil.

Doubts were entertained as to the accuracy of this information. The absence of any loss on the Egyptian side in operations of such magnitude was felt to be improbable. Further, it was recognized that on the date at which Hicks was stated to have entered Obeid he must, according to his calculated rate of progress, have been at least a week's march from that town. The report received no sort of confirmation, official or otherwise, and was soon generally disbelieved.

On the 18th November the French Consul-General received a short telegram from his agent at Khartoum, stating that, according to information from a private source, Hicks' army was surrounded and in want of provisions.

On the 19th two messengers arrived at Duem with letters. According to their statements, a fight had taken place between Egyptian troops and a great number of rebels at a place called Kaz. During the first two days' fighting the Dervishes suffered great loss. The *Mahdi*, seeing this, advanced with his regular troops from Obeid, all well armed. The fighting continued from the 2nd to 5th November, when Hicks' whole army was destroyed, all being killed but about fifty men.

This news was confirmed by other persons, including a Copt, who, disguised as a Dervish, arrived at Khartoum from Kordofan on the 21st November. He asserted that he was an eyewitness of the fight, in which, according to him, the Egyptian troops, with the exception of 200, were totally destroyed. The later accounts received contained more details; but as these are in many respects conflicting, it is proposed to give a short summary of one or two of the different narratives, omitting only such portions as would be mere repetition.

According to a camel-driver, who followed in the service of Kenaui Bey, the army, after leaving Duem, met the rebels, with whom some skirmishes took place, and arrived at Rahad without serious fighting. There was a lake at Rahad, from which they got a supply of water, and then started for Alouba. On this march the rebels attacked in great numbers, but were defeated. The army passed the night at Alouba. The next day (2nd of November), after three hours' marching through a forest, a large force of rebels suddenly appeared, and the Egyptians halted and formed square. Fighting went on all that day, and after an engagement, in which there were losses on both sides, the rebels were again defeated. Intrenchments were thrown up, and the night was passed on the field of battle.

On the 3rd the march was resumed. Again the rebels attacked in considerable numbers, endeavouring to surround the army, but after a serious engagement, in which both sides lost severely, they were once more defeated. The night was passed on this new field of battle. On the 4th the army directed its course towards Kashgil. After four hours' marching, the force was surprised by the rebels, who directed against it a well-sustained fire. The soldiers were halted in square, and returned the fire. They suffered terribly from thirst; nevertheless they continued to fight all that day and during the night.

On the morning of the 5th, the firing having ceased, the army advanced towards the wells. After half an hour's march, the Dervishes, who were hidden in the woods, surrounded the troops on all sides, and opened fire. The force replied with a strong fusillade, which was well kept up till towards mid-day, when the enemy made a general charge with guns, spears, and lances, and destroyed the whole army with the exception of 200 soldiers.

On the 1st December a telegram from Khartoum stated that for the last week there had been an Arab rumour that there were dissensions between Hicks and Al-ed Din Pasha prior to the battle, and that these dissensions were known to all. Hicks, according to the rumour, was weary of waiting near the water at Melbeis. Al-ed Din Pasha refused to move further, because there was no water, and half the army went over to him, and refused to obey Hicks. Hicks therefore pushed ahead with all his European staff, artillery, and seven or eight thousand men, was entrapped into an ambush, and fought for three days, not having a drop of water or a reserve cartridge. All his army was destroyed. The rumour added that Al-ed Din and his party, who stood by the water, were afterwards attacked, and that they were at the far side of Obeid, fighting every day, with large losses; and that there was with them a white officer, English or German, who escaped, badly wounded, from the massacre of Hicks and his army. There was also Mr. Vizetelly, an artist, a prisoner in El-Obeid.

The story of a Greek merchant who escaped from Obeid was that when Hicks started from Duem, large bodies of Arabs encamped each night on the place occupied by the army the night before. Hicks frequently wished to turn back and disperse these men, but Al-ed Din Pasha assured him that they were friendly natives following in support of the army.

On the sixth or seventh day Hicks sent back a small body of his men. These were fired upon by the Arabs, and Hicks then insisted that these should be dispersed. Al-ed Din refused, and Hicks then drew his sword and threw it on the ground, saying that he resigned, and would no longer be responsible if Al-ed Din did not permit his orders to be obeyed. Hicks also declared that from the time he left Duem Al-ed Din had caused his orders to be disobeyed. After some time Hicks was persuaded to resume the command; but things went on as before, the body of rebels in the rear always growing larger.

After some slight engagements, Kashgil was reached. Here an ambuscade had been formed some days before, the guide employed having been told to lead the army thither. When the Arabs opened fire it was from behind rocks and trees, where they were wholly covered, and could fire with impunity. The shells and bullets of the Egyptian force were harmless, so thick was the cover. Hicks wheeled his army to gain the open, but found the defile blocked by Al-ed Din's so-called friendly natives, who had so long been following him. They also had got under shelter, and opened fire on the army. The Arabs, from behind their protection, kept up the fire for three days, and in the whole affair lost only from 270 to 300 men.

The Egyptian soldiers were then lying on the ground, dying or in convulsions from thirst, and the Arabs found them in groups of twenty or more, unable to rise. They were all speared where they lay. Hicks' staff and escort alone had water, and were in a group on horseback. When the Arabs came out of cover, Hicks charged, leading his staff, and shooting down all the rebels in his way. They galloped past towards a *sheikh* (supposed by the Egyptians to be the *Mahdi*). Hicks rushed on him with his sword, and cut his face and arm. The man had on a Darfur steel mail shirt. Just then a thrown club struck Hicks on the head and unhorsed him; the horses of the staff were speared, but the officers fought on foot till all were killed. Hicks was the last to die.[2] The *Mahdi* was not in the

---

2. The account here given of Hicks' death is borne out to some extent by another version, according to which, the cartridges being all spent, Hicks put himself at the head of the army, and ordered bayonets to be fixed. When last seen he was with his staff. Sword in one hand and revolver in the other, he charged in the midst of the enemy, and was in a few moments overpowered. Another report contains the following:—"Surrounded by his staff, who dropped around him one by one, Hicks fought like a lion, emptying his revolver thrice, and then hacking with his sword, till a lance-thrust stretched him beside his slaughtered companions." So impressed, according to one narrative, were the Arabs by Hicks' gallantry that they resolved to build a tomb over his body in recognition of his bravery. Klein, the German servant to one of Hicks' officers (already referred to), and who managed to escape, reported that Hicks was taken prisoner in the second day's fighting, and afterwards killed at a place three days distant from Obeid. He adds that the *pasha's* hands were cut off, and he was cut to pieces afterwards.

battle, but came to see Hicks' body. As each *sheikh* passed, he pierced it with his lance (an Arab custom), that he might say he assisted at his death.

Later still, a boy who had been with Hicks' army, made a statement to the following effect:—At Lake Rahad Hicks made a fort and mounted twenty-three guns. The troops rested there for three days. The enemy was hemming them in, and Hicks determined to push on to Obeid. The army advanced at daybreak. It had not marched an hour when the enemy for the first time opened fire, at long range. Some camels only were wounded. The army halted for the night, intrenched itself, making a *zeriba*. For two days the army remained in camp. It then marched to Shekan, where it again halted for two days in consequence of being surrounded by the enemy, whose fire began to kill both men and camels.

Leaving Shekan, the force marched till noon. It then halted, as the enemy were firing from the bushes on all sides. On the third day the cavalry made a sortie, and encountering the enemy's horsemen, put them to flight, capturing several horses. This was early in the day. The square then resumed its march. Shortly after, the galloping of horses was heard, and countless Arabs appeared on all sides, waving their banners and brandishing their spears above the bushes. The square was halted, and, opening fire, killed a great many, whilst the Egyptians at the same time lost heavily. The bushes were too thick for the Krupp guns to do much execution, but the machine-guns were at work day and night. Next morning Arabs were seen lying six deep killed by these guns. There were nine Englishmen with the force besides Hicks. The Egyptians lay down to hide, but Hicks ordered his English officers to go round and make them stand up.

At noon he sounded the assembly, to ascertain who was left alive. The force was shortly after joined by Al-ed Din and his division. The next morning the entire force marched together through a forest. Through field-glasses an immense number of the enemy could be seen. The men insisted on continuing their march to the water instead of halting to fight. Hicks, yielding to their remonstrance, continued to march in square. Before noon, Melbeis, where there was abundance of water, was in sight. About noon the Arabs in overwhelming numbers burst upon the front face of the square. It was swept away like chaff before the wind. Seeing this, the other sides of the square faced inwards, and commenced a deadly fusillade, both on the enemy and crossways on each other. Terrible slaughter ensued.

Seeing that all hope of restoring order was gone, Hicks and the few English officers who remained then spurred their horses and sprang out of the confused mass of dead and dying. The officers fired their revolvers, killing many, and clearing a space around them till all their ammunition was expended. They had then got clear outside the square, and took to their swords, fighting till they fell. Hicks alone remained. He was a terror to the Arabs. They said his sword never struck a man without killing him. They named him "the heavy-armed." He kept them all at bay until a cut on the wrist compelled him to drop his sword. He then fell. The struggling and slaughtering went on for hours. The black troops forming the rear of the square remained in good order when all else was confusion. They marched some distance and formed a square of their own. They were pursued, and the Dervishes shouted to them to surrender. They replied, "We will not surrender. We will not eat the *effendina's* (*khedive's*) bread for nothing. We will fight till we die, but many of you shall die too!" Whilst the parleying was going on, an unexpected rush was made which broke the square, and the blacks were all killed.

This last account, which is the most circumstantial that has come to light, bears, it will be observed, a certain resemblance to the narrative of the camel-driver already quoted. In both, the serious fighting is made to begin at Lake Rahad. The advance, accompanied by frequent halts, was made through trees and bushes. The attacks made under cover were received in square formation, the men were suffering from want of water, and the final onslaught was made about mid-day. The final scene in which Hicks and his staff charged their foes also agrees with the previous accounts.

Of the number of Hicks' force which perished it is impossible to give a correct estimate. According to Gordon they were so numerous that the *Mahdi* made a pyramid with their skulls.

Of the number of the *Mahdi's* forces engaged no very accurate accounts exist. The Copt whose narrative has already been referred to put it at the preposterous figure of 300,000. The soldiers who brought the news of Hicks' pretended victory put the *Mahdi's* forces at from 25,000 to 30,000, but Orientals, in the matter of numbers, are notoriously inexact. The Greek merchant, whose account has been quoted, mentioned the *Mahdi's* whole standing army as 35,000 men. Gordon Pasha, on the other hand, expressed the opinion that the enemy did not exceed 4,000 in number. It is certain that a considerable portion of the *Mahdi's* forces consisted of the trained soldiers, formerly belonging to Arabi's army, and who had surrendered at Bara and Obeid. These alone amounted to 5,500, and were provided with Remington rifles and an ample supply of ammunition. It is said that these soldiers were placed in the front rank, with the Soudanese behind to prevent their running away.

There is reason to believe that Adolf Klootz,[3] a late sergeant of the Pomeranian Army, who was servant to Major Seckendorff, and deserted some days before the Battle of Kashgil, took part in the action, and commanded the *Mahdi's* artillery. A Christian lay-sister of the Austrian Convent at Obeid, who succeeded in escaping a month later, reported that this man was then with the *Mahdi*, and was the only European saved from Hicks' army.

Of the *Mahdi's* losses in the battle with Hicks no record exists.

The *Mahdi*, after his victory, returned to Obeid, where a great religious ceremony took place to celebrate the event. The heads of the European officers were cut off and placed on spikes over the gates of the town.

Of the crushing nature of the blow inflicted by the defeat of Hicks' army it is scarcely necessary to say more than a few words. It destroyed the only army which Egypt had ready to put in the field. It increased the prestige of the *Mahdi* enormously, and placed all the country south of Khartoum at his mercy.

Khartoum itself was in a situation of very great peril. Its garrison numbered only some 2,000 men to defend four miles of earthworks and keep in order 60,000 natives, of whom 15,000 were avowed rebels.

Measures for the defence of the town and the calling in, as far as possible, of the outlying garrisons were at once taken, and reinforcements were demanded from Cairo. In the meantime a panic prevailed, and all the Europeans began to take flight.

Happily the *Mahdi* did not follow up his success, but remained in the neighbourhood of Obeid for several weeks, occupied, probably, in dividing with his followers the spoils of victory.

---

3. Klootz is the person referred to in many of the reports as Vizetelly.

CHAPTER 30

Abandonment of the Soudan— Osman Digna

On the 31st of October, 1883, at the suggestion of Cherif Pasha, it was resolved that the British Army of Occupation, which now numbered 6,700 men, should be reduced to a total force of 3,000 men and six guns, to be concentrated in Alexandria. Speaking of the change proposed, ministers declared, at the Guildhall banquet on Lord Mayor's day, that by the 1st of January, 1884, the last British soldier would have left Cairo. How far this prediction was verified will be seen later on.

On the arising of trouble in the Soudan the question was submitted in Parliament to Mr. Gladstone whether or not Her Majesty's Government regarded the Soudan as forming part of Egypt, and, if so, whether they would take steps to restore order in that province. Mr. Gladstone enigmatically replied that the Soudan "has not been included in the sphere of our operations, and we are by no means disposed to admit without qualifications that it is within the sphere of our responsibility."

On the 19th November Sir Evelyn Baring wrote to Lord Granville that bad news was expected from Hicks Pasha, and if his force were defeated Khartoum would probably fall into the hands of the rebels. The Egyptian Government had no funds to meet the emergency, and it was not improbable that the Egyptian Government would ask Her Majesty's Government to send English or Indian troops, or would themselves send part of Sir Evelyn Wood's army to the front.

On the 20th Sir Evelyn Baring was informed that the British Government could not lend English or Indian troops, and advised the abandonment of the Soudan within certain limits. This was at once communicated to Cherif Pasha.

On the 22nd news reached Cairo of the destruction of Hicks' army. The political consequences of this disaster will be seen from what follows.

On the 24th Sir Evelyn Baring telegraphed that the recent success of the *Mahdi* was a source of danger to Egypt proper, and that the danger would be greatly increased if Khartoum fell, which seemed not improbable. On the 25th Lord Granville replied that under existing circumstances the British force in Egypt should be maintained at its then present strength, and, in view of the alarming condition of the Soudan, informed Sir Evelyn Baring that the Egyptian Government must take the sole responsibility of operations in that country.

On the 3rd December Sir Evelyn Baring expressed a hope that Her Majesty's Government would adhere steadfastly to the policy of non-interference in the affairs of the Soudan. As a natural outcome of this policy, it appeared to him that neither English nor Indian troops should be employed in the Soudan, and that Sir E. Wood's army, which was officered by English officers on the active list, should, as was originally intended by Lord Dufferin, be employed only in Egypt proper. On the 13th Lord Granville again telegraphed that Her Majesty's Government had no intention of employing British or Indian troops in the Soudan. They recommended the *khedive*'s ministers to come to an early decision to abandon the territory south of Assouan, or at least of Wady Halfa.

On the 14th Sir Evelyn Baring reported as to the immediate steps necessary if the policy of abandonment were carried out. As it was impossible to say beforehand what the effect on the population of Egypt proper would be, he recommended that Her Majesty's Government should be prepared at a short notice to send a couple of battalions from the Mediterranean garrison, and that immediate steps should be taken to bring the force of the Army of Occupation up to its full strength.

On the 16th Sir Evelyn Baring informed Cherif Pasha that Her Majesty's Government had no idea of sending English or Indian troops to the Soudan, that Her Majesty's Government would not object to the employment of Turkish troops exclusively in the Soudan, with a base at Souakim, if they were paid by the Sultan. He added that Her Majesty's Government recommended the abandonment of all the territory south of Assouan, or at least of Wady Halfa, and that they were prepared to assist in maintaining order in Egypt proper, and in defending it and the ports of the Red Sea.

On the 20th Sir Evelyn Baring was authorized to inform Cherif Pasha that Her Majesty's Government adhered entirely to the policy which they had laid down with regard to Egyptian affairs, which had been interrupted owing to the destruction of Hicks' army, and they were of opinion that ineffectual efforts on the part of the Egyptian Government to secure their position in the Soudan would only endanger its success. Her Majesty's Government adhered to the advice given on the 13th inst. with regard to the course which should be pursued by Egypt in view of the disaster which had occurred in the Soudan.

The advice given to yield up the Soudan was most unpalatable to the Egyptian Government, and Cherif Pasha communicated to Sir Evelyn Baring his objections in a *note verbale* dated 21st December. In forwarding the note Sir Evelyn added he felt sure that under no amount of persuasion or argument would the present ministers consent to the adoption of the policy of abandonment. The only way in which it could be carried out would be for him to inform the *khedive* that Her Majesty's Government insisted on the adoption of this course, and that if his present ministers would not carry out the policy, others must be named who would consent to do so.

On the 2nd January, 1884, Cherif wrote to Lord Granville that the former had already pointed out the necessity imposed on the Government of His Highness of retaining the Upper Nile, and the pressing need they had of obtaining the temporary assistance of an armed force of 10,000 men, with a view to opening up the Souakim-Berber road. The news which reached them from Baker Pasha confirmed the opinion that the means at their disposal were inadequate for coping with the insurrection in the Eastern Soudan. Under these circumstances, and taking into consideration that they could not get any help from Her Majesty's Government as regarded the Soudan, the Government of His Highness found themselves compelled to apply to the *Porte* without delay for a contingent of 10,000 men to be sent to Souakim.

The reply was not long in coming. On the 4th January Sir Evelyn Baring was informed that in important questions, where the administration and safety of Egypt were at stake, it was indispensable that Her Majesty's Government should, as long as the provisional occupation of the country by English troops continued, be assured that the advice which, after full consideration of the views of the Egyptian Government, they might feel it their duty to tender to the *khedive*, should be followed. It should be made clear to the Egyptian ministers and governors of provinces that the responsibility which for the time rested on England obliged Her Majesty's Government to insist on the adoption of the policy which they recommended, and that it would be necessary that those ministers and governors who did not follow this course should cease to hold their offices. The alteration in the tone adopted by Lord Granville will not fail to strike the reader. Formerly it was advice, now it was command.

On Lord Granville's despatch of the 4th January being communicated to Cherif Pasha, he at once resigned.

Some difficulty arose as to how he was to be replaced. Riaz Pasha was still sulky at not having been allowed when last in power to hang Arabi, and would not accept office, but eventually Nubar Pasha agreed to undertake the formation of a native ministry, and declared that he accepted the policy of Her Majesty's Government in regard to the Soudan.

The late Nubar Pasha, the new President of the Council of Ministers, was one of the most conspicuous characters in modern Egyptian history.

He came to Egypt some fifty years ago, as a *protégé* of Boghos Bey, the Minister of Mehemet Ali. After accepting various minor posts under the Government, Nubar in 1865 became the chief of the Railway Administration. Nubar, however, possessed talents which were destined to raise him to a position more exalted than the comparatively obscure one of head of the Railways, and he speedily became Ismail Pasha's prime minister, and must with him share a fair proportion of praise and blame.

An Armenian by birth and a Christian by religion, Nubar possessed an intelligence far superior to that of other Egyptian statesmen. That he should have found himself able, in spite of his independent ideas and somewhat dictatorial habits, to accept the formation of a Cabinet at this epoch, is a proof of his far-seeing capacity and sound judgment.

Regarding Nubar's history impartially, it is difficult to deny that while more in earnest and far-seeing in his projects than Ismail, he was equally indifferent as to the means by which the money was obtained to carry them out. At the same time it is certain that the execution of nearly every good project that nominally emanated from Ismail was due to Nubar. He was the minister by whose agency Ismail, after difficult and intricate negotiations, succeeded in obtaining the title of *khedive*, the change in the order of succession, and practical independence at the price, nevertheless, of a large increase in the annual tribute paid to the *Porte*.

Nubar, however, has a still greater claim to fame, in having brought to a successful issue the scheme for the International Tribunals, whereby the exclusive jurisdiction of the Consular Courts in civil cases was abolished, and natives in dispute with Europeans were made subject to the new courts.[1]

During the course of the preceding events troubles were arising in the Eastern Soudan.

Early in the month of August, 1883, considerable excitement was caused at Souakim by the news that some emissaries of the *Mahdi* had arrived near Sinkat, and were raising the tribes. At the head of the movement was a man destined to play an important part in the succeeding operations. This was Osman Digna.

Osman Digna was the grandson of a Turkish merchant and slave-dealer, who settled in the Eastern Soudan in the early part of this century. Osman and his brother Ahmed for some time carried on a thriving business in European cutlery, cottons, ostrich feathers, and slaves, and their head-quarters were at Souakim. Ahmed managed the business at home, while Osman, of a more restless and adventurous spirit, was the travelling partner, and journeyed far and wide, for the Dignas had branches or agencies at Jeddah, Kassala, Berber, Khartoum, and other places.

His visits to the Soudan enabled him to become acquainted with the leaders of the anti-Egyptian movement, which, though not culminating in rebellion until the years 1881-2, was recognizable at least as early as 1869-70. About the last-named period the fortunes of the house of Digna began to decline. Osman and his brother sustained serious losses in the capture by a British cruiser of one or two cargoes of slaves on their way to Jeddah. Then came the Anglo-Egyptian Slave Convention, which completed the alarm and disgust of the slave-dealers, and the commercial ruin of his house led Osman to schemes of rebellion.

In 1882 he went to the Red Sea coasts, in the vicinity of Sinkat, thence inland to Khartoum, and threw in his lot with the new prophet. Eventually all the tribes in the Eastern Soudan went over to Osman Digna, who was named *emir* to the *Mahdi*.

---
1. He died in France, January, 1899.

On the 16th October, 1883, 160 Egyptian troops, on their way to reinforce Sinkat, were attacked in a defile by 150 men belonging to the rebel tribes near Sinkat, and, with the exception of twenty-five, were all killed.

Osman, leaving Sinkat to be besieged by the tribesmen, who, after this success, were joining his cause day by day, moved down to Tamanieb, about nineteen miles from Souakim. Osman then commenced operations with a view to the capture of Tokar, sixteen miles from Trinkitat, on the Red Sea coast.

On the 3rd November Mahmoud Talma Pasha, who had been appointed to the command of the troops in the Eastern Soudan, left Souakim with 550 men in two Egyptian gunboats for Trinkitat. The object of this expedition was the relief of Tokar, which was also besieged by the rebels. The force landed on the 4th of November, and set out on the march at eight a.m., the cavalry in advance, and a mountain-gun in the centre. After an hour and a half's march the troops rested for twenty minutes, and when marching recommenced they were attacked by the enemy. The Egyptian soldiers formed a square and commenced firing. The left side of the square was broken into by eight or ten men. This created a panic amongst the troops, many of whom threw away their rifles without firing a shot, and a general stampede ensued. The Egyptian loss was eleven officers and 148 men. Amongst the killed was Captain Moncrieff, R.N., the British Consul at Souakim, who had joined the expedition. When last seen Moncrieff was stabbed in the thigh by an Arab, whom he afterwards shot, but the captain was at that moment struck fatally in the back by a spear. The singular part of the affair is that the attacking force only amounted to 150 or 200 men.

This disaster created a panic at Souakim, where only a thousand troops remained for the purposes of defence. So little confidence was felt in them, that arms were served out to the civil population.

On the 17th November Suleiman Pasha, who had been named Governor-General of the Eastern Soudan, left for Massowah to obtain 400 black soldiers to be employed for the relief of Tokar and Sinkat.

On the 2nd December the black troops, having arrived, were sent with an expedition, comprising a total force of 700 men and one mountain-gun, to Tamanieb, between Souakim and Sinkat, about three hours' march from the former place. At noon, when passing through a defile, the Egyptian force was surrounded and cut to pieces. On being attacked the Egyptians formed a square, but after firing only ten rounds the square was broken. The black soldiers, fighting back to back, made a desperate resistance, but, being unsupported by the rest of the force, their efforts were unavailing. Out of 700 men comprising the expedition only thirty-five escaped. The rebel force was probably not less than 2,000 to 3,000.

Information was now received that Osman had concentrated a force 7,000 strong on the Tamanieb road, that Sheikh Taka had surrounded Sinkat with 11,000 men, and that the rebels at Tokar numbered 3,000. Fears began to be entertained for the garrisons of Tokar and Sinkat, as they were known to be in want of provisions.

In this threatening state of affairs no alternative remained but to despatch reinforcements from Cairo and Alexandria. The difficulty, however, was how to provide them; after much consideration the Egyptian Government decided to make the attempt.

General Valentine Baker was appointed to command the expedition. Amongst his officers were Colonel Sartorius, Chief of the Staff and Second in Command; Lieutenant-Colonel Harrington, Lieutenant-Colonel Hay, Majors Harvey, Giles, and Holroyd, Morice Bey, and Dr. Leslie.

On the 11th of December Colonel Sartorius arrived at Souakim with 650 *gendarmes*. In order to protect the place some English vessels of war, under the command of Rear-Admiral Sir W. Hewett, were stationed off the town, and from time to time fired a few rounds of shell at the rebels' position.

On the 16th the first battalion of blacks, organized by Zubehr Pasha, left Suez to join Baker.

A few days later orders were given to send down the second battalion. This one was in a worse condition than the other. The officer commanding protested against going, as he said many of his men did not know how to put a cartridge in their rifles; but as Baker had written on January 8th asking for the immediate despatch of troops, drilled or undrilled, no delay was allowed, and the second battalion left on the 20th.

Further reinforcements were brought up to swell Baker's force from the Berber and Somali territories, by another battalion of Turks from Cairo, and some 200 *bashi-bazouk* cavalry.

Baker had by this time collected a force of nearly 4,000 men, with some Krupp and Gatling guns and rocket tubes. Part of his men were policemen in uniform, ignorant of the rudiments of military drill, many were simple *fellaheen*, whose unfitness as soldiers has been already referred to, and the rest were the sweepings of the streets of Cairo and Alexandria. The native officers were as disappointing as the men. With an army thus composed, it is not surprising if gloomy forebodings prevailed as to the result of the expedition.

Leaving a force to garrison Souakim, Baker on the 1st February moved the rest of his army to Trinkitat.

By the 2nd the last of the troops and transports arrived at Trinkitat. On the same day a fort was constructed about three miles beyond Trinkitat to protect the guns and transports whilst crossing a morass lying between the sea and the mainland. This was occupied by Sartorius with 600 blacks, the remainder returning into camp.

On the 3rd the whole of the troops, with the guns, marched out to the fort and bivouacked for the night. The force then consisted of 3,746 men.

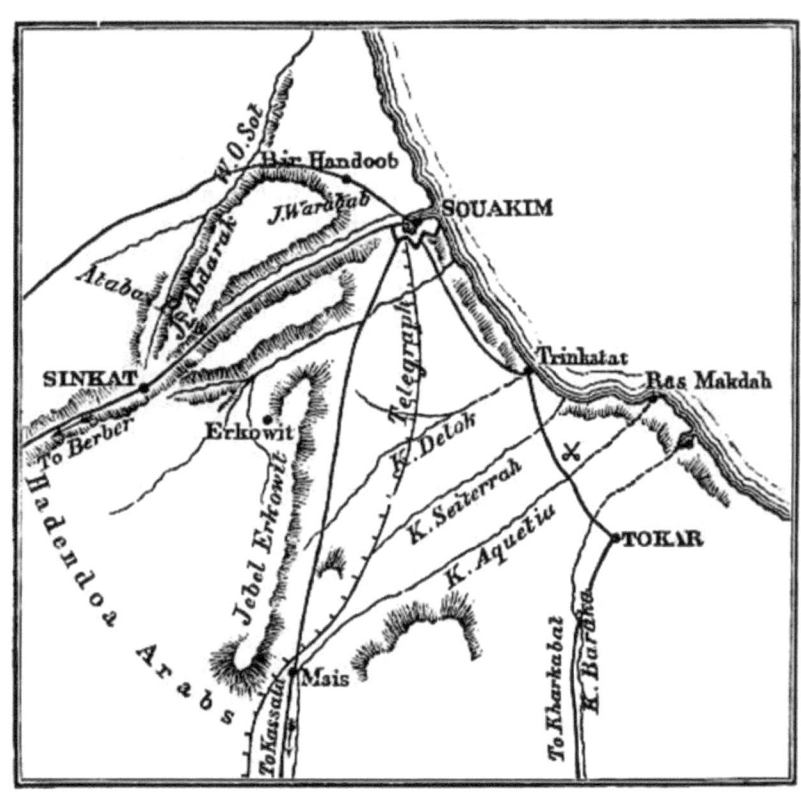

Chapter 31
Baker's Defeat at El-Teb.

The morning of the 4th February, 1884, was dull with heavy showers. The troops were paraded before daybreak. At 6.30 the force marched in the direction of Tokar. The formation was as follows:—Three infantry battalions in echelon, and marching in columns of companies; artillery and cavalry on the front and flanks, and cavalry vedettes extending all round at points a mile distant from the main body. The baggage, transported by 300 camels, was in the rear, guarded by 200 blacks.

The country was open, but scattered here and there were patches of scrub and thorny mimosa bushes. The scrub grew thicker as the force advanced; but the ground was still sufficiently open for the operations of cavalry.

After the force had marched about six miles, shots were heard from the vedettes on the left front, and small numbers of the enemy were sighted in the distance right ahead. A halt was at once called. The scouts reported that the enemy was concealed in some bushes in advance of the left front. Twice a Krupp gun was brought up and some shells fired amongst them, causing them to fall back. The march was then resumed.

Bands of Arabs were next seen on the ridges, both in front and towards the right, and in the latter direction a small body of horsemen, apparently scouts, appeared in sight about a mile off. Major Giles was ordered to charge them with the cavalry. This he at once did; but after dispersing them, and wheeling towards the front, he suddenly came upon a large number of spearmen, who sprang up from out of the brushwood. Major Giles would have charged them, but his men, after their long gallop, were in too loose order; there was no time to form, and nothing remained but to fall back upon the main body. As the cavalry retired, the mounted skirmishers joined them, and the Arabs followed close upon their heels.

In the meanwhile, the enemy opened a musketry fire simultaneously on the front and both flanks. The force was taken by surprise, though warnings of what was coming might have been detected previously, as the vedettes on the left had for some time been drawing nearer to the main body. This, however, seems to have been overlooked. The scouts were now seen hastily retreating, and a large body of the enemy came swarming over the hills. The intention seemed to be to rush upon the army on all sides.

To repel the impending attack, Sartorius Pasha, who was in advance with Baker, was sent to form the infantry into a single large square, with the camels and baggage in the centre. Two companies of the Alexandria battalion at first refused to obey orders, and stood like a panic-stricken flock of sheep; but at length the infantry formed in front, on the left flank, and also on part of the right flank. On the remaining part, however, and also along the whole of what would have been the rear of the square, the companies were a noisy, confused rabble, the soldiers being mixed up with the camels and baggage in wild disorder.

This was the state of things when the enemy, numbers of whom had been concealed in the brushwood, rushed on with loud yells, delivering their chief attack upon the left side of the force, and upon the left portion of the front line.

The frantic efforts of the Egyptians to get into proper formation, the confused din of orders, and the chaos in the rear, where 300 camels with the whole of the transport were struggling to force their way into the interior, defy description. The square was formed eventually, but the rear side was but an irregular outbulging mass of horses, mules, camels, and men, tightly wedged together, and extending towards the centre. The confusion was increased by the cavalry skirmishers, who, when the rush came, charged panic-stricken right into the square, many of them being shot by their comrades, who by this time were firing wildly in all directions.

The enemy were now rapidly encircling the entire force, which was delivering a tremendous fire mostly into the air. Under cover of the smoke the rush was made. The Egyptian infantry on being attacked broke almost at once, falling back into the centre of the square, and forcing the transport animals upon the rear of the Soudanese black troops. These last stood well for some time, but after a while became demoralized by the rush of fellow-soldiers and camels from behind.

The right of the square was not at first assailed, and here the men for some time kept up a continuous fire towards the front, with the result of killing many of their own cavalry.[1] Into the gaps made in the square the enemy now poured in hundreds, and all became panic and confusion. Sartorius, who, with his staff, was inside the square, tried to rally his men. The task was a hopeless one.

At the time the charge was made on the left flank of the column, Baker with Colonel Hay and the rest of his staff were out with the cavalry in front. Upon riding back they found that the enemy had already got between them and the square. They succeeded in cutting their way through, though the general and Hay had narrow escapes from the spears thrown at them. On nearing the square they had to run the gauntlet of the fire of the Egyptians in front, who, regardless of what was going on around, were blazing away before them. When Baker reached the square the enemy had already broken it up, and it was clear that all was lost. In eight minutes from the time of the rush the whole force was in hopeless flight.

The scene on all sides baffles description; of those inside the square very few escaped, they got jammed in amongst the mass of baggage-camels and had but a poor chance of firing or defending themselves.

The Egyptian cavalry were the first to run. They fired off their carbines into the air without taking aim at anything, and then bolted at full speed. Sartorius and his staff, who with difficulty succeeded in extricating themselves from the square, were sent off by Baker to endeavour to get the flying cavalry to halt and make a charge. After shooting two of his men, Sartorius succeeded in effecting a momentary halt; but the instant his back was turned they were off again in full flight.

The Soudanese warriors displayed the most reckless bravery. One of them was seen charging alone a whole company of infantry. The Egyptians offered no resistance, and the rebels with their two-edged swords and spears were slaughtering them by hundreds. What had been the square was now a seething, surging mass of men and camels.

The Turks and the European Police, who, in spite of the rush, had managed to get together near the guns, alone made a stand, and were annihilated almost to a man. The European officers, cut off from the

---

1. Lieutenant Cavalieri, and probably also many other officers, were killed in this way.

main body by the rush of the enemy, formed a little group apart, and were bravely defending themselves with their swords and revolvers. Morice Bey, after he had received a spear-thrust through the side, killed no less than three of his assailants. When last seen alive, he was standing in the left front face of the square alongside the camel conveying the £400, of which he was in charge, and reloading his revolver, whilst he waved on his men. Near Morice Bey, and close to the guns,[2] were Surgeon Leslie, Captain Forrestier-Walker, and Lieutenant Carroll. When last seen Dr. Leslie was sabering the Arabs who swarmed over and under the wheels of the Gatlings, and Forrestier-Walker was shooting his men as they attempted to run from the guns. All four remained at their posts until speared by the rebels.

All around, the scene was simply one of savage massacre. The Egyptians, paralyzed by fear, turned their backs, submitting to be killed rather than attempt to defend their lives; hundreds threw away their rifles, knelt down, raised their clasped hands, and prayed for mercy.

The Arabs displayed the utmost contempt for their opponents. They seized them by the neck, or speared them through the back, and then cut their throats. One was seen to pick up a rifle thrown away by a soldier and brain him with his own weapon. Another rode in among a crowd of retreating Egyptians, hacking and hewing about him with his long sword. An Egyptian officer whom he attacked, instead of defending himself, raised his shoulders to his ears, and lay down over his horse's neck. In that position, with his hands grasping the mane, he meekly took the blows of his assailant until the latter was killed by a shot from an English officer's revolver. The yells of the savages and the cries of the victims are described as appalling.

After having made his ineffectual effort to stop the cavalry, Sartorius ordered Lieutenant Maxwell to gallop after them, already in full flight to Trinkitat, and try to rally them. Maxwell overtook them. He gave his instructions to the Egyptian officer in command. The latter would not even try to get his men together. He refused thrice. Maxwell then shot him through the head. He succeeded in rallying some forty or fifty men; but another band of fugitives coming up, swept them off as in a deluge.

The road back to Trinkitat became nothing but a long line of fugitives. The men not only threw away their arms and accoutrements, but even great part of their clothing, in order to get away the faster.

---

2. So sudden and rapid was the enemy's onset that only a single round was fired, the Egyptian gunners bolting instantly afterwards.

Officers were seen to shoot their own men for the sake of obtaining their horses.

A large body of Arabs followed the flying soldiers at a steady pace, stabbing them through the back as they overtook them. Some few of the Soudanese troops who had retained their rifles occasionally turned and fired as they retreated, but most of the fugitives were too overcome by terror to resist. As the pursuers neared them, they threw themselves screaming on the ground, and were speared or sabred one after another. This carnage lasted during a pursuit of upwards of five miles.

The enemy pursued right up to Fort Baker, as the fortification on the mainland side of the lagoon was called. The garrison left to defend the work had long since taken flight. Sartorius and the surviving English officers formed a cordon across the narrow neck of land. Their purpose was to stop all but the wounded, but the endeavour failed. The fugitives in hundreds rushed on, many of them in a state of absolute nudity. The cavalry positively refused to obey the orders of the English, their own officers having already fled to Trinkitat. They even threw away their saddles, and turned their horses loose, making the rest of their way to the beach on foot, in order that they might not be sent out to fight again.

Fortunately, the enemy did not follow up the pursuit beyond Fort Baker, otherwise scarcely any of the army would have escaped. Baker was one of the last to return to the fort. Finding it impossible to rally any of the men at the fort, Sartorius was sent on to man the lines of Trinkitat, in order to protect the embarkation. Arrived at Trinkitat, he succeeded to some extent in manning the lines with the few men in whose hands rifles remained.

The fugitives ran pell-mell towards the boats, which, had they not already been aground, would have been sunk by the numbers who crowded into them. Many of the men waded into the sea in their eagerness to get off to the transports, and it was only by firing upon them with revolvers that the officers could induce them to return to the shore, and wait for their turn to embark. The first troops ordered on board were those who possessed no arms. Stores and horses were embarked during the night on board the various steamers waiting. Baker and Sartorius, and the other English officers, remained on shore to superintend the embarkation. Although there were indications of the presence of the enemy no attempt at attack was made.

The total number on the Egyptian side killed in the battle was

2,373, out of a force numbering altogether 3,746.

The following European officers were killed:—

Morice Bey, Captains Forrestier-Walker and Rucca, Lieutenants Carroll, Smith, Watkins, Cavalieri, Bertin, Morisi, de Marchi, and Dr. Leslie.

Four Krupp guns and two Gatlings were left in the hands of the enemy. As each man carried 100 rounds of ammunition, and 100 more were in reserve, at least half a million cartridges, as well as 3,000 Remington rifles and carbines, were also lost.

The enemy's losses were at first estimated at about 1,000, but it is obvious that they must have been much under that figure, for there was little real resistance. A later estimate of 350 would probably be nearly correct. Indeed, the whole of the rebel force was reckoned by the English officers as not more than 1,200, and Baker Pasha has put them as low as 1,000.

It is difficult to avoid seeing that some blame for the disaster attaches to Baker. He knew, or ought to have known, the composition of the troops he commanded, and that the short training they had undergone was insufficient to render them fit to take the field. There was, indeed, the pressing necessity for relieving the garrisons of Tokar and Sinkat, and this is about the only thing to be said in his justification.

The question whether or not Baker was surprised has been much discussed. One thing is clear. If he were not surprised, his army undoubtedly was. As already mentioned, the enemy rushed in before there was time to form the square properly. It has been argued that it could not be a surprise, because the enemy were sighted more than a mile off, and fired at as well. The obvious answer is, that if they had been sighted and fired at twenty miles off, it would have made the matter no better, if after all, the rush found Baker unprepared. The more abundant the warning, the heavier the blame upon those who failed to profit by it. There may possibly have been no surprise, in the sense of the enemy jumping up out of the bush when nobody dreamt of their existence. But to deny that the enemy were upon the force before the latter was prepared to receive them—that, in short, the battle was lost before the men had time to defend themselves—the most ardent admirer of the general will hardly attempt.

Further, military critics are of opinion that even with disciplined troops the formation of 3,000 men into a single square was a hazardous experiment. The infantry might have been drawn up in three echeloned squares. Each of these would then have been capable of giving support to the others. If one square had been broken, the others might have stood firm. The Turks, as their behaviour showed, might have been trusted to hold fast in a square of their own. A large proportion of the blacks would certainly have had more confidence had they been drawn up by themselves. But the mixture of Turks and blacks with the cowardly Egyptians was inevitably fatal. Even with good troops, Baker's arrangements would probably have led to failure. But with an army mainly composed of impressed slaves and the sweepings of the Cairo and Suez bazaars, the only result could be destruction.

Disastrous as the result was, it is probable that had the Arab assault been delivered five miles further on the march toward Trinkitat, the annihilation of the Egyptian force would have been as complete as that which befell Hicks Pasha's ill-fated column.

On the night of the 5th February, the transports, with Baker, Sartorius, and the remainder of the troops, arrived at Souakim, where the news of the disaster created a panic. In order to provide against an attack by the rebels, and also preserve order in the town, Admiral Hewett, on the 6th, landed a party of bluejackets and marines with Gatling guns. With the remnant of Baker's troops, nearly 3,000 men were available for the defence of the town, but the majority were completely demoralized. In every part of the town and on the road to the camp were heart-rending scenes, women and children weeping for husbands and fathers killed in the late battle. Even for the purpose of holding Souakim, the Egyptian troops could not be relied upon, whilst the townspeople, infected with religious mania, threatened to turn on the Europeans.

On the 9th it was decided to declare Souakim in a state of siege, and to give the British officers full powers, military and civil, over the town. The Egyptian Government were at the same time notified that in the event of Souakim being attacked it would be defended by a British force.

On the same day spies from Sinkat brought a letter from Tewfik Bey to the effect that the garrison having eaten the camels, and even the cats and dogs, were subsisting on roots and the leaves of trees.

The force at Souakim was now employed working day and night strengthening the intrenchments and fortifications. A further force of marines and bluejackets landed from the fleet, occupying the new barracks which had been made in the centre of the lines. This post was surrounded by a trench, and made impregnable. The advanced lines, about a mile in length, were to be manned by Egyptian troops in case of an attack. As a means of preventing the latter from running away, the communication between the lines to be held by them and the rest of the works was so arranged that it could be immediately cut off, in which case it was hoped that the Egyptians, having no alternative, might be induced to stand their ground.

On the 10th the charge of Souakim was handed formally over by Baker to Admiral Hewett, and the troops, numbering some 3,800 strong, were paraded. At the same time a proclamation was posted in that town announcing that the admiral had taken over the command.

On the 12th the news reached Souakim of the fall of Sinkat. It appears that the rebels surrounded the place and demanded the submission of the garrison. Tewfik Bey, with the courage which had marked his conduct throughout, declined to lay down his arms, replying that he preferred death to submission. He then sallied forth with 450 half-starved men, and attacked the rebels, killing a large number. He was finally overpowered, and the whole of his force annihilated. Tewfik seemed to have fought bravely himself, and after expending all the cartridges of his Remington carbine, defended himself with his sword. Only five men escaped the general massacre, and all the women except thirty were sold as slaves.

CHAPTER 32

Gordon's Mission

We now arrive at the period when the abandonment of the Soudan having been decided upon, the British Government confided to General Gordon the task of extricating the Egyptian garrisons scattered throughout the country. In dealing with this part of the subject the space available in the present work will not admit of more than a concise summary of events. The subject has, however, been so exhaustively dealt with by other writers, that the abbreviated account given in the following pages will probably be found sufficient for the general reader.

Charles George Gordon was born on the 28th January, 1833. Gazetted to the Royal Engineers in 1852, he took part in all the operations in the Crimea, including the first assault of the Redan. In 1860 he went to China, where he shared in the advance on Pekin. In the spring of 1862 he was summoned to Shanghai to check the advance of the Taepings, and in March, 1863, was appointed to the command of "the ever victorious army."

Of Gordon's exploits in the Chinese service it is unnecessary to dwell at any length. The Emperor bestowed on him the post of Commander-in-Chief, with the decoration of the yellow jacket and peacock's feather. The British Government promoted him to the rank of Colonel, made him a C.B., and in 1865 he returned to England.

In 1874, as already stated, Colonel Gordon succeeded Sir Samuel Baker in the Soudan. Offered £10,000 a-year salary, Gordon would only accept £2,000. Landing at Souakim, he crossed the desert to Berber, paid his first visit to Khartoum, and pushed up the Nile to Gondokoro, in September. He began by conciliating the natives and by breaking up the slave-stations. He continued Governor-General for a period of eighteen months, during which time he accomplished miracles.

When he arrived, there was a fort at Gondokoro, and one at Fatiko, 200 miles to the south, miserably garrisoned by soldiers, who dared not venture out half a mile for fear of being slaughtered the natives. When he left he had established a chain of stations from the Soudan up to the Albert Nyanza, and rendered the communication between them perfectly safe. He had, moreover, succeeded in restoring peace to the tribes of the Nile Valley, who now freely brought their produce to these stations for sale. He had checked the slave trade on the White Nile, and secured a revenue to the *khedive*'s exchequer, without having recourse to oppression. He had been the means of establishing satisfactory relations with King M'tesa, the powerful ruler of Uganda, had mapped out the White Nile from Khartoum almost up to the Victoria Nyanza, and had opened water communication between Gondokoro and the lakes.

In October, 1876, Gordon, judging that he had done enough for the Soudan, started northward, halted at Cairo to request Cherif Pasha to inform the *khedive* that he intended quitting his service, and on the 24th December reached London.

Egypt, however, had not yet done with him. Gordon remained only a short time in retirement before he was again called to Egypt. In February, 1877, Ismail Pasha made him not only Governor-General of the Soudan, but also of Darfur and the Equatorial Provinces, a country 1,640 miles long and 660 miles broad.

Gordon hastened to Khartoum, the seat of his new government. It was time. The Soudan had been drained of Egyptian troops for the support of the *sultan* in his war with Russia. Darfur was in revolt, and its garrisons were beleaguered.

Arrived at Khartoum, he at once set to work to overthrow every tradition of Oriental rule. In less than a month he revolutionized the whole administration, abolished the *courbash*, checked bribery, arranged for a water-supply to the city, and commenced the disbandment of the Turks and *bashi-bazouks*, who, instead of acting as a frontier guard, favoured the passage of slave-caravans.

In February, 1878, he was summoned by telegraph to the Egyptian capital to lend his aid in arranging the finances of the country, which had fallen into hopeless confusion. Reaching Cairo on the 7th March, he was received with every honour, and placed at table on the *khedive*'s right hand. He now fell into disfavour with the Egyptian Government. He was too much in earnest and spoke out too openly, and within a month started off in quasi-disgrace to inspect the south-eastern provinces of his government. After dismissing an old enemy, Reouf Pasha, from the governorship of Harrar, he made his way back to Khartoum by Souakim and Berber, and for months remained engaged in settling questions of finance and the affairs of the province.

In July, 1879, Gordon received the news of the *khedive* Ismail's deposition, and started at once for Cairo. He told Tewfik, the new *khedive*, that he did not intend to go back to the Soudan, but he nevertheless accepted a mission to Abyssinia to settle matters with King Johannes. Physically worn out by his exertions, he came to England for a time, visiting on his way thither the ex-*khedive* at Naples.

On the appointment in May, 1880, of Lord Ripon to the Governor-Generalship of India, Gordon accepted the post of private secretary to the *marquis*, but resigned it on the 3rd of June, feeling, as he expressed it, "the hopelessness of doing anything to the purpose."

On the invitation of the Chinese authorities he soon afterwards left India for China, between which country and Russia differences had arisen, and after successfully exerting his influence in the maintenance of peace, left China the following August.

In the spring of 1881 Gordon went to the Mauritius as Commandant of the Royal Engineers, remaining for a year, when he was made Major-General. In the following May he proceeded to the Cape to aid the Colonial authorities in solving the Basuto difficulty.

Shortly after his return to England he left for Palestine, where he spent a year in retirement outside Jerusalem, devoting much time to proving, to the horror of pious tourists, that the commonly received "holy places" were not the right ones after all, and working out the scheme for a Jordan Canal.

He then undertook a mission to the Congo River for the King of the Belgians, and only relinquished his post on the British Government requiring his services in the Soudan.

Opinions in Egypt were much divided on the subject of Gordon's mission and his chances of success. His courage, energy, and disinterestedness were beyond all doubt. There were, however, uncertainties, not to say eccentricities, in his character, which led many persons to question whether he was a fit person for the task to which he was called. That he had formerly an immense influence over the tribes of the Soudan was unquestionable. But people remembered that years had passed away since that period, and argued that Gordon, returning to the Soudan with half-a-dozen followers, would not be the Gordon of Ismail's time, backed by his prestige and at the head of a powerful armed force. The difficulty, however, was to find anyone else. It was Gordon or nobody, and the critics were compelled to shake their heads and hope all would be for the best.

Gordon's original instructions were dated the 18th January, 1884. He was to proceed at once to Egypt, to report on the military situation in the Soudan, and on the measures which it might be advisable to take for the security of the Egyptian garrisons and for the safety of the European population in Khartoum. He was to consider and report upon the best mode of effecting the evacuation of the interior of the Soudan, and upon the manner in which the safety and the good administration by the Egyptian Government of the ports on the seacoast could best be secured. He was also to give especial consideration to the question of the steps that might usefully be taken to counteract the stimulus which it was feared might be given to the slave trade by the insurrectionary movement and by the withdrawal of Egyptian authority from the interior. He was to perform such other duties as the Egyptian Government might desire to intrust to him. He was to be accompanied by Colonel Stewart.

Gordon received new and more extended instructions from Sir Evelyn Baring, at Cairo, on January 25th. The following are their salient passages:—

> It is believed that the number of Europeans at Khartoum is very small, but it has been estimated by the local authorities that some 10,000 to 15,000 people will wish to go northward from Khartoum only, when the Egyptian garrison is withdrawn. These people are native Christians, Egyptian *employés*, their wives and children, &c. The government of His Highness the *khedive* is earnestly solicitous that no effort should be spared to insure the retreat both of these people and of the Egyptian garrison without loss of life. As regards the most opportune time, and the best method for effecting the retreat, whether of the garrison or of the civil populations, it is neither necessary nor desirable that you should receive detailed instructions.
>
> You will bear in mind that the main end to be pursued is the evacuation of the Soudan. This policy was adopted, after very full discussion, by the Egyptian Government, on the advice of Her Majesty's Government. It meets with the full approval of His Highness the *khedive* and of the present Egyptian Ministry.

You are of opinion that the 'restoration of the country should be made to the different petty *sultans* who existed at the time of Mehemet Ali's conquest, and whose families still exist;' and that an endeavour should be made to form a confederation of those *sultans*. In this view the Egyptian Government entirely concurs.

A credit of £100,000 has been opened for you at the Finance Department, and further sums will be supplied to you on your requisition when this sum is exhausted.

Gordon's final instructions were given him by the Egyptian Government in a *firman* appointing him Governor-General. By this *firman* he was empowered to carry into execution the evacuation of the respective territories and the withdrawal of the troops, civil officials, and such of the inhabitants as wished to leave for Egypt. He was, if possible, after completing the evacuation, to take steps for establishing an organized government in the different provinces.

The significance of the alteration in Gordon's instructions will be perceived from Lord Granville's remark at the close of his summary of Gordon's new duties, in a despatch of March 28th, that "Her Majesty's Government, bearing in mind the exigencies of the occasion, concurred in these instructions," which virtually altered General Gordon's mission from one of advising and reporting to that of directing the evacuation not only of Khartoum, but of the whole Soudan, and also of establishing an organized government.

Gordon left Cairo on January 26th, 1884, and arrived at Khartoum on the 18th February. He held a *levée* at the Mudirieh, the entire population being admitted. On his way between the Mudirieh and the palace about 1,000 persons pressed forward, kissing his hands and feet, and calling him "*Sultan*," "Father," and "Saviour of Kordofan." General Gordon and Colonel Stewart at once opened offices in the palace, granting admittance to everyone with a grievance and giving all a careful hearing. The government books, recording from time immemorial the outstanding debts of the overtaxed people, were publicly burned in front of the Palace. The *courbashes*, whips, and implements for administering the bastinado, were all placed on the blazing pile. Gordon created a native council of the local notables. Then he visited the hospital and arsenal.

With Colonels Stewart and De Cöetlogon and the English Consul he visited the prison, and found it to be a perfect den of misery. Two hundred beings loaded with chains lay there. They were of all ages, boys and old men, some having never been tried, some having been proved innocent, but left in prison, some arrested on suspicion and detained there more than three years, others merely prisoners of war. Gordon at once commenced to demolish this Bastille. Before it was dark scores of prisoners had had their chains struck off. In the evening the town was in a blaze of illumination, the bazaar being hung with cloth and coloured lamps and the private houses decorated. There was also a display of fireworks by the population, who indulged in rejoicings till after midnight.

Gordon's next act was to issue a proclamation repealing the existing laws against slavery. As a good deal of indignation has been expressed at this step, it is only fair to give his explanation.

Gordon in his *Diary* says:

> Was it not announced that the Soudan was going to be abandoned, and consequently that the Soudanese were going to be allowed to follow their own devices (which are decidedly slave-huntingly inclined)? What possible influence could my saying that that feeble Treaty of 1877 was not going to be enforced have on people who were going to be abandoned?

Chapter 33

Souakim Expedition, 1884

The defeat of Baker's force, following, as it did, the annihilation of Hicks' army, created a most painful impression in England.

The situation was this—two armies led by English commanders and officered in great measure by Englishmen had been successively destroyed. Of the garrisons of Sinkat and of Tokar, one was known to have been sacrificed, and the other might share its fate any day. Besides this, Souakim itself was seriously threatened.

With regard both to Hicks' and Baker's expeditions the government was severely attacked both in and out of Parliament.

Of the character of the force which Baker had assembled at Trinkitat, the British Ministers had full information. Before it started there was a consensus of opinion that it was foredoomed. The special correspondent of the *Daily News* telegraphed on February 1st, 1884, that:

> Baker Pasha's force is unequal to the task of the relief of Sinkat, and if the troops whose chiefs have visited our camp prove faithless, Sinkat will be lost.

The *Standard's* correspondent sent telegrams to the same effect. On February 1st the *St. James's Gazette* said "there was a very bad chance for Baker Pasha;" while the *Spectator* declared that "the chances against the success of the expedition were as three to one." The *Times* did not think Baker Pasha's enterprise a too hopeful one, considering the class of men of which his force was composed, and added:

> .... that it would be a calamity if the fate of Hicks' expedition were to be risked again after a warning so recent and solemn.

Opinion amongst military men, both in Egypt and at home, was to the same effect.

And yet Baker, like Hicks, was allowed to lead his rabble on to destruction. England, it was true, had declared that it took no responsibility as regards the despatch of Hicks' army; but England at the time of both disasters was omnipotent in Egypt. The country, bound hand and foot, was in the hands of the British Government. Under these circumstances, to permit was to do. The existence of power involved responsibility. The government of the *khedive* after the events of 1882 was little more than a shadow. England had only to advise, and Egypt to obey. Nevertheless, the Egyptian Government was permitted to send forth two wretchedly equipped expeditions, one to Kordofan and another to Souakim, both almost inevitably doomed to destruction.

The matter was not rendered more pleasant by the reflection that whilst Baker was sent with an impossible army to perform what, with his force, was a hopeless task, a British Army capable of accomplishing with ease all that was wanted remained idle in its barracks at Cairo. The shortsightedness of British policy was shown by the fact that this very force had after all to be despatched to accomplish what Baker had failed in. Unfortunately, however, it was destined, like many other operations recorded in this work, to be too late.

Public opinion had been especially moved by the news of the fall of Sinkat and the massacre of its brave defenders, and it was felt that an effort should be made to save, if possible, the garrison of Tokar from a similar fate. For this purpose it was decided that a British force should be sent to Souakim.

The force to be employed was to be chiefly drawn from the Army of Occupation in Egypt, and General Stephenson was instructed by telegraph to make the necessary preparations. He was informed that the object of the expedition was to relieve the Tokar garrison if it could hold out, and, if not, to take any measures necessary for the safety of the Red Sea ports. He was to select the three best battalions under his command, and these, with the Royal Irish Fusiliers (then on their way from India), the York and Lancaster Regiment from Aden, and a battalion of Marines, were to form an infantry brigade. The garrison of Alexandria was to be removed to Cairo while the expedition lasted, and orders were sent to the fleet to hold Alexandria temporarily.

The 10th and 19th Hussars, the Mounted Infantry, and any trustworthy native horsemen at Souakim, were to constitute the mounted force. The 19th Hussars were to be mounted with native horses taken from the Egyptian cavalry under Sir Evelyn Wood. The baggage was to be on the lowest possible scale, as the troops were to be back in

Cairo in three weeks. Tents were to accompany the force to Souakim or Trinkitat, as the case might be. The greatest publicity was to be given to the determination to relieve Tokar by British soldiers.

Messages were despatched to the garrison at Tokar, urging them to hold out, as relief was on the way, and the expedition was hurrying forward with all possible speed.

The command of the expedition was given to Major-General Sir Gerald Graham, who had led the Second Brigade at Tel-el-Kebir. Generals Davis and Redvers Buller were to accompany him.

Every effort was made to send off the expedition as early as possible. The troops from Egypt embarked at Suez and proceeded to Souakim and Trinkitat. Between the 16th and 18th February the 10th and 19th Hussars, two batteries of Royal Artillery, the 3rd Battalion of the 60th King's Royal Rifles, the 42nd Royal Highlanders (Black Watch), the 75th Gordon Highlanders, the 65th York and Lancaster Regiment, the 89th Royal Irish Fusiliers, the 26th Company of the Royal Engineers, and 100 Mounted Infantry left for the scene of operations. Detachments of Marines from the vessels of the Mediterranean Squadron were also told off to accompany Graham's force.

The reorganized Egyptian Army under Sir Evelyn Wood was anxious to take part in the expedition, but the British Government had declined to sanction this, on the ground that the Egyptian army was expressly raised for the defence of Egypt proper, excluding the Soudan.

General Graham left Suez with his headquarters on the 18th February and proceeded to Souakim.

Meanwhile Admiral Hewett had communicated with Osman Digna and warned him that a British force was going to relieve Tokar, and at the same time informed him that the English Government wished to avoid useless bloodshed, and would not interfere with the tribes if they did not oppose the expedition. Osman Digna replied that he felt himself obliged to take Tokar, and must, therefore, fight the English, and the responsibility for any bloodshed, he added, would rest with the latter.

On the 22nd of February an Egyptian soldier, who escaped from Tokar, stated that the garrison was then going over to the rebels, and that the commandant was treating for capitulation on the following day. Spies who arrived subsequently said that they could not approach Tokar owing to the presence of rebels in the vicinity, and on the 24th, whilst the British forces were disembarking at Trinkitat, news was received that Tokar had already fallen.

As to the precise manner in which this was brought about some little mystery exists, but so far as can be ascertained the circumstances attending the fall of Tokar appear to have been as follows. The garrison had for some time been harassed by a continual fire kept up by the Krupp guns and rifles in the hands of the rebels. The soldiers were despairing of relief, and the officers more or less disaffected. The bulk of the inhabitants were in favour of a surrender. According to some accounts, the governor for some while resisted their importunities; according to others, he was only too willing to hand over the town to the besiegers. In any case, negotiations were on the 19th opened with them through a merchant in Tokar, who had been imprisoned by the authorities as a sympathiser with the *Mahdi*, and who was now despatched as an emissary to the rebel camp. The surrender was fixed for the next day.

The emissary returned to Tokar the same evening accompanied by 100 rebels, who were admitted to the town. One officer and a few soldiers still wanted to fight, but they were over-ruled by the others, who preferred ceding the town to Mussulmans rather than to Christians. During the night such soldiers as remained loyal escaped from the town, and several of them, journeying by night, made their way to Souakim. The next day the town was finally surrendered.

There seems to have been no valid reason for giving up Tokar, there being an abundance of provisions, and 45,000 rounds of ball cartridge left. Although the town had been shelled and exposed to a heavy rifle fire for five days, the total loss suffered during the bombardment was only two men killed and twelve wounded out of a garrison of 300 men. The rebel force numbered less than 1,000.

Some doubt was at first felt as to the correctness of the news of the surrender of Tokar. In any case the expedition was now at Trinkitat, and it was resolved not to countermand it.

On the 26th Graham was instructed that, in the event of Tokar having fallen, the main object would be to protect Souakim. The next day Mr. Gladstone stated in Parliament that the Cabinet saw no reason to doubt the accuracy of the report of the fall of Tokar. Notwithstanding this, it was decided to continue to push on with Graham's expedition.

The real reason for this decision is not altogether clear. Probably the truth is that the British Government was unwilling that the preparations which had been made should be in vain. Possibly, also, it was desired that the army, being on the spot, should strike a blow at Osman Digna before coming away. From a despatch sent to Graham on the 24th February it would seem that the objects to be attained by persevering with the expedition were to march on El-Teb, to protect any fugitives, and to bury the English dead, after which it was to return by land to Souakim. These objects it was still in General Graham's power to attain.

On the 26th, after a preliminary reconnaissance by the Hussars and Mounted Infantry, the Gordon Highlanders and Royal Irish Fusiliers moved across the lagoon and took possession of Fort Baker. From early morning the enemy had shown in considerable numbers in the vicinity of the fort, but as the troops advanced the former fell back. A number also showed in force on the ridge nearly two miles distant. Upon the cavalry advancing, they still held their ground and opened fire at long range; but it being evident that a yet larger force was still behind the ridge, it was not considered advisable to charge.

The two succeeding days were occupied in transporting a supply of water and three days' provisions for the whole army.

On the 27th the enemy massed some two miles off, and numbering about 2,000 strong, kept up continuous firing on the English sentries and outposts. A last effort was now made to treat with the rebels. Major Harvey, accompanied by Colonel Burnaby, rode with an escort to the rising ground two miles distant. Here he planted a white flag with a letter attached to the staff, enjoining the troops to disperse and to send delegates to Khartoum to consult with General Gordon as to the settlement of the Soudan provinces. The enemy maintained continuous firing at the party, but, after it had withdrawn, took the flag and letter, but left no reply.

On the afternoon of the 28th Graham and the remainder of the force proceeded to the fort and bivouacked for the night. Each man carried seventy rounds. No transport was taken.

The two infantry brigades were disposed as follows:—1st Brigade under General Redvers Buller—2nd Brigade under General Davis. For transport there were 600 camels, with 350 mules, and 100 camels for ambulance work. There was also a camel battery of 80 animals and 100 men.

CHAPTER 34

Graham's Victory At El-Teb.

On the morning of the 28th February the bugles sounded the *reveillé* about five, and instantly all were on the alert. The camp fires were relighted, breakfast was got ready, and although the men had been drenched by the rain which fell during the night, everyone was in excellent spirits. At 8 o'clock the order was given to advance, the men having fallen in some time previously.

The force, though nominally in square, was formed in a long rectangle, having an interior space of about 500 yards by 150 yards. The Gordon Highlanders, in line, were in front; in the rear the Royal Highlanders (Black Watch); on the right the Royal Irish Fusiliers, with four companies of the King's Royal Rifles; and on the left the York and Lancaster Regiment and the Royal Marines. Intervals were left at the angles for the guns and Gatlings, the Naval Brigade occupying the front and the Royal Artillery the rear angles. In the centre were the staffs of Generals Graham and Buller, the officers of the Royal Engineers, and the medical department. The front and left of the square were covered by a squadron of the 10th Hussars, the right by a troop of the 19th Hussars, and the rest of the cavalry were in the rear, under the command of General Stewart. The total force, including the officers and men of the Naval Brigade, was a little under 4,000 in number. The accompanying diagram over the page shows the formation:—

The men marched off with their water-bottles filled and one day's rations. The only transport animals were those carrying ammunition and surgical appliances; all these were kept together in the centre of the square.

The rain which had fallen caused the ground for the first two miles to be very heavy. The Naval Brigade and the Royal Artillery dragged their guns by hand, so that frequent halts had to be made to rest the

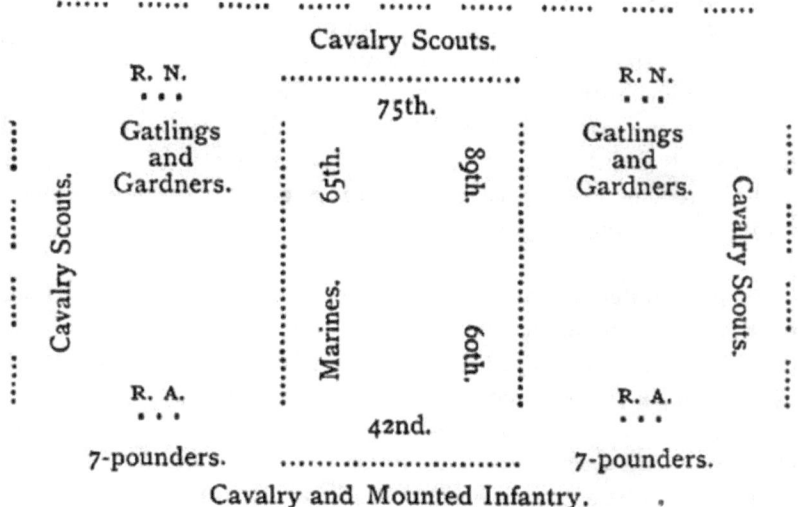

men. The force kept well to the north, and when about a mile from Fort Baker, amidst low sand-hills thick with scrub, the enemy opened fire with their Remingtons. The range, however, was too great, and no damage was done. A few hundreds of the assailants were seen on the high ground on the front and flanks. They retired very slowly before Graham's force, keeping within 1,200 yards.

The route taken was somewhat to the left of the site of Baker's defeat, which therefore lay between the squares and the enemy's position. The infantry were thus spared the unpleasant sight which the remains of his army presented. The Hussars, however, rode over the very spot. The air was polluted with the smell of the decomposed bodies, the first of which was met with about a mile from Fort Baker. The course taken by the fugitives from the scene of the battle was marked by a belt about three miles in length and a hundred yards in breadth. Here and there a few of the runaways had straggled from the line of flight, only to leave their bones in the adjoining bush. Most of the victims appeared to have fallen on their faces, as if speared or cut down by their pursuers from behind.

On the spot where Baker's square had been destroyed, the dead, in every attitude of painful contortion, lay piled in irregular heaps, literally two or three feet deep over an area of at least 300 yards. The bodies were all stripped, scarcely a vestige of clothes remaining. Of some only the bare skeletons were left, but for the most part the remains had not been attacked by vultures or wild animals, though all, or nearly all, had been savagely mutilated. Just beyond this spot was a low mound of earth, covered with sticks, from which waved strips of calico of different colours, marking the graves of the fallen rebels.

During the march, H.M.S. *Sphinx*, off Trinkitat, at about 9.30, fired four rounds, but the range was far too great to be effective, and as her shells were falling more than a mile short of the enemy's position, and, moreover, coming dangerously near the cavalry, she was signalled to cease firing.

The Mounted Infantry were now sent forward on the left to get in touch with the enemy, who appeared obstinate about moving, although not wholly inclined to fight. About 10 o'clock reports came in from the front that the enemy were intrenched on the left.

The defences consisted of shallow earthworks facing west by north, somewhat semi-circular in shape. These were defended on the south-west side by a battery on a mound (marked "A" on the plan), mounting two Krupp guns and a brass howitzer; and on the north-east side by another battery ("G" on the plan) armed with two Krupp guns, two brass howitzers, and one Gatling. All these guns had been taken from Baker's force, and, as was afterwards ascertained, were worked by Egyptian gunners from the garrison of Tokar. Half-way between the two batteries was a brick building, the remains of a disused sugar factory, and also, lying on the ground, an old iron boiler. Rifle-pits were scattered about on two sides of the position. These pits were constructed to hold about twenty men each, and were scooped out of the sand in such a way that an attacking force in front might get right up to them before becoming aware of their existence. In the rear of the position were the wells, some twelve in number, and the buildings forming the village of El-Teb.

At 11.20 Graham found himself, at a distance of 800 yards, immediately opposite the south-west battery ("A"). Not caring to attack the position in front, he moved his force off to the right, on which the enemy opened fire with case and shell. Fortunately their aim was bad, so that few casualties occurred, and Graham, moving steadily on without returning their fire, succeeded in getting his force round on the left flank of the work, which was on the proper left rear of the enemy's line.

Here the square was halted, the men were directed to lie down, and four guns of the Royal Artillery and the machine-guns were brought into action at a range of about 900 yards. The practice from

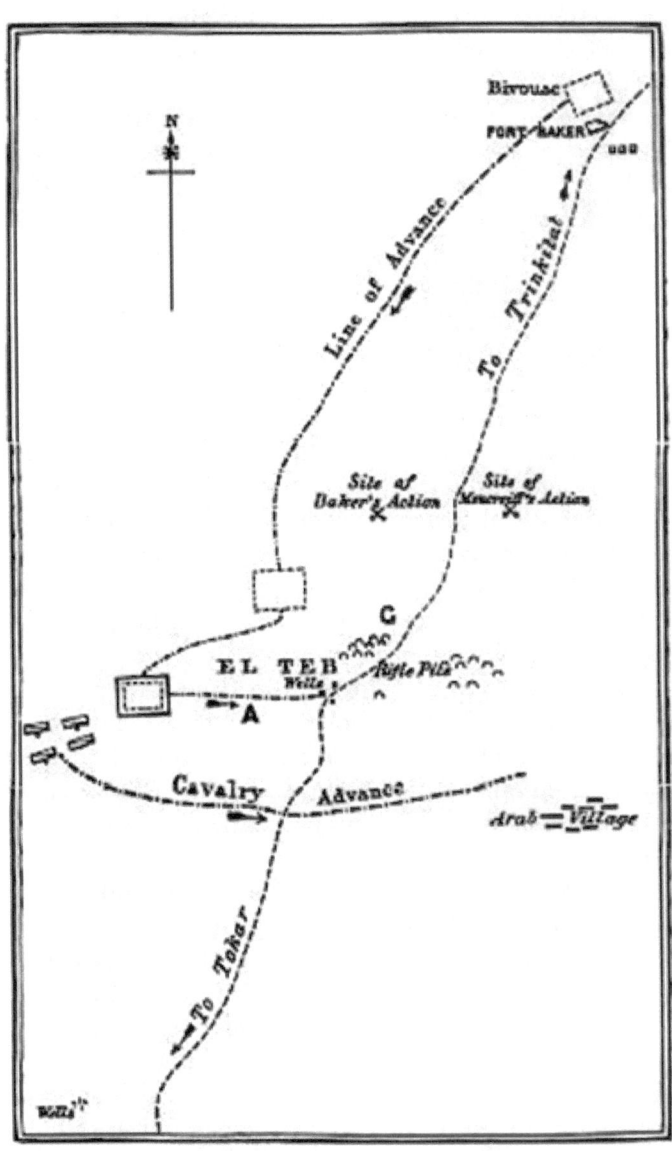

BATTLE OF EL-TEB.

the guns was carried on with remarkable accuracy and deliberation, and with the help of the machine-guns of the Naval Brigade, which poured in a stream of bullets, the two Krupp guns in the battery, taken as they were slightly in reverse, were speedily silenced, and their gunners driven off.

The bugles then sounded and the infantry advanced, the square moving by its left face, which by the flank movement was opposite to the work attacked. The fighting line was thus composed of the York and Lancaster, supported by the Marines, the Gordon Highlanders and Royal Highlanders, with bagpipes playing, moving in columns of fours on either flank, the rear of the square being formed by the King's Royal Rifles and the Royal Irish Fusiliers. The York and Lancaster advanced steadily, firing with their Martinis as they did so, till within a short distance of the works, when, with a cheer, they and the bluejackets on the right carried them with a rush, and captured the guns.

This, however, was not accomplished without the most determined resistance on the part of the enemy. The Soudanese clung to their position with desperation. They were in no military order, but scattered about, taking advantage of the abundant cover which the ground afforded. They made several fierce counter-attacks, sometimes singly and sometimes in groups, on the advancing line, many hand-to-hand fights taking place.

It was marvellous to see how the Soudanese warriors came on, heedless and fearless of death, shouting and brandishing their weapons. To the right and left they fell, but those who survived, even when wounded, rushed on. A few, notwithstanding the rifle fire, got within five or ten paces of the square, thus proving how many bullets it takes to kill a man.

When the York and Lancaster made their rapid advance, they were met by a rush of several hundreds of the enemy, before which the battalion at first recoiled some thirty or forty yards (the distance they had outrun their comrades), thereby leaving a corner of the square open. The regiment fell back a little, and the Marines advanced to their support; the square was quickly closed, and in a few minutes all was well again, the troops being as steady as possible. The check was but momentary, and they again advanced, firing with great precision.

The ground at this place was broken and difficult. The formation of the troops consequently became irregular, and gaps were here and there left in the square. A halt for a few minutes had therefore to be called before the final rush, in order to re-form the column and also to distribute fresh ammunition.

Colonel Burnaby was the first to mount the parapet of the battery, with some men of the Black Watch. He was armed with a double-barrelled shot-gun, a deadly weapon when used at close quarters.

Captain Wilson, of the *Hecla*, seeing a marine closely pressed in front of the battery, rushed to the man's assistance, and whilst surrounded by five or six of the enemy, broke his sword over one of them. The others closing round him, he tackled them with his sword-hilt, and escaped with only a sword-cut through his helmet, which wounded the scalp.

No sooner was the south-west battery taken than the Krupp guns in it were wheeled round and directed upon the other battery to the north-east of the position, which they soon silenced.

At this period General Stewart, apparently under the impression that the infantry had finished their part of the work, moved his cavalry round the present right flank of the square, and executed the charge referred to later on. But the fight was not yet over: the enemy was still in possession of the village and wells of El-Teb, as well as of the north-east battery, to capture which the force had to fight its way to the left across the intrenchments from the southern to the northern extremity. By this movement the Black Watch entered into the front or fighting line. But, in reality, the square formation was broken up so that the whole infantry division became an irregular semi-circular line, with the Black Watch and York and Lancaster in the central and more advanced position of it, and the Royal Irish Fusiliers and Gordon Highlanders on the wings.

The enemy defended their remaining position with extraordinary determination. In front were the brick sugar factory and iron boiler already described, and all round were the rifle-pits, to which they clung with desperate energy. This position the Black Watch, which, in General Graham's despatch, were described as being at this moment "somewhat out of hand," were ordered to charge, a movement which would have caused great loss of life. The regiment, instead of at once obeying, advanced with deliberation, and irregularly forming up, poured a converging fire upon the factory. Several shells were also fired into it to dislodge the enemy, but the guns were too small to effect a breach. At length the Naval Brigade, with the Gatlings, took the building, the sailors firing their revolvers through the windows whilst the Highlanders shot down the enemy as they tried to escape. The building was found full of bodies, and round the boiler no less than a hundred Soudanese lay dead.

During the whole time of the attack the enemy never seemed to dream of asking for quarter. When they found their retreat cut off they simply charged out, hurled their spears at the attacking force, and fell dead, riddled with bullets.

About 2 p.m. the force advanced upon and occupied the northeast battery without resistance. The last work on the right of the position was occupied by the Gordon Highlanders. The enemy had, by this time, given up all idea of further fighting, and as the smoke rolled away the defeated Soudanese were seen streaming away in the direction of Tokar and Souakim, and the battle of El-Teb was won.

To return to the cavalry under Brigadier-General Stewart. His instructions were "to avoid engaging the enemy until their formation was broken, and until they were in full retreat." Bearing this in mind, the question may well be asked, Why did the cavalry charge at that particular stage of the action when the enemy's force was neither broken nor in retreat?

As, when the artillery have produced the first effectual impression on an enemy, the infantry advance to perform their task, so the cavalry strike in to complete the confusion and ruin caused by the infantry. But in this case, not only were the enemy not half beaten, but the charge was made, according to Graham's despatch, "against masses of the enemy not yet engaged."

To describe the charge: after the storming of the battery "A" the cavalry was massed behind the left rear of the square, ready to act at any given point when necessary. At 12.20 p.m., as the square advanced, numbers of the enemy were visible in a plain beyond the ridge, and Stewart, swinging his force round the infantry's right, gave the order to charge. The cavalry were in three lines, the 10th Hussars, under Colonel Wood, forming the first; the 19th Hussars, under Lieutenant-Colonel Barrow, the second; and one hundred of the 10th, under Lieutenant-Colonel Webster, formed the third. This formation was maintained when the cavalry began to gallop, causing the enemy to split into two large bodies right and left.

After a gallop of three miles the first two lines overtook some of the Soudanese. Amongst them was a woman, who miraculously escaped through the first line unhurt. Being perceived and spared by the second, she showed her gratitude by firing a rifle after the men who had saved her.

There was now only a small party of the enemy in front, and a halt was sounded. At this moment an orderly overtook Barrow, informing him that Webster, with the third line, was being "cut up." That officer, after the first two lines had passed, had suddenly discovered away on his right a body of the enemy appearing out of the brushwood; a hundred, or, according to another account, two hundred, of these were mounted. They carried two-handed swords, and rode barebacked. In their rear were numbers of spearmen on foot. Webster wheeled his squadron to the right, and in a moment found himself engaged with a large force of the enemy.

On receipt of the orderly's report the word was instantly given "Right about wheel." Barrow's two squadrons then became the front line, and Wood's the rear. As the two lines rode back to Webster's assistance they found themselves confronted by some hundreds of Soudanese, mounted and on foot. Some thirty horsemen rode with full force boldly against the first line of the advancing squadron. Three of them came straight through safely, and, undismayed either by the shock they had survived, or the equal peril of the second line sweeping down upon them, wheeled their horses with wonderful rapidity, not hesitating to follow in full pursuit the squadrons from which they had so narrowly escaped.

Very little harm, however, resulted from this attack. The real opposition came from the spearmen, who lay scattered among the hillocks and mounds of sand, and who, rising at the precise moment, attempted to hamstring the horses of the cavalry, or else drove home their heavy spears, throwing them whenever they were unable to reach their foe by hand. The spears were like Zulu *assegais* in form, except that, being weighted with a roll of iron at the extreme end of the shaft, they had a greater momentum and piercing power. The Soudanese also threw boomerang-like clubs of mimosa wood at the horses' legs, thus bringing many of the animals to their knees.

Barrow, whilst leading the charge, was struck by a thrown spear which pierced his arm and side. He, nevertheless, rode on until his horse was brought down in the manner above described.[1]

---

1. Colonel Barrow's life was saved by Quartermaster-Sergeant Marshall, who caught him as he was falling, and seizing a loose horse belonging to a dismounted trooper, was, with the assistance of the latter, placing the colonel on it, when it fell. Marshall and the trooper then supported the colonel through the scattered masses of the enemy. The danger run may be imagined from the fact that Barrow and a corporal of the 19th, named Murray, were the only two who, when unhorsed, escaped with their lives. Murray had no less than four horses either speared, hamstrung, or clubbed—a circumstance almost unexampled.

The first line, missing its commander, and not fully realising the position, swept straight on, whereas Barrow would no doubt have wheeled it to the right. Stewart, who was riding somewhat in advance of the left flank of the second line, noting at once the flaw, drove spurs into his horse, and with his staff galloped hard to bring round the erring squadrons. It was a race between this small band, the general and Staff, and a number of the enemy rushing from the right. The former won, and caught up the first line; but in this conflict, during the sweep of the 10th Hussars, as they followed, wheeling with admirable precision to the left, the chief casualties of the day occurred. Lieutenant Probyn, of the 9th Bengal Cavalry, attached to the 10th Hussars, was among the first to fall. Of the General's four orderlies one was killed and two were wounded. Major Slade fell dead, pierced with spear-wounds, and his horse hamstrung to the bone.[2] Another officer killed at the same time was Lieutenant Freeman.

After the 10th and 19th had charged again and again through the scattered groups of spearmen, doing but little execution on account of the unsteadiness of the Egyptian horses,[3] each line dismounted one of its squadrons, and poured volley after volley into the enemy; after which the Hussars rode back to El-Teb, having lost heavily, in fact, one man for every eight engaged.

The loss in killed on the British side was 4 officers and 26 men; in wounded, 17 officers and 142 soldiers and marines. The officers killed were Lieutenant Freeman, 19th Hussars; Major Slade, 10th Hussars; Lieutenant Probyn, Bengal Cavalry; and Quartermaster Wilkins, King's Royal Rifles.

The magnitude of the loss sustained in the cavalry charge will be apparent when it is considered that out of a total of thirty killed no less than thirteen, or nearly half, belonged to the small force under General Stewart. It is singular that, with the exception of the loss sustained by the cavalry, all the casualties during the fight were caused by the enemy's bullets.

Of the enemy's force several estimates were made. It is obvious that their total number was much under the figure of 10,000 originally reported by General Graham. Another authority puts the numbers who

---

2. Major Slade was not missed until the cavalry had for some time been returning to the square. He is supposed to have been killed in an attempt to help Lieutenant Probyn. Twelve spear wounds were found on his body. 3. Most of these were wholly untrained, and the rest only understood one movement, *viz.*, that of retreating in the presence of the enemy.

fought at the intrenchments and wells at 3,000. In addition to these was the force held in reserve, and attacked by the cavalry. These were probably 2,000 or 3,000 more.

It is stated in some of the accounts that 2,000 were slain and 5,000 put *hors de combat*. Unfortunately it is impossible to arrive at strict accuracy in such matters, but it is a fact that 825 bodies were counted on the field of battle.

In any case the defeat was a conspicuous one, more especially considering the comparatively small loss sustained by Graham's force.

The chief lesson taught by the engagement is the tremendous power of the breechloader in steady hands. Against such weapons, carried by British soldiers, all the courage of the Soudanese was of no avail. With the exception of one moment, when the hurried advance of the front line threatened to imperil the square, the enemy never succeeded in getting near enough to be a source of serious danger; and but for the cavalry attack, the utility of which, as already remarked, is open to considerable doubt, the victory would have been won with almost a total immunity from loss.

Of the tribes who fought against Graham one is said to have been totally exterminated. Their reckless courage in action was the theme of general admiration. Both during and after the fight their principal aim seemed to be to sell their lives as dearly as possible. Lads of twelve, after fighting desperately, fell dead into the shelter-trenches, with their teeth set and their hands grasping their spears.

It was almost impossible to save the wounded or to take prisoners, as the dying, even in their last moments, strove to thrust or cut with knife, spear, or sword. The troops as they pressed forward had to shoot or bayonet all they came near, for the wounded would start up and strive to kill or maim their foes, a grim pleasure lighting up their faces whenever they could bury their weapons in a soldier's body.

A marine roving about among the enemy's dead, behind the boiler more than once referred to, was killed by a wounded Soudanese hidden among the slain. The Arab with a knife fairly disembowelled the English soldier, and was himself bayoneted on the spot almost immediately afterwards.

Sometime after the battle, and when the troops were searching about the enemy's works, a boy of about twelve years of age, unobserved among a heap of dead and dying, started up and rushed with a drawn knife on two soldiers, who, taken aback at first, ran some yards, and then turned and shot him. At some distance outside the lines a

Soudanese sprang like a cat upon the back of one of the soldiers and tried to cut his throat; an officer, rushing up, shot the savage through the heart with his revolver, barely in time to save the soldier's life.

The coolness of the British soldier seems never to have deserted him, and gave rise to some scenes which might almost be described as humorous. When the rush was made and the bulk of the assailants either killed or driven back, one Soudanese warrior, spear in hand, dashed singly forward. With a "hop, skip, and a jump," he cleared the front rank of the square, only, however, to be adroitly caught on the point of the bayonet of a soldier behind. "How's that, sir?" said the soldier, turning to his officer. "Well caught," said the latter, involuntarily reminded of the game of cricket.

After the fighting was over, and in a comparatively quiet corner near the wells, one of the Soudanese suddenly went for a black sergeant belonging to the Egyptian army. The latter, unprepared for the onslaught, sought refuge behind his camel. Here he was pursued by his enemy, who tried every means to get at the sergeant. The latter was chased round and under his animal several times, to the amusement of a group of Highlanders, who looked on unwilling to spoil the sport. On went the chase, the two dodging round the sheltering camel, and it was uncertain who was to win when the Soudanese, with his long knife, proceeded to stab the camel. This attempt to secure an unfair advantage was too much for the Highlanders, two of whom took aim at the Soudanese. Their rifles went off at the same moment, and the man fell. It was impossible to say which shot proved fatal, and a lively discussion ensued as to "whose bird" the Soudanese was to be considered.

When the square was being assailed, a Soudanese, after being hit by a rifle-bullet, suddenly swerved towards one of the guns. A gunner saw him coming, snatched a rammer, and knocked him down with a blow on his head. Before he could rise the Soudanese was bayoneted. A trooper of the Hussars, named Hayes, after his squadron had passed ahead of him, attacked a spearman, who parried his sword-thrusts with one of the hippopotamus-hide shields carried by most of the enemy. The trooper tried in vain to cut the man down, but his horse was too restive to render this practicable. Hayes then coolly dismounted, and after parrying a spear-thrust, killed his opponent with a sword-cut.

Admiral Hewett, who had accompanied the force, as well as Baker Pasha, who was wounded by a piece of shell, returned to Trinkitat late in the afternoon with a small escort of cavalry. Graham, with the army, bivouacked at the wells that night, and started the next morning for Tokar, leaving behind 500 of the 42nd to guard the wounded and the supplies which had been brought up.

On the Mounted Infantry and a squadron of the 10th Hussars nearing Tokar they were fired on from some huts in the town and had to retire to the main column, which was some way behind; on its coming up Colonel Clery, the Chief of Graham's Staff, rode forward towards the town, when he discovered that the rebels had all fled; a soldier bearing a white flag came out, and it was found that the Egyptian garrison had, as had been reported, capitulated previously, but their lives had been spared, and some of them even bore arms. On the English troops coming up the townspeople professed to be overcome by delight and came out dancing and shouting, and kissed the soldiers' feet.

The same day a party of the 42nd Regiment was sent out to bury the Europeans who fell in Baker's defeat. All the bodies being stripped of every particle of clothes, it was most difficult to identify them; but twenty-five were distinguished, and of these the following could be identified with certainty, *viz.*, Morice Bey, Dr. Leslie, Captain Forrestier-Walker, Lieutenants Watkins, Carroll, Smith, and Morisi.

Of the Egyptians who fell, only Abdul Rassak Bey, Chief of the Staff, could be recognized. Morice Bey and Dr. Leslie were both lying side by side inside the left front of the square with their faces towards the front. Walker and Watkins were also close together in the opposite corner.

The troops bivouacked in the plain in front of Tokar, supplies being brought forward from Fort Baker.

On the 2nd March the cavalry rode out to the encampment of the enemy at a place called Dubba, about three miles distant: here was found inside a *zeriba* a pile of 1,500 Remingtons, 200 boxes of ammunition, one 7-pounder gun, and one Gatling. Outside was a hut, in which was stored the loot taken at Baker's defeat, a miscellaneous assortment, gun-cases, portmanteaus, writing-cases, surgical instruments, &c. A party of Hussars broke up the whole of the rifles, and the other things of value were loaded on mules.

The day following the arrival of the troops many of the inhabitants who had fled when the rebels were fighting at El-Teb, or had gone off in company with them, returned with their families and property. A wounded Egyptian artilleryman said that he and seven others had been dragged with ropes from Tokar to El-Teb to work the guns. All the others were killed, and he, on trying to escape, was shot in the back by the Soudanese, but managed to crawl to Tokar during the night. He stated that a great number of the enemy escaped from the fight in a wounded condition. According to this man and others, the rebel leaders alleged that they were deceived by Osman Digna, who told them it was untrue that the English were coming, and assured them that they would only have to meet and defeat another Egyptian army.

The troops then returned to Trinkitat, accompanied by 700 of the survivors from Tokar, and commenced to re-embark for Souakim on March 5th.

CHAPTER 35

Graham's Victory at Tamaai

By the 9th of March the change of base from Trinkitat to Souakim had been completed.

On the same day the Black Watch marched out and occupied a *zeriba* constructed by Baker some weeks before, and distant about eight miles on the road from Souakim to Sinkat.

According to the account given by a correspondent, before they moved off the ground Graham addressed them on parade. To the amazement of everyone who heard him, he said that, although he claimed to have the reputation of the Black Watch as much at heart as any of them, he could not say that he was altogether pleased with their performance the other day at El-Teb. He was understood to refer to the fact that the regiment had not broken into the double when amongst the enemy's rifle-pits, and to the rate at which they had fired away their ammunition. But to show that he had not lost confidence in them, he went on to say he was going to place the Black Watch in front throughout the coming operations.

With that unfortunate speech rankling in the minds of both officers and men, the General sent the regiment on its way. Not only was the speech ill-advised, but, as ever one knew except Graham himself, it was unjust. Its effect was apparent later on.

Owing to the absence of a breeze and the intense heat, the men were unable to proceed except at the slowest rate and with frequent halts. Even then there were hundreds of stragglers from the ranks. The officers did all in their power to keep the men together, but it was nearly 1 p.m. before they were all got to the *zeriba*. Five men suffered attacks of sunstroke, and many others were temporarily disabled by heat and exhaustion.

Camels and mules conveying water and stores kept arriving from

Souakim during the 9th and 10th, by the end of which time a large quantity of water, ammunition, and provisions had been collected at the *zeriba*. At 6 p.m. on the 11th the artillery and infantry advanced to the *zeriba*, which they reached at midnight. There was a bright moon, and the night air was soft and pleasant, so that the march did not distress the men, although it was hard work for the Naval Brigade.

The strength of the force was as follows:—

Royal Artillery, 176 men.

1st Infantry Brigade, under General Buller: Royal Engineers, 62 men; 3rd Battalion King's Own Rifles, 565 men; Gordon Highlanders (75th), 712 men; Royal Irish Fusiliers (89th), 343 men.

2nd Infantry Brigade, under General Davis: Royal Highlanders 42nd Black Watch), 623 men;[1] York and Lancaster (65th), 435 men; Royal Marine Artillery and Light Infantry, 478 men.

At daybreak on the 12th the cavalry, comprised of 251 men of the 10th Hussars, 362 men of the 19th Hussars, and 124 of the Mounted Infantry, arrived at the *zeriba*, where the total force now amounted to 4,069 men.

About 10 a.m. it was reported that the enemy was in force some six miles distant. Accordingly, the troops were ordered to advance towards Tamaai as soon as the men had had their dinners. About 1 p.m. the force began to move.

The following diagram explains the formation:—

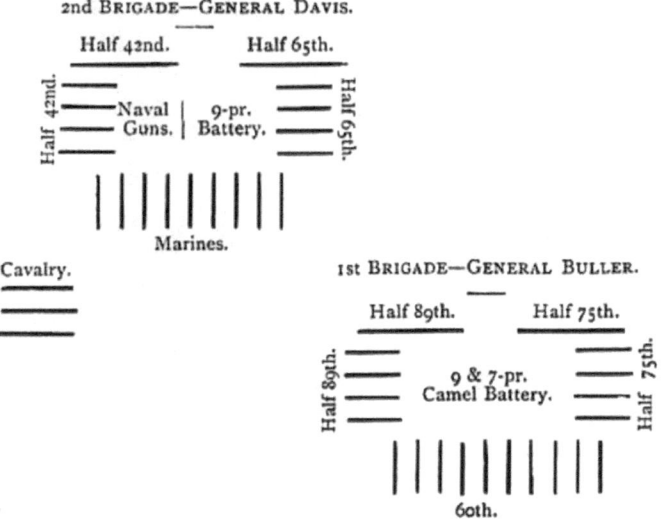

---

1. Already in *zeriba*.

The 1st Brigade, under Buller, marched on the right rear of the other, at a distance varying from 600 to 900 yards in an oblique line. In military language the two brigades moved in echelon, the 2nd Brigade leading, the object being to expose the enemy, in the event of his charging one brigade, to a raking or flank fire from the other. The rear battalions and the half-battalions on either flank of each brigade marched at wheeling distances, so that on the word to form outwards being given, two complete squares could be formed. The two brigades were thus placed so as to form two independent oblongs, the front face or line of each brigade being about 200 yards in length, the sides about 100 yards. The main body of the cavalry was echeloned on the left rear of the 2nd Brigade.

It will be seen that, although the force at Tamaai was about the same as that at El-Teb, a different formation was adopted. The unwieldiness of a single great square had been shown by experience. It had the further disadvantage that, in the event of an attack on one side, the fire of at least two of the other sides could not be utilized. There was, moreover, the old adage against *"putting all one's eggs in one basket."* The comparatively difficult ground which had to be got over at Tamaai was probably another reason for the change.

The line of march was about south-west. The Mounted Infantry having reported that the low hills, six miles in front, were clear of the enemy, it was deemed advisable to gain and occupy them before dark, and, if possible, attack the enemy and drive them from their position near the wells. The afternoon was hot, and frequent halts were necessary. The ground was covered with grass knee-deep, scrub and brushwood, and in some places the prickly mimosa and cactus were seven feet high.

By 3.30 the highest hill of the range was reached by the cavalry scouts, and the broad intervening valley of Tamaai could be seen from its summit through the haze. About four o'clock the infantry squares reached the base of the hill and halted for a few minutes, whilst the scouts were pushed forwards. At five o'clock they came in and reported that the enemy, estimated at 4,000 men, were advancing to the attack.

The force was at once formed up in a defensive position on a favourable piece of ground, having a clear space of 100 yards to the front, and, as there was now barely an hour of daylight left, the Engineers and pioneers were set to work to form a *zeriba* round the camp by cutting down the mimosa bushes which grew plentifully about.

Before this the enemy had fired a few rifle shots and had shown in some numbers on a ridge about 1,200 yards distant. By way of checking this, and to show the power of the guns, two of the 9-pounders and a Gardner gun fired a few rounds, and the enemy disappeared.

The operations of the day thus closed, the cavalry were sent back to Baker's *zeriba* to water their horses, and, tired with their day's exertion, the infantry lay down within the irregularly-shaped square formed by the mimosa bushes. The men lay two deep and slept with their greatcoats on and their arms beside them. Orders were given that all lights should be extinguished at nine.

About a quarter to one on the morning of the 13th there was an alarm, and the enemy opened a distant dropping fire, which continued throughout the night, causing few casualties, but disturbing the men's rest. One man of the York and Lancaster was killed, and five, including an officer, were wounded, as well as some camel drivers and horses.

At sunrise a 9-pounder and the Gardner gun were run out and made some excellent practice at a range of 1,300 yards, dispersing the enemy, who retired to their main position near the wells of Tamaai. About 7 a.m. Stewart arrived with his cavalry, and at 7.30 ordered out the Mounted Infantry to feel the enemy. At 8 o'clock the whole force moved out from their bivouac. A native who accompanied the troops, and who had lately been a prisoner in Osman Digna's camp, informed General Graham that the bulk of the enemy's force would be in a deep *khor*, or watercourse, the sides of which would serve as an intrenchment. Graham therefore directed the advance to be made to the left of this position, where the ground rose a little, intending (as he stated in his despatch) to sweep the ravine with artillery fire before attacking.

The advance was made by the two brigades in squares marching in echelon. Owing to some slight delay in getting the 1st Brigade forward, the 2nd (which General Graham and his staff now joined) was somewhat further in advance than was intended when they first came in contact with the enemy. The route lay towards the south-south-east, across a sloping plateau intersected by dry watercourses, towards a deep ravine, full of boulders and huge detached rocks.[2] The morning was bright and clear, with a brilliant sun, but there was no wind, as at El-Teb, to carry off the smoke. This, as will be seen, became important.

As the brigades advanced the black forms of the Soudanese were

---

2. This was the *khor* already spoken of.

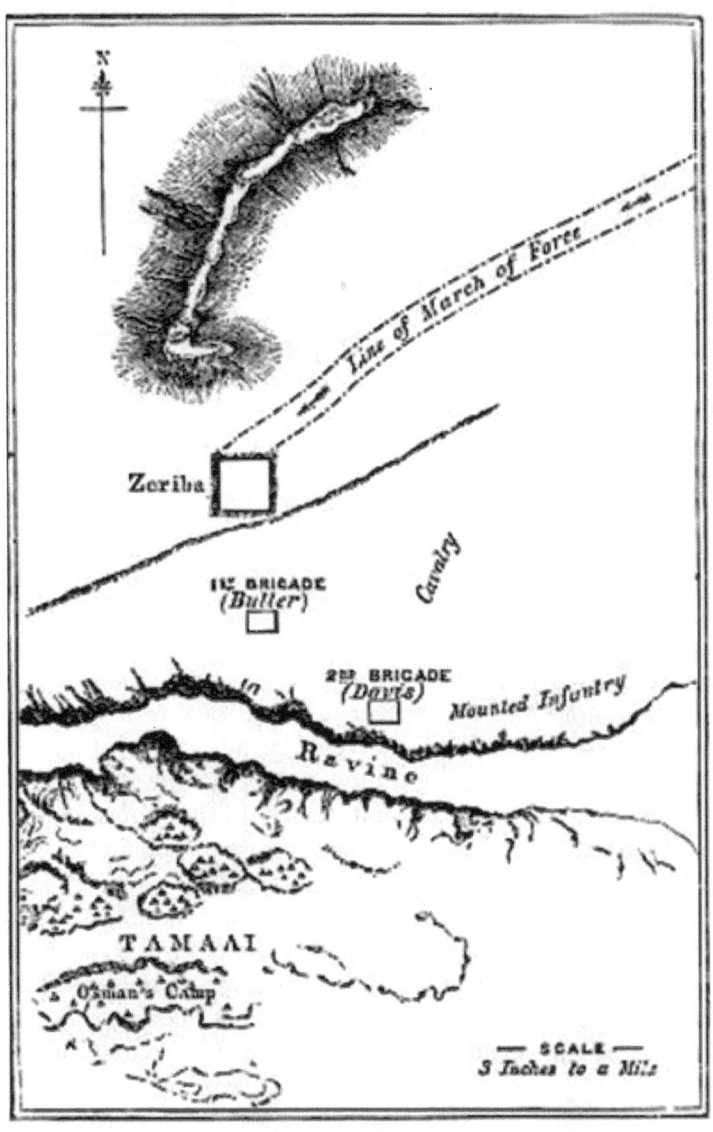

BATTLE OF TAMAAI.

seen ranged along the hills on the front and right of the British force. Two squadrons of cavalry, together with some Abyssinian scouts, were sent forward to skirmish and endeavour to clear the bushes through which the infantry had to advance. The skirmishers had not gone far before they became hotly engaged. Captain Humphreys, in command, sent back word that the ravine was occupied in force. Although this was only a few hundred yards in front, it was so hidden by bushes as to be invisible to the infantry.

About twenty minutes after starting, the 2nd Brigade was halted to re-form itself from the somewhat loose order into which it had fallen in its advance over the rough ground. At half-past eight it was moving slowly towards the ravine, which extended itself irregularly all along the front, and was from 900 to 1,000 yards off. The 1st Brigade, 700 yards distant to the right and rear, was timing its movements and taking its ground step by step with the 2nd Brigade.

Some 5,000 or 6,000 Soudanese were now visible, the greater part being on the south, or more distant, side of the ravine, here about 50 to 100 yards wide. Some hundreds of them were also among the bushes to the right as well as in the immediate front. They opened fire on the 2nd Brigade, but the greater part of the bullets flew harmlessly overhead. The skirmishers were withdrawn, and as soon as they were out of the line of fire, the brigade replied, the men firing independently as they advanced. When the square got within 200 yards of the ravine, a series of broken and irregular rushes was made by the Soudanese on the front; but the fire of the Martinis prevented any of the enemy getting at this time within twenty yards of the British line

The front became soon comparatively clear of foes, and then (about 9 a.m.) Graham[3] gave the order, "Forty-second, charge!" and the Black Watch, forming the left half face of the square, remembering the General's speech of two days before, cheered, and, regardless of consequences, broke away at the double. The 65th half battalion, on the right face of the square, had no order given to them, but seeing the Highlanders dash ahead, they too rushed on. The front rank of the square charged up to within thirty yards from the edge of the ravine, then slackened speed, and, though still advancing, recommenced firing. The order was given to "Cease firing," but the men, seeing armed natives spring up in every direction right and left, were not to be controlled, and continued to blaze away.

---

3. General Graham, who had taken the command of the brigade out of the hands of General Davis, gave the order personally.

The enemy were now swarming on the ridges on the opposite side of the ravine, and the Gatling and Gardner guns, which had been run out a few yards in front of the right corner of the square, were turned upon them. Many were observed running down the slopes, and disappearing among the rocks in the little valley intervening. In the absence of any wind, the smoke from the guns hung around the column in thick folds, totally obscuring the view. Under cover of this smoke, hundreds of the Soudanese crept up the near side of the ravine, and threw themselves upon the right front and right flank of the square, which fell back in disorder. The 65th, unable to resist the onslaught, were thrown back in confusion upon the marines in the rear, numbers being knocked off their legs in the rush. Their colonel (Byam) and four of his officers were thrown down. Soldiers and savages alike went trampling over them. As the colonel lay, he was assailed by four spearmen, but with his revolver he shot one at each touch of the trigger. The colonel rose up, and whilst the main body of his regiment was breaking up, rallied some thirty of his men, who, standing back to back, repelled with bayonet-thrusts the assaults of the Soudanese who encircled them. Fifteen of the men of the 65th fell where they stood.

As the 65th on the right face and corner were borne back from the edge of the ravine, the right wing of the 42nd became exposed, and the enemy, rushing in at the gap, were among the Highlanders on their flank and rear, cutting and spearing in every direction. The 42nd then recoiled several paces, the movement, according to one correspondent, "resembling the slow swing of a door on its hinges."

The condition of the column was something like this:—

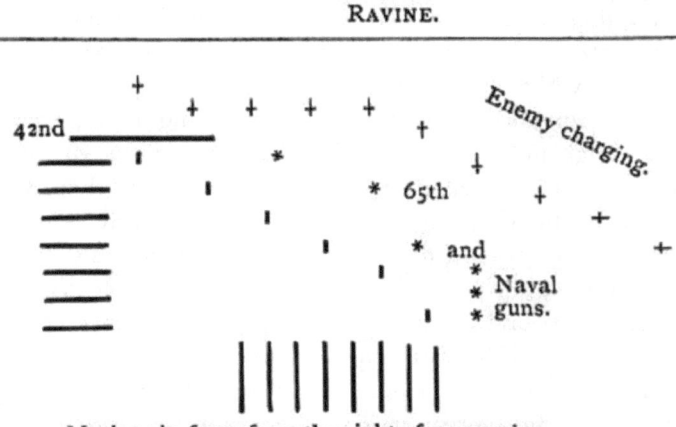

An officer appropriately compared the appearance of his part of the yielding line to the scramble in a game of football. The men were so huddled together that many of them were unable either to fire their rifles or use their bayonets. Captain Scott Stevenson, of the 42nd, was suddenly seized by the legs by some Soudanese, who were crawling on the ground. One of them dragged at the frogs of his kilt, and then at his "sporran." The captain, who was one of the best boxers in the army, literally kicked himself clear, and his claymore being too long a weapon to use at such close quarters, he laid about him with its hilt and with his fists.

The marines in rear of the brigade were wheeled up to support the 65th and close the gaps left in the formation, but it was too late, and they too were thrown into confusion, and borne away on the line of retreat. Graham and his staff tried their best to check the movement and rally the men. As the Marines were being swept away, Major Colwell shouted in stentorian tones, "Men of the Portsmouth Division, rally," which they did, 150 of them closing together in a compact body, forming a little square. The Highlanders also formed one or two such groups, and materially assisted in bringing about the general rally which soon followed. In spite of every effort, however, the whole force fell back about 800 yards, in a direction to the eastward of that taken in the advance.

The Naval Brigade, which had been sent to the front with the machine-guns, during the rush lost three of their officers, Lieutenants Montresor, Almack, and Houston Stewart, and many of their men. The guns had to be abandoned, partly owing to the hurried retreat, and partly because of the nature of the ground. Before retiring, the Naval Brigade found time to lock the guns, so as to prevent the enemy, who immediately captured them, from making any use of the weapons in the short interval which elapsed before they were retaken.

Instances of individual heroism were not wanting at this trying moment. One Highlander, seeing three or four mounted *sheikhs*, who were hounding on their men, rushed out at the leader of them and bayoneted him on his horse. Whilst the Black Watch were retiring, hard pressed, a private rushed at one of the enemy who was slashing right and left, and ran him through with his bayonet, so violently that he had to drag the wounded man with him for some distance before the soldier could extract the weapon. Every soldier who stumbled or fell during the retreat was at once done for, the enemy darting forward in squads and thrusting their spears into him as long as a sign of life remained. The nature of the struggle may be gathered from the fact that of twenty men who formed a section of a company of the Black Watch when charging up to the ravine, only three escaped alive, and they were badly wounded.

As has been related above, the formation of isolated groups among the retreating soldiers assisted to bring about the rally which took place in about twenty minutes. But a more powerful aid, and one without which Davis's square might have shared the fate of Baker's force at El-Teb, was at hand. The 1st Brigade, under Buller, had been attacked at the same time as the 2nd Brigade, and from its position at some 400 to 500 yards distance from the ravine, it had the advantage of a wider fire radius. The men were formed in square, the 75th on the right, and the 89th on the left being the leading regiments with the 60th in the rear and the 9 and 7-pounder guns in the centre.

Whilst the narrowness of the space between the slope and the 2nd Brigade enabled the enemy to "rush" the square before the infantry had time to fire more than a round or two, the distance between the slope and Buller's troops rendered it impossible for the enemy to reach them in face of a well-directed fire. Not one of the Soudanese who ran nearer than eighty yards to Buller's square lived to tell the tale. There was no hurry, no flurry in the handling of this brigade. The men formed up, shoulder to shoulder, in leisurely order when they saw the enemy coming on. Their deliberate volleys sounded like the harsh grating sound of the sea on a shingly beach, and when the smoke drifted slowly away the plain reappeared black with the bodies of the dead and dying.

Not content with attacking Buller's square in the front and on the flanks, the enemy even passed round to the rear, so that, at one time, all four sides were engaged. So well, however, was the brigade handled, and so steady were the men, that this made no difference. Buller was able, not only to hold his own ground, but also to assist the 2nd Brigade. As this fell back, it got to the left of Buller's square, and the general, seeing that something was wrong, moved up a short distance, and began pouring in a heavy cross fire upon the Soudanese who were assailing the other brigade. At the same time Stewart, moving his cavalry round to the left flank of Buller's square, dismounted his men, and fired a volley into the enemy's right flank. The Soudanese were thus between two fires.

Now, covered by the fire of the 1st Brigade and by the cavalry, Davis's square rallied. The retreating troops were halted and re-formed, this time in line with the Marines on the right, the 65th in the centre, and the 42nd, with 160 of the Naval Brigade in their rear, on the left. After a quarter of an hour's halt, a fresh supply of ammunition having been served out to each man, the 2nd Brigade went once more to the attack.

The soldiers were forbidden to fire until the enemy should come well within range, and on this occasion they obeyed orders more faithfully, marching slowly and clearing the ground of the enemy as they advanced. Thanks to the position taken by the 1st Brigade, which had now moved up 200 yards closer to the ravine and halted, Buller was able to pour a raking fire into the enemy, and so prevent any attempt to again "rush" Davis's flank.

The position was thus:—

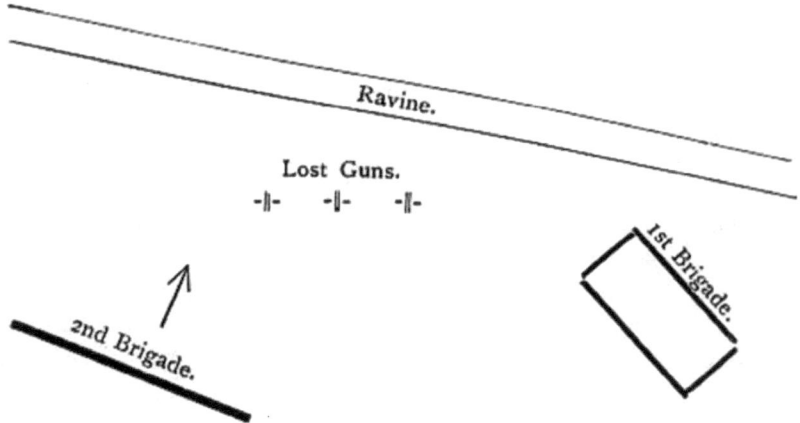

In ten minutes the lost ground was regained and the guns recaptured. They were immediately hauled into position, and fired a few rounds at the enemy, who began to move off to the opposite slopes of the ravine, within twenty paces of which Davis's force halted at 11 a.m.

It was now the turn of the 1st Brigade, which, still in square formation, was sent off to take a second intervening ridge some 800 yards off. Forward down and across the ravine went the brigade. With a cheer the men took the first ridge, firing as they went along occasional shots at the enemy's main body, who could be seen gathered on the second ridge beyond. The Soudanese, disheartened, kept up a feeble fire, retreating as the brigade advanced. The defence of the second ridge was insignificant, and it was carried without difficulty.

From the top Tamaai could be seen in the valley 180 feet below, with the tents and huts of Osman Digna's camp. By 11.40 a.m. these were in the possession of the British forces.

Osman Digna was not present at the battle, preferring to watch the action from the top of a neighbouring hill. His cousin, Mohammed Mousa, commanded the enemy's forces, and was shot at the commencement of the engagement.

Squads of men were told off to search for the wounded, a task of some danger, on account of the number of partially disabled Soudanese lying in the bush. Here, as at El-Teb, wounded Arabs refused to accept quarter, but waited an opportunity to spring out and attack any of the soldiers who came sufficiently close. An eyewitness wrote as follows:—

> One wounded savage lay half reclining on a sloping bank near the spot where the Gatling gun had been rolled into the ravine. He was badly wounded in the leg, a bullet having shattered his knee. Grasping his heavy broad-bladed spear, he looked defiance and mischief at the soldiers as they approached. A bluejacket was the first to venture near him, and although Jack had his rifle and cutlass attached, he liked not the far-reaching spear. The troops were forbidden to fire, and there was nothing for it but to tackle the man with steel. The deft handling of the spear, wounded as the foe was, made Jack cautious. I looked and watched. A soldier now stole up on the opposite side of the Hadendowa, but even then the savage, like a wounded stag at bay, was not to be trifled with. A mean subterfuge, cunning stratagem, or what you will you may call it, prevailed. A stone thrown at the Arab's head stunned him for the moment, and before he recovered the bluejacket had plunged his cutlass into him, bending the weapon into such a hoop shape that he could barely withdraw it.

The British losses were as follows:—Killed: Lieut. Montresor, *Euryalus*; Lieut. Almack, *Briton*; Lieut. Houston Stewart, *Dryad*; Capt. H. G. W. Ford, York and Lancaster; Major Aitken, Royal Highlanders; and 86 non-commissioned officers and privates. Wounded: Seven officers and 103 non-commissioned officers and privates. Missing: Nineteen men. Of the above, three officers and eleven men were killed at the taking of the guns, and the loss of the 2nd Brigade at the time of the square being broken was 70 in killed alone. The number of the enemy was originally reported by Graham as being from 10,000 to 12,000, and the loss as over 2,000 in killed. According to one account, over 1,500 lay dead in an area of 200 yards; 600 of these were counted on the spot where the square was broken. Another account puts the total number of the enemy's forces engaged at 9,000, and the loss in killed and wounded 2,400. No prisoners were taken.

Of the nature of the surprise intended for him at the ravine, Graham had ample warning beforehand. Nevertheless he moved his men almost up to the brink of the spot where the enemy lay in ambush, and very nearly brought about a disaster.

As to the order given to a part of the front rank to charge, it is unnecessary to say anything in its condemnation. The charge was made at nothing. The front rank of the square doubled, whilst the sides and rear only followed at quick time. It was, as a critic remarked, taking the lid off the box.

Of the conduct of the soldiers of the 2nd Brigade it is impossible to speak too highly. It was in consequence of a sheer military blunder that the front of the square got separated from the rest, and that the men were driven back by the surging mass of Soudanese; but it was proof of the highest discipline and coolness that under these circumstances the men, compelled to retire, kept their faces steadily toward the enemy, and were able to re-form without panic or confusion.

The feeling of the troops, or at all events of the 2nd Brigade, after the battle, was that they had been victorious, in spite of the mismanagement of their superiors. The men of the Black Watch were especially sore at what had occurred. Their idea was that they had been needlessly exposed. They had a grievance ever since the beginning of the campaign. At El-Teb they had been expected to charge rifle-pits in which hundreds of the enemy were concealed. As this movement would have caused great loss, the advance was made deliberately. For this the regiment had, as has already been mentioned, been severely taken to task. To enable them to retrieve their supposed loss of reputation, the Black Watch were placed in the position of honour and danger at Tamaai, and when the order to double against the enemy, thus, as it turned out, breaking the square, was given, they obeyed promptly, though, as they said, "We knew the order was foolish, but we were put on our mettle." "It was of no use," they argued, "to form a square if it was to rush at the enemy in fragments."

Before returning to Souakim on the 15th of March, parties of engineers were told off to complete the destruction of Osman Digna's camp at Tamaai. This extended over a level plain two miles in length, surrounded by naked rocks. The camp, as well as the huts and stores, were soon in a blaze in scores of different places, the flames shooting up to a great height, and volumes of smoke obscuring the view between the camp and the distant hills. One feature of the scene was the explosion of the magazines, containing about 600,000 rifle cartridges, captured from Baker at El-Teb, besides a large quantity of Krupp and machine-gun ammunition.

The British forces being once more concentrated at Souakim, Admiral Hewett issued a proclamation offering 5,000 dollars for the head of Osman Digna. Whether this step was in accordance with the rules of civilized warfare or not may well be doubted. At all events, it created a strong feeling of indignation in England, and in three days the admiral, acting under instructions from home, withdrew the objectionable document.

On the 18th the 19th Hussars, the Mounted Infantry, and the Gordon Highlanders made a march to the wells of Handouk, a few miles from Souakim. They found them all deserted, and no signs of the enemy. A *zeriba* was formed at the base of a detached hill held by a company of the Highlanders. News was brought to the camp that Osman Digna's force was increasing, and that he had announced his intention of renewing the fighting. He was reported to have 2,000 men with him.

On the 19th General Stewart, with two squadrons of Hussars, went to Otao, eight miles further west, in search of the enemy, but in vain. A squadron was also sent to Tamanieb, where Osman was reported to be, but found no traces of him.

On the 21st two batteries of artillery and also the 10th Hussars were moved out to Handouk.

On the 23rd the Gordon Highlanders were sent to a point near the entrance of the Tamanieb valley to form a new *zeriba* in conjunction with a company of the 89th, which marched from Souakim to join them, with water and stores.

On the 25th General Graham marched with two brigades, under Buller and Davis respectively, to a *zeriba* eleven miles from Souakim.

The march-out was a most exhausting one on account of the heat, and between 300 and 400 men fell out of the ranks. There were numerous cases of sunstroke. According to one account, the number of men who fell out was equal to one-fourth of the whole force, the rear of which, it is said, resembled a routed army. Many of the sick found room in the ambulances, and others trudged along as best they could on foot. The men were now becoming tired and disgusted with the campaign, and there was a good deal of grumbling and dissatisfaction in the ranks.

The whole force bivouacked when nine miles from Souakim, and the night's rest restored the men who had fallen out during the march, and all but four returned to duty on the morning of the 26th.

Stewart's brigade of cavalry left the camp shortly after 9 a.m. for Tamanieb. Graham's orders were that operations should be confined to reconnoitring, the troops to fall back on learning the enemy's position. For the first five miles the route lay across a plain through patches of mimosa. After this, the hills were reached. Small parties of the enemy were seen mounted on dromedaries, watching the force. On a hill 600 feet high Stewart established a heliograph station for signalling to the *zeriba* in the rear. After another five miles' march, a second signal station was placed among the hills. From this point the enemy's position could be seen two miles distant. Behind them were the wells of Tamanieb. The number of the enemy appeared, at first, to be about 3,000, though it subsequently turned out much less. It was now half-past one, and the Mounted Infantry advanced to within 700 yards, keeping up a fire meanwhile.

This skirmishing was continued till 3 o'clock, when, the object of the reconnaissance having been attained, General Stewart withdrew to the first signal station. Here he was met by General Buller, who had advanced with the 75th and 89th Regiments, having left camp at ten. In the afternoon the remainder of the force, with the exception of the 65th Regiment and the sick, also advanced, and joined Buller at the first signal station, where a new *zeriba* was formed. A quiet night was passed at the advanced *zeriba*.

Shortly after 5 a.m. on the following day, the entire force, numbering 3,000 men, marched out. The Mounted Infantry scouted along the ridges to the right and left flanks, but there was for some time no sign of the enemy.

It was cool at first, owing to the early hour at which the march commenced, and there were no sick. The men were in the best of spirits, not only at the prospect of offering the enemy battle, but because they believed that the impending engagement would end the campaign. The troops went forward very slowly on account of the rocky nature of the ground. About fifty men fell out owing to the heat. As the hostile position was approached, the Mounted Infantry and a squadron of hussars were sent forward to occupy the ground held during the skirmish of the previous day. When they advanced the enemy opened a fire, to which the troopers replied.

At nine Graham brought up the reserve of the Mounted Infantry, leaving the two Infantry Brigades in the rear. Shortly after this, the enemy's fire slackened. Half-an-hour afterwards the 1st Brigade had advanced far enough for the 9-pounders to open fire on the enemy, of whom only small bodies could be seen.

At ten the cavalry skirmishers were within 100 yards of the Tamanieb Khor, and the Soudanese were seen retreating *en masse* to the right and left. Close at hand were the wells, and the troops, instead of pursuing, were halted for a quarter of an hour to water the horses, which were suffering greatly from thirst. The soldiers, too, drank copiously after their march. When the cavalry formed up and moved along the wells to the village the enemy had disappeared. There was no resistance, and Graham ordered the burning of the village. This was immediately carried out, and the huts, some 300 in number, were soon in a blaze.

There were no casualties on the side of the British, nor do any of the accounts refer to any loss on the part of the enemy, who, according to one report, did not number over 100 altogether.

After this achievement the troops started on the return march to Souakim.

The whole of the force reached Souakim on the 28th, and with the exception of a battalion left to garrison that place was at once broken up, the troops from Egypt returning to Cairo, and the remainder proceeding to England. No trustworthy information was obtained as to the position or force of Osman Digna, though the village of Tamanieb showed signs of a recent occupation by his army. Under these circumstances, to attempt to pursue Osman further into the interior was considered to be impracticable. The troops, too, were again suffering from the heat, and it was deemed best to close the campaign for the season.

The rapidity of Graham's campaign was one of its most striking features. The orders for the expedition were received in Cairo on the 12th February. By the 1st of March a force of over 4,000 men had been assembled at Trinkitat, had fought the battle of El-Teb, and had brought away the fugitives from Tokar. Starting from Souakim on the 11th March, the expedition had by the 28th fought the Battle of Tamaai, occupied the enemy's position at Tamanieb, and terminated the campaign.

Besides serving to develop the admirable qualities of the British soldier under trying conditions, the campaign cannot be said to have achieved any permanent result, it having only shattered and not annihilated, Osman Digna.

The ill effects of the withdrawal of Graham's force upon the rebellious tribes cannot well be exaggerated. Notwithstanding their repeated defeats they easily persuaded themselves that they had driven the English out of the country, and the policy of "Rescue and retire" pursued by the British Government was the means of laying up a store of future trouble for Souakim and the neighbourhood.

Although there was no further opportunity of fighting Osman Digna at this period, the question naturally arises, whether at all events part of Graham's force might not have been usefully employed in assisting Gordon in withdrawing the Egyptian garrisons.

One pretext for the battles of El-Teb and Tamaai was the necessity for opening the road to Berber. On March 25th Lord Edmond Fitzmaurice said:—

> One thing was perfectly certain, that it was of the very greatest importance, with a view to keeping open communications with Khartoum, that the road between Souakim and Berber should itself be open.

As the road between Souakim and Berber was the short cut out of the Soudan, the importance of keeping it open could hardly have been ignored by a government concerned in the task of extricating from the Soudan an army of 29,000 men with all the civil *employés* and their wives and families. Gordon could hold Khartoum, but by no possible miracle could he keep open the road hundreds of miles in his rear by which he had to send the troops and refugees down to Egypt. Hence, he suggested to the government that if they wished to intervene, they should open up the Souakim-Berber route by Indian Moslem troops.

After the victory at Tamaai Graham could have sent a few squadrons of cavalry through to Berber with ease, and he was anxious to do so. Two squadrons would, in the opinion of all the authorities in the Soudan, have sufficed to open the road and to save Berber, which was the key of the Soudan, and without the retention of which evacuation was hopeless. General Stephenson and Sir Evelyn Wood both agreed that the move was possible, although Stephenson disliked it, owing to the scarcity of water on the road.

On February 29th Gordon had telegraphed:—

> There is not much chance of the situation improving, and every chance of it getting worse; for we have nothing to rely on to make it better. You must, therefore, decide whether you will or will not make an attempt to save the two-thirds of the population who are well affected before these two-thirds retreat. Should you wish to intervene, send 200 British troops to Wady Halfa, and adjutants to inspect Dongola, and then open up Souakim-Berber road by Indian Moslem troops. This will cause an immediate collapse of the revolt.

On March 2nd he telegraphed:—

> I have no option about staying at Khartoum; it has passed out of my hands, and as to sending a larger force than 200, I do not think it necessary to Wady Halfa. It is not the number, but the prestige which I need. I am sure the revolt will collapse if I can say that I have British troops at my back.

On the 5th Sir Evelyn Baring wrote to Lord Granville:—

> General Gordon has on several occasions pressed for 200 British troops to be sent to Wady Halfa. I agree with the military authorities in thinking that it would not be desirable to comply with this request.

On March 11th Lord Granville replied to Gordon's urgent entreaties that:

> Her Majesty's Government are not prepared to send troops to Berber.

Sir Evelyn Baring, who had opposed the despatch of troops to Wady Halfa and to Berber, on March 16th recognized the necessity for action. On that day he telegraphed home:—

> It has now become of the utmost importance not only to open the road between Souakim and Berber, but to come to terms with the tribes between Berber and Khartoum.

But Lord Granville still felt unable to authorize an advance of British troops.

On March 24th Sir E. Baring telegraphed:—

Under present circumstances, I think that an effort should be made to help General Gordon from Souakim, if it is at all a possible military operation. General Stephenson and Sir Evelyn Wood, whilst admitting the very great risk to the health of the troops, besides the extraordinary military risks, are of opinion that the undertaking is possible.

Mr. Power, British Consular Agent, telegraphed from Khartoum on March 23rd:

We are daily expecting British troops. We cannot bring ourselves to believe that we are to be abandoned by the government. Our existence depends on England.

It was in vain; notwithstanding every appeal the British Government determined to refuse, until too late, the assistance asked for.

Chapter 36

The Gordon Relief Expedition

Gordon's situation at Khartoum in the meantime may be learned from what follows.

On the 27th February, 1884, he issued a proclamation to the inhabitants of the Soudan, stating that he would be compelled to use severe measures against those who did not desist from rebellion, and also that "British troops are now on their way, and in a few days will reach Khartoum."

In a despatch, on the same day, to Sir E. Baring, Gordon said:—

> You must remember that when evacuation is carried out the *Mahdi* will come down here, and by agents will not let Egypt be quiet. Of course my duty is evacuation, and to do the best I can for establishing a quiet government. The first I hope to accomplish. The second is a more difficult task, and with care and time can be accomplished. Remember that once Khartoum belongs to the *Mahdi*, the task will be more difficult.
>
> If you decide on smashing *Mahdi*, then send up another, £100,000, and send up 200 infantry troops to Wady Halfa, and an officer to Dongola under pretence to look out quarters for troops. Leave Souakim and Massowah alone. I repeat that evacuation is possible, but you will feel the effect in Egypt and be forced to enter into a far more serious affair to guard Egypt.

While Gordon was sending almost daily expressions of his view as to the only way of carrying out the policy of eventual evacuation, it was becoming clear to him that he would very soon be cut off from the rest of Egypt. His first remark on this subject was to express "the conviction that I shall be caught in Khartoum;" and he wrote:— "Even if I was mean enough to escape, I have no power to do so."

The accuracy of this forecast was speedily demonstrated. Within a few days communications with Khartoum were interrupted, and although subsequently restored for a time, the rising of the riparian tribes rendered the receipt and despatch of messages exceedingly uncertain. On the 8th of April, however, Gordon succeeded in getting the following message through to Sir Evelyn Baring:—

> I have telegraphed to Sir Samuel Baker to make an appeal to British and American millionaires to give me, £300,000 to engage Turkish troops from the *sultan* and send them here. This will settle the Soudan and the *Mahdi* forever. For my part I think you will agree with me. I do not see the fun of being caught here to walk about the streets for years as a dervish with sandaled feet; not that I will ever be taken alive.

Eight days later he wrote as follows:—

> As far as I can understand, the situation is this—You state your intention of not sending any relief up here or to Berber. I consider myself free to act according to circumstances. I shall hold out here as long as I can, and if I can suppress the rebellion I shall do so. If I cannot I shall retire to the Equator.

The complete investment or siege of Khartoum may be considered as having commenced about this time.

When Gordon first began to perceive that he would get no material help from his government, he made several propositions which would, if adopted, have relieved them from further responsibility. As indicated in the foregoing telegrams, one was to make an appeal to international philanthropy, and by employing Turkish troops to smash the *Mahdi*. Another was that he should steam up the Nile, and taking Bahr Gazelle and the Equatorial Province in the name of the King of the Belgians, join hands with Stanley, or whoever else might represent the king, on the Congo.

While communications were still maintained, Gordon sent his account of his first action with the rebels, which showed not only the kind of enemy he had to deal with, but also the sort of men on whom he had to depend for the defence of Khartoum. On the 17th of March he described in the following words an action on the previous day:—

> At eight a.m. on the 16th two steamers started for Halfiyeh. *Bashi-bazouks* and some regulars advanced across plain towards

rebels. At ten a.m. the regulars were in square opposite centre of rebels' position, and *bashi-bazouks* were extended in their line to their right. A gun with the regulars then opened fire. Very soon after this a body of about sixty rebel horsemen charged down a little to the right of centre of the *bashi-bazouks*' line. The latter fired a volley, then turned and fled.

The horsemen galloped towards the square, which they immediately broke. The whole force then retreated slowly towards the fort with their rifles shouldered. The horsemen continued to ride along the flanks cutting off stragglers. The men made no effort to stand, and the gun was abandoned, with sixty-three rounds and fifteen cases of reserve ammunition. The rebels advanced, and retreat of our men was so rapid that the Arabs on foot had no chance of attacking. Pursuit ceased about a mile from stockade, and the men rallied. We brought in the wounded. Nothing could be more dismal than seeing these horsemen, and some men even on camels, pursuing close to troops, who, with arms shouldered, plodded their way back.

In fact, this fight was a massacre, as the Egyptian soldiers did not attempt the least resistance. Colonel Stewart, who commanded in person, was wounded. The two *pashas* under him were subsequently convicted of treachery and shot.

On the 25th of June the garrison heard of the fall of Berber. The news was brought by the English Consul, Mr. Cuzzi, who was sent in by the rebels to inform Gordon that the one connecting link between him and the outer world had fallen into the hands of the *Mahdi*.

Long before the summer of 1884, it was evident that the position of Gordon at Khartoum had become so critical that, if he were to be rescued at all, it could only be by the despatch of a British force. As far back as April 23rd, Earl Granville telegraphed to Mr. Egerton at Cairo, instructing him to forward a cipher message to Gordon asking what would "be the force necessary to secure his *removal*, its amount, character, the route for access to Khartoum, and time of operation."

Early in May, war preparations were commenced in England, and on the 10th of the month the military authorities in Cairo received instructions to prepare for the despatch in October of an expedition for the relief of the Soudanese capital. Twelve thousand camels were ordered to be purchased and held in readiness for a forward march in the autumn.

On the 16th May a half-battalion of English troops was moved up the Nile to Wady Halfa. A few weeks later some other positions on the Nile were occupied by portions of the Army of Occupation. Naval officers were also sent up the river to examine and report upon the cataracts and other impediments to navigation. Still it was not till the 5th August that Mr. Gladstone rose in the House of Commons to move a vote of credit of £300,000 to enable the government to undertake operations for the relief of Gordon, "in case it might be necessary."

The government policy on the subject of Gordon had been repeatedly attacked in Parliament. On July the 8th Lord Hartington formally declared to the House of Commons that it was not the intention of the government to despatch an expedition for the relief of Gordon, unless it was clearly shown that such was the only means by which Gordon and those dependent on him could be relieved. "We have received," added the Secretary of State for War, "no information making it desirable that we should depart from that decision." Urged on, however, by the public press, and plied day after day with questions in the House of Commons, the government at last brought forward the vote of credit. The money was granted, and the War Office then began to take action.

Lord Wolseley had as early as April 8th pressed the Government on the subject, and on the 24th July he wrote that he thought no time should be lost in pushing up a small brigade of 3,000 or 4,000 British troops to Dongola. He believed that such a force would most probably settle the whole business, adding:

> But you must know that time presses. I believe that such a force could be sent from England and reach Dongola about October 15th if the government is in earnest, and acts at once. Remember we cannot command things, and all the gold in England will not affect the rise and fall of the Nile, or the duration of the hot and cold seasons in Egypt.
>
> Time is a most important element in this question, and indeed it will be an indelible disgrace if we allow the most generous, patriotic, and gallant of our public servants to die of want, or fall into the hands of a cruel enemy, because we would not hold out our hands to save him. Dongola can be reached without fighting, and our presence there in force might secure for us all the objects we wish to obtain.

On the 20th July Gordon sent a message asking where the reinforcements were, and what was their number. On the 30th he announced, "Retreat is impossible. I recommend as a route for troops Wady Halfa, but fear it is too late." On the 31st he expressed himself to Sir Evelyn Baring as follows:—

> You ask me to state cause and intention of staying at Khartoum. I stay at Khartoum because Arabs have shut us up and will not let us out.

The views of the British Government as to the rescue of Gordon were communicated by the Marquis of Hartington to General Stephenson, commanding the Army of Occupation, on the 8th August. The government, the former wrote, were not convinced that it would be impossible for Gordon to secure the withdrawal from Khartoum, either by the employment of force or by pacific means, of the Egyptian garrisons, and of such of the inhabitants as might desire to leave. Nevertheless, he added, "Her Majesty's Government were of opinion that the time had arrived when some further measures for obtaining accurate information as to his position, and, if necessary, for rendering him assistance, should be adopted."

As to what "further measures" were to be adopted considerable difference of opinion existed amongst the advisers of the government. It was agreed that there were but two routes by which Khartoum could be approached by an expedition, one by way of the Nile, and the other *viâ* Souakim and Berber, but which of the two presented the least difficulty was a point upon which the highest authorities differed.

The first involved sending the force a distance of 1,650 miles from its base at Cairo, by a river in which were innumerable obstacles in the shape of cataracts, rocks, and shoals. The expedition would have to proceed against the stream, thus making progress slow, and in boats, every one of which would have to be specially constructed for the purpose.

The second necessitated a march from Souakim to Berber of some 280 miles over a country furnished only with a few wells, the supply from which might have to be supplemented by water to be carried by the expedition, in addition to a journey of 200 miles from Berber to Khartoum.

In the last case there was an almost absolute certainty that the march would have to be made in the face of an opposing force.

General Stephenson, who may be considered as the highest authority on the subject, was in Cairo, and therefore in a certain sense on the spot. He had, moreover, the advantage of conferring with Commander Hammill of the *Monarch* and other officers, who had for weeks previously been engaged on the Nile in examining into the facilities for getting steamers and boats past the cataracts, and other obstacles in the way of river navigation. His opinion was strongly adverse to the Nile route, and in favour of that by Souakim and Berber.

Lord Wolseley, however, basing his calculations on the success of the Red River Expedition, had formed an opposite opinion to that of General Stephenson, and Lord Wolseley being all-powerful at the War Office, his views were adopted by the government.

On the 15th of August Lord Hartington further explained his views of the measures to be adopted, insisting that the movement must be made by the Nile Valley, instead of by the Souakim-Berber route, with the sole and exclusive object of relieving Gordon, adding:

> This renders it essential that, in framing any plans for the movement of troops south of Wady Halfa, the possibility of being obliged to advance as far as Khartoum itself should be included in and form a necessary part of such plans.

His Lordship at the same time declared it to be essentially necessary to provide for the return of the troops before the end of the winter season.

Lord Hartington telegraphed to Stephenson to report fully as to what he proposed, and to state the number of the force and of camels which would be required. On the 21st General Stephenson telegraphed to Lord Hartington, with the information asked for, adding:

> My own opinion still is in favour of the Souakim-Berber route:—
> Should this be adopted, Egyptian troops should be sent to New Dongola, consisting of two battalions, one regiment of cavalry, one battery of artillery; one English battalion retained at Wady Halfa; half battalion Egyptian, Korosko; and one English and one and a half battalions Egyptian at Assouan, leaving about 2,000 Egyptians with Marines available for garrisoning Souakim and line of communication to Berber.

But Lord Hartington was evidently too much impressed by the arguments of Lord Wolseley to be inclined for further discussion. On the 22nd August he wrote:—

> I gather from the telegraphic correspondence which I have had with you since my despatch of the 15th instant that, in acting on the instructions communicated to you in my despatch of the 8th instant, you have to this date based your preparations on a scheme of operations which is substantially that sketched out in the report of Commander Hammill, dated 4th August. I also learn from your telegram of the 21st instant that, while it is in your opinion possible by the means indicated in that report to send the small force described in my despatch of the 8th to New Dongola, it would not be practicable by those means to push forward such a force as would in your opinion be required to reach Khartoum, and to bring it back within the next winter. Influenced by this consideration, you state that your opinion is still, if such an operation should be undertaken, in favour of the Souakim-Berber route. For the reasons stated in my despatch of the 8th, I am not now prepared to authorize a movement on that line.

Then came the intimation that Wolseley was to command the expedition.

> To Lieut.-General Stephenson.
> War Office, August 26, 1884, Midnight.
> After anxious consideration, Her Majesty's Government have come to the conclusion that it is unjust to you to ask you to be responsible for directing an operation which, after full knowledge of the plan, you consider to be impracticable. They have, therefore, decided to send Lord Wolseley to take temporarily the chief command in Egypt. Government highly appreciate the manner in which you have carried out the important and difficult duties of your command, and earnestly hope that you may feel yourself able to remain in Egypt while Lord Wolseley is there, and assist him with your advice.

In making the choice of routes, the one vital question of time seems to have been insufficiently considered. Gordon was known to be hard pressed, and the object should have been for the expedition for his rescue to arrive at its destination with as little delay as possible. From Souakim to Berber occupied Hicks Pasha less than three weeks, and from Berber to Khartoum five or six days more; of course, it is not pretended that a force so large as Wolseley had under his orders could march nearly as rapidly as Hicks' small detachment. But it may be argued that assuming that the route by Souakim was *possible*, and of this there seems no doubt, the relief expedition, even if it had to fight its way step by step, must eventually have arrived in much less time than the many months occupied by Wolseley on the river route.

Chapter 37

Progress to Dongola

The Nile route having been decided on, preparations on a large scale were begun.

The first thing was to obtain boats for the transport up the Nile; and for these, contracts were at once entered into with various firms in England. Eight hundred in all were ordered. From their shape they were called whalers, and they were to be each thirty feet in length, with six feet six inches beam, and a draught of two feet six inches. Each was to weigh nine hundredweight, and was to be fitted with twelve oars and two masts with lug sails. Every boat was to be fitted to carry a dozen men, *viz.*, two boatmen and ten soldiers, besides provisions and ammunition. The price of each boat was £75.

Eight steam pinnaces were equipped for the expedition, as well as two stern-wheel paddle-boats.

At the same time a contract was entered into with Messrs. Thos Cook and Son, the well-known tourist agents, for the transport of the entire force as far as Sarras, just above the Second or Great Cataract.

To assist in the Nile navigation 380 boatmen, called *"voyageurs"* were engaged; 290 of them were French or English-speaking Canadians, with a few half-breeds, all from the St. Maurice or Ottawa districts, and about fifty were Iroquois Indians from Caughnawanga. The remainder were Salteaux from Manitoba.[1] In addition to the Ca-

---

1. It subsequently transpired that many of the *"voyageurs"* had absolutely no experience in the management of boats, and were worse than useless. There were some excellent men amongst them, and more particularly among the Indians, but the general opinion was that the bluejackets from the fleet could have performed the work far more efficiently, besides being sober and amenable to discipline. When, in addition, it is stated that the Canadians received very high salaries, the wisdom of engaging these men for the Nile expedition appears open to much doubt.

nadians 300 *kroomen* were obtained from the West Coast of Africa to carry stores round the cataracts.

All the Nile steamers in serviceable condition belonging to the Egyptian Government, including those under contract to Messrs. Cook and Son, were requisitioned for the transport of the whalers and men of the expedition.

It next became requisite to fix the numbers of the force to be placed under Wolseley's command. In doing this allowance had to be made for the many posts which it would be necessary to establish in order to keep up the line of communication.

It was at first arranged that not more than 5,000 men should form the expedition, but later on the number was raised to 7,000. Two regiments were ordered from India, three battalions from Gibraltar, Malta, and Cyprus, one battalion from Barbadoes, and several companies of the Royal Engineers and some batteries of the Royal Artillery, with drafts of the Commissariat Transport and Army Hospital Corps, from England.

These, with the troops already in Egypt, and a contingent of seamen and Marines, made up a total force of 14,000 men, from which Lord Wolseley was to select the 7,000 required for the expedition. Colonels Sir Charles Wilson, Brackenbury, Harrison, Henderson, and Maurice, and Lord Anson, were appointed to the force for special service. General Sir Redvers Buller was named Chief of the Staff, and General Earle was told off to command a brigade.

The instructions given to Lord Wolseley stated that the primary object of the expedition was to bring away Gordon from Khartoum; and when that purpose should be effected, no further offensive operations of any kind were to be undertaken. The government even questioned the necessity of advancing as far as Khartoum, and expressed a desire that the sphere of military operations should be limited as much as possible.

Throughout the month of August the arsenals in Great Britain were in full activity, and every effort was made to get the expedition forward in time to take advantage of the high Nile. During the latter part of the month, and during September, troops and stores were arriving almost daily in Alexandria and were being forwarded at once to the front.

One may judge of the measures taken from the fact that on the 1st September, within sixteen days after the order for the Nile boats had been given, many of them were already shipped, and a fortnight later

400, or half the total number, had been sent off.

The whalers on arriving in Egypt were at once forwarded by rail and river to Assiout. Thence they were towed by steamer to Assouan, over 300 miles further, and just below the First Cataract. Here most of them were placed upon trucks for conveyance by a railway eight miles long to Shellal, on the south side of the cataract. Some few were hauled through the rapids and past the Isle of Philæ. Once through the cataract all was fair sailing as far as Wady Halfa, 200 miles further, where the Second Cataract forms another obstacle to Nile navigation.

Lord Wolseley arrived at Alexandria in company with Lord Northbrook on the 9th September, and left the same day for Cairo.

Meanwhile the Nile, from Assiout to the Second Cataract, presented a scene of unwonted bustle and activity. Posts were established at Assiout, Assouan, Wady Halfa, and other places for the purpose of forwarding supplies. Coaling stations were provided for the steamers, and almost interminable processions of steamers, barges, whalers, and native craft passed up daily with men, horses, and stores.

Prior to Lord Wolseley's departure from England, Sir Evelyn Wood and Commander Hammill had started up the Nile to superintend the operations. The 1st Battalion of the Royal Sussex was conveyed from Assouan to Wady Halfa by the *Benisouef* steamer, and then hurried on to Dongola with three months' rations for a thousand men on board some of the boats which the *mudir* had in the meanwhile despatched to Sarras. The Royal Sussex was replaced at Wady Halfa by the Staffordshire Regiment, and then the Mounted Infantry came up by water to Sarras and proceeded to Dongola. Throughout the earlier part of September troops were constantly advancing, Lord Wolseley having expressed the desire that they should be pushed on to Dongola without waiting for his arrival. The men were conveyed by train to Assiout, and thence by steamer to Assouan.

A large number of the whalers had already arrived at Wady Halfa, when, on September 27th, Lord Wolseley, who had completed his plan of operations, left Cairo with his staff for Upper Egypt. Journeying along the Nile in the yacht *Ferouz*, he made frequent halts on the way, inspecting the military arrangements and visiting various points of interest. Arriving at Assouan on October 1st, he inspected the Egyptian and British troops encamped there, and, after visiting the Temple of Philæ, again embarked with Sir Redvers Buller and his staff.

Even before Wolseley had left Cairo Generals Earle and Sir Herbert Stewart had already reached Wady Halfa. The latter at once set out for Dongola, and arrived at his destination on September 30th, at the same time as two hundred and fifty men of the Mounted Infantry, who made the journey up the Nile from Sarras in "*nuggars*," or native boats.

On the 5th October Wolseley reached Wady Halfa. This had become temporarily the base of the British operations as well as the permanent chief *depôt* of commissariat and ordnance stores for the expedition. The railway at Wady Halfa, running for a distance of thirty three miles along the east bank of the Nile, was utilized for forwarding stores, &c., to Sarras. Some of the whalers were landed at Bab-el-Kebir ("The Great Gate") and carried overland above the Second Cataract, whilst others were hauled through it. A good number of the whalers had already passed prior to the arrival of Wolseley at Wady Halfa. The first boat, indeed, was hauled up the rapids on September 25th without any other appliances than its own gear and some towing ropes, the operation occupying but a quarter of an hour. The second boat was then hauled up by means of Commander Hammill's cleverly-arranged tackle, and the operation was carried out even more rapidly and safely.

At Wady Halfa, Wolseley got news respecting Colonel Stewart, which he telegraphed as follows:—

Wady Halfa, October 5, 1884.
Stewart bombarded Berber, and, taking one steamer and some of the boats, with forty soldiers, proceeded down the river. Other steamers continued bombardment of Berber, and then returned towards Khartoum. Stewart's steamer struck on a rock at El-Kamar, one day's journey above Merawi. They arranged for camels to continue journey with Suleiman Wad Gamr, who went on board to undertake to supply camels and guide them, and received a sword and dress; when they went ashore to start, they were set upon and killed. Suleiman afterwards took the steamer, and killed all but four on board. Express sent out to find out who those four are.

The statements made by different natives, who subsequently reached Dongola with reports of the murder, varied considerably as to date, time, and place, but as the informants one and all spoke from hearsay, this was not surprising. It was ultimately ascertained that the rumours were perfectly true, and that Stewart, after accomplishing two-thirds of his journey from Khartoum to Dongola, had been murdered, together with Mr. Power, the British Consul at Khartoum and correspondent of the *Times*; M. Herbin, the French Consul at Khartoum, and a number of Greeks and Egyptians.

From Gordon's despatches and Sir Charles Wilson's subsequent report, it appears that the expedition, consisting of three steamers, left Khartoum on the night of September 10th, and proceeded to Shendy. The steamers then went on to Berber, and, after shelling the forts, two of them returned southward under the command of Gordon's man, Khasm-el-Mus, while Stewart and his companions tried to reach Dongola with the steamer *Abbas*, which carried one gun, and had in tow two boats full of men and women. All went well with the party until they approached Abu Hamid, when the rebels swarming along the shore opened so severe a fire that those on board the steamer had to cast the boats adrift. The boats fell into the hands of the rebels below Abu Hamid, and the Greeks and Egyptians they contained were taken in captivity to Berber. The *Abbas*, however, with forty-four men on board, pursued its course through the country inhabited by the Monassir tribe.

On the 18th September, while the steamer was approaching the village of Hebbeh, it ran upon a hidden rock, got caught when partly over, and was badly injured towards the stern. What afterwards occurred was subsequently related by an Egyptian stoker, named Hussein Ismail, who, taken prisoner at the time, ultimately escaped from the rebels and joined General Earle's column.

He said as follows:—

> We were passing at the time through Sheikh Wad Gamr's country, and had seen the people running away into the hills on both sides of the river. When it was found that the steamer could not be got off the rock, the small boat (a dingy with which the launch was provided) was filled with useful things, and sent to a little island near us. Four trips were made. Then Colonel Stewart drove a nail into the steamer's gun, filed off the projecting head, and threw both gun and ammunition overboard. The people now came down to the right bank in great numbers, shouting, 'Give us peace and grain.'
> We answered, 'Peace.' Suleiman Wad Gamr himself was in a small house near the bank, and he came out and called to Colonel Stewart to land without fear, but he added that the soldiers

must be unarmed or the people would be afraid of them. Colonel Stewart, after talking it over with the others, then crossed in the boat, with the two European Consuls (Mr. Power and M. Herbin), and Hassan Effendi, and entered a house belonging to a blind man named Fakri Wad Etman, to arrange with Suleiman for the purchase of camels to take us all down to Dongola.

None of the four had any arms, with the exception of Colonel Stewart, who carried a small revolver in his pocket. While they were in the house the rest of us began to land. Shortly afterwards we saw Suleiman come out of the house with a copper water-pot in his hand and make signs to the people who were gathered near the place. They immediately divided into two parties, one entering the house and the other rushing towards us on the banks, shouting and waving their spears. I was with the party which had landed when they charged down. We all threw ourselves into the river, whereupon the natives fired, and killed some of those in the water; several others were drowned, and the rest were speared as they approached the shore.

I swam to the island, and hid there till dark, when I was made prisoner with some others, and sent to Berti. I heard that Colonel Stewart and the two Europeans were killed at once, but Hassan Effendi held the blind man before him, so that they could not spear him. They accordingly spared his life, and he afterwards escaped to Berber. Two artillerymen, two sailors, and three natives, are, I believe, still alive at Berber, where they were sent by Suleiman. All the money found on board and in the pockets of the dead was divided among the murderers, and everything else of value was placed in two boxes and sent under a guard to Berber. The bodies of Colonel Stewart and the others were thrown at once into the river.

Hussein Ismail, the stoker, did not actually witness the death of Stewart, but heard of it from natives, who acknowledged that he fought desperately for his life, killing one of his assailants and wounding a second one with his revolver.

According to Gordon's *Diaries*, Stewart, Herbin, and Power left Khartoum of their own free will. The situation at the time was felt to be desperate. Herbin asked to go. Stewart said he would go if Gordon would exonerate him from deserting. Gordon, in reply, said that by remaining and being made prisoner Stewart could do no good, whereas by going down and telegraphing Gordon's views, Stewart would be doing him a service. The Greeks, nineteen in number, were sent as a body-guard, as Gordon subsequently stated. Stewart took with him the journal of events at Khartoum, from 1st March to 9th September, with the Foreign Office cipher, all the documents relating to Gordon's mission, and £60 in gold.[2] As to Gordon's reason for not accompanying the party, he stated in his *Diary* that "he couldn't if he would, as the people were not such fools as to let him, and that he wouldn't if he could, desert them." He added that it was generally believed that the passage of the *Abbas* down was an absolute certainty without danger.

Forty more whalers reached Wady Halfa in tow of the steamer *Ferouz* on the 16th October, and ten days later the Canadians also arrived. Wolseley now gave orders for the troops to hurry forward with all possible despatch. There was as yet but a mere advance guard at Dongola, including the Mounted Infantry, the first battalion of the Royal Sussex, some squadrons of the 19th Hussars and the Camel Corps; the main body of the expeditionary force being still at Wady Halfa, or even lower down the Nile. However, on November 2nd, the general advance practically commenced by the South Staffordshire Regiment embarking for Dongola.

The start of the South Staffordshire was followed by that of the Cornwall Regiment, some detachments of the Essex Regiment, the Royal Engineers, the West Kent, the Royal Irish, the Gordon Highlanders, and such portions of the Camel Corps, Artillery, and Transport Service as had not yet moved forward. While the mounted detachments proceeded by road along the western bank of the Nile, the foot-soldiers rowed up the river in the whale-boats.

From Wady Halfa to Dal, a distance of 123 miles, the course of the Nile comprises a series of dangerous rapids and intricate passages, the cataracts of Samneh, Attireh, Ambigol, Tangour, kasha, and Dal following each other in swift succession. The two first are not so difficult, but the rapids of Ambigol, which extend some four or five miles, are impassable at low Nile, and a severe trial even when the water is high. A short distance further, the Tangour Cataract bars the way, and it is as difficult of passage as that of Ambigol.

A quantity of dynamite had been sent out from England for blasting the rocks at this and other points, but when it reached Wady Halfa any such proceeding was impracticable, as the river was then too high. The dynamite being useless, the boats had either to be carried beyond

---

2. A letter from the *Mahdi* states that all these fell into his hands.

the cataracts or to ascend them, navigated by the Canadians or hauled along by natives specially engaged for the purpose. The difficulties of navigation between Wady Halfa and Samneh were illustrated by the experience of the Royal Engineers.

The detachment of engineers under Major Dorward, numbering fifty-seven, left Sarras in five boats at ten a.m., and by two o'clock next day had just succeeded in making the passage of the nearest cataract. For the greater portion of the distance, seven miles in all, the work was of a most difficult and exhausting description, the current being in some places exceedingly strong, and the banks rough and most unsuitable for towing. The boats proved to be not nearly strong enough for the work for which they were intended. The rudders, too, were found to be too small to be of use, and the Canadians found fault with the boats having been provided with keels, which were not only useless but in the way. The difficulties of the ascent were increased by the falling of the Nile, which, instead of running quietly and smoothly as before, now rushed in broken water over the shallows, and increased the number of rapids indefinitely.

Two new and formidable rapids made their appearance in two days between Sarras and Samneh. The passage of the rapids was aided by natives sent down from Dongola; without their help the soldiers could never have hauled the boats up; the cargoes had to be taken out at the foot of the cataracts and carried overland to the upper end; it was not till noon on the 5th of November that Major Dorward arrived at Ambukol, the voyage occupying over a month. Three of the boats which had been injured in the ascent were repaired with tin and lead plates and made ready to continue the journey. The work of navigation was described as most severe, beginning at daylight, and only ending when it became too dark for the men to see what they were doing; the crews were frequently breast-deep in water.

To provide for the wants and the relief of the men on the way, a series of stations had been established at Ambigol, Akasheh, Tangour, Zarkamatto (or Dal), Absarat, Kaibar, and Abu Fatmeh, there being on an average one for every thirty-three miles of the river's course between Sarras and Dongola. Each station was commanded by an officer, with a detachment of Egyptian soldiers under him and a commissariat *depôt*.

The hauling of the steamers sent up the river for the conveyance of stores or for towing purposes proved extremely difficult. It was necessary to sling them in cables passed under their keels, and secure them with steel hawsers round their hulls, and even then accidents frequently befell them. Some thousands of men were employed in hauling the vessels through the intricate and winding passages among the granite rocks that lie in the bed of the river. The s.s. *Ghizeh* passed successfully through the cataract of Akabat-el-Banet beyond Sarras, but on reaching Tangour she was wrecked and sunk, only her masts and funnel being above water. At one moment it seemed as if the *Nassif-el-Kheir* steamer would meet with a similar fate, and it was only by the greatest exertions and by a wonderful display of skill that she was eventually got past the rapids at Samneh.

About the same time the twin screw steamer *Montgomery* reached Samneh, having passed through the western channel, thus avoiding the full force of the cataract. The first of the steam-pinnaces from England was likewise launched at Sarras, being successfully hauled down an improvised slip from the railway to the river, although the drop was a steep one, and the engineers had no proper appliances for such work. One of the stern-wheel steamers built by Messrs. Yarrow and Co. was brought by barges in 700 pieces to Samneh, and riveted up and launched there. This vessel, which was 80 feet in length, 18 feet in beam, and only 16 inches in draught, was capable of carrying from 400 to 500 men and a machine-gun.

As may be supposed, there was no slight trouble in forwarding the stores which had been collected at Wady Halfa to Dongola. From Wady Halfa they went a little way by rail, and then to Ambigol by camel; between Ambigol and Tangour, and thence to Korti, by native boats and by whalers.

The Camel Corps,[3] above referred to, which had been formed in accordance with Lord Wolseley's instructions at an early stage, numbered in all some 1,500 men, and consisted of detachments from the Household Cavalry, and other mounted regiments, and from the Guards, each forming a separate division—Heavy Cavalry, Light Cavalry, and Guards, with a fourth regiment of Mounted Infantry. The detachment of marines was attached to the Guards.

The idea of forming such a corps was by no means novel, having been adopted by Napoleon I., who, when in Egypt, organized a similar force, mounted on dromedaries. This French Dromedary Corps, it is said, would march ninety miles in a day over the desert, without provisions or water. The practice, when in action, was for the animals

---

3. *With the Camel Corps Up the Nile: the 'Gordon Relief Expedition' Against the Mahdists, Sudan, 1885* by Lord Edward Gleichen also pub;ished by Leonaur.

to lie down, and for the men to fire over them.

Lord Wolseley's Camel Corps met on the road from Wady Halfa to Dongola with frequent mishaps and delays. The camels, only really at home on their native sands, often got so entangled amongst the rocks and blocks of granite that they could with difficulty be persuaded to advance. As the march was made along the east bank of the Nile, it became necessary to ferry the animals over the river at Dongola, and considerable time was spent in this operation, as boats were not always ready at the crossing places.

On the 28th October Wolseley and his staff left Wady Halfa by train for Sarras, whence they proceeded by camels to Hannek, escorted by a small detachment of Egyptian troops, and guided by Arab *sheikhs*. *En route* they met the Guards' Camel Corps, under Colonel Sir William Cummings, and pushed forward to the point where the steamer *Nassif-el-Kheir* was waiting to convey them to Dongola.

On the 3rd November Wolseley arrived at Dongola,[4] and was received by Sir Herbert Stewart and the *mudir*, or governor. The native troops lined the avenue from the river bank to the Mudirieh, and a detachment from the Sussex Regiment formed a guard of honour.

A *firman* from the *khedive* to the *mudirs*, the notables, and the people was read, ordering them to obey Lord Wolseley, "who had been sent to the Soudan to carry out such military operations as he might consider necessary."

His Lordship conferred on the *mudir* the Order of the Second Class of St. Michael and St. George. It is said that the *mudir* subsequently underwent a process of purification to rid himself from the contamination thus caused. The same *mudir* was afterwards found to be in direct communication with the enemy.

---

4. This is sometimes called New Dongola, and is not to be confused with Old Dongola, some 60 or 70 miles further south, on the east bank.

CHAPTER 38

Advance to Korti

Meanwhile disquieting rumours with regard to Gordon had reached Cairo, and Sir Evelyn Baring telegraphed to Lord Wolseley on November 3rd, asking him whether he had any reason to believe that there was any foundation for the reports which had been current in Cairo for the last few days, that Khartoum had been taken, and that Gordon was a prisoner.

Lord Wolseley telegraphed from Dongola the same day to the following effect:—

Major Kitchener telegraphs to Sir C. Wilson that he has seen a man named Ibrahim Wad-Beel, who recently came from the Arabs some distance south. He said all was quiet, and when Gordon received our messenger, he fired a salute, and held a parade of troops. A second telegram from Major Kitchener, dated November 3, announces that Haji Abdallah had arrived, and stated that a man from Shendy reported that the *Mahdi* came with a strong force to Omdurman and asked General Gordon to surrender. General Gordon replied that he would hold Khartoum for years.

The information as to the position of Khartoum up to this date was as follows:—

On the 8th October a letter had reached Cairo from M. Herbin, the French Consular Agent at Khartoum. It was as follows:—

Khartoum, July 29, 1884.
We are in a strong position at Khartoum. No need for alarm, unless it be the want of provisions (in two months our provisions will be exhausted). There is abundance of ammunition.

The least assistance would enable us to relieve the town. If at the moment of eating our last biscuit we were to attempt to retire in a body northwards, the retreat could only be effected at the cost of immense exertions and dangers (the means of transport are wanting). Besides this, the people would rise to a man to pillage the convoy. A few determined men might attempt to escape southwards to the Equator, but it would be necessary to abandon most of our soldiers, and all the women and children. Gordon Pasha has decided that he will share the fate of the town, and I think it my duty to share that of the few Frenchmen shut up here. Except for unforeseen circumstances, you can even now foresee what will happen.

On October 31st Sir E. Baring had received a telegram stating that an Arab of the Kababish tribe had brought the news that the *Mahdi's* troops had attacked Gordon's force at Omdurman opposite Khartoum, a few days before, but the attack was repulsed. In a telegram dated Debbeh, November 2nd, a correspondent gave the following additional news:—

Gordon attacked the rebels at Omdurman with a flotilla of twelve vessels, including steamers. For eight hours the engagement lasted. There were 25,000 rebels, and they had four Krupp guns. One gun burst. They retreated, leaving enormous numbers of dead behind them. The fugitives retired to Markeat, but were returning with an additional force.

On the 1st November, Sir E. Baring had received communications from Gordon to the effect that on the date they were sent off, *viz.*, 13th July, Khartoum was "all right and could hold out for four months."

The next letter received from Gordon appears to have been the following. Though dated in August, it was not received till the 23rd November.

It was as follows:—

General Gordon to Sir E. Baring.
Khartoum, August 5, 1884.
We are sending up steamers to Senaar, on Blue Nile, to open route. Arabs have left our vicinity in nearly all directions. When steamers come back we hope to recapture Berber by surprise, to place garrison in it, and Stewart and Power will descend

Nile to Dongola and communicate with you. The garrison of Berber (to which I shall give provisions for three months) will be the Egyptian troops from this place; and I also shall make the foreign consuls go down to Berber. I can look after security of Berber for two months, after which time I cannot be longer responsible for it, and you must relieve it from Dongola, or let the garrison perish and Berber be again taken by Arabs. You will dislike this arrangement, perhaps, but I have no option; and it would entail no risks to you, seeing that Berber will be held during your advance.

All well here, and troops elated at the result of their recent victories.

Notwithstanding every effort to get the troops up the river as rapidly as possible, so many difficulties intervened that the task occupied much longer than had been anticipated. Early in November Wolseley telegraphed that, owing to steamers breaking down, difficult coaling, and scarcity of native labour, he did not expect to concentrate his force at Ambukol, on the Nile just above Old Dongola, until the end of the year.

The necessity for pushing forward with all possible despatch was made clear to Wolseley by a letter of much later date, received from Gordon on the 17th November, saying that he could hold out for forty days with ease, but that after that time it would be difficult. The following is an extract:—

> Khartoum, 4th November, 1884.
> Post came in yesterday from Debbeh, Kitchener, dated 14th October, cipher letter from Lord Wolseley, 20th September last, which I cannot decipher, for Colonel Stewart took the cipher with him. No other communications have been received here since 31st, letter which arrived a week after Stewart's steamer left this.
> At Metammeh, waiting your orders, are five steamers with nine guns. We can hold out forty days with ease; after that it will be difficult. Terrible about loss of steamer. I sent Stewart, Power, and Herbin down, telling them to give you all information. With Stewart was the journal of all events from 1st March to the 10th September. The steamer carried a gun and had a good force on board.
> Since 10th March we have had up to date, exclusive of Kitch-

ener's 14th October, only two despatches; one, Dongola, with no date; one from Souakim, 5th May; one of same import, 27th April. I have sent out a crowd of messengers in all directions during eight months. I should take the road from Ambukol to Metammeh, where my steamers wait for you. Leontides, Greek Consul-General, Hanswell, Austrian Consul, all right. Stewart, Power, and Herbin went down in the *Abbas*. Your expedition is for relief of garrison, which I failed to accomplish. I decline to agree that it is for me personally. You may not know what has passed here. The Arabs camped outside Khartoum on the 12th March; we attacked them on the 16th March, got defeated and lost heavily, also a gun. We then from that date had continual skirmishes with Arabs.

★★★★★

The soldiers are only half a-month in arrears. We issue paper money, and also all the cloth in magazines. All the captives with the *Mahdi* are well. The nuns, to avoid an Arab marriage, are ostensibly married to Greeks. Slatin is with *Mahdi*, and has all his property, and is well treated; but I hear today he is in chains. A mysterious Frenchman[1] is with *Mahdi*, who came from Dongola. We have got a decoration made and distributed, with a grenade in the centre; three classes—gold, silver, pewter. Kitchener says he has sent letters and got none in reply. I have sent out during last month at least ten. Steamer with this leaves tomorrow for Metammeh. Do not let any Egyptian soldiers come up here; take command of steamers direct, and turn out Egyptian *fellaheen*. If capture of steamer with Stewart is corroborated, tell French Consul-General that *Mahdi* has the cipher he gave Herbin. Hassen Effendi, telegraph clerk, was with Stewart. You should send a party to the place to investigate affairs and take the steamer.

On the 15th November, Lord Hartington telegraphed to Lord Wolseley to know how the information in Gordon's letter affected his plans. In reply, his Lordship, who had gone back to Wady Halfa, to hurry forward the expedition, stated that Gordon's letter made no change in his plans, but that it seemed to indicate the almost impossibility of Gordon's relief without fighting, adding that he, Wolseley, had sent Gordon the following message:—

---

1. This was the notorious Oliver Pain.

Wady Halfa, November 17, 1884. Yours of 4th inst. received 17th; the first I have had from you. I shall be at Kasr Dongola in four days.

A few days later an Arab merchant who arrived at Dongola from Khartoum *viâ* Shendy and Ambukol, and who had come by the desert route, stated that both water and fodder were plentiful. This news was confirmed by a messenger who returned to Dongola from Khartoum on the 19th November.

On the 28th a messenger sent by Gordon arrived at Dongola with a letter addressed to the *khedive*, Nubar Pasha, and Baring, in cipher, and dated as far back as the 9th September. The letter began:—

> There is money and provisions in Khartoum for four months, after which we shall be embarrassed.

A telegram from Gordon to Sir E. Baring and Nubar Pasha, undated, but received 29th November, gave the following details:—

> Seeing now that the Nile is high, and steamers can go as far as Berber, I have formed an expedition of 2,000 men of the Khartoum garrison, which will proceed by steamers in order to rescue the Mudirieh of Berber from the hands of the rebels. After its recovery this force will remain at Berber with food for two months only, and if in that time the relieving army does not reach Berber in order to reinforce it, the Nile will have fallen and the islands will be dry, and the same result will ensue as before. Therefore it is to be hoped that the necessary troops will be sent to seize the Ghesireh of Berber while the Nile is high; and Stewart is going down in the small steamer, the *Abbas*, to proceed to Dongola by way of Berber, in order to communicate (with you) on the Soudan question.

On the 29th November a messenger who had been despatched with a letter to Gordon, but had been taken prisoner not far from Khartoum, and had subsequently made his escape, came into camp. He reported that the *Mahdi's* troops were suffering from disease, food was very dear, the Arabs were deserting, but the Kordofan men were faithful to him; that Gordon sent to the *Mahdi*, inviting him, if he were the real *Mahdi*, to dry up the Nile and cross over; that five hundred regulars recently went over to Gordon; that the regulars still with the *Mahdi* were discontented; that on the 14th he saw an attack made on Khartoum between the Blue and White Niles; that it was repulsed, and the *Mahdi*, who was looking on, was very angry because it had been made without his orders.

Aware that time was of paramount importance, Wolseley, in order to stimulate his men to exertion, offered a prize of £100 to the battalion which should make the quickest passage from Sarras to Debbeh, twenty miles further up the river, a measure which was much criticized by a portion of the British Press.[2]

Wolseley now gave orders for the formation of a small naval brigade, to be commanded by Lord Charles Beresford, his naval *aide-de-camp*.[3]

On the 23rd November, some cases of smallpox having occurred at Dongola, Sir Herbert Stewart started to select another camping-ground at Debbeh, a little further up the river.

All the remaining troops destined to take part in the expedition reached Wady Halfa by the end of November, with the exception of the 1st battalion of the Cameron Highlanders, which remained at Korosko.

The advance in force from Dongola commenced on the 2nd December, from which date the troops as they arrived were moved on beyond Debbeh to Ambukol, where a *depôt* for supplies had been formed and placed in charge of Stewart. The headquarters were established at the latter place on the 12th December. From Ambukol the force was moved a few miles further up the river to Korti, a much healthier spot.

Sir Herbert Stewart, with the Mounted Infantry and Guards' Camel Corps, reached Korti on the 15th December, after a march along the east bank of the Nile.

Wolseley's arrival at Korti on the 16th was followed by that of the South Staffordshire Regiment. The last companies of the South Staffordshire, with part of the Sussex Regiment, reached the front on the 22nd, and they were speedily followed by other detachments. The Light Camel Corps, under Colonel M'Calmont, arrived on the 24th, after a twenty days' march from Wady Halfa, and at the same time the Heavy Camel Corps came up from Debbeh. General Buller, the Chief

---

2. The prize, after a keen competition, was won by the Royal Irish Regiment, the Royal Highlanders coming in second, and the West Kent third.

3. The appointment of Lord Charles Beresford was perhaps justly regarded as a piece of favouritism. Commander Hammill, who had for months been engaged in the preliminary work on the Nile, and whose services in passing the steamers through the cataracts have been already referred to, was passed over.

of the Staff, reached the front soon afterwards.

Of the Nile journey Wolseley reported to Lord Hartington:

> The English boats have up to this point fulfilled all my expectations. The men are in excellent health, fit for any trial of strength, as the result of constant manual labour.

As a commentary on the above, it may be mentioned that nine out of sixteen boats which brought up some of the Duke of Cornwall's Regiment were lost, and the remainder, owing to the slightness of their build, had to be patched with tin to prevent their sinking—over fifty boats in all were lost. There can be no doubt as to the "constant manual labour" mentioned by Lord Wolseley. The men arrived in a deplorable plight, many of them without either boots or trousers. A more ragged set of soldiers never arrived at the seat of war. According to one account there was literally not a sound garment in the whole column, and the men resembled Falstaff's ragged regiment rather than a body of British troops.

By Christmas Day, a great part of the expeditionary force was concentrated at Korti.[4]

It now became necessary to decide upon the route to be adopted by the expeditionary force in order to reach Khartoum. The one important question to consider was that of time; already the journey up the river had taken much longer than was expected. The season during which military operations could be carried on was limited, and if, as had been intended, the expedition was to return before the hot weather there was not a day to spare. Moreover, Gordon's latest communications showed that he was rapidly running short of provisions, and if not speedily relieved Khartoum must fall.

As a military operation, the route by the Nile offered many advantages, and had time permitted there is no doubt that Wolseley's whole force would have gone that way. But the distance to be traversed requiring months for its accomplishment, rendered it imperative to adopt some other expedient if Gordon was to be relieved at all. Under these circumstances, it was determined to divide the expeditionary force into two columns, one to proceed across the desert to Metammeh, a distance of 185 miles, and thence to Khartoum, and the other to proceed by the river up the Nile Valley.

Shortly stated, Wolseley's plans for the campaign were as follows:—

---

4. The last whaler with troops did not arrive till 7th February, 1885.

1st. By despatching a column across the desert to Metammeh to secure the shortest passage to Khartoum, and at the same time to hold the wells at Gakdul and Abu Klea, and to occupy Metammeh whilst communications were maintained with Gordon.

2nd. By despatching a second column along the Nile Valley to disperse the rebels around Hamdab, fifty-two miles distant from Korti, to punish the Monassir tribes for the murder of Colonel Stewart, to leave Berti in safety, to rid Abu Hamid of the enemy, and to open up the desert route from thence to Korosko, whence stores and ammunition for an attack on Berber would be forwarded. Thus covering a great bend of the Nile, the column would operate on Berber, dislodge the rebels there, and join hands with the other column on the banks of the Nile at Metammeh.

In a letter to the Secretary at War, Wolseley gives the reasons for adopting the above plan of operations in the following words:—

> I had always thought it possible that upon arrival here I might find it necessary to operate beyond this point in two columns—one continuing up the river in our English-built boats, while the other pushed rapidly across the desert to Metammeh, and it was with the view of securing to myself the power of moving across this desert that I proposed the formation of a Camel Brigade.
>
> Any march across this desert with a small column, as an isolated operation, would be hazardous, and for the purpose of my mission a most useless undertaking. Such a column would most probably be able to fight its way into Khartoum; possibly it might fight its way out again; but it could never bring away General Gordon and his garrison in safety. Undertaken, however, under present circumstances, the march of a small force across this desert presents a very different aspect. The so-called *Mahdi* and his supporters are well aware that they have to deal not only with it, but also with the English Army, which they know is advancing up the Nile on Khartoum by Abu Hamid and Berber. Upon arrival here I had to decide whether I should keep all my force together and follow the Nile Valley to Khartoum, or to divide it into two columns—one following the river, while the other was pushed rapidly across to Metammeh.
>
> If I were not restricted by time, the first course would be by far the most satisfactory, the safest, and would insure the best

results; but I know that General Gordon is pressed by want of food, and the hot season is not far off, when military operations in this country are trying to the health of European soldiers. I therefore decided upon the last-mentioned course.

The first, or Desert column, was placed under the command of Sir Herbert Stewart, and consisted of men mainly belonging to different sections of the Camel Corps; a company of the Royal Engineers, part of the 19th Hussars, and detachments of the commissariat and medical corps. The force was to be accompanied by 2,000 camels for the purposes of transport. Sir Charles Wilson was to proceed with Stewart, and to the former was allotted the task of opening up communication with Gordon when once the Nile should be struck at Metammeh.

Lord Charles Beresford and a small body of seamen were told off to accompany the force, to take possession of any of Gordon's steamers which might be found at Metammeh. A detachment of infantry was to proceed to Khartoum by the steamers, and Sir Charles Wilson was empowered on entering Khartoum to march his men through the city to show the people that British troops were at hand, but he was directed only to stay long enough to confer with Gordon.

The Nile column was placed under Major-General Earle, and consisted of the Staffordshire and Duke of Cornwall's Regiments, the Black Watch, the Gordon Highlanders, a squadron of the 19th Hussars, a battery of Egyptian Artillery, an Egyptian Camel Corps, and the auxiliary native troops of the Mudir of Dongola. The whole, with transport, numbered about 3,000 men.

CHAPTER 39

Stewart's Desert March

The march across the desert being determined upon, the first step was to seize and hold the wells of Gakdul, some ninety-five miles distant, and there establish a *depôt* for ammunition, provisions, and stores. This being accomplished, and a garrison being left to guard the post, the remainder of the force, with the baggage animals, were to return to Korti and make a fresh start with further supplies. This somewhat cumbrous arrangement was necessitated by the insufficient transport at the general's disposal.

On the 30th December, Stewart's force, consisting of 73 officers, 1,032 non-commissioned officers and men, 2,099 camels, and forty horses, paraded for inspection on the rising ground south of Korti, preparatory to the march across the Bayuda Desert.

The baggage-camels were arranged in columns, with from twenty to thirty marching abreast, and with fifty yards interval between each troop. The Guards in front and the Mounted Infantry in the rear were in close companies ready to dismount and form square at a moment's notice. Wolseley inspected the whole, and in the afternoon the cavalry scouts, under Major (afterwards Sir Herbert) Kitchener with some Arab guides, moved off in front.

A little later the great column got in motion, striking straight off across the undulating and pebbly plain towards the distant horizon. It was a strange sight to see the camels, with their necks stretching out like ostriches and their long legs, moving off in military array, until the rising dust first blended desert, men, and camels in one uniform grey hue, and finally hid them from the sight of those who remained in camp. Scared gazelles rose from among the rocks and bounded away across the desert, from time to time, as the force advanced. Broad as was the face on which this column marched, it extended fully a mile

in length. The first halt was made at five p.m. with a view to ascertaining the whereabouts of the hussars, who had gone on in the morning to collect wood and light fires at the first halting-place. After some time it was discovered that they had taken the wrong route, and it was not till midnight that they joined the column. The halt lasted for an hour and a half. General Stewart then gave orders for the column to close up, and for the camels to proceed on a broader front.

When they moved on again in the bright moonlight, the length of the column was reduced to half-a-mile, and was not only under better control on the line of march, but more able to resist any sudden attack.

The march continued until early in the forenoon of the 31st, when a long halt was called, and the camels were unloaded. There was some excitement among the men when they halted for the first bivouac, owing to the uncertainty as to the whereabouts and disposition of the inhabitants. Only a few huts were visible, and these were deserted. Plenty of green fodder was obtainable, and the troops remained on the spot undisturbed until three in the afternoon, when a fresh start was made.

The force now marched through a beautiful country. Great spreading plains covered with mimosa and scrub succeeded one another, bounded by black rocky mountains, through the gorges of which the troops passed only to emerge on fresh tracts of the same character. The formation observed almost throughout the march was columns of companies, and the force was so distributed that in two minutes three squares could be formed in échelon to resist any attack.

At a quarter-past five the column again halted, and then, with a bright moon, resumed its way, passing the wells of Hambok, where only a small supply of water was found. After leaving Hambok the route was amidst verdant trees and long grass, forming quite a contrast to what one would expect in a so-called desert.

Shortly after midnight a halt was made at the wells of El Howeiyah. At 8.30 on the 1st January, 1885, the march was resumed till one p.m., when a halt was made during the heat of the day.

Thus far the column had met neither friends nor foes, but just before this halt the capture was made of a man and his family, who were watching their flocks. The man, who turned out to be a noted robber chief, was thenceforth made use of as a guide.

Later in the afternoon the column marched again until dark, then, waiting until the moon rose, resumed its way. Without any further halt the column continued its march throughout the night. During the night one or two prisoners were taken; one of them being an Arab from Metammeh, who gave important information.

At four a.m. on the 2nd the force was opposite the wells of Abou Halfa, three miles from the main track. A company of Mounted Infantry was sent to seize the wells. This was effected, only a few natives being seen, and these fled at the approach of the troops.

Three hours later the mouth of the gorge leading to Gakdul wells, distant 95 miles from Korti, was reached. The column had occupied forty-six hours and fifty minutes on the march, and been thirty-two and three-quarter hours actually on the move. There had been no casualties on the road, and the men, although they had remained almost without sleep since leaving Korti, were in the best of spirits.

The wells at Gakdul proved to be three in number, situated at the north end of a large circular plain or natural amphitheatre, surrounded by steep rocks of yellow sandstone some 300 feet in height. The day was occupied in watering the camels. At eight p.m. Sir Herbert Stewart, with all the camels and the whole force except the Guards and Engineers, started on the return journey to Korti.

The force, numbering in all about 400, which was left to guard the wells, set to work under Major Dorward, of the Royal Engineers, to construct three forts on the high ground, and made improvements in the arrangements for watering and in the means of access to the wells. Major Kitchener's Mounted Infantry captured a convoy of camels laden with dates for the *Mahdi*. The appearance of natives in the neighbourhood was reported, but otherwise the little party at the wells met with no excitement. On the 11th a convoy of stores and ammunition, under Colonel Clarke, arrived at the wells from Korti.

Stewart and the column which accompanied him back from Gakdul returned to Korti on January the 5th. Lord Wolseley rode out to meet the column and complimented the General on his achievement.

The prisoners taken stated that Metammeh was occupied in force by the *Mahdi's* army. Some put the fighting men there at 2,000, others said that there were 5,000. The enemy had thrown up an intrenchment and were prepared to receive an attack.

In the interval between General Stewart's departure from and return to Korti, Lord Wolseley (on the 30th December) had received from a messenger from Khartoum a communication from Gordon, showing the desperate condition of things there.

The messenger brought a piece of paper the size of a postage-stamp, on which was written:—

> Khartoum all right.
>   (Signed)   C. G. Gordon.
> December 14th, 1884.

It was genuine, as Gordon's writing was recognised, and his seal was on the back of it.

Gordon told the messenger to give Lord Wolseley the following message:—

> We are besieged on three sides, Omdurman, Halfiyeh and Khojali. Fighting goes on day and night. Enemy cannot take us, except by starving us out. Do not scatter your troops. Enemy are numerous. Bring plenty of troops if you can. We still hold Omdurman on the left bank and the fort on the right bank. The *Mahdi's* people have thrown up earthworks within rifle-shot of Omdurman. The *Mahdi* lives out of gunshot. About four weeks ago the *Mahdi's* people attacked Omdurman and disabled one steamer. We disabled one of the *Mahdi's* guns. Three days after fighting was renewed on the south, and the rebels were again driven back.
>
> (Secret and confidential.)—Our troops in Khartoum are suffering from lack of provisions. Food we still have is little; some grain and biscuit. We want you to come quickly. You should come by Metammeh or Berber. Make by these two roads. Do not leave Berber in your rear. Keep enemy in your front, and when you have taken Berber send me word from Berber. Do this without letting rumours of your approach spread abroad. In Khartoum there are no butter nor dates, and little meat. All food is very dear.

It is clear that the words "Khartoum all right" were simply intended to deceive in the event of the written communication getting into the wrong hands. This became evident later on from a letter which Gordon wrote to a friend in Cairo at the same date as he penned the words "Khartoum all right," but which did not arrive till the month of February.

> All is up I expect a catastrophe in ten days' time. It would not have been so if our people had kept me better informed as to their intentions. My *adieux* to all.   C. G. Gordon.

The latter part of the verbal message is significant, and seems to imply that Gordon anticipated that if the approach of the troops were to become known, the treachery which he had all along expected would be accelerated.

It is scarcely necessary to say that only the written portion of Gordon's communication, *viz.*, "Khartoum all right," was disclosed to the British public, who thus formed a very erroneous opinion as to his real position.

It does not appear that Wolseley's plans were changed by the receipt of Gordon's message; there was, in fact, nothing to be done but to push on with all possible speed.

On the 8th January Stewart, having strengthened his column, again set out for Gakdul.

On the 10th, the force reached the Hambok wells, whence Stewart pushed forward to Howeiyah. On arriving there it was found that the Engineers and Mounted Infantry, left behind on the previous journey, had sunk several holes to a depth of nine feet or so in the rough gravel soil near a dry watercourse, and that some of these holes contained about six inches of cold opal-coloured water with a chalybeate taste. Unfortunately the holes in question had been practically drained a couple of hours before by the men of the previous convoy; so that Stewart's troops had to content themselves with only a quart per head for the entire day.

Resuming their forward march, they reached a grassy plain to the south of the Galif range shortly after sunset, and here they bivouacked until the following morning. A fresh start was then made, but the heat and excessive thirst were beginning to tell both on men and camels, thirty of the latter dropping dead on the road. However, the column persevered in its course, and the wells of Abu Haifa were reached at three in the afternoon. Pannikins, canteens, water-bottles, and horse-buckets were soon at work, the men taking their turn until their thirst was quenched.

Early on the 12th the column was astir, and at eleven o'clock it defiled along a rocky gorge into the crater-like amphitheatre where the Gakdul reservoirs were situated. Here was found the force left to guard the wells when Stewart returned to Korti. It was ascertained that more wells were to be found across the hills at a distance of a mile or two, but the three natural receptacles at Gakdul itself were computed to contain among them nearly half-a-million gallons of water, so that for military purposes the supply was regarded as practically inexhaustible.

Colonel Burnaby arrived at Gakdul on the 13th with a convoy of grain. The following day, the march towards Abu Klea was resumed, Major Kitchener going back to Korti, and Colonel Vandeleur being left with 400 of the Sussex Regiment at Gakdul to hold that station, whilst the Guards who had previously protected the wells joined the column. The force was composed as follows—Three troops 19th Hussars; Naval Brigade, one Gardner gun; half battery Royal Artillery, *i.e.,* three (7-pounder) screw-guns; Heavy Camel Regiment; Guards' Camel Regiment; Mounted Infantry, Camel Regiment; Sussex Regiment; Naval Brigade Royal Engineers; Transport and Medical Corps; in all 1,581 men with 90 horses, 2,880 camels, and 340 drivers.

Beyond Gakdul, the road led across a more barren region than that which had been previously traversed. Only ten miles were covered on the afternoon of the 14th.

The following day the column was again on the move at 5 a.m. When opposite Gebel-el-Nil, a well-known mountain in the desert, a halt was made to allow of the stragglers coming up. The march was now telling severely on the heavily laden camels, which had been for several days on half allowance of forage. Numbers of them fell through sheer exhaustion, and had to be shot to put them out of their misery or to prevent their falling into the hands of the enemy. At noon the march was resumed until the evening, when, after going twenty-four miles since the morning, the column halted near another mountain, Gebel Serghain.

On the 16th the column started at 5 a.m. It was then too dark to see anything, and the force got into some confusion. This, however, was soon rectified on daylight appearing.

Whilst halted at half-past eleven for breakfast, a report was received from Lieutenant-Colonel Barrow, of the 19th Hussars, who had been sent forward with his squadron to reconnoitre the neighbourhood of the Abu Klea wells, stating that he had seen some fifty of the enemy standing in groups on the hills about four miles north-east of Abu Klea. Shortly after this the whole force was advanced. The ground now traversed was a vast flat plain favourable for military evolutions, and the Guards' Camel Regiment, the Heavy Camel Regiment, and the Mounted Infantry Camel Regiment moved in a broad front in line of columns at half distance. Before the column rose steep black mountains through which it had to pass, and in the centre, at a point where the ground slopes towards the Nile, were the wells of Abu

Klea.

It soon became evident that the enemy was in force, and looking to the hour (two p.m.) Stewart deemed it undesirable to attempt an attack that day. The column, therefore, was ordered to bivouac when about three miles from Abu Klea.

Abu Klea is an elevated spot in the desert, about 300 feet above the level of the Nile, distant above forty-three miles, on the caravan track, from Gakdul, and from Metammeh twenty-three miles.

On the troops bivouacking for the night the men were set to work cutting down brushwood, and forming a *zeriba* round, the baggage and camels. A stone breastwork with a frontage of about 150 yards was thrown up as an additional protection some 100 yards further to the front. Pickets were also placed on the hills to the left of the position.

From an advanced position occupied by the outposts the enemy's camp was sighted across a pass about two miles ahead, and in front of it a long line of flags marked the position. Meanwhile two troops of the enemy were watching the movements of the British force from the hills on the left front.

Towards six o'clock the enemy fired a few stray shots on the British right flank, to which three of the screw-guns replied with a few rounds. The enemy continued firing at intervals all night, with no results beyond one slight casualty.

Chapter 40

The Battle of Abu Klea

Upon the 17th inst. it was plain that the enemy were in force. During the night they had constructed works on the right flank of the column, from which a distant but well-aimed fire was maintained. Both on the right and in front the manoeuvring of their troops in line, with drums beating and banners waving, was apparent, and everything pointed to the probability of an attack being made. Under these circumstances Sir Herbert Stewart was in no particular hurry to advance, in the hope that his apparent dilatoriness might induce the enemy to make the attack.

The skirmishers had been engaged from early dawn, and bullets soon began to fall thicker and thicker around the British position; men who had jumped up to stretch their legs were not sorry to lie down again under cover of the little wall which surrounded the *zeriba*. After waiting some time for the attack which the enemy did not seem disposed to make, the general ordered breakfast to be served out at 9 a.m., and made his preparations for an advance. His intentions were, briefly, to fight his way to the wells of Abu Klea at any cost, leaving only a small garrison to protect the baggage and camels in the *zeriba*; the wells once won, to send back for the baggage, feed and water the column, and push on to Metammeh at once.

Meanwhile the fire became hotter and hotter. Stewart seemed a favourite target for the enemy's marksmen, and brought grief to several. The first to fall was Major Dickson, of the Royals, shot through the knee. Colonel Burnaby's horse next received a wound, and was led limping to the rear. Major Gough (commanding the Mounted Infantry) was knocked senseless by a bullet on the temple, and Lieutenant Lyall, R.A., was struck in the back by another.

The camp was now strengthened to admit of its being held by a reduced garrison of 40 Mounted Infantry, 125 Sussex, and details; and the rest of the force, with the exception of the Hussars and a few of the Mounted Infantry, proceeded to form square, in which formation the advance was to be made.

The square was formed as follows:—Left front face, two companies Mounted Infantry; right front face, two companies Guards, with the three guns Royal Artillery in the centre. Left face, two companies Mounted Infantry; one company Heavy Camel Regiment. Right face, two companies Guards, detachment Royal Sussex. Rear face, four companies Heavy Camel Regiment, with Naval Brigade and one Gardner gun in the centre. In the centre were some thirty camels for carrying water, ammunition, &c.

It will be noticed that each face of the square, except the rear, was made up of a composite force, the object being, probably, to provide against a break of corps at the angles. Thus the Guards held the right forward angle, and the Mounted Infantry the left; the Heavy Camel Regiment held the rear face and the left rear angle; the Sussex Regiment filled the gap in the right rear face between the Guards and the Heavy Camel Regiment. Thus there was a break of corps only at the right rear angle.

It should be stated that after various experiments all idea of fighting on the camels had been abandoned, and that in the operations of the column at this time and subsequently the camels were simply used for purposes of locomotion. This being so, the terms "Camel Corps" and "Mounted Infantry," when used must in most cases be understood as meaning dismounted troops belonging to those corps respectively.

At about 10 a.m. the force advanced, its front and flanks being covered by skirmishers who engaged those of the enemy. A square formation is unsuited for rapid movement, and the men went forward at a slow march to allow of the guns and camels coming up, keeping always on open rocky ground, so as to avoid spots where the enemy could collect unseen.

No sooner had the advance commenced, than a redoubled fire from the enemy showed that these movements had attracted their attention. The hills on each side were alive with their sharpshooters and spearmen, running parallel to the square and keeping up a hot fire all the time. The skirmishers had to do their utmost before they succeeded in reducing the fire which at this time poured down upon Stewart's men. The ground was rough and uneven, and intersected with ruts and water-courses, which it was difficult to get over without disarranging the square, so that frequent halts had to be made.

At 11 a.m. the column brought its left face opposite the left flank of the enemy's position, and it became necessary for him to attack in order to avoid being enfiladed.

When about 1,500 yards from a line of flags on the left front marking the enemy's position, the guns fired four or five shells, and hundreds of men were seen to rise up and bolt, leaving only their standards visible. Then on a sudden came the enemy's attack. To resist it the square was halted on the face of a hill sloping towards the enemy's position, and a hurried attempt was made to close up the rear. When the order to close up was given, the Naval Brigade had begun to move the Gardner gun from its position in middle of the rear face and put it at the left rear corner of the square. In order to do this it had to be taken through the camels, which were crowded together between the two positions, and in the confusion when the rear closed up the gun and the sailors round it were left outside the formation; they were thus at first dangerously exposed, but, happily, just before the rush the Gardner gun was drawn back, taken through the left face, and brought into action a few paces in front of it.

The first intimation of the impending charge was the running in at full speed of the skirmishers. They were followed by a black mass of Arabs, said to have been 5,000 in number, who, rising suddenly out of cover when the troops were at a distance of 450 yards from the flags, made straight for the square. Their shouts as they came on were described by an eyewitness as being like the roar of the sea. Headed by mounted *emirs* or *sheikhs* with banners in hand, they neared the left front of the square, where they were received with such a deadly fire from the (dismounted) Mounted Infantry that they swerved round the left flank and made a furious onslaught on the left rear of the square, where the Heavy Camel Regiment was stationed.

The rush was so sudden that the skirmishers had barely time to reach the square before the enemy fell upon the Heavy Camel Corps,[1] who, to avoid killing their own men, were for some minutes compelled to reserve their fire. Among the first to feel the effects of the charge were the Naval Brigade, which had, as already stated, put their

---

1. There was something anomalous in placing heavy cavalry in an infantry square, a formation altogether contrary to the spirit of their training and traditions. Notwithstanding this, the behaviour of the force in the *mêlée* which ensued, and the steadiness which enabled the square to be re-formed under circumstances which rendered disaster possible, were worthy of the finest traditions of the British Army.

gun outside of the square. After firing eight rounds at the advancing enemy, it was noticed that the elevation was too great. This was rectified, but after six more rounds the gun jammed and became useless. When Lord Charles Beresford was attempting to clear it with the assistance of his chief boatswain's mate, the enemy came on them, spearing the latter, and knocking Lord Charles down under the gun. His two officers, Lieutenants Pigott and De Lisle, were speared, whilst the rest of the Naval Brigade were driven back for a few minutes, when a rush was made, and the gun recaptured, Lord Charles then getting back unhurt into the square.

With such impetuosity was the charge made that the Heavy Camel Corps were borne back, and the square penetrated by the sheer weight of numbers.

Frantic shouts to the Guards to stand firm were heard. Both officers and men still faced the enemy, although the line of the Heavies was bent into an irregular semicircle extending into the square as far as the kneeling camels behind. These camels formed a useful breastwork, beyond which the assailants could not penetrate, and over and around the animals the battle raged, both parties fighting hand to hand, bayonet against spear.

For ten minutes a desperate struggle extended from the left rear to the centre. It was at this period that Colonel Burnaby fell, a spear having severed his jugular vein, but not until he had killed with his own hand more than one of his assailants. Stewart's horse was thrown off his legs and then speared, and his orderly was killed beside him. The general's life was only saved by the coolness and presence of mind of Sir Charles Wilson, who was standing next to him. A few of the enemy had crawled in between the camels, and one man who had succeeded in doing this was making, spear in hand, for the General. Sir Charles Wilson observed the move, whipped out his revolver, and shot the man dead.

Many of the camels were speared by the assailants, and the interior of the square formed a mass of falling camels and struggling combatants, half hidden amid dust and smoke. The issue could not, however, be said to have been a moment in doubt, for the Heavy Camel Corps were soon supported by soldiers from the other side of the square. These were in readiness to oppose any further advance had the line given way, though they were obliged to withhold their fire so long as the two parties were mingled in the strife. Later on they faced about and fired into the square, killing no doubt both friends and foes.

It was not long before every Arab who had entered the square was killed, the rest beaten back, and amid three hearty cheers the square re-formed on fresh ground away from the killed and wounded.

It was now half-past three, and as the enemy moved off the guns opened on them with grape at 500 yards range, and hastened their retreat.[2] They withdrew in a slow, sullen way, turning round from time to time as if anxious to come on again. Eventually the last of them disappeared over the sand-hills.

The rifles with which some of the enemy were armed were all of the Remington pattern, and formed part of the arms captured from Hicks Pasha's army. The rest of the enemy carried the heavy Soudan sword or a long spear, supplemented in most cases by a shield of tough hide. The Berber force, which had a contingent of 250 horsemen, retreated towards Berber after the action.

Throughout the battle the enemy fought with the most reckless courage and absolute disregard of death.

The troops on the right attack were led by Abu Saleh, Emir of Metammeh, on the left by Mahommed Khair, Emir of Berber. The latter was wounded, and retired early; but Saleh came desperately on at the head of a hundred fanatics, escaping the fire of the Martinis marvellously, until at last he was shot down in the square.

The loss of the enemy was not less than 1,200 killed and wounded, 800 bodies being counted on the open space flanking the square. The slaughter would have been greater still had the square been able to open fire as soon as the charge commenced, instead of having to wait till the skirmishers had run in. But for this, in spite of their bravery, comparatively few of the assailants would have succeeded in coming to close quarters.

The British loss, *viz.*, ten officers and sixty-five non-commissioned officers and men killed, and eighty-five wounded, was very heavy for a force whose total number was only 1,800 men. The following is the list of officers killed:—

Colonel Burnaby, Royal Horse Guards; Major Carmichael, 5th Lancers; Major Atherton, 5th Dragoon Guards; Major Gough, Royal Dragoons; Captain Darley, 4th Dragoon Guards; Lieutenant Law, 4th

---

2. The force opposed to Stewart was stated by the prisoners taken to consist of ten tribes of about 800 men each. According to the report of the Intelligence Department, their numbers were still greater, and were made up of Ababdeh, Bisharin, and other Arabs from Berber, soldiers of the old Egyptian army, Arabs and others from Metammeh, men of the *Mahdi's* regular army (400 armed with rifles), and Arabs of various tribes from Kordofan.

Dragoon Guards; Lieutenant Wolfe, Scots Greys; Lieutenants Pigott and De Lisle, Naval Brigade; Lord St. Vincent.[3]

The greatest loss on Stewart's side fell on the Heavy Cavalry Camel Corps, of whose officers six were killed and two wounded. The extraordinary disproportion of killed and wounded officers as compared with the rank and file is remarkable, and speaks volumes for the self-sacrificing devotion of the officers of both services.

The seizure of the Abu Klea wells was a matter of paramount importance, and the detachment of the 19th Hussars, which had come up too late to strike at the retreating foe, was pushed forward to perform this service. This they were able to accomplish without resistance, a fact which goes far to prove the demoralization of the enemy. The Hussars, as stated in Stewart's report, took possession of the wells at 5 p.m. They then sent back filled water-skins for their comrades at the *zeriba*. Jaded as the rest of the men were by marching, by night alarms, by a fierce heat, and an encounter with an enemy seven times their number, they reached the wells soon after.

The water was plentiful, and though of a muddy yellow colour, it was fit for drinking. At eight at night a portion of the Guards, with some of the Heavy Camel Corps and Mounted Infantry, were sent back to fetch the occupants of the *zeriba* in the rear. The force then bivouacked on the ground near the wells without tents, provisions, or baggage. The night was piercingly cold, and the men had to get between the camels, and cover themselves with the baggage nets for warmth and shelter.

Next morning the party despatched to the *zeriba* returned, and the whole column, including camels and baggage, was now concentrated at the wells. On the arrival of the *zeriba* detachment with stores and provisions, the force partook of its first meal since the morning of the previous day.

---

3. Died of his wounds subsequently.

CHAPTER 41

The Advance on Metammeh

Although active preparations were commenced at once for the march to Metammeh, the column was not ready to proceed till 3.30 p.m. on the 18th. The interval was occupied in loading up the camels, filling the water-bottles and constructing a fort to protect the wounded, who were to be left behind with a detachment of the Sussex Regiment. It had been hoped that the advance would be postponed until the following morning, in order that the men might have a rest, but General Stewart was resolved to push on before the enemy had time to recover from their recent defeat. So, as soon as everything was in order, the march commenced.

Stewart's intention was to proceed along the Metammeh road, and after passing the wells of Shebacat and getting within a few miles of Metammeh, to turn to the right and strike the Nile about three miles above the town. This he hoped to do before daybreak, and then to attack the town. The column moved off with the hussars in front, then the Guards, and after them the convoy, followed by the Heavies and the Mounted Infantry. The total number of camels was 2,500, of which 1,350 were ridden by the fighting part of the force, and the remainder were used for transport.

The force got on pretty well and with few halts until sunset, but as darkness came on the tall grass became thicker, and the ground more broken. Here the camels began to tumble about and get out of their places. After two hours of this work, the guide reported that they were getting near the wells, and the Guards dismounted so as to be prepared for an attack.

The trees now became more dense, and the tracks so diminished in number as to allow only room for a half section of cavalry to pass between the scrub on either side. Here the column fell into wild disorder; the baggage camels got entangled in the bush, and many of them had to be left behind.[1] The men, utterly worn out by want of rest, went to sleep, tumbled off, and their unguided camels wandered off the track. To show the confusion that existed, on several occasions the rear guard were found in front of the force, thus proving that the troops were going in a circle. The passage through the bush, difficult as it would have been for the men and transport by daylight, by night, and with no moon, became almost impossible, and the disorder was endless. Had the enemy attempted to rush the column in the darkness, the consequences might have been disastrous, more especially considering the exhausted condition of both men and animals.

Still the column blundered on till at last it got to open ground, where a long halt was made. At 1.15 a.m. on the 19th, the force again advanced over a fairly easy country, with a few scattered trees, but no path. Both men and animals were so worn out that continual halts had to be made. Directly the halt sounded the men laid down to snatch a few minutes' sleep.

Daylight found the column still some six or seven miles from the Nile, which, however, was nowhere visible. Stewart, suspecting the guide of treachery, now placed him in charge of a cavalry escort, and altered the direction of the column more to the eastward in the hope of striking the river. After going about two miles further, the town of Metammeh, with a broad tract of vegetation marking the presence of the Nile, came in sight.

There was no chance now of getting to the river without being seen, so the column kept on its way till about 7 a.m., when crowds of the enemy were observed swarming out of the town, some coming straight towards the British force, while others kept along the river bank as if to cut off the column from the Nile.

The troops had by this time reached an open piece of ground, where, on a low gravelly hill, they halted and formed square round the camels. It was evident that a fight was inevitable, and Stewart, determining that his men, exhausted by their long night march, should not fight on empty stomachs, ordered breakfast to be got ready.

Meanwhile the enemy were working round the position with great rapidity, and firing with their Remingtons into the square, where by 8 a.m. the bullets began to drop freely. The plain around was dotted with bushes, and there were many depressions, so that the enemy's marksmen, whilst concealed themselves, were able to keep up a steady

---
1. Over a hundred camels with their loads were lost in this way.

fusillade.

To protect the men, a *zeriba* of camel saddles, boxes, &c., was hastily constructed. The work was very trying, and the men fell fast whilst it was going on. As the fire became hotter, the parapet of the *zeriba* grew in height, and here and there traverses of boxes and packages were built up as a protection against the enfilading fire of the enemy's sharpshooters.

A little after ten General Stewart fell, severely wounded, and from this moment Sir Charles Wilson took over the command. Other casualties occurred about the same time, including Lieutenant C. Crutchley, of the Scots Guards, wounded, and Cameron, correspondent of the *Standard*, and Herbert, correspondent of the *Morning Post*, killed. Burleigh, of the *Daily Telegraph*, was also wounded. The British troops all this time were replying as best they could to the enemy's fire, but the men were gradually being worn out, and their shooting was comparatively ineffective. The enemy being concealed in the long grass, the men in the *zeriba* laboured under the disadvantage of being exposed as targets without being able to strike back. This went on for hours, the fire on both sides continuing without intermission, and men dropping fast. It became evident that this state of things could not last, and orders were given to construct works in which to place the heavy baggage and the wounded, in charge of a small detachment, whilst the square should take the initiative and march to the Nile.

Under heavy fire the works were completed, a redoubt being thrown up by Major Dorward and Lieutenant Lawson, of the Engineers, and the *zeriba* strengthened. This was not accomplished without loss, twelve men being killed and forty wounded up to this time. The baggage, camels, &c., were protected by the artillery and the Gardner guns which were left in the *zeriba*. With them were the 19th Hussars (whose horses were so done up as to render them useless as cavalry), the Naval Brigade, half the Heavy Camel Corps. Colonel Barrow was left in command under Lord Charles Beresford, who was the senior officer in rank.

During the forming of the square, so hopeless did the situation appear to some of the correspondents, that they started for Abu Klea, but were turned back, partly by the cavalry sent out by Colonel Barrow, and partly by the enemy's horsemen. Eventually all the correspondents remained in the *zeriba* except Villiers, the artist of the *Graphic*, who went forward with the column.

Owing to the delay caused by strengthening the *zeriba* and constructing the redoubt, it was three o'clock when the square moved slowly out from the *zeriba*. The object of the advance was not so much to attack as to gain the desired position on the river. The movement was a strikingly bold one, as the smaller force left behind was exposed to great risks, and the larger one was weakened by division. Everything depended on the steadiness of the advancing square. Were it to give way, the small party remaining in the redoubt could not hope to hold out for any length of time.

The column was about 1,200 strong. The front of the square was composed of the Grenadier Guards and Coldstreams, the right flank of the Scots Guards and part of the Heavy Camel Corps, and the left flank of the Mounted Infantry, while the Sussex Regiment and another part of the Heavy Camel Corps brought up the rear.

They moved at a slow march, keeping always in the open, covered by the fire of the Gardner gun in the redoubt, whilst flanking skirmishers threaded their way through the mimosas, for the ground was rough and irregular, with bushes in all directions.

For two miles the enemy, though visible in force, made no direct attack, but contented themselves with keeping up an incessant rifle-fire from a distance. However, on approaching a gravel ridge between the British force and the river, a body on foot, some thousands strong, was seen approaching in crescent formation. The square was at once halted, and the men lying down, delivered volley after volley with the utmost steadiness. Soon the critical moment came when the charge took place. Led by several emirs on horseback, 800 of the enemy's spearmen hurled themselves against the square. The troops never wavered for a moment, but cheered lustily when they saw the rush coming. The main body of the assailants made for the left angle of the front face, where the Guards and Mounted Infantry were posted.

The attack looked serious, but the Guards and Mounted Infantry received the charge with a fire so deadly at 300 yards, that all the leaders with their fluttering banners went down, and not one got within thirty yards of the square. The fight only lasted a few minutes; the Dervish front ranks were swept away, and then there was a backward movement as the whole of the assailants recoiled and, with the masses assembled on the adjoining hills, disappeared in the direction of Metammeh. They left 250 bodies on the field, including those of five of the emirs, whilst not a single British soldier was either killed or wounded in repelling the charge.

During the advance, the garrison in the *zeriba* had been engaging the enemy at long range. Though attacked by rifle-fire up to the time that the charge was made on the square, the assailants never came to close quarters. The garrison made effective use of the guns in shelling the masses of the enemy on the gravel hills in front of Wilson's advancing force. As the column moved forward, their shells were seen bursting and scattering the crowds, and it was mainly owing to the accuracy of the artillery fire that a larger number of spearmen did not join in the charge.

The British loss in the day's fighting was twenty killed and sixty wounded. The officers and newspaper correspondents killed were as follows: Officers, 19th Hussars, Quartermaster A. G. Lima; Commissariat and Transport Corps, A. C. Jewell; correspondents, Messrs. St. Leger Herbert and Cameron.

A few minutes' halt to enable the men to have a drink of water and fill up their ammunition pouches was allowed, and then the column continued its march towards the hill. When the gravelly ridge was occupied the sun was about setting, and the river, which had been so long looked for, was not yet in sight. Parties were pushed on in search of it in the darkness, and eventually, half an hour after nightfall, the Nile was reached.[2]

The wounded were at once taken to the most suitable place to be found on the river bank, whilst the men went down by companies to drink. The camels, which were by this time as worn out as the men, were turned adrift to graze in the surrounding vegetation. The men were so exhausted that when they came up from their drink they fell down like logs, and difficulty was experienced in rousing them and getting them into their places for the night.

The force was allowed to bivouac in peace on the Nile bank, and both officers and men, lying on the bare ground, found the rest of which they were so much in need. The only sign of the enemy's presence was the beating of the *"tom-toms,"* which went on all night.

On the 20th the adjacent village of Abu Kru (which for some unknown reason was called Gubat) was occupied, and a small garrison being placed there, the rest of the troops, recruited and refreshed, marched back to relieve the party at the *zeriba*. As the returning column neared the work, the small garrison greeted it with hearty cheers.

---

2. The story is told of one of the soldiers who on hearing the creaking and groaning of one of the *"sakheas,"* or waterwheels (a sound which the troops had not heard since leaving Korti), exclaimed, "We can't be far off now; I can hear them blooming musical boxes again."

The task of removing the wounded, together with the rest of the camels, the baggage, and guns, was then commenced, and continued until the whole were brought to the new position at Gubat.[3] The hussars' horses by this time had been two days and the camels five days without water.

Sir Charles Wilson's dash for the Nile was one of the most hazardous of military operations, and has been condemned by nearly all professional critics. He not only divided his already reduced forces in the face of the enemy, but cut himself off from his baggage, artillery, and supplies. On the other hand, there was an absolute necessity for gaining a position on the river with the least possible delay, and, if a further justification were wanted, Sir Charles can point to the complete success which attended the movement. If one regards closely the question of risk, it is impossible not to feel that the despatch of Stewart's column of only 1,800 men across the desert against an enemy of unknown strength was in itself a highly venturesome proceeding, and one which, if undertaken by a less able commander or with inferior troops, must have ended in disaster.

This, in fact, was very nearly being the case with the column at Abu Klea, where nothing but the steadiness of the men saved the day. "Success justifies all risks," but it is a curious circumstance that, whilst one argument against adopting the Souakim-Berber route was that it involved a long desert march with a fight at the end at Berber, this was practically what happened to Stewart's force, which, after a long and trying march, had to fight towards its end both at Abu Klea and Metammeh.

There was this difference, however, between the two, that the result of Stewart's operations was to open a line of communications from Metammeh to Cairo of more than 1,300 miles, instead of one of only 280 miles from Berber to the Red Sea. There was the further consideration that, from the disposition of the *Mahdi's* forces, less resistance would probably have been met with at Berber than was encountered in the Bayuda desert, whilst Khartoum being almost as accessible from Berber as from Metammeh, the former would have been nearly as important as the latter as an objective point for the purposes of the expedition.

On the 21st, a garrison having been left in camp to protect the

---

3. The men at the *zeriba* had passed an undisturbed night, part of which they spent in looting the stores; the camel-drivers, native boys from Aden, were the worst offenders.

wounded, the rest of the column marched towards Metammeh, which was found to be a long village of mud houses with loopholed walls and two or three mountain guns. If, as was thought possible after the events of the previous day, it was found to be undefended, Wilson's idea was to take possession of the place. The advance commenced at daybreak. On nearing the town it was found to be full of people and strongly held.

An adjoining village was occupied by Wilson's men, who had to sustain a well-aimed fire from the loopholed buildings, whilst they could hit nobody in return. Two of the British guns were brought up, but did little harm, the shell merely going through the mud walls without bursting. Wilson's force was too small and already too much incumbered with wounded to justify an attack at close quarters, and the town if taken was too big to hold. So he determined to retire without pressing the attack. The troops, whose casualties amounted to only one man killed and one officer wounded, now deployed and fell back covered by skirmishers and the artillery.

Just at the moment when the attacking force was nearest the town, and the guns were attempting to make a breach in the enemy's walls, four steamers flying the Egyptian flag came downstream and anchored. Everyone knew at once that they were from General Gordon, and greeted them with loud cheers. They were commanded by Nusri Pasha, and were sent by Gordon from Khartoum to communicate with the expeditionary force. They had on board some Soudanese and Egyptians and some brass howitzers. Four of the latter were at once landed and run into action by a force of Soudanese from the steamers under Khasm-el-Mus, a native *sheikh* with the rank of *bey*. These made excellent practice at the town up to the moment when the retreat sounded.

Khasm-el-Mus stated that he had seen a force under Feki Mustapha marching down the west bank from Khartoum, and that it would reach Metammeh by sunset or very early next morning. The camp at Gubat was therefore hurriedly placed in a state to resist an attack, and arrangements were made for bringing in such of the stores as still remained at the *zeriba*.

Chapter 42

Gordon's Journals

Gordon's journals began on 10th September, 1884, and continued to 14th December, 1884. Want of space renders it necessary to give but a few extracts.

Gordon seems to have felt the announcement that the object of Lord Wolseley's expedition was to relieve him not less acutely than the neglect with which he had been treated by the government. More than once he recurs to the subject, and the receipt of some newspapers mentioning the departure of the Gordon Relief Expedition drew from him the following comments:—

> I altogether decline the imputation that the projected expedition has come to *relieve me*; it has come to save our national honour in extricating the garrisons, &c., from the position our action in Egypt has placed these garrisons in. . . . *I came up to extricate the garrisons and failed; Earle comes up to extricate garrisons, and, I hope, succeeds. Earle does not come to extricate me.* . . . I am not the *rescued lamb*, and will not be.

In another passage he refers again to the personal question:—

> It may be said that the object of the present expedition is for my relief personally; but how is it possible for me to go away and leave men whom I have egged on to fight?

On the subject of how the expedition should advance, and of what it ought to do on arrival, he wrote the following:—

> My view is this, as to the operations of British forces. I will put three steamers, each with two guns on them, and an armed force of infantry at disposal of any British authority. Will send these steamers to either Metammeh, opposite Shendy, or to the

cataract below Berber to there meet any British force which may come across country to the Nile. These steamers with this force coming across country will (D.V.) capture Berber and then communicate with Khartoum.... When Berber is taken I should keep the bulk of the forces there, and send up the fighting column to Khartoum.

On the same subject he adds:—

> I cannot too much impress on you that this expedition will not encounter any enemy worth the name in a European sense of the word; the struggle is with the climate and destitution of the country. It is one of time and patience, and of small parties of determined men, backed by native allies, which are got by policy and money. A heavy lumbering column, however strong, is nowhere in this land. Parties of forty or sixty men, swiftly moving about, will do more than any column. If you lose two or three, what of it? It is the chance of war. Native allies above all things, at whatever cost. It is the country of the irregular, not of the regular. If you move in mass, you will find no end of difficulties, whereas, if you let detached parties dash out here and there, you will spread dismay in the Arab ranks.

Later on he wrote:—

> All that is absolutely necessary is for fifty of the expeditionary force to get on board a steamer and come up to Halfiyeh, and thus let their presence be felt; this is not asking much, but it must happen at once, or it will (as usual) be too late.

It will not excite any great surprise that Gordon should have felt bound to come to the conclusion that—

> We are wonderful people; it was never our government that made us a grand nation; our government has been ever the drag upon our wheels. It is, of course, on the cards that Khartoum is taken under the nose of the expeditionary force, which will be *just too late.*

As indicated in this last sentence, Gordon seems to have had a presentiment that the relief which he had been looking to, more for the sake of his followers than of himself, would fail to arrive in time.

Thus, on October 24th, he wrote:

If they do not come before the 30th November, the game is up, and Rule Britannia.

And then comes the following paragraph, in characteristic style:—

I dwell on the joy of never seeing Great Britain again, with its horrid, wearisome dinner-parties and miseries. How we can put up with those things passes my imagination! It is a perfect bondage. I would sooner live like a Dervish with the *Mahdi* than go out to dinner every night in London. I hope, if any English general comes to Khartoum, he will not ask me to dinner. Why men cannot be friends without bringing their wretched stomachs in, is astounding.

The variety of Gordon's ideas, military, political, and humorous, is forcibly illustrated throughout the journals. Now he is describing a battle with clearness and graphic power, now he is criticizing a government or a minister, and now and again he is indulging his love of fun, at one time in pure jest, and at others in brilliant satire.

Speaking of the tendency of his men to duck their heads in order to avoid the Arab rifle-fire, he says:—

In the Crimea it was supposed and considered mean to bob, and one used to try and avoid it. —— used to say, 'It is all well enough for you, but I am a family man,' and he used to bob at every report. For my part, I think judicious bobbing is not a fault, for I remember seeing on two occasions shells before my eyes, which certainly had I not bobbed would have taken off my head. 'And a good riddance, too,' the Foreign Office would say.

One of the most amusing passages is that in which he says, "I must say I hate our diplomatists." Here follows a rough sketch of two figures, one intended for Sir Evelyn Baring, and the other for Mr. Egerton, his deputy in Cairo. The former is represented as saying, "Most serious, is it not? He called us humbugs—arrant humbugs."

Egerton is made to reply, "I can't believe it; it's too dreadful."

Gordon, with characteristic candour, continues, referring to diplomatists in general, "I think with few exceptions they are arrant humbugs, and I expect they know it."

The foregoing is accompanied by one of the many extracts from the Scriptures, which abound. It is as follows: "*Blessed is the man who does not sit in the seat of the scornful*" (Ps. i. 1).

Hearing the news that to prevent outrage the Roman Catholic nuns at Obeid had been compelled to declare themselves married to the Greek priests, Gordon remarks:

> What a row the Pope will make about the nuns marrying the Greeks; it is the union of the Greek and Latin Churches.

On the 23rd of September Gordon says, that from 12th March till 22nd September the garrison had expended 3,240,770 Remington cartridges, 1,570 Krupp cartridges, and 9,442 mountain-gun cartridges. He calculated that of the Remington cartridges perhaps 240,000 had been captured by the enemy, so that the number fired away would be only three millions. As the rebels lost perhaps 1,000 men in all, he reckons that each man killed required 3,000 cartridges to kill him.

There is less in the Diaries than might have been expected in the way of personal attack on the government which sent Gordon to Khartoum. He says, indeed:—

> I could write volumes of pent-up wrath on this subject if I did not believe things are ordained and work for the best. I am not at all inclined to order half rations with a view to any prolongation of our blockade; if I did so it would probably end in a catastrophe before the time when, if full rations are given, we should have exhausted our supplies. I should be an angel (which I am not, needless to say) if I was not rabid with Her Majesty's Government; but I hope I may be quiet on the subject of this Soudan and Cairo business, with its indecision; but to lose all my beautiful black soldiers is enough to make one angry with them who have the direction of our future.

The diaries refer frequently to the Stewart incident, already mentioned in these pages. Gordon resolved to send the *Abbas* down, and upon his assuring Stewart, in reply to his inquiry, that he "could go in honour," Stewart left. Stewart asked for an order, but this Gordon refused, as he would not send him into any danger he did not share. It was the wish of Stewart and Mr. Power (the *Times* correspondent) to leave Khartoum and proceed down the Nile, and Gordon placed no restraint on their wish. Further, when they left he took every step in his power to provide for their security. He sent his river boats to escort them past Berber, and he gave them much advice, which, if it had been implicitly followed, should have brought them in safety to Dongola. Once reconciled to their departure and the despatch of some of his steamers northwards, he formed his plan for the co-operation of the latter with the Relief Expedition. It has been shown how this was actually carried out; but while thus endeavouring to facilitate the progress of the expedition, Gordon seriously weakened his own position in Khartoum.

That these steamers, each of which he considered worth 2,000 men, had to run no inconsiderable danger is shown by the following extract:—

> If any officer of the expedition is on board, he will know what it is to be in a penny boat under cannon-fire. The *Bordein* has come in; she has seven wounded and one woman killed.

The news of the loss of the *Abbas* was a terrible blow to Gordon, and although at the time he knew nothing certain as to the fate of those on board, yet he feared treachery. Many of his anticipations as to the ultimate fall of Khartoum and other events were prophetic; and although he did not foresee the exact circumstances of the loss of the *Abbas*, he foresaw the fate of Stewart and those with him. After he heard that the *Abbas* had been captured, but had received no information as to the circumstances of the loss, he writes:—

> Stewart was a man who did not chew the cud, he never thought of danger in prospective; he was not a bit suspicious (while I am made up of it). I can see, in imagination, the whole scene, the *sheikh* inviting them to land, saying, 'Thank God, the *Mahdi* is a liar!'—bringing in wood—men going on shore and dispersed. The *Abbas* with her steam down, then a rush of wild Arabs and all is over!

Throughout the journals reference is made to various important documents, the most notable of which is a letter from the *Mahdi* to Gordon, dated 2nd *Moharrem*, 1302 (22nd October, 1884). In it the writer says:—

> We have now arrived at a day's journey from Omdurman, and are coming, please God, to your place. If you return to the Most High God, and become a Moslem, and surrender to His order and that of His Prophet, and believe in us as the *Mahdi*, send us a message after laying down your arms and giving up all thought of fighting, so that I may send you someone with safe-conduct, by which you will obtain (assurance of) benefit

and blessing in this world and the next. Otherwise, and if you do not act thus, you will have to encounter war with God and His Prophet. And know that the Most High God is mighty for your destruction, as He has destroyed others before you, who were much stronger than you, and more numerous.

In reply, Gordon sent a telegram to the commandant of Omdurman, to be communicated to the *Mahdi*, with the memorable words:

I am like iron, and hope yet to see the English arrive.

The following passages record some of the later incidents of the siege:—

12th November, 10.20 a.m.—For half an hour firing lulled, but then recommenced, and is still going on. The *Ismailia* was struck with a shell, but I hear is not seriously damaged. The *Husseinyeh* is aground (I feel much the want of my other steamers at Metammeh). 11.15 a.m.—Firing has lulled; it was very heavy for the last three-quarters of an hour from *Ismailia* and Arabs. It is now desultory, and is dying away. *Husseinyeh* is still aground; the *Ismailia* is at anchor. What a six hours' anxiety for me when I saw the shells strike the water near the steamers from the Arabs; imagine my feelings! Noon.—The firing has ceased, I am glad to say. I have lived years in these last hours!

Had I lost the *Ismailia* I should have lost the *Husseinyeh* (aground), and then Omdurman and the North Fort, and then the town. One p.m.—The Arabs are firing on the steamers with their two guns. The *Husseinyeh* still aground; that is the reason of it. 1.30 p.m.—Now has ceased. The *Ismailia*, struck by three shells, had one man killed, fifteen wounded on board of her; she did really very well. This is our first encounter with the *Mahdi's* personal troops. 2.45 p.m.—The *Ismailia* tried to take *Husseinyeh* off and got struck twice, in addition to the three times before mentioned, with shells, so she desisted from the attempt. The Arabs are firing on the *Husseinyeh*. I have ordered the Krupp of (Fort) Mogrim to play on the Arab guns, and shall wait till night to take off the *Husseinyeh*. She is nearer to the left bank than to the right bank. It is not clear if she is aground or half sunk (equally a trouble). 3.30 p.m.—The Arabs are bringing their guns nearer to the aground or half-sunken *Husseinyeh*.

The *Ismailia* reports that the two last shells have done her no material damage. 4.30 p.m.—The Arabs have now three guns bearing on the *Husseinyeh*. Six p.m.—The firing has ceased. I hope to get the *Husseinyeh* off tonight. Seven p.m.—The Arabs keep up a dropping fire on the *Husseinyeh*, who, I hear, has two shell holes in her, and has six men, including the captain, wounded.

22nd November.—I am terribly anxious for the fort at Omdurman, and am trying to devise some means of occupying the Arabs and diverting their attention elsewhere. . . . The Arab camps are about five miles from the city.

5th December.—I have almost given up an idea of saving the town; it is a last resource we make to open the route to the Omdurman Fort.

6th December.—I have given up all idea of landing at Omdurman; we have not the force to do it. The Arabs fired forty-five rounds at (Fort) Mogrim and the steamers. We had two men wounded at Mogrim and one killed. This is most distressing, to have these poor fellows wounded and killed.

13th December.—The steamers went up and attacked Arabs at Buri. Certainly this day after day delay has a most disheartening effect on every one. Today is the two hundred and seventy-sixth day of our anxiety. The Arabs appear to have suffered today heavily at Buri. . . . . We are going to send down the *Bordein* the day after tomorrow, and with her I shall send this journal. If some effort is not made before ten days' time, the town will fall. It is inexplicable this delay. If the expeditionary forces have reached the river, and met my steamers, one hundred men are all that we require just to show themselves."

The latest entry in the *Diaries* is on 14th December, and is as follows:—

Arabs fired two shells at the palace this morning: 546 *ardebs dhoora* in store; also 83,525 *okes* of biscuits. 10.30 a.m.—The steamers are down at Omdurman engaging the Arabs. Consequently I am on 'tenterhooks.' 11.30 a.m.—Steamers returned. The *Bordein* was struck by a shell in her battery. We had only one man wounded. We are going to send down the *Bordein* tomorrow with this journal. If I was in command of the two hundred men of the expeditionary force, which are all that is necessary for the movement, I should stop just below Halfiyeh and attack the Arabs at that place before I came on here to Khartoum. I should then communicate with the North Fort, and act according to circumstances. Now, mark this, if the expeditionary force—and I ask for no more than two hundred men—does not come in ten days the town may fall, and I have done my best for the honour of our country. Goodbye.

C. G. Gordon.

It would be impossible to find words more simple and at the same time more pathetic than those contained in the concluding sentences of the man who so long held the attention of the world riveted upon him, and who, unaided and alone, maintained the highest traditions of British courage and fortitude.

CHAPTER 43

Wilson's Voyage to Khartoum

"*Khartoum all right, can hold on for years.*—C. G. Gordon, 29: 12: '84," was the cheering message, written on a tiny slip of paper, which reached Sir Charles Wilson by Gordon's steamers.

With this writing came Gordon's journals, containing a narrative of events from the 10th September to the 14th December, some private letters and also some despatches addressed by him to "the Officer Commanding H.M.'s troops," to Sir Evelyn Baring, and others.

In one of the despatches, dated 20th October, 1884, Gordon informs the officer in command of the British troops of the sending to him of the steamers, and advises the removal from them of all Egyptians, whether *pashas, beys,* or privates, all of whom Gordon terms "hens." The letter concludes:—

> If you do not use the steamers, at least take out the hens and send them back empty. If you choose to put black troops on board, they will be welcome, but not those heroes of Tel-el-Kebir.

In another letter, dated 21st October, addressed to "the Chief of the Staff, Soudan Expeditionary Force," Gordon wrote that he had tendered the resignation of his commission in the British Army, and requested that the general commanding Her Majesty's troops advancing for the relief of the garrison might be informed of this fact.

The letter addressed to Sir Evelyn Baring was dated the 12th December. In it Gordon stated that, having been sent to Khartoum to draw up a report on the state of the Soudan, and for this purpose having been placed under the orders of Her Majesty's Minister in Egypt, he now informed him that Colonel Stewart took down this report, and that consequently Gordon's connection with the Foreign Office and Baring had ceased.

The latest letter was dated the 14th December, and was addressed to the chief of the staff. Its contents were as follows:—

> I send down the steamer *Bordein* tomorrow with Vol. 6 of my private journal containing account of the events in Khartoum from 5th November to 14th December. The state of affairs is such that one cannot foresee further than five to seven days, after which the town may at any time fall. I have done all in my power to hold out, but I own I consider the position is extremely critical, almost desperate; and I say this without any feeling of bitterness with respect to Her Majesty's Government, but merely as a matter of fact. Should the town fall, it will be questionable whether it will be worth the while of Her Majesty's Government to continue its expedition, for it is certain that the fall of Khartoum will insure that of Kassala and Sennar.

The writing dated 29th December, 1884, containing the expression, "Khartoum all right, can hold on for years," was probably intended, like Gordon's previous message to the like effect, merely to convey the information that he was still holding out.

The wording of the document was simply a *ruse* in the event of the capture of the person who brought the message, on foot, to the steamer after she left Khartoum. This is apparent from the letter of the 14th December, as well as from the statements of the Egyptian officers who accompanied the steamers. They reported that they had been for some weeks stationed a short distance above Metammeh waiting for the arrival of the British column. They had assisted in getting messages into and out of Khartoum, where the situation was altogether most gloomy. Gordon himself was well, they said, but his soldiers were despairing of relief, and it was necessary that some Europeans should proceed with the utmost alacrity to Khartoum, in order to reassure the population and the troops.

Abdul Hamid Bey, who commanded one of the steamers, the *Bordein*, informed Sir Charles Wilson that he left Khartoum on the 14th in that vessel, and Gordon then told him that if he (Abdul Hamid) did not return with English troops within ten days it would be too late; and that in that case he had better not attempt to return at all.

The other three steamers had quitted Khartoum in September, and had been down to Shendy and other places looking for the expeditionary force.

On the 22nd January, 1885, it was decided to construct two forts—a village fort to be held by the Guards, and a river fort, containing the hospital, to be held by the remainder of the force. The three small guns of the column, together with some from the steamers, were put in position.

The same day, the steamers were utilized by Sir Charles Wilson for the purposes of another reconnaissance, this time towards Shendy, a town opposite to Metammeh on the right bank of the Nile. Only a small force, consisting for the most part of a detachment of the Mounted Infantry, was embarked. Shendy was found to be in the possession of the enemy, though they were not in overwhelming force. One Krupp gun was mounted there. The steamers contented themselves with throwing a few shells into the place and then retired.

It was found that a portion of the enemy had occupied a small island in the Nile just opposite the British camp. The guns of the steamers were speedily brought to bear on them, and the infantry opening a steady fire drove the intruders out of the island and across the river.

The whole of the 23rd was occupied in changing the crews and soldiers on board the steamers, fitting them up and loading them with supplies for Khartoum, and preparing for a start. Owing to the absence of coal, wood had to be substituted, and the latter commodity was scarce. It was only obtained by landing parties from the steamers carrying off the timber of which the *sakheas* or waterwheels were constructed. A convoy of camels under Colonel Talbot was sent back to Gakdul after dark with despatches for Lord Wolseley, and instructions to bring up provisions. The escort of 400 men accompanying the convoy reduced the little garrison at Gubat to a total of 922 all told.

The original plan was for Lord Charles Beresford to man two of the steamers with his naval brigade and, after putting fifty of the Sussex Regiment on board, to take them with Sir Charles Wilson to Khartoum. Unfortunately it was impossible to carry out this programme. All the naval officers were killed or wounded except Beresford, who was so ill as to be unable to walk, and many of the best petty officers and seamen were also gone. Beresford indeed offered to accompany the expedition, but, as he was clearly not in a fit condition, Wilson felt bound to decline the offer. After consultation with him Khasm-el-Mus was placed in command of the steamer *Bordein*, and Abdul Hamid Bey in command of the *Tala Hawiyeh*. It was Lord Wolseley's idea that the military escort should enter Khartoum in red coats. There was some difficulty in finding a sufficient number of coats for the purpose, but at the last moment they were obtained from the Guards, and the Sussex men were enabled to appear in tunics which were sadly wanting in point of fit, though correct in colour.

At 8 a.m. on the 24th Sir C. Wilson left for Khartoum in the *Bordein*, with Captain Gascoigne, Yorkshire Hussars, ten non-commissioned officers and men of the Sussex Regiment, and one petty officer, artificer, Royal Navy; the *Tala Hawiyeh* followed with Captain Trafford and ten non-commissioned officers and men of the Sussex, Lieutenant Stuart-Wortley, King's Rifles, and one petty officer, artificer, Royal Navy. Captain Trafford commanded the escort, and Captain Gascoigne and Lieutenant Stuart-Wortley accompanied Wilson for service with Gordon, at Khartoum.

No information has been given why only two of the four vessels were despatched, nor why only twenty British soldiers were embarked. Of course little more than a "demonstration" could have been made with any force such as the steamers could have carried, even if all of them had been employed. Still the singular reduction from 14,000, the total of the British Army in Egypt, to 7,000, the force told off for the expedition, then to 1,800, the number of Sir Herbert Stewart's column, and finally to twenty, the number of Sir Charles Wilson's forlorn hope, cannot fail to strike the reader.

Colonel Boscawen was left in command of the force which remained at Gubat.

When near Sheikeih, on the left bank, a portion of the force under Fiki-Mustapha, which, it had been reported, was marching on Metammeh, was seen in the distance. It was ascertained afterwards that this force, about 3,000 men, had halted on receiving news of the fight at Metammeh, and then retired to Wad-Habeshi.

On the 26th two Shukriyehs came on board and reported that for the last fifteen days there had been fighting at Khartoum, and on the 27th a man shouted out from the left bank, that a camel-man had just passed with the news that Khartoum had fallen, and that Gordon had been killed.

On the 28th, a Shukriyeh on the right bank stated that Khartoum had fallen two days previously, and that Gordon had been killed. The news was generally discredited, and the vessels prepared to force their way past the enemy's batteries into Khartoum, the *Bordein* leading and the *Tala Hawiyeh* following close astern. The orders to the detachment of the Royal Sussex were to fire volleys at the embrasures of the batteries, whilst the Soudanese troops kept up an independent fire and the four guns on the steamers replied to the fire of the batteries.

On approaching Halfiyeh it was noticed that the palm-grove there had been burned, and that three or four large *nuggers* were lying alongside the bank. On the attention of Khasm-el-Mus being called to this, he at once replied, "Gordon's troops must be there, as the *Mahdi* has no boats." Directly afterwards a heavy fire was opened upon the steamers from four guns, and from rifles at from 600 to 900 yards range. One gun was in a *sakhea* pit at the water's edge, two in an earthwork a little above the *sakhea*, and one in the village. After passing Shamba, two guns on the right bank opened on the steamers while a heavy rifle-fire came from both banks, and this was sustained until they came within range of the guns of Omdurman.

When abreast of Tuti Island, which it was expected to find in Gordon's possession, the vessels were received by a sharp musketry fire at from 75 to 200 yards range; three or four guns, of which one was a Krupp, opened fire from the upper end of Tuti, or from Khartoum, two guns from the fort at Omdurman, and a well-sustained rifle-fire from the left bank. The steamers returned the fire both with guns and rifles.

On reaching a point beyond Tuti, Wilson came to the conclusion that Khartoum was in the hands of the enemy, and that it would be a useless sacrifice of life to attempt to land or try to force a passage to the town itself; he therefore ordered the *Bordein* to turn and run down the river at full speed. The *Tala Hawiyeh*, which had grounded for a few minutes, near the upper end of Tuti Island, followed, and the steamers drew up for the night near Tamaniat.

Here Wilson sent out two messengers, one to go to Khartoum to ascertain the fate of Gordon, the other to collect information. The latter, on his return, stated he had met a Jaalin Arab, who told him that Khartoum had fallen on the night of the 26th, and that Gordon was dead. He also said that on the 27th the *Mahdi* had entered Khartoum, prayed in the principal mosque, and then retired to Omdurman, leaving the town to three days' pillage.

The reasons which led Wilson to the conclusion that Khartoum had fallen were:—The heavy fire brought to bear from Tuti Island; the absence of any fire from Khartoum in his support; the fact that no Egyptian flag was flying from any place in or near the town, though government and other houses were plainly visible; the presence of a large number of dervishes with their banners on a sandspit; and the fact that a number of Gordon's troop boats and *nuggers* were lying along the left bank of the White Nile under Omdurman Fort.

On the 29th the *Tala Hawiyeh* ran at full speed on a sunken rock in open water opposite Jeb-el-Royan and rapidly filled. The *Bordein* was brought up at a small island below the wreck, and before sunset Captain Trafford and Lieutenant Stuart-Wortley came down with a large *nugger*, in which they placed ever one on board the steamer, the two guns, and such of the ammunition as had not been damaged.

Fiki-Abd-Er-Rahman, who had come down to the river with a flag of truce at Omdurman, and followed down to the scene of the wreck, came on board with a letter from the *Mahdi*, which was addressed to the party. The letter stated that Khartoum had been taken and Gordon killed, and offered a safe-conduct to any one sent to verify the facts. The *Mahdi* enjoined the English to become Moslems if they wished for peace, and promised protection to Khasm-el-Mus and his followers if they submitted. The messenger, on the other hand, stated that Gordon was with the *Mahdi* at Omdurman, and that the garrison of Tuti having refused to submit had been put to the sword.

Wilson made no reply to the *Mahdi's* letter, but, to secure a safe passage through the cataracts, where the slightest opposition would have been fatal to ever one on board the steamers, Khasm-el-Mus, with Wilson's cognisance, answered that he would never give himself up unless the *Mahdi* sent him a special safe-conduct and promise of safety. If this were sent he would surrender to Fiki-Mustapha at Wad-Habeshi, where guns had been mounted to oppose the passage of the steamers.

On the 30th they passed the most difficult portion of the cataract without opposition (the result of Khasm-el-Mus' answer, for during several hours the soldiers and men on the steamer and *nugger* were at the mercy of a few sharpshooters).

The same day two Shukriyehs came on board with information that Gordon was shut up in the mission church at Khartoum with some faithful followers.

On the 31st, after the *Bordein* had been lowered down a difficult fall with great care, she was run on a sunken rock off the island of Mernat between two and three miles above the enemy's position at Wad-Habeshi. The steamer was beached on the sandspit of a small island, and everything landed. The island of Mernat, about forty yards distant, was occupied by a picket of the Royal Sussex and the crew and soldiers of the *Tala Hawiyeh*, and at nightfall the picket of the Sussex was withdrawn to the smaller island.

Stuart-Wortley was directed to proceed as soon as it was dark to Gubat, with information of the position of the expedition, and a request for assistance.

Wilson at first intended to cross to the right bank of the Nile and march as soon as the moon rose, but finding it impossible to move the Soudanese troops, he bivouacked with Khasm-el-Mus on Mernat, whilst Captains Trafford and Gascoigne remained on the smaller island to guard the stores.

On the 1st February a *zeriba* was made on Mernat Island; the four guns from the steamers were mounted, and all the ammunition and stores which had been saved were collected. Some Shukriyehs from the mainland visited the party, and said that since the fall of Khartoum they had determined to throw in their lot with the *Mahdi*; they advised Khasm-el-Mus to do the same, but he replied he would never surrender without a letter from the *Mahdi* promising safety.

When the *zeriba* was finished, Wilson called the men to arms and, during the inspection which followed, was able to assure himself that a large proportion of the soldiers would remain loyal and fight to the last. One soldier deserted during the day. Two messengers were sent to Halfiyeh to obtain news from Khartoum.

On the 2nd Fiki-Mustapha, from Wad-Habeshi, crossed to the island and tried to persuade Khasm-el-Mus to submit, but he returned the same answer as before. A friendly Shukriyeh brought news that a steamer had left Gubat for the relief of the force at noon the previous day. A sister of Khasm-el-Mus, who had followed the steamers down the river, also arrived, with news that the families of all the officers on board the steamers had been killed at Khartoum, and that Gordon was killed whilst coming out of his room in Government House. Khasm-el-Mus' sister was sent back to Khartoum to obtain further information, and to purchase back any of the family sold into slavery. During the afternoon Abdul Hamid Bey (who had brought a strong letter of recommendation from Gordon to Lord Wolseley) deserted, as well as some of the *"reises"* (pilots) and four soldiers. As soon as Wilson was aware of this, he placed the remaining *reises*, who were all Dongolawis, and friendly to the *Mahdi*, under a guard of the Sussex, with orders that they were to be shot if they attempted to escape.

On the 3rd, Wilson ordered all the troops to be confined to the *zeriba*, and, in the event of the non-arrival of the steamer, made arrangements to seize Fiki-Mustapha, who was again to visit the island, and keep him as hostage.

To return to Stuart-Wortley: he left the island at 6.45 p.m. in a small rowing-boat with four English soldiers and eight natives, and floated past the enemy's works, who did not see him until opposite their last bonfire, when they fired several shots without effect. He then ordered the men to row hard, and reached the camp at Gubat at 3 a.m. on the 1st February without any further opposition.

The news he brought placed the force at Gubat in a state of consternation. The first necessity was, of course, to get Wilson's party off the island. It was decided that Lord Charles Beresford should start early in the afternoon in one of the remaining steamers. It was also resolved to send off a convoy across the desert to bring up reinforcements in view of a probable advance of the *Mahdi* with the force which the capture of Khartoum had set free.[1]

Stuart-Wortley left Gubat at 2 p.m. on board the *Safiyeh*, with Lord Charles Beresford in command; a portion of the Naval Brigade, under Lieutenant Van Koughnet; twenty non-commissioned officers and privates of the Mounted Infantry, under Lieutenant Bower, King's Royal Rifles; two Gardner guns; and two 4-pounder brass mountain-guns.

On the 2nd a few shots were fired from the west bank. The vessel stopped for the night just past Gebel-Fangur. On the 3rd she started at 6.30 a.m. At 8 a.m. she came in sight of the enemy's works at Wad-Habeshi, where the Arabs could be seen running into the rifle-trench; fire was opened with the bow gun at about 1,000 yards range. On nearing the position, the enemy opened a heavy rifle-fire, and a gun, in an embrasure facing down the river, also opened fire. The steamer replied with the Gardners and rifles, and also with a 4-pounder. When opposite the central embrasure, the enemy moved their gun and fired, their shot passing over the steamer. The latter's fire was so rapid and well-directed that the enemy were shy of putting their heads over the parapet to take aim.

Having passed the embrasure facing up the river, where the enemy had their second gun, a round shot passed through the vessel's boiler and caused the steam to escape in a huge volume. She proceeded about 300 yards further, while the steam lasted, and then dropped anchor at 500 yards from the enemy's position. Van Koughnet was shot through the thigh when serving the Gardner, one bluejacket was mortally wounded, and two more were severely scalded. The Gardners

---

1. The command at Gubat was taken by Colonel Mildmay Willson, of the Scots Guards, in the place of Colonel Boscawen, who had fallen ill.

had to be moved abaft the battery, and a hole made in it to allow the gun and the Gardners to play upon the enemy's works. The boiler was found to be repairable. Firing continued very brisk until 10.30 a.m., when the enemy's fire was silenced.

Wilson's party heard the *Safiyeh* coming into action with the enemy's battery at Wad-Habeshi; but shortly afterwards Trafford, who was on the "lookout" at the end of the island, reported that he had seen the steamer enveloped in smoke, and feared she had met with a serious accident. As the steamer continued to fire on the battery, and could be seen swinging at anchor, it was determined to break up the *zeriba* at once and march down to her.

As soon as the order was given a scene of wild confusion arose, as it was impossible to keep the Soudanese soldiers under control, and the enemy opened a heavy rifle-fire when they noticed the movement. Eventually the guns, ammunition, stores, wounded, and women, were placed in a *nugger*, and the troops assembled on the island. Gascoigne, with a small guard of the Sussex, was put in charge of the *nugger* with instructions to stop at the nearest point he could reach on the right bank.

Wilson then marched the rest of the British and Soudanese troops to the end of the island, whence they crossed to the right bank in a small boat. The crossing was covered by the detachment of the Sussex.

On reaching the *nugger* Gascoigne proceeded down the river until he reached the right bank opposite the *Safiyeh*, whilst Wilson marched to the same place. Finding it difficult to communicate with Beresford by signal, he sent Gascoigne, who volunteered for the service, in a small boat to the *Safiyeh* with the two naval artificers, and a native crew; the boat was received with a sharp rifle-fire from the enemy going and returning, but fortunately no one was hit. In the meantime, Wilson had got one of the guns out of the *nugger* and brought it into action against the centre embrasure of the battery; whilst three marksmen of the Sussex made good practice at 1,100 yards range, and the remainder of the Sussex and the Soudanese were drawn up behind a *sakhea* channel.

Lord Charles Beresford having sent a message to say that his boiler, which had been pierced by a shot, would be ready by the evening, and that he would pick the party up at a more convenient place about three miles lower down next morning, Wilson directed Trafford to proceed down the river with the Sussex and a portion of the Soudanese under Khasm-el-Mus to form a *zeriba* at the selected point.

Wilson remained behind to cover the passage of the *nugger* with the gun and a detachment of Soudanese, but she unfortunately ran on a sandbank, and did not get off before sunset. In dragging the gun down through the tangled vegetation after dark, the men, who had had no food, became exhausted, and it was found necessary to abandon the gun, which was spiked and thrown into the river. After sunset Gascoigne endeavoured to run past the battery in the *nugger*, but she again grounded on two rocks opposite to and about 200 yards from the centre embrasure. Here she remained all night and until about 8 a.m. next morning, under fire from the battery and rifle-pits, but by most extraordinary good fortune no one was wounded.

On the 4th Beresford, having got up steam, ran past the battery, which now reopened on him, and brought to a short distance below; he then sent a party of bluejackets under Lieutenant Keppel, in a boat, to Gascoigne's assistance. For more than an hour the work of lightening the *nugger* had to be carried on under fire, and nothing could exceed the coolness and gallantry shown by Gascoigne and by Keppel, who was struck by a spent ball during this trying time. When the *nugger* was clear of the rocks Beresford proceeded downstream, and embarked the soldiers and crews of the steamers by 11 a.m. The camp at Gubat was reached at 5.30 p.m.

Though the members of Wilson's expedition were repeatedly under fire, their losses were only two Soudanese killed and twenty-five wounded. This was due to the excellent manner in which the steamers were protected, as well as to the enemy's bad shooting. The casualties on board Beresford's steamer have been already mentioned, and they also were comparatively small for the same reason.

It only remains to add that there are probably few more gallant achievements recorded than the successful rescue effected by Lord Charles Beresford in the face of difficulties.[2]

---

2. A court of inquiry was held at Gubat to investigate charges of treachery against the two captains and one of the "*reises*" (pilots) of the wrecked steamers. The pilot was sentenced to death, but recommended to mercy on account of his having brought down Stuart-Wortley in the boat.

Chapter 44

The Fall of Khartoum

Gordon's *Diaries* bring the history of the siege of Khartoum down to the 14th December, 1884. The relative positions of the besiegers and besieged at that date may be seen from the accompanying plan.

It will be observed that Khartoum was protected on the north and west sides by the Blue and White Niles respectively, and on the south and east by a line of intrenched fortifications, with intervening redoubts, running from Fort Buri, on the Blue Nile, almost to the White Nile. Unfortunately, at this time, the late high Nile had washed away portions of the parapet for a considerable distance from the western end, and, now that the river had fallen, there was a serious gap in this part of the defences. To remedy this, Gordon had for some time employed working parties to repair the demolished parapets, but as the work had to be conducted under fire from the enemy's troops at Omdurman, on the opposite bank, but little progress had been made.

The ditch at this point was also more or less damaged by the action of the river, and was never completely restored. To guard this, the weak part of the position, Gordon stationed armed barges and native boats on the river close by. He also placed mines there, but these were destroyed by the Nile. In the rear of the line of ramparts, and between them and the town, extended an open plain, a little more than a mile in breadth, on which stood barracks and slaughter-houses, and here and there an Arab cemetery. On the south and east sides, fronting the fortifications, were the camps of the besieging armies of Wad en Nejumi and Abu Girgeh.[1]

The army under the immediate command of the *Mahdi* was encamped on the west of Omdurman, where Mohamed Faragallah Bey,

---
1. Wad en Nejumi was subsequently killed at the Battle of Toski, and Abu Girgeh fell at Tokar.

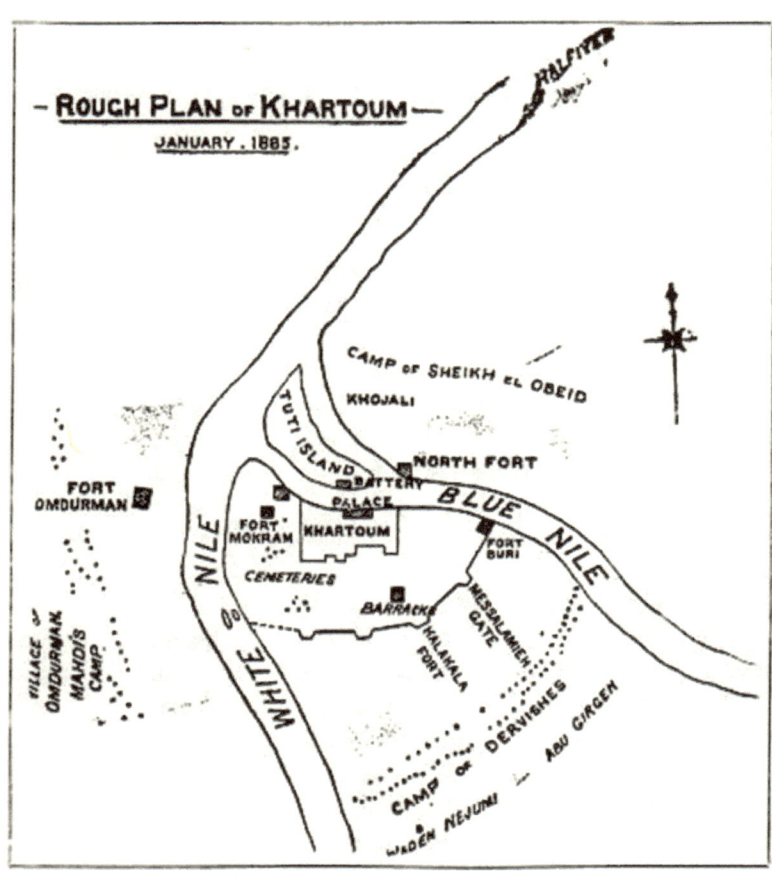

with some Egyptian soldiers, was still holding out, in a work called Fort Omdurman. A large force of Dervishes,[2] under Sheikh-el-Obeid, occupied a position at Khojali, on the north side of the Blue Nile, where Gordon also had a fort called "the North Fort," at a point named "Ras-el-Rasek," as well as a battery on Tuti Island, nearly opposite.

On the 14th December Gordon wrote, "In ten days the town may fall." There were then in store 83,525 *okes* (or 227,000 lbs.) of biscuit, and 546 *ardebs* (or 2,700 bushels) of *dhoora* (Indian corn), representing approximately eighteen days' rations for the troops alone. But Gordon had already, on the 22nd November, found it necessary to issue 9,600 lbs. of biscuit to the poor in the town, so great was the destitution which prevailed. As the siege progressed this state of things became more and more aggravated, and the government supplies had to be further drawn on for the benefit of the civil population.

Ever since the 3rd of November the Fort of Omdurman had been cut off from communication with Khartoum. It was then provisioned only for a month and a half, and at the end of the year the garrison was in great straits from want of food. Gordon made one or two efforts to relieve the garrison, but, having no longer his steamers, four of which had gone to meet the British expedition, and the fifth having been lost with Colonel Stewart, he was unable to open communication.

On the 5th January, 1885, Faragallah signalled that his provisions and ammunition were alike exhausted, and Gordon was compelled to reply that there was nothing for it but to surrender. Faragallah and the whole of the force at Fort Omdurman then capitulated, and were transferred to the *Mahdi's* camp, where they were well treated, as an encouragement to others to join the Dervish ranks.

On the 6th January, seeing that the garrison of Khartoum was becoming daily more and more reduced by want of food, and that existence for many of the inhabitants was almost impossible, Gordon issued a proclamation authorizing as many of the civil population as liked to leave the town and go over to the *Mahdi*. Some thousands of natives took advantage of the offer, and Gordon sent with them a letter to the *Mahdi*, asking him "to feed and protect these poor Moslem

---

2. It should be explained that the word Dervish is derived from the Persian language, and corresponds with the Arabic word "*fakir*," signifying "poor." Strictly speaking, "Dervish" applies to a member of a religious brotherhood or sect, but latterly, in matters dealing with the Soudan, the term has been used to indicate all those who have assumed the faith and uniform of the *Mahdi*.

people as he (Gordon) had done for the last nine months." After the fugitives had left, it was estimated that only about 14,000 remained in the town, out of a population shown by the census taken in the September previous as 34,000.

The fall of Omdurman was a great blow to the garrison of Khartoum, who thus lost the only position they had on the west bank of the White Nile. The Dervishes were thenceforth able to close the river to Gordon's two remaining steamers, and to establish ferries south of Khartoum, giving easy communication between the camps at Omdurman and those of Wad en Nejumi and Abu Girgeh. Khartoum was practically hemmed in on three sides.

The food difficulty became daily more serious. To make matters worse, those in charge of the biscuit and *dhoora* stole quantities of both, as occasion offered. The officer in charge of the stores was arrested and brought before a court of inquiry, but Gordon, realizing the emergency of the situation, had to point out to those conducting the investigation the necessity of not inquiring too critically into the matter.

The Island of Tuti was still held by Gordon's forces, and the crops there were reaped under the fire of the forts, and stored in the commissariat. This produced about 1,600 bushels of corn altogether, which, with the remaining biscuits, were served out to the soldiers. When this was finished, Gordon ordered a search to be made in the town, with the result that further quantities (32 bushels only) were discovered in some of the houses, and also buried in the ground. These also were taken to the government store, the owners being given, in every case, receipts for the quantities carried off. The search was conducted daily until there was nothing left in possession of the inhabitants.

Soon all that had been collected in the commissariat was finished, and then the soldiers and inhabitants were reduced to eating dogs, donkeys, skins of animals, gum, and palm-fibre. Then an actual famine prevailed. The gum produced diarrhoea, and the soldiers became so weak that they could scarcely man the fortifications.[3] The situation of the civil inhabitants was even worse. Many died of actual starvation, and corpses lay about the streets, no one having sufficient strength or energy to bury them.

All this time the enemy kept up a fusillade on the garrison, occasionally killing a few of their number. The soldiers were also harassed

---

3. During the last six days before the fall of Khartoum, the rations of the soldiers consisted of gum, and, when that failed, of palm-fibre only.

by repeated night attacks.[4]

Although it must have been evident to Gordon that the end could not be far off, he continued to encourage the people by proclamations announcing the near approach of the British Relief Expedition, and even went so far as to hire some of the principal houses on the river for the reception of the men belonging to it. Day by day he watched from the roof of his palace, in the hope of seeing them arrive. After awhile many of the inhabitants began to lose faith in him, and commenced opening communications with the *Mahdi*.

On the 20th January, the news of the battle of Abu Klea reached the *Mahdi's* camp, where it caused the greatest consternation. A council of *emirs* was thereupon held, at which there were great divergences of opinion. The *Mahdi* himself was strongly in favour of raising the siege. He told the *emirs* that he had been warned in a vision that he was to make a "*hegira*," or flight, to Obeid, whither he proposed to withdraw with his forces. He said, "If one Englishman had been able to keep us at bay for a year, what chance shall we have against thousands of Englishmen who have defeated our best men at Abu Klea?" All agreed except one *emir*, named Mohammed Abd el Kerim, who said that an attempt should be made to take Khartoum by assault, adding, rightly enough, that if it succeeded the English would not dare to come on, and that, if it failed, there would always be time to retreat. Abd el Kerim's views, for the time being, prevailed, and there was no longer any talk of raising the siege.

Before the meeting terminated it was decided to announce a great victory. Accordingly a salute of 101 guns was fired, the war drums were beaten, and every demonstration was made, as if in celebration of some great triumph. The stratagem failed to impose on Gordon, who had seen, through his glass, thousands of women in the camp, weeping and indulging in signs of despair. The actual news of the battle was conveyed to him shortly after by a female spy from Omdurman.

A council, composed of Farag Pasha, the military commandant, the chief government officials, the Greek Consul, and other leading members of the Greek colony, was hurriedly summoned to the palace. The meeting was then informed of the victory at Abu Klea, and that the English were approaching, and would arrive in two or three days. This

---

4. At a court martial held in Cairo on Hassan Bey, in June, 1887, on a charge of treachery in connection with the fall of Khartoum, one of the soldiers, being asked if the troops were exercised in "night alarms," naïvely replied "that there was no necessity for any such practice, as the enemy attacked every night."

intelligence inspired everybody with fresh hope, only, however, to give place to deeper despair when the next few days passed away without any signs of the relieving force. Gordon still struggled to keep up the spirits of his men, constantly saying, "They must come tomorrow," though few believed in him, and people began to say that, after all, the great battle which had taken place must have been a Dervish victory.

It is said that Gordon at this time took no sleep, but spent his days in watching the river from the roof of the palace, and his nights in visiting the various posts.

On the 23rd, he had a stormy interview with Farag Pasha, whom he reproached with having left one of the forts insufficiently guarded. It seems that Farag, on this occasion, proposed to surrender Khartoum to the *Mahdi*, and stated the terms which the latter was willing to accept. Gordon indignantly refused to listen to the proposition, and is even said to have struck Farag.

There is no doubt that, at this period, not only Farag, but many of the other officers and government officials, as well as some of the leading merchants, were in correspondence with the *Mahdi*, who was also kept posted up in the condition of the garrison by the deserters who, from time to time, left Khartoum. On one night alone, Omar Agha Ibrahim, a lieutenant of infantry, after taking the precaution of drawing half a month's pay for himself and his men, went over to the enemy with thirty of his comrades.

By the way of final preparations, Gordon had all the ammunition and powder not required for daily use removed from the arsenal and placed in the Catholic Church, a strong stone building near the palace, and commenced to lay a slow match train between the two buildings, so as to enable him to explode the whole supply, in the event of the Mahdists entering the town.[5]

To provide for the safety of the Europeans, he stationed the small steamer *Ismailia* just beyond the palace walls, with orders to the engineer to get up steam on a signal being made. The arrangement was kept secret, being communicated only to the principal Greek residents, who, it was proposed, should go on board with their families at the last moment and save themselves by the river.[6]

---

5. At the moment when the town was taken the train had not been completely laid.
6. The scheme fell through owing to a disagreement with the Greek Consul. There is every reason to suppose that Gordon never had any intention to escape himself in the steamer, although the Greeks formed the design of taking him with them by force.

Meantime the *Mahdi* had full information of the movements of the British expeditionary force. The delay in the advance from Metammeh inspired both him and his followers with fresh courage. It also gave support to Mohammed el Kerim's arguments, and when, on the 24th, intelligence was received that two steamers had started from Metammeh, a Council was held at which it was determined to act on his advice and make the attack before the vessels should arrive.

This decision was, to some extent, influenced by the circumstance that the *Mahdi* had opportunely had another vision, in which, this time, the prophet had assured him "that *Allah* had put the lives of the garrison into the *Mahdi's* hands, and that the attack should be made early on the morning of Monday, the 26th."

On the 25th Gordon was slightly ill, and, it being Sunday, he did not appear in public. Through mental strain and trouble his hair had grown completely white. Although he appeared to realize that the end could not be much longer postponed, he was repeatedly heard to say that, if he had only a couple of English soldiers to parade on the ramparts, he should not fear the enemy's attack.

In the morning he observed a great movement in the hostile lines, and called many of his officers, and the leading men of the town, to the palace. After telling them that he thought the attack was impending, he appealed to them to make a last effort, as he believed that the British troops would arrive in twenty-four hours. He called upon every male inhabitant—even the old men—to assist in manning the fortifications.

It was a gloomy Sunday in Khartoum, and as the day went by without any signs of the relieving force, despair settled down over all. When night came many of the famished soldiers left their posts on the ramparts and wandered into the town in search of food. Others were too weak, from want of nourishment, to go to their stations. Although this was not an unusual occurrence of late, the number of defaulters that night was so great as to cause the most serious alarm in the town, and many of the principal inhabitants armed themselves and their servants and went to the fortifications in place of the soldiers.

Gordon, who had established a complete system of telegraphic communication with all the posts along the lines, sat up alone writing in the palace till after midnight, and then, worn out with anxiety and fatigue, fell asleep.

In the early part of the night, which, after the moon had set, was dark and cloudy, the *Mahdi* crossed over from Omdurman with a huge mass of his followers and joined the armies of Wad en Nejumi and Abu Girgeh, drawn up on the south and east faces of the fortifications. After addressing the combined forces and giving his final orders, the *Mahdi* then returned to Omdurman, leaving Wad en Nejumi to conduct the attack.

At about 2 a.m. on the 26th, the entire force, under Wad en Nejumi, numbering from 40,000 to 50,000 men, began its advance. It moved in two divisions. The foremost was told off to attack the lines to the westward at the point between the Messalamieh Gate and the White Nile, where the defences had been partially destroyed by the river. The other division was to attack towards Buri, at the opposite, or eastern, extremity of the lines, or in the event of the attack on the White Nile side proving successful, to follow in the track of the foremost division and thus enter Khartoum. The instructions were to march as silently as possible, and not to fire until fired upon by the defenders.

Carrying "*angaribs,*" or couches of palm boughs, and bundles of brushwood, to throw into the trenches, under cover of the darkness the Dervishes marched noiselessly close up to the lines till the ditch was reached. This they found partly filled with mud and the parapet broken away. A few of the Dervishes fired in reply to the fire from the lines; the remainder, charging with spears, dashed into the trench and up the opposite side, shouted their war cries, and, meeting but little resistance, effected an entrance into the works.

The defenders only perceived the advance a few minutes before the actual attack, when the alarm sounded. The greater part of the troops were so tired and worn out that it was not till the sentries fired that the rest of the garrison started up, to find the enemy swarming across the ditch and up the broken parapet. When once the Dervishes were upon them, Gordon's soldiers made but little fight. Too feeble to withstand the rush, some were killed, and still more broke and fled.

In a few minutes all resistance at this part of the position was over, and whilst a stream of Dervishes from behind, pouring in through the place where the entry had been effected, pushed on and entered Khartoum, those in front rushed along inside the parapets and attacked the defenders in the rear. These last, stationed at distances of from three to four paces apart, and hopelessly outnumbered, could do but little. They fired a few shots and were then either killed or dispersed—leaving the enemy in undisputed possession of the fortifications. Over 150 soldiers' bodies were afterwards counted on the parapets alone.

The commandant, Farag Pasha, was at Buri, at the further end of the fortifications, when the assault was made, and at once rode down the lines, encouraging his men. When he reached the Messalamieh Gate, the Dervish horde had already crossed the ditch and were rolling up the line of the defenders on the parapets. Farag, seeing that resistance was useless, opened the Messalamieh Gate and surrendered himself prisoner. A great many of his followers also rushed out through the gate and threw down their arms. Charges of treachery have been brought against Farag for his conduct on this occasion, but, seeing that the enemy were well within the position when the gate was opened, this act could not have affected the issue one way or another. Farag's having been put to death in the enemy's camp three days later also tends to rebut the accusation of having betrayed his trust.

Mohamed Bey Ibrahim, who commanded at the same gate, formed his men, consisting of two companies, into a square, and, taking up a position on the plain between the lines and the town, fought courageously till he and nearly all his men were killed.

Bakhit Betraki was in charge at Buri, and held his ground till, seeing that the enemy had carried the works at the other end, and were inside the lines, he abandoned the fortifications. Then, rallying his men, he fought as long as any of them were left alive.

Notwithstanding the resistance offered in this and other instances, the Dervish loss was but trifling, only from 80 to 100 being killed in the whole operations, which, from the time the first gun was fired till Khartoum was taken, are said to have lasted three hours.[7]

The soldiers who had been placed on board the barges and armed boats on the White Nile, as already stated, made but very slight resistance. They did a little firing at the moment of the first assault, after which they forsook the boats and fled.

The garrisons at Tuti Island and at "the North Fort" were, from the nature of their positions, unable to take any active part in the fight; they fired occasionally from their guns, but when Khartoum fell they all surrendered without further opposition.

The party of Dervishes who, when the first attack succeeded, pushed on to Khartoum, at once took possession of the town and began massacring, pillaging and looting everywhere.

Their first thought was to rush for the palace, where they expected to find the treasure, as well as Gordon, the man who had so long and

---

7, For many of these details the author is indebted to *Mahdism and the Egyptian Soudan*, and to *Ten Years' Captivity in the Mahdi's Camp*, both by Sir Francis R. Wingate, the head of the Intelligence Department of the Egyptian Army.

so successfully resisted them.

Gordon, who had with him a company of black troops as a guard, on being aroused by the noise of the attack, went on the roof of the palace, which stood on the northern side of the town facing the Blue Nile, and, finding that the enemy had entered the works for upwards of an hour, kept up a hot fire in the direction of the attack. As dawn approached he could see the Dervish banners in the town. Soon the gun which he had mounted on the roof became useless, as it could not be depressed sufficiently to fire down upon the Dervishes, who were by this time crowding in thousands round the palace. Gordon, seeing that resistance was useless, then quitted the roof, put on his *pasha's* white uniform, and, with his sword by his side and his revolver in hand, placed himself at the door of his divan just at the top of the grand staircase. Here he stood and calmly awaited his fate.

A small band of Wad en Nejumi's followers forced their way into the building and dashed up the steps. Gordon asked them who was their leader. The only reply that he got was a curse, and one of the band plunged his spear into Gordon's body. Gordon made no attempt to defend himself, but turned away with a disdainful gesture, when he was again stabbed from behind and fell forward on the ground. Others of the party then rushed up and cut and hacked at the prostrate body until life was extinct. This was shortly before sunrise—whilst hundreds of Dervishes swarmed up to the palace roof and slaughtered the soldiers there.

Gordon's body was dragged down the steps to the garden, where the head was cut off, wrapped in a handkerchief, and taken to the *Mahdi*. The *Mahdi* is said to have been very angry at Gordon's death. His idea had been to convert him to Mahdism, and afterwards to hand him over to the government in exchange for Arabi Pasha. Gordon's head, after being shown to Slatin Pasha, then a captive in the camp, was hung on a tree at Omdurman, where multitudes of the *Mahdi's* followers cursed and insulted it. His body was left in the garden the whole day, and thousands of the Dervishes came up and plunged their spears into it. Later on it was thrown, with many others, into one of the wells adjoining.[8]

---

8. Though the above is the generally accepted version of Gordon's death, Mr. Charles Neufeld, in his published work *A Prisoner of the Khalifa*, gives the following narrative of the occurrence:—"Each day at dawn, when he retired to rest, he bolted his door from the inside, and placed his faithful body servant—Khaleel Agha Orphali—on guard outside it. On the fatal night Gordon had, as usual, kept his vigil on the roof of the palace, sending and receiving (continued next page)

The steamer which Gordon had placed near the palace was of no assistance at the critical moment. The captain saw the mob rushing to surround the building, and waited for Gordon to arrive. Later on, probably at the moment when Gordon met his end, a crowd of Dervishes made for the vessel, which, to escape being captured, steamed out into mid stream and moved backwards and forwards until the captain received a message from the *Mahdi*, offering him pardon if he would give up the steamer, which was thereupon surrendered.

After the palace had been taken the Catholic mission building and church were the next objects on which the mob directed themselves. The guards in the grounds outside were at once killed, and the assailants then broke into the building, killing and looting everywhere.

The massacre in the town lasted six hours, and 4,000 persons at least were killed. The black troops were spared, except such as resisted. The Bashi-Bazouks, fellaheen regulars, and the Shaggiah irregulars were mostly killed in cold blood after they had surrendered and been disarmed. Large numbers of the townspeople and slaves were either killed or wounded.

At 10 a.m. the *Mahdi* sent orders to stop the massacre, which then ceased, and the Dervishes devoted themselves exclusively to looting. The *Mahdi* had promised his followers as much gold and silver as they could carry when Khartoum fell, and immense disappointment was expressed when they failed to find the expected treasure, for which

telegraphic messages from the lines every few minutes, and as dawn crept into the skies, thinking that the long-threatened attack was not yet to be delivered, he lay down, wearied out. The little firing heard a few minutes later attracted no more attention than the usual firing which had been going on continuously night and day for months, but when the palace guards were heard firing it was known that something serious was happening. By the time Gordon had slipped into his old serge, or dark tweed, suit, and taken his sword and revolver, the advanced Dervishes were already surrounding the palace. Overcoming the guards, a rush was made up the stairs, and Gordon was met leaving his room. A small spear was thrown, which wounded him, but very slightly, on the left shoulder. Almost before the Dervishes knew what was happening, three of them lay dead, and one wounded, at Gordon's feet; the remainder fled. Quickly reloading his revolver, Gordon made for the head of the stairs, and again drove the reassembling Dervishes off. Darting back to reload, he received a stab in his left shoulder-blade from a Dervish concealed behind the corridor door, and, on reaching the steps the third time, he received a pistol-shot and spear-wound in his right breast, and then, great soldier as he was, he rose almost above himself. With his life's blood pouring from his breast—not his back, remember—he fought his way step by step, kicking from his path the wounded and dead Dervishes; ... and as he was passing through the doorway leading into the courtyard another concealed Dervish almost severed his leg with a single blow. Then Gordon fell."

Gordon's banknotes formed but a poor substitute.[9]

The bloodshed and cruelty which attended the massacre are said to be such as defy description. Nicola Leontides, the Greek Consul, had his hands first cut off and was then murdered. Martin Hansel, the Austrian Consul, and the oldest member of the European colony, was alive up to 2 p.m., when a party of Arabs, headed by his own *janissary*, entered his house and beheaded him, together with a man named Mulatte Skander, who lived with him. The two bodies were then taken outside, covered with petroleum and set fire to. The Austrian tailor, Klein, on making the sign of the cross, had his throat cut from ear to ear before the eyes of his wife and children. The savages then buried their lances in the body of his son, aged seventeen, who fell lifeless. The mother, a Venetian by birth, seized her son of five years old with one hand, and, holding her baby to her breast with the other, struggled heroically to prevent their taking her children from her. Eventually they seized her daughter, a girl of eighteen, who was carried off to add to the other booty taken.

Numbers of women, and even children, perished in the general slaughter. Of the survivors, all the young and good looking women and girls were taken off to the "*Beit el Mal*," the *Mahdi's* treasury, where the loot was ordered to be collected. There they lay exposed like cattle in a pen, awaiting their turn to be selected to fill the *harems* of the conquerors. The first choice lay with the *Mahdi* himself, then followed the various *emirs*, each in order of his rank. The women who were not chosen were distributed among the soldiers. The old women were given a few rags with which to cover themselves, and then sent to the Dervish camp to eke out a miserable existence by begging.

The number of Europeans made prisoners is stated to have been about ninety altogether, besides several thousands of natives. Most of these were removed to Omdurman, where they were left to get on as best they could, and exposed to many privations.

Only two days later, on the 28th, whilst the *Mahdi's* army was still engaged in celebrating the victory, Wilson's two steamers were observed slowly making their way up stream in the direction of the north end of Tuti Island, firing as they advanced both from guns and rifles. It was at once decided to oppose the landing of the red-coated soldiers who could be seen on board. All rushed to the river's bank,

---

9. There is an entry in Gordon's *Diary*, dated the 12th November, to the effect that the specie in the Treasury was then only £831, although there was paper representing £42,800 more.

the women shouting "*Môt lil Inglesi*" ("Death to the English").

After reaching a point mid-way between Tuti Island and the left bank of the White Nile, and apparently looking for indications as to the fate of Khartoum and Gordon, the steamers were seen to turn round and proceed down the river under a hail of bullets from the shore.

The news of the fall of Khartoum, after a siege of 317 days, or only nine days less than that of Sebastopol, reached the War Office in London at a quarter of an hour before midnight on the 4th February. It was communicated by a despatch from Lord Wolseley, sent from Korti, at 9.10 p.m. on the same day.

The War Office officials, many of whom were summoned on the receipt of the despatch, hesitated to believe the news it contained, until it should be confirmed by later intelligence, and the representatives of the Press Association were informed that nothing would be published till the following day. On the 5th the despatch appeared in the second edition of several of the morning papers, and England realized to the fullest extent the bitterness of a great national disappointment. All the gallantry and devotion of her officers and men had been unavailing; the costly Nile Expedition had proved a dismal failure; and Gordon had been allowed to perish.

The general feeling on the subject was intensified by the reflection that but two days elapsed between the fall of Khartoum and the arrival of the British troops before the town. The government of Mr. Gladstone was severely reproached with having been once more "too late."

As to the part taken by Sir Charles Wilson, there was a strong tendency to censure the delay which had occurred in the departure of the steamers for Khartoum. Sir Charles, in a letter to Lord Wolseley, gave full explanations on this subject. He based his reasons for not starting sooner on the following considerations:—

> 1st. The military situation. The force had been much weakened by its losses in the fighting on the 17th and 18th January, and would be further reduced by the convoy and escort which it was necessary to send back to Gakdul. The horses and camels were so "done up" from fatigue and want of food, as to be unable to reconnoitre any distance. Reinforcements for the enemy were reported as advancing both from Omdurman and Berber, and it was necessary for him, before leaving, to ascertain that

the small British force at Gubat was not liable to attack.

2ndly. The necessity of changing the men in the steamers (in accordance with Gordon's advice) and replacing them by Soudanese.

3rdly. The steamers' engines required to be overhauled, and the vessels themselves had to be prepared for resisting the batteries which it was known they would have to fight on their way to Khartoum.

4thly. Gordon was known to be still holding out, and there was nothing to show that the expected crisis, so long delayed, would take place in the next few days.

As a fact, the steamers from Khartoum reached Gubat on the 21st January, whilst the British were engaged with the enemy at Metammeh; and Wilson received the letters which General Gordon had sent down between three and four p.m. on that day. The earliest possible date for starting would, therefore, be on the morning of the 22nd, and Sir Charles pointed out that, if the steamers had left at that time and travelled at the same rate as they subsequently did, they would then only have reached Khartoum at mid-day on the 26th, when it had already fallen.

Sir Charles might, without exaggeration, have enlarged on the condition of his forces, which were so utterly used up—both men and animals—that a short interval of comparative repose was indispensable before anything further was attempted. That in spite of their condition they should have been able to undertake the abortive attack on Metammeh on the 21st, speaks volumes for their pluck and endurance.

Even if Wilson had disregarded all other considerations and pushed on at once with his handful of soldiers, there is every reason to suppose that the result would have been the same. From what has subsequently been ascertained, it is clear that for weeks previously the *Mahdi* had Khartoum at his mercy, and could have taken it at any moment, though he preferred that it should fall by the slower process of starvation.

He had full information of Wilson's movements, and had the latter started two days earlier, the only result would have been that the capture of the town would have been accelerated by precisely that period of time.

It would be too much to imagine that if the subaltern's guard which Wilson had at his disposal had reached Khartoum whilst it still held out, it could (notwithstanding Gordon's expectations to the contrary) have changed the fortunes of the day, or have induced the *Mahdi* to carry out his idea of raising the siege and retiring to Obeid. For this, the presence, or at least the advance, of the whole force at Gubat was necessary.

As it happened, the column at Gubat was not in a condition to advance, and the *Mahdi*, knowing that at the worst he had only the two steamers to reckon with, determined to risk an assault.

The responsibility for the disaster may be traced partly to the insufficient supply of camels to the Desert Column, owing to which Stewart, instead of pushing on at first straight across the Bayuda desert, was compelled to return from Gakdul Wells to Korti, and then make a fresh start, thus losing twelve days' valuable time. But after all, the main responsibility will always rest with the government which so long delayed despatching the Relief Expedition, and then, as if to make its failure the more certain, sent it by the wrong route.

CHAPTER 45

The Retreat from Gubat

The result of the taking of Khartoum was naturally to increase the renown of the *Mahdi* to a greater extent than ever in the Moslem world. His fame as a conqueror spread not only throughout the Soudan, but also in the towns and villages of Upper and Lower Egypt. Many of those who before had disbelieved in him, now became fully assured of his holy mission. Had he at once followed up his success by an advance down the Nile, the consequences to the British forces at Gubat and elsewhere might have been disastrous. As it was, he contented himself with staying with his followers in the neighbourhood of Khartoum, the pillaging of which no doubt afforded an agreeable relaxation after a long and arduous siege.

With Khartoum in the *Mahdi's* power, the whole situation was changed. His army instead of being concentrated before Khartoum, was set free to strike a blow at any point which he might think opportune for attack.

Not merely was the small force at Gubat in danger, but Wolseley's entire army was at this period divided and split up in fragments. One of these was at Gubat, in immediate proximity to the fortified town of Metammeh held by a superior force. Another was isolated near Kirbekan, where the enemy were reported to be in considerable strength; whilst a third remained with Wolseley at the headquarters at Korti. In addition detachments were scattered across the Bayuda desert at the different points of communication.

Though at first the capture of Metammeh and operations against Berber were contemplated, the question of the relief of Khartoum gradually resolved itself into the problem of extricating "The Relief Expedition" itself. Opinions differed greatly how this was to be effected. Some were in favour of the immediate retreat of the desert column to Korti. Others considered a march across the desert of so small a force, with the prospect of encountering hordes of Mahdists from Khartoum, anything but a safe operation. Other advisers were in favour of concentrating the whole of the expeditionary force on the capture of Berber and holding that place until the arrival of reinforcements from India or from home landed at Souakim, should either insure the safe retreat of the force, or allow of the recapture of Khartoum. That which was done will appear later.

During the absence of Sir Charles Wilson, the British force in the neighbourhood of Gubat, under Colonel Boscawen, was employed in improving and strengthening the works there. A triangular fort was erected, and earthworks with flanking trenches and parapets were thrown up both on the land side and towards Metammeh. Brushwood and wire entanglements were placed outside to impede the enemy in the event of their attempting to storm the position, and, in fact, every preparation was made to stand a siege.

Although an attack was constantly expected, the enemy, beyond beating *tom-toms* all night and making a parade every day, did nothing.

The force from time to time sent convoys of sick and wounded back across the desert to Abu Klea and Korti. To facilitate and guard the line of communications, the garrisons at the Wells were strengthened from time to time by detachments from Korti.

The whole country round Metammeh, except the village itself, where 2,000 to 3,000 of the enemy were quartered, remained quiet. At Metammeh, on the 28th January, there was a great firing of guns, with other signs of rejoicing over the news from Khartoum.

On intelligence of General Stewart's condition reaching headquarters, Sir Redvers Buller was appointed to succeed to the command of the Desert column, Sir Evelyn Wood becoming Lord Wolseley's Chief of the Staff, and Brigadier-General Grenfell succeeding Sir Evelyn Wood as "*Sirdar*" (Commander-in-Chief) of the Egyptian Army.

Buller left Korti on the 29th January for Gakdul by the Desert route. The Royal Irish and West Kent Regiments left at the same time to strengthen the garrisons at the Wells and reinforce Gubat.

On the 11th February, Buller, with six companies of the Royal Irish Regiment, which had marched on foot the whole way from Korti, reached Gubat. His instructions were to seize Metammeh and march on Berber, but on no account to let himself be hemmed in at Metammeh.

The programme was suddenly altered, and in lieu thereof a retreat was decided on. One reason for this change was the loss likely to be incurred in the taking of Metammeh, another consideration was the insufficiency of Buller's column to operate against Berber in the face of the large force, which, set free by the fall of Khartoum, the *Mahdi* would now have at his disposal.

Buller deemed it unwise even to attempt to hold the position at Gubat against the *Mahdi's* army reinforced by Gordon's captured soldiers, and supplied with the arms and ammunition taken at Khartoum. Reports of the *Mahdi* having commenced an advance with 50,000 men were received, and it was judged best to retire, and so avoid the risk of having the retreat cut off.

Under these circumstances preparations were made for the march back across the Bayuda desert.[1]

Before leaving, Gordon's two remaining steamers were rendered useless by removal of parts of the machinery.

On the 13th Buller evacuated Gubat. His force numbered nearly 1,600 rank and file, and consisted of the following corps:—Squadron of 19th Hussars, Naval Brigade with two Gardner guns, detachment of Royal Artillery with two guns, a portion of the Mounted Infantry, a portion of the Guards Camel Corps, a wing of the Heavy Cavalry Camel Corps, portions of the Sussex and Royal Irish Regiments, details from departmental corps, and 300 Soudanese.

The wounded were the first sent off, the escort of 300 men being placed under the command of Colonel Talbot. The bad cases were carried in litters by the Egyptians. Sir Herbert Stewart, by this time much changed for the worse, was among the sick.

On the march to Abu Klea, Buller met with no opposition beyond a skirmish which the advance guard had on the day of starting.

On the 16th the column arrived at Abu Klea, and at once set to work to strengthen the position against attack.

About thirty of the enemy's cavalry were seen scouting round the place all day. About an hour before sunset these were reinforced by some 400 infantry armed with rifles. They crossed the hills to the north-east and eastward, and having made a cover by throwing up a series of low stone walls, opened a well-directed fire at long range on the camp. The bullets fell all round and over the position. No lights or fires were allowed after dark, as the enemy kept up a dropping fire throughout the night. The British force made no reply. Up to the

---

1. Sir C. Wilson had left for Korti on the 5th.

morning of the 17th, two men had been killed, and four officers and ten men wounded.

On the 17th the guns of the Royal Artillery opened fire on the enemy's position with shrapnel. The Gardners were also turned on, but as the supply of ammunition was limited the fire had to be restricted. Still, slow as was the fire, it sufficed to check that of the enemy until eight a.m., when the cover they had been throwing up being completed, their fire became as heavy as before. Fortunately, the aim was somewhat interfered with by the high wind blowing, and by clouds of sand. Still, as Buller in his despatch to Lord Wolseley observed, to remain stationary subject to this unceasing pelting by bullets "was annoying."

The fire of the enemy did not interfere with the work of strengthening the camp. Three new forts mutually supporting one another were constructed. Buller placed the command of the principal and largest of them in the hands of Lord Charles Beresford, with his naval men and guns. The Royal Irish were ordered to hold the fort on the west of the camp, while the Sussex men garrisoned the fort on the east. The Engineers guarded the *zeriba* itself, in which the hospital was erected.

About noon a steady shelling of the enemy's position was commenced. The Gardner guns were at the same time again brought into use, and the Mounted Infantry also opened fire with Martinis. After about two hours of this long range fighting, the enemy's fire showed signs of slackening. Major Wardrop was then sent out to reconnoitre, and endeavoured to ascertain the actual strength and position of the enemy, up to this time unknown.

With one officer and three troopers the major crept round the enemy's right, under cover of some rising ground. Ascending a slight rise, he looked cautiously over, and observed that the enemy's riflemen on the hill were not numerous, and had no supports. He dismounted his men, and made them, without showing more than their heads, fire a volley. He then remounted and galloped off and repeated his tactics two or three times in different places, leaving one man in each place to fire as rapidly as possible, but without exposing himself to view. The Arabs were completely deceived by this manoeuvre, and imagining that large reinforcements of British troops had come up, became demoralized, broke off the fight, and retreated towards Metammeh, carrying with them their killed and wounded, and leaving only a few mounted scouts to watch the camp.

Buller's loss in this skirmish amounted to three men killed, and four officers and twenty-three men wounded. The enemy's losses were more severe. They were seen to carry off several bodies, and they left six on the field of battle. Owing to the nature of the ground it was impossible to form an estimate as to the strength of the enemy. Equally difficult was it to understand what their object was, but the better opinion seems to be that it was intended to try and engage Buller until the *Mahdi* should come up with his whole army.

Buller then sent off a detachment of the Light Camel Corps, with despatches for Gakdul, requesting that more transport camels with ammunition might be sent to him. His reasons for thus weakening his forces were twofold. In the first place, the water supply at Abu Klea was not sufficient for the whole force for many days. In the second, his means of transport were insufficient for the requirements of the marching column, in addition to those of the garrison at the Wells.

The night of the 17th was passed quietly at the camp. On the morning of the 18th Buller detached a party of infantry which moved southwards towards the hills which had been occupied by the enemy. Their position was found to be completely abandoned, and was taken possession of by the British force. A strong post was established on the principal hill, and scouting-parties were sent out, but nothing more could be seen of the enemy.

Sir Evelyn Wood, with three companies of the West Kent Regiment, was despatched from Korti to strengthen the force at Gakdul Wells, which they reached on the 17th, and from Gakdul a supply of transport camels with stores was sent on to Buller at Abu Klea.

During the march of the convoy from Gakdul nothing had been seen of the enemy until the neighbourhood of Abu Klea was reached, when suddenly a small body of armed men was observed watching the movements of the party. Some of the Camel Corps forthwith went in chase, and captured a half-dozen. These made no attempt to resist capture, but threw down their Remingtons, and begged for mercy. When interrogated the prisoners declared that there was no strong force of rebels anywhere near. There was, they said, a rebel camp on rising ground some two miles distant, but there were only 600 fighting men there, all of whom had recently come from Metammeh. The prisoners agreed in stating that none of the *Mahdi's* forces from Khartoum had yet reached Metammeh.

On the arrival of the camels and stores, Buller made his preparations for evacuating Abu Klea. His original intentions were merely to destroy the forts, and leave the wells untouched. But on the forenoon of the 23rd, he got information to the effect that the enemy had received a strong reinforcement, estimated at not less than 8,000 men. This compelled him to modify his plans, and he resolved to leave the forts standing, but to fill up all the larger wells.

The latter step was afterwards much criticized, and can only be justified by the extreme peril in which Buller's force might otherwise have been placed. To stop up a desert well is to the Oriental mind about the blackest crime that could be committed; and is a measure which is never adopted even in savage warfare. Buller, however, had no alternative.

The absence of water in his rear was the sole thing that could check pursuit by the supposed force in his rear. It was, in short, the only method of covering his retreat. Accordingly, regardless of Eastern traditions, heaps of stones and rubbish were piled into all the principal wells before leaving. It was foreseen that before the enemy could advance he must lose several hours, and perhaps days, in restoring the wells to their former state. This time Buller calculated on employing in getting a start over his pursuers.

At two p.m. all the baggage was sent on under convoy to camp on the Omit Handel plain out of gunshot range of the Abu Klea hills. At six the outposts were withdrawn, and an hour later the whole force, including thirty-two sick and wounded, was in retreat towards Gakdul. As they marched out, the troops were not interfered with by the enemy. The enemy's scouts appeared about midday on the 24th, and fired a few shots. After this they retired, and the column was no more molested, reaching Gakdul on the 26th.

There being barely sufficient camels for the supplies, all the men and officers had to march on foot. This, as Buller observed in his despatch, in the weather which prevailed, with an allowance of only three quarts of water per man a-day, was most exhausting. He adds, "Nothing could have been better than the spirit shown by all ranks."

At Gakdul Buller's force learned the news of the death on the 16th of their former leader, General Stewart, who, with the other wounded, had been sent on in advance.

The latest accounts of his condition had been such as to lead to hope of his recovery. It subsequently transpired that the nature of the wound he had received rendered this impossible, and after supporting the hardships of the desert march he finally succumbed the day before the convoy reached the wells of Gakdul, where a small force was left to bring on the stores.²

The column remained but a brief period at Gakdul, and on the 27th set out for Korti, which was reached on the 1st March, the last of the troops arriving on the 15th.

Of the march of Stewart's column across the Bayuda desert to Metammeh and back, it is unnecessary to say anything more. The highest military authority in Europe, Count Von Moltke, said of the men who took part in it, "They were not soldiers but heroes."

---

2. Major-General Sir Herbert Stewart was born in 1843, and was one of the youngest generals in the service. One of the earliest appointments made on the organization of the army for the first Egyptian campaign was that of Stewart as Staff officer to General Drury-Lowe, who was to command the cavalry division. He distinguished himself at Tel-el-Kebir, and took part in Drury-Lowe's brilliant ride to Cairo. When the Egyptians sent out a white flag to meet the advancing British force, General (then Colonel) Stewart at the head of a few lancers and dragoons, demanded, and received, the surrender of the Egyptians at Abbassieh. He accompanied General Graham to Souakim, and displayed conspicuous soldierly qualities at Tamaai.

CHAPTER 46

The Nile Column

The advance guard of the Nile column, consisting of 545 of the 38th South Staffordshire Regiment, left Korti for Abu Hamid in the whalers on the 28th December, 1884. Brigadier-General Brackenbury, second in command, with a troop of the 19th Hussars, followed the next day.

On the 3rd January, 1885, the force encamped at Hamdab, where General Earle and his staff arrived on the 4th. The remainder of the column was sent forward from time to time, as the regiments reached Korti.

On the 24th the force at Hamdab, having been in the meantime joined by the Royal Highlanders (Black Watch), a portion of the Gordon Highlanders, the Duke of Cornwall's Regiment, the Transport Camels and the Camel Battery, left camp and continued the journey up stream, the mounted troops proceeding along the banks, and the remainder going in the whalers as before. The enemy being reported to be in force at Berti, every precaution was taken to avoid a surprise, *zeribas* being formed each night, and a system of moonlight signalling was adopted.

Passing the Fourth Cataract and other formidable rapids, Berti was reached by the advance guard on the 1st February and found deserted. The enemy, according to the report of a deserter, had abandoned the place on the previous day, and retired up the river to Salamat. Suleiman Wad Gamr, the murderer of Colonel Stewart's party, it was reported, had fled beyond recall. The boat belonging to Stewart's steamer *Abbas* was discovered on the shore. Hussein Ismael, the stoker, whose account of the murder has been already given, presented himself and confirmed his previous story. The houses in Berti being searched, traces of Stewart's party were found in the shape of a number of papers, fragments of books, and a portion of a barometer.

On the 3rd the headquarters moved to Berti, where the rest of the troops encamped as they came up. On the 4th news was received of the fall of Khartoum by a telegram from Sir Evelyn Wood. The discouraging information was carefully kept from the knowledge of the men. The same message instructed General Earle to halt where he was until further orders. On the 8th the general was informed by telegraph that Lord Wolseley was communicating with the government as to future operations, but that the column was to push on to Abu Hamid. Orders for the troops to move up were thereupon issued.

On the night of the 8th General Earle received a report from Colonel Butler, who was in command of the advanced camp, that, in reconnoitring that day, he had found the enemy in a strong position, occupying some rocky knolls, and holding a high razor-backed ridge of hills behind. Earle then ordered the advance of the 1st Battalion South Staffordshire and 1st Battalion Royal Highlanders, in boats, to an open camping-ground which Colonel Butler had selected, about a mile short of the enemy's position, and ordered the squadron 19th Hussars, half of the Egyptian Camel Corps, and two guns of the Egyptian artillery, to advance to the same place.

On the 9th General Earle himself arrived on the scene, and having personally reconnoitred the enemy's position, and sent Colonel Butler with the cavalry to make a wide reconnaissance towards the enemy's rear, he decided to attack the position the next morning.

A company of the Royal Highlanders was left in a *zeriba* to guard the boats, baggage, and baggage animals, and at 7 a.m. on the 10th the advance commenced.

Two companies of the South Staffordshire and two guns were placed under the command of Lieutenant-Colonel Alleyne, who was instructed to take up a position on a rocky hillock facing the enemy's position, and, with the assistance of the Egyptian Camel Corps, to occupy the attention of the defenders in front, whilst, with six companies of the South Staffordshire and six companies of the Royal Highlanders, Earle marched about a mile and a half to his right front, thus completely turning the high ridge referred to in Butler's report, and the whole of the enemy's position.

Meanwhile fire was opened (at 8.30) by the two companies of the Staffordshire and the guns under Colonel Alleyne, the enemy replying with their Remingtons.

After turning the enemy's position, Earle's column, pivoting on its

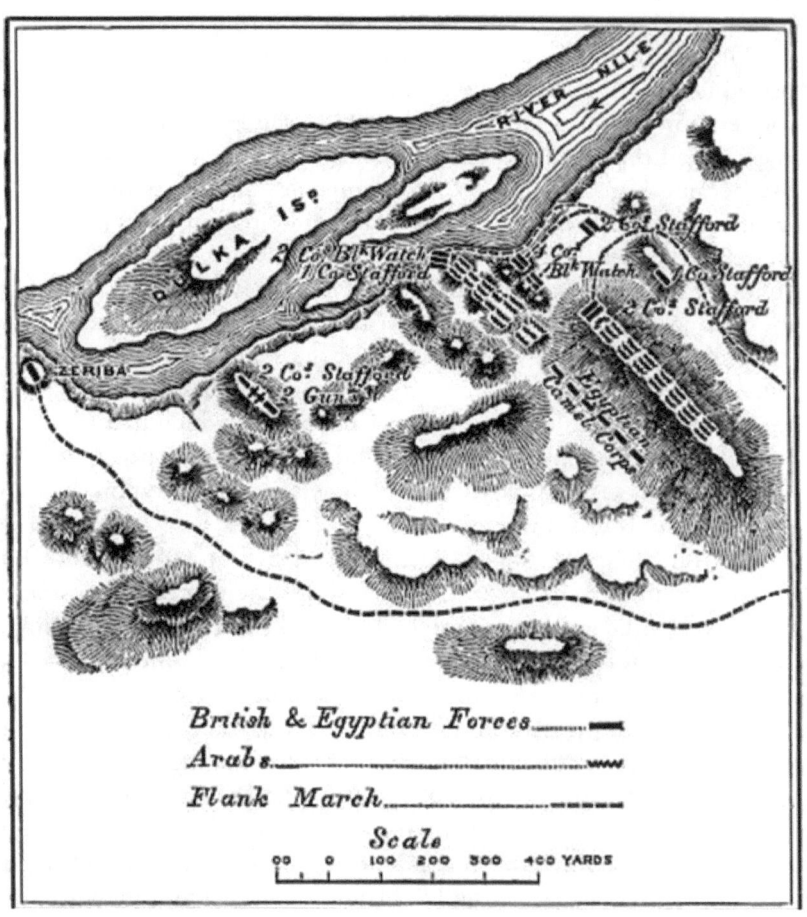

BATTLE OF KIRBEKAN.

left, brought the right of the column round till it reached the rear of the enemy's lines, and then marched over broken and rocky ground through a valley in the direction of the river, keeping the high ridge on the left. It was found that the column formation, ready to form square, was unsuited to the nature of the ground, and the further advance was made by companies, but not in extended order, points of vantage in the rocky ground being occupied in succession.

The enemy had been seen crowding the high ridge as the column passed its eastern end, but at first they appeared to take no notice. No sooner, however, had the force wheeled to the left than (at 9.15) fire was opened on it with Remingtons, hitting two or three men. As the fire became hotter Earle sent two companies of the South Staffordshire, under Colonel Eyre, to take the high ridge by working up its western shoulder. The men advanced under a heavy fire, and climbed about a third of the way up the shoulder, till they reached a cluster of rocks under which they obtained partial shelter.

At the same time, two companies of the Highlanders and a company of the Staffords were directed to advance under cover of the river bank and take the knoll nearest the river, towards which parties of the enemy were seen making their way, and swimming to the other side. This knoll was speedily captured, and the enemy's position on the two principal knolls was thus enfiladed.

The remainder of the Highlanders and Staffords then advanced from one cluster of rocks to another towards the rear of the position, firing as they did so, till they reached the rocks nearest to the enemy's position, about 400 yards distant. From behind the enemy's works, consisting of earthworks and loopholed buildings, a steady and well-directed fusillade was kept up on the attacking force. This continued for some time, till, difficulty being found in dislodging the enemy by musketry fire, the order was about to be given to assault the position and carry it at the point of the bayonet, when suddenly a body of the enemy abandoned their works, and with spears and banners charged down upon the nearest of the Highlanders, who were somewhat advanced towards the British left front under Colonel Green.

The Highlanders, without changing their formation, received the assault with a withering fire, killing many. The rest turned to their left and made for the river, where several of them were shot in the water as they attempted to escape.

After repelling this onslaught the Highlanders advanced with their pipes skirling, scaled the rocks, and stormed the main position from front and flank in gallant style, killing every one of the enemy, who were in great numbers among the rocks and boulders.

At this time General Earle, who had accompanied the advance up the ridge, was killed by a bullet from a hut in which several of the defenders had taken refuge.

Meantime the two companies of the South Staffordshire sent to take the high ridge had been received by a heavy fire; Lieutenant-Colonel Eyre had been killed, and their ammunition was exhausted. Lieutenant-Colonel Beale was sent by General Brackenbury, who had assumed the command, to reinforce the attack and take the ridge, which duty was successfully accomplished, and the enemy were driven from their last position by 1.30 p.m. Most of the defending force were armed with Remington rifles, and their position, which was a formidable one, was defended with desperate courage.

When General Earle made his turning movement, and so placed the detachment he was leading between the enemy and their camp, Colonel Butler, who had guided the column to the rear of the enemy's position, made a wide sweeping detour with the cavalry to the enemy's camp, three miles further on, which he captured. So rapidly was this operation conducted that the camp was in his possession before the Highlanders had captured the main position.[1]

Leaving two companies of the Highlanders to guard the captured position, the remainder of the troops were sent back to the camp they had left in the morning.

The Egyptian Camel Corps did excellent service in the fight. The position which they had taken up at the commencement of the day enabled them to protect the flank of the infantry in its advance. They remained in that position throughout the day, assisting by their rifles to keep down the fire from the high ridge and shooting, and in some instances pursuing and capturing, such of the enemy as attempted to escape towards the east on the southern slope of the hill. When

---

1. A private of the Duke of Cornwall's Regiment found in a donkey's saddle-bag a letter in Arabic from the Governor of Berber to the governor of the district, and which was as follows:—"I inform you that today, after the mid-day prayer, we received a letter from the faithful Khalifa Abdullah Eben Mohammed, in which he tells us that Khartoum was taken on Monday, the 9th *Rabi*, 1302, on the side of El Haoui, in the following manner:—The *Mahdi* prayed his dervishes and his troops to advance against the fortifications, and entered Khartoum in a quarter of an hour. They killed the traitor Gordon, and captured the steamers and boats. God has made him glorious. Be grateful and thank and praise God for His unspeakable mercy. I announce it to you. Tell your troops." Dated the 13th *Rabi*.

the Staffords stormed the shoulder of the hill one Egyptian soldier charged up alone on their extreme right and joined in the attack.

Besides forty-one donkeys and camels captured at Kirbekan, fifty-eight rifles, four fowling-pieces, two flint-lock muskets, one revolver, twenty-two swords, fifty-three spears, and ten standards fell into the hands of the English. Some prisoners were taken, and, according to their statements, the enemy were surprised by General Earle attacking their rear, and thought the soldiers who got behind their position were coming from Berber.

Owing to the way in which the position was surrounded, it is difficult to see how many of the enemy could have escaped. They lay thick in every nook and crevice, and on the open ground where they charged the troops, and the Staffordshires killed many on the main ridge of hills. Nevertheless, their losses are only put in the General's report as 200. As no account mentions more than 125 bodies having been counted on the field of battle, this appears a liberal estimate, even after allowing for the bodies swept away by the stream. The return of rifle ammunition expended gives a total of 24,040 rounds, or rather more than 120 for each man killed, leaving out of the calculation twenty-three shells fired from the Camel Battery. The English force engaged only numbered 1,200, owing to the Gordon Highlanders and the half battalion of the Duke of Cornwall's Regiment not having come up; the former, in fact, had not succeeded in getting further than Berti.

The enemy's force at Kirbekan was stated by prisoners as being from 1,500 to 2,000. General Brackenbury, however, has put the number who held the works at 800, and says that at least half of these escaped before the attack. The resistance made was due to the almost impregnable position taken up.

Owing to the excellent tactics adopted in taking the works in the rear, the loss of the attacking force was but small. The death of General Earle, however, made Kirbekan a dearly purchased victory. He met his death shortly after the assault which resulted in the capture of the ridges. The troops were at the time being collected and formed up. Between the crests of the two main knolls there was a depression forming a small flat plateau, on which stood a stone hut with a thatched roof. Earle was forming up the ranks only ten yards from the hut, when it was discovered that there were men in it. One of the latter fired from the hut and shot a soldier. The general thereupon ordered the roof to be set on fire, at the same time approaching the hut. The roof commenced to burn, and a native rushed out, and was at once bayoneted. At this moment a shot was fired from a window of the hut, and the general fell, shot through the head. The back of the skull was shattered, and he lived only a few minutes.

In addition to General Earle, the British and Egyptian loss was as follows:—

South Staffordshire Regiment—Killed, Lieutenant-Colonel Eyre and 3 men; wounded, 2 officers and 20 men.

Royal Highlanders—Killed, Lieutenant-Colonel Coveney and 4 men; wounded, 2 officers and 18 men; missing, 1 man.

Egyptian Camel Corps—Killed, 2 men; wounded, 1 man.

Total killed, 11; wounded and missing, 44.

On the 11th, General Brackenbury received further instructions, according to which the Expedition was to stay in the country till the *Mahdi's* power at Khartoum was destroyed, and arrangements were to be made for co-operation with General Buller in an attack on Berber. The instructions further stated that the column was to push on with all possible speed pursuant to orders.

On the same day, the column continued its progress, the wounded officers and men being conveyed in the boats. The difficult pass of Shukook was got through without opposition, though it bore signs of having been prepared for defence throughout its entire length of six miles.

On the 17th Salamat was occupied, and the force destroyed the house, palm-trees, and *sakheas* of Suleiman Wad Gamr, the chief author of Colonel Stewart's murder. Many relics of the murder were found, such as cards, papers, photographs, & c.

On the 20th, Hebbeh, close to the scene of the murder, was reached, and on that and the following day the 800 horses and camels of the force swam over to the opposite bank, the equipments and loads being ferried across in boats.

The wreck of Stewart's steamer was seen fixed upon a rock about 200 yards from the bank of the river. She was pitted with bullet-marks, and torn by fragments of shell. The natives had stripped her of everything useful.

The house of Fakri Wad Etman, where the murder was committed, was visited by General Brackenbury. Fragments of books, Stewart's visiting cards, and a shirt-sleeve stained with blood, were found close by.

Whilst the crossing was being effected, the troops, not otherwise engaged, were employed in destroying the houses and property of Fakri Etman. The force then advanced along the right bank towards Abu Hamid.

On the night of the 23rd, the whole column with 215 boats was concentrated at the last cluster of huts in the Monassir country, twenty-six miles from Abu Hamid, and the Cavalry, which had scouted six miles ahead, were still without touch of the enemy.

On the 24th, just as the further advance was being resumed, Brackenbury received Wolseley's instructions to discontinue the movement on Abu Hamid and return to Merawi. The despatch said, "Buller evacuated Gubat. His main body went to Gakdul with sick and wounded. He remains with 1,500 at Abu Klea. I have abandoned all hope of going to Berber before the autumn campaign begins." This was a bitter disappointment to both officers and men. A strong patrol was advanced to within sight of Mograt Island (just opposite Abu Hamid), after which the column was reversed, reaching Hebbeh again the same day.

On the 25th it remained at the halting-place the whole day, as the horses and camels absolutely required rest.

Continuing his movement down the river on the following day, Brackenbury reached a village opposite Salamat. Here, leaving the mounted troops and convoy to move independently on the right bank under the command of Colonel Butler, the general descended the river himself with the boats. On the 4th March Hamdab was reached, the force having descended with the boats in nine days, a distance that it had taken thirty-one days to ascend. On the following day the force arrived at Merawi. The crossing commenced at 2 p.m., and was completed at 11.30 a.m. on the 6th. On the 7th, Brackenbury, leaving the Black Watch, a troop of hussars, the Egyptian Camel Corps, and a detachment of engineers, to remain at Merawi under Colonel Butler, started with the rest for Korti, which was reached the following day.

Apart from the engagement at Kirbekan, the Nile column had no fighting exploit to boast of. The crushing effect of that action was, however, shown by the fact that after the fight, the enemy allowed General Brackenbury's force to march unmolested through the Monassir country, to take successively all the positions which had been prepared for defence, and subsequently to retire through the same positions without firing a shot or offering any opposition.

Credit is undoubtedly due to the column for the manner in which it triumphed over the difficulties caused by the nature of the river, which from a few miles above Merawi presented a succession of rapids. All these rapids, amongst the most formidable obstacles on the Nile, were ascended and descended at an unfavourable season, with a loss by drowning of only three lives throughout the entire operation.

CHAPTER 47

Wolseley and the Prosecution of the Campaign

To return to Lord Wolseley's headquarters at Korti.

There is no doubt that the news of the fall of Khartoum was a severe blow to Wolseley. It seemed as if, for once, his star had deserted him. All hope of adding the rescue of Gordon and the relief of Khartoum to his list of triumphs, was gone from the general who had so often been described as "the luckiest man in the British Army."

On the 4th February Wolseley had telegraphed the disaster to the War Office. On the 5th he sent another message, saying that he had directed all the wounded to be removed as soon as possible from Abu Klea and Gubat, and added, "I only await the decision of government to give further orders."

There is here a gap in the published Blue Book, some of the messages exchanged with the War Office being evidently suppressed. But in a despatch to Sir Evelyn Baring, dated the 6th February, it is stated that:

> Her Majesty's Government have given complete discretion to Lord Wolseley to take all such measures as he may deem necessary for the further conduct of his operations, and they have assured his Lordship that he will receive any further assistance which he may desire, either by the despatch of troops to Souakim and Berber, or in any other manner he may indicate.

That Wolseley, under the altered circumstances, was not prepared to advise an attempt to recapture Khartoum with the force at his disposal, appears clear from the following extracts from his despatch to Lord Hartington of the 9th February:—

I shall not attempt to disguise from Your Lordship how deeply the reported fall of Khartoum is felt by all ranks in the army under my command. If it be literally true—and it is difficult to disbelieve it—the mission of this force, which was the relief of Khartoum, falls to the ground.

The strength and composition of this little army was calculated for the relief, not the siege and capture, of Khartoum, the two operations being entirely different in character and magnitude. The former meant one or more engagements in the open with an enemy who, owing to the geographical position of Khartoum, could not concentrate his forces without raising the siege, and who, in order to concentrate, would have had to pass his troops, guns, ammunition, &c., over two unfordable rivers of considerable breadth, in the face of General Gordon's armed steamers.

If he opposed my advance along the right bank of the Nile upon Khartoum, he must have fought in a position where defeat would have been his destruction. I think I may say that, as long as Khartoum held out, he could not have prevented my entering it, although he might afterwards have awaited my attack in a selected position on the left bank of the White Nile to the south or south-west of the city.

With Khartoum in the enemy's possession, the whole conditions are reversed, and the *Mahdi*, strengthened by the large number of rifles, guns, ammunition, &c., taken in that place, and by the captured troops, who would certainly fight on his side, could concentrate an overwhelming force to oppose my advance; and, if defeated, could still fall back upon the city, the siege and capture of which, situated as it is in the fork of two unfordable rivers, would be an impossible operation for the little army under my command, more especially as it would then be incumbered by a large number of wounded men. As I have already said, the force under my command was not intended for any operation of that magnitude, nor was such an operation even contemplated in the instructions I received from Her Majesty's Government. Khartoum, in the hands of the enemy, cannot be retaken until the force under my command has been largely augmented in numbers and in artillery.

Although operations against Khartoum were for the moment out of the question, the necessity of doing something seems to have occurred both to the government and Lord Wolseley, if only for the sake of satisfying public opinion and restoring the prestige of the British army.

Seeing the position occupied by the British forces at this time, it is not surprising that Wolseley should have had the idea of seizing Berber by means of a combined attack by the River column under General Earle and by the Desert column from Metammeh under General Buller. It was intended that this operation should be accompanied by an onslaught upon Osman Digna in the neighbourhood of Souakim, which it was hoped would have the effect of keeping open the road between that place and Berber.

On 8th February, Wolseley telegraphed to General Earle as follows:—

> Government have decided that *Mahdi's* power at Khartoum must be overthrown. This most probably means a campaign here next cold weather, and certainly the retention in the Soudan of all troops now here. A strong force of all arms goes as soon as possible to Souakim to crush Osman Digna. We must now take Berber. Buller will take Metammeh. Let me know date you will reach Berber, so that Buller's force may co-operate with you.

The same day Wolseley telegraphed to Lord Hartington as follows:—

> The sooner you can now deal with Osman Digna the better. I should recommend brigade of Indian Infantry and one regiment of Punjaub Cavalry to be sent to Souakim as soon as possible to hold that place during summer, and co-operate with me in keeping road to Berber open; the English troops you send now to Souakim might then either go to mountains near there for summer, or to Egypt to be ready for autumn campaign.[1]

It is clear from the two preceding despatches that there had been some communication between the general and the government which has not been disclosed, on the subject of the English force which it was intended to send to Souakim.

---

1. There is an Arab proverb which here seems not inapplicable, "*Being worsted by his mother-in-law, he rounded on his wife,*" said of one who, having been beaten by a person stronger than himself, takes his revenge upon a weaker individual.

On 9th February, a further despatch from Wolseley to Earle stated that the government had decided that the troops were to stay in the Soudan till the *Mahdi's* power at Khartoum was destroyed; that if they could not do this before the hot weather they must wait till autumn; that Buller had left Gakdul on the 8th for Gubat, and would take Metammeh as soon as the Royal Irish reached Gubat; that on the River column reaching Berber, Buller, who would be in the neighbourhood with four or six guns and about 1,500 men on the left bank, would meet Earle and co-operate with him in the attack on Berber.

The government lost no time in carrying out the Souakim project, and on the 9th General Stephenson in Cairo received instructions to arrange for the immediate purchase of camels for the expedition,[2] and on the 9th February Lord Hartington telegraphed to Wolseley the composition of the force which the government proposed sending to Souakim, making altogether 9,000 men. The despatch added that the Indian Brigade and cavalry asked for had also been ordered. The general was asked to give his opinion as between this and the smaller force, which could move more quickly.[3]

On the 11th Wolseley's plans were so far matured that he telegraphed to Lord Hartington that he proposed leaving for Gubat to direct the operations himself.

To this Lord Hartington replied on the 13th that there appeared to be great advantages in Wolseley's present position for communicating with both columns, and with Souakim and Egypt, and stated that the government relied on him not to allow his natural wish to take an active part in the operations to influence his decision. The general replied that, as he did not expect to take Berber before the 16th March, there was no immediate necessity to decide the question of his leaving. He added that he proposed to leave General Dormer in command at Korti in case he (Wolseley) felt it desirable in the interests of the service to go forward.

On the 17th Lord Hartington telegraphed to Wolseley further details as to the Souakim force, and also the arrangements made with Messrs. Lucas and Aird for the construction of a railway from Souakim to Berber.

This seems to have been the first mention of the railway. Wolseley

---

2. It is said that the Mudir of Dongola being asked at this time if there was any prospect of good camels being obtained, answered that "he did not see why not, as the English had already bought up all the bad ones." 3. Lord Wolseley's reply did not appear in the Blue Book.

replied that if he could take Berber before the hot weather set in, which was very doubtful, the railway could then be made through to that place without any cessation of construction; but, if Berber were in the enemy's hands, in all probability it could only be made to the neighbourhood of Ariab. In the meantime, rails, sleepers, &c., for the construction of the desert section of 110 miles, from Ariab to Berber, should be collected at Ariab.

A few days later the news of Buller's retreat from Gubat apparently caused Wolseley to modify his plans.

Reporting that movement on the 18th, his Lordship added as follows:—

> I think he (Buller) acted with wisdom and discretion; for, since the fall of Khartoum, the whole of the *Mahdi's* army is disposable, and could have invested him at Gubat with a large force, not only of men, but of guns; this they cannot do either at Abu Klea or Gakdul. My instructions to General Buller were on no account to allow himself to be shut in near Metammeh; and, with the information he had of the *Mahdi's* movements, in proceeding to Abu Klea, he has rightly interpreted the spirit of these instructions. The fall of Khartoum set free for the *Mahdi* a considerable army; and furnished him with an arsenal containing a great number of guns and rifles, and about 1,000,000 rounds of rifle ammunition.
>
> Operations which before could be carried out under only the ordinary hazards of war cannot now be undertaken without incurring inordinate risks. When Khartoum fell, moreover, the main object for which General Stewart's force was sent to Metammeh ceased to exist. That object was to be prepared to march at once, even at considerable hazard, to the assistance of Gordon, should it be found that he required immediate aid.
>
> The capture of Khartoum left his force without an objective; while, at the same time, it greatly increased the insecurity of its position. Its isolated situation, separated from me by 180 miles of desert, and liable at any moment to have its communications cut by a movement of the *Mahdi* down the Nile, has latterly caused me considerable anxiety.

At the opening of Parliament on the 19th February the government announced that it had decided on going to Khartoum to break the power of the *Mahdi*. On the 20th February Lord Wolseley telegraphed that the state of his supplies would not admit of his going to Berber, even if he thought his lines of communication sufficiently secure, which he did not think they were, to warrant such a forward movement so late in the season. He would hold the line of river from Merawi to Dongola and Hanneck Cataract during the summer, and prepare for an autumn campaign. To do anything else would, he thought, be unwise.

With a view to carrying out the plan of holding the river as indicated, Wolseley now sent orders to Earle's Nile Column, to stop the advance upon Berber and to return to Merawi.

On the 21st, Lord Hartington asked Wolseley if anything more could be done for supplies for the summer.

Lord Wolseley replied on the 22nd as follows:—

When I have concentrated my force on this part of the Nile, I have no fear for my communications, so I do not want any more troops here now. It is important to thoroughly crush Osman Digna, and restore peace to the country now under his influence, in order to push forward the railway, and, by a brilliant success near Souakim, make the Soudanese realize what they must expect when we move forward in the autumn.

Wolseley's views on the military situation, and on the operations to be conducted, were communicated to Lord Hartington in a despatch dated 6th March, 1885, from which the following is an extract:—

In reply to my telegram, your Lordship informed me that my immediate duty was to protect the province of Dongola—the only province of the Soudan which is still clear of the enemy—and that, as soon as the necessary arrangements could be completed, Her Majesty's Government had determined to destroy the *Mahdi's* power at Khartoum, in order that peace, order, and a settled government might be established there. This I conceive to be in general terms a fair description of the new mission with which I have been intrusted, and which I shall endeavour to carry out next autumn.

I take this opportunity of congratulating Her Majesty's Government upon having adopted the Nile route as the line of advance for this force on Khartoum. Had this army been despatched from Souakim as a base, and upon arrival at, or near, Berber, learnt that Khartoum had fallen, it could not possibly have transferred its base to the Mediterranean, for it could not have been fed under those circumstances in this part of the Nile Valley. The province of Dongola would have been at the enemy's mercy, and the frontiers of Egypt would have been open to his attack.

As it is impossible for me to undertake any offensive operations until about the end of summer, it is important that in the meanwhile Osman Digna's power in the Souakim district should be crushed. The defeat will, in some measure, act as a counterpoise to the *Mahdi's* capture of Khartoum. This operation is not difficult, as the forces are near the seaboard, and it should be immediately followed by the occupation of the Tokar and Sinkat districts. A railway should also be begun without delay at Souakim in the direction of Berber. Your Lordship has informed me that a contract has been entered into for the construction of this railway on a gauge of 4 ft. 8-1/2 inches.

Although I do not for a moment entertain the idea that a railway of such a gauge can be completed over the 250 miles (about) of country lying between Souakim and Berber in time to have any very direct or immediate effect upon our operations towards Khartoum next autumn, I am convinced that active progress made upon it will bring home to Mohammed Ahmed, and to all intelligent Sheikhs, the fact that we are now in earnest, and do not mean to leave the country until we have re-established order and a settled government at Khartoum.

I am now engaged in distributing the army along the left bank of the Nile on the open reach of water that extends from the Hanneck Cataract to Abu Dom, opposite Merawi. There I shall be quite prepared to meet Mohammed Ahmed at any time during the summer, should he, by any good fortune, be tempted to advance in this direction. During the summer I shall collect the supplies which this army will require for its advance in the autumn. The railway from Souakim to Berber would take about two years and five months to complete.

In reading this despatch it will be seen that Wolseley lays stress upon the necessity of crushing Osman Digna's force at Souakim. He also recommends the immediate construction of the Souakim-Berber railway. But on the 20th February instructions had already been given to Graham to effect both these objects. Of this Wolseley was fully aware at the time, and it strikes one as singular that so late in the day he should be found advising the government to take two steps which had already been decided on.

Further, it will be noticed that His Lordship, whilst approving of the construction of the railway (which he reckons would require two years and five months) is careful to point out that he does not for a moment entertain the idea that it could be constructed in time to have any direct or immediate effect upon the operations towards Khartoum, to be undertaken in the autumn.

Another singular feature in the despatch is the complacency with which His Lordship, after the total failure of the expedition by way of the Nile, congratulates the government on having chosen that route.

The difficulties in the way of further operations during the summer now began to be apparent. The hot weather had set in at Korti. The thermometer on the 5th March registered 104 degrees under the shade of the trees. Later on it went up two degrees higher still. The wind blowing from the desert was like a blast from a furnace. Under these conditions the tents with which the soldiers were provided offered little or no protection. Sickness, too, began to break out, and several cases of enteric fever were reported.

The Nile Column, as already stated, got back on the 8th March, and the last troops of the Desert Column arrived from Abu Klea on the 16th, and, with the exception of the detachment left at Merawi, the whole of Wolseley's army was now assembled at Korti.[4]

---

[4] The troops at Korti about this time received a visit from some emissaries of the *Mahdi*, who interviewed General Dormer and pointed out the wonderful things which their leader could do. He could, they said, even interfere with the forces of nature, and drying up rivers and causing floods were only some of the trifling miracles which he was capable of bringing about. The general, who wore a glass eye, promptly took it out, spun it into the air, and replaced it. "Can the *Mahdi* do that?" he asked, at the same time winking with the restored eye. The astonished Dervishes made no reply, but quietly "*salaamed*" and retired, as if unwilling to continue longer in the society of one so evidently in league with evil spirits.

CHAPTER 48

The Souakim Expedition of 1885

The real object and intention of the Gladstone Administration in directing the despatch of the Souakim expedition of 1885 will probably remain forever a mystery.

Wolseley had, it is true, pointed out the necessity of losing no time in dealing a crushing blow to Osman Digna, and had suggested the sending of a brigade of Indian Infantry and a regiment of Punjaub Cavalry to Souakim to hold that place during the summer and to co-operate with him in keeping open the road to Souakim. He also approved the commencement of the Souakim-Berber railway. But his demands, so far as the published papers show, appear to have gone no further than that.

The expedition told off to Souakim was nevertheless fixed at 9,000 men, and comprised nearly every arm of the service. In addition, there were all the plant, materials, and labour required for the purpose of making the Souakim-Berber railway. The season chosen for the expedition, too, was singularly unfortunate, as it coincided with the precise time of the year at which, a twelvemonth before, the hot weather had compelled the withdrawal of Graham's army, and when even the one or two squadrons of Cavalry which Gordon had asked to be sent to Berber were refused him.

There is some reason to suppose that at the time the expedition was resolved upon the idea was that it should co-operate with Wolseley's forces in a movement upon Khartoum as soon as the Nile force should have succeeded in taking Berber, and that when the movement on Berber was postponed till the autumn the object of the expedition had to be limited to "the crushing of Osman Digna and the opening up of the Souakim-Berber route." At all events, this was announced as the official programme. It will not fail to strike the reader that this was to undertake in March, 1885, with troops from England, precisely the enterprise which the government, in March, 1884, declined to undertake with troops on the spot. The only change in the situation was that then the expedition would have been in time to have saved Khartoum, whereas now it was too late. It seems to have been fated that the policy of "Rescue and retire" should always be adopted, the former too late, and the latter too soon.

Probably the true explanation is to be found in the exigencies of the political situation. The Gladstone Administration felt the necessity for doing something, if only to satisfy public opinion, intensely excited by the news from Khartoum. The government had allowed Khartoum to fall and Gordon to perish. The result was neither creditable to the Ministry nor favourable to British prestige. On the 19th February Lord Salisbury, replying to Lord Granville's announcement that the government had "decided upon going on to Khartoum to break the power of the *Mahdi*," declared that "Gordon had been sacrificed to the squabbles of a Cabinet and the necessities of party politics."

This was followed on the 23rd by Sir Stafford Northcote moving a vote of censure in the House of Commons on the Soudan policy of the government. The motion was only lost by fourteen votes, a similar motion by Lord Salisbury being carried in the House of Lords by no less than 121 votes.

Whatever may have been the motives of the government in deciding upon the expedition to Souakim, no time was lost in making the necessary preparations. This time it was determined to carry out the operations on a grand scale.

The force was fixed at considerably more than double the number engaged in the Souakim expedition of 1884.

Amongst the troops ordered to take part in it were the 1st Battalion of the Coldstream Guards; the 2nd Battalion of the Scots Guards; the 3rd Battalion of the Grenadier Guards; the 1st Battalion of the Shropshire Regiment; the 2nd Battalion of the East Surrey; the 1st Battalion of the Berkshire Regiment; one Battalion of Royal Marines; one regiment of Australian Infantry; some batteries of Royal Horse Artillery, of Royal Artillery, and Australian Artillery; some companies of Royal Marine Artillery, and Royal Engineers, as well as squadrons of the 5th Lancers, and the 20th Hussars, and detachments of the Ordnance, Commissariat, and Medical Staff Corps. In addition to these, an Indian Contingent of over 2,000 men was provided. It comprised the 9th Bengal Cavalry, the 15th (Loodianah) Sikhs, the 17th Bengal

Native Infantry, the 28th Bombay Native Infantry, and some companies of Madras Sappers. Besides the above, several hundred labourers were ordered from England, and one thousand coolies from India to construct the railway to Berber.

The operation of crushing Osman Digna having to be performed, General Graham was selected as the "crusher."

This was a surprise to most people, and probably equally so to Graham himself. Military critics had not forgotten how, by his order to charge, given at an unfortunate moment, the general very nearly caused the wreck of the 2nd Brigade at Tamaai; nor the ill-feeling, bordering almost upon insubordination, which his treatment of the Black Watch had brought about in the Soudan army of 1884; and the appointment was freely criticized. The general, however, was a nominee of Lord Wolseley, and this, although it did not silence criticism, served in a great measure to satisfy public opinion.

Brevet-Major-General A. J. L. Fremantle was appointed to command the Brigade of Guards, and Major-General Greaves was named Chief of the Staff. The Infantry Brigade was placed under Major-General Sir J. C. McNeill, V.C.

General Graham's instructions, dated 20th February, were on arrival at Souakim to take command of the forces which were to be assembled there, to make the best arrangements which the shortness of the time at his disposal, before the hot weather commenced, would admit of to organize a field force, and to make such transport arrangements as were possible to enable it to secure the first and most pressing object of the campaign, *viz.*, the destruction of the power of Osman Digna.

The general was told that an agreement had been made with Messrs. Lucas and Aird to construct a railway from Souakim to Berber, and that on this he must greatly rely for his means of transporting supplies. It would therefore be of the first importance that every possible facility should be given to Messrs. Lucas and Aird in the conduct of their operations.

The pushing on of the railway from Souakim towards Berber was the next point to which he was to direct the greatest attention. By the agreement with Messrs. Lucas and Aird, the contractors were to construct for the War Department for the purposes of the expeditionary force, a 4 ft. 8-1/2-inch gauge single line of railway from Souakim, and thence in sections so far towards Berber as might from time to time be ordered in writing by the Secretary of State, and also an 18-inch gauge single line of railway in or about Souakim. The War Department engaged to keep the way clear and the working staff protected. The contractors were to supply plant and working staff, and, with regard to the latter, were to be at liberty, with the consent of the Secretary at War, to employ natives as labourers. The staff to be paid by the government, and rationed and clothed by the War Department. The contractors were to receive a commission of 2 *per cent.* upon all expenditure, from the War Department, such commission, however, not to exceed in the whole £20,000, and they were to be entitled to a further sum not exceeding £20,000 if the railway should be satisfactorily completed in the judgment of the Secretary of State.

On the 27th February, Lord Hartington again called Graham's attention to the necessity for rapidly constructing the railway from Souakim to Berber, and to the extreme importance of the services it would be required to perform, not only in connection with the advance of Graham's force, but also in connection with the troops under Wolseley's command when concentrated at Berber. His Lordship pointed out that by this route alone, when the railway should have been completed, could that force be supplied, re-equipped, and reinforced with that precision and certainty so essential to the future operations on the Nile. He continued:—

> When the first and essential operation of crushing Osman Digna and clearing the country sufficiently to make it safe for the constructors of the railway is accomplished, the next most important duty will be the pushing on of the railway, and I request that you will facilitate and aid this object by every means in your power. You will, of course, decide what military posts you will occupy.

Towards the end of February Graham's force began to assemble at Souakim, and from that date troop-ships and store-ships began to come in almost daily.

Early in March Graham reached Souakim, and assumed command of the force assembled there.

Considering the camp to be too extended, rendering night attacks too easy, he at once took steps to reduce the front occupied. The enemy had in fact for some time been in the habit of attacking in small bodies every night, and succeeded in killing or wounding many of the sentries. The camps were surrounded by *zeribas* and entanglements which were never attacked, the plan adopted being to creep in at unguarded points, and stab or spear the men as they slept. A large number of so-called friendly natives were employed about the camps in the daytime, and so acquired a knowledge of the localities. Returning at night, it was thus easy for them to choose positions which were unguarded, and so to murder the sleeping soldiers. That this was so, was shown by more than one native who had been shot down being found to be wearing the red badge given to the "friendlies."

On the 17th Graham's force amounted to 491 officers, 10,222 non-commissioned officers and privates, 1,616 horses, 2,759 camels, 791 mules, and 2,629 followers. At this date troop and store-ships were still arriving.

On the 19th Graham made a reconnaissance to Hasheen, about seven and a half miles from Souakim, with the Cavalry Brigade and Mounted Infantry, the Infantry of the Indian Contingent moving out about four miles in support. The enemy retired in front of the British force, evacuating the village of Hasheen, and making for the mountains, but not without first offering some resistance, by which one private was killed, and one officer and a sergeant were wounded. After this the whole force marched back to the camp.

On the 20th Graham determined on a general advance to Hasheen, and at 6.15 a.m., leaving only the Shropshire Regiment and details as guards, the whole force, numbering about 10,000 men, marched out from the camp. Making for the hills in front of Hasheen, the cavalry moved off at about 6.10 a.m., the infantry following at 6.25 in the following order:—The Guards in columns of companies, on the right; the 2nd Brigade (East Surrey Regiment and Marines), in line of company columns of fours; the Indian Brigade in column of companies on the left; the Horse Artillery Battery on the right of the line. The water camels and transport animals followed in rear of the 2nd Brigade.

The action is described in the general's despatch as follows:—

> The advance was made in a direction nearly due west. The Infantry reached the foot of the hills at about 8.25 a.m. The 17th and 24th Companies Royal Engineers, the Madras Sappers, and the 70th East Surrey Regiment, were ordered to commence work at once. The enemy had fallen back on Dihilibat and the Beehive Hill, exchanging shots with my advance guard at about eight a.m. I now determined to clear these hills, and gave orders to the Infantry to advance in the following order:—2nd Brigade in first line, Indian Contingent in support, Guards in

reserve; the Horse Artillery to take up a position on Beehive Hill.

At about nine a.m. the force had reached the foot of Dihilibat Hill. The Berkshire Regiment advanced up the steep slopes of the hill in attack formation, with one half battalion Royal Marine Light Infantry on the right rear, and the other half battalion in rear of the centre of the Berkshire Regiment as supports. The ascent was very steep and difficult, but the first spur was occupied without opposition. This spur is separated from the main edge by a deep ravine. The enemy now, however, opened a heavy fire from the summit, and from a position further to the right. The Berkshire Regiment replied by volleys, and the half battalion of Marines on the right was advanced to flank the enemy's position. The enemy then abandoned their position, and the Berkshire Regiment advanced to the summit, and detached one company to a spur on the left, from which an effective fire was opened upon the retiring enemy. Meanwhile the Indian Brigade had taken up a position between the foot of Dihilibat and the Beehive Hill; the Guards also were formed up near the foot of the north-east spur of Dihilibat Hill.

The Horse Artillery, which moved out with the Guards' Brigade as far as the first hills, received orders to follow the Indian Brigade in its further advance, and to take up a position on Beehive Hill. While passing under the Hill Dihilibat they were heavily fired upon, losing two horses. The slopes of Beehive Hill proving impracticable for the guns, the battery, after firing a few rounds of shrapnel into the bush, detached three guns to a position on a low spur to the west of Beehive Hill, where they remained in action for some time shelling parties of the enemy who were visible across the valley on the spurs of the Wharatab Range. The battery subsequently retired with the Guards' square, and took up a position on one of the hills reached at 8.25. Here several rounds were fired, subsequently to the retirement of the Infantry, at parties of the enemy which appeared on the low spur.

At about 9.40 a.m. two squadrons of the 9th Bengal Cavalry were detached by Colonel Ewart, commanding Cavalry Brigade, to pursue the enemy, who, driven from the Hill Dihilibat by the Berkshire Regiment, were retiring south in the direction of Tamaai. Colonel Ewart ordered two squadrons to dismount and fire volleys. These squadrons were charged by the enemy in considerable strength, and retired with loss on the square formed by the Guards at the foot of the Dihilibat Hill.

During the morning the 5th Lancers were employed in securing the right front. At about 10.45 a considerable force of the enemy endeavoured to advance down the Hasheen Valley from the north-west, apparently attempting to turn my right flank. Both the 5th Lancers and a portion of the 9th Bengal Cavalry were engaged with the small advanced parties of this force, and succeeded in checking the movement. During this time work was carried on by the Royal Engineers and Madras Sappers, assisted by parties of the East Surrey Regiment, and by about 2.30 p.m. four strong posts had been formed, and a *zeriba* commenced.

At 12.25 I recalled the Indian Brigade, the Berkshire Regiment, and the Marines covering the movement. The latter then joined the Indian Brigade, and, forming a single square, retired to the more open ground south. The Guards' square and the Artillery remained at the foot of the Dihilibat Hill till one p.m., and then retired, taking a direction somewhat to the south of that followed by the 2nd and Indian Brigades.

During the retirement of the Guards the right face of the square received a hot fire from parties of the enemy concealed among the bushes, and suffered some loss. By firing steady volleys into the bush the enemy's fire was effectually silenced, and the Brigade halted close to the south foot of the hills first mentioned. The general retirement of the whole force began about 4.30 p.m., and the camp was reached at 6.15.

The Dihilibat Hill was carried by the Berkshire Regiment with the greatest spirit, and the behaviour of the Guards' square under a heavy fire from an unseen enemy was marked by extreme steadiness. During the formation of the fortified posts, the presence of the enemy in rear rendered it necessary several times to order the East Surrey Regiment to stand to their arms. This was done without any confusion, and the Royal Engineers and Madras Sappers quietly continued their work on the defences.

It is impossible in such a country to estimate the numbers of an enemy who is able to remain completely concealed until he chooses to attack; but it is probable that on this occasion the number of Arabs present was about 3,000, of whom at least 250 were killed, much of this loss being caused by the fire of the Berkshire Regiment from the commanding position they had taken up on Dihilibat Hill. The scouting was very efficiently performed by the cavalry, considering the great difficulties of the country with which they had to contend.

The enemy, according to other accounts, seemed to have lost none of the daring with which they had met Graham's force a twelvemonth before. Instead of fleeing before the charge of the Bengal Lancers, the Soudanese actually charged the cavalry. The same tactics were practised as at El-Teb, the Soudanese throwing themselves on the ground at the critical moment of the charge, and slashing with their swords at the horses' legs. So badly were the lancers used that they had to fall back as stated n the despatch, losing one non-commissioned officer and four men, whose horses had been hamstrung in the encounter.

In the course of the fight, some 150 of the enemy sprang up from behind a hill 300 yards off, and had the audacity to charge the whole of the Guards' Brigade. The assailants were received by such a deadly fire from the face of the square that they never succeeded in getting nearer than fifteen or twenty yards of the line of bayonets. Those who survived at once turned and fled, leaving behind their wounded chief on a camel, within thirty yards of the square, where he was made prisoner.

The object of the recall of the Indian Brigade at 12.25 p.m., and the subsequent retirement towards the hill (then being fortified by the 70th Regiment) of that force, the Berkshire Regiment, and Marines, followed at one p.m. by the Guards and Artillery, practically the whole army, is not stated in the general's despatch. But from other reports it seems that the troops had got into a position where the thickness of the bush gave the enemy the advantage of pouring a heavy fire into General Graham's force, whilst the latter could only deliver an ineffective fire in return.[1] At the position to which the troops fell back, the ground was more open, and Graham's men could make better practice with their Martinis.

The apparent intention of the enemy to turn the right of the British line, also probably influenced the General in retiring.

After some hours' marching and fighting under a blazing sun the force set out on the return to Souakim, leaving a detachment to guard

---

1. According to the account of an eyewitness the Horse Artillery was stationed at one period at a point where the underwood grew so thickly that the gunners could not see seventy yards away from the guns.

the fortified posts made by the Engineers and Madras Sappers.

The following are the casualties as reported by telegram from Graham:—Officers killed, Lieutenant M. D. D. Dalison, Scots Guards; 1 native officer, Indian Contingent; 4 non-commissioned officers and privates, and 12 *sowars* of the Indian Contingent. Wounded, 6 officers, 26 non-commissioned officers and privates, 13 *sowars*, and 3 privates of the Indian Contingent.

The enemy's strength was, as usual, liberally estimated in the various newspaper reports of the action, some putting the number as high as 14,000 men. General Graham's original estimate was 4,000, but this he subsequently reduced to 3,000, a number probably much nearer the mark.

Graham's object in occupying a position at Hasheen was declared by him to be to protect his right flank in the impending advance on Tamaai, to obtain a post of observation near to the mountains, and to assist in overawing the tribes. How far this was effected may be judged from the fact that only five days later the works were dismantled and the place was abandoned.

CHAPTER 49

The Attack on McNeill's Zeriba

After the operations on the 19th and 20th March, 1885, preparations were made for the advance on Tamaai, Osman Digna's reputed headquarters and stronghold. Situated, as it was, some fourteen miles to the south-west of Souakim, the distance was deemed too great to be traversed in a single day's march. It became necessary then, as on previous occasions, to establish an intermediate position in which, as an advanced camp, the usual stores of water, provisions, and ammunition might be accumulated.[1]

About an hour after daylight on the 22nd March the force detached for this purpose started from Souakim. Ahead and on the flanks was one squadron of the 5th Lancers scouting; next marched the British regiments, the 49th Berkshire, and the Royal Marine Light Infantry, formed up in square under the command of Major-General Sir John C. McNeill. The Berkshire Regiment led the way, and the Marines brought up the rear, a detachment of the Royal Engineers occupying places in the flanks. The only representatives of the artillery arm were four Gardner guns with detachments of sailors and Royal Marine Artillery.

Outside the British square, but close to its left flank, moved the Field Telegraph waggon and party, which kept unrolling the telegraph wire and covering it with loose soil as it went on, so maintaining the communication with Souakim throughout the advance.

Formed up in a still larger square a short distance in rear of the right flank, the Indian Contingent marched in echelon under command of Brigadier-General Hudson. The 15th Sikhs formed the front face and a portion of the flanks. The remainder of the right flank and

---
1. Much of the narrative which follows is taken from *The Battle of Tofrek*, by William Galloway (1887).

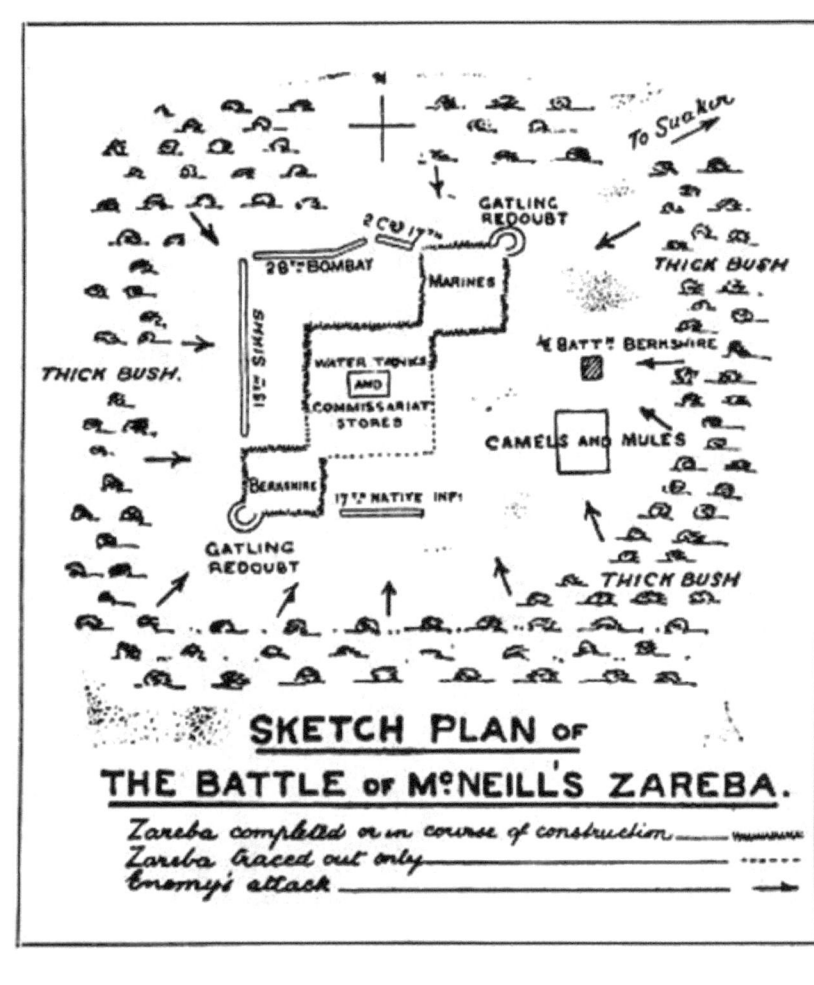

one half of the rear face were formed by the 28th Bombay Native Infantry. The 17th Bengal Native Infantry occupied a similar position on the left flank and rear face. In reserve, immediately within the rear face, marched a company of Madras Sappers. Within this square was inclosed a vast and miscellaneous array of laden camels, mules, carts, and conveyances of all kinds, forming the transport train. The camels alone numbered from 1,000 to 1,200, and there were in all some 1,500 animals. The combined British and Indian forces amounted to 3,300 men.

The orders were for the whole force to proceed to a point eight miles distant in the direction of Tamaai, there to form a *zeriba* (No. 2), in which the stores, &c., were to be deposited. When this was accomplished the lancers, Indian infantry, and empty transport train were to return, stop at a point five miles from Souakim, construct another *zeriba* (No. 1), and leaving it to be garrisoned by the 15th Sikhs, go back to Souakim.

General Graham accompanied the troops for about two and a half miles and then returned to camp, the chief of his staff warning McNeill to "look out for an attack," but, beyond this casual reference to the possibility of an attack, nothing more was said on the subject, although at headquarters information had several days previously been received that the force would be assailed by at least 5,000 of the enemy before there should be time to form the *zeriba*. The importance of this circumstance will be apparent later on in connection with the events which followed.

The route which the force was instructed to take was to the westward of the comparatively well-known road followed by Baker Pasha, and also by the British troops, in 1884, and though free from difficulty at first, later on led through thick bush of ever-increasing height and density. The rate of progress was necessarily slow, and frequent halts became imperative.

As the force advanced the Lancers began to report that parties of the enemy were seen hovering about.

The heat of the day, with a burning sun overhead, from which the bushes afforded no protection, now began to tell on the men, and at 10 a.m., when a little over five miles had been traversed, it was calculated by the two generals that, allowing time for the construction of the *zeribas* (Nos. 1 and 2) and the return journey, it would be well towards midnight before the Indian Brigade and transport train would get back to Souakim. Accordingly at 10.30 it was determined to halt the force and make the *zeriba* in an open space six miles from the camp at Souakim.

The spot selected formed a large oblong with very irregular outlines, presenting an area in the clearest portions about half a square mile in extent.

McNeill then telegraphed to headquarters at Souakim the change which the difficulties with the transport had necessitated, and received back in reply the message, "Go on if you can; if not, *zeriba*." The reply also stated that, as the halt had been made at only six miles distance, no intermediate *zeriba* would be required at the five-mile point previously ordered.

The site for the *zeriba* being fixed upon, no time was lost in making the necessary dispositions. The troops marched upon the ground in the same order in which they had advanced, and the British square, being the first to emerge upon the open, turning up a little to the left halted in its original formation, taking up a position on the north-east side of the open space. Past it came the Indian Brigade with the transport train under its charge, General Hudson disposing his troops so as to cover the ground on the three remaining sides.

On the side opposite the British square were posted the 15th Sikhs, to the right the Bombay Native Infantry, and to the left the Bengal Native Infantry. The bush in front of the Bombay Infantry being very dense, and comparatively open in front of the Bengal Infantry, two companies of the latter were moved across and placed on the right of the former to strengthen and prolong this face.

In order to protect the front of the various lines of infantry, small pickets of from four to five men each were thrown forward about 120 yards. A quarter of a mile further out in front of these pickets were the lancers, arranged as "Cossack posts" of four men each. Another "Cossack post," also of four men, was used as a connecting link, the remainder constituting the picket and visiting patrols.

At once the task of measuring and pegging out the site for the proposed works was taken in hand. The plan adopted was to form three separate squares placed diagonally like squares on a chess-board, or, as it is termed, "in echelon," the large or central square, intended to contain the stores, non-combatants, and transport animals, being between the other two. Attached to this, and communicating with it at its north-west and south-east angles respectively, were the smaller squares set apart for the north and south *zeribas*, of equal dimensions, with accommodation in each for a battalion and two Gardner guns.

By this arrangement every side of the central square or *zeriba* was capable of being swept by a flanking fire from the *zeribas* at the angles.

Working parties were organized for cutting down the bush and dragging it into position. The chief work of construction fell upon the Royal Engineers and the Madras Sappers, but to expedite matters working parties were drawn both from the British and Indian troops. The remainder of the British troops, retaining their original formation in square, piled their arms, and were ordered to lie down and rest. The Indian troops not engaged in cutting brushwood remained standing to their arms in lines two deep.

At 12.30 the Marines had their rations served out, the men dining by half-companies at a time.

At 1 p.m. Major Graves with a squadron of the 20th Hussars arrived from the camp at Souakim, and stated that he had been sent by General Graham to communicate with McNeill. The major reported that on the way out he had seen in his front stray parties of the enemy, who retired before the cavalry without coming into collision. On receiving a despatch for Graham's chief of the staff, stating that matters were proceeding satisfactorily, the major started with the Hussars on his return journey at 1.30.

As the most vital part of the defences, attention had been first of all directed to the formation of the north and south *zeribas*. Both of these were pushed on with the utmost expedition, but, as has been seen, the bush being thickest at the north side, in front of the Bombay Infantry, the *zeriba* at this angle was in a more advanced state than that on the south side. The former was completed shortly after 2 p.m., and the two Gardner guns designed for it were got into position. The battalion of Marines hitherto forming part of the British square was now transferred to this *zeriba*, together with the reserve ammunition and the telegraph waggon. With this transfer of Marines the Berkshire Battalion was contracted into a smaller square.

Meanwhile the south *zeriba* was also being rapidly proceeded with, and it being represented that the Berkshires had eaten nothing since 4 a.m., rations and water were ordered to be served out to them, the men taking their food by half battalions. As soon as the first of the half battalions had finished it was marched into the south *zeriba*, very soon after the Marines had occupied that on the north. The time was now getting on towards half-past two, and shortly after the half battalion had gone into the *zeriba* the soldiers piled their arms inside, part of the men going out in front of the *Sikhs* to cut bush in order to complete the defences.²

The camels had been unloaded in the central *zeriba*, and were filing out to form up for the return march, the bulk of them being collected on an unoccupied space to the south-east. The lines were being held by eight companies of the Bengal Infantry, by the 15th Sikhs, and by the Bombay Infantry.

This was the situation when shortly after 2.30 one of the Lancers rode up and informed McNeill that the enemy was gathering in front and advancing rapidly. Orders were at once given for the working and covering parties to come in and for the troops to stand to their arms. Whilst these instructions were being carried into effect, the cavalry were seen galloping up on every side with the Soudanese close at their heels.

The attack was delivered mainly on the southern and western sides, the Soudanese surging onwards in one vast impetuous mass, enveloped in clouds of dust and filling the air with shouts and yells as they made frantic efforts to storm the position. The Berkshires and Marines, as well as the Sikhs and Bombay Infantry, stood their ground, receiving and repulsing the attack with a heavy fire. The 17th Bengal Native Infantry, however, thrown into partial disorder by some of the cavalry riding through their ranks, fired one wild and scattered volley and fled for such cover as the *zeriba* might afford, many of them being shot down by the defenders. Every effort was made to rally the fugitives, and about 120 were got within the southern *zeriba*, where they fired another ineffectual volley and again broke and fled.

The assailants now crowded in by the uncompleted salient at a point where there was no brushwood, but merely a sandbag parapet, where the Gardner guns, not being yet in position, could not be got into action, and killed six of the sailors and four officers.

Other parties of the enemy following the retreat of the Madras Infantry dashed into the central *zeriba*, and caused a stampede among the animals there and a panic among the native drivers. A general rush of the latter took place both to the open side, and also through the north *zeriba*, where some of the marines were for the moment carried away by it. At this moment the rear rank of the Berkshire half battalion engaged in defending the western face of the south *zeriba*

---

2. The salient for the guns was so far advanced that the remaining Gardner guns had been brought up ready to be placed in position. The other half battalion of the Berkshires remained outside in its original position, the men engaged in having their dinners.

faced about and occupied the gap through which the Soudanese were now pouring. Meeting the enemy half-way, the Berkshires despatched every Arab who had entered, 112 bodies being counted within the limits of this *zeriba* alone. They also captured a flag which the enemy had planted on the sandbag parapet. In a few minutes this *zeriba* was cleared, and no further serious attack was made upon it.

The bulk of the enemy's force, repelled by the steady volleys from the troops on the south and west sides of the position, swept round by the great mass of the transport animals, gathered together outside and to the eastward for the return journey to Souakim. It was to cover this part of the ground that six companies of the Bengal Infantry had been drawn up in line. Their unfortunate collapse, however, gave the enemy an opportunity of which they were not slow to take advantage. With a wild howl, peculiarly alarming to the camel, they rushed upon the panic-stricken and helpless mass. Plying lance and sword, cutting, stabbing, hacking, and hamstringing the beasts, and slaughtering their drivers, the tribesmen of the Soudan drove before them an unwieldy and terrified body, heedless of everything but flight.

Thus driven, the transport train broke up and scattered itself in all directions. Impelled by the pursuers, part of it bore down upon the *zeribas* held by the Berkshires and Marines respectively, and part on the central *zeriba*. Mixed up as they were with the charging enemy, many of the animals were unavoidably shot down by the troops as a matter of self-preservation. The same thing happened in the attack made upon the half battalion of the Berkshires which remained drawn up outside in square formation, but, pursued by the Arabs, the great bulk of the baggage train went off in their mad flight in the direction of Souakim.

After the southern *zeriba* the two main points of attack were the northern zeriba, held by the Marines and the half battalion of the Berkshires. Both these positions were in the direct line of the camel stampede, and their occupants were placed at a serious disadvantage. In spite of the completed mimosa fences, trampling their way over all obstacles, a mass of the terror-stricken animals tore right through the northern *zeriba*, for the time seriously disorganizing the defence. As stated by Colonel Way, an eyewitness—

> Everything seemed to come at once, camels, transport of all kinds, including water-carts, ammunition mules, 17th Native Infantry, Madras Sappers, sick-bearers, Transport Corps, cavalry

and Arabs fighting in the midst. All these passed close by me, and went out on the other side of the *zeriba*, carrying away with them a number of the marines and some officers, who eventually got together and returned. The dust raised by this crowd was so great that I could not see anything beyond our *zeriba* for a minute or two, and it was impossible to say what might happen. The men behaved splendidly, and stood quite still. It was about the highest test of discipline I shall ever see, as in my opinion nothing could beat it.

The stampede of the transport train is thus described by another writer:—

> Suddenly from the bush all along the face of the *zeriba* fronting Tamaai burst out a clamour of savage cries, and the next instant the whole assemblage of transport animals plunged forward. There was a multitude of roaring camels, apparently heaped one upon another, with strings of kicking and screaming mules, entangled in one moving mass. Crowds of camp-followers were carried along by the huge animal wave, crying, shouting, and fighting. All these surged up on the *zeriba*, any resistance being utterly hopeless. This mass of brutes and terrified natives swept all before it, and a scene of indescribable confusion ensued.

Notwithstanding the rush of the transport which had passed through the marines' *zeriba*, comparatively few of the enemy seem to have penetrated it, only twelve bodies being counted there. Outside the dead were much more numerous, the position having been attacked on various sides. The men behaved with the greatest coolness, and, after being rallied by their officers when the living avalanche had swept past, were well in hand.

The naval detachment in this *zeriba*, more fortunate than their companions in the southern one, had their Gardner guns in action from the first, discharging at least 400 rounds and doing great execution.

The half battalion of the Berkshires remaining, formed up in the open at a distance of 250 yards east of the *zeriba*, had also a severe time of it. Falling in and standing to their arms at the first alarm, they formed a rallying square, and successfully defended themselves against the repeated attacks made on them. It was found that 200 of the assailants had fallen before the fire of their rifles, whilst amongst themselves there was only one slight casualty.

Other small bodies of men who were outside the *zeriba* at the moment of the attack, or had stampeded at its occurrence, were similarly collected by their officers, and succeeded in making their way back to the *zeriba*.

The whole affair lasted only about twenty minutes, after which the enemy, unable to stand any longer against the leaden hail of the Martini-Henry and Snider rifles, recoiled at every point, and at twelve minutes past three, as the assailants disappeared in the bush, the bugle sounded "Cease firing." Up to the last moment individual Arabs came forward, throwing up their hands above their heads, and facing the rifles as if bent on suicide, and courting the death which they received. Small groups of them also formed up as if to encourage each other for a renewed assault, but without effecting anything they melted away before the deadly fire of the soldiers.

When the smoke cleared away, and there was time to look around, a dreadful spectacle presented itself. The dead bodies of friends and foes lay thickly scattered within and about the *zeribas*. Everywhere were wounded and slaughtered men and animals, whilst groans and cries filled the air. Strewn upon the ground were arms and accoutrements of every kind, with all the usual accompaniments of a savage and sanguinary conflict.

The enemy's force was reported by General Graham in his despatch as not less than 2,000, although, as he states, it was impossible to form an accurate estimate.

The Soudanese as usual fought with the utmost courage. One man came rushing on to the *zeriba* holding by the hand a boy armed with a knife. Throwing the boy over the defensive works, he jumped in after him, and immediately both were killed. At another point there stood between the opposing forces another boy, apparently not more than twelve years old, actually throwing stones at the British troops in one of the *zeribas*.

Among various mischievous devices resorted to may be noted that of a Soudanese armed with a rifle, who during the attack managed to creep up close to the mimosa fence of the southern *zeriba*, and from this cover contrived in succession to shoot first one and then another of the Berkshires, and though fired at in return, was missed. His third shot was directed at a major of the regiment on duty inside the *zeriba*, who narrowly escaped, the bullet carrying away his trousers pocket and part of his coat, and not till then was the assailant shot. Another trick of the assailants was to bring hides, and throwing them on the top of the thorny bushes forming the fence, they would spring over into the *zeriba* and rush at the defenders and engage in a hand-to-hand fight.

During the assault on the southern *zeriba* an interesting adventure occurred to the colonel of the Berkshires. He was sitting on his horse close to his regiment when the attack took place, and was confronted by a gigantic Soudanese who appeared from behind a camel, brandishing a huge spear, and bent on slaughter. Their eyes met, and seeing the colonel's revolver levelled at his head, the expression on the countenance of the savage suddenly changed from triumph to horror as the colonel fired, and the Arab, with the upper part of his head blown away, fell to the ground a ghastly wreck.

McNeill's force suffered severely, having, exclusive of camp-followers, 6 officers and 94 men killed, and 6 officers and 136 men wounded, and 1 officer and 10 men missing. Amongst the killed were Captain Francis J. Romilly, and Lieutenant C. M. C. Newman, of the Royal Engineers; Lieutenant Montague H. M. Seymour, of the Naval Brigade; Major Von Beverhoudt, of the Indian Contingent; Quartermaster C. Eastmead, of the Ordnance Store Department, and Lieutenant George S. Swinton, of the Berkshire Regiment. The bodies of 8 British and 25 Indian soldiers were found in the bush away from the *zeriba*.

The loss in transport animals was enormous, over 900 camels alone being killed. Scores of them, which had been left outside the *zeriba*, were shot as the enemy swarmed on to the attack.

The enemy's loss was severe. Graham states that 1,000 bodies were found on the field. Besides the 112 bodies counted in the *zeriba*, there were the 200 found in front of the Berkshire Regiment. Near the redoubt held by the Naval Brigade, the dead lay in heaps. All around the ground was literally strewn with bodies; among them were several women and boys.

Throughout the entire conflict McNeill showed the greatest coolness and judgment, leading his men on with a courage oblivious of danger. During his preliminary efforts to rally the Bengal Native Infantry, the general, mounted on his grey Arab horse, found himself outside the defences, with the enemy streaming on full in front. Here, strange to say, he seemed to be entirely unnoticed, and, with revolver in hand ready to despatch any who might venture too near, he quietly turned his horse, and without difficulty made him cross the fence and step into the *zeriba*.

Later on, towards half-past three, there were circumstances which appeared to indicate that the enemy, notwithstanding the heavy loss they had sustained, were disposed to renew the attack, a large gathering of them presenting itself to the south-east of the *zeriba*. Their attitude was so threatening that McNeill resolved to make a sortie and endeavour to disperse them. Taking with him two companies of Marines, he led them straight for the enemy. As they advanced the little force was soon in front of the foe. Fire was at once opened, and the ground cleared; and though the men were anxious to make a charge with the bayonet, the demonstration having served its purpose, the troops were withdrawn without further fighting.

Notwithstanding McNeill's successful defence of the *zeriba*, and the heavy loss inflicted on the enemy in the action on the 22nd, Sir John has been the object of much adverse criticism. This criticism has been directed upon several points. It has been asked, Why were the fatigue men employed in cutting materials for the *zeriba* allowed to go into the bush unarmed? Sir John's answer is, that this was done designedly; the working parties were covered by the Cossack pickets of the Lancers; men incumbered with slung arms could not work to any good purpose in hot weather; in the event of attack, it was not desirable that the working parties should attempt to make a stand, as they would be of more service by running in and taking their places in the alignment marked by their piled arms, and they would thus avoid the danger of masking the fire of the troops in position.

The main charge, however, brought against the general is that he allowed himself to be surprised. This, however, if true at all, is so only in a limited sense of the term. That his force was attacked before the whole of it had time to form up in a fighting attitude is undoubted; but whether this was through any fault of his is quite another matter. The careful planning of the *zeribas*, the disposition of the troops, and the outlying pickets and vedettes have already been referred to. It is difficult to see what other precautions the general, with the means at his command, could have adopted. Not more than one-third of the British troops ever left their arms, and the Indians, minus their fatigue parties, remained throughout in position constantly ready for an attack. Whilst one half of the Berkshires moved into their completed *zeriba*, the remaining half was carefully re-formed in square outside. In the issue, as showing that a *zeriba* was little required for their protection, this last half battalion proved the strongest part of the position, and though subject to repeated attacks, lost not a man.

That Sir John was not informed in time of the impending attack was due to the insufficient number (one squadron only) of cavalry with which he was provided, and which were absolutely necessary for covering a frontage of over three miles. Here it may perhaps be remarked that, had this suggested itself to the general's mind, it seems strange that he did not take steps to detain and utilize the squadron of Hussars, under Major Graves, which visited the *zeriba* shortly before the attack was made.

The general had many difficulties to contend with. He was incumbered with a wholly disproportionate mass of transport; was directed on an impracticable line; was unsupplied with information of vital importance; and, finally, was sent to conduct an operation of which he strongly disapproved. To crown all, there was the flight of the Bengal Infantry at the very commencement of the fight, an event which the general could hardly have been expected to foresee. The result, however, was a signal victory, and practically the only successful operation of the campaign.

Graham was at Souakim whilst the attack was made on the *zeriba*. On first hearing the firing at 2.45 p.m., he ordered the Guards and Horse Artillery to go to McNeill's assistance. The force advanced two miles on the road when a message sent by the field-telegraph from the *zeriba* arrived, stating that the attack had been repelled, after which the proposed reinforcements returned to Souakim.

The following day Graham advanced to McNeill's *zeriba*. Here he sent off the following despatch, dated Souakim, March 23rd, 6.30 p.m.:—

> Advanced Zeriba, 12 noon.
> Arrived here with Guards and large convoy. Am sending in wounded and baggage animals with Indian Brigade and Grenadier Guards, under Fremantle, leaving two battalions of Guards here with McNeill's brigade. A strong *zeriba* has been constructed, and I consider position secure against any number of enemy. The attack yesterday was very sudden and determined, and came unfortunately on our weakest point. The *Sikhs* charged the enemy with bayonet. The Berkshire behaved splendidly, clearing out the *zeriba* where entered and capturing three standards. Marines also behaved well. Naval Brigade was much exposed and suffered severely. Engineers also suffered heavily, being out working when attacked. The enemy suffered very severely, more than a thousand bodies being counted.

Many chiefs of note are believed to have fallen. I deeply regret our serious losses, but am of opinion that McNeill did everything possible under the circumstances. The cavalry, 5th Lancers, did their best to give information, but the ground being covered with bush it was impossible to see any distance. The troops behaved extremely well. All the staff and regimental officers did their utmost. Enemy charged with reckless courage, leaping over the low *zeriba* to certain death; and, although they gained a temporary success by surprise, they have received a severe lesson, and up to the present time have not again attempted to molest the *zeriba*.

Of the scene round McNeill's *zeriba* some idea may be formed from the following description:—

When going from Souakim the last three miles of the march were marked at every step by graves, Arab and Indian, so shallow that from all oozed dark and hideous stains, and from many protruded mangled feet, half-stripped grinning skulls, or ghastly hands still clenched in the death agony, though reduced to little more than bone and sinew. Strewed around, thicker and thicker, as we neared the scene of that Sunday's fight, lay the festering bodies of camels and mules; and around them hopped and fluttered, scarcely moving when our column passed, hundreds of kites and vultures. The ground was also thickly sown with hands and feet dragged from their graves by the hyenas, and the awful stench and reek of carrion which loaded the air will never be forgotten by any of us. Day after day we passed and repassed over the same sickening scene with our convoys, in blinding dust and under a scorching sun, obliged to move at a foot's pace to keep up with the weary camels, and to pick our steps carefully for fear of suddenly setting foot on one of those dreadful heaps of corruption.

On the 25th March a convoy was sent out to McNeill's *zeriba*, under escort of the 15th Sikhs, 28th Bombay, and the Madras Sappers, with a few cavalry. When three miles from Souakim the convoy halted according to instructions, commenced cutting wood and forming a *zeriba*. A battalion composed of Guards and marines from McNeill's force marched towards them and was attacked on the way by a long range fire from the enemy, by which a lieutenant of the Marines and one private were wounded. At two p.m. the two escorts met, when the Guards and Marines taking over the convoy prepared to return to McNeill's *zeriba*. At this moment the enemy appeared in force and attacked the column. The Guards, Marines, and cavalry, moving out in four different detachments, fired into the attacking force and dispersed it.

The Guards and Marines then started again, but after ten minutes the enemy again appeared and fired a volley into them, which was at once returned. After less than a quarter of an hour a third attack was made. The Guards fired volley after volley, and once more drove back their assailants. The column then renewed its march, parties of the enemy still following them, and from time to time attacking their rear. Eventually the party got safely to the *zeriba*.

The result of the day's proceedings was to show that the enemy, in no way disheartened by the losses on the 22nd, were still in force, and ready to attack within four miles of Souakim. The attempt on the convoy was evidently made with the object of capturing the supplies destined for McNeill; and though it failed, it showed the increasing boldness of the enemy.

On the 25th, a war balloon which had been sent out to McNeill's *zeriba* made an ascent in charge of Major Templar. The same day, with a view to the advance, the headquarters camp was shifted to a spot two miles nearer Tamaai, and the East Surrey Regiment having destroyed the post on the hills near Hasheen, came in and joined the main body.

CHAPTER 50

Graham's Advance and Withdrawal from the Eastern Soudan

On the 26th March, another convoy was attacked, this time about two miles only from Souakim. The enemy on this occasion charged the head of the square, and were repulsed with considerable loss, none of them getting within five yards of the square. The British casualties were three wounded. It was said that 100 of the enemy were killed in this affair. The heat of the weather was now beginning to make itself felt, and several cases of sunstroke occurred amongst the troops engaged.

The first part of the Australian Contingent arrived at Souakim on the 29th March. The troops consisted of twenty-eight officers, 500 men of the battalion of Infantry, thirty men of the artillery, and thirty-three men of the Ambulance Corps. The contingent, which was commanded by Colonel Richardson, met with an enthusiastic reception from the naval and military forces at Souakim.

The railway was now vigorously pushed forward in the direction of Handoub, and on the 2nd April General Graham determined to advance and attack Osman Digna in his position at Tamaai, although there was some doubt whether he would accept battle.

Accordingly at three a.m. the general paraded his troops in the moonlight, and at four marched them to McNeill's *zeriba*. This *zeriba* (No. 1) was reached at 9 a.m., and the force halted until 10.15 a.m. for rest and refreshment. During this time arrangements were made for the defence of the *zeriba*, at which the 28th Bombay Native Infantry were left with two Gardner guns manned by marine artillery. The balloon was filled and made ready for use for reconnoitring purposes.

The troops were joined at the *zeriba* by the Grenadier Guards, the

Berkshire Regiment, the 24th Company of the Royal Engineers, two Gardner guns, manned by the Naval Brigade, the Mounted Infantry, and one troop of the 9th Bengal Cavalry.

A finer body of men than that which was now assembled was probably never got together. They were in the best of spirits, and looked forward with eagerness to meeting the enemy. The size and composition of the force were such as to render any possibility of it receiving a check from Osman Digna out of the question.

The place where it was hoped the engagement would come off was the spot where Graham had encountered such severe resistance just twelve months before. This time it was determined to be prepared to meet any number of the enemy.

The march was resumed at 10.15 a.m., the whole force marching in square. It was composed of 8,175 officers and men, 1,361 horses, 1,639 camels, 930 mules, and 1,773 camp-followers.

Soon after starting, an attempt was made to reconnoitre from the balloon, and parties of the enemy were reported to be discovered some miles in front. The wind, however, increased to such an extent as to render the balloon unserviceable, and at eleven it had to be packed up.

The following details of the operations are taken mainly from General Graham's despatch.

> The square advanced slowly with frequent halts, owing to the density of bush in the neighbourhood of the *zeriba*.
>
> "At 12.15 p.m., about three miles from *zeriba* No. 1, the cavalry and Mounted Infantry reported the presence of the enemy in the bush in scattered groups, a few being on camels and the main portion on foot. These appeared to be at first advancing through the bush, but gradually fell back before the advance of the cavalry.
>
> At 12.45 p.m. the force halted for a short time, and at 1.30 p.m. the enemy were reported as retiring towards the Teselah Hills and Tamaai. At 2 p.m., about three miles from the Teselah Hills, the force halted for water and food, and the Mounted Infantry and a squadron of the 9th Bengal Cavalry were ordered to reconnoitre the position on these hills, reported to be lined with the enemy.
>
> At first the enemy seemed inclined to defend the position, but their flanks being threatened they fell back on Tamaai. Teselah,

a group of bare rocky hills, about 100 feet high, but practicable for guns, was occupied by the Mounted Infantry and Bengal Cavalry at three o'clock. From these hills an excellent view was obtained of the scattered villages of New Tamaai, lying between the ridges of low hills beyond Teselah, and the deep ravine Khor Ghoub, beyond which the country becomes exceedingly mountainous and intersected by ravines with precipitous sides. The Mounted Infantry were ordered to push on to the village, find out if it was occupied, and then, if practicable, move on to the water and water the horses. One company advanced about a mile south through a village, when fire was opened on them from another village further south; while the company moving towards the water in the Khor Ghoub were fired upon by the enemy on the ridges near. The fire was returned, and the Mounted Infantry fell back to the Teselah Hill, where they were ordered to join the cavalry, and return to No. 1 *zeriba* for the night.

The main body of the force reached the Teselah Hills at 5 p.m., when the usual *zeriba* (2) was formed.

About 1 a.m., on the 3rd, shots were fired into the camp from about 800 to 1,000 yards. The moon was shining brightly, and the men at once stood to their arms, and the Grenadier Guards answered by a volley. This and a shrapnel shell silenced the enemy, not, however, before one of Graham's men had been killed and two wounded.

At 4.30, on the 3rd, the troops were aroused, and the *zeriba* being left in charge of McNeill with the East Surrey and Shropshire Regiments, the advance was resumed at eight.

Graham's object was to gain possession of a cluster of villages at New Tamaai which had long been Osman Digna's headquarters, and to secure the water supply, either by attacking the enemy's position, or by drawing them into an engagement on the open ground near the villages. The ground over which the men advanced was rough and broken. It was free from bush, but was intersected with deep gullies, and studded with jutting rocks and boulders.

At 8.45 fire was opened at long range by about 200 Arabs on the Mounted Infantry and Bengal Cavalry in front. This was replied to. It soon became evident that the enemy were unable to oppose any serious resistance to the advance of the column.

The force proceeded through the villages, which were found to have been recently deserted, and at 9.30 the crest of the north side of the Khor Ghoub was gained.

The Mounted Infantry and Bengal Cavalry were all this time engaging the enemy on the right flank, but were unable to draw them from their positions.

The 2nd Brigade, under General Hudson, now moved to the right, advanced across the Khor Ghoub, and ascended the hill on the opposite bank. The Berkshire Regiment, with the Marines on their right, opened fire from the highest point in the centre of the hill, and the Scots Guards threw out a company to fire up the *khor*. The Guards' Brigade and Australian Regiment moved forward in support of the 2nd Brigade, crowning the ridges on the north side of the *khor*. G Battery of the Royal Horse Artillery came into action on the left flank of the 1st Brigade, and opened fire on some parties of the enemy.

During those operations the enemy were keeping up a distant fire, which resulted in one man being killed, and one officer and fifteen men wounded. The enemy's numbers and loss it was impossible to estimate with any accuracy, but a steady, well-aimed fire was kept up on such bodies as showed themselves, and the effect of the fire was to overcome any opposition they may have intended to make.

On descending to the bed of the *khor* it was found that at the spot where the previous year was running water, there were no signs of water beyond a little moisture, and well-holes partly filled in. By digging about four feet down only a small supply of brackish water could be obtained, and at a short distance there was a shallow pool on a bed of black mud.

It is probable that this failure of the water supply had had much to do with the disappearance of Osman Digna's forces.

Graham's force had brought with it only three days' supply of water, and this failure of the wells at Tamaai rendered it dangerous to advance against Tamanieb, for should the wells there be found to be also waterless, the position of the army would become very serious.

Under these circumstances, and in view of the retirement of the enemy, and their evident inability or indisposition to meet the force, the general considered it best to withdraw, as it would have been fruitless to attempt to follow Osman Digna into the mountainous country with no water for the transport animals.

At 10.20 a.m. Graham ordered the withdrawal of the force, by alternate brigades, from the position which had been taken up. By 10.40 a.m. the troops had recrossed the *khor*, the movement being covered by two Horse Artillery guns on the ridge to the north, which fired a few rounds of shrapnel at detached parties of the enemy.

New Tamaai was ordered to be destroyed, and it was fired as the troops retired through it. Considerable quantities of ammunition were destroyed. Osman Digna's residence is believed to have been among the huts burnt.

At noon the force reached No. 2 *zeriba* at the Teselah Hill. As the troops fell back a handful of Arabs made their way, parallel to the line of march, along the distant hills to the right, keeping up a running fire on the British column. From *zeriba* No. 2 the force moved gradually back to the other *zeriba*, and thence to Souakim.

The total casualties were one man killed and six wounded. Only seven men fell out during the march.

It was a severe disappointment to the troops that, after all their exertions, the marches in the blazing sun to and from the *zeribas*, and the loss of life in previous engagements, the enemy should refuse to await the attack, and that the want of water should prevent the column following him up. The temporary occupation, followed by the destruction, of a wretched village, was a very inadequate result to show after such extensive preparation, and so much labour and effort.

From the 11th to the 20th April, Graham was occupied in making reconnaissances to Hasheen, Otao, Deberet, and Tambouk, taking a few prisoners, and capturing sheep and cattle.

The construction of the railway was at the same time pushed forward, till it was close to Otao, making altogether a total distance of eighteen miles.

Meanwhile, Osman Digna's followers amused themselves cutting the telegraph wires and damaging the railway works as opportunities offered.

They also made nightly attacks on Graham's camp. In order to check this, a series of automatic mines, to explode when trodden on, was placed outside the British lines. It does not appear that this measure answered the purpose intended, although an accidental explosion of one of the mines resulted in the loss of a promising young officer, Lieutenant Askwith, of the Royal Engineers.

Osman Digna's exact position at this period seems to have been somewhat of a puzzle to Graham, but on the 22nd he was able to telegraph that Osman was for the time without any large following, and that his people were greatly discouraged by their losses in the various engagements, and also in want of food.

The question of withdrawing the expedition now arose. Graham was most unwilling to retire without having achieved something decisive, and on the 26th he telegraphed that he strongly recommended crushing Osman before the expedition should be withdrawn. He added, that with Osman crushed, the country would be at peace, and the native allies safe; whereas if the British force were withdrawn he would soon become as strong as ever, would threaten Souakim, and punish the friendly tribes.

In the beginning of May Lord Wolseley arrived at Souakim and from that moment the question of what was to be done was taken out of Graham's hands.

The government had made up its mind, so far as such an operation was possible, not to go on with the railway to Berber at all events for the present, and the inutility of keeping the expedition in Souakim in face of the policy of abandoning the Soudan, referred to in the following chapter, generally, naturally struck Lord Wolseley.

On the 4th May he telegraphed to Lord Hartington that if it was positively decided not to push forward the railway as part of the campaign against the *Mahdi* at Khartoum, he advised the immediate embarkation of the Guards, the navvies, and Australians, leaving only the Indian Contingent and one British battalion for a garrison at Souakim. He added, on the 5th, that the heat was increasing, and the men of the expedition would soon become sickly; that he did not think the further operations wished for by Graham were, in face of the hot weather, desirable. Among other suggestions he proposed to the government to send back to England the ships laden with railway material, and to take up the railway before the troops fell back.

This despatch suggests the idea that Wolseley was beginning to get a little tired of giving advice to a government which was always asking his opinion and never acting upon it.

On the 8th he was instructed that the government adhered to the decision to adopt the proposal for defence of the frontier in his despatch of 14th April, but that the government did not approve of his suggestion to take up the railway and ship off the plant; but that he should arrange to hold the line, pending consideration whether it would be carried onwards.

This last despatch was too much for Wolseley, who appears to have thought it hard enough to have to carry out a policy of which he disapproved, without having the initiation of it attributed to himself; and in his despatch of the 11th he replied:

"What you term my proposals, were the military dispositions recommended in order to give effect to your policy at Souakim, to stop the railway, and send away as many troops as could be spared for service elsewhere. If the garrison here is to be seriously reduced, the railway must be either taken up or abandoned."

"Unless you have some clearly defined Soudan policy to initiate, any military operations, such as the extension of the railway would entail, would be to throw away uselessly valuable lives."

On the 13th Wolseley was instructed that the government adopted the dispositions recommended in his telegram of the 5th. This was followed by preparations for the immediate embarkation of the expedition.

Before this, Graham had on the 5th made a raid on Takool, a village ten miles south of Otao, and twenty west of Souakim, and driven out the enemy, reported to be 700 strong. Graham's force burnt Takool, and captured between 1,500 and 2,000 sheep and goats in this the last exploit of the campaign.

The railway works were now discontinued, the troops called in from Otao, and the navvies withdrawn. As the last truckload came in from the front, it was followed and fired on by jeering Soudanese.

The store-ships, which had for weeks been lying in the roads with rails, plant, and machinery not yet unloaded, were ordered back to England with their cargoes.

On the 17th May Graham and his staff left Souakim with the Coldstream Guards. The grenadiers, as well as the Australians and Scots Guards, sailed the following day.

The remainder of the troops followed shortly after, and before the end of the month the whole of the expedition, with the exception of the Shropshire Regiment and a portion of the Indian Contingent, had left Souakim.

Of the results obtained by the expedition, there is but little to say. Its departure left Osman Digna still uncrushed, and the Souakim-Berber route still unopened; and Osman was enabled in 1885 to boast, as he had done in 1884, that he had driven the British out of the country.[1]

This expedition was of far greater strength than its predecessor, and it is no disparagement to the officers and men engaged in it to say that their exploits did not equal those of the expedition of 1884.

---

1. Osman wrote to the *Mahdi* that "God struck fear into the hearts of the English, and they went away."

Tamaai, Handoub, and other positions had been taken and occupied temporarily, and a small portion of the railway had been made. This represented about the sum total of results.[2]

---

2. A return of the approximate cost, as nearly as can be ascertained, of the military expeditions, has been issued. The extra cost of the first expedition to Souakim, in 1884, was £352,352; the extra cost of the second expedition, in 1885, was £2,127,762; and the cost of the Souakim-Berber railway, including pipe line and water supply, was £865,369; making a total of £3,345,483. This is the cost incurred over and above the normal charge for the maintenance of the troops concerned.

CHAPTER 51

Evacuation

Towards the end of March, 1885, the force at Korti was gradually withdrawn to the town of Dongola, where Wolseley again fixed his headquarters. A small garrison of black troops only was left at Korti. The detachment at Merawi, under Colonel Butler, still remained there as a rear guard.

Although it had been decided to postpone further operations until the autumn, there is no reason to suppose that Wolseley entertained any idea that the enterprise against Berber and Khartoum was ever going to be abandoned. But early in April an unexpected contingency had to be reckoned with. On 9th April Mr. Gladstone announced to the House of Commons the Russian attack on the Afghan frontier, and the calling out of the Reserves in the United Kingdom.

This led the British Government to reconsider the whole question of the Soudan Expedition, and Wolseley was instructed to proceed to Cairo and confer with Sir E. Baring and General Stephenson on the military situation.

On 13th April, Lord Hartington telegraphed to Wolseley as follows:—

> In the condition of Imperial affairs it is probable that the expedition to Khartoum may have to be abandoned, and the troops brought back as soon as possible to Egypt. Consider at once what measures should, in that case, be taken for safe withdrawal of troops. This would involve stopping advance from Souakim, but not hurried withdrawal.

On the 14th April Wolseley telegraphed that in the event of the Government determining to withdraw the troops from the Soudan, before completion of arrangements he must know whether it was intended to retain Dongola, Wady Halfa, Korosko, or Assouan, as the frontier post. He said that if the position on the southern frontier of Egypt was to be exclusively one of defence, he would hold Wady Halfa and Korosko as outposts, with a strong brigade at Assouan. There would be no difficulty in withdrawing troops, but for the position in Egypt it was most essential that the announcement of withdrawal should be accompanied by an authoritative statement that the Government was determined to maintain a British garrison.

The next day Wolseley telegraphed his opinion on the question of withdrawal, strongly advising the retention of Dongola. His message, omitting irrelevant passages, was as follows:—

> At, and south of Assouan, I have about 7,500 British fighting soldiers. Retreat policy will require at least 2,500 on the frontier, leaving 5,000 available. For the sake of this handful, is it advisable to reverse Soudan policy? Retreat from Dongola hands that province over to the *Mahdi*, and renders loyalty of Ababdehs and other frontier tribes very doubtful. Withdraw Graham's force if necessary; this will not seriously disturb Egypt; but hold on to Dongola province.

There are few unprejudiced persons who will not agree in the soundness of the views above expressed. The reply was as follows:—

> War Office, April 15th, 1885.
> Your telegrams of the 14th and 15th received. Decision will probably be to adopt proposal for defence of Egyptian frontier at Wady Halfa and Assouan, as in your telegram of 14th. It is desirable that troops not required for this purpose should be concentrated as soon as possible, and available for any other service.

The government at this time had fully made up their minds to withdraw from the Soudan altogether as early as possible.

Wolseley, on the other hand, was anxious that before this step should be finally taken, the *Mahdi* should be crushed once for all, and in a very able despatch, dated the 16th April, set forth his views.

The document, which reads very like a protest against the policy of the Gladstone Cabinet, omitting some passages, is as follows:—

> Both from a military and financial point of view, and also with regard to the general well-being of Egypt proper, the growing power of the *Mahdi* must be met, not by a purely defensive

policy on the frontier, whether at Assouan or Wady Halfa, but by his overthrow in the neighbourhood of Khartoum.

The despatch concludes:—

> To sum up. The struggle with the *Mahdi*, or rather, perhaps, with *Mahdi*-ism, must come sooner or later. We can accept it now, and have done with it once and for all, or we can allow all the military reputation we have gained at the cost of so much toil and hard fighting, all the bloodshed and all the expenditure of the past campaign, to go for nothing, and try and stave the final struggle off for a few years. These years will be years of trouble and disturbance for Egypt, of burden and strain to our military resources, and the contest that will come in the end will be no less than that which is in front of us now. This is all we shall gain by a defensive policy.

The Afghan question still troubled the ministry, and on the 20th April Lord Hartington telegraphed that the:

> Government were about to announce that it was necessary to hold all the military resources of the Empire, including the forces in the Soudan, available for service wherever required. The government would not therefore make provision for further offensive operations in the Soudan, or for military preparations for an early advance on Khartoum, beyond such as could not be stopped with advantage, and did not involve hostile action, *viz.*, river steamboats contracted for, and the completion of the Wady Halfa Railway. As to ulterior steps, the government reserved their liberty of action. With the cessation of active operations on the Nile, any considerable extension of the Souakim-Berber Railway was to be suspended; but as Souakim must be held for the present, it might be necessary to occupy one or more stations in the neighbourhood, and the government would retain a garrison in Egypt, and defend the frontier.

On the 23rd April Wolseley proposed that he should go to Souakim in order to form an opinion on the spot as to the points which it would be desirable to hold.

This was approved by the government, and on the 24th Wolseley communicated the arrangements made for the disposition of the Nile force in his absence as follows:—

On 1st June, troops at Merawi start for Dongola, at which place and Abu Fatmeh I propose to concentrate force now up the Nile. This movement will be completed by 1st July.

In the meantime, railway to Ferket will be in a forward state, and able to assist greatly in the movement of troops and Civil Government officers on Wady Halfa. At present nearly all the troops are in huts; to move them in this present hot weather will be very trying to their health.

When troops are concentrated at Dongola and Abu Fatmeh I shall expect orders before I move them to Wady Halfa.

On the 27th April Wolseley was informed that he was to act in accordance with the proposals contained in his telegram of the 24th. The concentration, he was instructed, should be deliberate, but the movement from Merawi was to begin at once.

Wolseley and his staff left Cairo on April 29th and immediately embarked for Souakim.

General Buller and Sir Charles Wilson being asked their opinions, both reported strongly against a withdrawal from Dongola, and their views were supported by Sir Evelyn Baring.

All argument, however, was in vain. The government remained unconvinced.

In the beginning of May the Merawi detachment moved down to Dongola, and on the 13th the evacuation of the latter place commenced.

The Soudan having to be abandoned, the government evinced some desire to consider how far some sort of government could be set on foot for the province of Dongola.

Sir E. Baring, to whom a question was addressed on the subject, referred to Wolseley and General Buller. The former, regarding the matter from a military point of view, replied that a railway ought to be made to Hannek (just below the town of New Dongola), and the end of the line held by a British battalion, and Dongola itself should be garrisoned by 2,000 black troops. The present "*wekil*," according to Wolseley, should be appointed *mudir*. "It was safer," added his Lordship, "to attempt this than to hand Dongola over to the *Mahdi* and anarchy."

Buller replied that he did not think it possible to establish a government as proposed, and that the first thing to be considered was who was to take charge of it. His opinion was that no force of blacks that could be got together would be sufficient to hold the province. He added that he did not believe the railway to Hannek to be anything but a waste of money; it would besides require all the present force as a covering party; he believed the British were withdrawing just as the fruit was falling into their hands; concluding with the sentence, "I do not believe that when we leave Dongola anyone else will keep the *Mahdi* out."

Sir E. Baring, in forwarding the above opinions, said that "in view of the decision of the government he thought that instructions should be given to send down all troops, and as many of the civil population as wished to leave, to Wady Halfa," and concluded in the following words:—

> Your Lordship will understand that we make this recommendation only because we consider it to be the necessary consequence of the decision of Her Majesty's Government to abandon the province of Dongola at once, but that it must in no way be taken to imply our agreement with that decision.
> Nubar Pasha, on behalf of the Egyptian Government, requests me to make a final and most earnest appeal to the Government of Her Majesty to postpone the departure of the British troops from Dongola for, say, six months, in order that there may be at least a chance of establishing a government there.
> Nubar Pasha fears that the retreat of the British from Dongola will react on Egypt, and especially on the southern provinces, to such an extent as will render it impossible for the *khedive's* government to maintain order, and that they will be forced to appeal to Her Majesty's Government for help to preserve order in the country, and that thus the present system of government which Her Majesty's Government have been at so much trouble to maintain will be found no longer possible.

Nubar's appeal had no effect, and the question of the future government of Dongola occupied the British Cabinet no more. On the 14th May, Sir E. Baring was informed that it was the intention to withdraw the whole force to Wady Halfa.

On the 16th Wolseley telegraphed his idea as to the British force which should remain at Korosko and Wady Halfa.

This was approved by the government, and the troops continued their journey down the Nile.

The departure of the soldiers from Dongola was accompanied by the exodus of a large portion of the native population, who feared to be left exposed to the vengeance of the *Mahdi*.

Mr. Gladstone's Ministry retired from office on 12th June, and on the Conservative Cabinet coming into power, one of the first questions with which it occupied itself was that of Egypt.

It was impossible for the Ministry of Lord Salisbury to at once reverse the Egyptian policy of their predecessors, but the new premier declared that "England had a mission in Egypt, and that until it was accomplished it was idle to talk of withdrawal."

The evacuation of the Soudan, however, stood on a different footing. The steps taken by Mr. Gladstone's Government were so far advanced that the measure was already practically a *fait accompli*. As Lord Salisbury stated:

> . . . . the whole of the Soudan down to Dongola had been already evacuated, and the whole of the province of Dongola, with the exception of a rear-guard left at Debbeh, had been evacuated also; and 12,000 of the luckless population, to avoid the vengeance of the *Mahdi*, had fled from their houses and taken refuge in Upper Egypt.

It was not, however, without inquiry that Lord Salisbury's Cabinet determined to proceed with the evacuation. Wolseley was again consulted, and in a despatch of 27th June he wrote:—

> You cannot get out of Egypt for many years to come. If the present policy of retreat be persisted in the *Mahdi* will become stronger and stronger, and you will have to increase your garrisons and submit to the indignity of being threatened by him. Eventually you will have to fight him to hold your position in Egypt, which you will then do with the population round you ready on any reverse to rise against you. No frontier force can keep Mahdism out of Egypt, and the *Mahdi* sooner or later must be smashed, or he will smash you.
> To advance in the autumn on Khartoum and discredit the *Mahdi* by a serious defeat on his own ground would certainly finish him. The operation, if done deliberately, would be a simple one; and, as far as anything can be a certainty in war, it would be a certainty. Until this is done there will be no peace in Egypt, and your military expenditure will be large and increasing. My advice, therefore, is, carry out autumn campaign up the Nile, as originally intended. I would leave Souakim as it is.

On the 2nd July the government telegraphed that—

> Her Majesty's Government, after a full consideration of all the circumstances, were not prepared to reverse the orders given by their predecessors by countermanding the retreat of the force from Dongola.

Thus the policy of evacuation was affirmed.

General Brackenbury with the last of the rear-guard left Dongola on the 5th, and followed the rest of the troops down to Cairo.

On the 6th July Wolseley handed over the command of the British troops to General Stephenson, and in a few weeks the greater part of the officers and men forming the expedition had left Egypt.

The services of the officers and men forming the Gordon Relief Expedition were referred to by Lord Salisbury on the 12th August in moving in the House of Lords a vote of thanks in the following words:—

> In considering their merits you must keep out of sight altogether the precise results and outcome of the labours they have gone through and the dangers they have incurred. Of course this is not the moment at which to broach controversial topics, and I only wish to say that you must look upon this fact—that they failed to fulfil the main purpose for which they were sent out through no fault of their own. The prize of success was taken from them, as it were by an overmastering destiny, by the action of causes, whatever their nature, over which they themselves had no more control than they would have over a tempest or earthquake.[1]

There can be no doubt that Lord Salisbury's eulogium was well deserved.

The merits of the officers and men were unquestionable. That they did not succeed was owing to the incapacity of those who sent them, at the wrong time, by the wrong route, on their fruitless errand.

---

1. Lord Wolseley was created a viscount for his services with the expedition.

Chapter 52

Continuation

The preceding chapter brings the narrative down to the summer of 1885, at which period the First Edition of the present work was brought to a close.

In the final chapter the errors of British policy in Egypt were dealt with. It was pointed out how the dilatory fashion in which England intervened to suppress the Arabi revolt led to its indefinite prolongation; how when Alexandria had been destroyed, and massacres had taken place all over the country, a British Army was sent too late to avert these disasters; how when the Arabi insurrection had been put down, and that of the *Mahdi* took its place, England reduced the Army of Occupation, and left Egypt to attempt to cope single-handed with the revolt; how in 1884, when Tokar and Sinkat were cut off, England sent an army to the relief of those places only in time to find that they had already fallen; how when many British lives had been sacrificed, and thousands of Soudanese had been slaughtered in the Eastern Soudan, England, instead of crushing Osman Digna and opening the route to Berber, withdrew her troops only to send another expedition in the following year, when too late to accomplish those very objects; finally, how, having sent Gordon to bring away the garrisons in the Soudan, England, again too late, despatched an expedition to his rescue.

The feeble manner in which the reform of Egyptian institutions had been taken in hand was also indicated, and it was pointed out how England, by declaring that her stay in the country was only to be short-lived, added to the difficulty of carrying any of such reforms into effect.

With regard to the Drummond-Wolff Convention of the 24th October, 1885, it was foretold that the inquiry provided for into Egyptian affairs would be illusory, and the withdrawal of the Army of Occupation, which the convention was to effect, was one of those events which might safely be relegated to the remote future.

It was pointed out that, whatever the future of Egypt under British guidance might be, it was impossible that it could be marked by greater errors than had been witnessed in the past, and, in conclusion, advice was given in the words following:—

> Put the administration really, instead of nominally and half-heartedly, under English control. Discard all idea of going away in two years, or twenty years, or two hundred years, if the country is not brought to order and prosperity by that time. Declare that as long as England remains she will be responsible for Egyptian finances, and for the safety and property of Europeans. Simplify as much as possible the official staff and system, and take proper steps for securing whatever point may be needed as the frontier.

It is satisfactory to be able to observe that since the above was written much has been done in the way of following the author's recommendations. The firm attitude adopted with regard to Egypt by Lord Salisbury's Ministry on its accession to office in 1885 has been maintained by succeeding governments, and with the happiest results. One Egyptian administration after another has been taken in hand, abuses have been suppressed, corruption reduced to a minimum, and order and regularity introduced. The finances have been placed on a sound footing; reforms have been everywhere inaugurated; and tranquillity reigns throughout the country, which has arrived at a pitch of prosperity such as in modern times it has never before attained. In addition, as a result of the improvements made in her military system, Egypt, with England's aid, has been enabled to suppress a formidable insurrection, and to regain the most valuable of her lost provinces.

The different steps by which all this has been brought about may be gleaned, partially at least, from the following pages.

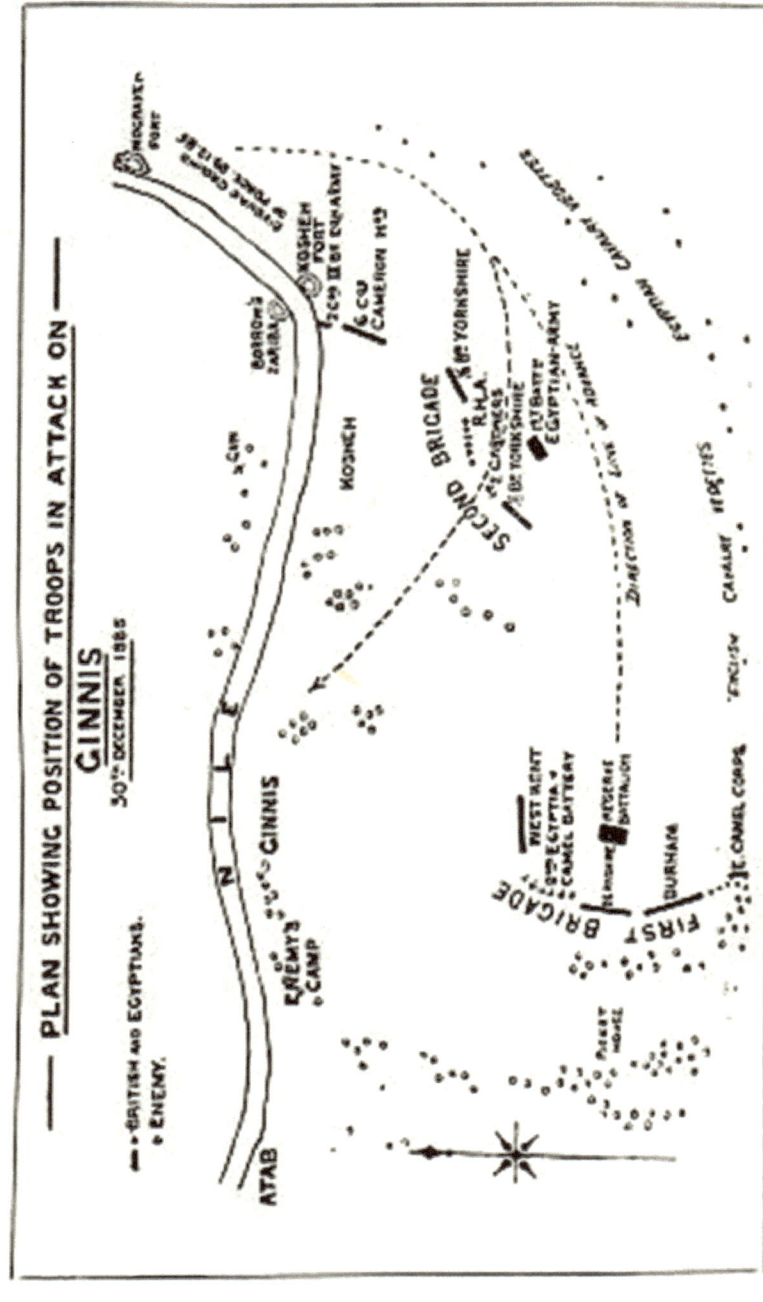

CHAPTER 53

The Mahdist Invasion

It was not unnatural that the retirement of the Gordon Relief Expedition, in 1885, should have inspired the *Mahdi* with the idea that the moment had now arrived for the fulfilment of what he regarded as part of his Divine mission, *viz.*, the invasion of Egypt. Two British armies had been sent, in two successive years, to the Eastern Soudan, and both, after a certain amount of fighting, had been withdrawn, whilst a third, despatched for the relief of Khartoum, had, when almost at the gates of Khartoum, been forced to retrace its steps, and retreat down the Nile. What ensued was only the result foretold by Lord Wolseley when he prophetically declared to Her Majesty's Government that "the struggle with the *Mahdi*, or rather with Mahdism, must come sooner or later. Eventually you will have to fight him to hold your position in Egypt. No frontier force can keep Mahdism out of Egypt, and the *Mahdi*, sooner or later, must be smashed, or he will smash you."[1]

When, as stated in another chapter, the last of the British troops left Dongola on 5th July, 1885, an Egyptian frontier field force, composed of British and Egyptian troops, was formed, and placed under the command of Major-General Grenfell, Sir Evelyn Wood's successor as Sirdar of the Egyptian Army. His headquarters were fixed at Assouan, whilst Brigadier-General Butler commanded the advanced brigade at Wady Halfa, with outposts at Kosheh, about forty-two miles south of the railway terminus at Akasheh.

The *Mahdi's* plans for the invasion of Egypt were formed as early as May, in fact, as soon as he was able to make sure of the break-up of the Nile Expedition.

---

1. For much of the information contained in the present chapter the author is indebted to the excellent work *Mahdism and the Egyptian Soudan*, already referred to.

The idea was to make the advance in two river columns, under the command of the Emirs Abd-el-Medjid and Mohammed-el-Kheir respectively, who were to march on Wady Halfa, whilst a third column was to cross the desert from Abu Hamid to Korosko, thus cutting the communications of the defensive force at Wady Halfa.

The death of the *Mahdi* in the month of June by no means interfered with the carrying out of this programme, his successor, the Khalifa Abdullah-el-Taaishi, being almost as capable a leader as his predecessor, and even more oppressive and unscrupulous.

Notwithstanding that Omdurman, which had become the *khalifa's* capital, was ravaged by famine and small-pox, the preparations for the advance continued, and by the early part of August Debbeh and Old Dongola were occupied by the forces of Abd-el-Medjid, numbering 4,000 men. By the end of the month the whole of the country south of Dongola was in the hands of the *khalifa's* troops. On the 24th, Wad-en-Nejumi, one of the chief *emirs*, was reported as having left Omdurman with a large force, going north. It must not be supposed that the expedition was popular with the *khalifa's* soldiers, but unfortunately they had no choice in the matter. They are said to have declared, "Our brothers are dead; the English shoot well, and we have nothing to eat."

From Dongola the invaders proceeded north along the Nile, till, on the 20th September, they had reached as far as Hafir. The Dervish forces at that place, and at Dongola, were estimated at 7,000 by the beginning of October.

Meanwhile, another army was marching on Abu Hamid, where 3,000 men arrived in the latter part of October.

Seeing that the Dervish attack was impending, steps were taken to meet the emergency. Two gunboats were sent to patrol the river above Akasheh, and the post at that place was strengthened by the sending of a force of Egyptian Mounted Infantry, and a half battalion of black troops.

On the 26th October General Grenfell telegraphed from Assouan to General Stephenson for another battalion to be sent him from Cairo, adding, "We should now look upon an advance on Egypt as merely a question of time, and be thoroughly prepared." On 4th November, Captain Hunter (now Sir Archibald Hunter), of the Intelligence Department, reported that 8,000 of the enemy had crossed to Abu Fatmeh, and that everything indicated an immediate advance. On the next day news was received that the enemy was advancing on both banks, Mohammed-el-Kheir on the east, and Abd-el-Medjid on the west, with the object of cutting off the communications of the advanced force, and preventing reinforcements reaching it.

A few days later, *viz.*, on the 17th, it became known that 8,000 Dervishes had reached Dulgo,[2] and that the advanced guard was at Absarat, whence it was to march on Khanak, to cut the Wady Haifa railway.

On the 27th, it was reported that 7,000 of the enemy were occupying the heights near Ammara, a few miles south of Ginnis, and that 4,000 more were now at Abu Hamid. Three days afterwards a spy gave information that 1,000 mounted men had left by the desert for the north of Akasheh, and that another thousand had crossed the river to the west bank, the intention being to make a simultaneous attack on Kosheh, Akasheh, and the railway.

The news of the Dervish advance now caused widespread alarm in Cairo, as well as in Egypt generally, and, to preserve public order, the police force had to be reinforced, more especially in the frontier provinces. Steps were, at the same time, taken to strengthen the Army of Occupation by sending two additional battalions from the United Kingdom.

On the 30th November, General Butler and his staff left Wady Halfa for the front at Akasheh, and General Grenfell moved up to Wady Halfa. At this date the frontier force was disposed as follows:— At Kosheh, 600 British and 300 Egyptians; at Mograkeh, 260 Egyptians; at Sarkamatto and Dal, 200 Egyptians; at Akasheh, 600 British and 350 Egyptians; and at Wady Halfa, 500 British and 350 Egyptians; total, 3,160 men. In addition to these, small detachments were posted at Ambigol Wells, Sarras, and other places.

A skirmish, which took place at Ginnis on the 29th, showed that the main body of the enemy was posted in front of Kosheh, where it had arrived on the previous day.[3]

On the 3rd December, Captain Hunter engaged the advance party of the enemy, with Gardner guns and rifles, with considerable effect, several horsemen and foot-soldiers being killed.

Meanwhile an attempt had been made by the Dervishes to cut the line of communications at Ambigol Wells, where a small post of only thirty men of the Berkshire and West Kent Regiments was established

---

2. Frequently spelt "Delligo."

3. Ginnis and Kosheh are two villages on the east bank of the Nile, and are only separated by a short distance.

in a fort. The Dervish force attacked with men, mounted and on foot, and one gun. They were driven off with some loss on the 2nd December, but on the two following days returned to the attack. Several sorties were made by the little garrison, until the arrival of reinforcements on the 4th caused the besiegers to retire.

At 6.15 a.m. on the 12th, 3,000 Dervishes attacked a fort constructed at Mograkeh, near Kosheh, and got within 100 yards of it. The garrison of the fort, consisting of 300 men of the Egyptian army, behaved with great steadiness, and repulsed the attack. After the skirmish, the enemy moved to the village of Ferket, a place on the river north of Ginnis, and occupied it, From this point they retired to the hills. Two men killed and half a dozen wounded represented the Egyptian loss.

This was followed, on the night of the 15th, by a further attack on Kosheh from a battery erected on sand hills on the western bank, which was silenced, and the attacking force driven off on the 16th.

All the posts were now rapidly reinforced. General Grenfell had already arrived at Wady Halfa on the 4th December, and on the 19th December General Stephenson came from Cairo and assumed the command of the frontier force, with Grenfell as Chief of the Staff.

Arrangements were promptly made to inflict a crushing blow on the enemy, who, encouraged by the slight resistance to their advance hitherto made, had pushed their foremost troops north of the village of Ginnis, where the main body was established.

At the same time, about 1,000 men, with a gun, threatened the *zeriba* on the west bank, held by the Egyptian troops.

On the 29th, Generals Stephenson and Grenfell marched from Ferket and bivouacked on the east bank below the fort of Kosheh, where the whole of the fighting force was by this time concentrated.

The troops consisted of—*Cavalry*, 20th Hussars; British Mounted Infantry and Camel Corps; Egyptian Cavalry and Camel Corps: *Artillery*, 1 battery Royal Artillery; 1 Egyptian camel battery and Gardner guns: *Royal Engineers*, 1 company: *Infantry*, 1st Brigade, under General Butler—Berkshire Regiment, West Kent Regiment, and Durham Regiment; 2nd Brigade, under Colonel Huyshe—Cameron Highlanders; Yorkshire Regiment; 1st and 9th Battalions (part only) of the Egyptian army. Total, about 5,000 men.

On the morning of the 30th, Stephenson attacked and defeated the *khalifa's* forces at Kosheh and the neighbouring village of Ginnis.

On the two preceding days, artillery fire had been kept up on the enemy's position. At 5 a.m. on the 30th, the whole force advanced.

By daylight the 2nd Brigade and the 1st Egyptian Battalion had taken up a strong position on the heights above Kosheh, at a distance of about 1,200 yards from, and directly opposite, the village. At 6.10 a.m. the British battery attached to this brigade began to shell Kosheh. A quarter of an hour later the Cameron Highlanders and two companies of the 9th Soudanese rushed the houses in gallant style.

The village was captured, together with a brass gun, at 6.50 a.m. The gunboat *Lotus* co-operated in this movement, and by her fire inflicted considerable loss on the retreating Dervishes.

Whilst this was going on, the 1st Brigade, under Butler, had swept round to the south end of the village of Ginnis, and by daybreak had gained a position on the hills about a mile from the river. Up to this time, the advance made along the flank of the enemy's position had escaped observation, but as the eastern sky behind the advancing troops brightened, the Dervishes, who were completely surprised, came out from the low ground along the river, and streamed to the front. Thence they opened an irregular fire, which, in spite of the Martini-Henrys of the brigade, was maintained for about forty minutes.

In the meanwhile, the Egyptian battery, attached to the 1st Brigade, had been brought into action on the right of the position, and was doing good service. The infantry deploying in line, the West Kent on the right, and the Berkshire and Durham Regiments on the left of the guns, kept up a steady fire, assisted by the Egyptian Camel Corps. Notwithstanding the volleys of the Martini-Henrys, a large body of spearmen managed to creep up unobserved, through a deep ravine in front of the line of infantry, to a spot where the dismounted camels of the Egyptian Camel Corps had been placed.

The spearmen then made so rapid a rush that the men of the Camel Corps had not time to mount, and so were driven back fighting hand to hand with their assailants, who pressed them closely. The West Kent Regiment, which on the attack developing had been moved to the left of the line, came to the assistance of the Camel Corps, and shooting down numbers of the enemy, the rest fell back and fled to the hills. The brigade, then swinging round to the left, was directed upon the village of Ginnis, and, though time after time attempts at a stand were made, the enemy were eventually all dispersed, and at 9.15 the village was occupied, the Dervishes fleeing south, in the direction of Atab.

The 2nd Brigade, after disposing of Kosheh, had continued its advance in the direction of Ginnis, which it entered on the eastern side, a quarter of an hour after the 1st Brigade had taken possession.

The cavalry went in pursuit of the fugitives until 10 a.m., and by that time the Dervish Army had been dissolved into a mass of disorganized and terror-stricken Arabs. Many of them crossed over to the west bank and escaped into the desert.

The camp at Ginnis was seized, and four guns and twenty standards captured.

The British and Egyptian loss in the fight was only seven killed and thirty-four wounded, and if, as estimated, out of a force of 6,000 men, the *khalifa's* troops had 500 killed and 300 wounded, it must be admitted that the engagement partook more of the nature of a *battu* than a battle.

After the fight, and on the same day, the 1st Brigade advanced to Atab, five miles to the west of Giniss, whilst the cavalry continued the pursuit to Abri, which on the following day was occupied by Buller's brigade.

The action at Ginnis was a serious check to the *khalifa*. Not only had his emir Abd-el-Medjid with eighteen minor chiefs been killed, but the prestige which the *Mahdi's* successor enjoyed amongst his followers had also sustained a severe blow.

The remainder of his scattered-forces was now collected at Kermeh, about 30 miles north of Dongola, where, under the command of Mohammed-el-Kheir, they awaited reinforcements.

CHAPTER 54

Finance, the Suez Canal, and the Army of Occupation

In the year 1885, each of the subjects mentioned in the heading of the present chapter came prominently to the front. In the following pages it is proposed to deal with the different matters in succession.

Finance. In July, 1885, Egypt, thanks to the good offices of Great Britain, was enabled to arrange a very thorny question which had arisen with regard to her finance. To explain what occurred, it is necessary to refer to the events which had previously taken place.

Under the financial decrees of Ismail Pasha, certain revenues were assigned to the Public Debt Commissioners to provide for the interest and Sinking Fund of the debt. Although, by the Law of Liquidation accepted by the Powers in 1880, the rate of interest was reduced, the provision for the Sinking Fund was left untouched, and the result was that the debt was gradually reduced by about a million. This, however, was too good a state of things to last. The expenses caused by the insurrection in the Soudan, the necessity of providing for the payment of the Alexandria indemnities, and other pressing claims, not only rendered it impossible for Egypt to continue the reduction of her existing debt, but made it indispensable to contract a fresh one in the shape of a new loan.

In March, 1884, at the invitation of Lord Granville, a conference of the Great Powers was held in London to discuss the situation. To purchase the goodwill of France, what became known as "The Anglo-French Convention" was entered into. By this, subject to the acceptance by the powers of the British financial proposals, the British troops in Egypt were to be withdrawn at a fixed date, unless the Powers, in the meantime, should agree to their remaining. Lord Granville pointed out the absurdity of Egypt continuing to pay off her old debts at a moment when the funds at her disposal were insufficient to meet her current expenditure. The British proposals, which involved not only a suspension of the Sinking Fund, but also a further diminution in the rate of interest, were opposed by the French representative; and Lord Granville, in a somewhat summary manner, dissolved the conference. Lord Northbrook was then despatched to Egypt as High Commissioner, and in September, 1884, no means having been discovered of relieving the financial tension, the Egyptian Government, under his advice, adopted the strong measure of directing the governors of the provinces, as well as the heads of the customs and railway administrations, to pay directly to the Treasury the balance of their receipts for the current half-year (which closed on the 25th October), instead of to the "*Caisse*" of the debt.

It is worthy of remark that there was at this time sufficient money in the "*Caisse*" to pay the interest on the debt, and the funds intercepted would simply have gone to swell the Sinking Fund. The step, nevertheless, was a clear violation of the existing arrangements between Egypt and her creditors, and naturally raised a storm. Protests rained in from all quarters; and some of the powers, notably France, Germany, and Russia, used strong language. The commissioners of the debt also attacked the *khedive*'s ministers in the Mixed Tribunals. The Egyptian Government, realizing that it had got into a "tight place," again by British advice, meekly bowed its head and directed the payments to the "*Caisse*" to be resumed. The Cairo Mixed Tribunal on the 18th December gave judgment directing the government to refund the money diverted.

This they were absolutely unable to do, and an appeal was lodged, partly to gain time and partly because the negotiations with the powers, abruptly broken off by Lord Granville, had been in the meantime renewed. At last, on the 18th March, 1885, "The London Convention" came to the aid of Nubar Pasha and his Cabinet. The effect of this agreement and the declarations dated the 17th March annexed to it was that the powers acquiesced in the issue of a new loan of £9,000,000. Foreigners were made liable to certain taxes, and the Law of Liquidation was modified. Further than this, the Mixed Tribunals were declared incompetent to proceed with the action against the government. On 27th July, 1885, a decree embodying these terms was signed, and a situation full of embarrassment was happily put an end to.

The Suez Canal. It should be mentioned that in the declarations annexed to "The London Convention" was one which provided that a commission composed of delegates of the Great Powers should assemble at an early date to consider the measures to be adopted to secure the free navigation of the Suez Canal in time of war. What possible connection there was between this question and that of Egyptian finance it is hard to say, but, the engagement having been made, it had to be carried out, and the negotiations were at once taken in hand.

The International Commission for dealing with the matter held its first sitting in Paris on the 30th March, 1885, and proceeded to discuss the various points involved.

As stated in a previous chapter, the attention of the powers had been called to the matter by Lord Granville, then Foreign Secretary, as far back as the 3rd January, 1883, though thus far no progress had been made.

By the 13th June, 1885, the commission had agreed on the text of a convention by which the freedom of navigation of the Canal in war-time was to be secured, and the commission then concluded its sittings.

It should be mentioned that the British delegates, in approving the arrangement, formally declared that they did so under express reservation against the application of any of the clauses which might be incompatible with the existing situation in Egypt, or which might fetter the action of Her Majesty's Government or the movements of Her Majesty's forces during the British occupation of Egypt. From the date last mentioned, the question was under discussion by the respective governments till more than three years later, when the Convention was concluded, and finally ratified by the Powers on the 22nd December, 1888.

The principal provisions of the convention were the following, *viz.*:—

That the Canal should be open to both merchant vessels and men-of-war both in time of war and peace; that the Canal should not be subject to the exercise of the right of blockade; that no act of hostility should be committed in the Canal, its ports of access, or within a radius of three miles; that vessels of belligerents should only take in supplies so far as they were actually necessary, and that their stay in port should be limited to twenty-four hours; that the like interval should elapse between the sailing of a belligerent vessel and the departure of a vessel of a hostile power; that no belligerent power should disembark or embark either troops or munitions of war; that no vessel of war belonging to the contracting powers should be stationed in the Canal, and not more than two at Port Saïd or Suez; that the restrictions imposed should not apply to measures which the *sultan* or the *khedive* might take for the defence of Egypt by their own forces or for the maintenance of public order; and that no fortifications should be erected.

Referring to a former chapter dealing with M. de. Lesseps' contention as to the neutrality of the Canal, it is worthy of note that in no part of the convention does the word "neutrality" occur, and it is a fact that in Lord Salisbury's instructions to the British delegates they were expressly warned to avoid using that expression and to substitute for it the term "freedom of navigation."

The Army of Occupation. In August, 1885, the continued presence of the Army of Occupation (then 14,000 in number) had for some time been producing increased irritation on the part of the *sultan*, and also of the French Government. Sir H. Drummond-Wolff was then sent to the East with the object of endeavouring to arrive at some understanding with regard to the withdrawal of the British troops. The British envoy was also, in combination with the Turkish commissioner Moukhtar Pasha, to consider the steps to be taken for tranquillizing the Soudan, and to inquire what changes might be necessary in the civil administration of Egypt.

The British commissioner was received by the *sultan* on 29th August, and having signed a preliminary convention with the Turkish Minister of Foreign Affairs at Constantinople, came on to Cairo two months later, where he was joined by his colleague.

Their joint inquiry lasted till the end of 1886, and resulted in various suggestions which were not adopted.

In January, 1887, the Sultan, backed by France, was pressing the British Government to name a day for the evacuation, and, with a view to meeting his views as far as possible, a definite convention on the subject was signed by the two commissioners on the 22nd May, 1887.

According to this agreement, the British troops were to withdraw at the end of three years, unless at the expiration of that period external or internal danger should render the postponement of the evacuation necessary, in which case the troops were to be withdrawn as soon as the danger should have disappeared. Two years after the withdrawal, the supervision exercised by Great Britain over the Egyptian Army was to cease. Thenceforward Egypt was to enjoy territorial immunity, and, on the ratification of the convention, the powers were to be invited to recognise and guarantee the inviolability of Egyptian territory. Nevertheless, the convention continued, the Turkish Government was to have the right to occupy the country militarily if there should be danger from invasion without, or if order and security were threatened within.

On the other hand, the British Government reserved the right to send, in the above-mentioned cases, troops which would take the measures necessary to remove those dangers. Lastly, both the Ottoman and British troops were to withdraw as soon as the causes calling for their intervention should be removed.

The essential point in the agreement was the recognition, by the Sultan, of England's right to reoccupy Egypt, on emergency, and this at once gave rise to trouble.

As soon as the terms of the convention were communicated to the French Government, the French ambassador was rampant everywhere, and both he and his Russian colleague at Constantinople made the most violent opposition. They lost no opportunity of putting pressure on the *sultan*, who at first was disposed to abide by the arrangement. They went so far as to declare that, if he ratified the convention, France and Russia would thereby have a right to occupy provinces of the Turkish Empire, and to leave only after a similar convention should be concluded with them. They also hinted that France might do this in Syria, and Russia in Armenia. Austria, Germany, and Italy, on the other hand, urged the ratification of the convention, but the poor *sultan* was too much alarmed to consent, and, on the 14th July, proposed to England to throw over the agreement which his ministers had signed, and to reopen negotiations for a new convention altogether.

This was a little too much for Lord Salisbury, then Foreign Secretary and Prime Minister. Needless to say the mission of the British envoy, upon which £25,046 in money and two years in time had been wasted, came to an end, and Sir H. Drummond-Wolff, who had already been waiting for a month to obtain the desired ratification, left Constantinople on the 15th. His colleague, Moukhtar Pasha, whose occupation was now gone, nevertheless remained in Egypt, where he is to be found at the present date, drawing a handsome salary, but with no defined duties.

The failure of the negotiations was probably as little regretted by

Lord Salisbury as it was by everybody else having the welfare of Egypt at heart. Although the time may arrive when that country will be in a position to walk alone, in 1890 (the period fixed for the withdrawal of the Army of Occupation) that time had not been reached. The reforms inaugurated were then only beginning to bear fruit, and, without the supporting influence afforded by the presence of British troops, ran the risk of being only imperfectly carried into effect, even if they did not perish altogether.

It must be conceded that, considered merely as a military force, the presence of the Army of Occupation has for years ceased to be necessary. British ministers have over and over again declared that England's intervention in Egypt was for the purpose of suppressing anarchy, supporting the authority of the *khedive*, and restoring public order. No one can deny that all these objects have long since been attained, and those who attempt to justify the retention of the British troops on the supposition that their withdrawal might be followed by fresh troubles adopt an argument similar to that of a person who, having extinguished a conflagration in his neighbour's house, should persist in occupying it on the pretence that the fire might break out again.

But regarded as a moral support to England in carrying out her extended programme of reforming Egyptian institutions, the presence of the Army of Occupation may be for some time to come a necessity.

Writing on this subject, Sir Alfred Milner, in his admirable work *England in Egypt*, remarks as follows:—

> The British troops have of course no sort of status in the country. They are not the soldiers of the *khedive*, or foreign soldiers invited by the *khedive*; they are not the soldiers of the protecting Power, because in theory there is no protecting Power. In theory, their presence is an accident, and their character that of simple visitors. At the present moment they are no longer, from the military point of view, of vital importance, for their numbers have been repeatedly reduced, and for several years past they have not exceeded, and do not now (1892) exceed, 3,000 men.
>
> It is true that their presence relieves a certain portion of the Egyptian army from duties it would otherwise have to perform, and that, if the British troops were altogether withdrawn, the number of Egyptian soldiers might have to be somewhat increased. But its value as part of the defensive forces of the

country does not, of course, constitute the real importance and meaning of the British Army of Occupation. It is as the outward and visible sign of the predominance of British influence, of the special interest taken by Great Britain in the affairs of Egypt, that that army is such an important element in the present situation.

Its moral effect is out of all proportion to its actual strength. The presence of a single British regiment lends a weight they would not otherwise possess to the counsels of the British Consul-General. Take the troops away, and you must either run the risk of a decline of British influence, which would imperil the work of reform, or devise, for a time at least, some new and equivalent support for that influence, a problem not perhaps impossible, but certainly difficult of solution.

Chapter 55

The Eastern Soudan

Any history of the military operations in Egypt, during the period comprised in the accompanying chapters, would be incomplete without a notice of the events which were in the meantime taking place in the Eastern Soudan.

In May, 1885, when Graham's force withdrew from Souakim, General Hudson took over the command. The troops left to protect the town consisted of 930 Europeans, 2,405 Indians, and the Egyptians forming the regular garrison.

Osman Digna, with the greater part of his followers, was again at Tamaai, and had also a small force at Hasheen. The fall of Kassala soon after, by setting free the besieging force, enabled Osman still further to strengthen his position in the neighbourhood of Souakim.[1] Under these circumstances, General Hudson was compelled to remain strictly on the defensive.

It would be both long and wearisome to attempt to describe the various incidents which occurred during many of the succeeding months.

Day after day the Dervish scouts approached the forts, and cavalry patrols went out and fired upon them; night after night parties of the enemy took up positions from which they fired on the town, and remained until dislodged by the shell fired from the forts and from the man-of-war stationed in the harbour. Thus Souakim continued to be besieged, the enemy refraining from any serious attack, and devoting themselves principally to raiding the friendly tribes in the adjoining territory.

---

1. Osman was reported as slain on the 23rd September, 1885, when the Dervishes were routed by the Abyssinians at Kufeit. So far from this being the case, he shortly after marched into Kassala, in triumph.

On 11th May, 1886, the remainder of the British and Indian troops left, and Major Watson took command as Governor-General of the Eastern Soudan. The garrison at this time consisted of 2,500 Egyptians.

In June, the prospect began to brighten. The Dervishes withdrew their patrols round Souakim, and evacuated Hasheen and Handoub. The friendlies then began to take courage, and made advances upon Tamaai, which they blockaded, and eventually occupied on 11th September, the Soudanese garrison retiring with loss into a fort near the village.

On the 7th October the friendlies scored a further success. After being twice repulsed, they assaulted and took the fort after an hour's fighting, killing some 200 of the defenders and capturing eighteen guns.

The redoubtable Osman Digna, being wanted at Omdurman, had previously withdrawn, and no hostile force now remained in the Eastern Soudan.

Two thousand pounds was paid to the friendlies by way of subsidy, and trade with the interior was opened.

In November, Colonel Kitchener, who had succeeded Major Watson, reported "the collapse of Osman Digna's power," and a season of greater tranquillity than Souakim had known for years was experienced.

In January, 1887, affairs at Souakim had even further settled down, and many of the hostile tribes expressed a desire to come to terms, but, in June, news arrived that from 2,000 to 3,000 Dervishes, mostly Baggaras, were advancing from Kassala to relieve Tokar, at that time besieged by the friendlies. The arrival of the Baggaras at Tokar tended to revive the fanatical spirit at that place, but had not much influence on the surrounding tribes, who refused to present themselves there when summoned by Osman Digna.

In July, Osman was again called to Omdurman, and in his absence nothing particular was done in the neighbourhood of Souakim. During the autumn, things looked so peaceful that the garrison was reduced by the withdrawal of two battalions, and news of this circumstance reaching Osman, who had then returned to Kassala, he at once collected some 5,000 men and marched to Handoub. By 18th December he was again master of the whole country up to the walls of Souakim, which once more was in a state of siege. On 17th December, an attack was made on the Water Forts, and repulsed. A deserter reported that at Handoub and Tamaai a fighting force of 5,000 men was preparing to capture Souakim by a rush, and that the scheme would be carried out at daybreak very shortly.

In January, 1888, frequent night attacks were made; but they were invariably repulsed by the fire from the men-of-war in the harbour. On the 17th, a party of friendlies attacked the Dervish camp at daybreak. Mounted troops from Souakim went in support. The friendlies surprised and captured the enemy's camp. Then the Dervishes scattered in the pursuit re-entered the position from the rear, and drove off the friendlies with considerable loss. The whole Egyptian force then retreated to Souakim, pursued for four or five miles by the victorious Dervishes. In this engagement Kitchener and Lieutenant McMurdo were wounded, and eleven soldiers and friendlies were killed. As a result of the engagement, Kitchener was warned that in future he should not take part in similar operations with British officers or Egyptian regulars.

The intention was to capture Osman Digna, but although seen in the distance, he succeeded in escaping at the moment when the fortune of war appeared to be going against him.

Emboldened by this success, the Dervishes began to display increased activity round Souakim, the neighbourhood of which was infested with marauding bands. On the 3rd March, a large party established themselves by night at a disused position called Fort Hudson, and kept up a continuous fire on the town. On the morning of the 4th, numbers of the enemy were seen advancing, and H.M.S. *Dolphin* opened fire at 10 a.m. The Egyptian forces, to the number of 450 men, advanced to endeavour to drive the enemy from Fort Hudson, the friendly Amarar tribe assisting. The position, however, was too strong, and they were repulsed.

To make matters worse, just at the moment when a reinforcement of the enemy necessitated the retirement a shell from the man-of-war, aimed at the Dervishes, burst among the friendlies, who, suddenly scared, fell back in disorder upon the regulars, who had nothing left to do but retreat with all possible speed. The Dervish force maintained its position during the remainder of the day under a heavy cross-fire. At nightfall the Dervishes drew off and made no further attempt to reoccupy the position. The Egyptian loss in this highly unsuccessful sortie was Colonel Tapp and eight men killed and seventeen wounded, without counting the poor friendlies.

After the affair of the 4th March things resumed a comparatively quiet condition for some months. The enemy's cavalry from time to time came within range, and a few shots were exchanged, but nothing serious was attempted on either side. The inaction of the blockading force was doubtless due in great measure to the dissensions which at this period broke out amongst the hostile tribes, some of whom were anxious to take Souakim by assault, whilst others deemed it useless to make the attempt. The result was a series of quarrels, which nearly led to actual fighting.

On the night of the 17th September, however, the aspect of things changed, and without any previous warning a force of some 500 men of the Jaalin and Baggara tribes intrenched themselves at a distance of 1,000 yards from the Water Forts, with the intention of cutting off the water supply, and commenced firing on the town. This was kept up continuously for some time by day and night, and frequent casualties occurred. On the 22nd the enemy placed a gun on the ridge between the Water Forts, and shelled the town until compelled by the fire from the lines to withdraw.

It was now evident that at any moment a determined attempt might be made to capture the town, and reinforcements were urgently called for. In response to the appeal, an additional vessel of war and another battalion were sent to Souakim.

Meanwhile, the besiegers still continued active in the trenches, which they pushed forward to within 600 yards of the defensive works. Their fire began to get exceedingly accurate, though but little harm was done.

Early in November General Grenfell arrived with two divisions of Horse Artillery and six mortars, which it was hoped would make the enemy's position in the trenches untenable. After taking a survey of the situation, Grenfell decided that it was necessary to drive the Arabs from their trenches as soon as a sufficient force should be assembled to make the operation practicable.

Two more Egyptian battalions, marching *viá* Keneh and Kosseir, reached Souakim in the beginning of December. In addition to this reinforcement, and in consequence of doubts being entertained at home as to how far the Egyptian troops could be relied on to face the Soudanese alone and unsupported, the 2nd Battalion of the Scottish Borderers and 100 of the British Mounted Infantry were sent from Cairo. This brought the entire force up to 750 British troops, 2,000 Egyptians, and 2,000 Soudanese.

A reconnaissance made by the cavalry on the 9th December having been forced to retire before a strong body of the enemy's horsemen, it was recognized that the cavalry force ought to be strengthened. In consequence of this, a squadron of the 20th Hussars was sent from Cairo.

Apprehension being still expressed as to the sufficiency of Grenfell's force, half of the 1st Battalion of the Welsh Regiment was also despatched.

By the 18th, the additional troops had all arrived, and everything was prepared for the impending attack.[2] The enemy's trenches were situated between 800 and 900 yards south-west of the two Water Forts, Ghemaiza and Shaata, and extended in a long irregular line. The ground to the west of the northern flank was clear and practicable for cavalry, while to the north of the northern flank was a depression which would enable the troops to form up for attack before coming under fire. This circumstance decided General Grenfell to attack on the north flank, whilst at the same time making a feint on the south flank.

It was arranged to make the attack a surprise, and with this object a naval demonstration was prepared at Mersa Kuwai, eight miles to the north of Souakim, and visible from Osman Digna's camp at Handoub. It was also decided that, previous to the actual attack, the trenches were to be vigorously cannonaded by the guns from the lines, and H.M.S. *Racer*.

At 6 a.m. on the 20th, the artillery fire commenced along the whole line of defence, and the troops marched out to the attack. The 1st Brigade, under Colonel Kitchener, was composed of the 9th, 10th, and 12th Soudanese Battalions; the 2nd Brigade, commanded by Lieutenant-Colonel Holled-Smith, consisted of the 4th Egyptian Battalion and the 11th Soudanese. The Scottish Borderers and the 3rd Egyptian Battalion marched out independently, and took up a position in the rear of the Water Forts at 6.30 a.m.

The two brigades now advanced to a position parallel to the extreme north flank of the enemy's trenches, where they formed front and moved steadily towards the works. When within 600 yards the troops came under fire. The advance was continued without replying until within 200 yards, when the brigades, advancing by quick rushes and opening a heavy fusillade, reached the trenches and captured them at the point of the bayonet. Here the greatest slaughter took place, and

---

2. Much of the narrative of the fight which follows is derived from *Mahdism and the Egyptian Soudan*.

the survivors, attempting to rally on their right flank, were dispersed by the 11th Soudanese, who, in their eagerness to fight, had broken their square and deployed.

During the attack on the trenches, the cavalry remained on the right of the infantry, guarding their flank. The Horse Artillery Battery at this period came up and shelled the redoubt on the south flank of the intrenchments, which had also been exposed to a heavy infantry fire from the Welsh Regiment and the 3rd Egyptian Battalion, which had advanced from their position behind the Water Forts. The two Egyptian brigades now cleared the whole line of intrenchments from north to south, and, with the Mounted Infantry on the north flank, poured steady volleys upon the Dervishes, by this time in full retreat upon Handoub.

An attempt made by the enemy's horsemen to work round the right flank of the attacking line at an earlier stage of the action was defeated by the 20th Hussars, who charged and drove them in disorder in the direction of Hasheen.

By 8 a.m. the whole thing was over, the position was taken, and the bugles sounded "Cease firing." The cavalry, however, continued to pursue the retreating enemy, whilst the rest of the troops intrenched themselves in *zeribas* on the captured position.

The defeat of Osman Digna's followers was most complete. Out of a force of a little over 1,500 men, they had 500 killed either in the fight or during the pursuit. On the other side the loss was insignificant, being only six killed and forty-six wounded. It must be admitted that the Dervish force was vastly inferior in point of numbers to their opponents,[3] who also possessed the advantages of superior skill and discipline. Even making every allowance for these circumstances, it is difficult to account for the trifling loss sustained by the Anglo-Egyptian troops, except on the hypothesis that they never, in point of fact, encountered any real resistance. Another circumstance was that the Dervish force was left to defend their position against greatly superior numbers without being reinforced. This may perhaps be explained by the diversion caused by the naval demonstration made at Mersa Kuwai, and which no doubt caused Osman Digna to imagine that a serious attack at that point was also contemplated.

The effect of Grenfell's victory on the local tribes must have been very great, and the idea naturally was that an immediate advance of the Egyptian troops would be made. This, however, formed no part of

---

3. Grenfell's fighting force amounted to over 5,000 men.

the general's instructions, which were simply to drive the enemy from their trenches, and on no account to advance against Osman Digna at Handoub.

Before leaving, Grenfell approved plans made for the construction of additional forts and redoubts, so as to prevent the enemy being able in future to intrench themselves within range of the town, and his mission being accomplished, he then returned to Cairo.

The British troops were next withdrawn, and Colonel Kitchener, who was left in command of the garrison of 2,000 men, maintained a purely defensive attitude.

CHAPTER 56

The Nile Frontier

At the end of March, 1886, Mohammed-el-Kheir was still at Kermeh, with a considerable force distributed between that place and Dongola. Although there was nothing to show that the contemplated invasion of Egypt had been abandoned, there is reason to believe that the *khalifa's* attention was at this time diverted by events which occurred in Kordofan, where many of the tribes broke out into open revolt against his authority. Probably from this cause, and from troubles which arose on the Abyssinian frontier, no further move in the direction of Egypt had been attempted since the fight at Ginnis.

Seeing no further prospect of fighting, General Stephenson had quitted the Anglo-Egyptian force, which, on the 18th January, was concentrated at Kosheh, and returned to Cairo. It was now determined to fix the frontier of Egypt once more at Wady Halfa, and to this point all the troops and stores were withdrawn by the 15th April, not, however, without the loss of two steamers which were wrecked in trying to pass the Cataract. The British troops were sent back to Assouan, and the defence of Wady Halfa was thenceforth left entirely to the Egyptian soldiers.

As soon as the news reached Omdurman that the Anglo-Egyptian forces had retired there was great rejoicing, and fresh impetus was given to the northward movement. The *khalifa* took steps to reinforce the various Emirs in command, and at same time sent proclamations by the hands of emissaries to Egypt. These proclamations called upon the people of Upper and Lower Egypt "to rise as one man and destroy the Turks and *infidels*." They also announced that "the *khalifa* of the *Mahdi* would shortly take Constantinople, Mecca, and all other parts of the world."

In pursuance of this programme, in the month of June the Dervish forces again began to advance on the Nile, and on the 15th occupied Akasheh once more, whilst a party advanced to Ambigol Wells and destroyed the railway between that point and Akasheh.

In July, the further carrying out of the project of invasion was suspended in consequence of the *khalifa* receiving news that his emir Mohammed-es-Sherif had sustained a most serious defeat in Darfur. For this, and other reasons, he was prevented from sending the reinforcements intended to his followers on the Nile. On 6th July, the commandant, Colonel Smith, reported from Wady Halfa that Mohammed-el-Kheir was retiring to Khartoum, and Wad-en-Nejumi was not coming to Dongola, whilst all the Dervishes were leaving that province and massing at Khartoum. The colonel added that "in this direction all heart appears to have died out of the movement."

In October, however, the situation took another turn, and General Stephenson, in a despatch to the British Government, reported that the force of the enemy in the Dongola district and to the north, including that on the way down from Berber, might be reckoned at from 7,000 to 10,000 fighting men, 1,500 of whom were armed with rifles; 5,000 of the number were already in Dongola and other places to the north. The force possessed two or three steamers and a fleet of native boats. The despatch stated that "a serious advance upon the frontier may be apprehended and should be guarded against."

On the 11th November, Major-General the Hon. R. H. de Montmorency (now Lord Frankfort), commanding the British troops in Alexandria, was sent to take command of the troops at Wady Halfa.

On the 29th, the advanced guard of the enemy, under Nur-el-Kanzi, was at Abkeh, eight miles south of Wady Halfa and was estimated at about 2,000 men. The intention of the Dervishes was not to attack Wady Halfa at first, but to make a descent on the river at Argin, a few miles to the north of Halfa, thus cutting the communications, whilst the main body would besiege that place. To frustrate this design a fortified post was established at Argin, and also at Deberra, ten miles to the north of Halfa.

On the 30th, having first repaired the break which had been made in the railway, Colonel Chermside advanced with the Egyptian Cavalry, Camel Corps, and a battalion of infantry to the enemy's camp at Gemai, which he found deserted, and occupied it.

At daybreak on the 1st December, the main body, consisting of two and a half Egyptian battalions, under General de Montmorency, left

Wady Halfa for Gemai, where it joined Chermside. The latter with his force then pushed on to the enemy's main position at Sarras, thirty miles south of Halfa. The Dervishes retreated across the desert before his advance, and he was only able to come up with a few stragglers. De Montmorency halted the main body at Gemai and went on with his staff to Sarras, where he arrived the same evening. His intention had been to break up Nur-el-Kanzi's force, but finding that the Dervishes refused to make a stand anywhere, after remaining at Sarras two days, the general returned with the whole force to Wady Halfa.

At the end of the year a band of Dervishes again gave trouble, occupying Sarras once more. From this point they threatened Wady Halfa and devastated the neighbouring country. They then retired, but only to return in April, 1887.

On the 27th April it was reported that the Emir Nur-el-Kanzi, with the advance guard of a formidable force, had occupied Sarras and pushed forward an outpost as far as Gemai.

Colonel Chermside, who commanded at Wady Halfa, at once despatched Major Rundle with 200 cavalry and two guns of the Camel Battery *en route* to Sarras, with orders to march by night and to prevent the natives giving notice of the advance of the main body.

The 9th Soudanese Battalion, under Captain Borrow, and the 1st Egyptian Battalion, under Major Lloyd, moved out soon after, and early next morning concentrated at Abkah.

The cavalry were directed to push on, and at daylight to engage the enemy and keep him occupied until the arrival of the infantry. These instructions were ably carried out, and a block-house situated on the hills overlooking Sarras was seized, as well as the railway station and a block of buildings adjacent. This operation was performed under fire from another block-house on the hills to the eastward, held by the enemy's riflemen.

At 5.15 a.m. a cavalry patrol was pushed along the destroyed railway line, but before it had advanced a quarter of a mile it came across the main body of the Dervishes, and retired to the railway station, from behind which a heavy fire was now directed on the enemy's position. Messages were at once sent back to Colonel Chermside, who was by this time advancing with all haste with the remainder of the column.

At 6.30 the two guns of the Camel Battery came up, and, after firing twenty rounds, breached the second block-house, which was then promptly stormed and taken. The guns were then turned on the enemy's main position, which was shelled with satisfactory results.

Chermside, with the infantry, had by this time arrived, and the enemy having evacuated their camp and retired into a narrow ravine about 200 yards from the river, two companies were detached to turn the left of their position, the remainder being retained as support near the railway station.

The cavalry had been previously sent to take part in the turning movement, and succeeded in doing this simultaneously with the front attack which was now made, driving in with considerable loss some fifty Arabs. The enemy's second line, seeing the cavalry in their rear, made no attempt to join the first line, but made straight for the river and escaped. In the meantime, as the two detached companies had neared the enemy's left, the spearmen with wild yells rose from the ravine, and dashed down the bank on them. The shock was so great that the small Egyptian force was compelled to fall back on its supports, nevertheless fighting all the way. They were promptly reinforced, and again advanced. The enemy contested every inch of the ground, fighting hand to hand, and falling almost to a man. Many of them were killed in the river, and others, in attempting to turn the left of the infantry, fell under the fire of the reserve of the fighting line. Here their leader, Nur-el-Kanzi, was killed.

At a quarter to 11 a.m. the enemy's whole position, with ten standards and a considerable quantity of arms and ammunition, was captured. Nearly their whole fighting force of 200 men was annihilated, whilst the Egyptian loss was but twenty-one killed and thirty wounded.

The Dervishes from the first were hopelessly outnumbered, and the fight was principally interesting as being the first action fought by the modern Egyptian soldier independent of British support.

After the action the whole of the Egyptian troops withdrew to Wady Halfa, where for a short time they were allowed to enjoy peace and tranquillity.

This state of things was not destined to last. On the 18th June another descent was made on Sarras, to which its former inhabitants had returned. The Dervishes, on this occasion, contented themselves with plundering the houses, and carrying off the women and any other objects of value they could lay hands on, after which they again retired south.

At a council of *emirs* held at Omdurman early in August, it was decided to resume the advance on Egypt. By the end of the month, a force of 2,000 men, under the Emir Mohammed Ahmed-el-Hashim, left Ferket for Sarras, which, on the 27th September, was again occupied. On the 19th October the Dervish force at Sarras, having been joined by reinforcements from Dongola, amounted to 2,500 men. On the 25th a message was received from Khor-el-Musa, the outpost fort, four and a half miles from Wady Halfa, that a body of 1,000 Dervishes was in sight and marching on Halfa. Colonel Wodehouse, then in command, advanced with the mounted troops and came in view of the enemy watering their camels near the Abka Pass. The 9th Soudanese Regiment had meanwhile taken up a position on the hills three miles south of Khor Musa.

The mounted force, having completed its object, prepared to fall back on the infantry. At this moment, it was sighted by the enemy's cavalry, which, followed by their infantry, approached and opened an ill-directed fire. Wodehouse's camels had difficulty in moving rapidly over the rocky ground, and delayed the retiring force. Taking advantage of this, the Dervishes dashed into the midst of the Egyptian mounted troops, and several hand-to-hand encounters took place. The retirement on the infantry supports was gradually effected, and the 9th Soudanese then checked and eventually drove them back with loss. The Egyptian casualties were one man killed and two wounded.

After this skirmish, the Dervish force retired to Gemai, which it adopted as a permanent outpost, the main body remaining at Sarras. The idea of a direct attack by the Mahdists on Wady Halfa seems to have been for the moment abandoned.

After a time the difficulty of keeping a large body, like that at Sarras, supplied with food became apparent to their leaders. Small-pox, too, broke out in their camp, and numbers of deaths occurred daily. Under these untoward circumstances, and with the continued troubles in Darfur on his hands, the Khalifa was once more obliged to postpone the execution of his project of invasion.

On the 4th June, 1888, the last detachment of British troops, *viz.*, one company of the Welsh Regiment, was withdrawn from Assouan, and the protection of the frontier was intrusted solely to the Egyptian army.

The skirmish in which Colonel Wodehouse defeated the enemy was followed by a series of desultory raids, not only in the vicinity of Wady Halfa, but at many points between that place and Assouan, raids which spread terror in the hearts of the villagers. The Egyptian troops, by establishing posts along the Nile and by patrolling the river by gunboats, did their best to repress and punish these forays. One of the most serious of these was the midnight capture and recapture of the Egyptian fort of Khor Musa on the 29th August, 1888. At this date, the Dervish force was still occupying Sarras, which had become a sort of central point for the raiders, and from this point the attack on the fort was directed. The fort itself was a native house on the river bank converted into a fortification.

In the darkness of the night, some 500 Dervishes arrived close to the fort, and a small party, detached from the main body, crept quietly up under the river bank unperceived until close under the walls. The sentry at the south-western corner, hearing a noise, challenged, and was immediately shot. The corporal of the guard, hearing the report of a rifle and a shout outside the walls, at once opened the western gate on the river, and was shot down. The assailants then streamed through the gate and killed the whole of the guard. The garrison, suddenly roused, turned out, and finding the south end of the fort full of the enemy, fought their way into the northern section.

Here, for two hours, they made a stubborn resistance, firing from every available spot, though without much effect, the enemy being protected by the intervening walls. The defence, thus far, had been conducted by a native major, who, on the first alarm, had telephoned to Wady Halfa for assistance. The news reached Colonel Wodehouse at 11.30 p.m., and, without delay, he despatched reinforcements by train, as well as a detachment of cavalry as a guard. The gunboat *Metemmeh* also got under way, and at 1.30 a.m. opened fire on the portion of the fort held by the enemy.

Lieutenant Machell, who arrived with the troops, posted his men in such a way as to prevent any possibility of the enemy escaping, and with fifty men crept stealthily round, until they arrived at the western gate, which had been left open. Here his men, rapidly forming up, fired a volley straight into the mass of the enemy collected inside. The latter, completely surprised, attempted to climb the wall, but only to be met at the point of the bayonet by the men waiting below to receive them. Machell then dashed in through the gate and, forming his men into a rough line, repulsed the assailants, who, finding their retreat cut off, fought with the energy of despair.

Soon all within the adjoining inclosure were either killed or wounded, and the fort was again in the possession of the Egyptians. The bodies of eighty-five, mostly Baggara and Jaalin Arabs, were found in and around the fort, and many others fell in the line of retreat. The

Egyptian loss was also severe, amounting to nineteen killed and thirty-four wounded.[1]

The reverse sustained by the Dervishes, on this occasion, was a serious discouragement to their leaders, whilst, at the same time, it gave increased confidence to the riverain population.

---

1. The author is indebted to *Mahdism and the Egyptian Soudan* for the greater part of these details.

CHAPTER 57

Wad-En-Nejumi and Collapse of the Invasion

After the repulse of the Dervish attack on Khor Mussa (in August, 1888), the southern frontier of Egypt was left for some time comparatively undisturbed, but, early in 1889, persistent rumours reached Cairo that the long-threatened invasion was at last to come off. This time it was to take place down the left bank of the river, the idea being to avoid Wady Halfa and the other fortified posts, and, by starting from a post opposite Sarras, to strike across the desert to Bimban, a place on the Nile, about twenty-five miles north of Assouan. The military authorities in Cairo, from the first, considered the project impracticable, seeing the difficulties which must arise in conducting an army of 5,000 men (the estimated number of Wad-en-Nejumi's force), with an equal number of camp-followers and without either adequate provisions or means of transport, across a waterless desert, only to fight a battle at the end. Nevertheless, it was deemed advisable to be prepared, and steps were taken to provide for the defence of the villages on the west bank in the neighbourhood of Wady Halfa, where block-houses were constructed at the various points most liable to attack.

The first indication of the forward movement of the Dervishes was in April, 1889, when the Emir Abd-el-Halim reached Sarras with 1,000 men. Wad-en-Nejumi at this period was at Hafir, thirty miles north of Dongola, with about 5,000 more, and with this force he calculated upon taking Egypt with a rush.

On the 5th May, a party of the Dervishes at Sarras, where by reinforcements the enemy's force had been increased to 2,500 men, crossed over to the west bank and set out for the village of Serra (north of Wady Halfa). Here, on the 9th May, they appeared to the number of

600 and commenced pillaging the houses, but, after a stubborn fight with a detachment of the 13th Soudanese, were driven off into the desert, taking with them some of the loot. In the fight, the marauders lost some thirty men, the Egyptian loss being only six wounded.

On the 22nd June, Wad-en-Nejumi reached Sarras, and, crossing the Nile, united his followers with those of Abd-el-Halim, who had already transferred his camp to the western bank. The combined forces, estimated at over 4,000 men, then marched to Matuka,[1] which they reached on the 28th.

To oppose the invaders, a flying column was organized at Wady Halfa. It consisted of two squadrons of cavalry, eight Krupp guns, two companies of the Camel Corps, and the 9th, 10th, and 13th Soudanese Battalions, in all 1,940 men. Colonel Wodehouse, in command, hearing from his scouts that the enemy might march at any moment on Argin, three miles distant, took his measures accordingly. To protect the village of Argin, there was at the south end, standing a little back from the river, a block-house held by a company of the Camel Corps and an infantry detachment.

At the extreme north end, three and a half miles distant, was a large building, the house of the "*omdeh*," or head man of the village, garrisoned by 250 more infantry. In the centre, between the two points, the 13th Soudanese, under Captain Kempster, took up a position in some detached houses, which they placed in a state of defence. All three positions were practically in a line, and, with the exception of the block-houses, on the river. On the east bank, facing the north end of the village, stood the fortified post of Ishkait, with one gun. Such were the dispositions made for the defence of Argin by Colonel Wodehouse, who had at his disposal four stern wheel gunboats, and a number of native craft for transport purposes. With these, his intention was to reinforce with the remainder of his flying column any point of the straggling line of defence which might be threatened.

On the 1st July, after sunset, Wad-en-Nejumi's force left Matuka in a vast crowd in a north-western direction, and making a detour into the desert, were seen at dawn on the 2nd at a distance of two miles from the forts of Wady Halfa. Colonel Wodehouse, sending the cavalry along the west bank, proceeded to Argin by steamer with half the 9th Soudanese and the 10th Battalion. Learning that the mounted troops were in touch with the enemy, he disembarked his men and guns on

---

1. Matuka is situated on the west bank of the Nile, five and a half miles south of Khor Mussa.

the east bank, opposite the centre of the village, and, after sending the gunboats to cruise in front, awaited events. Meanwhile, at 8 a.m., a portion of the cavalry had cut off a few stragglers in the enemy's rear, who were making for the Nile, until, faced by superior numbers, the Egyptians were forced to fall back.

The enemy, continuing the advance, occupied the hills west of Argin, about 5,000 yards from the village, driving in the 2nd Camel Corps, which had been reconnoitring from the southern post.

From a commanding position on the east bank, where Colonel Wodehouse had established his headquarters with two companies of the 9th Battalion and the artillery, the enemy were now perceived planting their banners on the hill-tops to mark their positions, and descending in numbers towards the north end of the village. The artillery immediately opened on them, and the 10th Battalion, under Major Hunter, was sent across in a gunboat to reinforce the central and northern posts. The enemy continued their forward movement in a north-easterly direction, though exposed to a flanking fire from the cavalry and Camel Corps, and at 8.30 a.m. three large parties of them approached within 1,000 yards of the 13th Soudanese in the central post, when the volleys they received from Captain Kempster's battalion forced them to sheer off and take cover behind a long ridge to the left of the position. From this point, they kept up a harassing rifle-fire until, the reinforcements having disembarked near the northern post, the rifles of the 10th Battalion, added to those of the 13th, compelled them to retreat.

Though this first attempt to seize the village failed, small parties of Dervishes continued to come down to the river between Kempster's position and the southern post, and occupying a portion of the houses, opened fire on the cavalry and Camel Corps, inflicting some loss.

Up to this time no serious attempt had been made to push home the attack, and the fighting had been of a somewhat desultory character. The Dervishes occupying the captured houses, continually receiving reinforcements from the main body, about noon placed a gun in position and opened fire on the artillery on the east bank, only to be silenced, however, by the latter after firing a few rounds.

One of the gunboats was then sent to drive the Dervish force out. In this she signally failed, and after a cannonade on both sides lasting for an hour, she had to return with the commander and two men wounded.

In the meantime there was, it seems, a disagreement between the

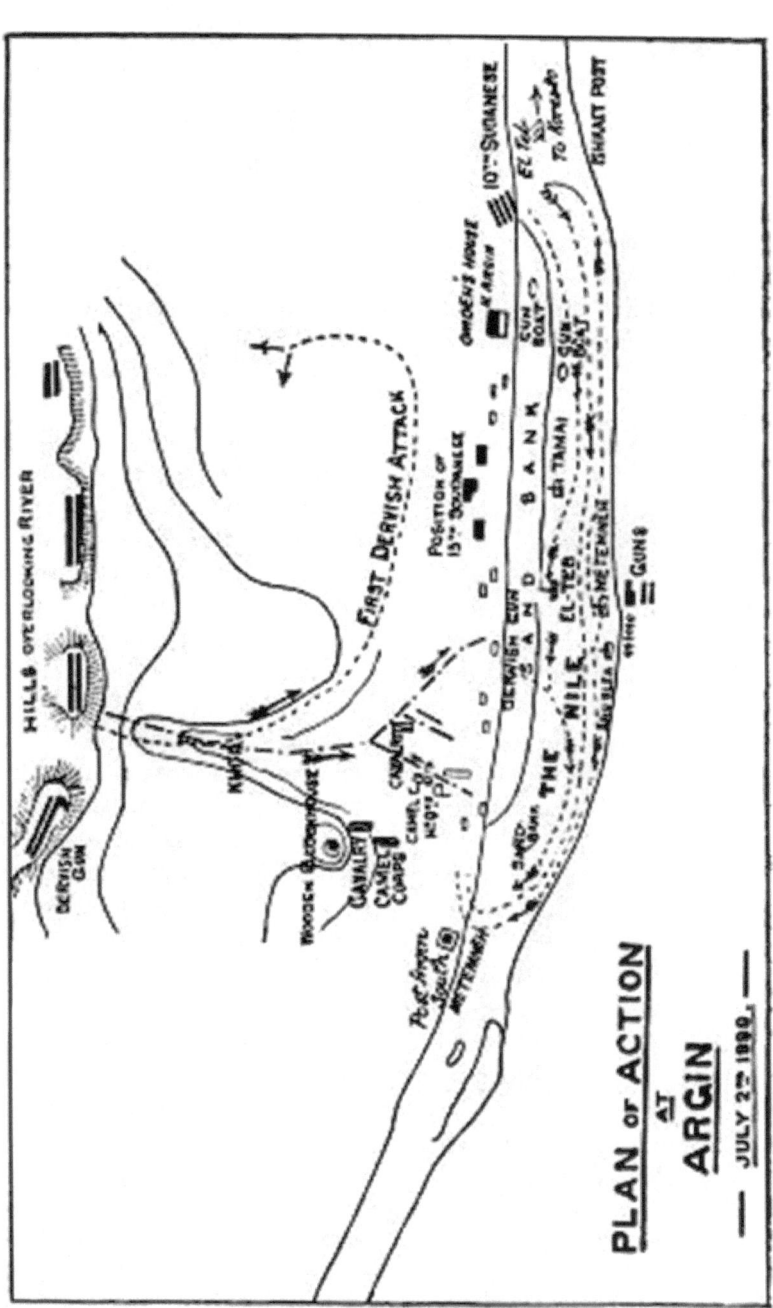

two *emirs*, Abd-el-Halim wishing to capture the village, and Wad-en-Nejumi refusing to consent. The dispute ended in Abd-el-Halim collecting his own men, and as many others as he could prevail upon to follow him. Then he advanced rapidly down a *khor* leading to the centre of the village, his left being protected by riflemen posted on the ridge behind, to which they had been driven in the morning, and his right being covered by the fire from the captured houses.

The movement being perceived from the eastern bank, Colonel Wodehouse again opened fire with his artillery, but the Dervishes nevertheless still came on, and divided into three groups, one of which was directed towards Captain Kempster's position, the second taking the centre of the village, and the third advancing to the southern post.

Seeing the nature of this new attack, Wodehouse promptly ordered the 10th Battalion, then stationed near the northern post, to embark and reinforce the troops to the southern end of the village. Two of the first companies to land from the steamer had hardly advanced any distance before they were charged by the enemy's cavalry and spearmen, and forced back to the water's edge. There, aided by the fire from the gunboat, they maintained their position against heavy odds, until help came in the form of two companies of the 9th Soudanese and some of the Camel Corps.

Major Hunter, the rest of whose battalion had by this time landed, now assumed command of these detachments, and, advancing steadily, drove back the assailants, who frequently charged him, only, however, to be shot down to a man. Seeing a number of horse and spearmen rallying on the left, Hunter now halted his men in a position which, with the adjacent houses right and rear, formed a square, and remained on the defensive.

In the meantime, Captain Kempster, observing the enemy streaming down into the village, kept up a steady fire from his loopholed houses, to which the Dervish riflemen on the ridge replied. Hearing that a gun had been brought into position on the river bank to his left, he went with a party of men to seize it, but, finding that the post was too strongly held, he retired after some fighting, in which he lost seven of his men. The gun was shortly after captured by a party of the 13th Soudanese, though not without a severe hand-to-hand encounter. Wodehouse had now arrived on the west bank, and sent Major Hunter with some companies of the 9th to clear the ground to his left front. Though three times charged by the Dervish spearmen, he succeeded, and drove the enemy back through the *khor* by which they had advanced. Some fifty of the Arabs who remained in the captured houses were surrounded, and the houses being set fire to, the unfortunate inmates had no alternative but to come out and be killed.

This completed the work of the day, and at 6 p.m. Argin was completely cleared of the Dervish force, which left some 900 men killed in and around the village, besides 500 prisoners, men, women, and children.

The Egyptians engaged amounted to less than 2,000 men, and their loss was eleven killed and fifty-nine wounded.

The enemy's camp was found the next day still in its original position, and although Wodehouse, with the object of drawing the Dervishes, placed the 10th Soudanese opposite the entrance to the *khor*, there was no response.

There was now another difference of opinion between Abd-el-Halim and his commander-in-chief, Wad-en-Nejumi, as to the further steps to be taken. The former, wounded in the engagement, and depressed by his recent defeat, wished to retreat to Matuka. To this Nejumi positively refused to consent, and, assembling his entire force, declared that he would never desist from what he regarded as a holy undertaking, and that the weak hearts who wished to retire to their homes might do so. The result was that over 500 of his followers seceded and made their way back to Matuka, whence they subsequently went further south. By this proceeding, Wad-en-Nejumi's force was diminished altogether by nearly 2,000 men.

At midnight on the 4th, the Dervish leader burnt his camp and moved still further north towards Serra.

Wodehouse, not feeling strong enough to attack now, contented himself with keeping in touch with the enemy, and heading them off the river. With the bulk of his flying squadron on the west bank, and his four gunboats in mid-stream, he was able to do this without running unnecessary risk.

The Dervish army continued its onward march, Wodehouse's force descending the river and keeping abreast of Wad-en-Nejumi all the time. Conflicts frequently occurred, and the enemy lost several men from the fire of the steamers, and by desertion.

This state of things continued till the 8th, when the Dervish force was discovered encamped behind the village of Faras. From this point they were shelled out by the artillery on the east bank, and on the 10th they took up a position on the hills two miles above Belanga, and

3,000 yards from the river.

Wodehouse concentrated his column at Belanga village, sending on the Camel Corps to Toski.

After the fight at Argin, it dawned upon the military authorities that if any stop had to be made to the advance of the Dervishes on the Nile, Kitchener's force would have to be supplemented by further troops. Accordingly the 1st and 2nd Egyptian battalions, a mule battery, and two squadrons of cavalry were despatched in hot haste to the front.

On 5th July, the *sirdar*, Sir Francis Grenfell, left Cairo, and a British brigade, under Brigadier-General the Hon. R. H. Montmorency, was moved up the river. It was composed of the 2nd Battalion Royal Irish Rifles, the 1st Battalion of the Welsh Regiment, with a squadron of the 10th Hussars, a detachment of Mounted Infantry, and a mule battery.

These forces were to be concentrated, in the first instance, at Assouan, and thence either to take up a strong position at Bimban, and there await the Dervish attack, or, in case Wad-en-Nejumi's advance should prove less rapid than was expected, to form a second column to join Wodehouse's force, and bring on a decisive action further up the river.

The British cavalry, artillery, and Royal Irish Rifles reached Assouan on 25th July, and the Egyptian troops having also come up, a column of the latter, composed of the 1st and 2nd Battalions of Egyptian Infantry, the 11th Battalion of Soudanese Infantry, with artillery and cavalry, was organized and placed under the command of Colonel Kitchener.

No time was lost in pushing them forward; and on the 19th two of the infantry battalions reached Toski, which they proceeded to put in a state of defence.

In the meantime, Wad-en-Nejumi's force at Belanga had been strengthened by the arrival of 500 men, with 100 camels, under the command of another emir, called Makin-en-Nur. This brought the number of Wad-en-Nejumi's troops up to a total of 3,300 fighting men and 4,000 camp-followers. With these, on the 28th July, he resumed his march to the north.

Pausing for one night at a distance of ten miles from the celebrated temple of Abu Simbel, they continued on their way till the 1st August, when they took up a position in the hills four miles to the south of Toski. On the same day Wodehouse's force, which step by step had

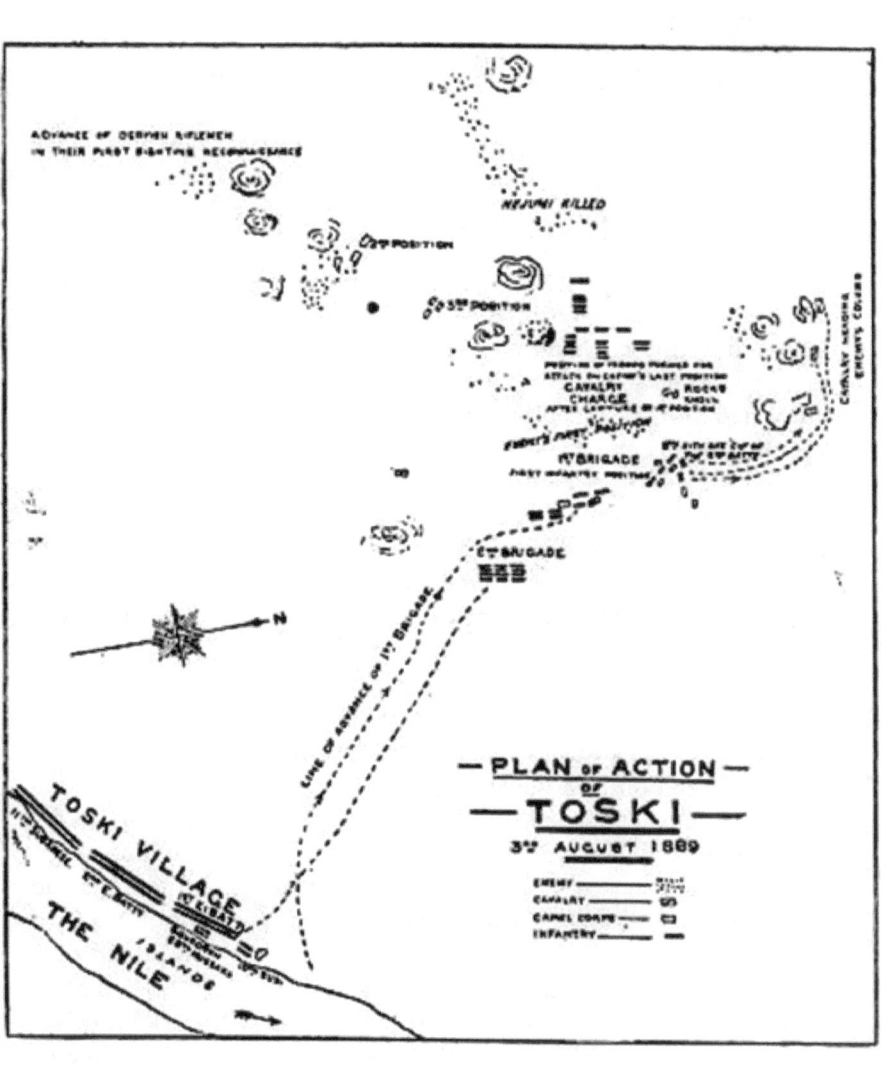

followed Wad-en-Nejumi's movements down the Nile, also reached Toski, where the whole of the Egyptian troops from Assouan, together with General Sir Francis Grenfell and the British cavalry, had concentrated the previous day.

With the exception of the British brigade, the entire Nile field force was now assembled, and General Grenfell took over the command.

On the 3rd the general, receiving information that Wad-en-Nejumi intended to resume his march northward, ordered all the mounted troops to make a reconnaissance in force, the object being to check the Dervish advance and keep Wad-en-Nejumi in his present position until the arrival of the British brigade.

Nejumi's camp was placed on the inner extremity of a range of granite hills, extending from the river inland in a westerly direction and situated about four miles south of Toski. The village consisted of scattered houses covering the land for about three miles from end to end and dotted in places with palm groves; 1,200 yards in the rear the cultivated ground disappeared in the desert which stretched away till closed in by a range of hills at a distance of six miles from the Nile. Behind these hills lay Nejumi's camp.

The desert was intercepted here and there by rocks and boulders of a height and size sufficient to afford cover to considerable numbers of men. Across this desert ground the British and Egyptian mounted troops advanced. They consisted of four squadrons of cavalry and a camel corps. Grenfell himself accompanied the force.

On nearing the enemy's position, it was seen that camels were being loaded up, and everything prepared for an immediate move. It was evident that if this was to be prevented no time was to be lost. The cavalry pushed on, and the enemy's riflemen, advancing in skirmishing order, at once opened fire. This was answered by the dismounted Camel Corps, which, taking up a position on a commanding ridge, poured volleys on the Dervishes, now coming on in considerable numbers. The fire of the latter, however, became too hot, and the Camel Corps, as well as the mounted troops generally, retired to a second position, which they were equally unable to hold. A third position, 900 yards off, was now occupied, and it being on a hill with clear ground intervening, the mounted troops were able for some time to hold their own and keep up a steady fire.

The situation at this moment was such that orders were sent back to bring up the 1st Brigade from Toski. At 8.30, before there was time for the reinforcements to arrive, the Arab spearmen in force emerged from two ravines and steadily advanced on the position. A further retirement then became necessary, and the troops took up a position at the foot of a conical hill two miles from Toski, where they were joined by two guns of the Horse Battery. At 9 a.m. the guns opened fire on the advancing column, which now, followed by a mass of camp-followers and baggage animals, turned to its left and marched steadily across the Egyptian front.

It then became evident that Wad-en-Nejumi did not mean fighting, and that his object was simply to get away, and continue his advance northward. To prevent this, which would have frustrated the whole object of the reconnaissance, Grenfell immediately sent off for the 2nd Brigade, and whilst the two guns continued their fire Colonel Kitchener, with the mounted troops, made a detour to the north and checked Nejumi's further advance. Finding that his march was opposed, the *emir* determined to accept battle, and placed his followers upon some semi-detached hills to the west of the ground occupied by the mounted troops.

The tops of these hills were by this time planted with standards and lined with riflemen, the spearmen being kept out of sight. The camp-followers and transport animals were placed in a temporary camp behind the hills in front.

In the meantime, the 1st Brigade, under Major Hunter, together with the artillery, had come up unseen under the cover of some rising ground, and stationed themselves on an eminence 800 yards distant from and exactly opposite to the enemy's position. The 2nd Brigade, arriving shortly after, was kept as a support on the left rear of the 1st.

The 1st Brigade then opened fire all along its front. This was kept up and replied to for half an hour. Colonel Wodehouse, who was in command of the infantry division, then proceeded to extend his line by moving the 9th Soudanese to the right with a view to enfilading the enemy's left flank. After the battalion had moved only 500 yards it was halted on a number of men on the first hill being observed preparing to charge. At this moment, emerging from their cover, on they came with wild cries, and charged down towards the battalion. The Egyptians never wavered, and maintaining their formation, by a steady fire drove the enemy back with a loss of some 150 of their men. The battalion, supported by a company of the 2nd Egyptian Regiment, then advanced and took possession of the hill, in spite of frequent isolated charges made by its defenders.

Under cover of a heavy cannonade kept up by the artillery, the whole line of troops then advanced towards the various points held by the enemy. On arriving in front of Wad-en-Nejumi's central position, another attempt was made to charge. It was directed this time against the 10th Soudanese, which, in combination with the 9th, had seized a ridge connecting two of the hills. The charge, however, collapsed under the well-directed volleys of the 10th.

During this period the 13th Battalion, supported by the 1st Egyptian, had been operating on a detached hill to the left and suffering from an enfilading fire from some concealed riflemen. The battalion had already lost seventy of its men, when General Grenfell ordered the hill to be stormed. The two battalions together then advanced, and, after a severe hand-to-hand fight with the Dervish spearmen, swarmed up the hill and captured the position.

Repeated attempts were made to retake the lost ground, and even after the Egyptian troops had gained the summit of the hill, small bodies of the enemy collected on the off side and charged upwards with the greatest determination. These attempts only ended when the last of the brave assailants was shot dead only a few paces in front of the Egyptian line.

Only one hill out of those chosen by Nejumi for his position was now held by the enemy, and this was soon stormed and carried at the point of the bayonet by the united 9th, 10th, and 13th Soudanese Battalions. By this operation, which was achieved at 11.30 a.m., the whole of the enemy's position was taken, and the two guns of the Horse Battery were occupied in shelling a defeated foe, in full retreat.

At this period, Wad-en-Nejumi personally made an heroic effort to rally his dispersed followers, and the cavalry, which, during the fight, had been stationed in the rear of the infantry, had to be sent to stop the movement. The Egyptian squadrons led the charge, followed by the British Hussars, and, dashing into the midst of such of the enemy as were collected, completed the rout. The Camel Corps assisted in the final fight by a carefully directed fire on the enemy's flank, and in a few minutes not an Arab was to be seen on the plain.

There was, however, reason to believe that Nejumi, so far from fleeing, had, with his defeated band, taken up a new position in the temporary camp formed for his camp-followers and baggage behind the hills. Therefore Grenfell, desirous of following up at once the advantage gained, at noon directed a general advance in that direction. The troops moved forward with the 11th Soudanese and 1st and 2nd

Egyptian Battalions in front, and the 2nd Brigade in support. The artillery shelled the enemy's position as the troops advanced. The resistance encountered was but trifling, the foe, by this time, being in full retreat, leaving his camp, with a large collection of arms and military accoutrements, to fall into the hands of the victors. The cavalry then pursued the defeated Dervishes for over two miles, and captured a great number of prisoners, and amongst them several women and children.

At the moment when the fighting was deemed finished, a loaded camel, surrounded by about forty men, was observed following the line of retreat, and was fired upon by a troop of cavalry. The camel and most of the men fell apparently killed. The cavalry then approached and summoned the survivors to surrender. This was met by the Arabs springing to their feet and making a charge on the cavalry, in which all the Dervish warriors were killed except one, who escaped on a stray horse. The load carried on the camel turned out to be the body of the brave Wad-en-Nejumi, who, though badly wounded early in the day, had refused to fly, and devoted his last moments to an heroic attempt to rally his dispersed followers.[2]

The defeat amounted practically to annihilation, and Wad-en-Nejumi's force as an army ceased to exist. On the day of the fight and during the three days following 4,000 prisoners were taken, and the enemy's loss in killed was estimated at over 1,200. The Egyptian loss was but 25 killed and 140 wounded.

In this, as in many of the other fights, it was simply the same old story: on the one side a mass of reckless, fanatical, and courageous savages; on the other trained and disciplined troops, acting under the orders of a skilful general. In a conflict conducted under such conditions, there could be but one result, and nothing remains but to regret the appalling loss of life which formed one of its inevitable concomitants.

On the 9th August, as soon as arrangements had been made for the disposal of the numerous prisoners, the troops returned to Assouan, and the Nile field force was distributed amongst the various points where it was deemed necessary to retain garrisons. The British brigade, which had not succeeded in arriving in time to participate in the fight, was gradually moved down to Cairo.

The victory at Toski marked the turning point in the invasion,

---

2. Alongside the camel was found the one-year-old child of the dead chief. The infant was duly cared for, and became an intelligent and well educated boy in Cairo.

and was a shock to the cause of Mahdism which it took years to recover. The reinforcements, which were on their way down the Nile to join Nejumi, beat an immediate retreat, and all further operations for the invasion of Egypt were suspended. Numerous deserters from the Dervish force, as well as hundreds of destitute refugees, crowded into Wady Halfa, and were provided with relief. Though there was no longer any talk of invasion, as a protection for the frontier a battalion of Egyptian infantry reoccupied and held Sarras, and peace and tranquillity now reigned once more.

CHAPTER 58

The Eastern Soudan Again

In January, 1889, things at Souakim had drifted back pretty much into the same old groove, and the petty attacks of Osman Digna's followers were constantly renewed. The enemy's mounted men used, time after time, to approach the outlying forts, fire a few shots, and then retire.

The military authorities, not feeling themselves equal to the task of clearing the neighbourhood of the hostile Arabs, hit upon the expedient of inviting the tribes suspected of being unfriendly to the Mahdist cause to do so. The invitation, which took the form of a proclamation issued by General Grenfell, was not favourably responded to. The attitude of the tribes was one of expectancy, and all the *sheikhs* who responded stated pretty much the same thing, namely, that they would come in and help as soon as Osman Digna's power should be broken, and that they were perfectly willing to assist in cutting off stragglers, but they declined for the present to compromise themselves further.

On the other hand, Osman Digna was not more successful in inducing the tribes to flock to his standard. On the 11th February, he burnt his camp at Handoub, and transported the remainder of his forces to Tokar, which now became the central point of rebel authority in the Eastern Soudan.

After Osman's departure, matters around Souakim visibly improved. The tribes brought in cattle frequently, a little trade sprang up, and things generally wore a more peaceful aspect.

By the month of August, the Haddendowa and Amarar tribes combined against the Baggara, who were Osman's chief allies, and, obtaining assistance, in money and food, from the Souakim authorities, advanced upon Sinkat, intending, if successful there, to attack Osman's position at Tokar. The united warriors, 700 strong, succeeded only in capturing some cattle at the former place, after which, meeting with a superior force, they were compelled to fall back on Tamanieb. No further assistance being given them, they then broke up and dispersed.

On the 7th October, Osman Digna departed from Tokar to attend a council held by the *khalifa* at Omdurman, in consequence of the defeat and death of Wad-en-Nejumi, which had meanwhile taken place at the fight at Toski.

In December, Osman left Omdurman, and proceeded by way of Gedaref and Kassala with the object of gathering followers with whom to renew the struggle in the Tokar district.

With great difficulty, owing to tribal dissensions, he after some months got together a force of 10,000, including women and children, which he conducted to the scene of his former exploits. Owing, however, to the grain supply from Souakim, on which he had relied for his requirements, being suddenly stopped, he had a difficulty in feeding his new levies. The result was that many of them left him and went in search of food and shelter elsewhere.

In November, 1890, Osman Digna was again at Tokar with a greatly reduced force, estimated indeed at only 1,000 men, whilst at Handoub but about 150 of his followers remained. From this last point they made occasional raids in the neighbourhood of Souakim, harassing the friendly tribes, and generally making things unpleasant so far as the limited numbers of the aggressors would allow.

The misery and starvation of the well-disposed inhabitants round Souakim at this time was intense, owing to the gates of the town being closed, and a cordon being drawn round the forts as a measure of precaution against the cholera, thus stopping all trade. The Haddendowa, Beni-Amer, and Amarar tribes implored the government to assist them in casting off the Dervish yoke.

This was the position when the moment was deemed favourable for striking a final blow at Osman Digna, taking Tokar, and pacifying the Eastern Soudan.

In January, 1891, the situation became all the more favourable for these operations inasmuch as Osman Digna, towards the end of the month, again left Tokar, taking with him many of his already reduced garrison.

On 27th January, Colonel Holled-Smith, then in command of the troops at Souakim, advanced to Handoub with the Egyptian cavalry and the 11th and 12th Battalions of Soudanese Infantry, and, after a short engagement, captured and occupied the place. Over forty of the

Dervishes fell in the fight, and the remainder dispersed and fled to the hills.

Handoub having fallen, the attack on Tokar was next taken in hand.

For this purpose, on the 8th February, an expeditionary force under Colonel Holled-Smith was formed. With the addition of some companies of the 1st Egyptian Battalion, which joined a few days later, it consisted of nearly 2,000 men, and was composed of 180 cavalry, two large Krupp guns, two mountain guns, and four battalions of infantry, *viz*., the 1st and 4th Egyptian and the 11th and 12th Soudanese. Following the course pursued in all the former campaigns, the force was sent by sea to Trinkitat, which was selected as the base of operations. At the same time a force of 500 friendly natives was raised and sent by land towards Temerin, to intercept the retreat of the Tokar garrison if opportunity offered.

By the 15th, the expeditionary troops had reached Trinkitat, and on the morning of the following day the advance, directed in the first instance towards the wells of El Teb, commenced. The line of march led over the site of General Baker's defeat exactly seven years before, and heaps of white bones still marked the spot. At 3 p.m., the column reached the wells without encountering any resistance. Here the troops bivouacked, every precaution being taken to guard against a surprise. On the 18th, a severe sand-storm prevented the march being resumed, and the troops remained in camp. In the interval news was received that Osman Digna was now at a place called Afafit, a village a mile and a half beyond the ruined town of Tokar, and had with him considerable reinforcements.

On the 19th, at daylight, the column, after leaving a small garrison at El Teb, advanced upon Tokar. The cavalry in advance first seized and occupied the ruined *Mamourieh* or government buildings, and then at 10 a.m. the infantry were brought up to the north-eastern side of the village, which consisted merely of crumbling walls. Scarcely was the place reached when the enemy were seen advancing through the bush surrounding the *Mamourieh*. There was no time to be lost, and the infantry moved up at the double and formed a semi-circular line of defence, the 4th Battalion lining the ruined buildings on the right, the 11th Battalion those on the left, whilst the 12th Battalion held those in the centre of the position. So rapidly was the attack developed that some Dervishes had actually taken possession of some of the ruins on the left flank of the Egyptian position before the 11th Battalion had taken up the defence assigned to them. The main body of the enemy, now only fifty yards from the front rank of the troops, proceeded to extend to the right and left to envelop the entire position.

Firing began along the whole line as the enemy came on. The bulk of their force was directed against the 12th Battalion, their attack being pushed home with the usual dash and fearlessness. The troops, however, stood their ground, and did not yield an inch throughout the whole line. Their firing settled down to steady volleys, which quickly began to check the onward rush. As soon as this was perceived, the 11th Battalion, moving from the left, advanced into the bush and cleared it of the attacking force, taking, at the point of the bayonet, some ruins occupied in front. The 11th then halted at a commanding point to the south-east of the original position. The 4th Battalion remained in position on the right of the line, and, with the transport escort column, protected the rear, which at one time was seriously threatened by the enemy's horsemen.

The Dervishes, after the charge of the 11th Battalion, at once commenced to retreat, followed closely by the cavalry, which, advancing into the bush on the right, found some open ground, where they did great execution.

This completed the rout of the Dervish attacking column, which gradually disappeared to the south in the direction of Temerin.

The troops then formed up on the high ground occupied by the 11th Battalion and halted for a rest prior to advancing on the Dervish headquarters at the village of Afafit. It was reported that Afafit was occupied in force, but as the troops advanced the enemy, who had occupied some intervening sand hills, hurriedly retreated, and at 4 p.m. the village was entered by the cavalry, the inhabitants coming out in numbers and welcoming the troops with many expressions of joy.

The strength of the Dervish force was estimated at 4,000, but this included 2,000 men whom Osman Digna kept in reserve, and who never came into the fight at all. The enemy's loss was put at as high a figure as 700 men, and it must have been considerable even allowing for bad shooting, no less than 60,000 cartridges having been fired away by the Egyptian force. This last lost Captain Barrow, of the South Lancashire Regiment, and nine men killed, besides forty-eight wounded.

On the morning of the following day it was ascertained by a cavalry reconnaissance that Osman Digna, deserted by all but 300 followers, had passed through Temerin, going off in the direction of Kassala.

Communication by land was now established with Souakim, and on the 22nd Afafit was visited by General Grenfell, who reviewed the troops and congratulated them on their victory of the 19th.[1]

On the 2nd March the expeditionary force was broken up, and after leaving garrisons at Afafit, El Teb, and Trinkitat, the rest of the troops returned in triumph to Souakim.

Disturbances in the Eastern Soudan then for a while ceased; a general amnesty was proclaimed; the tribes hastened to offer assurances of their loyalty; trade revived; and steps were taken to resume the cultivation of the fertile lands in the Tokar district.

The concluding events in the Eastern Soudan, though not chronologically in their place in the present chapter, are here inserted to avoid recurring to the subject. They may be briefly stated as follows:—

In 1892 the indefatigable Osman Digna once more appeared in the neighbourhood of Souakim, with a force varying in number from time to time. His principal object was to raid the local Arabs. In the summer of that year he attacked the Egyptian post established at Temerin, but was driven off by Major Hunter, with a loss of seventy men. This and other attempts led to the strengthening of the Souakim garrison, and Osman made no further attempts.

Although in 1893 Osman was reported to have received considerable reinforcements and to be contemplating a fresh advance, it did not come off.

After a long interval, in 1895, Osman, from his position in the hills, made a raid into the now cultivated lands of the Tokar delta.

On the 15th April, 1896, an Egyptian force of 1,000 officers and men, under Colonel Lloyd, left Souakim to co-operate with a detachment of 250 soldiers, under Major Sidney, from Tokar, in supporting a party of friendly Arabs, headed by a sheikh called Omar Tita, at Horasab, in the Erkowit Hills, where Osman Digna and a number of Dervishes had established themselves.

The column, which marched in square formation, arrived at the Teroi Wells in the afternoon, having covered a distance of nineteen miles. Here the force bivouacked, and the animals were watered.

The cavalry, under Captain Fenwick, was then ordered to reconnoitre and to endeavour to establish touch with the Tokar force and inform the commanding officer that the Souakim force would remain where it was for the night, so as to enable the Tokar contingent to join.

---

1. This engagement, which took place at Tokar, for some unknown reason is referred to by some writers as the Battle of Afafit.

It had been arranged previously with Omar Tita that he should hold the heights and the pass of Khor Wintri while the two Egyptian forces concentrated.

While the cavalry were proceeding towards the Khor Wintri they were suddenly attacked by a body of 200 horsemen, supported by a large force on foot. The men were ordered to trot, but it was soon seen that the Dervishes were gaining upon them. The reconnoitring party then galloped towards the open country. Some, becoming entangled in the bush, fell off their horses and were speared. Fenwick, with thirty-eight officers and men, retired to the left flank and ascended a hillock, where they kept the enemy off by firing volleys all night. The Dervishes made four attempts to storm the hill, but were on each occasion repulsed.

Meanwhile an officer and thirty-two men rode through the scrub and returned to Teroi Wells. Colonel Lloyd immediately despatched two volunteers from the mounted police to endeavour to discover the whereabouts of Captain Fenwick and the Tokar force, but both men were killed by the Dervishes.

On the morning of the 16th the Dervishes, hearing heavy firing during the night from the Khor Wintri, drew off, and Captain Fenwick's party was then able to make its way back to Teroi Wells and rejoin the force there.

The return of Captain Fenwick's reconnoitring party to the square at Teroi Wells was a great relief to the members of the column, who had entertained the gravest fears for their safety.

The cavalry having rested, the column left Teroi Wells and moved towards the Khor Wintri to join the Tokar force. Owing to the thickness of the bush and the roughness of the country, the troops were obliged to proceed on foot. The camels were not required, and the food and reserve ammunition were sent on towards the hills held by Omar Tita's men. The two forces joined in the evening at the Khor Wintri, eight miles from the bivouac at Teroi Wells.

The column, on arriving at the Khor Wintri, found Major Sidney there holding the wells, the Dervishes with whom he was in touch having retreated up the pass.

Major Sidney reported that he had arrived at the Khor Wintri on the previous afternoon and surprised the Dervishes there. On the approach of his force a party of Dervishes moved up the hill to the right, and Sidney sent a party up the hill to check them. The remainder then formed into square and opened fire upon the main body of the Dervishes, who were advancing and who numbered about 90 horsemen and 500 spearmen. The latter attempted to turn the right flank and rear by ascending the mountains, but in each instance they were met by a heavy fire and finally retreated up the pass, losing about thirty killed and many wounded. Only three Soudanese soldiers were wounded.

Shortly after the junction of the Souakim and Tokar forces Omar Tita arrived in camp. He reported that his tribesmen had abandoned the heights and pass to the enemy.

It was decided that the column should return to Souakim on the following day, the enemy having retreated bodily towards Horasab. The column bivouacked again at Teroi Wells on the 17th, and arrived at Souakim on the 18th, where it was enthusiastically welcomed by the inhabitants.

The effect of this engagement was that demoralization set in at Osman Digna's camp. It was known that he had lost over 100 killed and about the same number wounded. Nevertheless, by making a considerable detour the remainder of his fighting force managed to reach Horasab, whence they dispersed among the hills. Thus ended the last fight in the neighbourhood of Souakim.

The story has now arrived at the point at which the reconquest of Dongola was decided upon. For this undertaking every available Egyptian soldier was required, and the Souakim troops having to be withdrawn, a strong Indian contingent was once more despatched to protect Souakim.

The force, which arrived on the 30th May, consisted of 4,000 men, made up of the 26th Bengal Infantry, the 35th Sikhs, the 1st Bombay Lancers, the 5th Bombay Mountain Battery, and two Maxim guns, the whole under the command of Colonel Egerton.

The duty of the Indian Contingent was simply to act as a garrison for Souakim, where they remained, but saw no fighting.

A question as to whether the expenses of the Indian troops should be borne by the taxpayers of the United Kingdom or be thrown on the Indian Budget was raised soon after the Indian Contingent reached Souakim. The matter was warmly discussed in the House of Commons on the 6th July. Of the merits of the case there could hardly be a doubt. The force was sent to Egypt in order to set free the Souakim garrison which was required for the Dongola expedition, a matter in which India had not the remotest interest. It could not be pretended that the *khalifa* was in any way a source of danger to the Suez Canal, the great highway to India, or that he threatened the interests of that dependency in the slightest degree. Nevertheless on a division, by 252 votes to 106, the House decided that India was to bear the burden (about £5,000 a month), England paying only the expenses of the transport of the troops, a conclusion so obviously unjust that it shocked the national conscience, and for a time seriously endangered the popularity of Lord Salisbury's Government.

Chapter 59

In Lower Egypt

Whilst wars and rumours of wars prevailed on her frontiers, Egypt, internally, was enjoying peace and prosperity.

So completely tranquil was the condition of the country in January, 1887, that a considerable reduction in the strength of the Army of Occupation was decided on. This was effected gradually until the whole force numbered only 3,500 men. This had a double advantage. It not only set free the troops for service elsewhere, but it relieved Egypt from the burden of contributing to their support.[1]

The financial tension having been relieved by the London Convention of 1885, various reforms were taken in hand, and made steady, if not rapid, progress.

Amongst them the use of the "*courbache*" was abolished, and in criminal cases the punishment of imprisonment substituted—a humane and beneficent change, which nevertheless added to the difficulty of collecting the revenue, and led to a considerable increase of crime.

The *khedive*, Tewfik Pasha, was himself a moderate but sincere reformer. He quite realized that the state of things which under Ismail's rule had brought the country to the verge of ruin could not be continued, and gave a loyal support to his European advisers. His Prime Minister, Nubar Pasha, who had replaced Cherif in January, 1884, when the latter could not be brought to accept British advice with regard to the abandonment of the Soudan, was not unfavourable to the English, and for some time found himself able to work in harmony with the various British officials who were now introduced into the government service.

---
1. Egypt's contribution to the expenses of the Army of Occupation at this period amounted to £200,000 *per annum*.

Unfortunately certain elements existed which were certain to produce friction sooner or later. Nubar Pasha was a statesman of too much ability and with too important a history to be able for any great length of time to quietly sit down and play a secondary part. Hence he gradually grew restive under the advice which England from time to time felt bound to tender to him. He fell out first with Sir Colin Scott Moncrieff, the head of the Irrigation Department, then with Sir Edgar Vincent, the financial adviser, and finally with Sir Evelyn Baring himself.

In June, 1888, Nubar was dismissed on a personal question which arose between him and the *khedive*, and replaced by Riaz Pasha, who had been sulking in retirement ever since he was denied the pleasure of hanging Arabi in 1882.

Under Riaz's administration the work of reform continued. More particularly was this the case in the departments relating to finance and irrigation. Sir Edgar Vincent conferred a great benefit on the population by substituting a simple and convenient currency for the chaos of coins of all metals and all currencies which had for many years been in circulation.[2]

Extensive changes were introduced in the matter of irrigation. The work upon the "Barrage," which regulates the water supply of the Delta, was completed in 1890. A proper system of inspection was established, and the native cultivator was no longer compelled to rely upon the goodwill of a corrupt Egyptian engineer for the water for his lands.

The result was that increased areas of land were brought into cultivation, and the cotton crop in 1890-91 was nearly double that of the average for previous years.

The abolition of the ruinous system of forced labour for the execution of public works, begun in the days of Nubar, was completed during Riaz's term of office, notwithstanding the persistent obstacles put in the way by France. In 1890 the Egyptian finances had made such a recovery, and Egyptian stock stood so high, that it was found possible to convert the Privileged Debt and to reduce the interest from 5 to 3½ *per cent*. The net result of this and of the conversion of the Daira Loan was to relieve the Budget by £E.314,000 a year.

The English, whilst all these improvements were being made, had

---

2. The new coins, although "made in Germany," had impressed on them in Arabic characters the words "struck in Cairo," with the year of the *sultan's* reign in which they were made superadded.

not become more popular in Egypt, but their presence began to be tolerated by the natives, who could not but see, though they would not acknowledge, the benefits which it secured to them.[3]

In the civil service the Egyptian functionaries commenced to know their British teachers, and to learn that as long as the former did their duty they would be supported against the tyranny or caprice of their official chiefs, and a feeling of security such as had never been known before was the result.

In 1889 the question of reforming the native courts of justice had been considered. Sir Evelyn Baring's proposal was to strengthen them by increasing the number of European judges. Riaz, on the contrary, was not too favourable to the appointment of foreigners, but he had to give way, and in November, 1889, two additional Englishmen had been nominated to the Court of Appeal, making in all three English and three Belgian judges. This, however, did not effect all that was required, and in the spring of 1890 Mr. (afterwards Sir John) Scott, a judge of the High Court of Bombay, with extensive Indian as well as Egyptian experience, was appointed temporary "judicial adviser" to the government.

Scott drew up a report, pointing out the defects of the existing system, and, above all, the necessity for a further improvement in the *personnel* of the courts. Riaz Pasha strenuously opposed this, and his nominee Fakri Pasha, Minister of Justice, wrote a counter-report, condemning all the changes which Scott had recommended. Sir Evelyn Baring promptly recognized which side was in the right, and that the question was whether there was to be a reform or not. Scott's proposals were accepted, and his appointment was made permanent, so as to enable him to superintend the carrying of them into execution. Riaz Pasha had to accept the inevitable, which he did with a bad grace, and in May, 1891, he resigned.

Riaz was succeeded by Mustapha Pasha Fehmi, the present Prime Minister, the first Egyptian Premier really in sympathy with the English, with whom he from the first has cordially co-operated. So effec-

---

3. An instance of this occurred to the author personally. On asking a native landowner if, under the new regime, his taxes were not lighter, and were not collected at a more convenient season than formerly, he replied in the affirmative. Interrogated further if his water supply was not more regular, and the increase of his crops was not also greater than before, he answered with an emphatic "Yes." When, however, the question was put to him, "To whom do you attribute these changes for the better?" the man simply replied, "'Tis the will of *Allah*."

tual had been the changes made in the administration of the finances, that, notwithstanding a considerable remission of the land tax, the revenue of the country had risen from £E.9,574,000 in 1886, the first year in which the benefit of "The London Convention" had been felt, to £E.10,539,460[4] in 1891, with a large surplus over expenditure, and besides this reserve funds amounting to £E.2,811,000 had been created.

Progress was also made in the work of putting down the slave trade, and in 1891 Sir Evelyn Baring was able to write that the traffic was practically extinguished. As a commentary upon this it may be mentioned that a few months later no less a personage than Ali Pasha Cherif, a large landed proprietor and the President of the National Assembly, was convicted in the native courts of law of, and sentenced to imprisonment for, being personally concerned in the purchase of slaves for his household.

Whilst events in Egypt were thus progressing the country sustained a severe loss in the death of the *khedive*, Tewfik Pasha, which took place after a short illness at Helouan, on the 7th January, 1892. His Highness' eldest son, Prince Abbas Pasha Hilmy, the present *khedive*, then seventeen years of age, succeeded to the throne of Egypt in virtue of the Imperial *firman* of the 8th June, 1873.

Upon the new *khedive's* arrival from Vienna, where he was completing his studies, he received a warm welcome, and by his subsequent acts created an excellent impression on all classes of society.

He at once confirmed the former ministers in power and lent his aid to the work of reform.

Although on the death of Tewfik the new *khedive* was *de jure* as well as *de facto* the ruler of Egypt, his recognition by an Imperial *firman* from the *Porte* was a formality which nevertheless had to be observed. The preparation of this important document was known to have been completed at Constantinople, and an envoy was told off to bring it to Egypt. Still for some time it did not come. To do honour to the occasion a division of the British Mediterranean fleet was despatched to Alexandria. It did not, however, please the *sultan* that his envoy should be thus received, and the official's departure from time to time was postponed. Then began a little game of "hide and seek."

It was given out that the *firman* would not be sent until after the approaching fast of "*Ramadan*," and the British admiral, as if tired of waiting, withdrew his ships and put to sea. No sooner was this known

---

4. The above figures represent ordinary receipts only.

to the *sultan* than the Imperial yacht conveying the envoy was despatched in hot haste to Egypt. The admiral, however, was not to be baffled. He had only steamed a hundred miles or so from land, and, with his ships in extended order, awaited the return of a fast vessel which he sent to Suda Bay for news. On her return with intelligence that the envoy had started, the fleet steamed slowly back to the coast of Egypt, where, on the arrival of the Turkish yacht, the stately ironclads, after saluting, formed in two lines dressed in colours, and escorted her into the harbour of Alexandria.

When the *firman* reached Cairo it somehow leaked out that it differed in important particulars from what it ought to have been, and before the precious document, for which £E.6,000 was paid, was read on 14th April, the mistake had to be put right by telegraphic communication with the *Porte*.

In June, 1892, the great services rendered by Sir Evelyn Baring in connection with Egypt received their recognition in the shape of a peerage which was conferred on the distinguished Minister Plenipotentiary and diplomatic agent for Great Britain in Cairo. Honours were never better deserved. Writing of Lord Cromer, as the new peer must henceforth be called, an eminent author (Sir Alfred Milner), more than once quoted in this book, says:—

> It would be difficult to overestimate what the work of England in Egypt owes to the sagacity, fortitude, and patience of the British Minister. His mental and moral equipment, very remarkable in any case, was peculiarly suited to the very peculiar circumstances in which he found himself placed. Perhaps the most striking feature about him has been a singular combination of strength and forbearance. And he needed both these qualities in an exceptional degree. On one side of him were the English officials, zealous about their work, fretting at the obstruction which met them at every turn; on the other side were the native authorities, new to our methods, hating to be driven, and keen to resent the appearance of English diplomatic pressure.
>
> The former were often inclined to grumble with him for interfering too little; the latter were no less prone to complain of his interfering too much. What a task was his to steer an even keel between meddlesomeness and inactivity! Yet how seldom has he failed to hit the right mean. Slowly but surely he has carried

his main points, and he has carried them without needlessly overriding native authority or pushing his own personality into the foreground. He has realized that the essence of our policy is to help the Egyptians to work out as far as possible their own salvation. . . . The contrast between Egypt of today, (as at time of first publication), and Egypt as he found it, the enhanced reputation of England in matters Egyptian, are the measure of the signal services he has rendered alike to his own country and to the country where he has laid the foundations of a lasting fame.

In January, 1893, an incident occurred in Cairo which attracted an amount of attention somewhat out of proportion to its real importance. The Prime Minister, Mustapha Pasha Fehmi, became so ill that his life was despaired of. The *khedive* thereupon informed Lord Cromer of his desire to appoint another Egyptian statesman, Tigrane Pasha, in Mustapha's place. This was discouraged by the British representative on the ground that Tigrane was a Christian. The next thing was that the *khedive* summarily dismissed Mustapha and three of his colleagues, and nominated Fakri Pasha, the late Minister of Justice, as Premier. Fakri had been dismissed shortly before, on Lord Cromer's suggestion, on account of his opposition to judicial reform.

At the same time Lord Cromer was informed that what was taking place was to be followed by a wholesale dismissal of English officials, a report, however, which the *khedive* has always denied. On the matter being telegraphed to Lord Rosebery, then British Foreign Secretary, His Lordship took the matter seriously and directed Lord Cromer to protest, and to inform the *khedive* that Her Majesty's Government expected to be consulted in such matters as a change of ministry, and that the appointment of Fakri could not be sanctioned.

The *khedive*, on this being pointed out to him, consented to cancel the appointment objected to, and to nominate Riaz Pasha as the substitute to Mustapha, which was accepted. The *khedive*'s nominations to the other vacant posts were not found fault with, and there the matter would have ended had not symptoms of an apparent anti-English feeling shown themselves in the capital, and in the tone of the native press generally. In consequence of this, it was determined to strengthen the Army of Occupation, then numbering only 3,000 men, by two additional battalions, which were promptly despatched to Egypt.

The amusing part of the incident was the interview which took place between Lord Rosebery and the French Ambassador on the 18th January, when the latter stated that he had called to protest against what he termed a high-handed proceeding which had occurred in Egypt. Lord Rosebery replied that he quite recognized that there was some high-handedness. It then turned out that they were not talking about the same thing, one referring to the action of Lord Cromer, and the other to that of the *khedive*. On matters being explained, Lord Rosebery scored off the ambassador by saying that he was at a loss to understand the latter's meaning, as he could hardly call Lord Cromer's making a protest a "high-handed proceeding," seeing that that was the express object for which the ambassador had sought the present interview.

The serious part of the incident was the view which the British Government took of it. Lord Rosebery, in a despatch dated the 16th February, declared that:

> ..... if the Prime Minister and the heads of other important departments were to be summarily dismissed in disregard of British advice, there was nothing to prevent the dismissal of any other functionaries, European or native, who might not have the good fortune to fall in with the tendencies of the moment, or whose prominence might afford a favourable opportunity for the display of autocratic power. It was not too much to say that, under these circumstances, the whole fabric so laboriously built up during the last ten years would have been at the mercy of caprice or intrigue, and would rapidly and necessarily have crumbled away.

Riaz Pasha on his return to power showed himself anything but disposed to work well with the *khedive*'s English advisers. His policy took the form of stubborn opposition rather than active resistance, and it required all the firmness and tact of Lord Cromer to keep things in the right path. With the promotion of Maher Pasha to the post of Under-Secretary at War, attempts were made to interfere with the authority of the *sirdar* in matters relating to the army, and hardly were these defeated than the further difficulty known as the "frontier incident" occurred.

The *khedive* on his visit to Wady Halfa in January, 1894, made some observations on the army which were taken by the British officers as a slight upon them, and the *sirdar*, General Kitchener, in consequence, resigned. He, however, withdrew his resignation almost immediately after, at the request of the *khedive*. The matter was regarded by the British Government as an attempt to discredit the English officers, and to undermine their authority with the troops, and Lord Cromer was instructed to ask that a general order should be issued expressing the *khedive*'s satisfaction with the army, and the officers generally, and also that Maher Pasha should be removed. Both these requirements were complied with and the incident was closed.

Riaz Pasha shortly after resigned, and Nubar again returned to power. Under his advice the relations of the *khedive* with the British Government became more cordial, and no further "incidents" such as those above recorded took place.

CHAPTER 60

The Dongola Expedition

In a previous chapter, the history of events on the Nile frontier was brought down to the month of August, 1889, when Wad-en-Nejumi's forces, after the crushing defeat they encountered in the engagement at Toski, were retreating southwards, and the projected invasion of Egypt was suspended. The incidents which marked the next few years may be related in a few words.

The years 1890 and 1891 passed almost undisturbed on the frontier. The chief military command in the province of Dongola was vested in one of the *khalifa's emirs*, called Mohammed Khalil Zogal, with a force and detachments at Sunnah, and at Suarda, fifty miles south of Akasheh. From this last point patrols occasionally went north to Akasheh itself, but the Nile frontier generally remained quite undisturbed.

From Korosko, Saba Bey, in the autumn of 1890, made a reconnaissance towards Abu Hamid, with some irregulars, and captured one of the Dervish outpost forts, which he, a few hours afterwards, was compelled to relinquish. The matter is only worth mentioning by reason of the fact that in the fight which accompanied Saba's retreat the notorious Suleiman Wad Gamr, Colonel Stewart's murderer, was killed.

In April, 1892, Colonel Kitchener succeeded Sir Francis Grenfell as Sirdar of the Egyptian Army. In the same year there were signs of increased activity in the Nile Valley, and between Dongola and Suarda some 5,000 fighting men were kept under arms.

In January, 1893, the Dervishes again became aggressive, and 600 of them advanced to cut the railway connecting Sarras and Wady Halfa. The raid failed, owing to the precautions taken by Colonel Wodehouse. The Dervishes, however, managed to surprise and outnumber

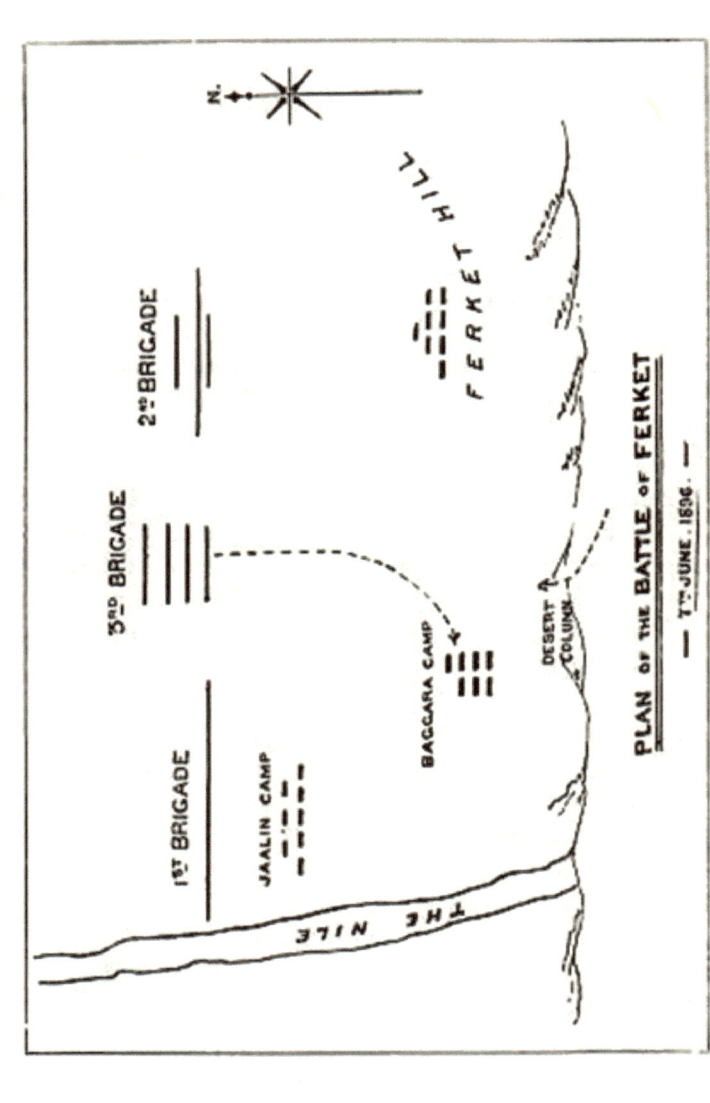

120 of the Egyptian Camel Corps, who had been sent to follow up the retreat. The Egyptians fought courageously, but, having lost their two senior officers, Captain Pyne and Major Fuad Effendi, were defeated, and had to retire with a loss of no less than thirty-four men killed and fifteen wounded. The Dervish loss was estimated at more than double that number.

In July of the same year, the Dervishes made a sudden descent on Beris, the southernmost village of the El Khargeh Oasis, to the northwest of Assouan.

In November, the enemy made an attack upon the desert outpost of Murad Wells, but were repulsed.

From this date, with the exception of a raid on a village in the Wady Halfa district in 1895, the Dervishes in the neighbourhood of the Egyptian advanced posts observed a strictly defensive attitude.

The year 1896 brought with it great changes in the entire situation. The reoccupation of the province of Dongola had for some time been in contemplation by the Egyptian Government and its advisers. It was felt that a blow must sooner or later be struck at the power of the *khalifa*, which, though it had succeeded in laying waste some of the most fertile provinces abandoned by Egypt, was known to be waning, if not dying, of its own unpopularity; but no one thought that the blow would be struck so soon. In choosing the moment for action, the British Government was influenced to a very large extent by a desire to assist a friendly power in a position of extreme difficulty. Only a short time before (29th February, 1896) a terrible disaster had happened to the Italian army in Africa, which had been defeated at Adowa with heavy loss by the Abyssinians under Menelik.

Driven back in the direction of Massowah, the remains of the Italian forces found it impossible to lend a helping hand to their comrades garrisoned at Kassala, who were threatened by the Dervishes, and in a situation of imminent peril. One object of the British and Egyptian advance which in March, 1896, was determined on, was, by making a diversion in the region of Dongola, to save Kassala, or at all events its garrison. It was not from purely disinterested motives that this step was decided upon. It was obvious that the moment when a large body of the *khalifa's* forces was occupied with the Italians would be a favourable one for a movement on Dongola, whereas if Kassala was to fall into the hands of the Dervishes, the latter would be let loose to overrun the Nile Valley. Everything in fact was ripe for the expedition.

There were, moreover, political reasons for not delaying it. In the valley of the Upper Nile, the race between the Powers for possession of that part of Africa was beginning to attract attention. The French were extending their influence from the south-west, and the Belgians were sending out expeditions from the south, and there was a general feeling that some corresponding action on the part of Great Britain was desirable, as soon as a favourable opportunity should occur.

Speaking in the House of Commons in March, Mr. Curzon, Under Secretary for Foreign Affairs, stated that:

> In view of the reported forward movements in various directions by the Dervishes and the threatened beleaguerment of Kassala, the government, acting in conjunction with the government of Egypt and their advisers, and in order to avoid danger to Italy, to Egypt, and to England, and in the interests of Europe, had ordered an advance to Akasheh.

He added that the advance might be extended to Dongola, and that the future action of the government was to be "regulated by considerations not merely military and strategical, but political and financial."

It was decided that the Dongola expedition should consist of about 9,000 Egyptian troops, under the command of the *sirdar*. In addition to these, the 1st Battalion of the North Staffordshire Regiment was to be moved from Cairo to Wady Halfa to relieve the Egyptian garrison there, and also to be at hand if required. The route chosen was by rail and river to Wady Halfa, and thence by a march along the Nile bank to the front.

The decision of the British Government was arrived at so suddenly that it was not even communicated to the *khedive* and his advisers. The news took Cairo by surprise. Without any previous intimation it became known at midnight on the 12th March that Colonel Hunter, who commanded the frontier force at Wady Halfa, had been ordered to advance and occupy Akasheh, that all available troops were to be pushed up the Nile with a view to an advance on Dongola, and that the 1st Battalion of the North Staffordshire Regiment (64th), then quartered in Cairo, was to leave immediately for Wady Halfa.[1]

---

1. It is said that Colonel Rundle, Chief of the Staff of the Egyptian Army, was aroused to hear the news by stones thrown at his window in the middle of the night, and that no one could be found bold enough to awake and inform the *sirdar*, who remained in ignorance until the morning.

Although the news took Cairo by surprise, it was the kind of surprise with which one hears that something long expected and long delayed has at last really come true. For years past the Egyptian Army had been steadily trained and prepared for the event which the disaster to the Italian arms in Abyssinia only precipitated.

A few words may here be said concerning the state of the army at this period. Its formation, begun by Sir Evelyn Wood soon after Tel-el-Kebir, had progressed slowly but surely. The men had been gradually disciplined under British officers and accustomed by degrees to meeting the Dervishes in the numerous frontier skirmishes of the past ten years. In 1884-5, Egyptian troops were employed upon the lines of communication of Wolseley's Nile expedition, and some of the Camel Corps were under fire at Kirbekan. Backed by British troops, they fought well at Ginnis, and they crushed Wad-en-Nejumi single-handed at Argin and Toski. At the beginning of 1896 the army numbered 18,000 men. It consisted of sixteen battalions of infantry, each battalion having six companies of from 100 to 120 men each, and about eight squadrons of cavalry, with camel corps, artillery, &c.

Of the infantry, ten battalions were composed of *fellaheen*, taken by conscription, and six of Soudanese blacks (volunteers enlisted for life). The *fellaheen* battalions numbered from 1 to 4 had British colonels and majors; those numbered rom 5 to 8 were officered only by natives. The Soudanese Battalions numbered from 9 to 14 (this last only in course of formation) had British officers, whilst the 15th and 16th Battalions, made up of reservists called out for the campaign, were also partly officered by Englishmen. There were in all about eighty British officers, a number increased to 120 by others sent out on special service in the course of the campaign.

A glance must now be taken at the means of transport at the disposal of the *sirdar*, and it will be seen that, as in Wolseley's expedition, the provisioning of the above force at a distance of nearly 1,000 miles from its base in Cairo formed one of the chief difficulties to be dealt with.

In March, 1886, the Upper Egypt Railway was open as far as Girgeh, 341 miles above Cairo, but it had been prolonged, for Government purposes only, to Belianeh, eight miles further on. Thence everything had to be carried in steamers and native boats to Assouan. Here men and stores had to be unloaded and conveyed overland by the eight-mile railway to Shellal, just above the First Cataract, where they were again shipped and taken on to Wady Halfa. From this last place to Sarras, a distance of thirty miles, a railway existed when the campaign began, and this line was continued as quickly as possible in the rear of the army as it advanced. It may here be observed that the rapid construction of this railway, under the direction of Nicour Bey and Captain Girouard, of the Royal Engineers, was not the least notable feature of the campaign. From the rail-head to the front stores had to be carried by convoys of camels and mules, aided on the less broken parts of the river by relief boats, as soon as the rising Nile had allowed them to be dragged up the cataract by steamers. The navigation of the Nile between Wady Halfa and Dongola is not easy, the broken water of the Second Cataract extending from Wady Halfa almost to Sarras, and at Hannek, 100 miles further on, the Third Cataract again obstructs the navigation.

On the 20th March, Mr. Morley moved a vote of censure of the House of Commons on the government in connection with the Dongola expedition, but on a division the motion was negatived by 288 votes against 143.

There was an incident in connection with the expedition which is of sufficient importance to deserve notice.

A few days after the expedition was decided on, the Egyptian Government, on the 19th March, applied to the commissioners of the Public Debt to advance towards the expenses the sum of £500,000, to be taken from what is known as the "Reserve Fund." This fund was created pursuant to the Khedivial decree of 12th July, 1888, under which the financial arrangements made by "The London Convention" of 1885, already referred to in a former chapter, were once more modified. The changes made comprised the suspension of the Sinking Fund of the Debt, and the application of the money to form a reserve fund, to meet unforeseen contingencies. One of these was declared to be "extraordinary expenses incurred with the previous sanction of the commission of the debt."

Four out of the six commissioners agreed in considering the Dongola expedition as coming under the above category, and advanced the money. The French and Russian commissioners dissented. This led to a lawsuit in the Mixed Tribunal of Cairo, which later on, viz., on the 9th June, ordered the government to refund the money with interest. The judgment being confirmed on appeal on the 2nd December, 1896, the *khedive's* advisers might have found themselves in a position of some difficulty had not Lord Cromer vigorously taken the matter in hand, and induced the British Government to lend the sum which had to be refunded. The amount due under the judgment, £515,600, was repaid to the "*Caisse*" on the 8th December, and the *khedive*'s Ministers expressed their lively gratitude. This was still further earned when later on the British Government released their claim to be repaid the sum advanced.

On 21st March the *sirdar*, with Major Wingate and Slatin Pasha, and the 1st Battalion of the North Staffordshire Regiment, 917 strong, left Cairo for Assouan and Wady Halfa. At the same time the various Egyptian battalions were hurried up the river with all possible despatch.

As usual the enterprising firm of Messrs. Thomas Cook & Son came in for the principal part of the river transport work. All their steamers, except those engaged in the postal service, were requisitioned by the Egyptian Government, and, deprived of their handsome fittings and luxurious accommodation, now figured as troopships between Belianeh and Assouan. Between the 21st and 26th March, these steamers shipped from the former place no less than 4,500 men, besides 750 animals and an enormous quantity of stores. A detachment of the Connaught Rangers was stationed at Belianch in charge of the store *depôt* established there.

It should be mentioned that the 9th Soudanese Battalion, forming part of the Souakim garrison, marched from Kosseir, on the Red Sea, to Keneh, on the Nile, following the route across the desert taken by General Baird and his army in 1801.

Meanwhile Colonel Hunter with his frontier force moved on to Akasheh, which for some time past had been the advanced post of the Dervishes, and occupied it without opposition.

The Egyptian troops now concentrated as rapidly as possible at the various posts between Wady Halfa and Akasheh, the Staffordshire Regiment being left to garrison the former place.

The railway was now being pushed forward, and on 24th May it was completed to a point three miles beyond Ambigol, sixty-three miles south of Wady Halfa.

To guard against raids on either flank in the proposed further advance, the west bank of the Nile was patrolled by native irregulars, and the important post of Murad Wells had its garrison of Ababdeh "friendlies" strengthened by some two or three companies from one of the Egyptian battalions.

The post of Murad Wells, situated about half-way between Korosko and Abu Hamid, was by far the most important of the desert posts. No Dervish descent upon the east bank of the river was possible unless these wells had been first secured; consequently there had been repeated struggles for their possession. Their guardianship had at the time now referred to been intrusted to the Ababdeh Arabs in the pay of the government. The last attack on the wells was that made by the Dervishes as lately as November, 1893, but which was repulsed with severe loss. The chief of the tribe, Saleh Bey, who was in command of the defending force, lost his life on this occasion, but was succeeded by his elder brother, Ahmed Bey, an equally capable leader.

On the news of Hunter's advance to Akasheh, a younger brother, Abd-el-Azim, on the 11th April made a bold reconnaissance to the south. Crossing the desert with a party of his Ababdehs, he struck the Nile about forty miles south of Abu Hamid, and then continuing some eighty miles further along the river, he informed the people of the Egyptian advance. They received the news everywhere with the greatest delight, and expressed their joy at the prospect of being delivered from the *khalifa's* reign of terror. Abd-el-Azim was able to obtain some useful information of the Dervish movements. At Abu Hamid there were only about 400 fighting men, but Berber was held by 6,000 of the Jehadia, Jaalin and Baggara tribes.

On the 1st of May the first fight of the season came off in the neighbourhood of Akasheh. About noon 240 of the Egyptian cavalry, under Major Burn Murdoch, when some four miles from Akasheh, suddenly came across 300 mounted Baggara, with a further force of about 1,000 men on foot, drawn up behind them. The odds being too great, the cavalry was ordered to retire. Seeing this movement, the Dervish horsemen, advancing amid a cloud of dust, charged down upon the rear troop just at the moment that the cavalry had entered a narrow defile. Several of the men were speared and stabbed in the back before the main body had time to wheel and in their turn charge the assailants.

This they quickly did in dashing style, and then ensued a hand-to-hand fight which lasted about twenty minutes, at the end of which the Dervishes wheeled about and galloped off to the rear of the spearmen on foot. The ground not admitting of another charge, the cavalry then dismounted and opened fire on the enemy. This was kept up till at 3 p.m., just as the 11th Soudanese Battalion was arriving in support, the Dervishes retired, to the great satisfaction of the small Egyptian force, which with jaded horses, and suffering intensely from want of water, had been fighting continuously for three hours under a burning sun.

The cavalry had two killed and ten wounded, against eighteen killed and eighty wounded on the enemy's side.

On the 2nd June the arrival of the 10th Soudanese Battalion at Akasheh completed the concentration necessary for the further advance.

From information obtained by the Intelligence Department it was ascertained that the Dervish force, though inferior in number to that of the Egyptians, was composed of good fighting material, Baggara, Jaalins, and Jehadias, and was led by the well-known Emir Hamuda. Their total number was estimated at 3,000.

On the evening of the 6th the Egyptian troops commenced the advance, quitting Akasheh on the march to Ferket, on the east bank, sixteen miles distant. The *sirdar*, who had shortly before reached the front, was in command. The force was divided into two parts, which may be called the River and the Desert Columns.

The River Column, under the command of Colonel Hunter, consisted of infantry and artillery. The infantry was divided into three brigades of three battalions each; the artillery was composed of two field batteries and two Maxims, the latter worked by thirty men of the Connaught Rangers.

The Desert Column, commanded by Major Burn Murdoch, consisted of seven squadrons of cavalry, the Camel Corps, one infantry battalion mounted on camels, one battery of Horse Artillery, and two Maxim guns. The total force of the two columns was not less than 9,100 men.

The *sirdar's* plan for the attack was for the River Column to proceed along the Nile bank, and the Desert Column to make a detour to the east, so timed that both columns should reach Ferket at dawn, the former attacking from the north whilst the latter cut off the Dervish retreat east and south. On the west of their position was the Nile, the further bank of which was guarded by Egyptian irregulars, so as to prevent the possibility of escape on that side. Thus the Dervishes were to be completely hemmed in on every side.

The River Column bivouacked at 11 p.m. at a place distant only about four miles from the enemy, every precaution being taken to prevent news of the advance reaching the Dervish force. There were no bugle calls, no lights, and no firing.

At 12.15 on the morning of the 7th June the march was resumed, the 1st Brigade taking the ground nearest the river, the 2nd being on the left, and the 3rd in the rear.

Meanwhile the Desert Column was skilfully guided in the darkness across the desert until it reached the point south of Ferket where it had been arranged that it should take up its position.

The enemy became aware of the approach of the two columns almost simultaneously, saw that all prospect of retreat was cut off, and hurriedly prepared for action. Their formation was largely governed by the position of their camps. Their left wing, or wing next the river, occupied the huts of the Jaalin camp, and was thrown forward beyond the centre, which was opposite the Baggara camp; the right wing again was slightly in the rear of the centre.

The engagement began by the Dervishes opening fire at 5 a.m. from an outpost on the Jebel Ferkeh, a mountain on the north side of the village close down by the river under which the River Column had to pass.

The 2nd Brigade brought a heavy fire to bear upon the hill, and quickly clearing it, the march continued. As the column reached the more open ground beyond Jebel Ferkeh, the troops opened out, and the brigades on the right and left got into fighting formation, with two battalions thrown forward and one in reserve. The 1st Brigade then moved towards the river to attack the enemy's left wing, whilst the 2nd Brigade advanced on the right wing near the Jaalin camp; the 3rd Brigade coming up from the rear to fill the intervening gap.

The entire force then steadily advanced, firing as they went, whilst the Desert Column shelled the enemy from the south and rear. The Dervishes fought with the courage of despair, and frequently charged the Egyptian troops. Small bodies of the enemy continued fighting in the huts forming the different camps long after any organized resistance had ceased to be possible, and obstinately refusing quarter. Hut after hut had to be cleared at the point of the bayonet amid vigorous hand-to-hand fighting, and in one hut alone eighty Baggara corpses were subsequently found.

Position after position was taken, and an utter rout ensued. Such of the Dervishes as survived the attack of the River Column fled to the south, only to find their retreat cut off by the Desert Column, which by this time had advanced on the flank of the enemy, who were thus effectually caught as intended. Many of their mounted men, finding themselves headed off by the cavalry, galloped back to die in front of the lines of infantry.

The footmen, too, were seen hurrying to and fro seeking a way through the encircling Egyptian forces. Such of them as succeeded were closely pursued by the cavalry, and least 150 were thus slaughtered within a few miles of Ferket.

The enemy's losses were estimated at 1,000 killed and wounded, and over 500 were taken prisoners. The Egyptian loss, on the other hand, was limited to twenty men killed and eighty wounded. The Dervish *emir* in command was Osman Azrak, who had lately superseded Hamuda; and the former and at least forty other *emirs* were among the slain.

The whole fight was but a short affair, the first shot being fired at 5 a.m., and two hours later the whole thing was over.

Burn Murdoch, with the Desert Column, continued to follow up the pursuit as far as Suarda, which he occupied the next morning.

The effect of the engagement at Ferket was that fifty miles of the Nile Valley were cleared of the Dervishes; that the only organized army of the *khalifa* near the frontier was destroyed; and that Suarda, which had for many years been the starting-place for raids on the Nile villages, became the advanced post of the *sirdar's* army.

CHAPTER 61

The Reconquest of Dongola

After the destruction of the Dervish force at Ferket and the occupation of Suarda, no further advance was undertaken for a period of three months. There was, however, plenty of hard work to do, and rarely has an army toiled through a long, hot summer in the way that the *sirdar's* troops worked in those trying months of June, July, and August. In the year 1896, the railway had to be pushed on, stores had to be concentrated at the front, and steamers to be dragged up the cataracts. In addition to this, there was a severe cholera epidemic to be fought and overcome.

The advance post of Suarda was fortified and strongly held by the 2nd Infantry Brigade, with some artillery. The cavalry and Camel Corps made reconnaissances further south, but no additional posts were occupied during the summer.

One particularly successful expedition was made. It had been ascertained that the Emir Osman Azrak, with a body of Dervish cavalry, had come north to Kidden, a village near the Kaibar Cataract, with the intention of collecting the entire male population in the district, and driving them south to Dongola to assist in the defence of that place. On June the 17th, two squadrons of Egyptian cavalry and a company of the camel corps, under Captain Mahon, arrived; and the Dervishes, though greatly superior in numbers, fled without fighting. Eleven boats loaded with grain were captured, and the unfortunate inhabitants of the village were enabled to make their escape to the Egyptian lines north of Suarda.

From these refugees a good deal of information was obtained as to what the Dervishes were doing. The news of the defeat at Ferket had been received in Dongola with consternation. Wad-el-Bishara, the governor, sent the intelligence on to the *khalifa*, asking at the same time for large reinforcements, if the town of Dongola was to be defended. In the meantime, he made preparations for defence, fortifying the place, enrolling all the able-bodied men in the province, and calling in from the desert such of the Bedouins as were friendly to the cause.

All this while the work of pushing forward supplies was rapidly continued. The field telegraph, laid for the most part in the desert sand, followed closely upon the heels of the army.

The railway was steadily pushed on by Captain Girouard, R.E., until it reached Kosheh (the scene of the engagement of 30th December, 1885), whither on July 5th the head-quarters camp had been moved for sanitary reasons.

During all this period the expedition was pursued by persistent ill fortune. The rise of the Nile was unusually late, and consequently the dragging of the gunboats over the Second Cataract was delayed. Heavy rain storms, most unusual in this part of the Soudan, occurred, and the last, on August the 25th, swept away part of the line near Sarras.

By far the worst visitation of all was the cholera. The disease was imported into Egypt in October, 1895, but made only little way during the winter. In the spring of 1896 it began to increase, and in the second week of June reached the first military post at Assouan. Here it was quickly stamped out, but was taken to Korosko by the men of the 5th Battalion, and shortly after appeared at Wady Halfa. Here the epidemic was very severe, and difficult to deal with, for Halfa could not be isolated, as all the troops and stores had to pass through it, and the epidemic followed them until it reached Kosheh. As soon as the cholera appeared at Wady Halfa the North Staffordshire Regiment was moved into camp at Gemai, six miles further off in the desert, but nevertheless many cases occurred among the men. The epidemic first reached Kosheh on July the 15th. The camp was at once moved back 2,000 yards into the desert, and the most stringent precautions were taken to insure the purity of the water supply, as well as to keep the men from bathing or washing clothes in the river.

With these precautions, the disease, which was of a very rapid and fatal type, was at last stamped out, but not until 235 Egyptian soldiers in all had fallen victims. Amongst others were four British officers and two English engineers, who had been sent to supervise the putting together of a new gunboat.

At the end of August, the concentration of the troops further south was begun, and begun badly. The 1st Brigade was advanced from Suarda, where it had been stationed, to Delligo, a distance of forty-five miles. To avoid a bend of the river the men were marched as far as Absarat, that is about half of the way straight across the desert. The heat was most oppressive, a scorching sand storm raged part of the time, and the men in heavy marching order, carrying two days' rations and 100 rounds of ammunition, were unaccompanied by water camels, but had to trust to two *depôts* which had been formed on the road. Out of 3,000 men no less than 1,700 fell out, and ten died and were buried, during this disastrous march, undertaken without any adequate motive.

On the 15th September the 1st Battalion of the North Staffordshire Regiment, which had moved up from Gemai, arrived, and the advance really began. Every available soldier being wanted, but small garrisons were left upon the line of communication. Kosheh, now the railway terminus, as the most important place, was guarded by the 6th Battalion, but the other posts northwards had only a few men each. The expeditionary force consisted of the North Staffordshire, the three brigades which fought at Ferket, and a fourth brigade, composed also of three Egyptian battalions.

With the artillery, Camel Corps, and infantry the total force amounted to nearly 15,000 men.

On the 14th the troops marched into Fereig, the North Staffordshires being conveyed by steamer. On the 17th the whole force moved on to Bargi, about ten miles further south, and on the 18th to a spot on the river bank opposite the island of Imbos. On the 19th the army started before daybreak to attack the Dervishes, who were reported to be strongly intrenched at Kermeh, but Wad-el-Bishara, who was in command, disappointed the *sirdar* by moving the whole Dervish force across to the west bank during the previous night, and was now holding the village of Hafir. Then at 6.30 a.m. commenced the little battle of Hafir, between the Egyptian artillery and gunboats and the Dervishes on the left bank. A long line of shelter trenches, with loopholed mud walls, ran along the river front of the position, and here five small guns, which had been captured at Khartoum, were mounted. These were served by ex-gunners of the Egyptian army.

The north and south sides of the position were protected by deep morasses, and on the left lay moored against the western bank a small gunboat built by Gordon at Khartoum, and some twenty-five large sailing vessels laden with grain. The engagement was opened at 6.30 a.m. by the Egyptian artillery, which was replied to by the Dervish guns and riflemen, but little damage was done on either side.

Half an hour later, Commander Colville, R.N., arrived with his steamboat flotilla, consisting of his flagship, the *Tamaai*, the *Abu Klea*, and the *Metammeh*.

The steamers then began to attack the forts, steaming up until they got abreast of them, pouring in their fire, and then dropping down stream until they were out of range.

The Dervish fire was wonderfully accurate, the ships being struck again and again by the shells while the rifle bullets pierced all the woodwork. One shell actually entered the magazine of the *Abu Klea*, but fortunately did not explode. There were several casualties. Two men were killed, and Captain Colville and twelve men wounded. This engagement lasted for hours, and though the practice made by the gunboats was good, and the enemy must have lost heavily, still their fire was not silenced.

About 1,200 yards from the enemy's position was a large island, called Artaghasi, joined by a swampy isthmus to the mainland, now that the Nile was falling. Three batteries of artillery and the Maxim battery were sent to take up a position on the island, just opposite the Dervishes. The guns were promptly brought into action, and about an hour later the Dervish fire was silenced. Nevertheless shots were fired intermittently during the afternoon and through the night, especially in the neighbourhood of the grain boats which the Dervishes were trying to discharge.

Meanwhile the steamers, delivering their parting shots as they passed the forts, went on to Dongola, which they reached before sunset.

Thus ended the fighting for the day. The casualties on the Anglo-Egyptian side, as already stated, were but trifling; those of the enemy, though reported as heavy, were never exactly ascertained. One writer estimates them at 200.

On the morning of the next day, the 20th, it became evident that the Dervishes had evacuated Hafir. Some of the inhabitants came out and waved a welcome to the Egyptians, while others brought all the boats across to the east bank, where they were immediately taken possession of. It was found that Bishara, misled by false information, had evacuated Hafir at three in the morning, and marched with all his force to Dongola to oppose the crossing which he had been led to expect would take place there. The *sirdar*, however, learning this, ordered that the river should be crossed at once at Hafir, and the movement was begun that very day.

It was no small undertaking to throw such a large force across a river a mile and a half wide, with only a few gunboats and sailing craft, and it is hardly surprising that the army was not ready to resume its march upon Dongola until the evening of the following day. In the meanwhile, Colville's gunboats returned, having thrown a few shells into Dongola, and captured several more boat loads of grain.

On the evening of September the 21st, the Anglo-Egyptian force marched twelve miles further south, and bivouacked on the river bank nearly opposite the island of Argo. On this day, too, the *Abu Klea* was sent on ahead to watch Dongola, where on the following day she was joined by the *Tamaai* and *Metammeh*.

Early in the morning of the 22nd, the force marched a few miles on to Zowerat and rested there.

At 4.30 a.m. on the 23rd, lighted by a brilliant moon, the Anglo-Egyptian force moved on Dongola. The gunboat *Zafir* arrived from the north, and was at once sent on to join Colville's command. The order of march was as follows:—The 1st Brigade was on the left near the river; on their right was the 3rd Brigade. Next came the artillery, Maxims, and North Staffordshire. On the right, next the artillery, was the 2nd Brigade with the Camel Corps, Horse Artillery, and cavalry on the extreme right, away in the desert. The 4th Brigade formed the rear guard. The force presented a front two miles in length. At seven o'clock the Dervishes came in sight, and the Egyptians briskly advanced to meet them. The former, however, would not fight. Time after time they halted in battle array as if to attack, but each time seeing the odds were so hopelessly against them, they suddenly retreated.

In the distance, the sound of guns from Colville's steamers was heard; but the troops on shore never got a chance of a shot. At 9.30 the force was abreast of the Dervish camp to the north of the town of Dongola, where they saw the Egyptian flag waving over the old Mudirieh and learned that the blacks garrisoning the place had surrendered to the steamers. Then it was seen that there could be no fight, and that all that remained to be done was to pursue the Baggaras, Jaalins, and others now in full retreat. This task was thereupon taken in hand by the cavalry, Camel Corps, and Horse Artillery, whilst the remainder of the force, skirting a morass which lay between the town and the western desert, marched on, till at 11 a.m. they turned the southern end of the swamp and entered Dongola.

The inhabitants crowded amongst the troops, seizing and kissing the hands of the soldiers and displaying the utmost joy at being delivered from the oppression of the Baggara.

The important part taken by the gunboats in the capture of Dongola may be stated in a few words. They steamed up abreast of the town in the early morning, the rearmost steamer being only a little ahead of the infantry advance. They then opened fire on the defences on the river bank, but there was no effective reply. They also kept up a steady fire on the Dervish camp in the desert, already referred to, and afterwards on the Baggara Arabs, now retiring before the advancing infantry. Again there was no reply. At 9.30 the blacks garrisoning Dongola hoisted the white flag, and the cannonade ceased. Commander Colville then landed with a hundred Soudanese soldiers and hoisted the Egyptian flag.

The close pursuit by the mounted troops which ensued compelled the Dervishes to abandon a large portion of their black foot-soldiers, who were only too glad to remain. Indeed, it was one of the most satisfactory features of the day's work that, owing to the absence of fighting by the force on shore, only a few lost their lives. Those were of the unfortunate native population, who are always placed in the front ranks of the Dervishes.

The Baggara, however, offered some resistance to the pursuit, and made several charges whilst endeavouring to cover the retreat of the main body. Some 900 prisoners, in all, were captured. These were shortly afterwards converted into a black battalion and added to the *sirdar's* forces.

On the night of the 24th, the Anglo-Egyptian force bivouacked in and around Dongola, or rather the ruins of that once flourishing town. The place was now practically deserted, and in the streets not a soul was to be seen. Everywhere was ruin and desolation.

On the 26th, there being no more work for the North Staffordshires to do, and the regiment suffering a good deal from sickness, it was sent back to Cairo.[1]

As a consequence of the fall of Dongola every Dervish fled for his life from the province. The mounted men made off across the desert direct to Omdurman, and the foot-soldiers took the Nile route to Berber, always being careful to keep out of range of the gunboats, which were prevented by the Fourth Cataract from pursuing them beyond Merawi.

---

1. In this short campaign the battalion lost no less than sixty-four of their number (including those who died in Cairo soon after their return, principally from enteric fever).

CHAPTER 62

The Advance to Berber

Preceded by the gunboats, the main body of the expedition after the capture of Dongola proceeded southwards, leaving detachments behind to guard the line of communication. Debbeh, Korti, and Merawi were successively seized and occupied.

The *sirdar* also went south to inspect the different positions and receive the submissions of the most important *sheikhs*, after which he returned to Cairo, leaving his forces stationed at the three strategic posts above mentioned.

On Kitchener's departure the province was placed under military law, Major-General Hunter, who had fixed his headquarters at Merawi, being in command.

Courts of justice and a police force were established in the province of Dongola, the rebuilding of the town was begun, and the railway was continued along the Nile to Kermeh, forty miles to the north, and which now became the southern terminus. The former inhabitants were invited to return to their lands, and cultivation was gradually resumed.

The principal difficulty in the way of progress was the lack of population, which since 1885 had fallen off from 75,000 to 56,000, and of these a large proportion consisted of women and children. The number of cattle had also diminished from 36,000 to less than 12,000 in the same period.

Whilst Dongola was being put in order, the *khalifa*, who expected that the capture of that province would be followed by a further advance, hastily took steps to fortify Omdurman, where he gathered all his available warriors, and awaited events.

This was the situation at the end of 1896.

We now arrive at the year 1897, when the intended reconquest of the Soudan, by the aid of British money and arms, was announced in the House of Commons. This took place on the 5th February, when the "Dongola Expedition vote" of £798,802 was moved by the Chancellor of the Exchequer.

Sir Michael Hicks-Beach declared on this occasion 'that, since the Dongola Expedition was undertaken, the British Government had never concealed, either from Parliament or the country, that, in their view, there should be a further advance in the same direction; that Egypt could never be held to be permanently secured so long as a hostile Power was in occupation of the Nile Valley up to Khartoum; and that England, having compelled the Egyptian Government to abandon the Soudan, had incurred towards its inhabitants responsibilities for the fulfilment of which the moment had arrived now that the baleful rule of the *khalifa* was crumbling to decay.'

The *sirdar's* policy of advancing gradually and consolidating at every step the authority of the Egyptian Government continued to be pursued in 1897.

The work of getting up supplies for the large force at the front occupied the first few months of the year, and this was a task of no small magnitude, considering that the country contained little or no produce, and that everything required had to be forwarded from the base in Cairo.

The necessity for the construction of a new railway for military purposes from Wady Halfa across the desert *viâ* Murad Wells to Abu Hamid now impressed itself on the *sirdar's* mind. Such a line was almost indispensable in the event of operations being extended in the direction of Berber and Omdurman. The existing line to Kermeh had served its purpose in bringing up supplies and otherwise until the time of the capture of Dongola, but its further extension would have to be made through a difficult country, and at a great sacrifice of time and money. It was therefore determined to discard it so far as the expedition was concerned.

The immense advantage of making a short cut across the eastern desert instead of following the tortuous windings of the Nile Valley will be evident to any one who studies the map and notes the respective positions of Wady Halfa, Kermeh, and Abu Hamid. The saving in distance is about 330 miles.

Influenced by these considerations, the authorities sanctioned the new line, and the materials having been got together at Wady Halfa, the work was promptly taken in hand.

Once commenced, the line, laid for the greater part on the desert sand by working parties from Wady Halfa, progressed with almost inconceivable rapidity, under the able direction of Captain Girouard. The country over which the railway passed consisted mostly of undulating desert. There were no bridges, and but few cuttings, and the average rate of progress was a mile and a half a day.

Although it was known that there was a Dervish force at Abu Hamid, no opposition was encountered from it.

In order to present the history of events in chronological order, it is here necessary to make a slight digression and refer to what happened about this period in another part of the Soudan.

In the month of June the *khalifa* was compelled to detach a portion of his army from Omdurman, and send it, under the orders of his cousin and principal emir Mahmoud, to suppress a revolt of the Jaalin Arabs at Metammeh. This tribe, which had long been kept under the *khalifa's* rule by the terrorism of the Baggara, was anxious to join hands with the Egyptians, and now struck for freedom. They fortified Metammeh, and courageously awaited Mahmoud's attack. On the 1st July it came, and, hemmed in and outnumbered by the Dervish horde, the brave Jaalins, after three days' resistance, in which all their ammunition was exhausted, were utterly routed. Metammeh was captured and burnt, and the country round devastated by the victors, who killed men, women and children indiscriminately.

The Jaalins had exasperated their foes by their determined resistance, and when the town was taken no less than 2,000 of its defenders were massacred. The prisoners were drawn up in line and treated thus: the first was beheaded, the second had his right hand cut off, the third his feet, and so on in succession until they had all been-dealt with. Their chief, Abdullah Wad Sud, the head of the Jaalin tribe, was taken a prisoner to Omdurman, and walled in in such a position that he could neither stand nor sit, and was thus left to die of hunger and thirst.

Such of the Jaalins as escaped declared their allegiance to the *khedive*, and, being supplied with firearms, and subsidized, joined the ranks of the "friendlies" and became useful allies. One of their first acts, when they had time to reorganize a little, was to seize and hold Gakdul Wells, a move which not only covered the Egyptian right on the subsequent advance, but also saved the province of Dongola from the danger of surprise by Dervish raiders.

Towards the end of July the desert railway line had advanced as far as it was deemed prudent to go whilst Abu Hamid remained in the enemy's possession, and it was determined to take the place by means of troops co-operating from what may be considered the opposite direction, *viz*., Merawi.

On the 29th July, General Hunter, with four battalions of Soudanese infantry and some artillery,[1] started from Merawi for Abu Hamid.

Following the route taken by the River Column under General Earle in 1885, and passing the battlefield of Kirbekan, Hunter arrived on the night of the 6th August within a few miles of Abu Hamid. The march, which covered 132 miles, made in the hottest time of the year, was accomplished in eight days.

At daylight on the 7th, the troops moved up to attack the enemy, who occupied an intrenched position in front of and within the village. Their centre was a rectangular mud-walled inclosure, extending over six acres, and in this were contained the wells, military stores, and quarters for the soldiers. The mud huts of the village were connected by walls, and these, as well as the walls of the inclosure, were loopholed for musketry. The whole position was held by about 1,500 men, one-third of whom were armed with rifles, and 150 were mounted.

The infantry deployed for the attack, and, as soon as the movement was completed, advanced in line covered by the fire of the artillery on their right. Some high ground overlooking the village was first carried with but little resistance. When the troops had approached within 300 yards of the walls they were met by a furious fusillade, and many of the Egyptians fell. The rest rushed onwards, and a stubborn house-to-house fight, in which several lives were lost, ensued. In some cases so determined was the resistance that the artillery were obliged to advance before a position could be carried. Eventually, when the enemy's mounted men had lost about half their number, the residue fled. They were followed by about 100 of the foot-soldiers, all that was left of the garrison, and Abu Hamid was then taken and occupied. Many prisoners were captured, including the Dervish leader, Mohammed Zein.

The serious nature of the fighting may be gathered from the fact that on the Egyptian side there were twenty-three killed and sixty-four wounded. Amongst the killed were two English officers: Major Sidney and Lieutenant FitzClarence. The Dervish loss must have been

---

1. Reckoning six companies to a battalion, this would make Hunter's force amount to about 2,500 men.

much heavier, quite four-fifths of the garrison being either killed or taken prisoners.

The fugitives continued their flight to Omdurman, spreading as they went the news of the defeat.[2]

Abu Hamid having fallen, every effort was now made to hurry up the rest of the army from Merawi, Debbeh, and Dongola with a view to an advance upon Berber, the next Dervish stronghold on the river.

The Nile having by this time risen sufficiently, the gunboats with further troops were enabled to pass the Fourth Cataract, and by the 29th August, with the exception of one which came to grief in the cataract, arrived at Abu Hamid. The sailing boats with more men and stores were also successfully hauled through, and reached Abu Hamid shortly after.

Before, however, they had time to arrive, intelligence was received to the effect that the Dervishes were evacuating Berber, the next stronghold on the river. The importance of this move was at once realized, and a party of "friendlies," under Ahmed Bey Khalifa, were sent on ahead of General Hunter's troops to seize the place. Meeting with no resistance, the "friendlies" entered Berber, where on the 6th September Ahmed was joined by the gunboat flotilla. Hunter, with the greater part of his army, entered Berber on the 13th. Berber, formerly a large and prosperous town and an important centre of trade, but now sacked and destroyed, was represented by a big Dervish village, built on a site some miles north of the original place, and some two miles from the river.

On the day that Ahmed Bey reached Berber, two of the gunboats went on to Ed Damer, a few miles beyond the junction of the river Atbara with the Nile. Here they exchanged some shots with the Dervish force which had retreated from Berber, and they also succeeded in capturing several boat-loads of grain.

Ed Damer, now become the Egyptian advanced post, was occupied by a half battalion of infantry; a fort was erected, and other steps were taken for putting the place in a state of defence.[3]

---

2. For a great part of the description above given the author is indebted to Mr. Bennett Burleigh's *Sirdar and Khalifa*.

3. Later on Ed Damer was disestablished, and Fort Atbara, at the northern angle of the two rivers, was substituted for it.

CHAPTER 63

On the River—Kassala

Whilst Hunter was making his advance upon Abu Hamid and Berber, the irrepressible Osman Digna, of Souakim notoriety, had collected a force of 5,000 men, besides a large following of women and children, at a spot called Adarama, on the bank of the Atbara River, about ninety miles above Ed Damer. Here Hunter proposed to attack him, but, owing to delays in bringing forward transport and supplies from Abu Hamid, he was not ready to advance till the 23rd of October. On this date, taking with him 400 of the 11th Soudanese, some detachments of the Camel Corps, and two guns, Hunter started. Marching by the Atbara river, the force reached Adarama on the 29th of October, only to find, to their disappointment, that Osman, hearing of the approach of the Egyptian troops, had evacuated that place only two days before, and crossing the river at Guidi, was now with his fighting men and followers making for Abu Deleh, 100 miles in the desert between Omdurman and Kassala.

Adarama was completely deserted, and on the 2nd November, after having set fire to the village, the expedition returned to Berber.

Osman Digna's retreat left the Eastern Soudan clear of Dervishes; and the Souakim and Berber route, after being so many years closed to trade, was now reopened. Amongst the first persons to take advantage of the reopening of the road was a batch of newspaper correspondents, who, being given to understand that no advance on Omdurman was likely to take place until the following year, chose that route for returning to Cairo. They met with no difficulty on the way, and reported that plenty of water was obtainable all along the route by merely improving the existing wells or digging new ones.[1]

---
1. This has an important bearing on the choice of routes on the occasion of the despatch of "The Gordon Relief Expedition," dealt with in a previous chapter.

The inaction of the Mahdist forces about this time is attributed to the differences which existed between the principal Dervish leaders. Mahmoud with 10,000 men was known to be in the neighbourhood of Metammeh, and, young, energetic, and full of ardour, was anxious to advance and meet the invaders. But between Mahmoud and Osman Digna, now at Abu Deleh, there was a feud on a question of women taken from Osman's tribe. Consequently Osman, like another Achilles, sulked in his tents and refused to co-operate in any way with Mahmoud. The *khalifa* at Omdurman, under the impression that the attack on his capital could not be much longer delayed, refused to weaken his forces by sending either men or supplies to enable Mahmoud to make a move, an operation of which, by the way, he strongly disapproved. Mahmoud, not feeling strong enough to risk an attack unaided, was thus constrained to remain on the defensive.

On the 15th October, three of the gunboats were sent, under Commander Keppel, to reconnoitre Mahmoud's position. Passing Shendy, on the east bank, they steamed on until they sighted Metammeh (the scene of the fight with Stewart's column in 1885), on the opposite bank. The town was found to be protected by seven circular mud forts, placed at intervals along the river for a distance of one and a half miles. The gunboats cleared for action, and, with the Egyptian flag flying, formed in line of battle in true naval style. As they advanced, keeping always on the eastern or opposite shore, Baggara horsemen were seen galloping from fort to fort as if to stimulate the defenders.

As the steamers approached they opened fire simultaneously on the two nearest forts at a range of 4,000 yards, making excellent practice with their quick-firing twelve and six-pounder guns. The Maxims were directed on the horsemen, and so effectively that in a few minutes they disappeared from the scene of action. The forts, mounting each one obsolete brass cannon, returned the fire, but their shell nearly always fell short. Two or three, however, struck the gunboats, and one man was mortally wounded.

After bombarding at long range for an hour, the flotilla moved up abreast of the position, and poured shell and shrapnel into any place where the enemy was supposed to be. The missiles burst in all directions, with the effect of causing the return fire to slacken perceptibly. As the gunboats passed the forts it was discovered that the embrasures existed only on the northern front, so that when once in the rear of the work no guns could be brought to bear.

Whilst steaming along the east bank and keeping a look-out for the enemy a party of riflemen opened fire on the vessels at a range of 100 yards. The bullets rattled against the sides of the gunboats, but no one was struck, and a few rounds from the Maxims speedily dispersed the sharpshooters, who fled amongst the scrub, leaving their dead behind them. The vessels then steamed past the town, firing as opportunities offered. They then turned and retraced their course downstream, shelling as they went till 2.30 p.m., when all firing ceased. The flotilla then dropped down to an island half a dozen miles to the north of Metammeh and made fast for the night.

On the morning of the 17th, the reconnaissance was resumed. During the night two additional guns had been mounted in the forts, making the total now nine instead of seven. The manoeuvres of the previous day were repeated, and after a few hours' shelling, the reconnaissance being completed, the gunboats proceeded to withdraw down the river. This being observed from the forts, they redoubled their efforts, and fired shell after shell at the retiring vessels, keeping it up long after they were out of range. At the same time a vast horde of Dervish warriors, probably Mahmoud's entire force, sprang into sight, streaming across the hills behind which they had fixed their camp.

Led by a chief on a white horse, they waved their banners and shouted in wild exultation at the supposed defeat of the attacking vessels. Keppel does not appear to have thought it worthwhile to take any notice of the demonstration and continued his course to Berber. Beyond the casualty above mentioned the Egyptians sustained no loss in the two days' engagement. There were no means of arriving at the number of killed and wounded on the Dervish side, though from the accuracy of the gunboats' fire and the fact that they expended no less than 653 shells upon the defenders it may be assumed that their loss was considerable.[2]

On the 1st November General Hunter made another reconnaissance with the gunboats, this time as far as the foot of the Shabluka, or Sixth Cataract. As on the previous occasions, the flotilla, both in going and returning, shelled the forts whilst passing Metammeh, where a large number of Dervishes, both mounted and on foot, showed themselves. The fire in reply from the enemy was ill directed, and the gunboats got back to Berber with only three men wounded.

The result of the reconnaissance was to show that Mahmoud was still in force at Metammeh and meant fighting. His men were nevertheless in great difficulty for want of the supplies asked for from

---
2. Many of the above details of the engagement are taken from the *Morning Post*.

Omdurman. To procure food they took to raiding the neighbouring Jaalin villages, a party of about 1,000 of them having the temerity to proceed close to Berber, despite the presence of the large Egyptian force there. Evading the vigilance of the gunboat patrol, the marauders, divided into five bands, proceeded to attack the like number of villages simultaneously. The inhabitants, consisting of "friendlies," had, however, been furnished by the government with Remingtons. Of these they made such good use that in each instance they beat off the Dervish attack and forced the aggressors to retire.

After the fall of Abu Hamid had insured the non-interruption of the work of constructing the military railway from Wady Halfa to Abu Hamid, the line was pushed on, and finally completed on 31st October. Abu Hamid was not, however, destined to be the terminal station. The advantage of continuing the railway to Berber for the purpose of bringing up supplies, as well as to facilitate the further advance in the direction of Omdurman was too obvious to escape attention. So, £200,000 being set apart by the Egyptian Government to meet the cost, the work was commenced and pushed forward with all possible rapidity.

Egyptian rule being now practically re-established in the Soudan, negotiations took place between the Egyptian and Italian Governments for the retrocession of Kassala, in accordance with the arrangement under which Egypt assented to the Italian occupation. The negotiations resulted in an agreement that the town and contiguous territory should be formally handed over to Egypt on the 25th December, 1897.

As the time drew near the *sirdar*, now Major-General Sir Herbert Kitchener, who had been absent at Merawi, proceeded to Cairo and thence to Souakim and Massowah, to arrange with the Italian military authorities for the passage through the Italian colony of Erythrea of the Egyptian troops which were to relieve the existing garrison of Kassala.

Kassala, which, after being for many years lost to Egypt, was now about to be restored, is a place of such interest that any history of the Soudan would be imperfect without a reference to its past and present position.

The situation of Kassala is somewhat remarkable. As will be seen on referring to the map, it forms one of the corners of what may be considered an equilateral triangle, the other corners being at Berber and Khartoum. The distances between the three places are approximately the same.

Originally constructed by Mehemet Ali in 1840 for the protection of the fertile province of Taka against the Abyssinians, Kassala gradually acquired a large trade, and developed into a town of 60,000 inhabitants.

On the 30th July, 1885, after a siege which lasted twenty months, it fell into the hands of Osman Digna's followers.

Kassala, as a Dervish stronghold, constituted a grave danger to Egypt, which in 1891, being equally unable "to take it or leave it," at the suggestion of the British Government, consented to its transfer to the Italians, then established at Massowah. By the terms of the agreement, Italy was to give back Kassala as soon as the *khedive*'s rule should be re-established in the Soudan.

It was not, however, till 1894, and then only after a hard fight between 2,600 Italian and the like number of Dervish troops, that the Italians, under General Baratieri, succeeded in occupying their new possession.

Even after Kassala had passed into their hands, the Italians had anything but a happy time there. The Dervish hordes were constantly raiding round the place, and, though beaten off by the superior discipline and valour of the Italian troops, the Dervishes invariably returned and at times inflicted severe losses on the Italians and their native allies. In 1896 Kassala was regularly invested for three months by the Dervishes, and in March the situation reached a most critical stage. The Italians, numbering with their native allies 37,000 men, had been hopelessly defeated by the Abyssinians at Adowa on the 29th February, with a loss of 7,000 killed, wounded, and missing. The Abyssinians also captured 1,500 prisoners and fifty-two guns. As ill-luck would have it, the Italians had not only the Abyssinians, but the Mahdists, on their hands, and Kassala was then hemmed in by an immense force of Dervishes, and no means existed of relieving the Italian garrison.

This was the moment when the British Government, in the hope of creating a diversion in their favour, hurried forward the Dongola Expedition in the manner referred to in a previous chapter. This was followed by the Italians inflicting a severe defeat on the Dervishes, 5,000 in number, on the 2nd April, 1896, at Mount Mokram, killing some 800, and compelling the rest to retreat beyond the Atbara river.

In January, 1897, Kassala was again threatened by Dervishes, but General Vigano once more caused them to retire.

The Egyptian troops told off to occupy Kassala consisted of the

16th Egyptian Battalion and some artillery, in all 850 men, under Colonel Parsons.

Arriving at Massowah from Souakim on the 29th November, 1897, they only waited long enough to be reviewed by the "*sirdar*," and then marched through the Italian territory of Erythrea to Kassala. They encountered the greatest consideration and kindness at the different Italian posts. On the force approaching Kassala on the 18th December, it was received by Major de Bernardis, the Governor, with a guard of honour; and a salute of twenty-one guns was fired from the fort as the Egyptian flag was hoisted side by side with that of Italy. Until the 25th, the date fixed for the formal cession, the Egyptians remained in camp about a mile from the fort.

Arrangements were now made for taking over a battalion of 700 natives which the Italians had raised from amongst the "friendlies," and who readily consented to take service under the *khedive*.

In the interval before the 25th Colonel Parsons, by way of trying the qualities of the new levies, indulged them in a little fighting. Two places held by the Dervishes, El Fashir and Osobri, situated on the Atbara river, and about fifty miles from Kassala, were attacked and taken, the latter only, however, after a siege of six days.

Whilst the "friendlies" were thus engaged, Kassala, on Christmas Day, was handed over to Colonel Parsons. As the Italian flag was hauled down the Egyptian artillery saluted it with twenty-one guns, and the Italians quitting a place the defence of which had cost the lives of so many of their brave companions, marched away across the desert.[2]

---

2. The new frontier was fixed at a spot called Zabderat.

Chapter 64

From the Nile to the Atbara

At the beginning of the year 1898, the position of the opposing forces was somewhat as follows:—The *khalifa's* principal army, numbering upwards of 40,000 men, remained concentrated at Omdurman. Mahmoud, who had by this time been joined by Osman Digna, was still holding Metammeh with a force which had been increased to 20,000 men.

The Egyptian Army was occupying Berber, with its most advanced post at Ed Damer. Abu Hamid, Merawi, Dongola, and all the other various positions along the line of communication down the river, were also held by Egyptian troops. Military posts had been established between Berber and Souakim, and Kassala was garrisoned by an Egyptian battalion and the "friendlies" taken over from the Italians. Progress had been made with the railway communications. The Egyptian line from Cairo had been extended to Luxor, and the military line across the desert from Wady Halfa had been brought forward from Abu Hamid to Abu Dis, or nearly a third of the distance to Berber.

On the last day of the previous year, the Intelligence Department learnt that Mahmoud, pressed, it was said, by the *khalifa*, either to advance and destroy the Egyptians, or to fall back upon Omdurman, contemplated moving down the Nile on Berber. The 10,000 highly trained Egyptian soldiers, whom the *sirdar* was able to put in the field, being deemed insufficiently strong to meet Mahmoud's undisciplined savages, a brigade of British troops was telegraphed for. In reply, Sir Francis Grenfell, commanding the Army of Occupation, gave orders on the 2nd January for the 1st Battalion of the Warwickshire Regiment, from Alexandria, and the 1st Battalions of the Lincolnshire and the Cameron Highlanders, from Cairo, to proceed up the river at once. The Seaforth Highlanders were also ordered to Egypt, from Malta. No time was lost in sending forward the reinforcements, and before the end of the month they had reached Wady Halfa, with the exception of the Seaforths, which it was intended to station, in the first instance, at Assouan. Major-General Gatacre, an officer who had seen much service in Burmah, was despatched from Aldershot to take command of the British brigade.

Whilst the British troops were finding their way to the front, the Nile Valley railway from Kermeh was being utilized for the purpose of bringing down as many of the Egyptian soldiers as could be spared from the Dongola district to Wady Halfa, whence they were rapidly transported across the desert by the military railway to Abu Hamid, and thence to Abu Dis.[1]

To give warning of Mahmoud's advance, the gunboats made frequent reconnaissances to Shendy and Metammeh, and parties of "friendlies" also patrolled the river banks above Ed-Damer, and the adjacent desert. The Dervishes, on their part, were not wholly inactive, and occasionally indulged in a little raiding, as opportunities offered.

On the 10th February, Mahmoud, probably considering that if he were to advance at all, he should do so before the Egyptian force was strengthened by the arrival of the British soldiers, commenced to move his army across the Nile to Shendy preparatory to marching them to attack Berber. The Dervishes having only a few native boats and some hurriedly constructed rafts as a means of transport, the crossing occupied an entire fortnight. During this period, Commander Keppel, with two gunboats, steamed to Metammeh, and on one occasion dispersed with his Maxims a party of riflemen stationed to cover the crossing.

No serious attempt, however, was made to oppose the movement of Mahmoud's force across the river, and by the 25th February the operation was completed. Apparently a great opportunity was thus lost. With the absolute command of the river which the Egyptians possessed in the gunboat flotilla, nothing would have been easier than to have taken advantage of the moment when Mahmoud's army was divided into two sections by the Nile, to fall upon and destroy each section separately. That something of the kind was not attempted has been explained on the supposition that it formed part of the *sirdar's* strategy to encourage Mahmoud to leave his fortified position at Metammeh, and attack the Egyptians on open ground.

Thanks to the facilities afforded by the railway, Gatacre's British

---
1. The trains attained a speed of twenty-five miles an hour.

brigade was, by this time, getting well forward. In the middle of February, the Warwicks, Lincolns, and Camerons were all assembled at Abu Dis, where they went into camp for some weeks. During this period, everything was done to get the men into good condition by means of route marching and field exercises. Following the precedent established by Lord Wolseley in previous campaigns, the most rigid abstinence in the matter of alcohol was enforced, even the use of the harmless and comforting beer being forbidden.[2] The result was that the men were in excellent condition, and, as Gatacre in one of his addresses to the soldiers told them, "there was an almost total absence of crime, and, he might say, of drunkenness also," the latter observation provoking roars of laughter.

The brigade was armed with the Lee-Metford magazine rifle. This weapon, though possessing great range and penetrating power, had, by reason of its small diameter (·303), the disadvantage of making so small a hole as to render it more than doubtful if it would be effectual in stopping the headlong rush which forms the principal feature of a Dervish attack. To remedy this defect, the tips of the bullets were scooped out at the pointed end to the depth of about half an inch. Experiments showed that a bullet treated in this manner expands like an umbrella on striking an object, and thus makes a sufficiently large hole for the purpose required. Whilst in camp at Abu Dis, details from each regiment were told off to conduct this operation, and over a million of bullets were subjected to this treatment. The result was that a thoroughly effective missile, appropriately named a "man-stopper," was created.

Curiously enough, at the moment when General Gatacre was preparing his dum-dum bullets for use against the Dervishes General Kitchener decided to discontinue the use of the dumb-dumb missiles which he had been employing against the correspondents of the press. These weapons, which were equally "man-stoppers," were in the form of general orders by which correspondents were forbidden to go beyond that ever-changing point known as "rail head." As "rail head" was necessarily always somewhat in the rear of the operations, the prohibition was considered a great hardship, as it curtailed the power of the correspondents to send the earliest intelligence of what was going on at the front. A great agitation was made in the English journals at the time, and before further operations were proceeded with the *sirdar*

---

2. A firm of brewers who had forwarded several hundred barrels of beer to Wady Halfa had them all returned on their hands.

modified the restrictions within certain reasonable limits. The prohibition thenceforth extended only to going out on reconnaissances, to going near the *sirdar*, not in itself a serious privation considering the past friction between him and the pressmen, and to standing in front of the firing line during general actions. This last, however, was, according to one writer, Mr. G.W. Steevens, the author of *With Kitchener to Khartoum*, not strictly insisted upon.

Space does not allow of entering into the merits of the controversy on the subject of the relations between newspaper correspondents and military authorities. At the same time it may be observed that a general who puts unnecessary obstacles in the way of the press, or exercises too rigid a censorship, always lays himself open to the remark that, like Cæsar, he prefers to write his own *Commentaries*.

On the 25th February, when Mahmoud had completed his crossing to the east bank, General Gatacre received orders to proceed at once with his brigade to Berber. The orders reached him after the troops had been out all day exercising in the desert. Nevertheless, tents were at once struck, and the same evening the advance began. As far as "rail head," now at Sheriek, the men were transported by train, after which they proceeded on foot, and marching partly by night and partly by day, on the 2nd March they reached Berber, where, in the absence of the *sirdar* at Wady Halfa, General Hunter had his headquarters with two Egyptian brigades.

On the British soldiers reaching Berber, the Soudanese battalions turned out in force, and gave Gatacre's men an enthusiastic reception. The next day the Egyptian massed bands played the new arrivals well on their way to their camp at Debeker, ten miles south of Berber.

The only things which gave out during the march were the regulation boots. Whether from inferior workmanship, or the effect of climate, the stitching failed, and the soles came off in great numbers. Two hundred of the men fell out from footsores, and many of the remainder had to tramp along to their destination barefooted.

On the 10th March the *sirdar* arrived at Debeker, and inspected the troops, which, two days later, moved camp into a healthier spot at Darmali.

On the 13th news was received that Mahmoud, leaving a garrison at Ben Naga in charge of his stores, had quitted Shendy the day before, and, after engaging Keppel's gunboats *en route*, had descended the Nile as far as Aliab, midway between Shendy and Berber.

All doubts as to his intentions being now at rest, a general advance

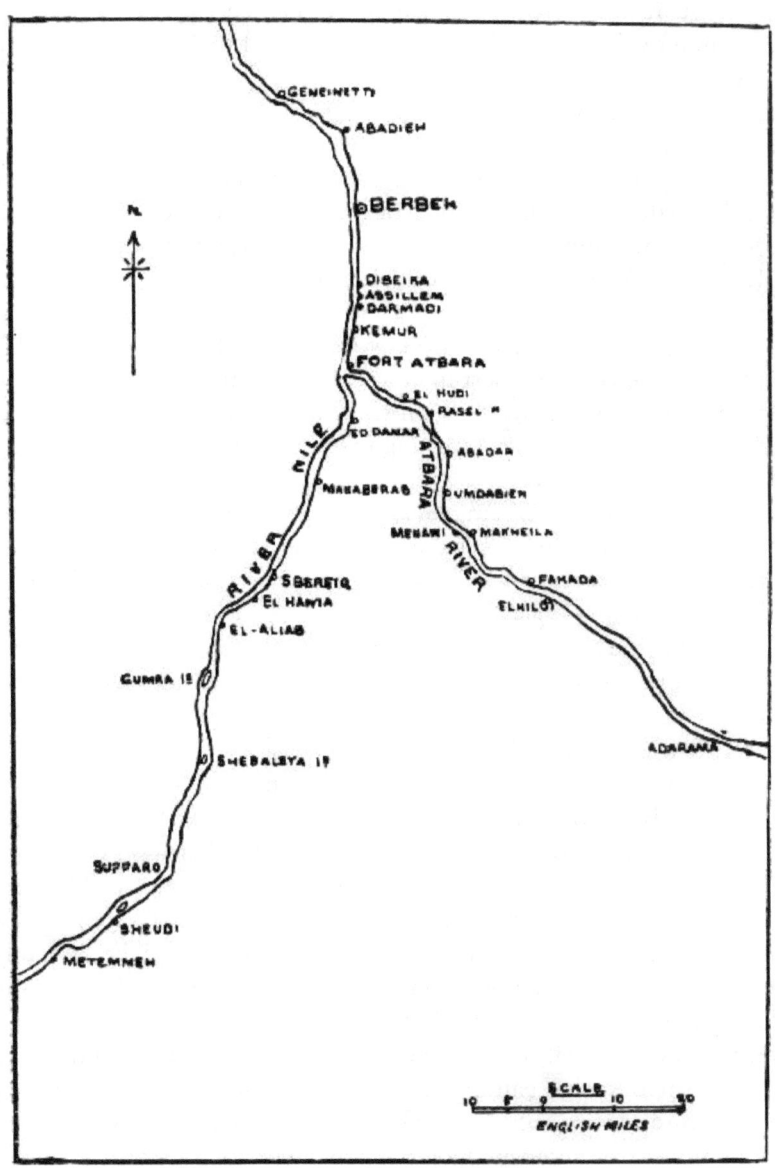

Map of the Nile and Atbara

of the *sirdar's* army was ordered to be made to Kenur, a deserted village about ten miles north of the Atbara. One Egyptian battalion was left to guard the store *depôt* at Berber, and a half battalion was placed in charge of the railway, by this time advanced to Geneinetti, twenty miles north of Berber.

The British troops at Darmali, on getting orders, at once set out, and marching amid intense heat and over trying ground, reached Kenur on the night of the 15th. On the following day they were joined by the Seaforths, which had been sent forward from Wady Halfa to Geneinetti by rail and thence by steamer. The Egyptian troops had been advancing meanwhile, and, with the exception of Lewis's brigade, the entire Anglo-Egyptian force was concentrated at Kenur on the 16th.

On the 19th March, Mahmoud with his whole army quitted Aliab, and started across the desert in an easterly direction towards the river Atbara. His intention was known to be to ford the river near a place called Hudi and then, after turning the Sirdar's left, to operate against Berber from the desert.

On the intelligence being received, it was determined to intercept, if possible, the Dervish forces, and the 20th saw the Anglo-Egyptian army on the march to Hudi, where, on its arrival, it was joined by the 3rd (Lewis's) Brigade, which had just come from Fort Atbara, a strongly fortified post at the confluence of the Nile and Atbara rivers.

The total force with the *sirdar* now amounted to about 13,000 men. It was composed of four infantry brigades, 800 cavalry, and four batteries of artillery with ten Maxims.

The British brigade, under Major-General Gatacre, consisted of the 1st Battalions of the following regiments: The Warwickshire (Colonel Quayle-Jones), Lincolnshire (Colonel Verner), Camerons (Colonel Money), and the Seaforth Highlanders (Colonel Murray). The Egyptian brigades were the 1st, under Lieutenant-Colonel Maxwell, formed by the 8th, 12th, 13th, and 14th Battalions; the 2nd, under Lieutenant-Colonel Macdonald, consisting of the 2nd, 9th, 10th, and 11th Battalions; and the 3rd, under Lieutenant-Colonel Lewis, composed of the 3rd, 4th, 7th, and 15th Battalions. To each of the four brigades an Egyptian battery of artillery was attached. The mounted troops consisted of eight squadrons of Egyptian cavalry, with Horse Artillery, under Lieutenant-Colonel Broadwood.

The Atbara at Hudi was at this season a narrow stream of clear water flowing slowly down a sandy valley, about a quarter of a mile wide, with steep banks covered with bush and Halfa grass. From Hudi the cavalry, with some Maxims under Colonel Broadwood, went forward to search for the enemy, whilst the remainder of the troops, after forming a *zeriba* from the surrounding mimosa bushes, bivouacked for the night. Each man lay down on the bare ground fully dressed with his arms and equipments beside him. The night, passed in the open air, was bitterly cold, and the dust permeated everything.

On the same day (the 20th) that the *sirdar's* army encamped at Hudi, on the north side of the Atbara, Mahmoud and his followers crossed the river from the south side near Nakhila, some thirty miles further up. Here he established himself, and commenced intrenching his position.

On the 21st, the *sirdar's* troops marched further up the Atbara, eventually halting at a spot marked in the maps "Ras-el-Hudi," where they were destined to remain for several days. The *sirdar* thus placed his force directly between the Dervish leader and Berber, effectually frustrating the intended move in that direction. There were no houses, huts, or habitations at Ras-el-Hudi, which derives its name from its geographical position, the Arabic word "*ras*" meaning "head." It was a pretty spot, green and fertile at this time of the year.

The Atbara here no longer flowed, but was represented only by a series of isolated pools of water, in which fish and an occasional crocodile were to be seen. A *zeriba* was at once made, and the camp generally put in a state of defence.[3]

Whilst the main body of the *sirdar's* force was advancing, the Egyptian cavalry under Colonel Broadwood, with the Horse Artillery and Maxims, pushed on as far as Abadar on the 22nd, and here the enemy were found in force. They consisted principally of Baggara horsemen, who charged with great gallantry a squadron of cavalry, under Captain the Hon. C. Baring, who had to fall back upon his supports.

Mahmoud's position having been by this time pretty well ascertained, a force consisting of a squadron of cavalry, with a batalion of infantry and Maxims in support, was sent on the following day, under the command of Major Collinson, to tempt the Dervish leader to come out. When the party had advanced about six miles in the direction of the enemy's camp, the cavalry met and opened fire upon a force of 300 or 400 Baggara horsemen who attempted to surround them. The cavalry, however, managed to get away, and fell back upon the infantry now formed up in square, which, with rifle and Maxim

---

3. During the stay of the troops, the heat was intense, the thermometer frequently standing at 117° in the shade

fire, eventually forced the Baggara to withdraw. The party then returned to the camp.

As already stated, Mahmoud had left a garrison close to Shendy, to enable him to keep up his communications with Omdurman, and as a guard for his *depôt*. On the 25th March, the *sirdar* detached one of his battalions, and sent it by Commander Keppel's steamers to take the position, capture the stores, and destroy Shendy. The expedition steamed past the last-named place to the *depôt* at Horh Ben Naga, and, on the following morning, disembarked the soldiers, who, encountering little resistance, drove out the Baggara garrison of 700 men, with a loss of 150 killed, seized the stores, and captured a large number of prisoners, including 650 women and children. Shendy was found to be in ruins. Such men as it contained gave themselves up. The forts were destroyed, and the place set fire to. The gunboats pursued the fugitives up to the foot of the Sixth Cataract, and then returned and re-embarked the soldiers, together with the booty, consisting of great quantities of grain, camels, donkeys, arms, and ammunition.

A reconnaissance made on the 30th March showed that Mahmoud occupied a strongly intrenched position, surrounded by brushwood, at Nakheila, on the north bank of the river, now quite dry, with his front towards the desert, and protected by a thorn *zeriba* running from his left, at right angles to the river, away to his extreme right. Deserters, who now came in daily, reported that Mahmoud was in great straits for food, his men existing principally on the nuts of the dôm palm, on cooked cabbage palms, and such other vegetables as could be found in the bush. Most of his warriors were disaffected, and were only prevented by strong measures from deserting *en masse*.

The Dervish chief was in a dilemma whilst the *sirdar* was in front of him; the projected move on Berber was impossible. On the other hand, the reports received of the strength of the Anglo-Egyptian force convinced him that to move out into the open and attack would be simply to court destruction. To leave the shelter of his intrenchments, and retire on Omdurman, was not only a hazardous operation, but one which must result in the demoralisation and desertion of his followers. Even if he succeeded in reaching Omdurman, Mahmoud may well have had misgivings as to the nature of the reception that he would meet with at the hands of the Khalifa. Under these circumstances, he decided that there was nothing for it but to remain where he was, and trust to the strength of his position to repel any attack the *sirdar* might make.

This was not at all what the *sirdar* wished for. It would have suited him much better to be attacked in the open desert, where his superior rifle and artillery fire would give him an immense advantage, than to have to attack Mahmoud in his *zeriba* in the bush, amid endless intrenchments and unknown obstructions. On the other hand, it was clear that something must be done. The Anglo-Egyptian force could not sit down or ever watching Mahmoud at a distance of only twenty miles. The difficulty of supplying 13,000 men by camel transport only was immense. The British troops, too, were beginning to suffer from the heat, inferior food, and inadequate shelter, and dysentery and enteric fever began to break out.

Realizing all this, the *sirdar* determined on a general advance, and on the 4th of April struck his camp at Ras-el-Hudi, and moved up the river to Abadar. Though this as a camping place much resembled the last, the troops, who had got tired of Ras-el-Hudi, with its endless sand storms and discomforts, rejoiced at the change, and the more so because it appeared to indicate fighting.

On the 5th, a final effort to draw Mahmoud was made. At daybreak General Hunter went out with eight squadrons of cavalry, eight Maxims, and a battery of horse artillery. When about 1,000 yards from the front of the enemy's position, the troops halted, and Hunter, with a few of his officers, went forward to obtain a nearer view.

The Dervishes showed themselves in no mood to be trifled with, and soon gave Hunter as much fighting as he wanted, for, at 9 a.m., two large bodies of Baggara horsemen came out of the bush right and left from the enemy's *zeriba*, and directed their efforts to getting round the flanks of the cavalry, whilst a third party fiercely charged them in front. Hunter, to avoid being cut off, had to gallop back to the main body, now engaged in repelling the attack.

In this they were assisted by the guns and Maxims on the left of the cavalry, and after a sharp struggle, in which the officers had to use their swords and revolvers, the Dervish onslaught was repulsed. A large body of footmen then streamed forth from Mahmoud's *zeriba*, and Hunter's force found it necessary to retreat to avoid being surrounded. As the cavalry fell back their retiring movement was covered by the Maxims, which continued firing, and practically saved the situation. The Dervish horsemen still followed, and pressed the rear and flanks of the retreating Egyptians, who more than once had to turn and charge to lessen the pressure.

When this had been effected, the retreat was continued more deliberately, two squadrons from time to time dismounting, and with their carbines keeping the foe in check, whilst other squadrons took up a position one or two hundred yards in the rear. At last, about 10 a.m., a combined charge of cavalry, headed by Colonel Broadwood, drove back the assailants, and both the opposing forces withdrew at 1 p.m. The Egyptian troops, without being further molested, got back to camp, where, the sound of the cannonading having been heard, the army had turned out ready for action.

The Egyptian loss in the fight was not heavy, being only eight men killed and fourteen wounded. The Dervish loss was put as high as 200. This, however, was only an estimate, as the retreating Egyptians did not stop to count the slain. At the same time, as the Maxims fired 6,000 rounds, it seems only reasonable to suppose that someone was hit.

Although the engagement on the 5th showed that Mahmoud meant fighting, it indicated that, so far as related to moving his army out into the open to be destroyed, he was still a "conscientious objector," and, with a view to attacking him in his position, the forward movement of the *sirdar's* army was resumed on the 6th April, when the troops brought up at the deserted village of Umdabbia, seven and a half miles from the Dervish camp. Here they remained for two days, whilst the final preparations for the attack were made.

At 5 p.m. on the 7th, after the stores and all superfluous baggage had been left in camp in charge of a half battalion of Egyptian infantry, the rest of the troops marched out into the desert. They moved in echelon, with the British brigade in front. Behind them was Macdonald's brigade; then came Lewis's brigade and the Camel Corps, Maxwell's brigade bringing up the rear. The route selected was parallel to the river, and over broken ground and desert sand. Although when night fell there was a bright moon, the sand, driven by a strong wind, obscured the view a good deal, and frequent halts had to be made to preserve the formation. When, after marching for three hours, a spot called Mutrus, three miles distant from the enemy, was reached, a halt was ordered, and the men, lying down in the desert, rested.

Chapter 65

The Battle of the Atbara

The *sirdar's* troops were left unmolested during the short rest which they took at Mutrus.

At 1 a.m. on the 8th April, the order was quietly given to fall in, and the men promptly obeyed without noise or bustle. Half an hour later the final march began, and the full moon being now well overhead, it was possible to see a considerable distance. There was no smoking or talking in the ranks, and the orders were given in a low voice or by a wave of the hand. The rumble of the gun-carriages and the dull thud of thousands of tramping feet were the only sounds which broke the stillness of the desert.

At 3 a.m. a huge column of flame was seen on the right. After burning a few minutes it dwindled away, and whether it was a beacon to notify to Mahmoud the approach of the army or whether it was the result of accident was never ascertained.

At 4 o'clock the troops were abreast of Mahmoud's position, where the camp fires could be seen burning. There was then a halt of half an hour. When the advance was resumed at 4.30, the men were no longer in square, but marched in attack formation, the British brigade on the left, Macdonald's in the centre, Maxwell's on the right, and Lewis's in reserve. The artillery and Maxims accompanied the infantry marching in the rear upon the right and left. The cavalry and Horse Artillery were away half a mile to the left.

In this formation the troops continued to advance till 6 a.m., when they halted in a commanding position 600 yards from the enemy's camp, which was plainly visible now that the sun began to rise. From the number of men seen running to and fro, and from other signs of activity, it was clear that the approach of the *sirdar's* force had been perceived.

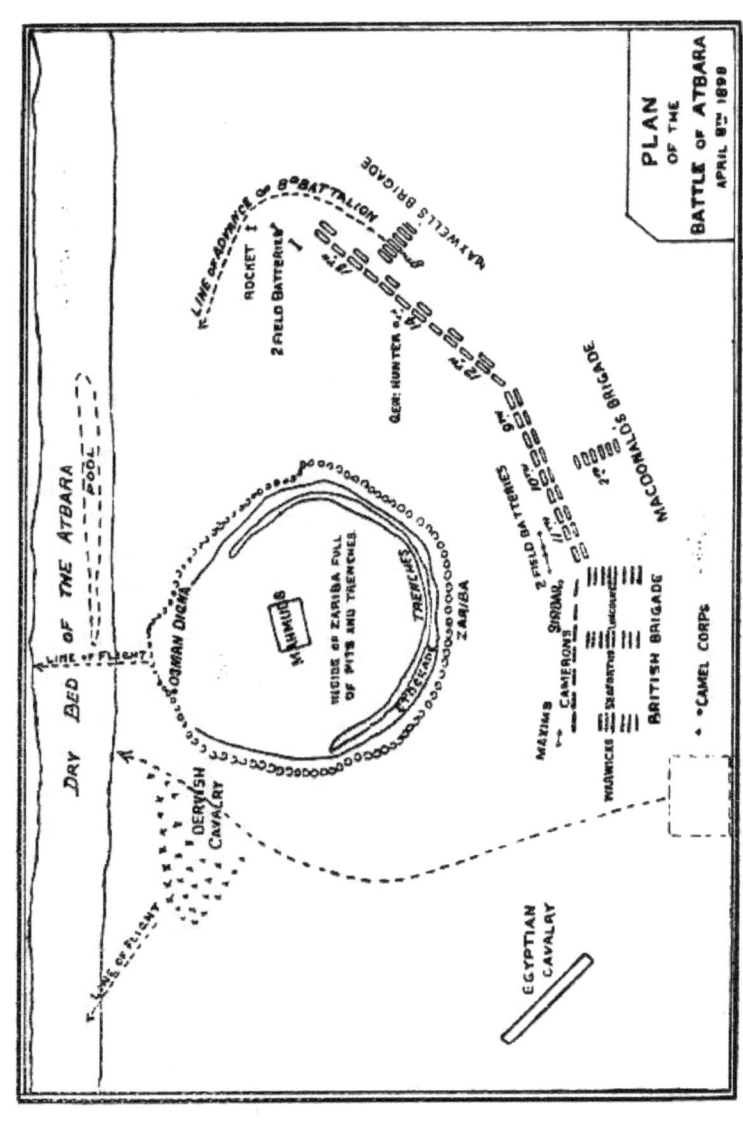

The enemy's works presented a sufficiently formidable appearance. Behind the long row of cut mimosa bushes forming the *zeriba*, and constituting the outer line of defence, were palisades of *dôm* palm logs stuck endways in the ground; and further back amongst the trees was an encircling trench, with numerous cross-trenches, a few earthworks, and a great many shelter huts made of palm branches and grass.

At 6.15, the guns were run into position, and opened fire. Two batteries of six guns each were placed on the extreme right of the Egyptians, and the like number on their left, at the interval between the Egyptian and British troops. In this way a cross-fire of twenty-four guns was brought to bear on the position.

The artillery was assisted by a rocket battery under Lieutenant Beatly, R.N.

The artillery fire, carefully directed, told with much effect on the *zeriba*, and soon many of the palisades were seen to be knocked away, whilst the shells at the same time made havoc with the earthworks. The rocket battery, after a few rounds, set fire to the grass huts forming the Dervish camp, causing a furious conflagration.

The Dervishes had hitherto kept well out of sight, but all at once, whilst the cannonade was in full operation, a large party of Baggara horsemen was observed galloping from the bush at the southern side of the *zeriba* and forming up, as if intending to charge the British left. On the Maxims opening on them, the Baggara at once turned and disappeared in the bush to the south.

The bombardment went on for an hour and a half, during which time there was no reply from the *zeriba* except a few bullets which were fired in the direction of Macdonald's and Maxwell's brigades, but, being aimed too high, the missiles passed harmlessly overhead.

The order to cease firing was now given, and the infantry, who had hitherto been lying down, interested spectators of the scene, formed up for the assault. The Camerons, extended in line, composed the front of the British brigade. Behind them, in column of companies, were the Warwicks on the left, the Seaforths in the centre, and the Lincolns on the right; continuing the line to the right was Macdonald's brigade, with six companies in line and the remainder behind in column of companies as a support. Still further to the right was Maxwell's brigade, with eight companies in line and four companies in support, and on the extreme right were one of Maxwell's battalions, the 8th, and one of Lewis's, the 15th Soudanese, also in column of companies. A squadron of cavalry was sent down towards the river on this flank. On the extreme left, in the rear of the Warwicks, Lewis's reserve brigade of two battalions was placed to prevent any flank attack on that side. The cavalry and Horse Artillery were placed half a mile off in the desert to the left of the whole force. The four batteries of artillery were posted on the right of the line, and the Maxims, twelve in number, were distributed between the right and left flanks and the centre.

At a quarter-past eight, the *sirdar* and his staff having selected a post of observation, about 900 yards from the *zeriba*, and General Gatacre and most of the field officers having dismounted and placed themselves at the head of their men, the "advance" sounded. Then the pipes of the Highlanders skirled, the bugles of the other British regiments and the bands of the native battalions played inspiring tunes, and the whole line, with bayonets fixed, advanced in quick time.

The Camerons, headed by General Gatacre and Colonel Money, and with a huge Union Jack (the regimental colours were all left in Cairo) in the centre, marched in advance of the British troops.

At intervals of every few yards the men halted, and "independent firing" was kept up. Then the line again moved forward, and the same thing was repeated. Suddenly, when the front rank had got within 200 yards of the *zeriba*, the return fire from the Dervishes commenced. It was mostly aimed too high, but here and there the bullets came dropping in, and the men in front began to fall, sometimes singly and sometimes in little groups of two or three together. Still the line swept onward, the troops, both British and Egyptian, preserving their formation as perfectly as if on parade.

As the Camerons reached some elevated ground sloping towards the *zeriba*, then only a hundred yards off, they became more exposed, and the bullets came more thickly. At last a halt was sounded, and for a minute or two "independent firing" was resumed with good effect, the Lee-Metfords making no smoke to obstruct the view, whilst, on the other hand, the little white wreaths from the Dervish fire indicated to the soldiers the points on which to direct their rifles.

The "advance" was then sounded, cries of "Come on, men!" were heard, and, amid ringing cheers, the Camerons rushed for the *zeriba*. The first to reach it were General Gatacre and Captain Brooke, his *aide-de-camp*. Seizing the bush with both hands, the general tried to pull it aside, nearly losing his life in the attempt. A Dervish rushed upon him with a spear; the general called out to his orderly, Private Cox, of the Camerons, "Give it to him, my lad!" and Private Cox bayoneted the Dervish, just in time.

Immediately after, the Camerons, closely followed by the Warwicks, Seaforths, and Lincolns, were up to the *zeriba*, and beginning to pull away the thorn bushes, being covered, as far as possible, by their comrades. Alternate companies dragged at the bushes, whilst the others replied to the Dervish fire. In a few minutes, the men succeeded in making gaps in the hedge sufficiently wide to allow of the troops entering, and, in a quarter of an hour from the advance being sounded, the *zeriba* was entered. It was found necessary to modify the original plan of attack. According to this, the Camerons having cleared a sufficient pathway, the battalions in their rear were to pass through their ranks, deploy, and join in a general advance by the whole line.

A deployment, however, in face of the rifle fire which was encountered, was not to be thought of, and it could hardly be expected that the Camerons, who had hitherto occupied the front rank, were going to stand aside and give place to the men of the other regiments. Realizing this, Gatacre called on the Camerons to push forward, and the battalion, headed by its officers, and with the Union Jack in front, dashed through the openings. Captain Findlay, a young officer of the Camerons, six feet two inches in height, was the first to enter the *zeriba*. With sword in one hand and revolver in the other, he sprang over the palisade and first trench, and fell mortally wounded.

The rush of the Camerons was closely followed by the Seaforths and the Warwicks, the men pushing on as nearly in line as the obstacles in their way would allow.

Here the real fighting began. The trenches were full of crouching Dervishes, firing point-blank as fast as they could load, and neither asking nor receiving quarter. It soon became, not so much a question of clearing the trenches as of killing every Dervish separately. The latter never lost an opportunity. Major Urquhart, of the Camerons, and one of the first to enter the *zeriba*, was shot dead, from behind, by a Dervish who, concealed amongst a heap of dead and dying, was waiting his chance to kill.

The enemy's riflemen were not particular in their choice of weapons, and Remingtons, Martinis, fowling-pieces, and elephant guns were brought into play indiscriminately. Major Napier, also of the Camerons, was so severely wounded with a shot from an elephant gun, as to have to be carried off the field. He died afterwards in Cairo. His regiment lost sixty men, either killed or wounded, in less than an hour.

The Seaforths also suffered severely. Lieutenant Gore, the first of his regiment to enter the enemy's lines, was shot through the heart, and Colonel Murray, of the same regiment, was shot in the arm by a round bullet from a fowling-piece.

Captain Baillie had his leg shattered, and died subsequently in Cairo. Sergeant-Major Mackay, also of the Seaforths, had an experience which is probably unique. When jumping the palisades, a Dervish spearman made a drive at him in mid-air, as he was, so to speak, "on the wing." Fortunately, the spear only tore the sergeant's kilt, and he then finished his assailant with pistol and claymore. The leading company of the Seaforths had eleven men killed or wounded.

Colonel Verner, of the Lincolns, a man of such gigantic stature that he could hardly be missed even by an indifferent marksman, had bad luck. One bullet cut his helmet strap and grazed his cheek, whilst a third hit him in the mouth, gouging away his upper lip, and taking off his moustache. The gallant officer refused to retire, and, with a bandaged head, continued with his men till the end.

As the men pushed on through the bush, several small mud-built forts had to be carried. Each of these mounted an old brass cannon, and was garrisoned by riflemen, who had necessarily to be slain.

Meanwhile, the Egyptians, away on the right, gallantly led by General Hunter, had entered a *zeriba* a little in advance of the British brigade, and steadily fought their way, step by step, across the trenches. Several of their English officers fell wounded, though, fortunately, none were killed. Some of their hardest fighting took place at a sort of inner *zeriba* or stockade, situated some thirty yards in the rear of the trenches, and strongly held. From this work a deadly rifle fire was directed upon the advancing troops, and one company of the 11th Soudanese, which was the first to try to take it, was nearly annihilated. Other companies of the same regiment then came on in support, and, after hard fighting, effected an entrance and occupied the place.

Once this position was taken, the combined troops had little difficulty in making their way across the entire *zeriba*, the Dervishes fleeing before them in scattered masses through the palm trees to the Atbara river.

Occasionally a group of fugitives would stop, under cover of the bank, and open a rifle fire on their pursuers, but after a few volleys all made off down the dry bed of the river, which formed the limit of the Anglo-Egyptian advance.

The battle of the Atbara was then won, and the order to cease firing was given. This was just twenty-six minutes from the final advance to the assault.

Then, on the banks of the river, the troops crowded together and indulged in mutual congratulations. The Soudanese soldiers wildly danced with joy, and, waving their rifles in the air, shook hands with every British soldier whom they came in contact with.

After a brief halt on the side of the Atbara, the force was re-formed, and marched back out of Mahmoud's works. As the troops returned, they were met by the *sirdar*, who was greeted with enthusiastic cheers. When he had addressed a few observations to the men, they formed up in squares of brigades to the right of the scene of the original assault.

The cavalry, directly the fighting was finished, had been sent off to pursue the Dervish horsemen, but they had got too long a start, so Colonel Broadwood's men only followed for about two miles, where the track was lost in the bush, and the force returned.

The losses of the British brigade were five officers (including three who died subsequently) and twenty-one men killed, and ninety-nine officers and men wounded. The Egyptian loss was much more severe, fifty-seven men being killed and 386 wounded, including ten of the British officers.[1]

The total, 568, though heavy enough, would doubtless have been greater had Mahmoud's forces been provided with anything like proper ammunition. As it was, their cartridges, originally of poor quality, mostly turned out from the arsenal at Khartoum, had much deteriorated; consequently the fire on the Dervish side was comparatively ineffective.

The enemy's loss could not have been much less than 3,000 men in killed and wounded; 2,000 bodies were counted in the *zeriba*, and about 500 more on the south side of the works and in the bed of the river. With the exception of Osman Digna, who escaped with the cavalry, and Mahmoud, who was made prisoner, all the principal *emirs* were killed. Mahmoud's ten guns (only two of which bore traces of having been fired), over 100 banners, together with an enormous quantity of rifles (including a Tower rifle of 1856), swords, spears, ammunition, and equipments, besides some grain and stores, fell into the hands of the conquerors; and 2,000 men were made prisoners.

---

1. According to a report to the War Department drawn up by Surgeon-Major Carr, out of the entire British force there were only three men whose wounds were caused by spears, all the rest being the result of gunfire. This would tend to show that the amount of hand-to-hand fighting engaged in was inconsiderable.

It is difficult to arrive at the exact numbers of the Dervish force engaged in the fight. Mahmoud was known to have left Shendy with 18,900 men, but some of these had been killed in the fights with the gunboats, and others in the various skirmishes and reconnaissances. His losses from deaths and desertions must have been even more considerable. All his cavalry, which, according to his statement referred to later on, numbered 4,000, were undoubtedly absent when the real fighting began.

After allowing for these deductions, it is improbable that the total of his force present at the fight could have exceeded 14,000, approximately the same number as his opponents.

The remains of Mahmoud's army, numbering probably about 8,000 men, continued its flight up the Atbara to Adarama, a distance of about fifty miles, losing many men on the way. Here the fugitives divided into two parties, one of which went to Gedaref, and the other, joined by Osman Digna, to Abu Deleh.

The Battle of the Atbara was a striking success. The Dervish force, like that of Arabi at Tel-el-Kebir, was broken up and dispersed. The Dervishes, opposed to an enemy nearly equal in point of numbers, fought well during the brief period that the engagement lasted; but, with their imperfect organization, insufficient artillery, and defective weapons, they would have stood no chance even against a smaller army than that which the *sirdar* brought against them. This, however, in no way detracts from the merit of the British and Egyptian troops, who, not less by their patient endurance and discipline than by their valour in the field, achieved so successful a result. But to go further, and, as many writers have done, to magnify a fight in which a disciplined army in less than half an hour routed a horde of starving savages, into a "brilliant victory," would be exaggeration.

No sooner was the fight over, than parties of men were told off to search the interior of the *zeriba*, which, from all accounts, presented a gruesome spectacle. Dead bodies, many of them mangled into mere fragments of humanity, were lying about everywhere. Not only men, but women also, were amongst the slain.

In the trenches, numbers of unfortunate black prisoners were found lifeless and chained hand and foot, with rifles in their hands. Others were discovered with forked pieces of timber round their necks, to prevent their escape. In one place the body of a Dervish chief was found pinned to the trunk of a tree by a rocket which had passed through his chest.

The slaughter was not confined to the human race alone. Hundreds of dead camels, donkeys, sheep, and goats had also fallen victims to the shell and rifle fire, and lay scattered about within the *zeriba*.

Whilst the search proceeded a party of the 10th Soudanese came upon the Emir Mahmoud, concealed in one of the grass shelter huts. He was at once seized, and limping slightly from a bayonet wound in the leg, was conducted before the *sirdar*. Throughout the interview Mahmoud, who was a man nearly six feet in height, wore an air of complete indifference. Addressing him in Arabic, General Hunter, pointing to Kitchener, said, "This is the *sirdar*," a piece of information which failed to produce any impression. The *sirdar* then asked, "Why have you come into my country to burn and kill?" To this wholly unnecessary question Mahmoud, with sullen dignity, answered, "As a soldier, I must obey the *khalifa's* orders, as you must the *khedive's*."

A few more questions were put as to Mahmoud's *emirs* and men, to which he gave curt replies. Being asked, "Where is Osman Digna?" Mahmoud replied, "I don't know. He was not in the fight; he went away with the cavalry.[2] All the rest of my *emirs* stayed with me. I saw your troops at five in the morning, and mounted my horse and rode round the camp to see that my people were in their places. Then I returned to my quarters and waited. I am not a woman to run away." Then, no one having any more conundrums to put, the prisoner was led off by an escort.

The same afternoon, as soon as the wounded had been collected, and the mournful duty of burying the dead had been performed, the *sirdar's* forces, less one Egyptian battalion, left to take charge of the spoils and to clear up the Dervish camp, marched back to the *zeriba* at Umdabbia, where they arrived before nightfall. From this point, all the troops, with the exception of Lewis's brigade, which returned to its former quarters at Fort Atbara, went, by easy stages, into summer quarters on the banks of the Nile. The British troops and those of Maxwell's brigade went into camp at Darmali, and Macdonald's to Berber, where on the 14th the *sirdar* made his triumphal entry.

The whole town was *en fête*, and the main thoroughfare was spanned with palm branches and banners. The route was kept by the troops of the garrison, and a salute was fired as the *sirdar* approached. The cavalry met him as he entered the town, and escorted him to an elevated platform, which had been erected in the centre of the town

---

2. Later on Mahmoud stated that 4,000 of his horsemen were half a day's journey distant on the occasion of the fight.

and draped with flags. Here the *sirdar* and his staff took their place, whilst the troops, with colours flying and bands playing, marched past in review order. Behind the cavalry came the captive Mahmoud on foot, with his hands tied behind his back.

The Dervish leader, though hooted by the crowd, showed no signs of depression, and walked with head erect, as if realizing that he was the most important feature in the show. An immense concourse of people witnessed the sight, and welcomed the troops with acclamations. The women were especially demonstrative, and many of them approached and threatened Mahmoud, to whom the expression "*Kalb!*" (dog) was freely used. When the display was finished, the troops went to their camp, and Mahmoud was sent down the river and interned at Wady Halfa.

Before leaving, Mahmoud had an opportunity of seeing an old acquaintance in Slatin Pasha, whom he had known in the days when Slatin was a captive at Omdurman. Slatin "had suffered many things" at the hands of Mahmoud, and their meeting, now that the relative positions of the two men were reversed, was mutually interesting.[3]

A week later the indefatigable gunboats, sent up the river, returned, and reported having fallen in with many of the fugitives from Nakheila at Aliab. The Dervishes refusing to surrender, an engagement ensued, in which 200 of them were killed and 70 made prisoners. Some of these reported that many hundreds of their number had died of thirst in the retreat across the desert after the battle.

---

3. Their conversation, which is too long to be reproduced here, after reference to old times, dwelt principally on the impending advance on Omdurman. Its substance was somewhat as follows:—Slatin: "Hullo, Mahmoud! Got *you* this time, dear boy!" Mahmoud: "Right you are, Slatin, but just you wait till you come across Abdullah! Then you will see what happens, and he may have you again."

CHAPTER 66

The Advance on Omdurman

In May, 1898, preparations began for the advance on Omdurman. The Egyptian headquarters were moved forward to Fort Atbara, where three months' provisions for 25,000 men were directed to be accumulated. Though every article had to be sent up from Lower Egypt, this was rendered less difficult by the recent completion of the railway (hitherto carried as far only as Luxor) connecting Cairo with Shellal, as well as by the prolongation of the military line to Abadieh, twelve miles north of Berber.

At Abadieh a naval arsenal, with workshops and factories, was established. Here the new screw gunboats *Sultan*, *Melik*, and *Sheikh*, which had arrived from England in sections, were put together and launched.

Meanwhile, pending the advance, Gatacre's brigade, in their summer camp at Darmali, were being exercised in route marching and manoeuvring, to keep them in training. The men had by this time got accustomed to the heat, and suffered but little sickness.

Early in June, there being no immediate fighting in view, the *sirdar* left for Cairo, and later on paid a flying visit to England. Several of the British officers also went on leave.

On the 22nd, the views of the British Government with regard to the impending advance were stated in the House of Commons by Sir Michael Hicks-Beach, in introducing the proposal to remit the loan contracted by Egypt in 1897 for the expenses of the Dongola Expedition. The Chancellor of the Exchequer declared that the government did not contemplate the undertaking of any further military operations on a large scale, or involving any considerable expense, for the recovery of the great provinces to the south of Khartoum. "What we do anticipate," he went on to say, "is that expeditions may be made by the gunboat flotilla, which will be at the disposal of the Administration, to free the waterway of the Nile from any interference with the perfect freedom of commerce with the interior, so far as it can be carried on by that waterway."

In July the British Government decided to strengthen the *sirdar's* force by additional troops, in the shape of another British brigade, together with cavalry and artillery. The British force which it was proposed to put in the field was a division consisting of two brigades, under General Gatacre. The 1st Brigade, commanded by Brigadier-General H. G. Wauchope, was formed of the battalions which had fought at the Atbara, viz., the Warwicks, Lincolns, Seaforths, and Camerons; the 2nd Brigade, commanded by Brigadier-General the Hon. A. G. Lyttelton, consisted of the 1st Battalion of the Grenadier Guards from Gibraltar, the 1st Battalion of the Northumberland Fusiliers and the 2nd Battalion of the Lancashire Fusiliers from Cairo, and the 2nd Battalion of the Rifle Brigade from Malta. In addition, there were the 21st Lancers from Cairo, a Maxim battery manned by a detachment of the Royal Irish Fusiliers from Alexandria, two field batteries (32nd and 37th) of the Royal Artillery, and details of Royal Engineers, Army Service and Medical Corps, making a total strength of about 7,500 men.

The Egyptian force which was to co-operate was also increased by another brigade. The whole was to consist of a division, under the command of Major-General Hunter, composed of four brigades, *viz.*, the 1st, 2nd, and 3rd, under Macdonald, Maxwell, and Lewis respectively, and a 4th brigade under Major (now Lieutenant-Colonel) Collinson, composed of the 1st, 5th, 17th, and 18th Battalions. The cavalry were to be ten squadrons, besides eight companies of the Camel Corps. The artillery force was to consist of one horse and four field batteries, and one Maxim battery.

The total Egyptian force represented about 12,500 men.

Fort Atbara was the point upon which, early in August, the British and Egyptian troops began to concentrate. Lewis's (3rd) brigade had already gone on ahead to cut firewood for the steamers, and establish *depôts* of stores at Nasri Island, ten miles below the Sixth Cataract. From there Lewis went on to Wad Habeshi, where the rapids commence.

The Egyptian troops were the earliest arrivals at Atbara, which soon became a scene of bustle and activity. The railway, by this time extended to within a short distance of the camp, lent important aid in bringing forward both men and supplies. The gunboats, increased by the new additions to ten in number, also materially assisted in the work of transport.

The Nile had risen superbly, and no difficulty was experienced in passing up the cataracts.

The next point of concentration was fixed at Wad Hamid, a short distance from Wad Habeshi, already mentioned, and but little time was lost in sending the troops forward.

On one day, *viz.*, the 3rd August, no less than six Soudanese battalions left Atbara. The cavalry and transport animals went forward along the western bank of the Nile. As the black soldiers left, the white ones began to arrive. Even before the last of the steamers conveying the six Egyptian battalions had started, the first half of the Rifle Brigade appeared, the remainder turning up on the following day. The regiment had left Cairo on the 27th and 28th July, proceeding by rail to Shellal, above the First Cataract, thence by steamer to Wady Halfa, and then by rail *viâ* Abu Hamid to Atbara. General Wauchope and his staff came up on the 5th, closely followed by the artillery, the Grenadier Guards, the Northumberland Fusiliers, the 21st Lancers, and the rest of the 2nd British brigade.

It is worthy of observation that, notwithstanding the railway connection established between Cairo and Assouan, recourse had once more to be had to the steamers of Messrs. Thomas Cook & Son for the transport of the horses belonging to the British brigade from Khizan, on the river just below Luxor, to Assouan. (See note following).

> Note:—As this is the last occasion on which it will be necessary to refer to Messrs. Cook & Son, it may not be out of place to recall some of the services rendered by that firm in the various operations on the Nile in which British troops participated. The important part taken by Messrs. Cook in regard to the "Gordon Relief Expedition" in 1884 has been already mentioned in these pages. On that occasion the firm transported Lord Wolseley's entire force from Assiout to the Second Cataract. In pursuance of their contract, on this occasion the firm's steamers transported altogether no less than 11,000 British and 7,000 Egyptian troops, 800 whalers, and 130,000 tons of stores and war material. When the melancholy failure of the expedition is contrasted with the admirable manner in which Messrs. Cook performed their contract, one is tempted to regret that

the latter was not made to include the rescue of Gordon and the Soudan garrisons. In the disturbances on the Nile frontier in 1885 and 1886, Messrs. Cook's fleet was again occupied in satisfying the military requirements of the British and Egyptian Governments. In the spring of 1896, when the hurried advance to Dongola was made, all of Cook's steamers were once more requisitioned for the purpose of conveying troops, both British and Egyptian, from Belianah to Assouan.

Nor were the services of the firm of a military character only. The late Mr. John Mason Cook, the managing partner, was a man of a singularly benevolent character. The founding of the Luxor Hospital for Natives was only one of many charitable works due to his liberality and energy. When the fighting at Tel-el-Kebir was over, he undertook the transport of the wounded to Cairo by water, and later on, when Wolseley's army was decimated with enteric fever, Mr. Cook conveyed the convalescents by special steamers up the Nile, in each case making no charge beyond that of the actual cost of running the vessels.

Probably few men have done better work in the cause of humanity and civilization than the late head of the firm of "Thomas Cook & Son." His influence with the natives, particularly on the Nile, was immense. He was, in fact, regarded as the "King of Upper Egypt." This is illustrated by at least two good stories told in Cairo. One relates to a native schoolboy, who, with a view to testing his proficiency, being asked to name the greatest personage in Egypt, replied, "The *Khedive*." He was then asked to name the second, and promptly answered, "Mr. John Cook." The other anecdote is that of the provincial governor, who when introduced by Cook's chief dragoman to Lord Cromer, then visiting Upper Egypt, said, "I never heard of Lord Cromer, but I am very happy to know any friend of Mr. Cook."

John Mason Cook died at Walton-on-Thames on the 4th March, 1899, after having enjoyed the unique distinction of being honoured and decorated by the sovereigns of almost every country in Europe but his own.

On the 13th steamers with the 1st (British) Brigade (Gatacre's) from Darmali passed Atbara, going direct to Wad Hamid. The same day, whilst many of the troops were still waiting for the means of transport, the *sirdar* took his departure for the front. After he left, and up to the 21st, more Egyptian troops continued to arrive. Some of them had marched all the way from Souakim, and others had toiled up against the stream from Merawi.

All were hurried forward from Atbara as fast as the means of transport would allow. No sooner did a steamer return from the front than she was refilled and sent off again packed to overflowing with a fresh batch of men.

By the 23rd August all but the last boat-load of soldiers had arrived at Wad Hamid. The Camel Corps, following the route taken by the Desert Column under Stewart in 1885, had marched across the Bayuda desert to Metammeh, and thence to the front. Abu Klea was found still white with Dervish bones. Metammeh, the scene of the slaughter of the Jaalins in 1897, presented an aspect of utter desolation. When first visited by Englishmen after the Jaalin massacre, human remains lay about the town in heaps, but the tribe had since removed and buried these. One ghastly souvenir still existed in the shape of a gallows, with portions of eight men suspended thereon.

Meanwhile from Wad Hamid reconnaissances had been pushed on as far as Shabluka, at the southern end of the Sixth Cataract, which place, as well as the gorge leading to it, was found to be evacuated. The entrance to the Shabluka gorge, where the river is only 300 yards wide, was defended by four forts with embrasures, and might have formed a strong position against any force approaching by the river. It had, however, the disadvantage of being liable to be easily turned by troops operating on land, and probably for this reason the *khalifa*, instead of making a stand at Shabluka, as had been expected, had left the place to take care of itself.

The reconnaissance was continued to the island of Jebel Royan, about thirty-four miles from Khartoum, whence, from an elevated position, a distant view of Omdurman and the white tomb of the *Mahdi* was obtained. The first person to set eyes on the spot which formed the object of the expedition was Major Staveley Gordon, the nephew of Gordon Pasha.

An advance post was established at Jebel Royan, and thither the stores which had been accumulated at Nasri Island were now transferred.

On the 23rd, preparatory to the further advance, the *sirdar* held a review of the assembled forces, British and Egyptian, and the next day the troops began moving off in successive divisions. The cavalry and Camel Corps were the first to start, closely followed by General

Hunter and the whole of the Egyptian division. On the 25th the British division marched out, and Wad Hamid was evacuated. The heat that day is described as most oppressive, and the march over the loose sand told severely on the men, and especially on those of the newly-arrived 2nd Brigade, who fell out in numbers. The steamers, most of them towing long trains of lighters, accompanied the force, whilst others scouted ahead. There being plenty of water in the cataract, the flotilla passed up without trouble.

After halting by the way the whole force, on the 27th, was assembled at El Hajir, opposite Jebel Royan. Whilst there news arrived of a disaster which had occurred to the gunboat *Hafir*. The vessel, when near Shendy, sprang a leak, and suddenly sank within a few yards of the shore. Fortunately no lives or stores had been lost.

The troops rested at El Hajir till 5 p.m. on the 28th, and then marched to Wady Abid, where a *zeriba* was made. The whole of the next day was spent at Wady Abid, where, on the night of the 29th, a terrific storm broke over the camp, deluging everything, and causing considerable discomfort. At 3 a.m. on the 30th the reveille was sounded, and soon after the men, drenched to the skin, set out for Sayal. On the 31st Sayal was evacuated, and the troops moved on to Suruab. The same day the gunboats shelled the Dervish advance camp at Kerreri.

On the night of the 31st another storm of wind and rain was experienced, which destroyed the field telegraph in places, and interrupted the telegraph communication for some days.

On the 1st September, the final advance was made to Egeiga, a village only six miles north of Omdurman. The troops started early, amid heavy rain. Several deserted villages were passed, and a little after midday a short halt for refreshments was made, at a place called El Gubeih, not far from Egeiga, which was reached an hour later.

Patrols of Dervish horsemen had been frequently seen during the march, falling back before the cavalry, and their outposts were driven in beyond Egeiga.

Some time before the main body of the army had reached Egeiga, the cavalry, striking off in a south-westerly direction, reached the slopes of Jebel Surgham, nearly a mile beyond. From this point, at noon, the entire Dervish army was seen drawn up in battle array in the desert outside the city. They were in five divisions, and their numbers were estimated at 35,000 men.[1]

---

1. It subsequently appeared that the actual numbers were between 40,000 and 50,000.

It soon became evident that this huge force had not come out for the mere purpose of being looked at. It began steadily to advance, with a line in front extending over three miles. At one time the enemy halted, and then again moved forward.

The cavalry then proceeded to fall back on Egeiga, where the main body of the army, receiving news that the Dervishes were advancing to the attack, had hurriedly moved out and formed up in position.

After following the retiring troops for some time, the vedettes at 2 p.m. reported that the enemy had halted, and later on it was observed that they were preparing bivouacs and lighting fires. So rapid was the Dervish advance that they all but came into action with the rear squadrons of the reconnoitring force.

Beyond a few shots exchanged between the Lancers and the enemy's scouts nothing further happened, and the *sirdar's* troops, after remaining in position all the afternoon, retired at nightfall to their camp.

Meanwhile the gunboats, under Commander Keppel, had proceeded at daylight on the 1st towing the 37th Howitzer Battery Royal Artillery in barges. Steaming up the east bank, with the aid of a party of friendlies, they cleared that side of the river. Several villages were found occupied, but these the friendlies took one after another.

On the steamers approaching Halfiyeh three forts opened on them. The gunboats returned the fire and soon silenced the works, which were then occupied by the friendlies. As the steamers, proceeding in line ahead, rounded Tuti Island, at the confluence of the Blue and White Niles, they were fired on by the forts, both at Khartoum and at Omdurman. The fire, though fairly heavy, was ill directed, and did no harm. A suitable spot having been found on the east bank, the howitzer battery was landed and at once brought into action.[2] After a few rounds at a range of 3,000 yards, the dome over the *Mahdi's* tomb was partially destroyed. The superior weight and accuracy of the steamers' guns ended the naval part of the fight almost as soon as it was begun, and the flotilla, leaving the *Tamaai* and *Nazir* to guard the battery, returned downstream to rejoin the army at Egeiga.

The night of the 1st September was an anxious one for everybody in the *sirdar's* camp. Less than five miles separated the opposing armies. Information had been received that the *khalifa* contemplated a night attack upon the position, and preparations to repel it were made. The men all lay down fully dressed on the sand with their arms and accou-

---

2. These guns fired 50 lb. shells with the new explosive called "Lyddite."

trements beside them. Though the moon was at its full only twenty-four hours before, the night being cloudy, there was not much light. The gunboats from time to time flashed their electric rays on Jebel Surgham and the surrounding country with a view to discovering any signs of a Dervish advance.

At the same time, natives from the village of Egeiga were sent out in the direction of the enemy's camp to obtain information, so as to give the idea that the *sirdar* intended to make a night attack, and in the expectation that this, coming to the *khalifa's* knowledge, would decide him to remain in his position. As a result the *ruse* succeeded perfectly, and, with the exception of two false alarms which occurred, the night passed away tranquilly enough.

In not making a night attack the *khalifa* lost a grand opportunity. Had he taken advantage of the comparative obscurity to hurl his enormous force upon the *sirdar's* position there is no saying what might have been the result. The rifle fire of the British and Egyptian troops, which was the thing the Dervish leader had most to fear, would have been far less effective than by daylight, and might not have been successful in stopping at all points the Dervish rushes. Had the enemy once succeeded in breaking the line of troops and engaging hand to hand with, say, the Egyptian divisions, the difficulty of coming to their aid in the darkness and confusion would have been considerable, and though the ultimate result might have been favourable, it could only have been attained by an enormous loss of life.

CHAPTER 67

The Battle of Omdurman

The force under the *sirdar's* command on the 2nd September, was thus composed:—

British Troops: 21st Lancers; 32nd Field Battery Royal Artillery; 37th Howitzer Battery Royal Artillery; two forty-pounders Royal Artillery.

Infantry Division, 1st Brigade (Wauchope's): 1st Battalion Warwickshire Regiment; 1st Battalion Lincolnshire Regiment; 1st Battalion Seaforth Highlanders; 1st Battalion Cameron Highlanders; six Maxims; detachment Royal Engineers.

2nd Brigade (Lyttelton's): 1st Battalion Grenadier Guards; 1st Battalion Northumberland Fusiliers; 2nd Battalion Lancashire Fusiliers; 2nd Battalion Rifle Brigade; four Maxims; detachment Royal Engineers.

Egyptian Troops: Nine squadrons cavalry; one battery Horse Artillery; four field batteries; ten Maxims; eight companies Camel Corps.

1st Brigade (Macdonald's): 2nd Egyptian Battalion; 9th, 10th, and 11th Soudanese Battalions.

2nd Brigade (Maxwell's): 8th Egyptian Battalion; 12th, 13th, and 14th Soudanese Battalions.

3rd Brigade (Lewis's): 3rd, 4th, 7th, and 15th Egyptian Battalions.

4th Brigade (Collinson's): 1st, 5th, 17th, and 18th Egyptian Battalions.

The gunboat flotilla, under Commander Keppel, consisted of the twin screw steamers *Sultan*, *Sheikh*, and *Melik*, each carrying two twelve-pounder quick-firing guns, one four-inch howitzer, and four Maxims; the large stern-wheelers *Fatteh* and *Nazir*, each armed with one twelve-pounder quick-firer, two six-pounder quick-firers, and three Maxims; and the small stern-wheelers *Tamaai*, *Hafir* (formerly *El Teb*), *Abu Klea*, and *Metammeh*, armed with one nine-centimetre

Krupp and two Maxims.

Each vessel was commanded by a British officer, with a non-commissioned officer of the Royal Marine Artillery as gunnery instructor.

The total force, naval and military, may be put down as a little over 22,000 men.[1]

The position occupied by the *sirdar's* force was a favourable one for defensive purposes. It stood on slightly elevated ground with a clear open space of desert dotted with scrub directly in front, and extending for five miles to the base of a group of hills to the westward. In a northerly and southerly direction was a series of hills of moderate elevation, culminating on the north at a distance of about two miles in the Kerreri Hill, and on the south at a distance of 1,200 yards in that of Jebel Surgham. Behind the position was the broad expanse of the Nile.

The camp formed a sort of angular crescent or horse-shoe, with the ends, practically the flanks of the position, resting on the river, and protected by the gunboats. In the centre were a few mud huts, and within the position, but a little to the north, stood the small village of Egeiga.

The troops were disposed as follows:—On the left was the 2nd British Brigade, composed of the Rifles, the Lancashires, the Northumberlands, and the Guards, with the Maxim battery worked by the Irish Fusiliers. Then came the 1st British Brigade, consisting of the Warwicks, the Camerons, Seaforths, and Lincolns, with a battery of Maxims manned by a detachment of the Royal Artillery. The Soudanese and Egyptian Brigades, under Maxwell, Macdonald, and Lewis, continued the fighting line round to the right, Collinson's Egyptian brigade being kept in reserve in the rear of Lewis's and Macdonald's. Maxims were placed between Lewis's and Macdonald's brigades. The 37th Howitzer Battery of the Royal Artillery had been detached and placed on the opposite bank of the Nile, as stated in the last chapter.

The 32nd Field Battery of the Royal Artillery, under Major Williams, was posted, with two Egyptian batteries and Maxims, on the extreme left of the position close to the river. The two remaining Egyptian batteries were put on the north or right side of the position. The 21st Lancers were picketed at the south end of the camp, and the Egyptian cavalry and Camel Corps occupied a position away to the

---

1. The British were armed with the Lee-Metford magazine rifle, and the Egyptians with the Martini-Henry.

north in the direction of the Kerreri Hill. Along the front of the British line a breastwork of bushes was placed, whilst the Egyptian line was defended by a shallow trench.[2]

Of the gunboats, two remained to support the howitzer battery opposite Omdurman, three others guarded the camp, and the rest were stationed at various points between Egeiga and Omdurman.

At 3.30 a.m. on the 2nd September the bugles sounded the reveille, and the troops all stood to their arms, the hour before dawn being the most usual for a night attack. After waiting an hour, there being no signs of the expected assault, the *sirdar* resolved to take the initiative and march out against the Dervish forces. At 5.30 the booming of the guns of the howitzer battery on the east bank and of the gunboats in front announced that the bombardment of Omdurman, which had begun the previous day, had recommenced. Before the cannonade had lasted many minutes the patrols reported the enemy to be advancing to attack. At 6.30 the Egyptian cavalry on the right were driven in and posted themselves with the Horse Artillery, Camel Corps, and four Maxims on the Kerreri ridge, on the right flank of the position. The British infantry were led forward a few paces, and formed up in double rank in the rear of their *zeriba* defences, the Egyptian battalions doing the same behind their trenches.

At 6.40 the shouts of the advancing Dervishes became audible, and a few minutes later their flags appeared over the rising ground, which formed a semicircle round the front and left faces of the position. They came on in an immense mass, composed apparently of five divisions, with ranks well kept, and marching with military regularity. As they advanced they chanted, "*La Ilah illa' llah wa Mohammed rasool Allah*" ("There is but one God, and Mohammed is His prophet"). *Emirs* and *sheikhs* led the way, and Baggara horsemen trotted abreast of the men on foot.

At 6.45 Major Williams's battery of Royal Artillery, on the left of the position, opened fire at a range of 2,800 yards. The guns made good practice, the shells bursting in the midst of the Dervish ranks. The enemy replied with a few rounds from some guns on the *khalifa's* left, but their shells all fell short. The intention appeared to be to cross the *sirdar's* front, but, suddenly swerving to their right, the main body of the Dervish forces bore down towards the southern face, where

---

2. The bush defence turned out a mistake, as the men had to stand up to fire over it, and thus exposed themselves to the enemy's bullets, whereas the Egyptian troops were able to lie down under the shelter of their trench.

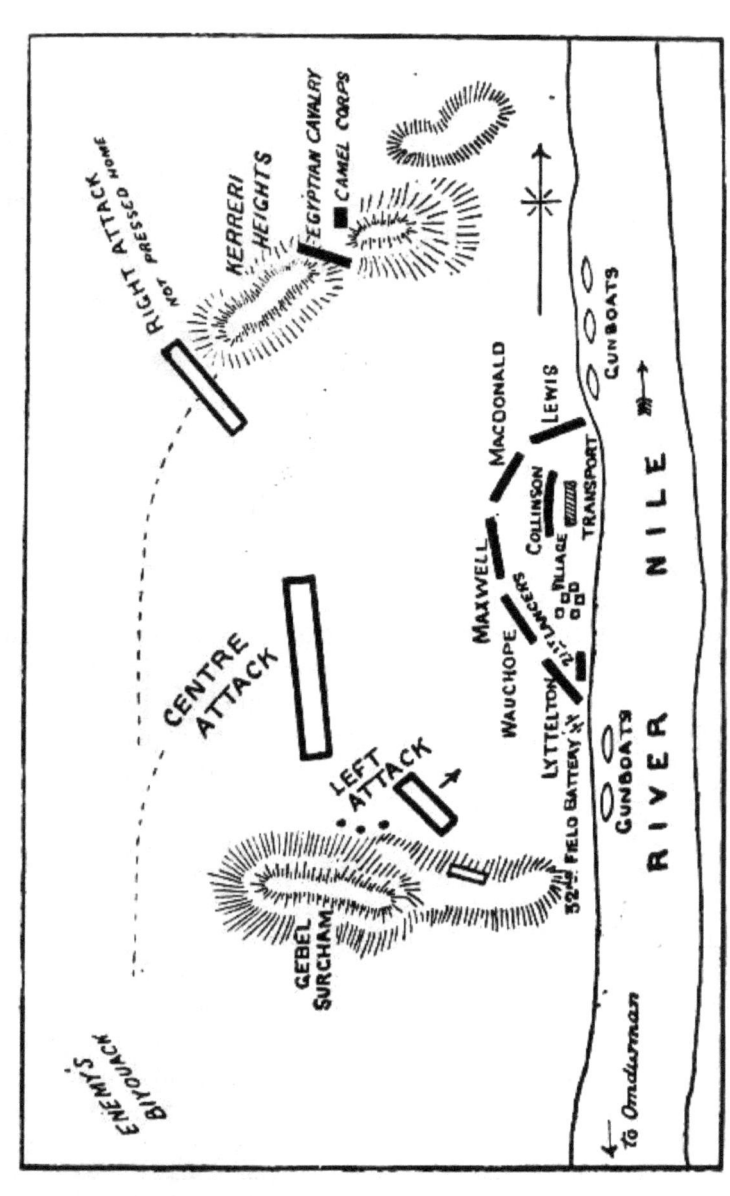

the British division was posted. Simultaneously with this movement another mass of Dervishes swarmed out from behind Jebel Surgham, to assail the left flank of the position. Though their riflemen, mounting the hill, opened a long range fire on the *zeriba*, this attack, being checked by the fire of the gunboats, was not pressed home.

Thus far the fire of the artillery, which had been supplemented by that from the Maxim-Nordenfeldts, though it thinned the enemy's ranks, failed to stop their advance, and in a short time the troops on the left and front were hotly engaged.

The Guards, who were the first of the British infantry to engage, opened with section volleys from their Lee-Metfords at a range of 2,000 yards. Then, as the range diminished, the fire ran along to the Warwicks, the Highlanders, the Lincolns, and later on to Maxwell's brigade. From one end to the other there was a continuous blaze of flame, the men firing both in volleys and independently. The Lee-Metfords grew so hot that the men in the firing line had to change them for others held by their comrades in the rear. The weapons gave out no smoke, so the view was uninterrupted. The Dervishes were seen falling in heaps, whilst the ground in front was white with dead men's clothing. Constantly reinforced from the rear, the assailants made repeated efforts to reach the lines of infantry, and as whole ranks went down others rushed in to fill their places.

When the front rank got within 800 yards of the British force, the fire became even more deadly, and the further advance was practically arrested. Even at this range, here and there, small bodies of Dervishes continued to make isolated attempts to reach the lines, but only to perish in the effort. What took place became less a fight than an execution. One old *sheikh*, bearing a banner, headed one of the rushes. In a few seconds he was left with but five comrades, who in their turn all dropped, and he alone charged to within 200 yards, at which point he folded his arms across his face and fell dead.

Up to this period there had been but few casualties, and the fight had been for the *sirdar's* force about the least dangerous that a soldier ever took part in. While the original advance was being made, a few only of the Dervish riflemen paused to fire, and, more for the purpose of working up their martial ardour than anything else, discharged their weapons in the air. Even when they took the trouble to aim, the bullets from their Remingtons all fell short. As soon as the opposing forces got closer together, things changed, and the enemy's fire began to tell. At the moment when the Dervish spearmen were being shot down in their mad rushes, a party of 200 of their riflemen managed to get within about 300 yards of the front, from which point, under cover of a bank, they opened fire.

The riflemen on Jebel Surgham, though shelled by the gunboats, persisted in their fusillade, and casualties became frequent. Captain Caldecott, of the Warwicks, was shot through the head, and died an hour later. One or two other officers, as well as two newspaper correspondents, were wounded, and twenty-five of the Camerons and over a dozen of the Seaforths had to be carried to the rear. Eventually the riflemen in front were dislodged by Major Williams's battery, which, firing shell among them, caused them to get up and run, only, however, to be shot down by the Warwicks, Camerons, and Lincolns, not a single rifleman being left alive.

The attack had hitherto been almost entirely directed on the British troops, but as the fight proceeded the enemy were gradually driven more and more to the right, thus leaving the 2nd Brigade (Lyttelton's) out of action, and giving the 1st Brigade (Wauchope's) and Maxwell's Egyptians all the work to do. Seeing this, Lyttelton moved up the Lancashires and the Rifles in support of the 1st Brigade.

After a while the enemy's onrushes began to diminish. It was not so much that the charging spearmen were driven back, as that they were all killed. The fire of the troops then slackened. Just before it ceased altogether a last Dervish effort was made. This time it took the form of a cavalry attack. A party of Baggara horsemen, about 200 in number, formed up at a distance of about 1,200 yards and gallantly charged Maxwell's whole brigade. A more hopeless enterprise could scarcely be imagined. Nevertheless, though swept down by rifle and Maxim fire, the remnant courageously dashed on till within 200 yards of the fighting line, when all that was left of them was a struggling mass of men and horses lying on the ground.

It was now about 8 a.m., the main attack was finished, and the great body of the enemy was gradually retiring in a westerly direction toward some hills three miles distant.

Whilst the *khalifa* was delivering his first attack on the front and left of the *sirdar's* position, a large and compact body of Dervishes, under the *khalifa's* son, Sheikh-el-Din, and the Emir Wad Helu, marched round to attack the right of the position. Here, posted on the Kerreri ridge of hills, were the Egyptian mounted troops, under Colonel Broadwood, with whom, at 7 a.m., about 10,000 of the enemy, advancing rapidly, soon became engaged. On the approach of the Dervish force, the guns of the Egyptian horse battery at once opened fire at a range of 1,500 yards, and the cavalry and Camel Corps dismounting, joined in with their Martini-Henry carbines. The Dervishes, however, continued to advance, firing as they came on. The force was in far too great a number for Broadwood to hope to operate against it alone with any prospect of success, and seeing that the intention was to surround him and cut him off from the *zeriba*, he directed the Camel Corps and guns, covered by the cavalry, to fall back upon the right flank of the position.

There was some delay in getting the camels to move, and afterwards in taking them and the guns over the rough and broken ground. The Dervishes pursued closely, firing all the while. The Egyptians from time to time halted, and fired volleys in return. So hardly was Broadwood's force pressed at one moment, that two of his guns had to be abandoned. For some minutes the fighting was most severe, hand-to-hand encounters took place, and over sixty of his men fell.

The Egyptian force had by this time fallen back to a point not far distant from the river, and fortunately at the critical moment one of the gunboats told off to protect the flanks steamed down to afford assistance. It at once opened with shell fire at close range, and inflicted heavy loss on the enemy, upwards of 450 bodies being afterwards counted within a comparatively small area. The intervention of the steamers effectually checked the onslaught, and enabled the Camel Corps to get to the *zeriba*, although the Dervishes for some time continued the pursuit of the cavalry. After this encounter the Dervishes made no attempt to push home their attack on the right, but drew off in good order and retired under cover of the hills. This, with the repulse of the Dervish attack already recorded on the left flank, terminated the first stage of the fight.

All attacks on the position having now failed, the 21st Lancers, about 320 in number, under Colonel Martin, were sent out to clear the ground on the left front, and to head off any retreating Dervishes from the direction of Omdurman. They moved off about 9 a.m., and after crossing the eastern slopes of Jebel Surgham perceived what looked like a force of from 250 to 300 of the enemy concealed in a *khor* or ravine, from which a few scattered shots were fired. The Lancers then wheeled into line and charged. When they got to a distance of only 200 yards from the position, a body of Dervishes, variously estimated at from 1,500 to 3,000 in number, suddenly rose from the *khor* and opened fire. The trap laid was now evident enough, but the

Lancers continued the charge, and, headed by their colonel, dashed on into the *khor*, fought their way through the Dervish ranks, and out at the opposite side.

This was not accomplished without the loss of several of their comrades. There was a three-foot drop into the ravine, and this caused many disasters. Colonel Martin's horse fell at this point, but, with the spearmen cutting and slashing all around him, he managed to get his charger on its legs again, and, with only a stick in his hand, rode through the fight uninjured.

The Dervishes made a desperate resistance. They reverted to their usual tactics of first hamstringing the horses and then spearing their riders.

Of the troopers who were unhorsed, hardly a man escaped alive. Lieutenant Grenfell was killed by a sword-cut received early in the fight, when charging by the side of his men. As soon as he was missed, Captain Kenna and Lieutenant de Montmorency rode back to search for him. Finding Grenfell's body, de Montmorency dismounted and proceeded to put it on his horse, which unluckily bolted, leaving him alone to face the Dervishes with his revolver. Happily Captain Kenna, with the aid of Corporal Swarbrick, succeeded in catching the animal, and De Montmorency was enabled to join his troop.

Major Wyndham's horse, after carrying him clear of the Dervishes, fell dead as he was mounting the slope of the *khor*. Captain Kenna, who was at the moment on foot searching for Grenfell, put the Major on Kenna's own horse and mounted behind him, and though the horse kicked them both off, they got safely out of the *mélée*.

When the lancers had reached the opposite side they continued their gallop for a distance of about 400 yards, when they rallied. Then taking up a position whence they could fire down the *khor*, they dismounted, and with their carbines opened fire on the enemy, eventually driving them off to the westward. As soon as the Dervishes had retired, a party of troopers advanced and recovered the bodies of Lieutenant Grenfell and others who had fallen. They were hastily buried on the spot.

The loss of the lancers in the charge was one officer and twenty men killed, and four officers and forty-six men wounded. Besides this, there were 130 horses either killed or injured. The charge itself has been the subject of much criticism. Most military men appear to consider that for cavalry to charge unbroken infantry of unknown quantity, over unknown ground, was, to put it mildly, a mistake. Its result, so far as the enemy was concerned, was practically nil. By the loss which the cavalry sustained in horses alone they were put out of action, instead of being reserved for the moment when they were required for the purpose of pursuing the fugitives. With the public, however, these considerations were lost sight of in the gallantry displayed by both officers and men, and the charge has long been one of the most popular episodes of the fight.[3]

Meanwhile the *sirdar* about 8.30 a.m. had given orders to evacuate the camp and march upon Omdurman. The army advanced *en échelon* of brigades from the left, Collinson's brigade in reserve covering the rear of the transport column, and the Egyptian cavalry and camel corps on the right and left rear.

At 9.30, the front brigades having reached the sand ridge running from the west end of Jebel Surgham to the river, a halt was ordered to enable the rear brigades to get into position.

Information was then received that the *khalifa*, with a large force, was present on the left slopes of Jebel Surgham, from the summit of which a party of the enemy were now firing.

It appears that the Dervish army had not returned to Omdurman on the previous night, but had bivouacked, some 40,000 strong, behind Jebel Surgham. When daylight appeared, and no attack was made on the *khalifa*, he divided his forces into three sections. One of these, as already related, attacked the front and left of the *sirdar's* position, the next moved towards the Kerreri heights with the object of enveloping his right, whilst the third, under Abdullah himself, remained concealed behind Jebel Surgham, ready to fall on the *sirdar's* flank in the advance upon Omdurman.

The *sirdar* realized the situation at once, and a change of front half right of the three leading brigades was ordered, whilst two companies of Maxwell's brigade stormed and occupied Jebel Surgham.

When the change of front was being effected, the sound of heavy firing on the right was heard, where Macdonald's brigade was by this time hotly engaged.

To enable Macdonald's men to take up position on the right of the echelon, his brigade had to change places with that of Lewis, and to move out to the right, so as to allow the latter to come into position on Macdonald's left front. Whilst carrying out this movement, and at the moment when he was separated by about a mile from the rest of

---

3. Captain Kenna and Lieutenant De Montmorency received the Victoria Cross for their gallantry on this occasion.

the army, Macdonald found himself faced by a strong body of Dervishes, advancing from the west, from the direction of Jebel Surgham. He at once halted and deployed into line to the front to meet the attack. It was not long coming. The Dervishes, estimated at 20,000 in number, commanded by the *khalifa* himself, made a determined onslaught on the brigade. The main attack was preceded by a charge of between 300 and 400 mounted Baggara, who, advancing in loose order, made straight for the long line of rifles which awaited them. The evident intention was to break Macdonald's line and give the men on foot an opening. The attempt was hopeless from the first; it was simply riding to certain death. Then the fusillade began, and horseman after horseman rolled in the dust.

Undismayed by the fate of their comrades, the Dervish footmen next came on, only to see their front ranks swept away by Maxim and rifle fire. Not a man got within 300 yards of the fighting line. The plain became dotted with white figures and black upturned faces. The Dervishes planted their banners in the ground and gathered round them, only to fall lifeless immediately after. At length the men behind, seeing the slaughter of those in front, stopped at a distance of about 400 yards, whence they continued firing, though assailed by the rifles of Lewis's brigade, which by this time was advancing to Macdonald's support.

The *sirdar*, learning from General Hunter of Macdonald's position, despatched Wauchope's (British) brigade to his assistance, and ordered the remaining brigades to make a further change of front half right. Before, however, the reinforcements reached Macdonald, he had practically disposed of the first great attack.

Still, the fight was not nearly over. Whilst Macdonald was yet engaged with the *khalifa's* force, and just at the moment when the order to advance was about to be given, the Dervishes behind the Kerreri heights emerged into the plain, and moved rapidly forward to deliver a second attack.

This new onslaught necessitated a further complete change in the disposition of Macdonald's brigade. Seeing his front and rear both threatened, and finding himself also in danger of being outflanked, he moved some of his battalions to the right, and deployed them into line, so as to form with the remainder of his brigade a sort of arrowhead, one side facing north and the other west.

The Dervishes came on in two masses, one commanded by Sheikh-el-Din, and the other by Wad Helu, and spread themselves out

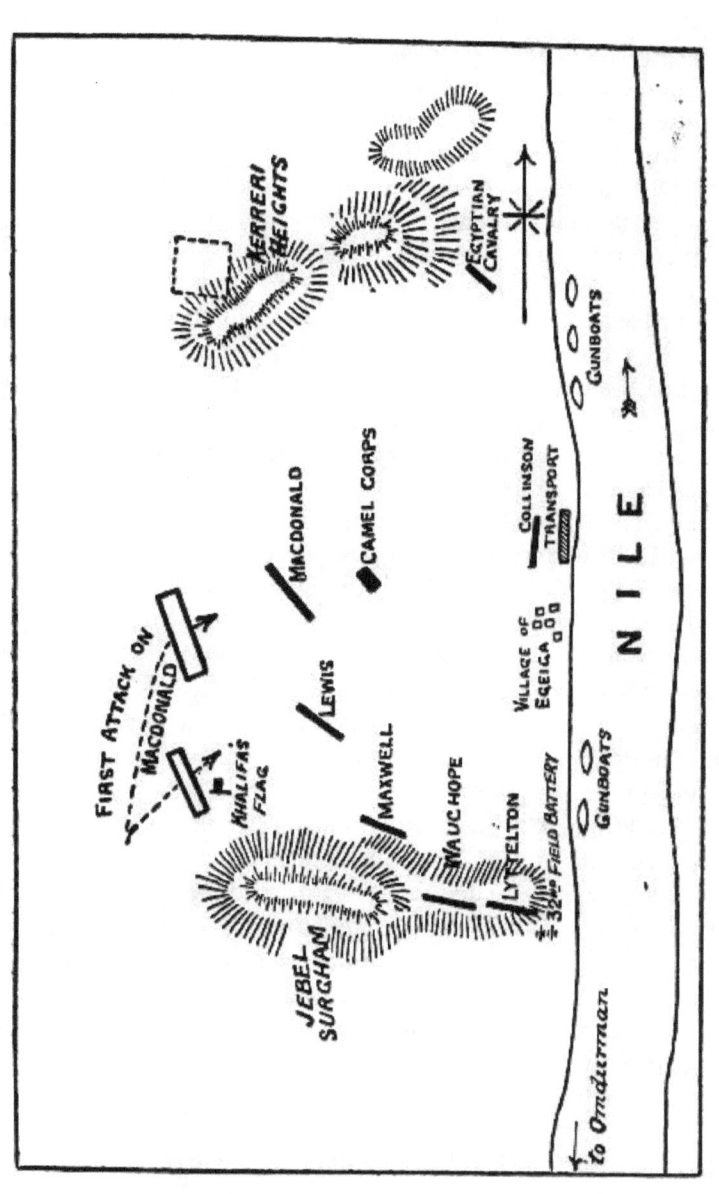

as if to envelop Macdonald's brigade. Between this and Lewis's there was a gap, into which the Warwicks, the Seaforths, and the Camerons were now rushing at the double, whilst the Lincolns hurried off to complete the line on Macdonald's right. As the Dervishes advanced, Macdonald's Soudanese received them with a fire so deadly, delivered in the open ground, that nothing could live in the face of it.

Whilst Macdonald was repelling the new assault on his right, Lewis's brigade was enfilading the *khalifa's* attack on the left.

The Dervish onslaught now began to weaken, and shortly after, as Wauchope's brigade came up, ceased altogether. The enemy, who had made their last despairing effort without having been able to push home, now broke and fled.

Thus Macdonald, with the aid of Lewis's and Wauchope's brigades, crushed this second and determined attack. The masterly way in which he handled his force was the theme of general admiration.

The slaughter which took place is described as something appalling, and the ground around the scene of the fight was literally strewn with dead and dying Dervishes.

Meantime Maxwell's and Lyttelton's brigades, accompanied by the 32nd Field Battery, had been pushed on over the slopes of Jebel Surgham, and driving before them the Dervish forces under Sheikh-el-Din, they established themselves in a position which cut off the retreat on Omdurman of the bulk of the *khalifa's* army, who were soon seen streaming off in a disorganized mass towards the high hills many miles to the west, closely pursued by the mounted troops, who cleared the right and front flanks of all hesitating and detached parties of the enemy.

The battle was now practically over, and Lyttelton's and Maxwell's brigades marched down to Khor Shambat, in the direction of Omdurman, which spot was reached at 12.30 a.m.; and here the troops rested and watered. The remainder of Hunter's division and Wauchope's brigade arrived at the same place an hour and a half later.

The result of the fight before Omdurman was declared in the Sirdar's despatch to be "the practical annihilation of the *khalifa's* army, the consequent extinction of Mahdism in the Soudan, and the submission of nearly the whole country formerly ruled under Egyptian authority."

The *sirdar*, for the skilful generalship and judicious disposition of his forces, which secured him the victory, is entitled to the highest praise, and no one will grudge him the honours with which his serv-

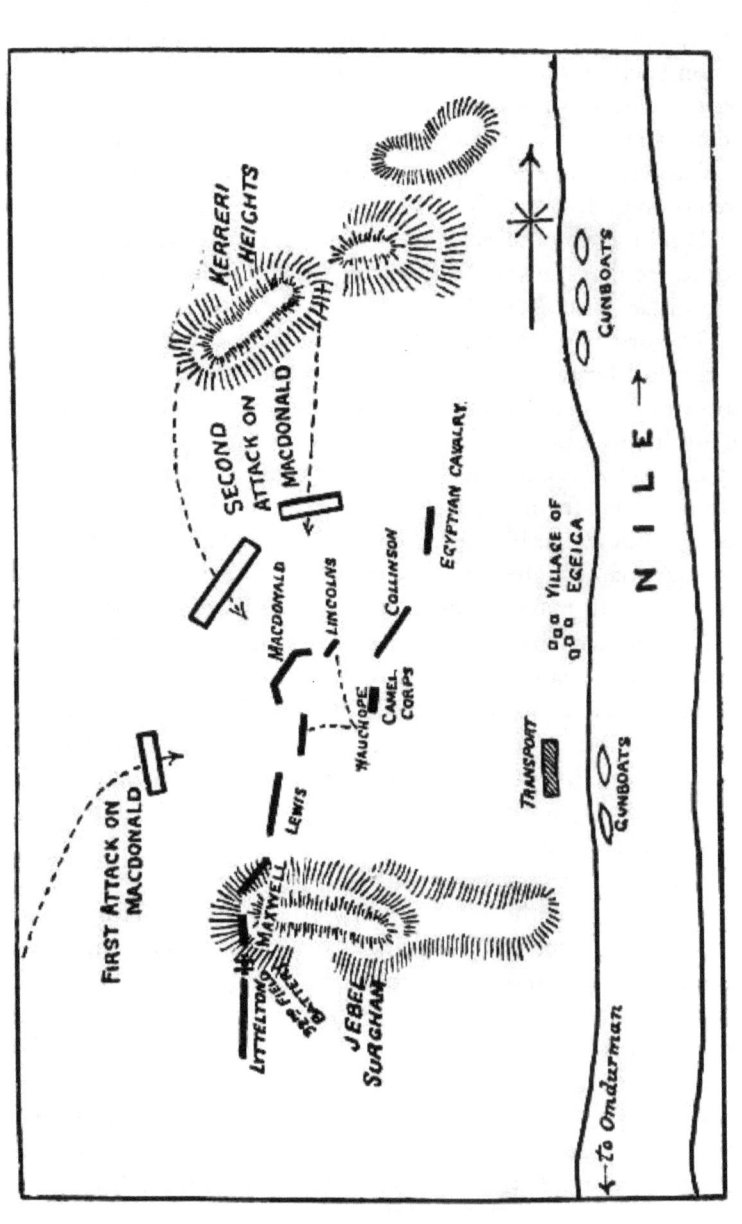

ices were recognised.[4]

As to the fight itself, it was in many ways, no doubt, a walkover. At the same time it was a lesson in the power of modern arms such as had never been seen before. It showed that against weapons of precision such as those carried by the Anglo-Egyptian troops even an overwhelming superiority of numbers is not in itself of any avail. It demonstrated once more the pluck and endurance of the British soldier, as well as the good fighting material of which his Egyptian allies are composed.

Whilst giving the *sirdar* every credit for his victory, it is impossible not to see that the *khalifa*, by his repeated blunders, completely played into his adversary's hands.

The first mistake of the Dervish leader was in not remaining within the fortifications of Omdurman, from which it would have been impossible to have dislodged him, except at a great sacrifice, instead of advancing out into the open and exposing his imperfectly armed legions to the deadly fire of the *sirdar's* rifles. In doing this the *khalifa* chose the one form of attack which gave him the least chance of success. He knew that his men had on other occasions broken the British and Egyptian squares, and was desirous of seeing if it could not be done again. In making this calculation the Dervish leader totally lost sight of the fact that his enemies possessed both better weapons and superior organization than in days gone by.

A second and fatal mistake was in not making a night attack on the *sirdar's* position, where, if the Dervishes had attacked in the darkness with the same impetuous courage which they displayed in daylight, it is by no means impossible that they might have got within the Anglo-Egyptian lines.

A third error was in not originally occupying Jebel Surgham, which, situated on the left front of the Anglo-Egyptian force, possessed for defensive purposes unquestionable advantages. Had the *khalifa* occupied this commanding position, the *sirdar* would have been left with two alternatives. He might either have accepted the challenge, and have taken the hill at a heavy loss, or he might have elected to pass it by, and by making a wide detour in the desert so reach Omdurman. This last operation, with the *khalifa's* forces still unbroken in the Anglo-Egyptian rear, would have been a hazardous undertaking, and would, moreover, have left the *khalifa* free to continue his resistance.

---

4. Sir Herbert Kitchener was created Baron Kitchener of Khartoum, and a sum of £30,000 was awarded him.

A further fault was in directing the first attack mainly on the *sirdar's* left, where the British troops were posted, instead of assailing the Egyptian and Soudanese battalions on the front and right. By adopting these tactics the *khalifa* attacked his enemy at the very strongest instead of the very weakest point.

In short, the *khalifa*, as a general, may be said to have been a complete failure, leaving undone those things which he ought to have done and doing those things which he ought not to have done, and there was no skill in him.

The Dervish loss was immense. No less than 10,800 bodies were counted on the field of battle in addition to over 300 in the town of Omdurman. Their wounded, estimated from the number who crawled down to the river and into the town, was 16,000 more, making a total of 27,000 altogether out of a fighting force of 52,000 men.[5] Besides these, 4,000 black troops surrendered and were made prisoners, and three of Gordon's old steamers were captured.

Bearing in mind the nature of the fight, the Anglo-Egyptian losses were remarkably slight.

The British killed were but two officers and twenty-five men; of these no less than twenty-one fell in the mistaken charge of the Lancers. The British wounded were eleven officers and 136 men. Of the Egyptian force one officer and twenty rank and file were killed, and thirteen officers and 222 rank and file were wounded. The total number of casualties in the *sirdar's* entire army was forty-eight killed and 382 wounded.

The *sirdar* in his despatch reporting the victory did full justice to the officers and men under his command, upwards of 300 of whom were specially mentioned for good service. Indeed, so long was the list that it excited a good deal of comment when the nature of the contest and the character of the enemy were taken into account. As a contrast to the above it may be mentioned that in Wellington's despatches after Waterloo, a fight in which the loss of the British alone was 1,759 killed and 5,892 wounded, only the names of thirty-two officers are specially mentioned.

---

5. Sir F. R. Wingate says in his report of 3rd March, 1899:—"Of the 4,000 Dervish black troops who surrendered 1,222 were wounded; there were wounded in almost every house in Omdurman; and, in view of the fact that almost every able-bodied man in the town had been forced to take part in the battle, it is fair to conclude that the number of wounded (16,000) as telegraphed was not over-estimated."

CHAPTER 68

The Capture of Omdurman

At 2 p.m. on the day of the fight, the *sirdar*, having ascertained that little or no resistance was to be expected in the town, advanced, with Maxwell's brigade and the 32nd Field Battery of Royal Artillery, through the suburbs of Omdurman to the great wall forming the *khalifa's* inclosure.

On their way the force was met by a number of *sheikhs*, bearing a flag of truce, who informed the *sirdar* that the inhabitants desired to surrender. This was accepted on condition that all the fighting men at once laid down their arms, and gave themselves up. The inhabitants then swarmed out in thousands from their houses, and cheered the troops.

Leaving two guns and three battalions to guard the approaches, the 13th Battalion and four guns of the field battery were pushed down by the north side of the wall to the river, and, covered by three gunboats, which had been previously ordered to be ready for this movement, the troops penetrated the breaches made in the walls by the howitzers of the 37th Battery, stationed on the opposite bank, marched south along the line of forts, and, turning in at the main gateway, found a straight road leading to the *khalifa's* house and the *Mahdi's* tomb. The gates of the *khalifa's* house were found to be barred, and the gunboats proceeded to shell the building from the river. In doing this they narrowly escaped killing the *sirdar*, who had taken up a position close by. The Hon. Hubert Howard, one of the newspaper correspondents, was struck by a fragment of one of the last shells fired into Omdurman, and killed on the spot. The house was shortly after entered, but not without resistance from some of the Baggaras concealed there, and who had to be killed.

On the house being taken, a move was made on the mosque containing the tomb of the *Mahdi*. Here a couple of Dervishes rushed out and charged Maxwell's men, killing one, and wounding another. Both the assailants were bayoneted. The mosque was then entered, and found to be quite deserted.

The portion of the mosque in which was the wooden sarcophagus containing the *Mahdi's* remains was thirty-six feet square, and was surmounted by a dome some seventy feet in height. The building was much damaged by the fire from the howitzer battery and gunboats.

To the great disappointment of every one, there were no signs of the *khalifa*, whose capture was the only thing necessary to complete the *sirdar's* triumph. It appears that the Dervish leader had quitted the town only a short time before the entry of the troops, and after he had made a vain effort to collect his men for further resistance. So rapid was his flight that some of the least attractive of his wives, and other incumbrances, were dropped on the road, and over 100 of the baggage camels, which had been told off to accompany him, fell into the hands of the victors.

On the subject of the *khalifa's* last days at Omdurman and his subsequent flight, Mr. Charles Neufeld (a German subject, who after eleven years' captivity was found and released by the *sirdar*), in his published book, *A Prisoner of the Khalifa*, writes as follows:—

> "The *khalifa* had been sitting for eight days in the mosque in communion with the Prophet and the *Mahdi*, and it was either on the Tuesday night or Wednesday morning immediately preceding the battle that the decision to move out of town was arrived at. On the Wednesday afternoon a grand parade of all the troops was held on the new parade ground, and, while it was being held, alarming news was brought by Abd-el-Baagi's messengers. . . . That night the rain came down in torrents, and the following day the army arose uncomfortable, and maybe a little dispirited, but Abdullah restored their good spirits by the relation of a vision. During the night the Prophet and the *Mahdi* had come to him and let him see beforehand the result of the battle; the souls of the faithful killed were all rising to paradise, while the legions of hell were seen tearing into shreds the spirits of the *infidels*.
> But all the time the gunboats were approaching, and soon shells were screeching through the air over the little shuddering group of prisoners. At night the soft thud of thousands of feet told of

the host of fugitives entering the town. It was all very well for the *khalifa* to order a salute to be fired in honour of a victory; other messengers were hurrying in with grave faces, and desiring to see one of the subordinate *emirs* before facing Abdullah. Between ten and eleven at night a riderless horse from the British or Egyptian cavalry came slowly moving, head down, towards the Dervish lines. The *khalifa* had related how, in one of his visions, he had seen the Prophet, mounted on his mare, riding at the head of the avenging angels, destroying the infidels. The apparition of the riderless horse was too much; at least one-third of the *khalifa's* huge army deserted, terrified.

When Yakoub told him of the desertions, Abdullah merely raised his head to say, 'The prophecy will be fulfilled, if only five people stay near me.' His Baggara and Taaishi stood by him, but they, too, were losing heart, for the *khalifa*, on his knees, with head bowed to the ground, was groaning, instead of, as customary, repeating the name of the Deity. However, he pulled round a little as the night progressed, and invented visions enough to put spirits into the remaining but slightly despondent troops.

"When the day had gone hopelessly against him, and he had been persuaded to enter the town, he ordered the drums and *ombeyehs* to be sounded, and endeavoured to make a final stand at the large praying inclosure. But few obeyed the summons, and of those that came some slunk away, and others jeered at the disconsolate and discredited prophet. Finally he sent his secretary to collect his household, but the secretary did not return. Stopping two fugitives, he sent them to ascertain the whereabouts of the enemy, and they came upon the *sirdar* and his staff not 1,200 yards away. Abdullah, warned in time, contrived to slip away, whilst the *sirdar* changed his direction and made the complete circuit of Omdurman.

The gunboats which had been employed in clearing the streets having returned, the remainder of Maxwell's brigade, which had been left at the corner of the wall, was now pushed forward, and occupied all the main positions of the town. Guards were at once mounted over the principal buildings and the *khalifa's* stores, and the *sirdar* then proceeded to visit the prisons and release the European prisoners.

Amongst the captives liberated, besides Neufeld, were Joseph Ragnotti, Sister Teresa Grigolini, and thirty Greeks. Neufeld was in chains, which had to be filed off before he was restored to liberty.[1]

In the arsenal were found large stores of ammunition, with thousands of weapons of all sorts, including some sixty cannon, also Dervish spears, swords, banners, drums, flint-lock muskets, rifles, camel equipments, and military odds and ends of various kinds, many of them captured from Hicks's army nearly fifteen years before.

Whilst Maxwell's brigade was thus occupied, the British brigades and the remainder of the *sirdar's* army had moved up from Khor Shambat, which they quitted at 4.30 p.m. On arriving at the wall they met with no opposition, and shortly after sunset marched into the town, amidst shouts of welcome from the populace. They continued their march, amid sickening stenches and scenes of misery and desolation, till they reached the open ground on the west side of the town. Here, as the various troops came up, they bivouacked for the night.

There was a certain amount of street fighting in the darkness, when isolated bands of Dervishes from time to time fired upon the Soudanese, who could not be restrained from retaliating. These struggles were attended by some loss of life, and no doubt partly account for the 300 or 400 dead bodies found in the town.

Of the services rendered by the gunboats during the day's it is difficult to speak too highly. During the battle they guarded the left flank of the army, doing great execution with their guns on the dense masses of the enemy. As already related, when the Camel Corps were so hard pressed, one of the vessels was able, by dropping down stream, to turn back a large body of Dervishes coming round Kerreri Hill. As the *sirdar's* victorious army advanced, the gunboats likewise pushed on, and went alongside the walls of Khartoum, helping to silence the fire from the houses near the river. Their services, however, did not end there, and at 8 p.m. they, together with the Egyptian cavalry and Camel Corps, started south in pursuit of the *khalifa*, the gunboats proceeding up the White Nile. Unfortunately, they were unable to render much assistance owing to the state of the river, which, having overflown its banks, was, though two miles in breadth, only navigable near the middle.

In consequence of the flooded state of the country, which prevented the troops from communicating with the gunboats conveying the

---

1. The total number of prisoners eventually set free at Omdurman was no less than 10,854, of whom 8,667 were civil and military employés of the Egyptian Government, taken captive when Khartoum, Obeid, and other places fell into the hands of the *Mahdi*.

forage and rations of the troops, the latter were compelled to abandon the pursuit after following up the flying *khalifa* for thirty miles over marshy ground.

The gunboats continued their course south for ninety miles, but were obliged to return without being able to come in touch with the *khalifa*, who left the river and fled westward towards Kordofan.

At 4 a.m. on the 3rd September, the Anglo-Egyptian Army marched out and bivouacked at a spot four miles south of Omdurman, whilst parties were told off to bury the soldiers who had fallen in the battle of the previous day.

The battlefield presented a sickening sight. The effect of the expanding bullet had been most deadly. The bodies of the slain lay closely strewn over acres and acres of ground, which were white with their calico uniforms. Some of the dead lay composedly with their slippers placed under their head for a last pillow; some knelt as if cut short in the middle of prayer; others were found literally torn to pieces by fragments of shells and by Gatling bullets. Mingled with the bodies were some seemingly as dead as the rest, but who sprang up when approached, and with sword or spear rushed at the nearest foe. These had in every case to be bayoneted or shot.

Incidents like those last referred to occurred not only during the search of the battlefield, but also at the period when, the Dervish attacks having been successively repulsed, the advance on Omdurman was resumed. They were taken advantage of to bring charges of cruelty against the Sirdar and his men, which on inquiry proved to be grossly exaggerated in those cases where they were not entirely unfounded.

It was alleged that the *sirdar* ordered, or gave it to be understood, that the Dervish wounded were to be massacred; that the troops wantonly killed or wounded unarmed Dervishes when no longer in a position to do injury; that Omdurman was looted for three days after its occupation; that when the *sirdar's* force was advancing on the town fire was opened by the gunboats on mixed masses of fugitives, including women and children, in the streets.

To these charges the *sirdar* subsequently gave a categorical denial, which, so far as the allegations related to himself personally, was wholly needless.

Captain Adolf von Tiedemann, of the Royal Prussian General Staff, writing on the subject, says:—

As regards the conduct of Lord Kitchener, I rode on the day of the battle from beginning to end—*i.e.*, from 5.30 a.m. till 9 p.m.—with very short interruptions, in his immediate vicinity, and heard and saw everything ordered or done by him. It would be an insult to Lord Kitchener if I attempted to contradict the insinuations made against him personally; such evident calumnies would never be given credence to for a moment in the mind of any intelligent man possessed of common sense. If the *sirdar* had been so bloodthirsty as the writer of the article in question[2] wishes us to believe, he would have found opportunities enough at every step during his entry into Omdurman to gratify his desires, for, after the *khalifa* had fled from the town, crowds of unarmed Dervishes rushed towards him, and it would have been easy enough for his escort to have cut them down. Lord Kitchener received them with kindness, and, as every one on his staff can testify, he did all in his power to put a stop to the street fighting which broke out here and there in the town. Putting aside all regard for his personal safety, he, as I saw several times, rode into narrow streets and courtyards, with uplifted hand, calling out to the inhabitants gathered there, '*Amân!*' ('Peace!').

As regards the killing of the wounded on the battlefield, that was a necessary measure which was as regrettable as it was indispensable. After the first attack of the Dervishes had been repulsed, and when the Anglo-Egyptian Army was moving off by brigades to its left towards Omdurman, I myself left the staff and rode over a great part of the battlefield, but I registered a mental vow never to do so again. A wounded and apparently defenceless Dervish lying on the ground is much more dangerous than his fellow with a whole skin and arms in his hand rushing against one. One knows perfectly what to expect from the latter, while the apparent helplessness of the former makes one forget the necessary caution and also the fact that a bullet fired by a wounded man makes quite as big a hole as one fired by an unhurt person.

During my ride over the battlefield I several times saw Dervishes who had been lying on the ground suddenly rise and fire off their rifles into the ranks of the troops marching near them or who had already passed by them, and for these latter

---

2. Mr. Bennett in the *Contemporary Review*.

it was simply demanded, as a measure of self-preservation, that they should secure themselves against such attacks by a chain of scouts pushed to the front. It is not only the moral right, but the duty, of the soldier to make use of his arms against an enemy from whom it is to be expected that he will use his weapons to inflict loss on the troops to which he (the soldier) belongs, and the behaviour of the wounded Dervishes was such as to justify this belief. It is quite possible that here and there some wounded enemies may have been shot who had no hostile intentions, and who were only intent on saving their lives, but it is difficult to realize the peaceable intentions of such. To make out a few such isolated instances and accusations of useless cruelty against a whole army appears to me absurd.

Besides, one heard of a large number of cases in which not only British, but also black, soldiers received and treated their wounded enemies with great kindness, although at times they had but a poor reward for it. I myself saw a man of the 32nd Field Battery giving a wounded Dervish a drink out of his water-bottle, holding up his head the while with his hand, and then leaving a piece of bread, which he took out of his own haversack, on the ground beside him.

It may be admitted that in the heat of the battle some of the enemy were killed whose lives might have been spared, but this is no unusual occurrence in the best-disciplined armies, also that a number of wounded were killed after the fighting was over. But in all or nearly all such cases it appears that these acts were dictated by necessity, on account of the Dervish habit of pretending to be dead, only to make a last and unexpected onslaught on his enemy. Such tactics were common at the battle of Omdurman, and many of the *sirdar's* men fell victims in consequence. Mr. Bennett himself related how he saw with his own eyes a "slightly wounded man suddenly rise up and stab no less than seven Egyptian cavalrymen before he was finally despatched." That the troops had to adopt somewhat drastic measures in consequence is likely enough, though what took place was far from being the wanton cruelty and indiscriminate slaughter which was alleged.

That Omdurman was looted for three days was a charge with even less foundation, inasmuch as the morning after the battle the troops were marched out of the town before daylight to a position some miles distant, and from that time until they went down the river they were not permitted to enter the place, except on one occasion, to which reference is made later on. Between the place of bivouac and the town, a line of sentries was established, and through this none but officers were allowed to pass.

The charge that the gunboats fired on the fugitives is, if true, only partially so. The fugitives who fled from the battlefield into Omdurman were naturally shelled as long as they were within range, otherwise time would have been afforded them to organize a fresh resistance, in which case the town could only have been occupied with heavy loss. As regards the women and children, the *sirdar*, the day before he directed the gunboats to bombard, sent a warning to the *khalifa* to withdraw the women and children. More than one person who visited Omdurman has reported that, although several bodies of men were seen lying about, in no case was the body of a woman or child found.

Another accusation was that no attempt was made either on the day of the fight, or on the following day, to do anything for the wounded Dervishes, who were left without food, surgical assistance, or water. With reference to this, the *sirdar* states that, considering the condition of the troops and the means at his disposal, he did everything in his power to relieve suffering amongst the enemy. It must be remembered that the total number of Dervishes wounded was estimated at 16,000. To attempt the medical treatment of anything like that number was manifestly far beyond the capabilities of the field hospitals. Of these, the large hospital established at Khor Shambat administered first aid to the wounded, and passed them on to Omdurman; some were also treated in the smaller field hospitals in the camps; but in Omdurman itself great difficulty was experienced in attempting to administer aid to the large number of wounded, scattered as they were amongst the native houses and huts. To provide for this, an Egyptian doctor, Hassan Effendi Zeki, who had been a prisoner with the Dervishes, formed a hospital in a central position in the town where upwards of 400 of the worst cases were tended, many outpatients coming daily to have their wounds dressed. According to the *Daily News* correspondent, from 6,000 to 7,000 wounded Dervishes were treated in this hospital, to which, according to the same authority, the *sirdar*, on entering Omdurman, directed the inhabitants to bring the wounded. It is difficult to see what more could have been done under the circumstances.

Besides the matters already referred to, the *sirdar* was attacked in regard to a step which was taken by his direction, although in his absence (on the subsequent Fashoda Expedition), namely, the destruction of the

Mahdi's tomb and the disposal of his remains.

What occurred was that the tomb was destroyed by charges of guncotton, the body was disinterred, cast into one of the steamer's furnaces, and the ashes thrown into the Nile. The head, it is stated, was retained by a British officer in the Egyptian service.

As what happened excited a good deal of indignation in Europe, it is only just to give the *sirdar's* explanation. He stated that after the Battle of Omdurman he thought that it was politically advisable, considering the condition of the country, that the *Mahdi's* tomb, which was the centre of pilgrimage and fanatical feeling, should be destroyed; the tomb was also in a dangerous condition owing to the damage done to it by shell fire, and might have caused loss of life if left as it was. He was advised by Mahommedan officers that it would be better to have the body removed, as otherwise many of the more ignorant people of Kordofan would consider that the sanctity with which they surrounded the *Mahdi* prevented this being done. The *sirdar* added that "the skull of the *Mahdi* was now buried at Wady Halfa."

When to the above it is added that so high an authority as Lord Cromer has declared that, under the exceptional circumstances of the case, the destruction of the tomb and the removal of the body were "political necessities," there is little more to be said with respect to an act which, at first sight, every one was disposed to regard with abhorrence.[3]

On the morning of Sunday, the 4th September, the *sirdar* visited Khartoum, being transported across the Nile in the gunboat *Melik*. At the same time representatives of every corps belonging to the expedition passed over in the *Dal* and *Akasheh*. Khartoum, though in ruins, presented, as seen from the river, a picturesque and pleasing appearance, with its gardens and palm trees extending almost to the water's edge.

Gordon's palace, now a ruined mass of buildings, with the upper storey fallen in, was still conspicuous. The staircase in front, where he met his death, no longer existed. The adjoining grounds, long since fallen into neglect, were still full of blossoming shrubs, and orange, citron, and pomegranate trees.

As the troops disembarked, just thirteen years too late to save the man who had so long and so heroically defended Khartoum, a crowd of wondering natives assembled to watch what was about to take place.

No sooner had the troops landed than they were formed up into three sides of a square, facing the front of the ruined palace. In the cen-

---

3. See Lord Cromer's despatch to the Marquis of Salisbury, dated 12th March, 1899.

tre were the *sirdar*, his staff, and the general officers commanding the different brigades. At a signal from the *sirdar*, the British and Egyptian flags were simultaneously hoisted on flag-staffs erected on the palace, and the bands played "God save the Queen" and the Khedivial Hymn, whilst the gunboat fired a royal salute of twenty-one guns, the officers and men all standing at attention.

"Three cheers for the Queen" were then given, the men shouting enthusiastically and waving their helmets in the air. This was followed by "Three cheers for the *khedive*," and again all present heartily responded.

The various chaplains attached to the British division now came to the front. The Guards' band struck up the "Dead March" in *Saul*, followed by a funeral march from the Egyptian band. The chaplains then performed a short but impressive service, and the Soudanese band concluded the ceremony by playing Gordon's favourite hymn, "Abide with me."

The service finished, several of those present, guided by Slatin Pasha, walked through what were once the streets of Khartoum, now only a collection of rubbish heaps. All the stone and building material had been removed to construct the houses at Omdurman. The only edifices spared in any way were the palace, the arsenal, and the Austrian mission building. Only a few of the inhabitants remained in the place which was formerly the capital of the Soudan.

A detachment of the 11th Soudanese was left to guard the flags which remained floating over the palace, and the rest of the troops then returned to Omdurman.

On the following day, the whole of the *sirdar's* army was paraded and marched, with full military display, through the streets of Omdurman, as well to give the natives an idea of the strength of the Anglo-Egyptian force, as to impress on them that the Mahdist rule was a thing of the past. The place reeked with filth, and the smell was overpowering. Bodies of men and animals lay decomposing in the streets, and on every side was squalor and misery.

After this the British troops, with the exception of some companies of the Northumberland Fusiliers, were shipped off as rapidly as possible to Cairo. There was no more fighting to be done, and the men were beginning to feel the after-effects of the past week's marching and fatigue. In addition to this, enteric fever had begun to set in, and the hospital tents were crowded. However, by the end of the month, nearly the whole of the British division had left.

CHAPTER 69

Fashoda

On the 7th September a surprising and unlooked-for incident occurred. One of Gordon's old steamers, the *Tewfikeyeh*, which had been sent by the *khalifa* up the White Nile, unexpectedly returned to Omdurman, only to find that the place had changed hands.

On being boarded she at once surrendered to the *sirdar*. Her captain reported that on reaching Fashoda he had been fired on by a party of white men, and in support of his statement produced some nickel-plated bullets, of small calibre, and evidently of European manufacture.

There was no doubt that a European expedition of some kind had arrived at Fashoda, and opinions only differed as to its nationality and object.

The *sirdar's* first step was to order all the newspaper correspondents back to Cairo.

At 6 a.m. on the 10th he left Omdurman in the postal steamer *Dal*. The gunboats *Sultan*, *Nazir*, and *Fatteh*, all towing barges, accompanied him. Later on he was joined by the *Abu Klea*. He took with him an Egyptian field battery, one company of the Camerons, and also the 11th and 13th, Soudanese Battalions. The river was at its height and very full. Steaming with all possible speed against the stream, the flotilla on the morning of the 15th reached a point called Renkh, 310 miles south of Khartoum. Here they found the *khalifa's* steamer *Safiyeh* (the vessel employed in the rescue of Sir Charles Wilson in 1885) and eleven large *nuggers* with a party of Dervishes, who, it appeared, were awaiting reinforcements from Omdurman to renew an attack which they had already made on the white men established at Fashoda.

The vessels were lying on the east bank of the river close to a Dervish camp. The Dervishes resisted for a while and fired on the *sirdar's* fleet. The gunboats returned the fire, one of the shells bursting in the *Tewfikeyeh's* boiler and disabling her. The enemy's fire was soon silenced, and a party of the 11th Soudanese then landed and cleared the Dervish camp.

The steamer and the *nuggers* having been captured, the flotilla went on its way about noon. The river here continued very wide, with much vegetation on its banks, where crocodiles and hippopotami were seen in numbers.

On the 18th a stop was made for the night ten miles below Fashoda, and a letter from the *sirdar* informed the commandant of the post which was reported as being established there of the approach of the steamers.

Next morning, when the vessels were about five miles from Fashoda, a rowing boat flying a French flag was seen approaching. It contained one of the officers under the orders of Captain (afterwards Major) Marchand, the commander of a French exploring expedition, which it turned out had occupied Fashoda since the 10th July.

As Fashoda was neared the French flag was seen in the middle of the native village, and near the old Egyptian fort the captain's force, consisting of eight officers and 120 Senegalese armed with repeating rifles, and some Shilluks with native spears, was drawn up. On the steamers making fast, Marchand went on board the *Dal* to visit the *sirdar*, and remained in conference with him three quarters of an hour. The *sirdar* declared that the presence of a French force was an infringement of the rights of Egypt and of the British Government, and protested against the occupation of Fashoda and the hoisting of the French flag. Marchand stated, in reply, that he was acting under the orders of the French Government, and that without instructions it would be impossible for him to withdraw. He admitted that, in the face of a superior force, he was not prepared to resist the hoisting of the Egyptian flag.

When the conference was over the steamers proceeded some 300 yards up stream and landed the *sirdar's* troops. The Egyptian flag was then hoisted about 500 yards from the French flag, on a ruined bastion of the fortifications, and saluted with all ceremony by the gunboats. Marchand's force, which had been attacked by the Dervishes on the 25th August, was in great want of ammunition and supplies, and the captain, in expectation of a further attack, had sent his steamer south to bring up reinforcements.

Leaving the 11th Soudanese with two guns and the steamer *Nazir*, the remainder of the force re-embarked and proceeded south to Sobat, where they arrived on the 22nd, hoisted the Egyptian flag, and established a second post. The *Abu Klea* remained with part of the 13th Soudanese Battalion, and the other steamers then proceeded down the Nile to Omdurman without further adventure.

On the *sirdar's* arrival, he at once communicated to the Foreign Office the result of his mission.

Although want of space renders it impossible to deal fully with the diplomatic incident to which the French occupation of Fashoda gave rise, a few particulars may, nevertheless, be given.

In the beginning of 1898, a Cairo telegram coming through Paris announced, somewhat prematurely, that a French expedition, under Captain Marchand, had arrived at Fashoda, and letters from his officers and men, written on their journey, expressed their anxiety to reach the Upper Nile before the British, and "to display the French flag between Khartoum and Gondokoro."

Although little notice was taken at the time of these announcements and aspirations, the knowledge of the Marchand expedition was undoubtedly one of the causes which determined the British Government to hasten the advance on Khartoum.

What subsequently occurred seems to have been in great measure foreseen by Lord Salisbury, who appears to have anticipated that difficulties might arise, not only with regard to France, but with Abyssinia as well.

In a despatch dated the 2nd August, 1898, communicating to Lord Cromer the views of the British Government as to the line of action to be taken after the occupation of Khartoum, the British Premier stated that the *sirdar* was authorized to send two flotillas, one up the White and the other up the Blue Nile. The flotilla up the White Nile was to be commanded by the *sirdar* as far as Fashoda, and the officer in command of the Blue Nile flotilla was to go as far as the foot of the cataract commencing about Rosiéres. Should he before reaching that encounter any Abyssinian outposts, he was to halt and await further instructions. The despatch added that:

> In dealing with any French or Abyssinian authorities who might be encountered, nothing should be said or done which would in any way imply a recognition by the British Government of a title to possession on behalf of France or Abyssinia to any portion of the Nile Valley.

It was scarcely to be expected that at the moment when the Anglo-Egyptian operations, undertaken mainly with the object of restoring her lost provinces to Egypt, had been crowned with success, England could acquiesce in the occupation of any portion of them by a foreign Power, and frequent exchanges of views took place between the British and French Governments.

The British Government asked for the withdrawal of Marchand, whom the French Minister had termed an "emissary of civilization." This demand the French Government was disinclined to agree to.

The French contention was that the country bordering the White Nile, though formerly belonging to Egypt, had by abandonment become *res nullius*, and that the French had as much right to a position on the Nile as the Germans or the Belgians.

The British case was that the valley of the Nile still belonged to Egypt, although her title had been rendered dormant by the successes of the *Mahdi*; further, that whatever title the latter might have acquired passed on the 2nd September by right of conquest to the British and Egyptian Governments.

Lord Salisbury declared on the 9th September that Her Majesty's Government did not consider that this right was open to argument. Nevertheless, the discussions on the subject, to which the Foreign Office declined to give the name of "negotiations," continued for two whole months, and were marked throughout by great firmness on the part of the British Cabinet.

Lord Salisbury, besides being backed by the British nation generally, was supported by the leading men amongst the Opposition, including Lord Rosebery, who, in the middle of October, made a speech in which the following passage occurred:—

> Great Britain has been conciliatory, and her conciliatory disposition has been widely misunderstood. If the nations of the world are under the impression that the ancient spirit of Great Britain is dead, or that her resources are weakened, or her population less determined than ever it was to maintain the rights and honour of its flag, they make a mistake which can only end in a disastrous conflagration.

Simultaneously quiet but effective steps were taken to put the defences of the United Kingdom in order, and to prepare the fleet for any emergency.

In the end the French Government, seeing that England was in earnest, made up its mind to retire from an untenable position. The good news was appropriately communicated to the nation by Lord Salisbury on November 4th at the Lord Mayor's dinner to the *sirdar*, and gave general satisfaction.

Shortly after, Marchand and his force returned to France, and an incident which had seriously threatened the good relations existing between England and France came to an end.

Whilst the *sirdar* was making his excursion to Fashoda, General Hunter, accompanied by a small force, proceeded up the Blue Nile. Here he met no Abyssinian Marchand disguised as an "envoy of civilization," and returned without having encountered any serious opposition from the tribes along the river.

Notwithstanding the blow suffered by the Mahdist cause at Omdurman, there was still some fighting to be done in another quarter. This time the scene of operations was in the neighbourhood of Gedaref, about 130 miles south-west of Kassala and 180 from the Blue Nile. This place had, previously to the fall of Omdurman, been held by an emir called Ahmed Fedil with upwards of 5,000 men.

Ahmed, with the object of assisting the *khalifa*, had withdrawn the greater part of his force from Gedaref, and on the 7th September, Colonel Parsons started from Kassala with 1,300 men composed of the 16th Egyptian Battalion and some irregulars to dislodge the garrison remaining at Gedaref.

On the 22nd Parsons arrived in front of the place, and, after defeating some 3,000 Dervishes, succeeded in occupying it. The fight was severe, the Egyptian losses being no less than thirty-seven killed and fifty-seven wounded. Meanwhile Ahmed Fedil, who had failed to reach Omdurman, was making his way back towards Gedaref, where, on the 28th, he turned up with 3,500 men. He made a determined assault on the town, but his Dervishes were defeated by Parsons with heavy loss. On the 1st October they withdrew to some distance, and the Egyptian force not being strong enough to pursue, occupied themselves in strengthening their defences.

General Rundle was then sent up the river to Parsons' assistance. Rundle reached Abu Harras, on the Blue Nile, whence Colonel Collinson, with the 12th Battalion, started across the desert and joined Parsons just in time to see Fedil's forces in full retreat in the direction of the river. At Rosiéres they found Colonel Lewis, who had been for several weeks on the look-out to intercept Fedil's crossing. A severe fight ensued between the Dervishes and the 10th Battalion under

Lewis, aided by some of the gunboats told off to patrol the river. Many of Fedil's force were killed and many more surrendered. Out of Lewis's 400 soldiers, no fewer than 159 were either killed or wounded. The enemy were utterly routed, but Fedil succeeded in crossing the river with a few of his followers. Several days later he passed over the White Nile and joined the *khalifa* in Kordofan.

The action at Rosiéres was the last fight of the campaign of 1898 which the *sirdar* had so successfully carried on against the Mahdists.

If there is one thing more remarkable than another in the campaign, it is the excellent administration by the *sirdar* of the force under his command. The construction of the railway, the management of the commissariat, the slow, sure, and irresistible advance, and the avoidance of accidents or reverses—all these constituted a triumph of administration. The manner in which the transport of the largest force ever sent into the Soudan under civilized conditions was effected will bear comparison with any campaign in modern times.

Another important feature was the comparatively small cost. According to Lord Cromer's report of the 26th February, 1899, the total expense from the spring of 1896, when the expedition to Dongola was decided upon, till the close of the operations in the Soudan, was only £E2,354,354. This included the construction of no less than 760 miles of railway at a cost of £E1,181,372, of 2,000 miles of telegraphs at a cost of £E21,825, and the building of six gunboats at an expense of £E154,934, thus leaving the military expenditure only £E996,223.

Whilst giving Lord Kitchener the fullest credit for the success achieved, it would be unjust not to refer to the powerful and steady support which in his task he received throughout from England's representative in Egypt, Lord Cromer, who, happily combining in himself the qualities of a soldier and a diplomat, was in a position to give most valuable advice in either capacity.[1]

---

1. Lord Cromer, as a recognition of his services in Egypt, was created Viscount Cromer in January, 1899.

CHAPTER 70

Destruction of the Khalifa

With regard to the further movements of the *khalifa*. As already stated, after leaving Omdurman Abdullah fled in the direction of Kordofan. Following the course of the White Nile, he proceeded, with only a few followers, to Duem, whence, quitting the river, he struck off in a south-westerly direction to Lake Sherkeleh, about 120 miles further. There he was joined by some of his shattered forces. Subsequently an Egyptian fort was established at Duem and occupied by the 2nd Egyptian Battalion.

Towards the end of 1898 it was reported that the *khalifa* had with him only a few hundred followers, and against these, in January, 1899, Colonel Kitchener, a brother of the *sirdar*, was despatched with 900 men belonging to the 2nd and 14th Battalions, and about fifty irregular Cavalry.

Starting from Duem in the following month, Colonel Kitchener's troops arrived at the *khalifa's* supposed position only to discover that he had evacuated his camp, which bore traces of having been occupied by some thousands of men, instead of the few hundreds reported as composing the Dervish force.

A reconnaissance was then made to within three miles of Abdullah's new position, and here Kitchener, having placed his men in a *zeriba*, sent out his scouts.

They reported that the *khalifa* had with him a force of about 7,000 men, of which more than half were armed with rifles, and that they were drawn up in fighting order.

Kitchener, realizing the insufficient number of his troops for an attack, and running short of water, abandoned the *zeriba* and fell back upon the river.

The *khalifa* followed him as far as the deserted *zeriba*, but, fortunately for the small Egyptian force, did not pursue further. The expedition was then abandoned, and Colonel Kitchener returned to Cairo.[1]

In the subsequent month of June the *khalifa* was still in the neighbourhood of Lake Sherkeleh, and raiding the tribes in that vicinity. According to later reports he had been attacked by the Tagalla tribe and had sustained heavy losses, by which, and by other causes, his adherents were reduced to as few as 4,000 men.

On this intelligence reaching Cairo it was determined that another attempt should be made against him as soon as the rainy season, then impending, should be over.

In September, news arrived that the still uncaptured Abdullah, with an army increased to 10,000 men, had established himself near Jeb el Gheddeer, a mountainous spot 100 miles north-west of Fashoda. A powerful *emir* named Arabi Dafalla, with a numerous following, was reported to be on his way to Darfur, with a view to joining hands with the *khalifa*. The military authorities then decided that the moment had come for finally crushing the *khalifa*.

On the 26th September, the *sirdar* reached Cairo from Europe, and proceeded at once to Omdurman, where the arrangements for a further expedition were being rapidly pushed forward. The greatest care was taken to ensure secrecy, but it became known that the force, which was to be under the personal command of the *sirdar*, would consist of about 6,000 men, including four battalions of Egyptian Infantry, with cavalry, camel corps and artillery, besides irregulars.

The troops were to concentrate at Kaka, on the White Nile, whence they were to march upon Jeb el Gheddeer, 90 miles distant from the river, at which place it was hoped the fight would come off. The expedition, which was to proceed partly by land and partly by river, was so far advanced that by the end of September the cavalry, camel corps, and artillery had already been sent off from Omdurman, and they were joined soon after by the Infantry, and on the 11th October the *sirdar* and his staff followed in the steamer *Dal*.

If the War Department was reticent with reference to Colonel Kitchener's expedition, it was even more so with regard to that of the *sirdar*. Of the doings of the latter nothing was permitted to be made public until the 26th October, when it was officially announced that

---

1. The Egyptian War Department was signally reticent with regard to this expedition, and for most of the foregoing particulars the author is indebted to a work recently published called *Sudan Campaigns, 1896-1899*.

the *khalifa* had fled from Jeb el Gheddeer, and, it being impossible to pursue him at that time, the *sirdar* had given orders for the troops to return to Omdurman. It was added that a reconnaissance to Jeb el Gheddeer would be made by the cavalry and camel corps before their return.

The *sirdar's* force, after leaving the river at Kaka, marched on the road to Jeb el Gheddeer as far as a place called Fungar. Here it was found that the *khalifa* had got thirty hours' start and was moving in a northerly direction across a waterless district, where it would have been very difficult to follow him, and the evasive Abdullah was therefore allowed to go his way.

Notwithstanding that the official announcement was followed by the return of many of the troops to Omdurman, and by the appearance of the *sirdar* in Cairo, people were reluctant to believe in the final abandonment of the expedition, and further developments were expected; nor were such expectations doomed to be disappointed.

On the 12th November it became known that the *khalifa* was seven days' journey from Jeb el Gheddeer and was making his way towards Abba Island, on the Nile, with a force estimated at considerably over 3,000 men.

In consequence of this information the Sirdar, on the 14th, suddenly started on his return to Omdurman, and the British troops in Cairo were ordered to prepare detachments to proceed to garrison Omdurman.

During the *sirdar's* absence Colonel Sir F. R. Wingate, then in command at Khartoum, learning that Dervishes had been seen in the neighbourhood of Abba, despatched Colonel Lewis, with two battalions of infantry and a flotilla of gunboats, to operate along the river and prevent raiding.

On Lewis reaching a place called Alobe, he found that a large Dervish force, under Ahmed Fedil, was encamped close by, but, at daylight, before Lewis was able to attack, they had all disappeared.

The *sirdar*, on reaching Khartoum, at once ordered Wingate to follow up Abu Fedil.

On the 20th, Wingate, with 3,700 men, composed of the 9th and 13th Soudanese Battalions, one Battalion of Irregular Infantry, some Maxims, and fifty Cavalry, arrived at Faki Shoya, to the west of Abba Island, where he was joined by 250 of the Camel Corps, who crossed over from the right bank of the Nile.

On the evening of the 21st, the Egyptian troops marched towards

Nefissa, 23 miles from the river, whither it was reported that Ahmed Fedil had retired. Nefissa was reached before daylight on the 22nd, and it was then discovered that Fedil had moved on to Abu Aadil, four miles further, where he was encamped with about 2,500 men.

The mounted troops, with guns and Maxims, were at once sent forward to engage the Dervishes and hold them in check until Wingate's main body should come up. This movement was ably carried out. The mounted force promptly attacked the enemy's camp with gun and rifle fire, meeting with a warm but badly-directed fire in return. The Dervishes rushed from the wood and charged up to within sixty yards of the guns, only, however, to be shot down in hundreds. Wingate then brought up the infantry in support, and, making a general advance, cleared the whole position. The Dervishes, utterly routed, bolted through the bush, followed by the cavalry. Four thousand of the enemy are said to have been killed in the fight and pursuit. After the action, which began at 10 a.m. and lasted only about an hour, the troops halted to rest.

It now remained to find the Khalifa Abdullah, who was known to be advancing towards El Ghedid, with the object of joining his forces with those of Ahmed Fedil. Thither it was resolved to push on, and at midnight on the 22nd the troops again started, reaching El Ghedid about 10 a.m. on the 23rd. Here water, of which they were much in need, was found, and news came that the *khalifa* and his army were encamped only seven miles off at Om Debrikat.

The cavalry and Maxims were immediately sent out to reconnoitre, and having ascertained the Dervish position, the whole of Wingate's force, at 12.20 a.m. on the 24th, advanced by moonlight to within three miles of the enemy, when a halt was called, and the troops deployed into attack formation. The advance was then resumed. Although strict silence was kept in the ranks, it soon became evident, from the sound of drums and horns, that the *khalifa* was aware of Wingate's approach. At 3.40 a.m. a gentle, rising slope, which laid between the troops and the Dervish camp, was reached; here the force halted and the men were allowed to sleep.

Soon after five, when only a faint light indicated the approach of day, numerous white figures, moving towards the Egyptian position, were recognized as Dervishes advancing to the attack. Wingate's troops were at once on the alert, and opened fire on the indistinct mass. The fire was returned by the enemy's riflemen, and in a few minutes the action became general. Half an hour later the enemy's fire got slacker and slacker, and Wingate's whole line advancing, swept through the Dervish position for two miles till the enemy's camp was reached.

As the troops passed over the field of battle, the deadly effect of the Egyptian fire was shown by the heaps of dead strewing the ground. Amongst them was the *khalifa* himself, who, surrounded by his bodyguard and principal *emirs*, made a gallant stand, but fell riddled with bullets. He seems to have met his fate with dignity. Seeing that he was defeated, he resolved to die, and gathering his *emirs* around him, they fell together. With him died Ahmed Fedil and Ali Wad Helu, also the *khalifa's* two brothers; Sennoussi Ahmed and Haroun Mohamed, as well as Sadik, the son of the Mahdi. The *khalifa's* son, Sheikh el Din, was amongst the wounded.

Wingate was leading the pursuing party of cavalry in front when the dead body of the *khalifa* was discovered, and a little boy advanced towards Watson Bey, who was following with the other troops, took Watson's hand, led him to a group of three dead bodies, and, pointing to a figure in the centre of the group, said, "That is my father." The other two were the *emirs* Abu Fedl and Ali Wad Helu. On this being reported to Wingate, he directed that the burial of the dead *khalifa* and his two companions should be carried out by their own people, with all due pomp and ceremony.

As soon as the news of the death of the *khalifa* was spread the greater part of his followers laid down their arms and surrendered. Every man of importance, except Osman Digna, who left soon after the firing began, was either killed or made prisoner. The total number of prisoners taken was about 3,000, besides a crowd of women and children found in the Dervish camp. The victory was complete; the enemy, out of a force of from 5,000 to 6,000 men, lost over 1,000 in killed, as well as a vast collection of arms, grain, and munitions. Wingate's losses were inconsiderable, amounting only to three men killed and twelve wounded.

After Wingate's brilliant achievement his men moved back to the river. Between the 21st and the 24th they had marched more than sixty miles over trying ground, had fought two decisive engagements, and destroyed the last army which the *khalifa* was able to put into the field.

To Sir F. R. Wingate is due the conspicuous merit of effectually suppressing Mahdism for ever in the Soudan.

Conclusion

It may reasonably be expected that the present work, a considerable portion of which is devoted to the intervention of England in Egypt, should not be brought to a close without some reference to the results attending it.

The military incidents, including the suppression of two formidable rebellions, the abandonment and reconquest of extensive territories, and the creation of a new national army, have already been mentioned.

Such of the political occurrences as were of sufficient general interest have also been touched upon. The effect of England's action in the Valley of the Nile, so far as it relates to the moral and material condition of the country, has yet to be dealt with.

It is no exaggeration to say that never in the pages of history has there been an instance of such rapid recovery as that of Egypt during the last seventeen years. Unfortunately the exigencies of space will not admit of more than a brief reference to the work which has been accomplished. For further and more complete information the reader would do well to consult Sir Alfred Milner's *England in Egypt*, a book already more than once quoted in these pages. In every direction a transformation has taken place. Finances have been put in order; revenue has increased; taxation has diminished; additional land has been brought into cultivation; the cotton crop (Egypt's most valuable product) has been doubled; foreign trade has augmented; railway, postal, and telegraph services have been developed; the administration of justice and the prison system have been reformed; sanitary matters have been taken in hand; education has progressed, and lastly, the population has increased to an extent hitherto unknown.

In support of the preceding statements a few figures may ere be given with advantage.

The augmentation of the revenue may be seen from the following table:—[1]

	£E.			£E.
1882	8,852,857	1891	... ...	10,828,733
1883	8,934,675	1892	... ...	10,475,766
1884	9,403,294	1893	... ...	10,425,353
1885	10,169,678	1894	... ...	10,444,650
1886	9,726,937	1895	... ...	10,698,023
1887	9,774,684	1896	... ...	11,015,702
1888	9,868,124	1897	... ...	11,442,937
1889	9,992,758	1898	... ...	11,347,980
1890	10,432,889	1899	(estimated)	10,600,000*

A noteworthy circumstance in connection with the growth of revenue is that it has been accompanied by an important diminution of taxation. Taxes to the annual amount of £E.1,132,666 have been remitted since the commencement of the Occupation, and the burden of taxation per head of the population has been reduced from £E.1 2s. 6d. to 17s. 9d., a diminution of 20 *per cent.*

Whilst the revenue was steadily increasing, the expenditure was so well kept in hand that the chronic deficit which so long figured in Egyptian Budgets was replaced in 1887 by a surplus, and this, with the exception of the year 1888, has continued ever since.

The following table shows the general financial results obtained since the commencement of the British occupation:—

	SURPLUS. £E.	DEFICIT. £E.			SURPLUS. £E.	DEFICIT. £E.
1883 ...	—	920,000	1891	...	951,000	—
1884 ...	—	460,000	1892	...	769,000	—
1885 ...	—	697,000	1893	...	720,000	—
1886 ...	—	684,000	1894	...	785,000	—
1887 ...	111,000	—	1895	...	1,088,000	—
1888 ...	—	1,000	1896	...	630,000	—
1889 ...	160,000	—	1897	...	690,161	—
1890 ...	591,000	—	1898	...	1,376,000	—

Out of the surpluses thus arising a "General Reserve Fund" has been created, by which the stability of the finances has been secured, and a fund provided for expenditure on productive public works, and for other beneficial objects. On the 31st December, 1898, the sum to the credit of the "General Reserve Fund" amounted to £E.3,893,000, of which £E.2,616,000 was pledged for the execution of public works.

---

1. These figures, which include both ordinary and extraordinary receipts, are, with the exception of those relating to the years 1898 and 1899, taken from statistical tables compiled by Sir Elwin Palmer, late Financial Adviser to the Egyptian Government. It should be added that the Egyptian pound may be regarded as the equivalent of £1 0s. 6d. in English money.

In addition to this Fund there is another Reserve Fund, consisting of the accumulated economies resulting from the partial conversion of the Public Debt, and destined to form eventually a Sinking Fund. This amounted at the last-mentioned date to £E.3,218,000.

The increase in the cotton crop, due mainly to extended irrigation, has been from 2,846,237 *kantars*[2] in 1882, to 5,954,000 *kantars* in 1898.

The improvement in the Foreign Trade is shown by the fact that the value of the exports of merchandise increased from £E.10,418,213 in 1888 to £E.11,706,258 in 1898, and the value of the imports during the same period from £E.7,738,343 to £E.10,811,151. The Customs Revenue (which amounted in 1882 to only £E.624,312) was more than doubled between the dates above given, the returns in 1888 being £E.959,939, and in 1898; £E.2,040,000.[3]

The progress made by the railways, post office, and telegraph administrations since the commencement of the Occupation is shown by the following figures:—

Receipts.[4]

	RAILWAYS. £E.	POST OFFICE. £E.	TELEGRAPHS. £E.
1883	1,213,000	102,000	67,000
1898	2,031,569	122,867	60,685[4]

According to Sir Elwin Palmer, 212 miles of new railways were opened between 1881 and 1897.

The advance made in regard to education appears from the fact that the expenditure on Public Instruction in the fifteen years ending in 1897 increased by over 37 *per cent.*, the number of government schools rose from 29 to 51, and the number of pupils from 2,000 to over 11,000.

The increase in the population, before referred to, is the more remarkable when the drain occasioned by the repeated wars in the Soudan is taken into account. In 1882 the inhabitants of Egypt numbered 6,813,919, and in 1897, when the last census was taken, the population had risen to 9,734,405, showing an augmentation of no less than 2,920,486, or 43 *per cent.*, in the space of 15 years.

It may be observed that Lane gives the population of Egypt in

---

2. The *kantar* is equal to 101lbs. 5oz.
3. These figures are taken from Mr. A. Silva White's lately published work called *The Expansion of Egypt*.
4. The diminution in the telegraph receipts is due to a large reduction in the tariff.

the time of the Pharaohs as between six and seven millions. A French historian, M. Mengin, puts the population in the time of Mehemet Ali as only 2,900,000.

Hitherto, mention has only been made of the advantages actually accrued to Egypt under British guidance. But if the gigantic irrigation works recently undertaken in Upper Egypt, known as "The Reservoir Scheme," fulfil only partially the expectations formed with regard to them, the benefits which the country will receive in the future will far exceed anything in the past.

These works, the foundation stone of which was laid in January, 1899, will consist of a huge dam and lock across the Nile at Assouan, and a similar, though less extensive, construction at Assiout—the whole to be completed in five years from 1st July, 1898, at a cost of £4,800,000—spread over 30 years.

By these works, the design for which, in its present modified form, is due to Mr. W. Willcocks, C.E., late of the Egyptian Irrigation Department, it is calculated that the failure of the cotton crop by reason of a low Nile will in future be avoided; 774,000 acres of land now imperfectly irrigated will receive perennial irrigation, other lands will get additional water, and 172,000 acres will be reclaimed from the desert.

The yearly increase to the wealth of the country is estimated at £E.2,608,000, and the direct annual benefit to the State at £E.378,400. In addition to this it is reckoned that the sale of such of the reclaimed land as belongs to the government will realise a sum of £E.1,020,000 to the exchequer.[5]

Whilst dealing with prospective benefits, it is impossible to avoid some reference to the advantages to Egypt which may eventually arise from the opening up of the reconquered provinces of the Soudan to trade and commerce.

The future government of these vast regions was provided for by the Soudan Convention, made between the British and Egyptian Governments in January, 1899. Under this the British and Egyptian flags are to be used together, both on land and water, in the Soudan, and the supreme military and civil command is to be vested in an officer termed the governor-general, nominated by Khedivial Decree, on the recommendation of the British Government. The governor-general is alone to have power to make laws, and until otherwise provided the

---

5. See Memorandum by Sir W. E. Garstin, C.E., dated 19th November, 1897, *Parliamentary Papers, Egypt No. 1, 1898*.

whole country will be under martial law.

The orderly administration of the country having been thus provided for, it only remains to wait and see the results. Though years may elapse before these realize the hopes formed, it is impossible not to believe that a territory which, under the most adverse circumstances, has produced such riches in the past, should not, under the present improved conditions, develop into a prosperous dependency of Egypt. Even should this not prove to be the case, the mere rescue of such a vast territory from barbarism will ever remain a triumph for the cause of civilization well worth the cost.

Whilst everyone must recognise the beneficent work which has been accomplished in Egypt under England's guidance, there may be persons inclined to doubt whether it can be regarded as permanent. To this there is but one answer, *viz.*, that England can never permit the country which she has rescued to drift back into a state of ruin and chaos. This may be thought to imply an indefinite prolongation of the Occupation. Such, however, does not of necessity follow. It may well be that the direction of Egyptian affairs will have to be left for some time in the hands of the power under whose influence so much has been accomplished. Until the reforms effected have had time to consolidate, withdrawal would jeopardize the edifice so laboriously erected, and be the worst of calamities. But the progress which the country, under an enlightened ruler, is daily making, joined to the growing intelligence of the people, encourage the belief that the moment will arrive when England may declare her mission on the banks of the Nile at an end, and leave to a regenerated Egypt the control of her own destinies.

ALSO FROM LEONAUR
AVAILABLE IN SOFTCOVER OR HARDCOVER WITH DUST JACKET

LIFE IN THE ARMY OF NORTHERN VIRGINIA *by Carlton McCarthy*—The Observations of a Confederate Artilleryman of Cutshaw's Battalion During the American Civil War 1861-1865.

HISTORY OF THE CAVALRY OF THE ARMY OF THE POTOMAC *by Charles D. Rhodes*—Including Pope's Army of Virginia and the Cavalry Operations in West Virginia During the American Civil War.

CAMP-FIRE AND COTTON-FIELD *by Thomas W. Knox*—A New York Herald Correspondent's View of the American Civil War.

SERGEANT STILLWELL *by Leander Stillwell*—The Experiences of a Union Army Soldier of the 61st Illinois Infantry During the American Civil War.

STONEWALL'S CANNONEER *by Edward A. Moore*—Experiences with the Rockbridge Artillery, Confederate Army of Northern Virginia, During the American Civil War.

THE SIXTH CORPS *by George Stevens*—The Army of the Potomac, Union Army, During the American Civil War.

THE RAILROAD RAIDERS *by William Pittenger*—An Ohio Volunteers Recollections of the Andrews Raid to Disrupt the Confederate Railroad in Georgia During the American Civil War.

CITIZEN SOLDIER *by John Beatty*—An Account of the American Civil War by a Union Infantry Officer of Ohio Volunteers Who Became a Brigadier General.

COX: PERSONAL RECOLLECTIONS OF THE CIVIL WAR--VOLUME 1 *by Jacob Dolson Cox*—West Virginia, Kanawha Valley, Gauley Bridge, Cotton Mountain, South Mountain, Antietam, the Morgan Raid & the East Tennessee Campaign.

COX: PERSONAL RECOLLECTIONS OF THE CIVIL WAR--VOLUME 2 *by Jacob Dolson Cox*—Siege of Knoxville, East Tennessee, Atlanta Campaign, the Nashville Campaign & the North Carolina Campaign.

KERSHAW'S BRIGADE VOLUME 1 *by D. Augustus Dickert*—Manassas, Seven Pines, Sharpsburg (Antietam), Fredricksburg, Chancellorsville, Gettysburg, Chickamauga, Chattanooga, Fort Sanders & Bean Station.

KERSHAW'S BRIGADE VOLUME 2 *by D. Augustus Dickert*—At the wilderness, Cold Harbour, Petersburg, The Shenandoah Valley and Cedar Creek..

AVAILABLE ONLINE AT **www.leonaur.com**
AND FROM ALL GOOD BOOK STORES

ALSO FROM LEONAUR
AVAILABLE IN SOFTCOVER OR HARDCOVER WITH DUST JACKET

THE ART OF WAR by *Antoine Henri Jomini*—Strategy & Tactics From the Age of Horse & Musket.

THE ART OF WAR by *Sun Tzu and Pierre G. T. Beauregard*—*The Art of War* by Sun Tzu and *Principles and Maxims of the Art of War* by Pierre G. T. Beauregard.

THE MILITARY RELIGIOUS ORDERS OF THE MIDDLE AGES by *F. C. Woodhouse*—The Knights Templar, Hospitaller and Others.

THE BENGAL NATIVE ARMY by *F. G. Cardew*—An Invaluable Reference Resource.

ARTILLERY THROUGH THE AGES—by *Albert Manucy*—A History of the DEvelopment and Use of Cannons, Mortars, Rockets & Projectiles from Earliest Times to the Nineteenth Century.

THE SWORD OF THE CROWN by *Eric W. Sheppard*—A History of the British Army to 1914.

THE 7TH (QUEEN'S OWN) HUSSARS: Volume 3—1818-1914 by *C. R. B. Barrett*—On Campaign During the Canadian Rebellion, the Indian Mutiny, the Sudan, Matabeleland, Mashonaland and the Boer War Volume 3: 1818-1914.

THE CAMPAIGN OF WATERLOO by *Antoine Henri Jomini*—A Political & Military History from the French perspective.

RIFLE & DRILL by *S. Bertram Browne*—The Enfield Rifle Musket, 1853 and the Drill of the British Soldier of the Mid-Victorian Period *A Companion to the New Rifle Musket* and *A Practical Guide to Squad and Setting-up Dtill*.

NAPOLEON'S MEN AND METHODS by *Alexander L. Kielland*—The Rise and Fall of the Emperor and His Men Who Fought by His Side.

THE WOMAN IN BATTLE by *Loreta Janeta Velazquez*—Soldier, Spy and Secret Service Agent for the Confederancy During the American Civil War.

THE BATTLE OF ORISKANY 1777 by *Ellis H. Roberts*—The Conflict for the Mowhawk Valley During the American War of Independenc.

PERSONAL RECOLLECTIONS OF JOAN OF ARC by *Mark Twain*.

CAESAR'S ARMY by *Harry Pratt Judson*—The Evolution, Composition, Tactics, Equipment & Battles of the Roman Army.

FREDERICK THE GREAT & THE SEVEN YEARS' WAR by *F. W. Longman*.

AVAILABLE ONLINE AT **www.leonaur.com**
AND FROM ALL GOOD BOOK STORES

ALSO FROM LEONAUR
AVAILABLE IN SOFTCOVER OR HARDCOVER WITH DUST JACKET

OFFICERS & GENTLEMEN *by Peter Hawker & William Graham*—Two Accounts of British Officers During the Peninsula War: Officer of Light Dragoons by Peter Hawker & Campaign in Portugal and Spain by William Graham.

THE WALCHEREN EXPEDITION *by Anonymous*—The Experiences of a British Officer of the 81st Regt. During the Campaign in the Low Countries of 1809.

LADIES OF WATERLOO *by Charlotte A. Eaton, Magdalene de Lancey & Juana Smith*—The Experiences of Three Women During the Campaign of 1815: Waterloo Days by Charlotte A. Eaton, A Week at Waterloo by Magdalene de Lancey & Juana's Story by Juana Smith.

JOURNAL OF AN OFFICER IN THE KING'S GERMAN LEGION *by John Frederick Hering*—Recollections of Campaigning During the Napoleonic Wars.

JOURNAL OF AN ARMY SURGEON IN THE PENINSULAR WAR *by Charles Boutflower*—The Recollections of a British Army Medical Man on Campaign During the Napoleonic Wars.

ON CAMPAIGN WITH MOORE AND WELLINGTON *by Anthony Hamilton*—The Experiences of a Soldier of the 43rd Regiment During the Peninsular War.

THE ROAD TO AUSTERLITZ *by R. G. Burton*—Napoleon's Campaign of 1805.

SOLDIERS OF NAPOLEON *by A. J. Doisy De Villargennes & Arthur Chuquet*—The Experiences of the Men of the French First Empire: Under the Eagles by A. J. Doisy De Villargennes & Voices of 1812 by Arthur Chuquet.

INVASION OF FRANCE, 1814 *by F. W. O. Maycock*—The Final Battles of the Napoleonic First Empire.

LEIPZIG—A CONFLICT OF TITANS *by Frederic Shoberl*—A Personal Experience of the 'Battle of the Nations' During the Napoleonic Wars, October 14th-19th, 1813.

SLASHERS *by Charles Cadell*—The Campaigns of the 28th Regiment of Foot During the Napoleonic Wars by a Serving Officer.

BATTLE IMPERIAL *by Charles William Vane*—The Campaigns in Germany & France for the Defeat of Napoleon 1813-1814.

SWIFT & BOLD *by Gibbes Rigaud*—The 60th Rifles During the Peninsula War.

AVAILABLE ONLINE AT www.leonaur.com
AND FROM ALL GOOD BOOK STORES

www.ingramcontent.com/pod-product-compliance
Lightning Source LLC
Chambersburg PA
CBHW032100230426
43662CB00034B/70